W9-BMO-383

The **Rough Guide** to

Ecuador

written and researched by

Harry Adès and Melissa Graham

with additional contributions from
**Carlos Villafuerte, Matthew L. Goldman, Louise Williamson
and Sarah Lazarus**

www.roughguides.com

Contents

Crafts and markets colour section following p.184

Galápagos field guide colour section following p.472

www.roughguides.com

3

◀◀ Cotopaxi summit ◀ Marching band in front of Catedral Nueva, Cuenca

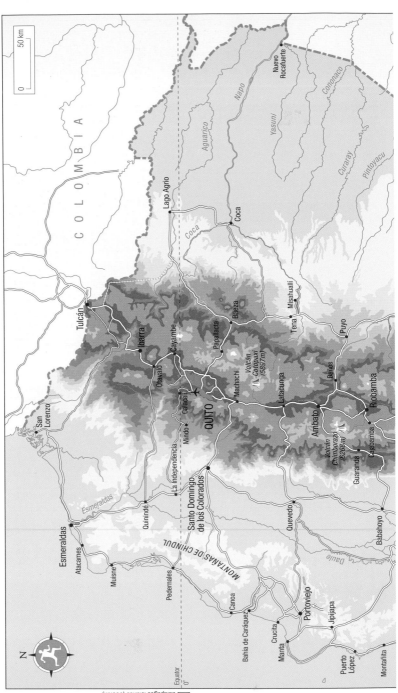

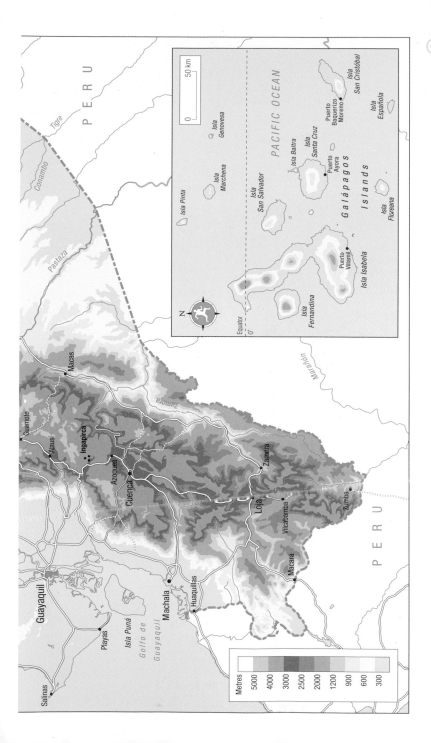

PERU

Tigre

Conambo

Pastaza

PERU

Macas

Zamora

Guamote

Alausí

Ingapirca

Azogues

Cuenca

Zamora

Loja

Vilcabamba

Zumba

PERU

Macará

Marañón

Guayaquil

Playas

Isla Puná

Golfo de
Guayaquil

Machala

Huaquillas

Salinas

PACIFIC OCEAN

Isla Pinta

Isla
Marchena

Isla
Genovesa

Isla
San Salvador

Isla Baltra

Isla
Santa Cruz

Puerto
Ayora

Puerto
Baquerizo
Moreno

Isla
San Cristóbal

Isla
Española

Galápagos Islands

Isla
Floreana

Puerto
Villamil

Isla Isabela

Isla
Fernandina

Equator
0°

N

50 km

0

Metres								
5000	4000	3000	2500	2000	1200	900	600	300

Introduction to
Ecuador

"Ecuador, so tiny on the map of the world, has always possessed the grandeur of a great country to those who know her well."

Albert B. Franklin, *Ecuador: Portrait of a People*

Sitting on the equator between Colombia and Peru, Ecuador may be the smallest Andean nation but it's packed with the most startling contrasts of scenery. With its astounding biodiversity, impressive historical legacy, stunning colonial architecture, bustling highland markets and diverse mix of people – blacks, whites, indigenous and *mestizo* – it's easy to see why this friendly and exotic destination is regarded as a microcosm of South America. From the icy pinnacles of Chimborazo, to the tropical forests of vast reserves like Parque Nacional Yasuní, to the palm-fringed beaches of the Pacific coast, Ecuador hums with life – all within easy reach of Quito, its jewel of a capital.

The steamy jungle wilderness of the Oriente and the mist-shrouded lowland cloudforests hold and protect just some of the country's mind-boggling array of flora and fauna: there are more bird species per square mile in Ecuador than any other South American country and more orchids than anywhere else on the planet. The country's greatest draw, though, are the captivating Galápagos Islands, nearly 1,0000km from the mainland, whose extraordinary wildlife inspired Charles Darwin and changed the world.

Ecuador's mainland divides neatly into three distinct regions running the length of the country in parallel strips. In the middle is the **sierra**, formed by the eastern and western chains of the Andes, which are punctuated by more than thirty volcanoes and enclosed by a series of high plateaux at around 2800m above sea level, themselves divided by gentle *nudos*, or "knots" of hills. This is the agricultural and indigenous heartland of Ecuador, a region of patchwork fields, stately haciendas and remote farming villages, as well as the country's oldest and most important cities, including Quito. East of the sierra is the **Oriente**, a large, sparsely populated area extending into the upper Amazon basin, much of it covered by dense tropical rainforest – an exhilarating, exotic region, though under increasing threat from the oil industry and colonization. West of the sierra, in the **coastal region**, banana, sugar, coffee, rice and cacao crops line a fertile alluvial plain that is bordered on

Fact file

• Ecuador is around 285,000 square kilometres in area - roughly equivalent to the US state of Nevada, or the United Kingdom combined with Belgium.

• Spanish is the official **language** of Ecuador, but there are more than twenty other native tongues, including several dialects of Kichwa, the language of the Inca Empire.

• The majority of Ecuador's 14.5 million **people** are *mestizos* (mixed spanish and indigenous blood), a quarter are indigenous people from more than a dozen native groups, seven percent are white, mainly of Spanish extraction, and three percent are black.

• The Spanish first established the boundaries of what roughly now corresponds to Ecuador in 1563. It became an **independent republic** in 1830, when it was officially named after the equator, which passes through it. Voting is compulsory for any literate person aged between 18 and 65, and optional for other eligible citizens.

• Ecuador's **main exports** are petroleum products, bananas, coffee, cacao, cut flowers and shrimp. Despite its large oil reserves and rich farmland, the economy is often severely affected by fluctuations in world commodity prices and around 38 percent of its people live below the poverty line.

▲ Saquisilí local

Volcanoes

Ecuador is one of the most volcanically active areas on the South American continent, and the highlands are studded with snow-crested cones looming into the sky either side of a broad central valley, which the explorer Alexander von Humboldt grandly called the "avenue of the volcanoes". Though many of the country's 55 volcanic peaks are extinct, eight remain active, while another nine have erupted in the last few thousand years and are classified as "potentially active". Anyone who stays for a few months is likely to feel a small tremor or see puffs of volcanic ash curling into the air from  a summit on the horizon. Every now and then volcanoes near population centres, such as Guagua Pichincha above Quito or Tungurahua by Baños, rumble into life triggering civil safety precautions. Nevertheless, Ecuador's volcanoes – which include the furthest point from the centre of the Earth (Chimborazo), the highest point on the equator (Cayambe), and one of the highest active peaks in the world (Cotopaxi) – are spectacular fixtures, attracting mountaineers from across the globe and awe in all who see them.

its Pacific seaboard by a string of beaches, mangrove swamps, shrimp farms and ports. Almost a thousand kilometres of ocean separate the coastline from the **Galápagos** archipelago, famed for its wondrous endemic birds, mammals, reptiles and plants.

Ecuador's regions provide a home to almost fifteen million people, the majority of whom live on the coast and in the sierra. For the most part, they are descendants of the various **indigenous groups** who first inhabited Ecuador's territory twelve thousand years ago, **Incas** who colonized the land in the late fifteenth century, **Spaniards** who conquered the Incas in the 1530s and **African slaves** brought by Spanish colonists. Although the mixing of blood over the centuries has resulted in a largely **mestizo** (mixed) population, the indigenous element remains very strong, particularly among the Kichwa-speaking communities of the rural sierra and the various ethnic groups of the Oriente such as the Shuar, Achuar, Huaorani and Secoya, while on the north coast there's a significant black population. As in many parts of Latin America, **social and economic divisions** between *indígenas*, blacks, *mestizos* and an elite class of whites remain deeply entrenched, exacerbated by a slew of recurrent economic and political crises. Despite this, the overwhelming majority of Ecuadorians remain resilient, remarkably cheerful, and very courteous and welcoming towards visitors.

Where to go

T hanks to its compact size, travelling around Ecuador is easy and relatively fast, with few places more than a day's bus ride from the capital. Unlike the attractions found in larger South American countries such as Brazil, Argentina and Chile, Ecuador's contrasting regions and highlights are within easy reach of each other, allowing for a more flexible approach to route-planning.

The majority of visitors fly in to **Quito**, whose glorious colonial centre – a maze of narrow streets and exquisite monasteries and churches – demands at least a couple of days to explore. Its modern **new town** is packed with hotels, restaurants and services that make it a convenient base for excursions. Striking north from Quito, the **northern sierra**'s green valleys are dappled with glistening lakes and crested by volcanic peaks, and the area is famed for its **artesanías**, centres of native craftwork, leather goods and woodcarving, all within a short bus ride of each other. Of these, **Otavalo** is undoubtedly the biggest attraction, thanks to its enormous Saturday market – one of the continent's most renowned – and flourishing weaving

▲ Direction signs, Cotopaxi

◄ Río Napo, Oriente

industry. The region also offers plenty of scope for walkers and horseriding enthusiasts, who should consider splashing out on a stay in any of several beautifully converted **haciendas**. South of Quito, the **central sierra** is home to the most spectacular of the country's volcanoes, including the snowcapped cone of **Cotopaxi**, and **Chimborazo**, Ecuador's highest peak at 6268m. Also in this rural region are some of the more exciting markets in the sierra, such as those of the villages of Saquisilí and Zumbahua, and the small town of Guamote. Rewarding off-the-beaten-track destinations include the dazzling crater lake of **Laguna Quilotoa**, with its remote páramo setting, while more established attractions include the busy little spa town of **Baños**, framed by soaring green peaks, and the **train** ride down the **Nariz del Diablo** ("the Devil's Nose") from **Riobamba**, the most fetching of the central sierra's cities. In the **southern sierra** lies the captivating colonial city of **Cuenca**, a UNESCO World Heritage Site and a convenient base for visiting **Ingapirca** – the country's only major Inca ruins – and **Parque Nacional Cajas**, a starkly beautiful wilderness. Further south, the charming city of **Loja** is a jumping-off point for visits to the **Parque Nacional Podocarpus**, whose humid lower reaches are particularly sumptuous, and the easy-going mountain village of **Vilcabamba**, a popular gringo hangout.

The **Oriente** embodies one of Ecuador's greatest wildernesses, a thick carpet of **tropical rainforest** unfurling for almost 300km, which was home only to isolated indigenous groups and the odd Christian mission until the discovery of oil here in the late 1960s. Since then, the region's infrastructure has developed apace, allowing easier access to the **Amazonian jungle** than any other Andean country. Two of the country's largest wild areas – the **Reserva Faunística Cuyabeno** and the **Parque Nacional Yasuní** – and a number of private reserves protect substantial forest tracts that have so far survived the incursions of the oil industry and colonists. Jungle lodges, many of them a canoe ride down the **Río Napo**, make for the most comfortable way of experiencing the thrill of this diverse and exciting habitat, but you can't do better than staying with an indigenous community for a glimpse into the lives of the jungle's resident peoples; some of the more isolated destinations can be reached only by light aircraft.

A few hours' drive northwest of Quito on the way to the coast, a number of private **reserves** showcase the country's beautiful **cloudforests** – otherworldly gardens of gnarled and tangled vegetation, wrapped in mosses and vines, and drenched daily in mist – and provide accommodation and guides for exploring or birdwatching, with some of the best sites on the western slopes of the Andes. The village of **Mindo**, enveloped in richly forested hills brimming with endemic species, is the birding capital of the country. Continuing westwards, Ecuador's varied coastline begins at the Colombian border in a profusion

Flora and fauna

Unmatched by any country of its size, Ecuador's considerable biodiversity includes more than 25,000 plant species, or ten percent of the world total, compared to around 17,000 for all of North America. Its 1600 types of birds are about twice as many as all of Europe, and half the total for all South America. The country also holds more species of mammals and amphibians per square metre than any other country on Earth.

This extraordinary concentration of wildlife is largely due to Ecuador's unique geography, its position on the equator and the geologically recent appearance of Andean cordilleras, which divide the coastal and Amazonian basins and provide an array of habitats and isolated areas for the evolution of new species. The country's highly varied terrain encompasses Andean mountains, parched semi-desert scrub, chilly high-altitude grasslands, subtropical cloudforests, tropical rainforests, dry forests, mangrove swamps, warm Pacific beaches and the unique environment of the Galápagos Islands.

of mangrove swamps, protected by the **Reserva Ecológica Manglares Cayapas-Mataje** and best visited by canoe from **San Lorenzo**, a down-at-heel town rich in Afro-Ecuadorian culture. The surrounding **north coast** is best known, however, for its **beaches** and the boisterous resort at **Atacames** is one of the most popular, though there are quieter places to enjoy the warm Pacific waters, including **Súa**, **Same**, **Muisne** and **Canoa**. Among the chief attractions of the **southern coast** is **Parque Nacional Machalilla**, with its dry and humid

forests, superb beaches and impressive birdlife on its offshore island, **Isla de la Plata**. Further down the coast, **Montañita** is rapidly gaining popularity with surfers and backpackers, while **Salinas** is perhaps the country's most prestigious seaside resort. **Guayaquil**, the region's main port and the largest city in Ecuador, is a frenetic and humid spot that's emerging as a tourist destination, while quieter attractions include the mangrove forests of the **Reserva-Ecológica Manglares Churute**, the warm, picturesque hill village of **Zaruma** and the petrified forest of **Puyango**.

Finally, the **Galápagos Islands** are for many visitors the initial lure to the country, and arguably the most compelling nature spot in the world. Ever since Darwin dropped anchor at these forbidding volcanic islands and unlocked the enigma of their motley creatures, they have enchanted all who come.

When to go

There's no real summer and winter in Ecuador, and its **weather** generally varies by regional geography, with temperatures determined more by altitude than by season or latitude. The warmest and driest months in the sierra are June to September, though this is complicated by various microclimates found in some areas. Outside these months, typical **sierra** weather offers sunny, clear mornings and cloudy, often wet, afternoons. In the **Oriente**, you can expect it to be warm, humid and rainy throughout the year, though there are often short breaks from the daily rains from August to September and December to February. In the **lowlands** it can get particularly hot on clear days, with temperatures easily topping 30°C. The **coast** has the most clearly defined wet and dry seasons, and the best time to visit is from December to April, when frequent showers alternate with clear blue skies and temperatures stay high. From May to November it's often overcast and relatively cool, especially in the south, with less chance of rainfall. The **Galápagos** climate

▲ Quito, old town

▲ Fisherman taking his catch into Puerto Lopez

sees hot, sunny days interspersed with the odd heavy shower from January to June, and dry and overcast weather for the rest of the year, when the *garúa* mists are prevalent. **El Niño** years can bring enormous fluctuations in weather patterns on the coast and at the Galápagos archipelago, when levels of rainfall can be many times the norm.

Average temperatures and rainfall

	Jan	Feb	Mar	Apr	May	Jun	Jul	Aug	Sep	Oct	Nov	Dec
Quito (sierra)												
Max/min (°C)	19/10	19/10	19/10	19/11	19/11	19/9	19/9	19/9	20/9	19/9	19/9	19/10
Max/min (°F)	66/50	66/50	66/50	66/52	66/52	66/48	66/48	66/48	68/48	66/48	66/48	66/50
Rainfall (mm)	114	130	152	175	124	48	20	25	79	127	109	104
Guayaquil (coast)												
Max/min (°C)	31/23	31/24	32/24	32/24	31/23	29/22	29/21	29/21	30/21	29/22	30/23	31/23
Max/min (°F)	88/73	88/75	90/75	90/75	88/73	84/71	84/70	84/70	86/70	84/72	86/73	88/73
Rainfall (mm)	224	279	287	180	53	18	3	0	3	3	3	30
Puyo (Oriente)												
Av daily (°C)	21	20	21	21	21	20	19	20	20	21	21	21
Av daily (°F)	88	88	90	90	88	84	84	84	86	84	86	88
Rainfall (mm)	302	297	429	465	409	457	389	345	366	381	363	333
Nuevo Rocafuerte (Oriente)												
Av daily (°C)	26	25	25	25	25	24	23	24	25	25	25	26
Av daily (°F)	70	77	77	77	77	75	73	75	77	77	77	79
Rainfall (mm)	160	188	206	284	356	320	295	224	241	229	198	152
Puerto Ayora (Galápagos)												
Max/min (°C)	28/23	30/23	31/23	30/23	28/22	26/21	25/20	24/19	24/19	25/20	26/20	27/21
Max/min (°F)	82/73	86/73	88/73	86/73	82/72	79/70	77/68	75/66	75/66	77/68	77/68	80/70
Rainfall (mm)	44	56	80	73	70	49	25	8	10	11	11	41

22

things not to miss

It's not possible to see everything that Ecuador has to offer in one trip – and we don't suggest you try. What follows is a selective and subjective taste of the country's highlights: fun festivals, outstanding beaches, spectacular wildlife and extraordinary landscapes. They're arranged in five colour-coded categories, so you can browse through to find the very best things to see, do, buy and experience. All highlights have a page reference to take you straight into the Guide, where you can find out more.

01 Otavalo market Page **135** • Even hardened skinflints won't be able to resist bagging a few of the fabulous handicrafts and weavings on offer at one of the largest and most colourfull artesanía markets on the continent.

02 Quito Page **71** • A mixture of church spires, tiled roofs and skyscrapers glinting in the sunlight against the brooding backdrop of Volcán Pichincha, the second highest capital in the world is an enthralling blend of urban and traditional indigenous cultures.

03 Climbing Cotopaxi Page **181** • Ecuador is a big draw for experienced climbers, but even novices, if fit, fully acclimatized and under professional guidance, can have a crack at Cotopaxi, one of the highest active volcanoes in the world.

04 **Laguna Quilotoa** Page **191** • This glittering green crater lake sits at the heart of the Quilotoa loop, a popular scenic diversion through the beguiling landscapes and villages of the rural central highlands.

06 **Orchids** Pages **337**, **338** & **342** • A miracle of biodiversity, Ecuador has more orchid species than any other country on Earth.

05 **Malecón 2000** Page **398** • A triumph of urban renewal, this landmark transformation of a dangerous and dilapidated riverside walkway into the cultural and recreational heart of the city, has been a leading force behind the renaissance of Guayaquil.

07 **Atacames** Page **362** • Kick back and relax on beautiful Atacames beach by day, because you'll need all your energy after sundown for its beachfront bars which throb with music and rum-swilling revelry well into the small hours.

08 **Mama Negra Fiesta** Page **184** • One of the country's best-loved festivals features a carnival of dazzling costumes, dancing troupes and marching bands parading through the streets of Latacunga.

10 Colonial Cuenca Page **239** • Pristine colonial architecture, cobbled streets, illustrious churches and flowering plazas give Cuenca a distinguished air and the well-deserved reputation of being the country's most enchanting city.

09 Ceviche Page **43** • The bright, zesty flavours and tender textures of ceviche, seafood marinated in lime juice, have made it a national obsession, especially on the coast, where it makes the perfect accompaniment to sun, a cold beer – and a bowl of popcorn.

11 The páramo Pages **129**, **135** & **163** • High-altitude grassland wildernesses rolling uninterrupted for miles between lonely, mist-shrouded lakes in many of the country's highland reserves, the páramo is bleak, cold and wet, but hauntingly beautiful.

12 **Nariz del Diablo train ride** Page **213** • Experience one of the world's great feats of railway engineering from the roof of a train as it descends the Andes over the "Devil's Nose" in a sequence of thrilling switchback turns.

13 **Galápagos wildlife** Pages **522** & the *Galápagos field guide* • The fearless creatures ekeing out an existence on a few scarred volcanic islands that inspired Darwin still give an unparalleled insight into the mechanics of nature at one of the world's most treasured wildlife destinations.

14 Isla de la Plata Page **432** • A short jaunt by boat from the mainland gives access to large colonies of sea birds, such as blue-footed boobies and waved albatrosses – a flavour of the Galápagos at a fraction of the cost.

15 Horseriding Page **51** • Brought by the conquistadors, horses may be late arrivals to Ecuador, but they are uniquely suited to in-depth exploration of the country's sweeping highland landscapes.

16 Museo del Banco Central Page **99** • See the riches of more than five thousand years of Ecuadorian culture at the country's top museum, which features some of the oldest ceramics discovered on the continent, exquisite pre-Columbian worked gold, and masterpieces of colonial and modern art.

17 Whale watching Pages **365**, **418** & **422** • The heart-stopping sight of a 36-tonne humpback breaching and flopping back into the ocean amid towers of spray can be experienced between June and September, when they come to the Ecuadorian coast to breed.

18 Jungle observation towers Page **302** • From the rainforest floor it's sometimes difficult to discern wildlife in the treetops, but several jungle lodges feature observation towers that rise above the vegetation to give unbeatable views across the forest canopy.

19 Contemporary art Pages **102**, **103**, **124**, & **190** • Ecuador's great modern artists are like the conscience of the nation, influential social commentators whose work, on view at several impressive galleries, shouldn't be missed.

20 Baños Page **199** • Whether it's nibbling on the local specialty, *melcocha* (a sticky toffee made in shop doorways), wallowing in thermal baths, or hiking, biking or rafting in the surrounding countryside, there's plenty to keep you occupied in this charming spa town.

21 Ingapirca Page **232** • Perched on a hillside overlooking serene pastoral countryside, Ecuador's best-preserved Inca ruins exhibit the fine stonemasonry and trapezoidal doorways that were the hallmarks of the empire's architecture.

22 La Compañía Page **91** ● Quito's centre is packed with magnificent churches, monasteries and convents, but few can match La Compañía's outstanding Baroque facade and sumptuous interior.

Basics

25

Basics

Getting there

Direct flights to Ecuador's international airports in Quito and Guayaquil depart from a relatively small number of places outside of Latin America. In the United States, regular services leave from Miami, Houston and Atlanta; in Europe, they go from Madrid and Amsterdam. Higher prices are likely in the July to September high season and during December.

If you're planning to include Ecuador as part of a South American tour, consider an "open-jaw" ticket, which lets you make your own way overland between your arrival and departure points. Popular combinations are Quito and Lima, or Quito and La Paz, and tickets cost about the same as a normal return.

Ecuador is too small to warrant its own **airpass**, but is included in larger networks, such as the LAN airlines Airpass (@www.lan.com), which links LAN destinations and offers further discounts if you have a transatlantic ticket with them.

Flights from the US and Canada

While there are few direct routes to Ecuador, it's easy to pick up connecting flights to the main hubs.

From the US, direct routes to Quito and Guayaquil are operated by American Airlines, LanEcuador and Aerogal from Miami; Continental from Houston; and Delta Air Lines from Atlanta. Avianca Airlines, Copa Airlines and Taca operate routes from other cities such as Los Angeles, New York and Miami, with changes in their respective hub airports at Bogotá, Panama City and San José.

Approximate flying times from the US to Quito without stops are four hours from Miami, and around five hours from Houston and Atlanta. Quito is about seven and a half hours from Toronto and Montreal, or about ten hours from Calgary and Vancouver. Prices range from around US$450 return from Miami, US$700–900 from Houston and CAN$900 from Toronto, but shop around, as prices can vary greatly.

Flights from the UK and Ireland

There are no direct flights to Ecuador **from Britain and Ireland**, but there are plenty of indirect flights to both Quito and Guayaquil involving a change of plane in either a European or American city. The US airlines fly via their respective hubs as discussed, while Iberia and Air Cornet offer services via Madrid, and KLM via Amsterdam (stopping at Bonaire, in the Dutch Antilles). Other possibilities include taking a flight to South American hubs, such as Bogotá or Caracas, from where connections to Ecuador can be made.

Typical journey times are between fifteen and seventeen hours, with Iberia and American Airlines offering marginally faster services. You can expect to pay around £550–800 return including tax in the low season and £650–900 in the high.

Flights from Australia and New Zealand

There are no direct flights to Ecuador **from Australia or New Zealand**, though there are two main indirect routings, one via Santiago in Chile, the other via the US. The most straightforward is the Qantas/LanChile route from Sydney to Quito and Guayaquil, stopping in Auckland and changing in Santiago. Travelling to Ecuador by way of the US means changing in Los Angeles and then Miami or Houston. Another option is to fly from Sydney or Auckland to Buenos Aires with Aerolineas Argentinas and to pick up a connection from there. There are no real bargains on either routing, and connections can be complicated. Typical travel times are around 25 to 40 hours. Expect to pay at least A$1700 from Australia, and NZ$1800 from New Zealand.

Flights from South Africa

To get to Ecuador **from South Africa**, you're best off flying to a South American hub, such as São Paulo, Buenos Aires, Santiago or Lima, from where there are ongoing services to Quito. Johannesburg to São Paulo with Varig is a ten-hour flight costing upwards of around ZAR5000. From São Paulo there are direct flights daily to Quito with Taca, which take another eight to nine hours.

Airlines, agents and operators

Airlines

Aer Lingus ⓦ www.aerlingus.com
Aerogal ⓦ www.aerogal.com.ec
Aerolineas Argentinas ⓦ www.aerolineas.com.ar

Air Canada ⓦ www.aircanada.com
Air Comet ⓦ www.aircomet.com
Air New Zealand ⓦ www.airnewzealand.co.nz
American Airlines ⓦ www.aa.com
Avianca ⓦ www.avianca.com
British Airways ⓦ www.ba.com
British Midland ⓦ www.flybmi.com
Continental Airlines ⓦ www.continental.com
Copa Airlines ⓦ www.copaair.com
Delta ⓦ www.delta.com
Iberia Airlines ⓦ www.iberia.com
KLM ⓦ www.klm.com
Lan ⓦ www.lan.com
Qantas ⓦ www.qantas.com
Taca ⓦ www.taca.com
Santa Barbara Airlines ⓦ www.sbairlines.com
South African Airways ⓦ www.flysaa.com
Varig ⓦ www.varig.com

Agents and operators

Abercrombie & Kent US ☎ 1-800/554-7016, UK ☎ 0845/618 2201, Australia ☎ 1300/851 800, New Zealand ☎ 0800/441638;

Six steps to a better kind of travel

At Rough Guides we are passionately committed to travel. We feel strongly that only through travelling do we truly come to understand the world we live in and the people we share it with – plus tourism has brought a great deal of **benefit** to developing economies around the world over the last few decades. But the extraordinary growth in tourism has also damaged some places irreparably, and of course **climate change** is exacerbated by most forms of transport, especially flying. This means that now more than ever it's important to **travel thoughtfully** and **responsibly**, with respect for the cultures you're visiting – not only to derive the most benefit from your trip but also to preserve the best bits of the planet for everyone to enjoy. At Rough Guides we feel there are six main areas in which you can make a difference:

- Consider what you're contributing to the **local economy**, and how much the services you use do the same, whether it's through employing local workers and guides or sourcing locally grown produce and local services.
- Consider the **environment** on holiday as well as at home. Water is scarce in many developing destinations, and the biodiversity of local flora and fauna can be adversely affected by tourism. Try to patronize businesses that take account of this.
- Travel with a purpose, not just to tick off experiences. Consider **spending longer** in a place, and getting to know it and its people.
- Give thought to how often you **fly**. Try to avoid short hops by air and more harmful night flights.
- Consider **alternatives to flying**, travelling instead by bus, train, boat and even by bike or on foot where possible.
- Make your trips "**climate neutral**" via a reputable carbon offset scheme. All Rough Guide flights are offset, and every year we donate money to a variety of charities devoted to combating the effects of climate change.

www.abercrombiekent.com. Upmarket tours of Ecuador and the Galápagos Islands.

Adventure Associates Australia ☎02/8916 3000, www.adventureassociates.com. A variety of mainland tours involving markets, the Devil's Nose train ride, Amazon lodges, volcanoes and Galápagos cruises.

Adventure Center US ☎1-800/228-8747, www .adventurecenter.com. Hiking and "soft adventure" specialists with a number of tours to Ecuador and Galápagos.

The Adventure Company UK ☎0845/609 1137, www.adventurecompany.co.uk. Group tours of the highlands, the Amazon and the Galápagos.

Adventure Travel New Zealand ☎09/355 9131, www.adventuretravel.co.nz. New Zealand-based agent for a number of package and adventure companies, including Peregrine, Exodus and Dragoman.

Adventure World Australia ☎02/8913 0755, www.adventureworld.com.au; New Zealand ☎09/524 5118, www.adventureworld.co.nz. Agent for a vast array of international adventure travel companies that operate trips to every continent, including tours of Ecuador and the Galápagos Islands.

Adventures Abroad US & Canada ☎1-800/665-3998, www.adventures-abroad.com. Adventure specialist giving general tours to Ecuador.

Andean Treks US ☎1-800/683-8148, www .andeantreks.com. For Ecuador, Andean Treks offers customized tours including one or more of four "segments": Amazon, highlands and haciendas, cities and the Galápagos Islands.

Austral Tours Australia ☎1800/620 833, www .australtours.com. Central and South American specialist offering trips to *Kapawi Lodge* and Galápagos cruises.

Bales Worldwide UK ☎0845/057 1819, www .balesworldwide.com. Family-owned company offering mainly Galápagos tours as well as tailor-made itineraries.

Discovery Initiatives UK ☎01285/643 333, www.discoveryinitiatives.com. Conservation-minded outfit that organizes group and talior-made trips to the Galápagos, rainforests, cloudforests and volcanoes.

Dragoman Overland UK ☎01728/861 133, www.dragoman.com. Adventurous small-group overland trips in a special truck including one of nine weeks from Quito to Santiago or Quito to Rio, and a 27-week trip around the entire continent, starting in Quito.

Elderhostel US ☎1-800/454-5768, www .elderhostel.org. Educational programmes for seniors, exploring the culture, geography and ecology of Ecuador.

Footprint Adventures UK ☎01522/804 929, www.footprint-adventures.co.uk. A company with a conservation ethos offering a good choice of small-group tours, including trekking, rafting, birding and climbing holidays.

Intrepid Travel UK ☎0203/147 7777, www .intrepidtravel.com. Small-group tours with the emphasis on cross-cultural contact and low-impact tourism.

Journey Latin America UK ☎020/8747 8315, www.journeylatinamerica.co.uk. Specialists in flights, packages, adventure tours and tailor-made trips to Latin America.

Mountain Travel Sobek Check website for your country's toll-free number www.mtsobek.com. Hiking tours, visits to haciendas, rafting on the Upano and Galápagos cruises.

Myths and Mountains ☎1-800/670-MYTH or 775/832-5454, www.mythsandmountains .com. Socially responsible tours visiting indigenous communities in the highlands and Oriente, meeting shamans and exploring local medicine.

Nature Expeditions International US ☎1-800/869-0639, www.naturexp.com. Tours combining the Galápagos with highland markets and horse rides.

Naturetrek UK ☎01962/733 051, www .naturetrek.co.uk. Specializes in birdwatching and botanical holidays, with cloudforest tours, and trips to the Oriente and Andean páramo.

North South Travel UK ☎01245/608 291, www.northsouthtravel.co.uk. Competitive travel agency, offering discounted fares worldwide. Profits are used to support projects in the developing world, especially the promotion of sustainable tourism.

On the Go Tours UK ☎020/7371 1113, www .onthegotours.com. Runs four different group-only tours to Ecuador and the Galapagos, from 10–24 days long.

Ornitholidays UK ☎01794/519 445, www .ornitholidays.co.uk. Specialist birding tours of Ecuador and the Galápagos.

Overseas Adventure Travel US ☎1-800/493-6824, www.oattravel.com. Small-group tours of the jungle and Galápagos, with add-ons to northern Ecuador.

Penelope Kellie UK ☎01962/779 317, www .pkworldwide.com. Agent for Galápagos cruises on a selection of top-class boats.

Quasar Expeditions US ☎1-866/481-7790, UK ☎0800/883 0827, www.galapagosexpeditions .com. Well-respected Galápagos specialist, owning a range of luxury and first-class yachts. Also arranges high-quality tailor-made land tours.

Reef and Rainforest UK ☎01803/866 965, www.reefandrainforest.co.uk. Trips to the Galápagos, plus birding groups in the Amazon basin and cloudforests.

Select Latin America UK ☎020/7407 1478, www.selectlatinamerica.co.uk. Specializes in Galápagos cruises on a variety of yachts, but can combine these with treks and jungle trips.

South America Travel Centre Australia ☎03/9642 5353, ⓦwww.satc.com.au. A 26-day tour including the Galápagos Islands and Otavalo in Ecuador. "Short tours" of the mainland including Devil's Nose, Ingapirca and Cuenca also available.
STA Travel US ☎1-800/781-4040, UK ☎0871/230 0040, Australia ☎134 782, New Zealand ☎0800/474 400; ⓦwww.statravel.com. Worldwide specialists in independent travel; also student IDs, travel insurance, car rental, rail passes and more. Discounts for students and under-26s.
Sunbird UK ☎01767/262 522, ⓦwww .sunbirdtours.co.uk. Specialist birdwatching tours to Ecuador, the Oriente, Podocarpus and the Santa Elena peninsula.
Trailfinders UK ☎0845/058 5858, Republic of Ireland ☎01/677 7888, Australia ☎1300/780 212; ⓦwww.trailfinders.com. One of the best-informed and most efficient agents for independent travellers.

Tribes UK ☎01728/685 971, ⓦwww.tribes.co.uk. Environmentally and culturally sensitive operator offering a range of small-group and special-interest tours around Ecuador.
Wilderness Travel US ☎1-800/368-2794, ⓦwww.wildernesstravel.com. Established adventure company offering Galápagos trips combined with hiking, kayaking and snorkelling options, plus trips to the highlands.
Wildland Adventures US ☎1-800/345-4453, ⓦwww.wildland.com. Conservation-minded operator offering hacienda tours of the highlands, jungle treks in the Amazon lowlands and Galápagos wildlife and diving packages.
Wildlife Worldwide UK ☎0845/130 6982, ⓦwww.wildlifeworldwide.com. Offers an 18-day "Complete Ecuador" package, in which you choose components such as jungle lodges, cloudforest trips and the Galápagos.

Health

Ecuador has its fair share of scary-sounding tropical diseases, but there's no reason to be paranoid. Most are rare and pose much more of a threat to residents – especially those from poorer communities with limited access to clean water and health care – than tourists. The two illnesses you should be especially vigilant against, however, are stomach upsets caused by contaminated food and water, and malaria. You can dramatically cut the risks of getting either through simple, practical steps.

Before you go

Consult your doctor or a travel clinic at least **two months before** you leave to discuss whether you need vaccinations or malaria prophylaxis. If you're travelling for more than a few weeks, it's also worth having a dental check-up. Spectacle and contact lens users should bring spare glasses and their prescription.

The only **inoculation** you are required to have by Ecuadorian law is for yellow fever – but only if you're coming from a tropical African or South American country, when (in theory, at least) you're supposed to show a vaccination certificate. It's a good idea to have the jab anyway if you're planning to visit the Oriente, where the disease is rare but present. The vaccination lasts for ten years. You should also make sure you're up to date with your vaccinations and boosters for polio, tetanus, diphtheria, hepatitis A and typhoid. Also consider jabs for rabies, tuberculosis and hepatitis B if you anticipate spending a long time in rural areas or with animals, if you're doing work in health care, or if you're planning on lots of long hikes in the wild; those consistently occupationally exposed to wild rodents for long periods in Loja, Tungurahua or Cañar provinces might also ask their health professionals about a plague vaccine.

Food and water

The traveller's commonest health complaint is an **upset stomach**, usually caused by contaminated food or water. Tap water is unsafe to drink in Ecuador; bottled water and soft drinks, widely available in all but the remotest places, are safe alternatives, but always check that the seal is intact. Wash your hands before meals and use bottled or boiled water to clean your teeth. You can also pick up stomach upsets from swimming in unclean water; only use chlorinated swimming pools and avoid beaches near large population centres or sewage outlets.

For **food and drink**, avoid the following: ice made from tap water; fruit juices with tap water added; raw vegetables and salads; undercooked, partly cooked or reheated fish, crustaceans, meat or eggs; dairy products and ice cream made from unpasteurized milk; and food that's been lying around uncovered where flies can get at it. Food that's freshly prepared and hot, and fruit and vegetables that you can peel yourself, rarely cause any harm.

If you plan to visit remote areas or want to avoid relying on bottled water, you may have to **purify your water**. Bringing water to a good rolling boil for a minute (3min at altitude) is extremely effective, though anyone travelling without cooking equipment will find chemical purification is simpler. Chemical and iodine tablets are small, light and easy to use, and iodine tincture is particularly effective against amoebas and **giardia**; iodine is unsafe for pregnant women, babies and people with thyroid complaints. Portable water purifiers give the most complete treatment but are expensive and relatively bulky to carry.

A bout of **diarrhoea**, sometimes accompanied by vomiting and stomach cramps, is an annoyance most travellers have to suffer at one time or another. In most cases it passes within a couple of days and is best remedied by resting and taking plenty of fluids. Avoid milk, alcohol and caffeine-based drinks; still drinks are preferable to fizzy. Rehydration salts are widely available in Ecuadorian pharmacies and are very helpful in replenishing lost salts. You can make your own solution by adding a generous pinch of salt and three to four tablespoons of sugar to a litre of clean water – aim to drink at least three litres a day if you're unwell, or a couple of glasses for every loose movement. Current medical opinion is that you should continue to eat normally as opposed to fasting, if you feel like eating. Anti-diarrhoeal drugs only suppress symptoms rather than solving the underlying problem, but can be useful when you're on the move and don't know when the next toilet stop might be.

Consult a doctor if symptoms last for longer than five days, there is blood in your stools, you also have a high fever or if abdominal pain is severe and constant. Most towns have facilities for testing stool samples; tests often only take a matter of hours, cost a few dollars and are invaluable for diagnosis. You'll usually have to buy your own sample pot (*caja de muestra*) from a pharmacy.

Diarrhoea caused by bacteria can be treated with a course of **antibiotics** like Ciprofloxacin (available over the counter in most Ecuadorian pharmacies). Ciprofloxacin does not work against **amoebic dysentery** (amoebiasis), which can become very serious if it's not treated with metronidazole (Flagyl) or **giardia**, a parasitic infection that induces sudden, watery and extra-bad-smelling diarrhoea, bloating, fatigue and excessive rotten-egg-smelling gas. Symptoms wax and wane but can last for weeks if left untreated with a course of metronidazole or tinidazole (Fasigyn); you should avoid alcohol if taking either of these medications.

Cholera – transmitted through contaminated water – occasionally breaks out in rural areas, but tends to be very localized and restricted to poor communities with inadequate sanitation. It's unlikely you'll go anywhere near these places, but if you suspect you're infected (symptoms include profuse watery diarrhoea, explosive vomiting and fever) it's easy to treat, provided you get to a doctor immediately and keep rehydrating by drinking large quantities of bottled or boiled water.

Insect-borne diseases

Heavy rains can trigger a sharp increase in **insect-borne diseases** in Ecuador, particularly malaria and dengue fever in the coastal provinces. The best way of avoiding such diseases is not to get bitten in the first place. Straightforward **precautions** include using insect repellent, covering up as much skin as possible with light-coloured, loose-fitting but tight-cuffed clothing and sleeping in screened rooms with a mosquito net, preferably treated with permethrin repellent.

Tens of thousands of people contract **malaria** every year in Ecuador, about a third of them with the very serious *falciparum* variety. The worst-affected areas are below 1500m, especially in or around population centres and when there's plenty of stagnant water for the mosquitoes to breed in. Above 1500m the risk falls substantially, and above 2500m the malaria mosquito cannot survive. Quito and the Galápagos Islands are free of malaria, and if you're keeping to the highlands, the risk is extremely small. The malarial *Anopheles* mosquito bites between dusk and dawn, so dress and protect yourself appropriately before sunset and sleeping.

Consult your doctor if travelling in malarial areas and follow a course of **prophylactic medication**. There are chloroquine-resistant strains of malaria in Ecuador, meaning you'll probably use Lariam (mefloquine), Malarone (atovaquone and proguanil) or Vibramycin (doxycyline). Malarial tablets need to be taken prior to arriving in risk areas and also after leaving them, as directed. These drugs do not completely wipe out the risk of the disease, and you should always take care to avoid being bitten. Symptoms include fever, diarrhoea, joint pain, shivering and flu-like symptoms; if you suspect you've caught the disease, see a doctor immediately and have a blood test. Symptoms can appear several months after leaving a malarial area.**Dengue fever** is a painful and debilitating disease spread by the *Aedes* mosquito, which bites during the day. There's no vaccine against dengue fever and there's not a lot you can do should you contract it, except resting and taking painkillers (avoid aspirin) and plenty of fluids. Symptoms include headaches, severe joint pain (its other name, "breakbone fever", is indicative) and high fever, though it's usually only fatal if caught repeatedly.

Avoiding insect bites will also provide you with protection against a number of rarer diseases such as: **leishmaniasis**, a parasitic disease spread by the bite of infected sand flies present in lowland Ecuador; **river**

blindness (onchocerciasis), spread by the bite of black flies found around fast-moving water, mainly in parts of Esmeraldas province; and **Chagas disease** (or American trypanosomiasis), which is carried by bugs found in rural mud, thatch and adobe buildings in coastal areas, and transmitted when the bug's faeces are unwittingly rubbed into its bite wound.

Altitude and hypothermia

If you've flown to Quito from sea level, you may feel a bit woozy, sleepless and lethargic – normal symptoms of the **acclimatization** process the body undergoes over a few days as it adjusts to reduced levels of oxygen at altitude. Symptoms, which might also include breathlessness, needing to urinate frequently, fatigue and strange dreams, will abate naturally if you rest and avoid alcohol and sleeping pills.

Acute Mountain Sickness (AMS), known as *soroche* in Ecuador, occurs when your acclimatization process does not keep pace with your rate of ascent. It's a debilitating and potentially dangerous condition caused by the reduced oxygen levels and atmospheric pressure at high elevations, and if you're going to go much above 3000m you should be aware of the risks. Your gender and fitness have no bearing on whether you will develop AMS, but children are known to be more susceptible to AMS than adults, and, if young, may not be able to tell you they're feeling sick, in which case they shouldn't be taken to high altitudes at all. Young adults (in their teens or even early twenties) are also more susceptible and should allow extra days for acclimatization. Symptoms include headaches, nausea and extreme tiredness, dizziness, insomnia, confusion and a staggering gait. The best way to relieve the condition is also the simplest – **lose altitude**.

You can minimize the risks of developing AMS by ascending to high elevations slowly and allowing yourself to **acclimatize** – don't be tempted to whizz straight up the nearest volcano without spending a night or two at altitude first. You should also avoid alcohol and salt, and drink lots of water or try the local remedy for altitude sickness, **coca-leaf tea** (*mate de coca*). A course of acetazolamide (Diamox) speeds up the acclimatization process, but this is a prescription-only drug in most countries, as it can be dangerous for people with heart conditions. It's unlikely you'll need this drug in Ecuador, but if you're planning to go to very high elevations, you might consider it as a precaution.

If you develop AMS, it is essential you do not ascend any further. Your condition will worsen and may become life-threatening. There are two severe forms of AMS. **HAPO** (high altitude pulmonary oedema) is caused by a build-up of liquid in the lungs. Symptoms include fever, an increased pulse rate and coughing up white fluid; sufferers should descend immediately, whereupon recovery is usually quick and complete. Rarer, but more serious, is **HACO** (high altitude cerebral oedema), which occurs when the brain gets waterlogged with fluid. Symptoms include loss of balance and coordination, severe lassitude, weakness or numbness on one side of the body and a confused mental state. If you or a fellow traveller displays any of these symptoms, descend immediately, and get to a doctor; HACO can be fatal within 24 hours.

Decompression sickness is a more oblique problem associated with gaining altitude quickly. If you have been scuba diving in the Galápagos or on the coast, wait at least 24 hours before coming to the highlands or flying.

Another concern for people at altitude is **hypothermia**, an underestimated enemy responsible for more deaths among trekkers and climbers than anything else. Brought on by exposure to cold and when the body loses heat faster than it can generate it, hypothermia is greatly accelerated when you're wet, tired and in the wind. Because early symptoms can include an almost euphoric sense of sleepiness and disorientation, your body's core temperature can plummet to danger level before you know what has happened. Other symptoms are violent shivering, erratic behaviour, slurred speech, loss of coordination and drowsiness, and are much easier to spot in other people than yourself. Victims should be given dry clothes, warm drinks (slowly) and kept awake and warm.

The sun

It's not a good idea to strip off and soak up the rays of the **equatorial sun**. Serious sunburn and sunstroke are real risks, particularly at altitude, when the temperature is not necessarily that high but the thin air amplifies the harm done by the sun's ultraviolet rays. Jungle and coastal boat rides can also be dangerous, as cool river or sea breezes disguise the effects of the sun as it is reflected off the water. Use a high-factor sunscreen on all exposed skin, reapplying after bathing or exertion, and wear a wide-brimmed hat. Drink plenty of water, particularly if you're exercising, and consider taking a rehydration solution or adding more salt to your food to counterbalance the effects of excessive sweating.

Animals

At some point you're bound to come across unfriendly **dogs**, especially if you're a hiker, as they're often used in rural communities to deter thieves. If a dog snarls and bares its teeth at you, back off slowly, without turning your back on it, staring at it, or showing any fear. Picking up a stone and pretending to throw it sometimes works, but you don't want to provoke an attack either. **Rabies**, though only a remote risk, does exist in Ecuador, with a couple of hundred cases a year: if you get bitten or scratched by a dog, cat or most other mammals you should wash the affected area thoroughly with soap and clean water and seek medical attention *immediately*.

Stings and bites from other creatures such as scorpions, spiders and snakes are very uncommon but can be terribly painful and, in rare cases, fatal. It's good practice to go through your clothes, socks and shoes before dressing, and to check your bedclothes and under lavatory seats. In the rainforests, watch where you put your feet and hands, and don't lean against trees. Walking around barefoot is an invitation to get bitten or stung and opens the door to hookworm.

Ecuador does have its share of venomous **snakes**, but bites are rare, and even if they do strike, there's every chance they won't inject any venom. In the unlikely event of snakebite, keep still. If possible, get someone to kill the snake for identification purposes, and get medical help as quickly as possible. In remote rainforest communities, following local knowledge may sometimes be better than spending hours getting to a hospital. Village doctors (*curanderos*) may know effective antidotes, and be able to prepare them quickly.

Volcanoes

Ecuador has several **active volcanoes**, some of which periodically belch clouds of ash over the surrounding countryside. In recent years the ones causing most disruption have been Guagua Pichincha near Quito, Reventador in the Oriente, and Tungurahua, which has been threatening the town of Baños for years. These are not the only active volcanoes in the country; you can keep abreast of any volcanic activity at Ecuador's Instituto Geofísico website ⓦwww.igepn.edu.ec (in Spanish), the Smithsonian Global Volcanism Program ⓦwww .volcano.si.edu (in English), or through local media, authorities and your embassy.

Other health hazards

Sexually transmitted diseases are as much a threat here as in any country. **Condoms** (*condones* or *preservativos*) are not as widely available as in Western countries – it's a good idea to take your own supply if you're worried about the safety of unfamiliar brands.

Car crashes cause more injuries to travellers in Ecuador than anything else. Minimize your risks by travelling on roads only during the day, wearing seatbelts in cars or helmets on motorbikes, avoiding overloaded buses and changing vehicle if you think the driver is drunk, fatigued or unduly reckless.

Medical resources for travellers

US and Canada

Canadian Society for International Health ☏613/241-5785, ⓦwww.csih.org. Extensive list of travel health centres.
CDC ☏1-800/232 4636, ⓦwww.cdc.gov/travel. Official US government travel health site.
International Society for Travel Medicine ☏1-770/736-7060, ⓦwww.istm.org. Has a full list of travel health clinics.

UK and Ireland

Hospital for Tropical Diseases Travel Clinic ☏0845/155 5000, ☏020/7388 9600 (Travel Clinic), ⓦwww.thehtd.org.
MASTA (Medical Advisory Service for Travellers Abroad) ☏0870/606 2782, ⓦwww .masta.org for the nearest clinic.
Travel Medicine Clinic ☏028/9031 5220, Belfast.
Tropical Medical Bureau ☏1850/487 674, ⓦwww.tmb.ie. Republic of Ireland.

Australia, New Zealand and South Africa

Travellers' Medical and Vaccination Centre ☏1300/658 844, ⓦwww.tmvc.com.au. Lists travel clinics in Australia, New Zealand and South Africa.

Getting around

Ecuador's inexpensive and generally reliable buses are the country's preferred form of public transport, and trundle along just about anywhere there's a road. By contrast, the train network covers only a small fraction of the country.

The road network is limited by North American and European standards, but expanding and improving all the time thanks to recent investments in the country's infrastructure, supported by the introduction of road tolls. Less than twenty percent of the highways are paved so expect a bumpy ride if you're going on any but the most important routes. The **Panamericana** (Pan-American Highway, often called *la Pana* by locals) forms the backbone of the country's road network, linking all the major highland towns and cities from Tulcán to Loja and on to Peru. A handful of other good roads spill down the Andes to important coastal cities including Guayaquil, Manta and Esmeraldas, while in the Oriente the road system is the least developed and exists almost entirely to serve the needs of the local oil industry.

The network's biggest problem has always been the **weather**, with floods and landslides both common, knocking out roads sometimes for weeks at a time. Even in fine conditions, rough terrain means travelling in the country's highland regions is often much slower than you might expect: going the length of the country by bus from the Colombian border to Peru, a distance of 818km on mostly paved roads, takes around 18 hours – an average speed of 45kmh.

By bus

Ecuador's comprehensive bus service makes getting around simple. Hundreds of companies ply the country's roads, often with dozens competing on the most popular routes, transporting people at little cost to all but the remotest regions. Levels of comfort can vary widely between companies: some have fleets of air-conditioned buses with TV, toilet and on-board snacks, while others run beaten-up old monsters with cracked windows, growling gears and belching exhausts. As a general rule, **luxury buses** (ask for an *autobús de lujo*) travel the most popular long-distance routes, leaving regularly all day and night, and require passengers to have a pre-booked ticket. They won't allow standing passengers on board, and only stop at scheduled destinations, reducing journey times.

The further into the backwaters you go, the more the comfort level is likely to drop. **Standard buses** will stop anywhere for anyone who wants to get on until every available crack of space has been filled. Obviously, the remoter the area, the less frequent the buses will be and most local and provincial services won't run much after nightfall. At the margins of the bus network, pick-up trucks (**camionetas**), minibuses (**busetas**) and open-sided trucks converted to hold wooden benches (**rancheras** or **chivas**) often fill the vacuum. If you're unsure of the area you're travelling to, note that most drivers know their routes well and are happy for you to ask them to stop at your destination – they'll let you know when you've arrived. For reasons of safety, **avoid travelling at night** on buses, when hold-ups and accidents are more likely.

Larger towns usually have a main **bus terminal** (*terminal terrestre*), where all the long-distance bus companies are based. In smaller towns, company offices and departure points may be scattered around, though they're usually never very far from the central square or main thoroughfare. Out of town, it's easy to hail non-luxury buses if you stand in a place where they have plenty of time to spot you; the standard gesture to flag one down is an apathetic point to the ground in the middle of the road next to you.

You can buy your **fare** from the conductor (*ayudante*) on board, who will come and collect it. Generally speaking, bus journeys cost roughly $1 per hour of travel. Overcharging is uncommon, but keep an eye on what others are paying. To get off, make for the door and say *"bajo"* or *"gracias"*. Alternatively, if you can, it's a good idea to buy your ticket at the company office in advance to guarantee yourself a seat, something you can do on all long-distance buses whether luxury class or not – seats towards the front lurch less.

Local **city buses** in the larger towns generally carry a board in the window showing their route, with a list of street names and key landmarks. There's normally a flat fare (currently around $0.20), which you pay as you enter. Local buses often stop to pick up and put down anywhere on request, though in some city centres proper **bus stops**, marked *"parada"*, are respected.

By train

The old traveller's adage, that all the fun is in the getting there, is never truer than with Ecuador's **trains**. A train ride here is a real treat – you can sit on the roof enjoying the scenery (do take care of overhead cables and tunnels), while the train slowly rattles down the track – but not a way to travel the country.

The network currently comprises three short tourist routes: Riobamba to Sibambe, down the vertiginous Nariz del Diablo (Devil's Nose; see p.213); Quito to El Boliche (by Cotopaxi national park; see p.120); and Ibarra to Primer Paso in the northern highlands (see p.156). Work is currently ongoing to restore the Quito–Durán (near Guayaquil) line.

At the time of writing, the section from Quito to Latacunga was near completion; check the website of the Empresa de Ferrocariles Ecuatorianos (EFE) Ⓦ www.efe.gov.ec for the latest.

By air

Flying within Ecuador is a quick, convenient and relatively inexpensive way of bypassing the country's serpentine and often crude road network. Those short on time can cut an all-day bus journey down to a 30-minute hop – and if the weather's clear, enjoy wonderful aerial views of volcanoes and rainforests in the process. **Domestic carriers include**: TAME (Ⓦ www.tame.com.ec), Icaro (Ⓦ www.icaro.com.ec), Aerogal (Ⓦ www.aerogal.com.ec), LanEcuador (Ⓦ www.lan.com), VIP (Ⓦ www.vipec.com), and Saéreo (Ⓦ www.saereo.com), plus a number of small-scale and local charter companies, particularly on the coast and in the Oriente. TAME offers the most extensive service, flying to most of the country's major centres, with ticket **prices** between $50 and $90 one-way, apart from flights to the Galápagos Islands, which are disproportionately expensive (see the Galápagos chapter on p.450 for full details). Busier routes should be booked days, if not weeks, in advance and it's important to **reconfirm** as **overbooking** is not uncommon. The weather can be a problem, particularly in Quito and the Oriente, resulting in fairly frequent delays, cancellations or diversions. Details of the various airline offices and destinations are given in the relevant chapters.

Driving

If you intend to zoom around the country in a short space of time, or want to get to really off-the-beaten-track destinations, **renting a car** is a worthwhile option. You will need to be at least 21 years old (extra charges are often payable if you are under 25) and have a major credit/debit card for the deposit. Theoretically, you only need your national licence to rent a vehicle, but you're strongly advised to bring an **international licence** as well – the Ecuadorian police, who frequently stop drivers to check their documents, are often suspicious of unfamiliar foreign licences and much happier when dealing with international ones. The national **speed limit** is 100kmh on highways (or less if indicated), and usually around 50kmh in towns or urban areas. Note that there are some draconian penalties for minor **motoring offences**, such as not wearing your seat belt; driving the wrong way down a one-way street is supposedly punishable by a fourteen-day mandatory jail sentence.

Rental outlets, costs and vehicles

For convenience's sake, you might want to arrange your car rental in advance through your nearest branch of an international rental company (see below), but it nearly always works out cheaper to sort it out when you get there, typically at the airport in Guayaquil or Quito. **Costs** are comparable to Europe or North America: in general, expect to pay around $35 a day or $230 a week for a small hatchback, and from around $80 a day or $550 a week for a mid-sized 4WD, including **insurance** and IVA (tax) – always make sure you're clear whether a price quoted includes insurance (generally around $5 a day), IVA and unlimited mileage. Check, too, what the **excess** is on the insurance (that is, the amount up to which you are liable in the event of an insurance claim). This is known as *el deducible* and is usually frighteningly high – around $1000 in the case of damage to the vehicle, and around $3000 for theft or "total destruction", as the rental companies alarmingly put it. It might be a wise precaution to use agencies such as ⓦ www.insurance4carhire.com, which provide year-long cover for rental vehicles, pay all excess costs and cover anyone named on the rental agreement.

When choosing which type of vehicle to rent, remember only a small portion of the country's roads are paved, and those that are surfaced can be in an atrocious state of disrepair. **Four-wheel-drive**, or at least high clearance and sturdy tyres, definitely comes in handy on unpaved roads, especially in the rainy season, but isn't necessary for the big cities and better-maintained parts of the road network. Air conditioning is another consideration for long journeys in the lowlands and Oriente.

On the road

Ecuadorian drivers tend to be undisciplined and sometimes downright dangerous; aggressive overtaking is particularly common, as is abruptly veering over to the wrong side of the road to avoid potholes. As long as you **drive defensively** and keep your wits about you, however, it's perfectly possible to cover thousands of kilometres without running into problems. **Never drive at night** if you can avoid it, as this is when most accidents occur, in part due to the absence of decent road markings, lighting and the lack of signs alerting drivers to

hazards. In addition, although **ambushes** against drivers are extremely rare, when they do happen it's most often at night.

Never leave valuables in your car at any time, or your car on the street overnight, as it will almost certainly be broken into; try to stay in hotels with a garage, or else leave your vehicle overnight in a securely locked *parqueadero*.

In the event of an **accident**, you should try to come to an agreement with the other party without involving the police if you can. This may not be possible if it is serious, and the upshot often is that both parties are detained until one admits liability. Unsurprisingly, hit and runs are common in Ecuador.

Car rental agencies

Avis ⓦ www.avis.com
Budget ⓦ www.budget.com
Hertz ⓦ www.hertz.com

Hitchhiking

Hitching is not recommended as a safe way of getting about, but it's widely practised by Ecuadorians, particularly in rural areas. For backpackers, the bus service is such that you'll only really need to hitch in the remoter places – you're most likely to get a ride in the back of a pick-up truck. The etiquette is to ask "*¿Cuánto le debo?*" ("How much do I owe you?") at the end of the journey, at which point you may be asked to pay a small amount, rarely more than the bus fare would have been, or let off for free. If you're worried about being overcharged, ask "*¿Cuánto sería?*" ("How much would it be?") before climbing aboard.

By taxi

Most towns in Ecuador have a fleet of yellow **taxis** – in some Oriente towns, white pick-up trucks (*camionetas*) take their place. Only in Quito are you going to find metered taxis; everywhere else taxis operate on a fixed-fare system, with a standard short journey typically costing around $1. For longer distances and in larger towns, such as Guayaquil, the fixed rate doesn't apply, and it's far more difficult to know what the fares should be. Most drivers are honest, but the best way to avoid being ripped off is

Addresses

Written addresses appear as a street and a number (Sucre 353), a street and the nearest intersecting street (Sucre y Olmedo) or all three (Sucre 353 y Olmedo). The number is often hyphenated – such as Sucre 3-53 – so that there's no confusion between the first digits (the block number) and the last digits (the house number). Post is kept in boxes and not delivered to the door in Ecuador, so many people understandably have no idea what their number is, or don't have one at all (written *s/n* for *sin número*). Note that the ground floor (US first floor) is known as the *planta baja*, while the first floor (US second floor) would be the *primer piso*.

to ask locals what the standard fares are to various destinations. Always agree on the price with the driver beforehand, and don't be afraid to haggle. Tipping isn't necessary, but it's common to round fares up for friendly service.

Taxis are also sometimes the best way of getting to out-of-the-way places such as national parks or mountain refuges, particularly if you're in a group and can share the cost. Hiring a taxi by the day could cost anywhere between $40 and $60; some taxi drivers will increase the price for bigger groups, but there's always room for negotiation.

By boat

Unless you're on a private boat transport to a smart jungle lodge, seats are invariably wooden and thoroughly uncomfortable. Bring something to sit on and keep food and water with you, as the bulk of your luggage will usually be put under wraps at the front of the boat.

The most likely place you'll end up in a boat is in the **Oriente**, where the best of the jungle is often a boat ride away. On the **coast**, the coastal highway now runs the entire length of the Ecuadorian seaboard, meaning you're less likely to need to travel by boat, but it's still fun to tour through the mangroves around San Lorenzo or Muisne. A few communities in the northern lowlands are still only reachable by river boat.

A **chartered boat** (*flete*) is more expensive than going on a public one, though you can reduce costs by gathering a group; the fare is usually fixed for the journey regardless of the number of passengers. Travel around the Galápagos Islands is almost exclusively by boat; refer to that chapter for details.

By bicycle

Even if Ecuador's chaotic roads don't always make the ideal cycleways, **cycling** can offer unrivalled closeness to the land and its people. For proper **cycle touring**, you're best off bringing your own bike and equipment from home. The best cycling is off the busy paved roads, so you'll need wide tyres, decent pannier clearance, plenty of low gears, and preferably 36-spoke wheels. It's good to know that once you're out of the scrum of Quito, the busy Panamericana is often paralleled by unused dirt and cobbled roads. A good rack, fully waterproof panniers and a secure bike lock are essential. Bicycle **repair shops** (*talleres de bicicletas*) are far more widespread than bike shops, but will only have parts for rudimentary repairs – bring a comprehensive toolkit and a selection of essential spares. When **planning your route**, don't forget that at this altitude you won't be able to cover anywhere near the distances per day that you do at home: reckon on about half.

In the UK, the CTC (Cyclists' Touring Club; ☎01483/238 337, ⓦwww.ctc.org.uk), is an excellent source of information for cycle tourists, and has factsheets on a range of subjects including recommended itineraries for touring in Ecuador, Peru and Bolivia.

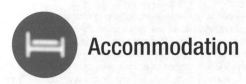

Accommodation

You can get good value for money across the accommodation spectrum in Ecuador: at the high end, you'll find beautiful haciendas, rich in history, which have lost none of their period charm, or the famous international luxury hotel chains. In the mid-range there are hotels as good as any in North America or Europe, but for a fraction of the cost. For travellers on a tight budget, just about every town in Ecuador has a hotel offering clean double rooms, often with a private bathroom, for $5–15 per person.

Supply is such that it's unlikely you'll have any trouble getting a cheap room, though coastal resorts can get very crowded during holidays, and city accommodation tends to fill for major fiestas. Except for the Galápagos Islands, the top jungle lodges and the most popular seaside resorts such as Atacames and Montañita, there's not much of a price difference between **seasons**, but broadly speaking the high season is mid-June to August and December to January, and at beach resorts during national holidays. Choices at the top end are always going to be fewer, so if you're on a higher budget, it's a good idea to phone ahead if you're set on one. **Discounts** are sometimes negotiable out of season too. The more expensive hotels are likely to add **22 percent** onto your bill: 12 percent for the IVA (value-added tax), plus a service charge of 10 percent. We have included the total amount in the price where relevant.

Hotels masquerade under a variety of names in Ecuador; generally, in increasing order of comfort, they are: *pensión*, *residencial*, *hostal*, *hotel* and *hostería*. Beware of anything calling itself a *motel*, which in Ecuador indicates the sort of place that charges guests by the hour. Some *hoteles* are as bad as the worst *pensiones*, however, and there's no substitute for having a good look round the rooms yourself before you sign in. Within any establishment, you'll often find wide variation in the quality of the rooms even though they may be priced the same: for example, you might be suffering in a dank, windowless room while across the corridor is something bright and clean with a balcony and views. You won't necessarily be given the best room available, so if you're not happy, say something.

There are differences between the highlands and lowlands, too. In the highlands, you can hope for **hot water** in all but the cheapest places, but in the lowlands, where people largely consider it unnecessary, only the more exclusive hotels will offer such a luxury. Conversely, **air conditioning** and fans are more common at a cheaper level in the lowlands than in the highlands.

Accommodation price codes

Unless otherwise indicated, **accommodation** in this book is coded according to the categories below, based on the price of a **double room in high season**, including tax and service if appropriate. Seasonal differences, usually found in tourist centres and coastal resorts, when prices can rise or fall by as much as fifty percent, are signalled in the text. In lodgings at the lower end of the scale, **single travellers** usually pay half rate, but more expensive hotels often charge close to or the same as the full double rate.

❶ under $10	❹ $21–25	❼ $51–80
❷ $11–15	❺ $26–35	❽ $81–120
❸ $16–20	❻ $36–50	❾ over $121

Mosquito nets are usually only in evidence on the coast and in jungle lodges; consider bringing one from home if you plan to spend time in remote lowland areas. Across the country in almost all hotels you'll rarely find a bathtub. A shower, sink and lavatory make up the standard bathroom.

Pensiones and residenciales

The humblest type of accommodation is the pensión, usually a simple family home around a small courtyard with a couple of basic rooms and a cold-water shared bathroom. At $10 and under for a double, this is about as cheap as you can go without being in a tent. At these prices *pensiones* tend to be either great value or uninhabitable. In some cases they won't even supply lavatory paper. Residenciales are larger, slightly more comfortable versions of the *pensión*, on the whole offering simple, modestly furnished rooms, often arranged around a courtyard or patio. They usually contain little more than a bed (or up to four single beds), and a bedside table, though some provide more furniture (perhaps a writing desk, chair and lamp), and a few more comforts, such as towels and soap. Most, but not all, have shared bathrooms – not necessarily with hot water (and sometimes it's only on for an hour or two a day), even in the highlands.

Hostales and hoteles

A hostal or hotel can be anything from attractive nineteenth-century family houses with waxed wooden floorboards, floor-to-ceiling windows and courtyards draped with flowers, to the generic, uninspiring hotel block to a fabulous luxury chain hotel. Facilities, on the whole, are better than in a *residencial*, with more likelihood of private bathrooms, hot water, clean towels, soap and, increasingly, cable TV. They'll typically cost anywhere between $10 and $80 for a double. Above around $35 a double, you should really start to notice the difference in comfort. Rooms should be well kept, clean and fresh, have good mattresses, phone, cable TV, air conditioning in the lowlands and all-day hot water powered by a *califón* (water heater) rather than an electric shower

– a terrifying looking contraption bolted on to shower heads with wires dangling around everywhere (touching the pipes can give you a mild shock when it's on). The pricier places often have their own restaurant and bar, and perhaps a laundry service. The best luxury hotels have all you'd expect of such anywhere in the world and charge prices to match.

Haciendas and lodges

Among the accommodation treats of highland Ecuador are the haciendas, grand farming estates of colonial times, converted into magnificent, out-of-the-way hotels. Many are truly luxurious, with all the period details, such as open fires in each room, and augmented by modern comforts and conveniences, including plush carpets and thundering hot-water showers. Some are still working farms, making their own produce and keeping stables and horses both for farm work and for guests. They're sometimes called hosterías, which signifies a large country hotel, but this category also includes the far less charming out-of-town tourist complexes with concrete rooms and a large swimming pool.

Lodges, most normally found in the country's forested regions and often made from natural materials, serve as bases for exploring the surrounding environment. The top-end ones have all the modern comforts allowed by their isolated locations. Most, though, won't have electricity, and some are lodges only in name, perhaps little more than open-sided shelters with raised platforms, mattresses and mosquito nets. Lodges usually consist of a collection of cabañas, simple cabins with thatched roofs and wooden walls and floors. These are also popular on the coast, particularly at beach resorts.

Camping and youth hostels

With so few designated campsites in the country and accommodation being so cheap, not many people bother with camping, unless they're out exploring Ecuador's wildernesses. Generally, you'll be allowed to pitch a tent inside most parks and reserves, where you can sometimes use the facilities of a nearby guard post or refuge, but on the whole you'll have to be entirely self-sufficient. On private land, you should seek permission from the owner, but bear in mind that camping near towns is uncommon and not regarded as particularly safe. A few hotels mentioned in the guide allow you to pitch a tent on their grounds and use their facilities at cheap rates. See the relevant "Listings" sections for individual cities and towns for advice on where to find **camping equipment**. For **stove fuel**, white gas (Coleman fuel) is available at hardware stores, while gas canisters can be bought at

camping outlets in the larger cities. Unleaded petrol/gas is also widely available at filling stations; note that "super" is likely to burn better at altitude.

Ecuador has a handful of **youth hostels** accredited with Hostelling International (HI). They're often quite comfortable, with dorms as well as double rooms. Discounts of a few dollars are available to HI members, but if you're on a budget, there's no great advantage of being one in this country, since many hostels charge around $10–15 per person – substantially more than perfectly adequate non-hostel accommodation.

Food and drink

It's easy to eat well for little in Ecuador, whose three distinct geographical regions produce a startling array of foods, including exotic fruits you'll never have seen before, and three regional styles of cooking.

Despite this variety, there's surprisingly little variation between the standard restaurant menus in these areas, with either fish (usually *trucha* or *corvina*, trout or sea bass), chicken or beef served with rice, chips or *patacones* (fried plantain), topped off with a smidgen of salad. Though the fish or chicken may be fried, boiled or breaded, it's easy to get tired with the overall monotony of the cuisine, meaning you'll want to be on the lookout for the more exciting **comida típica**, the traditional food of each region, cropping up on menus.

Eating out

Ecuador's restaurants range from those charging Western prices for top-class international cuisine to the grimiest roadside diner serving chicken, rice and little else besides. The majority of **restaurants**, however, are clean but modest and offer decent food at low prices. Most of them simply call themselves **restaurantes**, but others you might encounter are **cevicherías** (for *ceviche*), **asaderos** (usually roast chicken),

pizzerías (pizzas), **marisquerías** (seafood), **comedores** (usually for cheap set-meals), **picanterías** (cheap snacks and sometimes spicy food), **parrilladas** (grillhouses) and **paradores** (roadside stophouses). The Chinese restaurant, or **chifa**, is to Ecuador as the curry house is to Britain; *chifas* are found in just about every town in the country, dishing out tasty, inexpensive food to a loyal local following. The typical *chifa* dishes are *chaulafán* (fried rice) and *tallarines* (noodles), both mixed with meat and vegetables and served in large helpings.

Vegetarians are likely to become well acquainted with *pizzerías* and *chifas* for their *tallarines con verduras* (noodles and veg), among the few hot veggie meals available across the country. There's no shortage of vegetarian food in the main tourist centres, but away from those, the cry of "*soy vegeteriano*" or "*vegeteriana*" for a woman ("I'm a vegetarian"), will sometimes be met with offers of fish or chicken. A quick discussion with the staff usually ends with them finding something appropriate for you, even if it's just egg, chips and rice – and even the blandest food can be enlivened by *ají*, the chilli sauce found on most restaurant dining tables, one of the few spicy-hot elements of Ecuadorian cooking.

Many **restaurants** open early in the morning and serve **breakfast** (*desayuno*) in either the *continental* or *americano* varieties, the former being bread (*pan*), butter (*mantequilla*) and jam (*mermelada*), accompanied by coffee (*café*) and juice (*jugo*); add *huevos revueltos* or *fritos* (scrambled or fried eggs) to this and you've got an *americano*. In the Oriente, you'll come across the *petrolero* (oil man), which is all this plus a chunk of meat. Fruit salad, granola and yogurt also make appearances on breakfast tables in tourist centres.

Eating out can be very economical if you stick to **set menus**; at **lunch** this is called *almuerzo* and at **dinner** *merienda*, which consists of two or three courses and a drink for about $1–3. **À la carte** and individual **main courses** (*platos fuertes*) are typically $3–6 – you're probably in a smart place if it's much more than $7. Remember, better places will add twelve percent **tax** (IVA) and ten percent service to your bill.

Markets are among the cheapest sources of food, not only because of the range of nutritious fruits and produce on offer, but also the makeshift restaurants and **stalls** doling out fried meats, potatoes and other snacks. Although some stallholders may not be overly scrupulous on the hygiene front, sizzling-hot food prepared and cooked in front of you should be fine. **Street vendors** also supply **snacks** such as corn-on-the-cob or *salchipapas*, a popular fast food comprising a bag of chips propping up a sausage, all doused in ketchup. Vendors often carry their wares onto buses and parade the aisles to tempt passengers; as you haven't seen how or where these have been prepared, you should probably resist their advances.

Comida típica

In the **highlands**, a typical meal might start off with a *locro*, a delicious **soup** of potato, cheese and corn with half an avocado tossed in for good measure. This is great for vegetarians, who'll want to steer well clear of

its relative, *yaguarlocro*, which swaps the avocado for a sausage of sheep's blood, tripe and giblets. Other soups might be *caldo de patas*, cattle hoof soup; *caldo de gallina*, chicken soup; or even *caldo de manguera*, which literally means "hose pipe soup", a vague euphemism for its pork sausages made from viscera. A number of different grains, such as *morocho*, similar to rice, and *quinoa*, a small circular grain, are also thrown into soups, along with whatever meat and vegetables are available. Other possible **starters**, or snacks in their own right, include *empanadas*, corn pasties filled with vegetables, cheese or meat.

For a **main course** you might go for *llapingachos*, cheesy potato cakes – cheese, corn and potatoes are big in the highlands – often served with *chorizo* (sausage), *lomo* (steak) or *pollo* (chicken) and fried eggs. The famous *cuy*, guinea pig roasted whole, has been for centuries a speciality of the indigenous highlanders, and is rather good, if a bit expensive. Another traditional dish is *seco de chivo*, a stew usually made out of mutton in the highlands, and goat on the coast. The unappetizing-looking *guatita*, tripe smothered in peanut sauce, is actually much better than it sounds.

Mote, a hard corn peeled with calcium carbonate solution and then boiled in salt water, is frequently served as accompaniment to main courses, particularly *fritada*, seasoned pork deep-fried in lard, and *hornado*, pork slow-roasted in the oven. *Motepillo* is a Cuenca speciality, in which the *mote* is mixed with eggs to make corn-filled scrambled eggs. Another common side dish is *tostado*, toasted maize, or *canguil*, popcorn that often comes with soups and *ceviches*.

If you still have space left then there's *morocho de leche*, similar to rice pudding flavoured with cinnamon and often served cold; *quesadillas*, baked cheese doughballs brushed with sweet syrup; *humitas*, ground corn mixed with cheese, sugar, butter and vanilla, wrapped in banana leaves and steamed; or *quimbolitos*, which are similar but more spongy. *Higos con queso*, figs with cheese, is another common highland dessert.

Coastal delicacies, unsurprisingly, centre on **seafood**. The classic *ceviche* is prepared by marinating raw seafood in lime juice and chilli, and serving it with raw onion. It can be dangerous to eat uncooked seafood, so it's worth knowing shrimps (*camarones*) and king prawns (*langostinos*) are usually boiled for ten minutes before they're marinated. If a *cevichería* (*ceviche* restaurant) looks unhygienic, skip it. On the north coast, *encocados* are fantastic fish dishes with a Caribbean flavour, cooked in a sauce of coconut milk, tomato and garlic and often served with a huge mound of rice. Bananas and plantain often replace the potato, appearing in many different forms on the side of your plate. *Patacones* are thick-cut plantains fried up in oil and served with plenty of salt, while *chifles* are thinly cut plantains cooked the same way. *Bolón de verde* is a rather stodgy ball of mashed baked plantain, cheese and coriander traditionally served as a snack with coffee.

The **Oriente** has rather less well-defined specialities, but you can count on *yuca* (a manioc similar to yam) making an appearance, alongside rice, bananas and river fish (including the scrawny piranha). As a guest of a forest community, you may eat game such as wild pig or *guanta*, a large rodent not that different to *cuy*.

Drinks

Ecuador has more types of **fruit** than you can imagine – certainly far more than there are English names for – and just about all of them are made into mouthwatering **juices** (*jugos*). The most common fruit juices are made from *maracuyá* (passion fruit), *tomate de árbol* (tree tomato, also known in the West as tamarillo; it's orange and more fruity than a tomato), *naranjilla* (native to Ecuador, sweet and tart at the same time), *piña* (pineapple), *naranja* (orange), *guanábana* (a very sweet white fruit), *taxo* (another kind of passion fruit), *mora* (blackberry) and *babaco* (indigenous relative of the papaya, juicy and slightly acidic), but there are many others. Juices can come pure (*puro*) or mixed with water (make sure it's purified). When they're mixed with milk they're called *batidos*.

Bottled **fizzy drinks** (*colas* or *gaseosas*) can be obtained all over Ecuador, particularly Coca-Cola, Sprite, Fanta and 7-Up (which is called "*eseven*"). If you want to take your pop away with you, you'll have to pay a deposit on the glass bottle; a more common solution is to get it put *en bolsa*, in a small plastic bag with a straw. Plastic bottles and cans are becoming more common, but they are more expensive. Bottled **mineral water** can be bought throughout the country in still (*sin gas*) or sparkling (*con gas*) varieties. Home brands, such as Güitig from the mineral springs at Machachi, are facing stiff competition against plastic-bottled imports.

Considering Ecuador is a major **coffee** producing country, it's a shame there's not more of the real stuff about. Most cafés and restaurants will have a jar of Nescafé on the table, though a few places have *esencia de café*, a liquid coffee distillate. You'll get a cup of hot milk if you ask for *café con leche*, and hot water for black coffee if you specify *café negro* (sometimes simply called *tinto*). Only well-to-do places are likely to be able to get you a *café pasado* or filter coffee. **Tea** (*té*) is served without milk and usually with a slice of lemon. Asking for *té con leche* is likely to get you a cup of hot milk and a teabag. For just a dash of milk, it's best not to say anything until your (milkless) tea arrives, and then ask for a little milk. **Herbal teas** (*aromáticas* or *mates*) come in a variety of flavours, some of which are familiar, while others are made from native plants.

Apart from the output of a few small micro-breweries in the biggest cities, Ecuadorian **beer** essentially comes in two forms: Pilsener is the people's beer, weak, light and in big bottles; Club is a bit stronger, a bit more expensive and also comes in an export-strength green-bottled variety. South American imports like Brahma are increasingly common, but to sip European and US beers, available in some city bars, you'll have to pay for the privilege. You'll find good Chilean and Argentinian **wine** in the better restaurants for less than you'd pay at home.

The local tipple, especially in the sierra, is **chicha**, a fermented corn drink of which there are many varieties. Buckets – literally – of the stuff do the rounds at all highland fiestas. In the Oriente, the *chicha* is made from *yuca*, which is chewed up, spat in a pot and allowed to ferment. *Aguardiente* (also called *caña* or *punta*) is a sugar-cane **spirit**, sharper than rum (*ron*), that will take off the roof of your mouth. In fiestas they might mix it with fruit juices, or in the sierra drink it as *canelazo*, adding sugar, cinnamon (*canela*) and hot water to make a traditional highland warmer. On the coast it stars in many cocktails, the most ubiquitous being *caipiriña*, in which it (or rum) is combined with lime juice, sugar and ice.

The media

The media in Ecuador is torn between its great cities, with ownership of the main nationals and television stations based in Quito and Guayaquil. Even on the televised nightly news, coverage is split equally between newsdesks based in each city.

Newspapers run the gamut from national broadsheets offering in-depth reporting to tabloids revelling in lurid tittle-tattle. **Television**, on the whole, has a smattering of quality news and documentary programmes, but is dominated by imports, soaps and game shows. Ecuador has many local **radio** stations, which are considered the glue that binds remote communities together.

Newspapers

Ecuador produces several high-quality daily **newspapers**. Leader of the pack is the Quito-based *El Comercio*, a traditional **broadsheet** that has good coverage of home and international news, and comes with supplement sections on sport and business. The more progressive *Hoy*, again from Quito, also enjoys a high standard of writing, particularly in its robust editorials. The Guayaquil broadsheets, *El Universo* and *El Telégrafo*, are solid publications, the latter printing a news summary in English. There are a number of **regional newspapers** too, such as *El Mercurio* in Cuenca, and *La Hora*, with twelve regional editions. Just about all of these major dailies also have their own websites.

The gravity of the broadsheets is counterbalanced by a racy **tabloid** press, the most visible being Guayaquil's *Extra*, available across the country, which manages to plumb the depths of tabloid journalism with an unsavoury mix of sex and violence.

A few **English-language** pocket-sized city guides are published in Quito and have tourist information and the odd article in English and Spanish; these include *The Explorer* and *This is Ecuador* (Ⓦ www.thisisecuador.com). Imported news magazines are usually only found in the tourist centres, where you're also likely to get copies of the *International Herald Tribune* and the overseas edition of the *Miami Herald* newspaper.

Radio

Radio is an important part of community life, particularly in Ecuador's rural regions where **local stations** are used to pass news and messages between villages. There are hundreds of such stations across the country, the majority broadcasting on AM, with a significant minority on shortwave frequencies. **Religious broadcasting** from evangelical Christians is also widespread and can be picked up across the country; the best known station, **HCJB** (Ⓦ www .vozandes.org), features programmes and **news** in English and Spanish. With a shortwave radio, you'll also be able to pick up **BBC World Service** (Ⓦ www.bbc.co.uk /worldservice), **Voice of America** (Ⓦ www .voanews.com) and **Radio Canada International** (Ⓦ www.rcinet.ca).

Television

Ecuador has five main **national television** stations, and several other **regional channels**. Of the nationals, Ecuavisa and Teleamazonas are the most highbrow, with the best news bulletins and the occasional quality imported documentary. At the other end of the spectrum, there's Gamavision, based in Quito, which has a penchant for screening soaps (*telenovelas*), and Telesistema, from Guayaquil, which favours epic-length game shows, over-dubbed US imports and home-grown comedy. Telecentro holds the middle ground with a balance of popular programming interspersed with news and sport.

Cable TV has made big inroads in Ecuador, and even the cheaper hotels are getting it installed. The number of channels you'll get depends on how much the hotel owner has paid in subscription, but you'll almost always have an English-language film channel and a music channel. Only the top-end places are likely to have Direct TV, a satellite setup with dozens of familiar channels in English and Spanish.

Festivals

Ecuador has a long tradition of festivals and fiestas, dating from well before the arrival of the Spanish. Many of the indigenous festivals, celebrating, for example, the movements of the sun and the harvests, became incorporated into the Christian tradition, resulting in a syncretism of Catholic religious imagery and older indigenous beliefs. Most national holidays mark famous events in post-Conquest history and the standard festivals of the Catholic Church.

Whether public holiday or fiesta, Ecuadorians love a party and often go to much trouble and expense to ensure everyone enjoys a great spectacle, lubricated with plenty of food and drink. For most Ecuadorians the big fiestas are community-wide events that define local and national identity. If you get the chance, you should get to a fiesta at some point during your stay; these are among the most memorable and colourful expressions of Ecuadorian culture – not to mention plain good fun.

Carnaval is one of the more boisterous national festivals, culminating in an orgy of water fights before Lent. **Local fiestas** can also be fairly rowdy, and are reasonably frequent with even small places having two or three a year. Most towns and villages have a foundation day or a saint-day festival, and then maybe another for being the capital of the canton (each province is divided into several cantons). Provincial capitals enjoy similar festivals. You can expect anything at these celebrations: music, dance, food, plenty of drink, gaudy parades, beauty pageants, bullfights, marching bands, tournaments and markets. In the remoter highland communities, they can be very local, almost private affairs, yet they'll usually always welcome the odd outsider who stumbles in with a few swigs from the *chicha* bucket. They'll be much more wary of ogling, snap-happy intruders, who help themselves to food and drink – sensitivity is the key.

Public holidays and major festivals

On public holidays just about all shops and facilities are closed all day.

January

New Year's Day (*Año Nuevo*), January 1. Public holiday.
Epiphany (*Reyes Magos*), January 6. Celebrated mainly in the central highlands, most notably at

Píllaro in Tungurahua, but also in Montecristi on the coast.

February/March

Carnival (*Carnaval*). The week before Lent is marked by nationwide high jinks, partying and water-throwing. Beach resorts can get packed to the gills. In Ambato, it's celebrated by the grand Fiesta de las Frutas y las Flores, with parades, dancing, bullfights and sporting events – water-throwing is banned here. Two days' public holiday.

March/April

Holy Week (*Semana Santa*). Religious parades take place across the country during Holy Week, when many shops and services close and lots of people head to the beach. The big processions in Quito are on Good Friday. Public holidays for Maundy Thursday and Good Friday.

May

Labour Day (*Día del Trabajo*), May 1. Public holiday.
Battle of Pichincha (*La Batalla del Pinchincha*), May 24. Public holiday commemorating a famous 1822 battle.

June

Corpus Christi A moveable festival sometime in mid-June, on the first Thursday after Trinity Sunday. Celebrated in the central sierra, particularly Salasaca and Pujilí with *danzates* (masked dancers), wonderful costumes and, in the latter town, 5–10m poles people climb to get prizes at the top.
Festival of the Sun (*Inti Raymi*), June 21 and onwards. A pre-Conquest festival celebrated on the solstice at important ancient sites such as Cochasquí. Also subsumed into the Catholic festivals of San Juan, San Pedro and San Pablo, collectively known as "Los San Juanes" in the Otavalo and Cayambe regions.
San Juan June 24. John the Baptist's saint day, celebrated particularly heartily in the Otavalo region, beginning with ritual bathing in Peguche and ending with *tinku* – ritual fighting – in San Juan on the outskirts of Otavalo (now discouraged). Outsiders should avoid these two activites, but there is plenty of music, drinking and dancing to take part in.
San Pedro and San Pablo June 29. Celebrated across the country, though particularly in Cayambe and the northern sierra.

July

Birthday of Simón Bolívar July 24. Countrywide celebration of the birth of El Libertador. Public holiday.
Foundation of Guayaquil July 25. The festivities here often blur with those of the previous day.

August

Independence Day (*Día de la independencia*) August 10. Public holiday commemorating the nation's first independence (and thwarted) uprising in Quito in 1809.
Fetsival of the Virgin of El Cisne August 15. The effigy of the virgin is paraded 72km from El Cisne to Loja followed by thousands of pilgrims.

September

Yamor Festival A big shindig in Otavalo for the first two weeks of September.
Mama Negra de la Merced September 24. The religious one of two important fiestas in Latacunga, marked with processions and focusing on the Virgen de la Merced.

October

Independence of Guayaquil October 9. Big celebrations in Guayaquil. Public holiday.
Columbus Day (*Día de la Raza*), October 12. Marks the discovery of the New World. Rodeos held in Los Ríos, Guayas and Manabí provinces, an expression of *muntuvio* culture.

November

All Souls' Day/Day of the Dead (*Día de los Difuntos*) November 2. Highland communities go to cemeteries to pay their respects with flowers, offerings of food and drink, and incantations. *Colada morada*, a sweet purple fruit drink, and *guaguas de pan*, bread figures, are eaten and drunk. Public holiday.
Independence of Cuenca November 3. The city's largest celebration, which merges into the preceding holidays. Public holiday.
Mama Negra First Friday or Saturday of November. Famous fiesta in Latacunga with colourful parades and extravagant costumes, centred around the Mama Negra – a blacked-up man in woman's clothing – thought to be related to the town's first encounter with black slaves. Events continue up to November 11 celebrating the Independence of Latacunga.
Festival of the Virgin of El Quinche November 21. Pilgrims celebrate at the famous church outside Quito.

December

Foundation of Quito December 6. Festivities across the capital, with parades, dances, bullfights and sporting events. Public holiday.
Christmas Day (*Navidad*), December 25. Public holiday.
New Year's Eve (*Nochevieja*), December 31. *Años viejos*, large effigies of topical figures representing the old years are burnt at midnight.

Sports and outdoor activities

Having so much untamed wilderness within easy striking distance of major population centres, Ecuador is a superb destination for outdoor enthusiasts. Traditionally it's been a target for climbers, boasting ten volcanoes over 5000m, including the beautifully symmetrical Cotopaxi, and the point furthest from the centre of the Earth, the summit of Chimborazo. Ecuador has been making a name for itself in international rafting and kayaking circles and has a broad range of exciting runs packed into a small area. Hiking, mountain biking, surfing, diving, fishing and horseriding are all also widely available. Birdwatching is one of the biggest draws, with Ecuador's extraordinary biodiversity supporting more than 1600 bird species, almost a fifth of the world's total.

Climbing

Ecuador's "avenue of the volcanoes", formed by the twin range of the Andes running the length of the country, offers numerous **climbing** opportunities, from relatively easy day-trips for strong hill-walkers to challenging technical peaks for experienced climbers. The most popular **snow peaks**, requiring full mountaineering equipment, include **Cotopaxi** (5897m), **Chimborazo** (6268m), **Cayambe** (5790m) and **Iliniza Sur** (5263m). Lower, less demanding climbs, not requiring special equipment and suitable for acclimatizing or simply enjoying them in their own right, include **Guagua Pichincha** (4794m), **Sincholagua** (4893m), **Corazón** (4788m), **Rumiñahui** (4712m), **Imbabura** (4609m) and **Pasochoa** (4200m).

Not all of the higher peaks require previous mountaineering **experience**; many beginners make it up Cotopaxi, for instance, which demands physical fitness, stamina and sheer determination rather than technical expertise. Others, such as **El Altar** (5319m), are technically difficult and should only be attempted by climbers with experience behind them. It's

essential an experienced and utterly dependable **guide**, whose first concern is safety, accompanies climbers with limited mountaineering experience. Ecuador's best-trained mountain guides are those certified by an organization called ASEGUIM (Asociación Ecuatoriana de Guías de Montaña, Pinto E4-385 and J.L. Mera in Quito, ☎02/2234109, ⓦwww.aseguim.org), whose members have to pass exams and take courses spread over a three-year period before receiving the Diploma de Guía. It's always worth paying the extra for an ASEGUIM guide (usually in the region of $120–250 in total per person, per climb depending on length) – even relatively straightforward, non-technical climbs carry an inherent risk, and your life may depend on your guide. More experienced climbers should also seriously consider ascending with a guide, whose intimate knowledge of the route options, weather patterns, avalanche risks, glaciers and crevasses can make all the difference to the safety and success of an expedition, especially when the rapid melting of the glaciers is changing routes and climbing conditions at a pace. For

Ecuador's ten highest peaks			
Chimborazo	6268m	Iliniza Sur	5248m
Cotopaxi	5897m	Sangay	5230m
Cayambe	5790m	Iliniza Norte	5126m
Antisana	5758m	Tungurahua	5023m
El Altar	5320m	Carihuairazo	5020m

a list of recommended guides, see p.116 and p.216.

Practical considerations

December and January are generally regarded as the **best months** to climb, followed by the dry summer months of June to August. March, April and May are considered the worst months, but because of the topography and microclimates of the land, several mountains, such as Cotopaxi, are more or less climbable throughout the year. The **weather** is highly changeable, as are snow and glacier conditions. Unlike their alpine counterparts, Ecuadorian **glaciers** do not follow normal patterns of ablation and accumulation in summer and winter months respectively. Instead, glacier conditions can change from day to day, meaning the technical difficulty is also constantly changing; all the more reason to employ a properly trained guide who knows the mountain and its variable conditions well.

All your **equipment** will be provided by the guiding company if you're going with one, or can be **rented** from the listed companies or from specialist mountaineering outlets in Quito if you're not (see p.118). If you have your own plastic mountaineering boots, it's recommended you bring them with you; they will invariably be in better condition than most of the boots otherwise available. Check the equipment over very carefully before deciding which company to sign up with. Guides also provide all **food** on the climb, but you should take your own chocolate and nibbles to keep your energy levels up, as well as your own water bottle. **Accommodation** is usually in mountain refuges, which serve as the starting point of the climbs. You will typically only get three or four hours' sleep before a big climb, as it's common to set off around midnight or 1am to arrive at the summit around dawn, and descend before the sun starts to melt the snow.

One point that cannot be stressed forcefully enough is the **importance of acclimatizing** before attempting the higher peaks. This should involve spending a few days at the altitude of Quito (2800m), taking in a combination of rest and moderate exercise, followed by at least four or five days around 3500–3800m, interspersed with day-walks up some lower peaks. If you ignore this warning and try to shoot up Cotopaxi after a couple of days' hill-climbing around Quito, you may well find yourself vomiting every half-hour or so as you try to ascend, or simply too dizzy and nauseous to leave the refuge. See p.32 for more on the risks of **altitude sickness**. A couple of good bases for acclimatizing include the walker's refuge at La Urbina (3620m; see p.221) near Riobamba, hotels in and around Cotopaxi National Park (see p.178), and the tiny village of Salinas (3500m; see p.211), near Guaranda.

Several popular, though potentially hazardous, climbs are on **active volcanoes** – particularly Guagua Pichincha, Reventador, Sangay, Cotopaxi and Tungurahua – and you should be fully aware of the current situation before you ascend. You can check the latest volcanic activity news on the Instituto Geofísico website ⓦwww.igepn .edu.ec, or contact the SAE (see p.77) for up-to-date climbing conditions.

Hiking

Ecuador's great wilderness areas and striking landscapes offer fantastic opportunities for **hiking**, though a general absence of well-marked trails and decent trekking maps does mean a little effort is required to tap into the potential.

The widest choice of hikes is found in the sierra, where numerous trails lead into the mountains and up to the páramo, providing access to stunning views and exhilarating, wide-open spaces. The country's best-known long-distance hike is in the southern sierra: the **Inca Trail to Ingapirca** (see p.234), a three-day hike ending up at Ecuador's most important Inca ruins. Also down in the south, **Parque Nacional Cajas** (see p.248) provides some of the best hiking in the country, in a landscape strongly reminiscent of the Scottish highlands, while **Parque Nacional Podocarpus** offers a fabulous two-day hike across the páramo to the Lagunas del Compadre (see p.263).

Elsewhere in the sierra, rewarding possibilities include day-hikes in the area around **Laguna Quilotoa** (see p.191), and a wonderful two-day hike to El Placer hot springs in **Parque Nacional Sangay** (see p.224). There are fewer options for hiking in the **Oriente**, owing to dense forest cover; one notable exception is the two- to four-day **Reventador** trail, described on p.287, but hikes descending from highlands to lowlands, such as the one from **Oyacachi to El Chaco** (see p.135), are good for revealing Ecuador's various habitats and landscapes. **Cotopaxi** (see p.178) and **Machalilla** (see p.431) national parks also present good hiking possibilities, as do many areas of open country throughout the highlands. These suggestions are far from exhaustive, but provide a starting point for ideas should you want to plan your trip around a few hikes.

Hiking equipment

If you're thinking of going long-distance hiking without a guide, you should be competent at route finding and map reading, and equip yourself with the necessary IGM **topographical maps** (1:50,000 is the most useful scale) before you leave Quito (see p.61). You will also need a **compass** (GPS is also useful) and – for multi-day hikes – a waterproof **tent**, a warm **sleeping bag** (which needs to be good for –5°C in the sierra), a reliable **stove**, **candles** and waterproof **matches**. Other **equipment** essential for hiking in the sierra – whether you're on a day-hike or long-distance hike, and with or without a guide – includes: strong, water-resistant hiking boots; thermal underwear; warm layers such as a fleece or down jacket; waterproof jacket, trousers and gaiters; hat and gloves; water purification tablets; sunglasses; sun screen; spare boot laces; and medical kit. You might also consider taking **wellington boots** – widely available at market stalls in most towns – for wading through the deep mud that commonly blights mountain paths after rainfall. As a general rule, weather conditions in the sierra are driest from June to September and wettest from February to April.

Guided hikes

One way of getting around logistical diffi-culties is by **hiring a guide**, usually through a local tour operator. This solves the problem of arranging transport to the trailhead, and means there's far less danger of getting lost. A good guide can also enhance your enjoyment of the hike by sharing his or her knowledge of local flora and fauna with you, or of the history, legends and customs associated with the places you're hiking through. On the downside, if you're lumbered with a guide you don't get on with, or who wants to walk at a different pace from your own, this can really sour the whole experience. When booking a tour, it's always a good idea to ask to meet the person who will be guiding you before parting with your money, and it's essential to make clear what level of difficulty you're willing to tackle, and what pace you want to go at.

Typical **rates** for guided hikes are $20–40 per person per day, often with a minimum of three to four people per group. A selection of Quito companies offering this service is given on p.116, while provincial guides and tour operators are detailed throughout the Guide.

Rafting and kayaking

Whitewater rafting combines the thrill of riding rapids with the chance to reach some spectacular landscapes that otherwise can't be visited.

A small number of whitewater rafting and **kayaking** companies, mainly based in Quito, Tena and Baños, organize trips to dozens of rivers. Not far from Quito, on the way to Santo Domingo, the **ríos Blanco** and **Toachi** offer a selection of popular runs suitable for beginners and old hands alike. A high density of rivers around **Tena** has brought the town to the fore as a centre for the sport in Ecuador. Among the most popular is the **Upper Napo (Jatunyacu)**, a typical beginner's run, while the nearby **Río Misahuallí** is suitable for more advanced paddlers, weaving through a stunning canyon in a remote section of rainforest, described as the best rafting trip in the country. Other options from Tena include the **Río Hollín**, **Río Anzu**, and the **Río Quijos** and tributaries, all of which offer a range of possibilities. In the southern Oriente, the **Río Upano** is one of the most talked-about runs, involving a trip of several days with the spectacular Namangosa Gorge on the itinerary.

The rafts are heavy-duty inflatable dinghies that take six to eight people plus a guide. Rapids are categorized according to a **grading system**: beginners can happily handle waters of Class II and III rating, which usually involve substantial sections of quiet paddling between rougher and more exciting rapids; Class V runs are very difficult, sometimes dangerous, and can be terrifying for the non-expert.

Safety is the prime consideration before you choose to go whitewater rafting or kayaking. Rainfall can have a dramatic effect on a river, and an easy Class II in the dry months can turn into a swollen torrent too dangerous to run in the rainy season. A good rafting company will be on top of the situation and will not attempt to run unsafe water. A few shoddy outfits with untrained guides and inappropriate equipment do exist; only go rafting with a reputable company, those that have fully trained guides who know first aid, can supply good-quality life jackets and helmets and employ a safety kayak to accompany the raft on the run. For rafting companies operating out of Tena, see p.309; for runs around Quito, try Yacu Amu rafting (see box, p.117). Rafting companies in Baños are not as highly regarded as those listed in Tena and Quito. General **information** on river conditions and paddle sports in Ecuador can be obtained from the Ecuadorian Rivers Institute (ERI), based in Tena (☎06/2887438, ⓦwww .kayakecuador.com).

Birdwatching

With roughly as many species as North America and Europe combined crammed into a country smaller than Nevada, Ecuador arguably has the **best birding in the world**. There are hundreds of endemic species, and even some recent discoveries, such as the Jocotoco Antpitta found near Vilcabamba in 1997. The greatest **diversity** is in the transition zone habitats and montane forests, most famously on the **western flank** of the Andes, which forms part of the Chocó bioregion. The village of **Mindo**, west of Quito, is internationally recognized as an Important Bird Area, and there are several fine private reserves in

the northwestern forests renowned for their birdlife (see Chapter 6).

On the **eastern slopes of the Andes** (covered in Chapters 4 and 5) the Cosanga and Baeza areas are recommended, and, in the south, Podocarpus national park and the areas around Loja, Zamora and Vilcabamba. The most convenient way to watch birds in the **Oriente** is at one of the lodges, where ornithologist guides and bird lists, some recording well over 500 species, are provided. There are four main groupings of jungle lodges, each with slightly different species lists: the Cuyabeno area; around Misahuallí and Tena on the upper Río Napo or in Sumaco-Galeras reserve; on the lower Río Napo; and in Pastaza and the Southern Oriente. The best **highland and páramo** habitats are usually found in the national parks, for example El Ángel and Cajas, and the highland sections of Cotacachi-Cayapas and Cayambe-Coca reserves. On the **coast**, Parque Nacional Machalilla and Cerro Blanco hold interesting areas of dry forest, while the saltpans on the Santa Elena peninsula attract hundreds of sea and shore birds.

It's always worth getting a local **guide** to go birdwatching with you. They tend to know where to look and have a knack for picking out birds amid the undergrowth and greenery. Most of the better lodges and private reserves will have in-house guides, often trained ornithologists, or be able to get hold of one for you. For recommended field guides, see p.536.

Mountain biking

Mountain biking is more widespread in the sierra than in the lowlands, and rental companies in the main tourist centres can offer fairly cheap rates per day or half day; always check the bike's in good working order before you leave. Several specialist biking operators, mainly based in Quito (see p.114), also arrange single- or multi-day mountain-biking tours of diverse parts of the sierra, such as Cotopaxi National Park, the Papallacta area, or the Otavalo region, with both cross-country and downhill routes available. Being at altitude some trips can be hard work, but a reasonable level of fitness is generally all that's required. The better operators will be able to provide helmets. For general information on cycle touring see p.38.

Horseriding

Ecuador's sierra region offers numerous opportunities for **horseriding**, particularly at the many haciendas that have been converted into country inns, where riding has been a way of life for centuries. Riding up to the region's sweeping páramos framed by snowcapped volcanoes is undoubtedly a memorable experience, especially if you get an early start to catch the clear morning light and avoid the characteristic afternoon highland showers. Ecuadorian **horses** are very tough, capable of climbing steep slopes and trotting and cantering at high altitudes.

Most haciendas and reputable tour companies provide healthy, well-looked-after horses, but it's not unusual for cheaper outfits to take tourists out on neglected, overworked animals. If you sign up to a riding tour and your horse looks lame or ill, refuse to ride it and ask for another one. Check that the saddle is securely fitted, with the girth pulled tight, and take time to adjust your stirrups to the right length – they should be level with your ankles if you let your legs hang freely. Ecuadorian riding outfits hardly ever provide protective hats.

Two highly recommended dedicated **riding operators** are: the German-run Green Horse Ranch, north of Quito (☎08/6125433, ⓦwww.horseranch.de), which offers one- to nine-day rides throughout the sierra; and the excellent Ride Andes (ⓦwww.rideandes .com), run by a British woman who organizes riding holidays throughout Ecuador. Other outfits and guides are detailed throughout the text, including: *Hacienda Guachalá* (see p.132); *Hacienda Cusín*, *Hacienda Pinsaquí* and *Hacienda Zuleta* (see p.140); *Hacienda Yanahurco* and *La Ciénega* (see p.181).

Diving and snorkelling

Ecuador's top **scuba-diving** spots are in the Galápagos (see p.454), where there are good chances to see large sea fish as well as spectacular endemic reef fish. Most people arrange diving tours before arrival, but there are several operators on the islands who can arrange trips for you there and then. The Galápagos is not the easiest place for novices to learn to dive – mainly due to strong currents and cold temperatures – but it is possible. **Snorkelling** is likely to be an important part of a Galápagos cruise: bring your own gear if you have it; even though most boats can provide it, there may not be enough to go around and what there is may not fit. A **wet suit** is recommended between July and December. On the mainland, there's not a lot of scuba or snorkelling, apart from tours arranged in Puerto López (see p.430) for dives around the Isla de la Plata.

Surfing

There are at least 40 **surfing** spots on the Ecuadorian coast with the greatest concentration in Manabí and Guayas provinces between Playas and Manta. Laid-back Montañita in Guayas province has the reputation of being the leading surf centre, though quieter Canoa, and Mompiche to the north, also have a loyal, less hippy-ish following. There are some keen surfers on the Galápagos Islands, particularly at Puerto Baquerizo Moreno on San Cristóbal island. In all these locations, you'll be able to find places to hire a board and get a lesson. The surf **season** is at its height from December to March, when the waves are usually at their fiercest and the water at its warmest.

Paragliding

Paragliding, also known as parapenting, is free flight using a fabric "wing", which resembles a parachute, under which the pilot is suspended by a harness. It is a sport that has had a following in **Quito** (try the Escuela Pichincha de Vuelo Libre at Carlos Endara Oe3-60 and Amazonas; ☎02/2256592) and **Crucita** (see p.378) on the coast for some time, but which is now spreading to other highland towns, such as **Ibarra** (namely, FlyEcuador; see p.157), particularly places where there are good cliffs and ledges nearby to launch off. A few agencies offer tandem flights for beginners and courses for anyone interested in taking it further.

Fishing

Fishing (*pesca deportiva*) for trout (*trucha*) in the lakes of the sierra is quite a widespread local hobby. A couple of the national reserves are well-known fishing spots, namely El Ángel in the north and Cajas in the south (permits may be required). Few tours to the **Oriente** forgo the chance of fishing for what is reputedly the world's most ferocious fish, the piranha (*piraña*), with nothing more sophisticated than a line, hook and bait. Take care when de-hooking Oriente fish: some have poisonous spines discreetly tucked into their fins. **Deep-sea fishing**, a sport for the coast's wealthier people, is less widespread, with Salinas and Manta the main centres for hooking fish including marlin, tuna and dorado.

National parks and protected areas

Almost nineteen percent of Ecuador's territory is protected within 40 national parks, reserves, refuges and recreation areas, including 97 percent of the Galápagos Islands plus an ample marine reserve surrounding them. Encompassing mangrove swamps, dry and wet tropical coastal forests, cloud and montane forests, tropical rainforests, páramo and volcanoes, the protected areas represent a cross section of the country's most outstanding natural landscapes and habitats.

Some are so important they have earned international recognition – such as Sangay, a World Natural Heritage Site; Yasuní, a World Biosphere Reserve; and the Galápagos Islands, which are both. The principal aim of the **Ministerio del Ambiente**, which ultimately manages them, is to protect native flora and fauna from ever-increasing external pressures; few protected areas have the resources beyond this to invest in tourist facilities. Some parks might have a rudimentary refuge and a few trails, but for the most part these are pure wildernesses – areas that are primarily protected by virtue of their remoteness and inaccessibility – and exploring them is only possible with a guide and camping equipment or the logistical help of a tour operator.

Visiting national parks

No **permit** is needed to visit Ecuador's national parks; you simply turn up and pay your **entrance fee** if there's a warden (*guardaparque*) at the guard post (*guardería*) to collect it. Entrance to protected areas usually either costs $10 or $5, roughly according to their popularity, except for Cuyabeno ($20), Pasochoa ($7), Machalilla ($12–20), and the Galápagos Islands ($100). Nationals and residents pay substantially reduced rates in all cases.

Ease of **access** differs wildly from one park to the next, but most are reached via rough, bumpy dirt roads, and getting there often involves renting a vehicle or booking transport through a local tour company.

The *guardaparques* are the best people to speak to if you want **information**; they can also put you in touch with a good local guide, if not offer their own services. Alternatively, try the Ministerio del Ambiente office in the nearest town, which should have small leaflets (*trípticos*) about the park and basic maps. Finally, there's the head office in Quito (on the 8th floor of the Ministerio de Agricultura y Ganadería building on avenidas Amazonas and Eloy Alfaro; ☏02/2563429, ⓦwww.ambiente.gov.ec), which keeps information on all the parks and runs a library, though it can take time to track down what you want there.

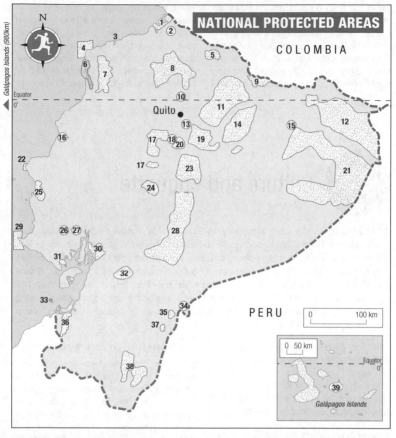

NATIONAL PROTECTED AREAS

COLOMBIA

Galápagos Islands (980km)

Equator
0°

Quito

PERU

0   100 km

0   50 km

Equator
0°

Galápagos Islands

NATIONAL PROTECTED AREAS

1. Cayapas–Mataje	**9.** Cofán Bermejo	**17.** Ilinizas	**25.** Machalilla	**33.** Isla Santa Clara
2. La Chiquita	**10.** Pululahua	**18.** El Boliche	**26.** Parque Lago	**34.** El Cóndor
3. Estuario Río Esmeraldas	**11.** Cayambe–Coca	**19.** Antisana	**27.** El Salado	**35.** El Quimi
4. Galera–San Francisco	**12.** Cuyabeno	**20.** Cotopaxi	**28.** Sangay	**36.** Arenillas
5. El Ángel	**13.** Pasochoa	**21.** Yasuní	**29.** Puntilla Santa Elena	**37.** El Zarza
6. Estuario Río Muisne	**14.** Sumaco Napo–Galeras	**22.** Pacoche	**30.** Churute	**38.** Podocarpus
7. Mache–Chindul	**15.** Limoncocha	**23.** Llanganates	**31.** El Morro	**39.** Galápagos
8. Cotacachi–Cayapas	**16.** Isla Corazón	**24.** Chimborazo	**32.** Cajas	

Few parks have provision for **accommodation**. Wardens are happy to let you **camp**, but there's rarely a designated camping area or camping facilities. Some reserves have a basic **refuge** (*refugio*); most of the volcanoes popular with climbers have these within a day's climb of the summit, usually a hut with a couple of rooms full of bunks, some simple cooking facilities and running water. They cost $5–20 a night and you should bring your own sleeping bag.

Private reserves

There is also a growing number of smaller **private reserves**, which have been set up for conservation, scientific research or ecotourism projects and managed by philanthropists, environmentalists or ecological foundations. Generally, these places are much better geared to receiving tourists than the national parks and many have a purpose-built **lodge** or accommodation within the main research station. They will often also have clear trails, equipment to borrow (rubber boots, binoculars), guides and information, such as bird lists. Yet all this convenience comes at a price – anything from $20 to over $100 a night, including meals, unless you're a volunteer, but it's well worth the extra cash for the chance to experience some of the most exciting ecosystems on the planet. The most obvious examples are the cloudforest reserves of northwestern Ecuador (see "Northern Lowlands" in Chapter 6) and the jungle lodges in the Oriente (see Chapter 5).

Culture and etiquette

A little politeness goes a long way in Ecuador, by nature a conservative and generally good-mannered country. An exchange of greetings is *de rigueur* before conversation, no matter how short or banal the subject; say *buenos días* before noon, *buenas tardes* in the afternoon, and *buenas noches* after nightfall. Shake hands with people you meet, and if it's for the first time, say *mucho gusto* ("pleased to meet you"); it's quite normal to shake hands again when saying goodbye. A more familiar greeting between women or between a man and a woman is a peck on the cheek.

Say *buen provecho* ("enjoy your meal") to your companions before a meal (not before your host if being cooked for), or to fellow diners when entering or leaving a restaurant, and use *con permiso* ("with permission") if squeezing past someone in a crowd.

Clothing and appearance

A dapper appearance, smart unrumpled clothes, brushed hair and polished shoes are unlikely to be achievable for most travellers, but are pretty well obligatory in business circles. Neatness in **dress** will always earn respect, particularly in the highlands, where sartorial norms are more formal than on the coast. Men should remove hats or caps indoors and short trousers or skirts shouldn't be worn inside churches (shorts for men on the coast are more forgivable), where scruffiness of any sort will be frowned on. Skimpy dress for women will probably draw unwanted attention (see p.65 for more), while topless or nude bathing on beaches is out of the question.

Dealing with bureaucracy

Politeness and tidy dress are particularly important when dealing with police or officials. Ecuadorian **bureaucracy** can be frustrating, but it's vital to maintain good humour; losing your temper will quickly turn people against you.

It's in this area you're most likely to encounter the darker side of Ecuadorian culture – **bribery**. While corruption is widely condemned, low-level graft is routinely practised, with minor officials sometimes asking for "a little something for a cola" (as the cliché goes) in return for a favour or to speed up paperwork. It's an art best left to locals; if you need a special favour, ask an Ecuadorian friend for advice on how to proceed and leave the negotiating up to them if possible. Never openly offer a bribe to anyone or you could end up in serious trouble.

Tipping

In smarter places, ten percent service charge will automatically be added to your bill; tipping above this is only warranted for exceptional service. Cheaper restaurants will not usually expect you to leave a tip, although it's very welcome if you do. Airport and hotel porters should be tipped, as should the people who watch your car for you if you've parked in a street. Taxi drivers don't normally get a tip, but will often round up the fare. Guides are tipped depending on the length of your stay or trip, from a couple of dollars to over ten. Tour crews in the Galápagos also receive tips (see p.451).

Toilets

In **toilets**, the bin by your feet is for your toilet paper – the plumbing can't cope with it being flushed. Public toilets are most common at bus terminals, where you'll see them signposted as *baños* or *SS HH* (the abbreviation for *servicios higiénicos*); women are *damas* or *mujeres* and men *caballeros* or *hombres*. Often there's an attendant who sells toilet paper at the door. It's a good idea to carry some paper (*papel higiénico*) with you, wherever you are.

A few other reminders

If arranging to meet someone or inviting someone out, remember **punctuality** obeys the laws of *la hora ecuatoriana* ("Ecuadorian time"), meaning Ecuadorians will usually arrive late, up to an hour being well within the bounds of politeness. The person making an invitation is usually expected to pay for everything, especially if it's a man entertaining a woman.

Pointing at people (not objects) with your finger is impolite; use your whole hand or chin instead. Beckon people towards you by pointing your hand downwards and towards you, not the other way round.

For more information on cultural questions, gay and lesbian travellers, see p.60; travelling with children, see p.65; tipping, see p.54; women travellers, see p.65.

Living in Ecuador

There's plenty of scope for spending fruitful time in Ecuador other than travelling. A huge number of possibilities exist for prospective volunteers, with a growing number of foundations and NGOs seeking outside help to keep running. Ecuador is also one of the top choices on the continent for learning Spanish. It's easy to enrol, lessons are good value and the language spoken in the sierra is clear and crisp.

Volunteering

Many opportunities exist for **volunteers**, though most require you to pay your own way for food and accommodation and to stay for at least a month, with a donation of around $250–450 going towards food and lodging. Reasonable Spanish skills will usually be needed for any kind of volunteer work with communities, and a background in science for research work.

Someone without these skills should still be able to find places with no trouble, especially in areas of conservation work demanding a degree of hard toil, such as reforestation or trail clearing in a reserve. In fact, short-term, unskilled volunteering has evolved into a kind of tourism in its own right in Ecuador, so-called "**voluntourism**". You can arrange to volunteer either from home – probably better for more formal, long-term posts – or on arrival in Ecuador, which is simpler and more convenient. The SAE in Quito (see p.77) keeps files on dozens of organizations looking for volunteers. We've listed below a few popular ones based in Ecuador, plus useful organizations abroad. If the **main purpose** of your trip is volunteering, you will need to have the appropriate **visa** before you go (see p.59); those planning to work with children should allow enough time for Ecuadorian authorities to carry out checks before travel.

Volunteer contacts in Ecuador

AmaZOOnico ☎09/9800463, ⓦwww .amazoonico.org. Volunteers needed to help tend to rescued forest animals and show guests around a jungle rehabilitation centre on a tributary of the Río Napo (see p.321). Best to book 6 months in advance.

Bospas Fruit Forest Farm El Limonal, Imbabura ☎06/2648692, ⓦwww.bospas.org. Welcomes interns to this organic, family farm in northwestern Ecuador (see p.161) to learn about sustainable farming, including planting, grafting and harvesting, to clear and maintain trails and occasionally to show visitors around.

Bosque Nublado Santa Lucía ☎02/2157242, ⓦwww.santaluciaecuador.com. Based in the cloudforests of northwestern Ecuador (see p.339), this organization seeks to protect community-owned cloudforest, establish sustainable sources of income and educate local people. Volunteers required to help with agroforestry, trail clearing, teaching local guides English and many other worthwhile projects.

Centro de Investigaciones de los Bosques Tropicales (CIBT) ☎08/4600274, ⓦwww .reservaloscedros.org. This organization manages the beautiful and remote Los Cedros reserve (see p.339) and needs volunteers to ensure its survival. Expect to work on reforestation, trail maintenance and general upkeep of facilities.

Centro de la Niña Trabajadora (CENIT) Huacho 150 and José Peralta, Quito ☎02/2654260, ⓦwww.cenitecuador.org. Helping children and families, especially working girls and women, overcome extreme poverty in Quito. Volunteers help in primary and high schools, a medical centre, production workshop or with outreach projects.

Colibrís Women's Artisan Cooperative ☎02/2157357, ⓦwww.colibrisecuador.org. Women artisans from the Marianitas community in the cloudforests northwest of Quito require help with arts and crafts design, production and sales, organic gardening, reforestation and English and environmental education.

Ecuador Volunteer Yánez Pinzón N25-106 and Colón, Quito ☎02/2557749, ⓦwww .ecuadorvolunteer.com. Can find you placements in social, community, ecological and educational projects throughout Ecuador.

Fundación Ecológica Arcoiris Segundo Cueva Celi 03-15 and Clodoveo Carrión, Loja ☎02/2572926, ⓦwww.arcoiris.org.ec. Based in Loja and most concerned with conservation and community projects in southern Ecuador.

Fundación Jatún Sacha Eugenio de Santillán N34-248 and Maurian, Quito ☎02/2432240, ⓦwww.jatunsacha.org. The foundation manages seven biological stations or reserves around the country, in the Oriente, highlands, coastal interior and the Galápagos, which require volunteers for conservation, education, maintenance, research and sustainable agriculture projects.

Fundación Maquipucuna Baquerizo E9-153 and Tamayo, Quito ☎02/2507200, ⓦwww.maqui .org. Researchers and volunteers are welcome at this reserve in the western flank cloudforests (see p.338), for work on conservation, maintenance, agriculture or education projects.

Fundación Sobrevivencia Cofán Mariano Cardenal N74-153 and Joaquín Mancheno, Carcelén Alto, Quito ☎02/2470946, ⓦwww.cofan .org. Volunteers needed at Cofán communities on the Río Aguarico deep in the Oriente for help on a number of ongoing projects.

FUNEDESIN Vicente Solano E12-61 and Av Oriental, Quito ☎02/2523777, ⓦwww.funedesin .org. Operates *Yachana Lodge* (see p.321) and works with Oriente communities to develop medical care, ecotourism, sustainable agriculture and education programmes, all with a view to conserving the rainforest. Needs volunteers for such projects, reforestation and trail maintenance, and professionals for the medical clinic and Yachana Technical High School.

Río Muchacho Organic Farm Guacamayo Tours, Bolívar 902 and Arenas, Bahía de Caráquez ☎05/2691107, ⓦwww.riomuchacho.com. Volunteers are needed to work on this ecological farm near the coast in Manabí province for reforestation, education in the local school and agriculture (see p.372).

In North America

AFS Intercultural Programs ⓦwww.afs.org. Runs summer programmes in Ecuador aimed at fostering international understanding for teenagers.

Earthwatch Institute ⓦwww.earthwatch.org. International non-profit organization with projects in Ecuador requiring volunteers to work in the field with research scientists.

Volunteers for Peace ⓦwww.vfp.org. Non-profit organization with links to "workcamps" in Ecuador, two- to four-week programmes that bring volunteers together from many countries to carry out needed community projects.

World Learning ⓦwww.worldlearning.org. World Learning's School for International Training runs accredited college semesters abroad, comprising language and cultural studies, homestays and other academic work in Ecuador. Its "Experiment in International Living" section offers summer programmes in Ecuador for high-school students.

Worldteach ⓦ www.worldteach.org. A non-profit organization placing volunteers as teachers in impoverished communities throughout the world. The Ecuador programme consists of about 75 volunteers a year who teach English, mostly at the university or mature student level.

In the UK and Ireland

Earthwatch Institute ⓦ www.earthwatch.org. See opposite.
i to i International Projects ⓦ www.i-to-i.com. TEFL training provider operating voluntary teaching, conservation, reforestation, health internships and work with children in Ecuador.
Rainforest Concern ⓦ www.rainforestconcern .org. British charity seeking to protect endangered rainforests with a particular focus on Latin America and Ecuador. It has many contacts here and elsewhere who urgently need volunteers.
Year Out Group ⓦ www.yearoutgroup.org. Full of useful information for students thinking of taking a gap year.

In Australia and New Zealand

AFS Intercultural Programs ⓦ www.afs.org.au, ⓦ www.afsnzl.org.nz. Runs summer programmes aimed at fostering international understanding for teenagers and adults.
Earthwatch Institute ⓦ www.earthwatch.org. As opposite.

Language schools

One-to-one **Spanish lessons** arranged in Ecuador cost around $5 an hour, offering tremendous value for money to prospective learners. Most language schools are based in Quito (see box, p.74), with a few others in Cuenca and the main tourist centres. You'll normally have lessons for the morning or afternoon (or both if you have the stamina), and there are often social activities arranged in the evenings and at weekends. To immerse yourself totally in the language,

homestays arranged through language schools are a good idea, sometimes costing as little as $10 a day for accommodation and meals. You can arrange Spanish courses in Ecuador from home, but it's unlikely to be as cheap as doing it when you get there. For arranging lessons and stays in advance, try **Amerispan** (ⓦ www.amerispan .com) or **CESA Languages Abroad** (ⓦ www .cesalanguages.com).

More adventurous linguists could also have a stab at learning an indigenous language, such as **Quichua**, which a few schools offer on the side. The reaction you'll get from native speakers, even with some elementary knowledge, is well worth the effort.

Work

Unless you have something arranged in advance with an international company or organization, you're unlikely to find much paid work in Ecuador. Being an English speaker, the only type of job you can expect to get with relative ease is as an **English-language teacher**, especially in Quito or Guayaquil. It's usually stipulated that English should be your native tongue for these posts, but completely fluent non-native speakers shouldn't have much difficulty. Don't expect to be paid very much, unless you have a TEFL (Teaching English as a Foreign Language) or similar qualification, which will give you greater bargaining power. You'll have to have a work visa, which can be expensive to get – enough to put most people off in the first place. If you have any training in ecology, biology, ornithology and the like, you could try to hunt around the jungle lodge operators asking if they need a **guide**. Fluent English speakers with such qualifications are often in demand.

Travel essentials

Costs

Although prices have risen since dollarization, those on a tight budget should be able to get by on about $15–20 (£10–14) per day, with the occasional treat. Spending $30–40 (£20–£27) daily will get you accommodation in more comfortable hotels, better food and the occasional guided tour. Those paying over $120 (£80) a day (travelling independently) are likely to find themselves in the country's best hotels and restaurants.

The most widespread **hidden cost** in Ecuador is **IVA** (*Impuesto al Valor Agregado*), a tax of twelve percent added to most goods and services. In lower-end restaurants and hotels it's taken for granted that IVA is included in the quoted price. Other places will add it to the end of the bill, often in tandem with a further ten percent service charge, making the final total 22 percent more than you might have bargained for. Car rental is almost always quoted without IVA. If in doubt, always clarify whether prices for anything from souvenirs to room rates include IVA.

Another unexpected cost is the **$40.80 airport departure tax**, payable in cash when you fly out of the country from Quito; at the time of writing, this was $27.17 if leaving from Guayaquil.

Crime and personal safety

Ecuador's reputation for being one of the safer Latin American countries has in recent years been tested by rising crime levels. Still, there's no need to be paranoid if you take sensible precautions.

Pickpockets and **thieves** favour crowded places, typically bus stations, markets, city centres, public transport, crowded beaches, fiestas and anywhere lots of people congregate to give them cover. When out and about, carry as little of value as you possibly can, and be **discreet** with what you have. Secret pockets or money belts are useful, but don't reveal hiding places in public. Split up your reserves in different places, making it less likely that you'll lose everything in one go.

On buses, keep close watch on your **bags**; don't put them under your seat or in overhead storage. The same goes for in restaurants – wrap the bag straps around your chair or leg. Be wary of people approaching you in the street, no matter how polite or smartly dressed. It's a common trick to use **distraction** to take your mind of your belongings; spilling something messy on you is a perennial favourite. Take care when withdrawing money from **ATMs**; you are particularly vulnerable from both robbers and card scammers if using machines on the street. Use machines inside banks and buildings where possible, during business hours.

Travelling at night, whether in your own vehicle or on public transport, is a bad idea whatever part of the country you're in. This is especially true in Guayas and southern Ecuador, where hold-ups have been an ongoing problem, as well as Esmeraldas province and the border regions with Colombia. In the big cities, especially Quito, **always take a taxi at night** rather than wandering the streets; it's safest to call a registered taxi through your hotel rather than hail one in the street.

Armed robbery is a problem throughout the country, and is on the rise in the Mariscal hotel district in Quito. Other danger spots are parts of the old town, the walk up to El Panecillo (always take a cab), Rucu Pichincha and Cruz Loma volcanoes (*not* including the TelefériQo complex itself), parques El Ejido and La Carolina. Security in Guayaquil is improving, but nevertheless you should be extra vigilant in the downtown areas, the dock and the airport.

Never accept food, drinks, cigarettes or other objects from people you don't know well, to minimize the risk of **drugging**. Chemicals have even been suffused into leaflets and paper, which when handled make victims compliant.

Border areas and crossings are always places to be extra vigilant. **Drug smuggling** and Colombian **guerrilla activity** along the northern border have made certain (remote) parts of Sucumbíos (capital Lago Agrio), Carchi (capital Tulcán) and Esmeraldas (capital Esmeraldas) provinces unsafe. San Lorenzo in the north has a problem with gun crime and "express kidnappings" have been reported in Huaquillas and Macará on the southern border. The Cordillera del Cóndor, southeast of Zamora, a region long involved in a border dispute with Peru, still contains unmarked **minefields** and should be avoided altogether.

Stay informed by referring to your government's website for the latest **travel advice** (see p.64).

Drugs

The possession of **drugs**, regardless of whether it's for personal use, is a very serious offence in Ecuador – one that can end in fifteen years in jail. People who've been charged may have to contend with the country's dilapidated and overcrowded prisons for more than a year before they're even brought to trial, not to mention being at the mercy of corrupt officials, who'll be aiming to bleed them for as much money as possible. If offered drugs in the street, walk away. Don't take any chances with drugs or drug dealers – setups have happened and raids are common in "druggie" places such as Montañita and certain Quito clubs. It's simply not worth the consequences. If you don't believe it, talk to any of the dozens of foreigners languishing in Ecuador's jails on drugs offences (the SAE arranges regular visits).

Police

The only contact you're likely to have with the **police** (*policía*) are at road **checkpoints** at various places around the country, mentioned in the Guide text, where you may be registered. Generally the police are polite and helpful, particularly the specially designated **tourist police** who patrol gringo-thick areas like La Mariscal, the Panecillo and the Mitad del Mundo

It's rare, but there are reports of corrupt or false police planting drugs in bags – the idea being to extract a large "fine" from the terrified tourist. Plainclothes "police" should always be dealt with cautiously; pretending you don't understand and walking away is a strategy.

If you are the victim of a crime, you should go to the police as soon as possible to fill out a report (*denuncia*). In an emergency call ☎911 in Quito, Guayaquil and Cuenca, or ☎101 elsewhere.

Electricity

110V/60Hz is the standard supply, and sockets are for two flat prongs. Fluctuations in the supply are common so you need to use a surge protector (*cortapicos*) if you're plugging in expensive equipment.

Entry requirements

Most nationals, including citizens of the EU, US, Canada, Australia and New Zealand, do not need a visa to enter Ecuador as tourists, and only require a passport valid for more than six months; in theory, you are also supposed to have a return ticket and proof of having enough money for the duration of the stay too, but these aren't often checked. Your passport will be stamped on arrival and you'll be issued with a **T-3 embarkation card**, which you should keep – it will be collected when you leave the country. The T-3 gives you **90 days** in Ecuador. If you want to extend your stay, you may need to get a **visa** (see below). People who **overstay** (or who don't have an entry stamp) are likely to get a $200 fine and deportation within 48 hours, and won't be allowed back into Ecuador for six months.

Visas

If you plan to stay in Ecuador more than ninety days or are visiting for some purpose other than tourism, you'll need a **visa**. Visas are divided between those for immigrants (10-I to 10-VI) and non-immigrants (12-I to 12-X), including those for study (12-V), work (12-VI), volunteering (12-VII), cultural exchanges (12-VIII), or business and tourism (12-IX and 12-X). Each has its own application procedure and **fee** which vary from $10 to $200 depending on type, plus $30 for the application form. For details, refer to the Ecuadorian Ministerio de Relaciones Exteriores website ⓦwww.mmrree.gov.ec or contact the Ecuadorian representatives in your country with ample time before you need to travel.

Rules for **extending a T-3 embarkation card** (see "Entry requirements" p.59) are regularly changing and are, at the time of writing, causing some confusion among both immigration officials and lawyers. At the moment, it seems a T-3 cannot be renewed, but there are reports it's possible to leave and re-enter the country and be issued with a new T-3 for another 90 days; however, this doesn't seem completely reliable and there have been cases of people being refused new cards. The other option is to get a 12-IX or 12-X visa from the Dirección General de Asuntos Migratorios y Extranjería, Edificio Solís, Av 10 de Agosto 21-255 and Carrión (ⓣ02/2227025). Allow at least a week, preferably more, on your T-3 card to obtain the visa. Whichever way you extend your visit, you will only be allowed to stay a total of **180 days** in any 12-month period.

Once in Ecuador, visa holders must **register** at the Dirección General de Extranjería at the corner of San Ignacio 207 and San Javier (ⓣ02/2221817; Mon–Fri 8am–12.30pm) in Quito, or the Sub-Dirección General de Extranjería in Guayaquil (ⓣ04/2322692) within thirty days of arrival in order to get a **censo** (resident identity card). The process takes several days and quite a bit of to-ing and fro-ing. Holders of immigrant visas will also need to get a *cédula* (national identity card); ask at the Extranjería for details.

If you're seeking to become a **long-term resident**, it pays to do plenty of research beforehand and to find trusted people to help you through the complicated legal process. Information and assistance can be found at ⓦwww.pro-ecuador.com.

Identification

The law requires you to carry "**proper identification**" at all times – for foreigners this means a **passport**. Visa holders will also need to carry their *censo* and any other relevant documentation. Photocopies of the

stamps and important pages are usually sufficient, so you can keep the original in a safe place. In the Oriente and border areas, only the originals will do. If the authorities stop you and you can't produce identification, you can be detained.

Ecuadorian embassies around the world

Australia 6 Pindari Crescent, O'Malley, Canberra, ACT 2606 ⓣ02/6286 4021, ⓕ6286 1231, ⓔembecu@bigpond.net.au
Canada 50 O'Connor St, Office 316, Ottawa, Ontario K1P 6L2 ⓣ613/563-8206, ⓕ235-5776, ⓔmecuacan@rogers.com
Ireland 27 Library Rd, Dun Laoghaire, Dublin ⓣ01/280 5917, ⓔcecudublin@mmrree.gov.ec
New Zealand Level 9, 2 Saint Martins Lane, Auckland ⓣ09/303 0590, ⓕ303 0589, ⓔlanglinks@aix.co.nz
UK Flat 3b, 3 Hans Crescent, London SW1X 0LS ⓣ020/7584 1367, ⓦwww.ecuador.embassyhomepage.com
US 2535 15th St NW, Washington, DC 20009 ⓣ202/234-7200, ⓦwww.ecuador.org

Gay and lesbian travellers

Ecuador took a leap forward in **gay and lesbian rights** by reforming its constitution in 1998 to outlaw discrimination on the basis of sexuality, and again in 2008 to allow same-sex civil unions. Yet it's still a very macho society and public attitudes have a fair bit of catching up to do. There is a blossoming gay scene in Quito and Guayaquil, but gay couples in Ecuador tend to avoid revealing their orientation in public places. Gay and lesbian travellers are probably best off following their example – overt displays of affection are likely to be met with stern disapproval, even abuse.

A good source of information on gay life in Ecuador, and in Quito in particular, including listings of gay-friendly clubs, restaurants, travel agencies and links to other local sites can be found at ⓦwww.quitoqueercity.info.

Insurance

It's essential to take out an **insurance policy** before travelling to Ecuador to cover against theft, loss and illness or injury. A typical policy usually provides cover for the loss of baggage, tickets and – up to a certain limit – cash or cheques, as well as cancellation or curtailment of your journey. Most of them exclude so-called dangerous sports unless an extra premium is paid: in Ecuador this can mean scuba diving, white water rafting, mountaineering and trekking. Many policies can be chopped and changed to exclude coverage you don't need. If you do take medical coverage, ascertain whether benefits will be paid as treatment proceeds or only after return home, and whether there is a 24-hour medical emergency number. When securing baggage cover, make sure the per-article limit – typically under £500/$750 – will cover your most valuable possession. If you need to make a claim, you should keep receipts for medicines and medical treatment. In the event you have anything stolen, you must obtain an official statement (*denuncia*) from the police.

Internet

In recent years there has been a rapid expansion of **internet** facilities across the country. Fierce competition keeps prices as low as $0.50–1 for an hour online in Quito and Guayaquil, and even in areas further afield it's rare to be charged more than $2–3 per hour. This means that unless you are staying for a long time or keeping to the cities and smarter hotels where wireless coverage is becoming more common, it's probably not worth the bother and risk of bringing your own **computer** to Ecuador.

Laundry

Most large towns and tourist centres will have an inexpensive **laundry** (*lavandería*) that charges by the kilo. Washing and drying are done for you and your clothes are neatly folded ready for collection – a wonderful service for travellers. In other areas, dry cleaners or laundries that charge by the item, which work out to be expensive, are more common. Many hotels offer a laundry service, or failing that are happy to let you use their laundry basin and clothes lines.

Mail

Letters and postcards **sent from Ecuador** can take anywhere from five days to a month

to reach their destination, though they're often faster to North America than anywhere else. If you need to send something of value or urgency, you're probably better off using a **courier**, such as DHL (many offices including in La Mariscal at Colón 1333 and Foch, and Avenida República 433 and Diego de Almagro; find your nearest on ⓦwww.dhl.com.ec), though this is much more expensive. Servientrega (ⓦwww.servientrega.com.ec) has been recommended as a fair-priced domestic courier.

The national post has three levels of service: ordinary, registered (*certificado*) and EMS (express, the national courier). To give some idea of **prices**, a postcard sent ordinary costs a little more or less than $1 depending on destination, a registered letter under 20g to Miami costs $2.14, while a packet under 2kg to Europe costs $39. Packets sent by surface mail are ten percent cheaper but much slower.

You can receive **poste restante** at just about any post office in the country. Have it sent to "Lista de Correos, [the town concerned], Ecuador", and make sure your surname is written as obviously as possible, as it will be filed under whatever the clerk thinks it is; you'll need to have photo ID to pick it up. If there's a return address on it, it will be sent back if you don't manage to pick it up. In Quito, Lista de Correos mail usually ends up at the main office on Espejo and Guayaquil in the old town; if marked "Correo Central", it could well go to the head office in the new town on Eloy Alfaro 354 and Avenida 9 de Octubre. The most convenient post office for people staying in La Mariscal is usually the Surcursal #7, at Torres de Almagro on Reina Victoria and Avenida Colón, which also has a poste restante service.

American Express card holders can make use of AmEx offices for mail services, and some **embassies** also do poste restante. **SAE** (see p.77) will take mail, phone messages (during club hours) and fax messages for members.

Maps

The widest selection of **maps** covering Ecuador is published by the Instituto Geográfico Militar (IGM) in Quito, up on the

Metric equivalent weights and measures

1km	=	0.62 miles	1 foot	=	0.3m
1m	=	1.09 yards	1 inch	=	2.54cm
1cm	=	0.39 inches	1lb	=	454g
1kg	=	2.2lbs	1 gallon (imperial)	=	4.55 litres
1 litre	=	1.76 pints (UK)	1 gallon (US)	=	3.79 litres
1 litre	=	2.1 pints (US)	°C	=	0.56 x (°F -32)
1 mile	=	1.61km	°F	=	(1.8 x °C) + 32
1 yard	=	0.91m			

hill overlooking the Parque El Ejido at Senierges and Paz y Miño (you'll need to bring your passport or ID along), which has maps on a variety of scales. The most useful maps for **trekking** are their 1:50,000 series, which show accurate contour markings and geographic features and cover most of the country except for remote corners of the Oriente. Unfortunately, popular maps are often sold out, in which case you'll be supplied with a difficult-to-read black-and-white photocopy. Maps are also available in a 1:250,000 series for the whole country, and a 1:25,000 series for approximately half of it. You may need a supporting letter from a government agency if you require maps of sensitive border areas and the Oriente.

Quito's best bookshops stock general maps of Ecuador as well as a series of blue **pocket guides** to Ecuador by Nelson Gómez E. published by Ediguías, which have reasonable fold-out colour maps of the country and major cities, local tourist guides and a country road map of mixed reliability.

Money

The **US dollar** is the official currency of Ecuador. Bills come in denominations of $1, $5, $10, $20, $50 and $100. Coins come in a mixture of US- and Ecuadorian-minted 1, 5, 10, 25 and 50 cent pieces, plus $1 coins only minted in the US; Ecuadorian coins can't be used abroad. The $50 and $100 bills are rarely accepted at most shops and restaurants, and small change is often in short supply, so bring plenty of low-denomination bills from your home country if possible.

Take a mixture between cash (in US dollars; other currencies are difficult to change), traveller's cheques (again US dollars; American Express has widest coverage) and bank cards when travelling to Ecuador; credit cards have the security of payment protection insurance and are one step removed from your bank account in the event of theft, while debit cards are cheaper and more convenient to use. Although it's common now to use ATMs to access the bulk of your travel money, don't rely solely on plastic – quite apart from loss or theft, Ecuador's electronic banking systems frequently go down too.

ATMs are widespread in Ecuadorian cities. Many machines are connected to the worldwide Visa/Plus and MasterCard/Cirrus/Maestro systems and a smaller number accept American Express and Diners Club cards. Usually, you won't be able to withdraw more than around $300–500 from an ATM in a day (depending on the bank), and a **handling charge** of around 1–3 percent will be deducted from your account if using a credit card (check interest rates before you travel for cash advances as these can be high) or typically a small flat fee for a debit card.

Traveller's cheques are getting difficult to change, even in Quito, Guayaquil and Cuenca, where most banks are currently not taking them; *casas de cambio* are your best bet, but the commission is sometimes unfavourable.

Full-time students should consider getting the **International Student ID Card**, or "ISIC card" (Wwww.istc.org), which in Ecuador is the only widely recognized student identification entitling the bearer to discounts at museums, some attractions and hotels, and occasionally with airlines and tour agencies, as well as to many other benefits. In some cases, only students at Ecuadorian institutions are eligible for the discounts.

The same organization offers the **International Youth Travel Card** to those who are 26 or younger and the **International Teacher Card** for teachers, offering similar discounts. All these cards are available from affiliated offices around the globe; check their website for your nearest branch.

Opening hours

Most **shops** are open Monday to Saturday from 9am to 6pm. Many occupy the family home and, outside the biggest cities, open every day for as long as someone is up. Opening hours of **public offices** are generally from 9am to 5 or 6pm Monday to Friday, with an hour or so for lunch. In rural areas, the working day often starts earlier, say at 8am, and a longer lunch of a couple of hours is taken.

Banks do business from 8 or 9am to 1.30pm, Monday to Friday, sometimes closing at 1pm on Saturdays. Some banks extend business to 6pm during the week, though with reduced services. **Post offices** are open Mondays to Fridays from 8am to 7pm, closing at noon on Saturdays, and **telephone offices** are open daily from 8am to 10pm; in rural regions and smaller towns, expect hours to be shorter for both services. **Museums** are usually closed on Mondays.

Phones

Many Ecuadorians make their calls from the numerous public phone offices in every town and city in the country, which are usually the cheapest and most convenient places for you to make local and national calls too. The nationalized telephone service is operated by **CNT** (Corporación Nacional de Telecomunicaciones), though you might still find offices with the old livery of Andinatel (in the north) and **Pacífictel** (in the

south and Galápagos); and **Etapa** for Cuenca. Inside the phone office you'll normally be allocated a cabin (*cabina*) where you make the call, and then you pay afterwards. In many cities, the nationalized phone offices are quickly being superseded by private and franchise offices, which often have longer opening hours and better rates for both domestic and international calls. The mobile phone companies Movistar and Porta (see below) also operate phone offices and card-operated phone kiosks, which can receive incoming calls; cards specific to each company are bought at nearby shops. These tend only to be economical to use if calling mobile phones of the same company.

There's a three-tiered tariff system for **domestic calls with CNT**: local calls from the state services cost around $0.11 per minute, regional calls $0.15, and national calls $0.22. Calls to mobile phones are charged at $0.25 a minute. **International calls** from CNT offices are $0.18 per minute to the US, $0.28 to Canada, $0.40 to the UK, $0.57 to Ireland, and $0.87 to Australia. It's usually a lot cheaper to make international calls from **internet cafés** using Skype or other similar internet telephone services.

Calling from hotels is convenient, but usually involves a big surcharge; check prices before using a hotel phone.

Mobile phones

The three Ecuadorian networks use GSM 850 (Movistar and Porta) and GSM 1900 (Alegro) and soon 3G 850. However, roaming is not cheap, so if you expect to use your **mobile** or **cell phone** often, you should consider getting a phone and

Calling home from abroad

The initial zero in omitted from the area code when dialling the UK, Ireland, Australia and New Zealand from abroad.

Australia international access code + 61

New Zealand international access code + 64

UK international access code + 44

US and Canada international access code + 1

Republic of Ireland international access code + 353

South Africa international access code + 27

account in Ecuador. The SAE (see p.77) sells secondhand phones, or if you need one for a short period only, you could rent with ⓦwww.rentacellular.net.

Useful phone numbers and area codes

Emergencies and information

Police ☎101
Fire ☎102
National operator ☎105
International operator ☎116 & 117
Emergency ☎911 (Quito, Guayaquil, Cuenca)

Area codes

Only use the prefix when calling from outside the area. Drop the zero if calling from outside Ecuador.

☎**02** Quito and Pichincha, Santo Domingo
☎**03** Bolívar, Chimborazo, Cotopaxi, Tungurahua, Pastaza
☎**04** Guayaquil and Guayas, Santa Elena
☎**05** Manabí, Los Ríos, Galápagos
☎**06** Carchi, Imbabura, Esmeraldas, Sucumbíos, Napo, Orellana
☎**07** Cuenca and Azuay, Cañar, El Oro, Loja, Morona-Santiago, Zamora-Chinchipe
☎**08 & 09** Mobile phones
☎**593** Ecuador country code

Photography

If you're using an **analogue** (**film**) camera, consider bringing fast film (400ASA and above) for the gloom of **jungles** and forests, while 200ASA is more appropriate for the brighter conditions elsewhere. It's best to bring your own film and batteries from home, but both are available in the bigger cities; check the expiry dates before purchase. You can transfer pictures taken with a **digital camera** onto disk or have them printed in the larger tourist centres to free up space on memory cards. Rechargeable batteries are ideal as the shelf-life of batteries bought in the Oriente or coast is often badly affected by heat and humidity.

You'll get best results when the sun is lowest in the sky, as you'll lose detail and nuance in the high contrasts cast by harsh midday light, though you can reduce heavy shadows using fill-in flash. Mountaineers with digital cameras should take their batteries out while climbing and carry them somewhere warm under their clothes; cold batteries lose power in seconds, usually just when you want to take that spectacular mountaintop sunrise. Always respect people's **privacy** and **never take someone's photograph without asking first**; usually they will be flattered or sometimes ask for a small fee or for you to buy something.

Time

Ecuador is 5 hours behind GMT (the same as US Eastern Standard Time), and the Galápagos Islands are 6 hours behind GMT (or one hour behind US EST).

Tourist information

There's a Ministry of Tourism **information office**, sometimes labelled "iTur", in every provincial capital and the main tourist centres. Some offices won't have an English-speaker on hand, but almost all have rudimentary maps, lists of hotels and restaurants, leaflets and probably basic information on any sites of interest in the area. Many regional centres also have tourist offices run by the municipality, which can be as good or better than their government counterparts.

Travel websites

ⓦwww.ecuador.com
ⓦwww.ecuadorexplorer.com
ⓦwww.ecuaworld.com
ⓦwww.ecuador-travel-guide.org
ⓦwww.exploringecuador.com
ⓦwww.goecuador.com
ⓦwww.purecuador.com

Government websites

Australian Department of Foreign Affairs
ⓦwww.dfat.gov.au, ⓦwww.smartraveller.gov.au.
British Embassy in Quito ⓦwww.ukinecuador .fco.gov.uk.
British Foreign & Commonwealth Office
ⓦwww.fco.gov.uk.
Canadian Department of Foreign Affairs
ⓦwww.voyage.gc.ca
Irish Department of Foreign Affairs ⓦwww .foreignaffairs.gov.ie.
New Zealand Ministry of Foreign Affairs
ⓦwww.mft.govt.nz.
US State Department ⓦwww.travel.state.gov.
South African Department of Foreign Affairs
ⓦwww.dfa.gov.za

Embassy of Ecuador in Washington Ⓦ www
.ecuador.org.
Quito Ⓦ www.quito.com.ec
Ministerio de Turismo Ⓦ www.vivecuador.com.

Travelling with children

Ecuadorians love children and will usually go out of their way to make life as easy for you as they can. Tourists per se can be a bit of a puzzle to the many Ecuadorians who have never left the country, but parents and their children represent something everyone understands – a **family**. Gringo children are something of a novelty, particularly outside the big cities, and will usually quickly attract the attention of local kids, who'll want to have a look and a chat. Before long, the whole family will be out too, and social barriers will crumble away much faster than they would under normal circumstances.

You and especially your children will get the most out of such openness if you take some time to learn some **Spanish**. You'll be amazed at how quickly children can pick it up when properly immersed for a week or three, and most language schools are very accommodating of their needs You'll also be amazed at the heart-melting effect it will have on even the surliest Ecuadorian when your child speaks to them in their own tongue.

For most **travel**, children pay half-price, and on a few things, such as **trains**, they go for free. Long-distance **buses** are an exception and full fares have to be paid for each seat, though if the trip isn't too long and the child not too big, they can sit on your lap without charge and even be plonked on a chair whenever the bus clears. Longer bus journeys can be very wearisome for children, but with forward planning it should be possible to break up any lengthy hauls into smaller chunks, which will allow you to see more on the way. If a big trip is unavoidable, consider taking an internal **flight** as these are relatively cheap for adults, while children under 12 go for half-price and under-2s pay just ten percent. In rural areas, you'll often find people will offer you a ride, through kindness, when they see you walking with a child.

Children will also regularly get half-price rates for their **accommodation**, and

occasionally be let off for free, particularly if young. Teenagers often appreciate hotels with plenty of secure outside or communal space, so they can have some freedom for a wander.

Ecuadorian **food** doesn't tend to be a big issue for children; old favourites like fried chicken or breaded fish and french fries are available just about everywhere. Experimenting with exotic fruits and juices can be a sneaky way to get youngsters interested in trying new foods, and if they hate everything bar the most familiar brands, these are available across the country, too.

Travellers with disabilities

South America is not the friendliest of destinations for **travellers with disabilities**, and sadly Ecuador is no exception. In all but the very newest public buildings, you're unlikely to find much in the way of ramps, widened doorways or disabled toilets. Pavements are often narrow and full of obstructions.

About twelve percent of Ecuadorians have a disability, and many manage with the assistance of others. Some of the smarter city hotels do cater for disabled guests and Quito's segregated bus systems afford access too, at least outside rush hour when it's not too crowded to get on in the first place. Travelling further afield in Ecuador is likely to throw up difficulties, and you may have to forego the idyllic rustic cabañas in the middle of nowhere for a luxury chain hotel, or substitute local buses for taxis or internal flights.

Women travellers

Travelling as a **lone woman** in Ecuador presents no major obstacles and can be very rewarding – if you are prepared to put up with the occasional annoyance and take a few simple precautions. **Unwanted attention** is the most common irritation and usually has to be borne most often by fair-headed women or those who most obviously look like *gringa*; dressing or behaving provocatively is only likely to make the situation worse. Being whistled, hissed or kissed at is part of the territory, but these situations are more a nuisance than a danger and the accepted wisdom is to pointedly ignore the perpetrators – shouting at them will only encourage them.

More serious cases of sexual assault are a concern in Ecuador for lone women; minimize risks by treating known danger situations with caution. Beaches are regarded as unsafe for women alone; generally anyone, even in groups, should stay off beaches at night. Avoid walking alone after dark anywhere and hiking alone. Hotspots for the latter include Rucu Pichincha and Cruz Loma near Quito, and Laguna Mojanda and El Lechero near Otavalo; if you want to hike in quiet places near tourist centres, go in groups. If you become the victim of rape or sexual assault, report the incident immediately to the police and your embassy in Quito. It must be stressed most Ecuadorians are friendly and respectful of solo female travellers, and few experience problems while travelling through the country.

Sanitary protection comes most commonly in the form of towels, with tampons being hard to get hold of outside the cities.

Guide

Guide

Quito and around

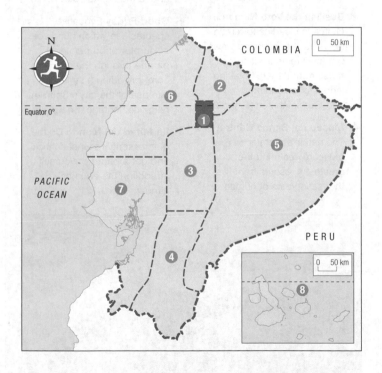

CHAPTER 1   # Highlights

* **Colonial Quito** Quito's magnificent historic quarter, holding some of the continent's best-preserved and most beautiful Spanish colonial architecture, all in an area easily explored on foot. **See p.86**

* **Basílica del Voto Nacional** Quito's concertinaed terrain lends itself to stunning views, but few are as exciting as those from the breathtaking ledges of this quirky neo-Gothic church. **See p.95**

* **Museo del Banco Central** The nation's premier museum, featuring the greatest treasures from five thousand years of human history in the region, including pre-Columbian ceramics and gold artefacts. **See p.99**

* **TeléfériQo** A swish gondola ride which effortlessly whizzes passengers high up the slopes of Volcán Pichincha above the capital. **See p.100**

* **Good Friday** Evocative spectacle in which hundreds of purple-robed penitents parade through the historic core, providing a striking glimpse of the city's Spanish religious heritage. **See p.111**

* **La Mitad del Mundo** Do the quintessential tourist schtick and get a photo of yourself straddling the equator – almost. **See p.121**

▲ Plaza de la Independencia, old town, Quito

Quito and around

igh in the Andes, Ecuador's capital, **Quito**, unfurls in a long north–south ribbon, more than 35km top to bottom and just 5km wide. To the west, the city is dramatically hemmed in by the steep green walls of **Volcán Pichincha**, the benign-looking volcano which periodically sends clouds of ash billowing into the sky and over the streets. Eastwards, Quito abruptly drops away to a wide valley known as the **Valle de los Chillos**, marking the beginning of the descent towards the Amazon basin. It's a superb setting, but apart from in July and August it can be bone-chillingly cold, with its much-vaunted "spring-like climate" all too often giving way to grey, washed-out skies that somewhat undermine the beauty of the surroundings.

Central Quito divides into two distinct parts. The compact **old town**, known as the *centro histórico*, is the city's undisputed highlight, a jumble of narrow streets and wide, cobbled plazas lined with churches, monasteries, mansions and colourful balconied houses. A UNESCO World Heritage Site, the old town contains some of the most beautiful Spanish Colonial architecture on the continent and the frenetic crowds of *indígenas* and *mestizos* that throng its streets give it a tremendous energy. A reputation for poverty and crime has traditionally discouraged tourists from actually staying here, but a sustained regeneration effort is turning it into a genuine alternative to the neighbouring, bland and modern **new town**, whose concentration of banks, shops, bars, hotels, restaurants, tour operators and internet cafés is convenient, if a little characterless.

As a major crossroads with 1.8 million residents, Quito is a busy **transit hub** to which travellers usually return between forays to the jungle, the coast, the Galápagos Islands and the northern and southern sierra. Featuring dozens of language schools, it's also a good place to learn Spanish, and many visitors spend several weeks or longer here mastering their *castellano*. It's an easy city to spend time in, even with the inevitable pollution and screeching horns, but when you fancy a break there's plenty nearby to keep you occupied.

The most popular **day-trip** is to the **Mitad del Mundo** (Middle of the World) on the equator, marked by a massive monument and several museums, a trip often combined with a visit to the giant volcanic crater of **Pululahua**. Other attractions in the area include the market at **Sangolquí**, Eduardo Kingman's house in nearby **San Rafael** and the **Pasochoa** forest reserve half an hour to the south, one of many protected areas nearby offering great birdwatching and hiking. Lesser-known attractions can be found northeast of Quito, including the religious sanctuary of **El Quinche**, the little town of **Calderón**, where curious dough figurines are made, and the zoo at **Guayllabamba**, featuring a host of native species.

Quito's **altitude** (2800m) can leave you feeling breathless and woozy when you first arrive – most visitors adjust in a couple of days, often by resting, drinking plenty of water and avoiding alcohol.

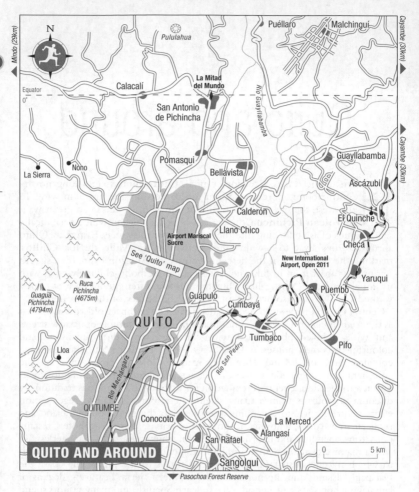

N

Mindo (29km)

Cayambe (30km)

Pululahua

Puéllaro

Malchinguí

Equator
0°

Calacalí

La Mitad
del Mundo

San Antonio
de Pichincha

Río Guayllabamba

Cayambe (30km)

La Sierra

Noño

Pomasqui

Bellavista

Guayllabamba

Ascázubi

Calderón

El Quinche

Airport Mariscal
Sucre

Llano Chico

Checa

See 'Quito' map

New International
Airport, Open 2011

Yaruqui

Ruca
Pichincha
(4675m)

Guagua
Pichincha
(4794m)

Guápulo

Puembo

QUITO

Cumbayá

Lloa

Tumbaco

Río San Pedro

Pifo

Río Machángara

QUITUMBE

Conocoto

La Merced

San Rafael

Alangasí

QUITO AND AROUND

Sangolqui

0   5 km

Pasochoa Forest Reserve

Quito

Although second to Guayaquil in population and economic clout, **QUITO** is
the political and cultural hub of a highly centralized country, where power is
wielded by an elite class of politicians, bankers and company directors, often
from old, moneyed families. Far more conspicuous than these sharp-suited
executives are the city's eye-catching *indígenas*, who make up a large part of its
population; Quito is still a place where Quichua-speaking women queue for
buses in traditional clothing with metres of beads strung tightly around their
necks, and where it's not uncommon to see children carried on their mothers'
backs in securely wrapped blankets, as they are in the rural sierra. All this makes
for a somewhat exotic introduction to the country, though the proliferation of

ragged shoeshine boys and desperate hawkers is a sobering reminder of the levels of poverty in the city, and its considerable social inequalities.

The key to **orientation** in Quito is to see the city as a long, narrow strip. At the southern end is the **old town**, focused on three large squares: the **Plaza de la Independencia** (also known as the Plaza Grande), **Plaza San Francisco** and **Plaza Santo Domingo**. The street grid around these squares comprises a small, compact urban core dominated to the south by the hill of **El Panecillo** (the Little Bread Roll), crowned by a large statue of the **Virgen de Quito**. Fanning north from old Quito towards the new town is a transitional stretch around **Parque La Alameda**, while the **new town** proper begins a few blocks further north at **Parque El Ejido**. Known by Quiteños simply as **El Norte**, the new town stretches all the way north to the airport, but the only parts you're likely to visit are the central areas of **La Mariscal**, just north of Parque El Ejido, where most accommodation and tourist facilities are located, and the business district further north, around **Parque La Carolina**.

Some history

Little is known about the indigenous people who, until the fifteenth century, inhabited the terrain Quito now occupies. Archeologists believe that by about 1500 a number of *señoríos étnicos* ("lordships" or "chiefdoms"), including that of the obscure **Quitus**, from whom the present-day city takes its name, inhabited the Quito basin. Quito was an important settlement and a major trading centre where visitors from the sierra, the coast and the Oriente came to exchange their produce. After the **Inca** expansion north into Ecuador during the late fifteenth century, the last great Inca emperors, **Huayna Capac** and his son **Atahualpa**, chose Quito as the political and ceremonial centre of the northern part of their empire.

The Spanish subsequently chose Quito as the capital of their newly acquired territory, despite the Inca general Rumiñahui burning it to the ground five days before its capture in 1534. The colonial city was founded as **San Francisco de Quito** on August 28, 1534, and its governor **Sebastián de Benalcázar** established the proper workings of a city on December 6 of that year, which is still celebrated as its official foundation date (see "Fiestas" box on p.111). The major squares and streets were soon marked out and lots were granted to the 204 colonists present. It wasn't long before the main religious orders moved in, including the Franciscans, Dominicans, Augustinians and Sisters of Mercy, all of whom immediately set to work building their own churches and monasteries with Indian labour. Within thirty years, the **cathedral** was finished, the main streets were paved with stone, irrigation channels supplied the city with water, and the city council established regulations for slaughterhouses and markets. By the end of the sixteenth century, most of the great churches, monasteries and public buildings were in place, making Quito one of the great cities of Spanish America, and one of its great centres for religious learning.

During the **seventeenth** and **eighteenth centuries**, there was no real departure from the city's early model: more houses and churches were built, along with modest public works. The population increased moderately, but not dramatically, and by 1780 Quito was home to just 25,000 inhabitants (a figure already reached by Lima, Peru, in 1610). Quito remained something of a backwater, its quiet pace of life interrupted only by the petty quarrels and rivalries between clerics, Creoles (Spaniards born in the Americas) and public officials.

This sleepy state of affairs ended abruptly in the early **nineteenth century** as the tide of revolution swept over the continent. Most of the important events marking Ecuador's struggle for **independence** took place in or around Quito, and in 1830 the city became the capital of the newly declared **Republic of Ecuador**, the seat of national government, congress and the supreme court. The following decades would see prestigious buildings (including the Teatro Sucre and astronomical observatory) constructed, statues of revolutionary heroes erected, new bridges built and streets paved, and running water provided in many homes. Yet growth was still slow and by the end of the nineteenth century, Quito's population was just 50,000.

As Quito entered the **twentieth century** it finally outgrew its original boundaries and slowly expanded north and south. The construction of new buildings became easier with the 1909 arrival of the **Quito–Guayaquil railway**, which facilitated the transport of heavy building materials and new machinery to the capital. Yet even by 1945, there had still been little fundamental change to Quito's long-standing physical and social landscape: the wealthy still lived in the colonial centre, the working class occupied a barrio near the railway station to the south, and farms and countryside still mostly surrounded the city.

All this changed dramatically in the **postwar** years, fuelled initially by the **banana boom** of the 1940s, which turned Ecuador into an important exporting country and gave it the resources to pay for new infrastructure in Quito, including hospitals, schools, universities, prisons and an airport. When the city's wealthy moved out to the fashionable new barrio of Mariscal Sucre (La

Learning Spanish in Quito

Home to more than seventy **language schools**, Quito is the most popular place in South America to learn Spanish, partly because rates are so cheap – $4–10 per hour for one-to-one classes – and partly because Spanish is spoken much more clearly here than in many other countries, or even in Guayaquil and the coast. Ecuadorian *serranos* (highlanders) tend to speak slowly and pronounce all the letters in each word (elsewhere, consonants are frequently dropped), making them easy to understand.

Nearly all schools offer **one-to-one lessons** or classes in small groups, but not all use books or visual aids. It's a good idea to ask if you can rotate your teachers, as this keeps the lessons fresher and allows you to compare techniques and decide what suits you best. Visiting a school and enquiring about facilities or methods, or perhaps even asking to sit in on a lesson, will give you the best idea if it's right for you before enrolling.

Some schools will encourage you to sign up for seven hours a day, but most students find that exhausting – four hours a day is a better bet, whether studying for just a few days or several weeks. The majority of schools offer the option of **staying with a family** (usually $10–15 per day, with meals included), while others now offer daily classes as part of full tours to the jungle or coast. Many schools also offer **activities** such as cookery classes, dancing lessons or day and weekend trips – all good ways to meet other students. The following institutions are established and reputable; South American Explorers (see p.77) and many embassies also supply lists of language schools.

Language schools

Academia Latinoamericana de Español Noruega 156 and 6 de Diciembre ☎02/2250946, ⓦwww.latinoschools.com. Well-structured courses, complete with homework and testing, with most teaching in small groups of four students or fewer, though one-to-one lessons are also offered. More expensive than most.

Amazonas Jorge Washington 718 and Amazonas, Edificio Rocafuerte, third floor ☎&℻02/2504654, ⓦwww.eduamazonas.com. Large, long-established school, also with a branch in the Oriente. Students are offered use of pool, sauna and jacuzzi at the *Hilton Colón* (see p.82).

Mariscal), Quito's social geography underwent a fundamental change as well. Further transformations followed the **oil boom** of the 1970s, which funded the construction of high-rise offices, new residential districts and public buildings, including the Palacio Legislativo. Accordingly, the population exploded and passed the **one million** mark in 1990 – due in part to the migration of workers from the countryside to the capital. Since then, Quito's boundaries have been spreading farther outwards, literally stretching the city's resources to their limits; at 1.6 million people and rising, the population boom shows no signs of fading, putting an ever-greater strain on housing, employment, transport and even sanitation and water supplies. Yet the metropolitan authorities have made real progress in developing a cross-city bus system and rejuvenating the historic centre – the architectural jewel of the capital and spiritual heart of the country – meaning Quito is more than ever a city to explore and enjoy.

Arrival

Quito is at the heart of Ecuador's national transport network and offers **bus** access to just about every corner of the country, along with regular intercity **flights**. Arrival in Quito can be a little unnerving, with huge crowds pressing around the

Bipo & Toni's Carrión E8-183 and Leonidas Plaza ⓣ&ⓕ 02/2547090, ⓦ www.academia.bipo.net. Excellent school with great teachers, plus a lovely garden with barbecue facilities, video room, library and café. Regularly donates a portion of its profits to environmental projects.

Galápagos Amazonas 884 and Wilson, first floor ⓣ&ⓕ 02/2565213, ⓦ www.galapagos.edu.ec. As well as ordinary language lessons, offers courses in literary analysis and business-oriented Spanish. Has a large reference library and arranges weekly activities.

Instituto Superior de Español Darquea Terán 1650 and 10 de Agosto ⓣ 02/2223242, ⓦ www.instituto-superior.net. Well-regarded school in a renovated Spanish Colonial house, with an on-site gym and garden, just north of La Mariscal. Other branches are in Otavalo and the Galápagos.

La Lengua Colón 1001 and Juan León Mera, Edificio Ave María, eighth floor ⓣ&ⓕ 02/2501271, ⓦ www.la-lengua.com. Friendly, centrally located school with a range of good-value, flexible programmes, including some on Latin American history, economics, politics, literature and culture. They also offer Quichua classes and have a branch on the coast in Puerto López.

Ruta del Sol 9 de Octubre N21-157 and Roca, Edificio Santa Teresita, third floor ⓣ&ⓕ 02/2562956, ⓦ www.rutasolacademy.com. Courses include cultural lessons, literature discussions and museum visits, with diplomas offered for some classes on completion. South of Parque El Ejido.

Simón Bolívar Mariscal Foch E9-20 and 6 de Diciembre ⓣ&ⓕ 02/2544558, ⓦ www.simon-bolivar.com. Dynamic young school, offering daily classes and a wide range of activities and tours, including six-day trips to the jungle or coast. Also has a branch in Cuenca.

South American Language Center Amazonas N26-59 and Santa María ⓣ 02/2544715, ⓦ www.southamerican.edu.ec. Long-established school with a good reputation and facilities. Popular with Ecuadorians for English lessons, making for a pleasant intercultural exchange.

exit gate at the airport and a confusing layout and menacing atmosphere at the bus terminal. The best thing to do is jump in a **taxi** and get to your hotel, where you can get settled. (For details of air, bus and train services leaving the city, see "Moving on from Quito", p.119.)

By air

The city's **airport**, Aeropuerto Internacional Mariscal Sucre (☎02/2944900, ⓦwww.quitoairport.com), serves both national and international flights, and is located in the northern part of the new town, 6km from the hotel district of La Mariscal. Facilities include a **tourist information desk** (daily 8am–midnight), **casa de cambio** (daily 4.30am–9pm; better rates in town) and several **ATMs**; a new, more spacious airport 18km east of the city is scheduled to open at the end of 2010.

It's best to take a **taxi** direct to your hotel. Paying the fixed fare at the official taxi desk in the airport of $5 to La Mariscal or $7 to the old town (typically bumped up by a dollar or so at night – ask to see the *tarifas de taxis* if you think you are being overcharged), is often better than trying to haggle directly with the driver. There are also booths for **minibus** companies, which are economical if you are in a group. If you have a reservation, it's worth asking your hotel before flying whether they offer a **pick-up service**. In light traffic, your driver should be able to get you to your hotel in less than twenty minutes.

Flights from North America usually arrive late at night after **bus** services have finished, but even in daylight, this is not a safe way to travel with your bags. Standard city buses pass outside the airport and the Metrobus stop is a block south on Avenida de la Prensa (both $0.25).

By bus

Quito's main **bus terminal** at the time of writing, the Terminal Terrestre Cumandá at Av Maldonado 3077 on the southern edge of the old town, makes for a rather dismal point of entry; this is not a place to linger, especially after dark. There's an **information desk** near the pedestrian entrance (8.30am–5.30pm; ☎02/2289047 or 2289049), an **ATM** and, right where the buses arrive, a long line of **taxis** – which you should take if you're arriving at night, early in the morning or if you have luggage. Establish a price with the driver before you get in, as many will refuse to use the meter from the bus station. You shouldn't have to pay more than a few dollars to get to the hotel district (La Mariscal) in the new town.

By the time you read this a new terminal should be in full operation, the **Terminal Terrestre Quitumbe**, at Avenida Cóndor Ñan and Avenida Mariscal Sucre, about 10km south of Cumandá (which will be turned into a giant car park). This will deal with the bulk of Quito's interprovincial bus services, although those heading north are destined to leave (at an unspecified date) from another new terminal being constructed at **Carcelén** in the far north of the city; some buses heading northwest of Quito already leave from the **Ofelia** station (off the Av de la Prensa on Diego Vásquez de Cepeda), as indicated in the text. As departure points are likely to change because of the new terminals, ask around for the best place to catch your bus. A small number of bus companies also have their own separate terminals in the new town (for details, see p.120).

The Cumandá bus terminal is a short distance from the trolley stop of the same name (see "City Transport", opposite), but beware of pickpockets in the few minutes it takes to walk there, not to mention petty thieves on the crowded trolleybuses themselves. Quitumbe terminal is also linked to the trolley system and will eventually be linked to Ecovía too. Ofelia is a few stops before Carcelén on the Metrobus system; the plan is to link the trolley to Carcelén one day as well. In all cases, a taxi's the best choice for travelling to or from a bus terminal if you have luggage or after dark.

Information

The **Corporación Metropolitana de Turismo**, a metropolitan body known as the Quito Visitors' Bureau in English, has maps, leaflets, brochures on Quito, English-speaking staff and an informative and regularly updated website, ⓦ www.quito.com.ec. They have four key offices around the capital: the head office in the old town inside the Palacio Arzobispal on the Plaza de la Independencia (Mon–Fri 9am–8pm, Sat 10am–8pm & Sun 10am–4pm; ⓣ02/2281904); at international arrivals in the airport (daily 8am–midnight; ⓣ02/3300163); at the Parque Gabriela Mistral, wedged between Luis Cordero, Diego de Almagro and Baquerizo Moreno in the new town (daily 9am–5pm; ⓣ02/2551566); and inside the Museo del Banco Central, at avenidas Patria and 6 de Diciembre (Mon–Fri 9am–5pm, Sat & Sun 10am–4pm; ⓣ02/2221116).

In the north end of town opposite the Parque Carolina at Av Eloy Alfaro N32-300, the **Ministerio de Turismo** (Mon–Fri 9am–5pm, with a lunch break; ⓣ02/2507555, ⓦ www.purecuador.com) has a small office on the ground floor, equipped with glossy **brochures** and fold-out **maps** of Quito and Ecuador. The **Ministerio del Ambiente** nearby, on the seventh and eighth floors of the high-rise at the corner of avenidas Amazonas and Eloy Alfaro (Mon–Fri 8.30am–4.30pm; ⓣ02/2563429, ⓦ www.ambiente.gov.ec), is less geared to the walk-in visitor, but with persistence can be a potential mine of facts on the country's **national parks and reserves**.

South American Explorers

At Jorge Washington 311 and Leonidas Plaza, **South American Explorers** (Mon–Wed & Fri 9.30am–5pm, Thurs 9.30am–6pm & Sat 9.30am–12pm; ⓣ02/2225228, ⓦ www.saexplorers.org) is a rich source of information on Quito and Ecuador, and is run with formidable efficiency. Non-members can pick up numerous **information sheets** on subjects as diverse as accommodation, restaurants, wi-fi access, climbing guides, outdoor-equipment suppliers, banks, embassies and doctors. Check the website for a full rundown of members' benefits (best to join in Quito for the discounted rate of $50), which include the "**Volunteer Resource Center**", possibly Ecuador's most comprehensive list of non-governmental organizations and community-based projects seeking volunteers, **trip reports** (mainly recommendations or warnings) filed by other members, social events, lectures and special member excursions.

City transport

Since most visitors stay in the new town and do their sightseeing in the old town, you'll probably end up using **public transport** as a means of shuttling between the two (the alternative is a 45min walk of some 3km). The superb **El Trole**, **Ecovía** and **Metrobus** systems are efficient and easy to use; ordinary **buses** are a bit more daunting for first-time passengers. **Taxis** are relatively cheap, convenient and plentiful, so you may find yourself in one for most city journeys; at night, or if you are carrying valuables or luggage, you should use nothing else.

Trole, Ecovía and Metrobus

Three modern, eco-friendly, wheelchair-accessible **bus networks** service Quito, running north–south on broadly parallel routes. The systems are segregated from the general chaos of ordinary traffic, feature clean, weatherproof bus stops, and provide a fast and quiet ride – no wonder they're often so crowded. The flat **fare** is $0.25; change is usually available at the kiosk alongside so you can pay the fare into the machine by the entrance barrier, where you can also buy books of tickets at slightly discounted rates. Each system is augmented by feeder buses (*alimentadores*), which branch off into the suburbs from the main terminals.

The **Trole** (Mon–Fri 5am–midnight, Sat & Sun 6am–10pm) is a little different from the other two lines in that it uses electric trolleybuses. It runs for about 16km from its northern terminus (Terminal Norte) along the Avenida 10 de Agosto into the heart of the old town, past the Terminal Terrestre Cumandá and deep into southern Quito, finishing at Quitumbe, by the new terminal there. Not every trolleybus serves the entire line, with different route numbers and colour codes indicating where they begin and end, but unless you're travelling outside the central areas – including the old town and the La Mariscal hotel district – it shouldn't make any difference which bus you take. There's a **one-way system** through the old town: southbound buses go along Guayaquil, while those returning north use Flores and Montúfar.

The **Ecovía** (Mon–Sat 5am–10pm, Sun 6am–9.30pm) runs for 9km between La Marín in the old town and the Río Coca transfer station in the north, mainly along the **Avenida 6 de Diciembre**, and operates in much the same manner as the Trole, except that it uses a fleet of articulated, low-emission **buses ecológicos**.

The **Metrobus** (daily 6am–10pm) is the latest addition to the system, running similar *buses ecológicos* between La Marín in the old town and Carcelén in the north, passing the airport and the Ofelia transfer station, mainly by way of **avenidas América** and **de la Prensa**.

Buses

Quito's ordinary **buses** operate from about 6am to 9pm and screech to a halt whenever anyone wants to get on or off. There's no route map available to make sense of the 134 different lines, but main stops and final destinations are marked on the front window – and as most of Quito is laid out in a grid and most buses ply the main arterials including 12 de Octubre, Amazonas, 10 de Agosto and Colón, it's not difficult to get where you want to go.

The flat **fare** is usually $0.25, but there are a few very beaten-up *populares* that cost only $0.18; use coins or small-denomination notes to pay. Although there are designated **bus stops**, it's normally possible to flag down a bus wherever you are, and to get off at any street corner (shout "*en la esquina, por favor*" or "*parada*" to the driver).

Green **interparroquial** buses service outlying suburbs and districts such as Calderón and La Mitad del Mundo. Many city buses pass through Plaza Marín (known simply as "La Marín"), a chaotic and none-too-safe bus station at the east end of Chile in the old town.

Taxis

Quito swarms with thousands of yellow **taxis**, from the immaculately cared-for to hunks of junk, but regardless of quality, you can usually flag one down in seconds wherever you are. Make sure you pick one with a four-digit code plastered on its doors and windscreen, which signifies a legal, registered taxi. Quito is the only city in Ecuador where taxis use a meter (*taxímetro*), and fares normally work out to be cheap. Check that your driver resets the meter when you get in; it should flash "LIBRE" and display the **starting fare**, currently $0.80, and then increase by a cent every three seconds or so. If he doesn't turn it on, a polite "*ponga su taxímetro, por favor*" should jolt his memory; if he claims it's broken, either set a price immediately or get out and take another cab. Some drivers are fond of rounding the fare up with tourists, but there's no obligation to pay any more than the price on the meter; the **minimum fare** is $1.

Even though they're legally required to do so until 10pm, many taxi drivers don't use their meters at night, when fares can be a dollar or two more than in the day – so agree on a price before you set off. Try also to carry small notes and coins to pay the fare exactly, as *taxistas* have an uncanny knack of running out of change when you need it the most.

If you want to **book** a taxi, try any of the following 24 hour radio taxi companies: Americantaxi (☎02/2222333), City Taxi (☎02/2633333) or Taxi Amigo (☎02/2222222). Booking a taxi for the day costs $50–70, something your hotel can easily arrange for you.

Accommodation

The majority of visitors to Quito stay in the **new town**, where there's a huge choice of **accommodation** in all price ranges. The area is also lively after dark, and convenient for changing money, booking tours and sorting out laundry. Many streets are noisy, so it's always worth asking for a back room.

Thanks to its ongoing regeneration, staying in the **old town** is becoming a genuine alternative, especially if you have the money to splash out on one of several new luxurious colonial conversions. Just accept that you can't explore freely after dark beyond the central heart in the blocks around the Plaza Independencia.

Wherever you stay, it's always best to take a taxi from your arrival point straight to your hotel and to avoid wandering the streets with your luggage. The following accommodation is marked on the maps on pp.80–81, p.87 (old town) and p.98 (new town).

Quito addresses

Quito is currently caught between two **street-numbering** systems. A few years ago, an attempt was made to modernize **addresses**, whereby north–south streets would be prefixed by the letter N (for *norte*) if north of Calle Rocafuerte at the edge of the old town, while addresses on east–west streets would be prefixed by E (*este* – east) or Oe (*oeste* – west) to indicate their orientation to Avenida 10 de Agosto. Following these letters come street number, a dash and then house number. However, both old and new systems are currently in use, with many people being slow to adopt their new numbers, so throughout the chapter we provide the form of address used by the establishments themselves.

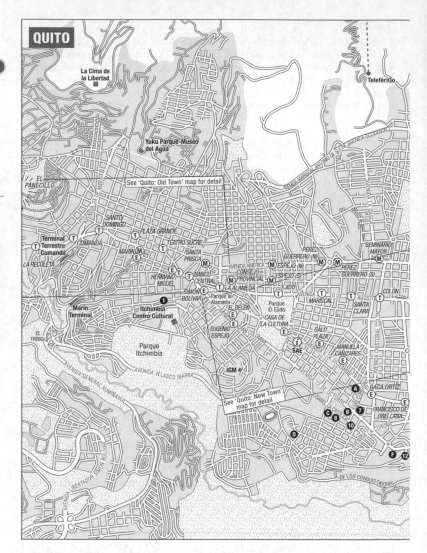

The new town

Most **new town** accommodation is in the downtown zone of **La Mariscal**, with the biggest concentration on the streets around José Calama, where new *hostales* keep springing up all the time. There are lots of restaurants, internet cafés and a steady stream of backpackers around here too.

Alcalá Luis Cordero E5-48 and Reina Victoria ☎02/2227396, ⓦ www.alcalahostal.com. Newer, more spruced-up version of its sister hostel, *Posada del Maple*, offering rooms with private bath and cable TV, with breakfast, unlimited tea, coffee

and hot chocolate all included. Rooms upstairs are fresher and brighter. ⑤
Amazonas Inn Joaquín Pinto E4-325 ☎02/2225723. Modern hotel with a pleasant street-level café. Some rooms are small, but all are

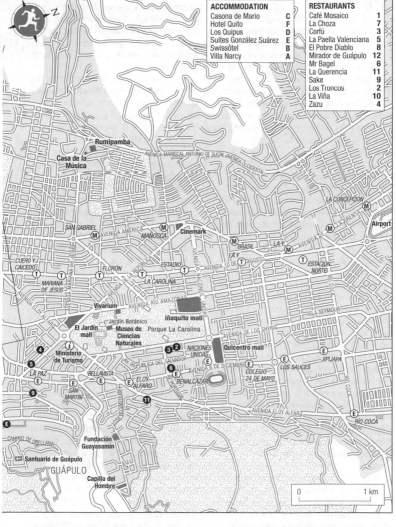

ACCOMMODATION	
Casona de Mario	C
Hotel Quito	F
Los Quipus	D
Suites González Suárez	E
Swissôtel	B
Villa Narcy	A

RESTAURANTS	
Café Mosaico	1
La Choza	7
Corfú	3
La Paella Valenciana	5
El Pobre Diablo	8
Mirador de Guápulo	12
Mr Bagel	6
La Querencia	11
Sake	9
Los Troncos	2
La Viña	10
Zazu	4

spotless and have private baths, cable TV and decent carpets. **❸**

Antinéa Juan Rodríguez 175 ☎02/2506838, ⓦwww.hotelantinea.com. Elegant French-run villa on a central leafy street, containing a mix of en-suite rooms, suites and mini-apartments, all tastefully furnished and equipped to a high standard. Also has a very pretty interior patio with lots of flowers, a gym and sauna, high-speed internet and includes a sizeable French breakfast. **❼–❽**

L'Auberge Inn Av Colombia 1138 and Yaguachi ☎02/2552912, ⓦwww.auberge-inn-hostal.com.

Situated between old and new towns, this pleasant Swiss-owned hotel has clean and comfortable rooms equipped with firm mattresses and soft duvets, a soothing garden patio, kitchen facilities, a restaurant, laundry service and luggage storage. **❷–❸**

Café Cultura Robles 513 and Reina Victoria ☎02/2564956, ⓦwww.cafecultura.com. Exuberantly decorated old house with high ceilings, big stone fireplaces and bright walls with frescos of parrots, flowers, dolphins and cherubs. Rooms on the ground and first floors are best, along with the three suites, each with a Victorian cast-iron bath. ❾

El Cafecito Luis Cordero E6-43 and Reina Victoria ☎02/2234862, Ⓦwww.cafecito.net. Nice clean dorms for four to five people, with spacious bunks and swept wooden floors, plus a single and a double room. The disadvantage of the late-night noise from the café below is offset by a ten percent discount on food and drink. Dorms $7, double ❹

Calama José Calama E7-49 ☎02/2237510. Popular budget hotel offering neat, square rooms with white walls, clean floors and private baths. Not much character, but central, functional and good value. ❷

La Cartuja Leonidas Plaza 170 ☎02/2523577, Ⓦwww.hotellacartuja.com. Excellent little hotel with stylish rooms offering TVs, safes, parquet floors and beautiful ceramic tiles in the bathrooms. Best of all is the interior garden with deckchairs and parasols – a real oasis of tranquillity. Breakfast and internet access included. ❼

Casa Bambú Solano E527 and Av Gran Colombia ☎02/2226738, Ⓦwww.hotelbambuecuador.com. Tucked away on a hillside above Parque El Ejido, this quiet little hostel features a roof terrace, open kitchen, internet access, DVD library and luggage storage. Rooms come en suite or with shared bath, and there are substantial discounts for monthly rates. Dorms $6, doubles ❷–❹

🏃 **La Casa Sol** Calama 127 and 6 de Diciembre ☎02/2230798, Ⓦwww .lacasasol.com. Lovely guesthouse with comfortable, neatly decorated en-suite rooms set around a pretty little courtyard; run by a cheerful staff, mainly from the Otavalo region, who are unfailingly polite and helpful. Features a sitting room with fireplace, luggage storage, laundry, library, good showers, tour services and lounge with cable TV, plus a tasty breakfast. SAE and long-stay discounts. ❼

Casona de Mario Andalucía 213 and Galicia ☎02/2230129, Ⓦwww.casonademario.com. A good-looking house surrounded by ample gardens in the quiet residential district of La Floresta, offering clean rooms with shared bath, kitchen, garage, laundry and storage facilities. Discounts for long stays. ❸

Cayman Juan Rodríguez 270 and Reina Victoria ☎02/2567616, Ⓦwww.hotelcaymanquito.com. Renovated old house with pleasant rooms with wooden shutters, firm mattresses and a fireplace in the sitting room. Breakfast included. ❻

Centro del Mundo Lizardo García 569 and Reina Victoria ☎02/25229050, Ⓦwww.centrodelmundo .com. Packed with character, this old house seems to have a permanent array of long-limbed

backpackers sprawled out in the sitting room. Most accommodation is in 8- to 12-bed dorms, all with lockable trunks, but there are also private rooms. Offers free breakfast, laundry facilities, use of a kitchen, stacks of information on local activities, and free drinks several nights each week. Dorms $4–6, doubles ❷–❸

🏃 **Crossroads** Foch E5-23 ☎02/2234735, Ⓦwww.crossroadshostal.com. Popular and friendly American-run hostel with a range of dorm and private rooms (some en suite) in a rambling old house, with a café, TV room with a huge DVD collection, kitchen, storage facilities and free wi-fi. The plentiful shared spaces, patio, garden and roof terrace make it a great meeting place. Dorms $7–8, doubles ❸–❺

Hilton Colón Amazonas 110 and Av Patria ☎02/2560666, Ⓦwww.quito.hilton.com. Luxurious international hotel boasting stylish modern decor, well-appointed rooms and a great fitness centre, including pool, gym and sauna. ❾

HotHello Amazonas N-20-20 ☎02/2565835, Ⓦwww.hotelothello.com. Small European-style hotel with immaculate en-suite rooms, all with floor-to-ceiling windows, cable TVs and plug-in heating. Full breakfast included and served in bed on huge wicker trays, if you wish. An excellent choice for this price range. ❻

JW Marriott Orellana 1172 and Amazonas ☎02/2972000, Ⓦwww.marriott.com. Unmistakable ziggurat of cream stone and green glass, Quito's plushest and best-appointed luxury hotel boasts all the facilities you would expect, including spa, pool, quality restaurant, airport shuttle and brisk room service. Discounted rates at weekends. ❾

Magic Bean Foch E5-08 ☎02/2566181, Ⓦwww .magicbeanquito.com. A handful of rooms above the popular café, some with bunks and shared baths, others with double beds and en-suite baths. All are spotlessly clean, light and airy, and come with free luggage storage, breakfast and wi-fi access. Dorms $10, doubles ❺

Mansión del Angel Wilson E5-29 ☎02/2557721, Ⓦwww.mansiondelangel.com.ec. Superb old mansion lavishly decorated with crystal chandeliers, gilt cornices, chaises longues and dark oil paintings. Most beds are four-posters, adding to the sense of luxury. Great place for a splurge. Breakfast included. ❼–❾

Nassau Pinto E4-342 and Amazonas ☎02/2565724, Ⓦwww.nassauhostal.com. Offering clean, fuss-free rooms with or without bath in a surprisingly quiet location just off Amazonas. The upstairs rooms feel more airy, and there's cable TV on the landing. ❷

Nü House Foch E6-12 and Reina Victoria ☎02/2557845, Ⓦwww.nuhousehotels.com.

Luxury boutique hotel with two restaurants in the heart of La Mariscal, whose snazzy contemporary furnishings are complemented by 32-inch TVs and fast wi-fi. Comfortable and highly regarded. ❾

Posada del Maple Juan Rodríguez E8-49 ⓣ02/2544507, ⓦ www.posadadelmaple.com. Relaxed and friendly house, offering rooms of varying shapes and sizes for a wide range of budgets. Use of kitchen, plus tea, coffee and breakfast included. Dorms $7.50, doubles ❹–❺

Hotel Quito González Suárez N27-142 and 12 de Octubre ⓣ02/2544600, ⓕ2567284. Landmark hotel with spectacular views over La Mariscal from the hills to the east. The building itself is past its prime, but it has more character than many of the contemporary luxury chains, and service and facilities are excellent. ❾

Hostal de la Rábida La Rábida 227 and Santa María ⓣ02/2221720, ⓦ www.hostalrabida.com. Charming Italian-owned hotel on a quiet residential street, providing the feel of a converted period house with its wooden floors, crackling fire and elegant rooms. Excellent service and good food in its cosy restaurant. ❼

Raices Tamayo N21-255 and Carrión, ⓣ02/2559737, ⓦ www.hostal-raices.com. Occupying a peaceful spot a few blocks from the Mariscal bustle, this assiduously tidy house has had a paint job to keep its guests cheerful. All rooms come with private bath and breakfast is included. ❺

Suites González Suárez San Ignacio 2750 and Av González Suárez ⓣ02/2232003, ⓦ www .hotelgonzalezsuarez.com. In a quiet district east of town, a comfortable mid-range hotel whose standard rooms offer cable TVs, spacious bathrooms and sofas. Pricier options include jacuzzis and balcony views over Guápulo. Buffet breakfast and airport transfers included. ❽

Swissôtel 12 de Octubre 1820 and Luis Cordero ⓣ02/2567600, ⓦ www.swissotel.com. Deluxe five-star hotel boasting five top-class restaurants, plush rooms, a wonderful spa and gym complex and all the facilities you would expect for the price. Buffet breakfast included. ❾

El Taxo Foch E4-116 ⓣ02/2225593. A large house on a quiet street featuring inexpensive rooms with shared or private baths and polished wood floors, a sitting room with big wood fire, kitchen facilities and internet. Friendly owners. ❸

Titisee Foch E7-60 and Reina Victoria ⓣ02/22529063, ⓦ www.hostaltitisee.com. Assiduously swept floorboards, pastel colours and straightforward but perfectly pleasant rooms feature in this spacious hostel. It's friendly, cheap and cheerful and often full, so book in advance. Breakfast included. ❸

Villa Nancy 6 de Diciembre 1934 between Cordero and Baquerizo Moreno ⓣ02/2563084, ⓦ www.villa-nancy.com. Agreeable Swiss–Ecuadorian bed and (buffet) breakfast with nine spacious rooms (six with private baths), kitchen and roomy lounge with a fireplace and cable TV.

Long-term accommodation

The best place to look for **long-term accommodation** is in the classified section of the daily newspapers *El Comercio*, especially on Sundays, and *Hoy*; conveniently, they both post classifieds (*clasificados*) on their websites (ⓦ www.elcomercio.com, ⓦ www.hoy.com.ec). You might also try the notice boards of South American Explorers (see p.77), which also keeps lists of families offering **homestays**. **Rates** average $175–300 per month for a two-bedroom apartment in the new town, but prices tend to increase if the landlord senses you're a foreigner; try to get a local friend to come along to negotiate the price.

For medium-term stays **apart-hotels** are a good option. They're a bit more expensive than renting your own apartment, but are comfortable, furnished and straightforward to arrange. *Antinéa* (see p.81) offers several luxurious apartments and duplexes for up to six people ($80–145 per night), while the more economic *Los Quipus*, Lérida E14-55 and *Lugo* in the Floresta district (ⓣ02/2224037, ⓦ www.losquipus.com; from $45 per day double occupancy or one- to six-person apartments for $800–1450 per month), also offers discounts for longer stays. One convenient option is *Casa Oriente*, Yaguachi 824 and *Llona*, near the Parque La Alameda (ⓣ02/2546157), a block of eighteen apartments whose one- or two-bedroom units have private bathrooms and small kitchens (doubles $120, two-bedroom apartments $130–150 per month). Those on the higher floors also have great views, and the rooftop terrace has laundry facilities. It's popular, so book as far in advance as possible.

Free airport pick-up for those staying more than one night. **⑤**

Villantigua Jorge Washington E9-48 and Tamayo ☎02/2528564, ✉alariv@uio.satnet.net. Family-run hotel in an attractive house in a quiet part of town, offering en-suite rooms with colonial reproduction furniture. Some rooms have balconies and

fireplaces, and interconnecting sets are popular with families. Breakfast included. **⑥**

Windsor Roca 668 and Amazonas ☎02/2224033, ⓦwww.windsorhotel.com.ec. Comfortable, modern six-storey hotel boasting a jacuzzi in every room, full cable TV, free internet, breakfast and airport transfer at a competitive price. **⑦**

The old town

Accommodation in the **old town** can be less expensive than in the new town, though many of the cheapest places are quite unsavoury, particularly those around the bus terminal. Yet the recent smartening up of the colonial centre has seen the appearance of a new generation of luxury hotels and exclusive restaurants in refurbished historic buildings, outstripping anything the new town has to offer for antique charm with both comfort and location. Still, the old town remains behind the new town in terms of quantity and variety of services – but the reward is waking up in the very heart of things and not feeling as if you're surrounded by hundreds of gringos.

Huasi Continental Flores 332 ☎02/2957327. It doesn't look like much from the outside, but the rooms are surprisingly nice, all with plenty of light, little noise and some with polished parquet floors and clean en-suite baths. **③**

Internacional Plaza del Teatro Guayaquil N8-75 ☎02/2959462, ⓕ2519462. Distinctive green-and-white building with its own parking. Rooms are a little dowdy, but large, clean and comfortable, and all have private baths. Room 202 has an enticing balcony with views of El Panecillo. **④**

Patio Andaluz García Moreno N6-52 and Olmedo ☎02/2280830, ⓦwww.hotelpatioandaluz.com. In a fabulous old building, parts of which date from the sixteen century, with colonnaded courtyards and balconies, complemented by twenty-first-century comforts, including cable TV, spa and internet. There's the *Rincón de Cantuña* restaurant (see p.109), a library and gift shop. Breakfast included. **⑨**

La Posada Colonial Paredes 188 and Rocafuerte ☎02/2282859, ⓕ2505240. Located in a not-great area near the bus terminal, but still a secure and friendly hotel with clean and spacious rooms, offering two to six beds in each. **②**

🏃 **Plaza Grande** García Moreno N5-16 and Chile ☎02/2510777, ⓦwww.plaza grandequito.com. This gorgeous, recently restored luxury hotel enjoys an unrivalled location on the Plaza de la Independencia. Within its striking Neoclassical walls, 3 of 15 suites overlook the square, but all come with internet, whirlpool and climate control. Sumptuous – and great dining, too (see p.108). **⑨**

Real Audiencia Bolívar Oe3-18 and Guayaquil ☎02/2952711, ⓦwww.realaudiencia.com. Rooms are a little ordinary for the price, but do come with

cable TV and private baths. What you're really paying for is the wonderful view over Plaza Santo Domingo, so don't miss out by getting a room on the wrong side. Breakfast and airport pick-up included. **⑦**

El Relicario del Carmen Venezuela 1041 and Olmedo ☎02/2289120, ⓦwww.hotelrelicario delcarmen.com. New hotel in a sensitively renovated building dating back to 1705, which trades easy hotel glitz for authentic detailing. Efficient service and breakfast included. No smoking. **⑧–⑨**

San Francisco de Quito Sucre 217 and Guayaquil ☎02/2287758, ⓦwww.sanfranciscodequito.com .ec. A beautiful colonial building, with modest but clean en-suite rooms around a charming, geranium-filled courtyard with a fountain. Breakfast and use of sauna and steam room included. **⑥**

Secret Garden Antepara E4-60 and Los Ríos ☎02/2956704, ⓦwww.secretgardenquito.com. On the fringes of the old town, this popular Ecuadorian-Australian hostel has a friendly vibe and a haven of a roof terrace, which is also a fantastic place to mingle while enjoying city views and inexpensive food. Spanish classes, travel services and airport transfers offered. Dorms $9, rooms **④**

Residencial Sucre Bolívar 615, Plaza San Francisco ☎02/2954025. Very basic and faintly squalid hotel on the corner of the plaza; rooms are just about passable though, and those directly on the corner have fantastic views over the square. **①**

Viena Hotel Internacional Flores 600 and Chile ☎02/2954860, ⓕ2954633. Handsome building with rooms around a patio, which is filled with potted ferns and a shrine to the Virgin. Slightly faded but still clean, with comfortable beds. **④**

Outskirts of Quito

If the hurly-burly of the city centre is too daunting, you could consider lodging in any of several good hotels on the **outskirts** of town, where you'll have the benefits of a more peaceful and spacious setting, but still be within range to visit the city sights.

La Carriona 2.5 km vía Sangolquí–Amaguaña, Sangolquí ☎02/2332004, ⌨www.lacarriona.com. An attractive, converted hacienda from the early 1800s with a grand cobbled courtyard, colourful gardens, swimming pool and spa, well-appointed rooms and delicious food. The staff can organize tours to Pasochoa with horses and guides, and trips to a dairy farm near Papallacta. Breakfast included. ⑧

Cuevas de Álvaro 32km east of Quito on the road to Papallacta, reservations at Carrión N21-01 and Juan León Mera ☎02/2228902, ⌨www .cuevasdealvaro.galeon.com. An eccentric subterranean bolt hole where the rooms and corridors have been hewn out of the rock, set in a ring around a central patio. Packages are offered including meals, hikes and horse rides. ⑨

Hacienda Chillo-Jijón vía Amaguaña, in the Valle de los Chillos ☎02/2331632, ⌨www.hacienda -ecuador.com. A 30min drive from town, this beautiful hacienda – once one of the largest textile mills in the country – has been in the same family since its construction in 1730 and is elegantly decorated with lavish original paintings and furniture. Horseriding, cycling, tennis, golf or just strolling in the expansive grounds are among the activities on offer. Distinguished and luxurious. By advance reservation only. ⑨

San Jorge 4km west of Av Occidental on the Nono road ☎02/3390402, ⌨www.hostsanjorge.com.ec. Only 20min from the new town on the northeastern foothills of Volcán Pichincha, this country hacienda has comfortable rooms with stone fireplaces, plus a swimming pool, sauna, whirlpool and steam room; there's also a private nature reserve ideal for hiking, biking, horseriding and birdwatching. ⑦–⑨

Sommergarten Chimborazo 248 and Riofrío, Sangolquí ☎02/2332761, ⌨www.ecuador -sommergarten.net. A haven set in pleasant gardens with a swimming pool and sauna. Tours are offered to many destinations, including sister hotels in El Ángel and the northern lowlands. Breakfast included. ⑥

Quito city tours

Numerous operators, including most of those listed in the "Tours from Quito" section on p.114, offer tours of the city itself. **Standard tours** ($25–35) last about three hours and usually include a mix of riding in a vehicle and walking around the old town, visiting a few churches and museums, and then taking a trip to the top of El Panecillo for great views of the city. Many operators also make tours of the old town **by night**, when the churches and monuments are illuminated to stunning effect. Others feature **special-interest** tours, such as the contemporary-art tour offered by Enchanted Expeditions, Av de las Alondras N45-102 and Los Lirios (☎02/3340525, ⌨www.galapagosenchantedexpeditions.com), which looks at the works of Oswaldo Guayasamín and other modern Ecuadorian artists. **Transport** on most city tours is in small minivans, but Klein Tours, Av Eloy Alfaro N34-151 and Catalina Aldaz (☎02/2267000, ⌨www.kleintours.com), drives its clients around in a splendid 1950s wooden bus.

One recommended – and less expensive – alternative to these private tours is to take a municipal **walking tour** of the old town (Tues–Sun 10am, 11am & 2pm; $12; 2hr 30min–3hr 30min), led by multilingual guides from the metropolitan police, which leave from the tourist information office in the Palacio Arzobispal (☎02/2586591; see p.88). Six walking tours are offered, which together cover most of the old-town sights. Two shorter tours (2hr) are also offered at night, when the historic centre looks its floodlit best, and they leave from the same place at 7pm (Tues–Sun; $7).

Finally, a quick and fun way of acquainting yourself with the main points of interest is to take a **horse-drawn carriage** (Sun–Wed 10am–10pm, Thurs–Sat 10am–midnight; $5 per person or $14 for a four-person carriage) on a 20-minute tour of the old town plazas and sights. The *carrozas* or *coches de la colonia* depart from a stand on García Moreno and Sucre opposite La Compañía.

The old town

Quito's chief attraction is the **old town** and its dazzling array of churches, monasteries and convents dating from the early days of the colony. Known to Quiteños as **el Centro Histórico**, the old town falls into a fairly small area that can be comfortably covered on foot in a day; trying to take in the forty-odd churches and assorted museums will quickly leave you feeling swamped and exhausted, so try to single out a few highlights. These should definitely include the three main squares – **Plaza de la Independencia**, **Plaza Santo Domingo** and **Plaza San Francisco** – as well as the charming little **Plaza del Teatro**. Of the city's churches (most daily 8–11am & 3–6pm), the most impressive are **San Francisco**, **La Compañía** and **La Merced**, along with **El Sagrario** and **San Agustín**.

The old town's most rewarding museum is the excellent **Museo de la Ciudad**, while the **Museo Alberto Mena Caamaño** and its waxworks set in evocative surroundings is also worth a visit. A short walk away, the **Museo Manuela Sáenz**, part shrine to the love between two of South America's heroes of the Independence era, and the **Museo Camilo Egas**, a permanent retrospective of one of Ecuador's greatest-ever artists, are fascinating. For a glimpse inside the best-preserved old-town houses, head for the **Casa de María Augusta Urrutia** or the **Casa de Sucre**, while for sweeping views of the city, a short taxi ride up to the summit of **El Panecillo** is highly recommended, or to the **Parque Itchimbía** – though the panoramas from the precipitous ledges on the spires of the **Basílica del Voto Nacional** can hardly be bettered.

Orientation in the old town can sometimes be confusing, as many streets have two different **street names**: the official name on green plaques, and the historical one painted on ceramic tiles; Calle Sucre, for instance, is also signed as Calle de Algodón (Cotton St). Only the official names appear on the maps and in the text of this guide; for information on how to read Quito street addresses, see box on p.79.

Plaza de la Independencia and around

The **Plaza de la Independencia**, or **Plaza Grande**, was first laid out with a string and ruler in 1534 and still preserves its original dimensions. Surrounded by the city's most important civic and religious buildings – the cathedral, Government Palace, Archbishop's Palace and City Hall – the plaza has always been the city's focus. On Sundays, when traffic is prohibited from the surrounding streets (9am–4pm), the square is at its best, offering a great place for **people-watching**, especially the permanent array of dapper old men out for a stroll in their Sunday best, and the school kids, grandmothers and sweethearts sitting on benches amid the spindly palm trees and flowerbeds.

The cathedral and Palacio de Gobierno

The sturdy horizontal outline of the **cathedral** (Mon–Fri 10am–4pm, Sat 10am–2pm; $1.50), with its gleaming white walls, grey-stone portals and terracotta-tiled roof, dominates the south side of the square. Constructed in 1678 and restored in 1806, its interior is not especially impressive, though it does contain the remains of Ecuador's most famous historical figure, **Field Marshal Sucre** (see p.493). More interesting are the details of the sensational murder that took place here during the Good Friday Mass of 1877, when the Bishop of Quito was poisoned with strychnine dissolved in the holy wine.

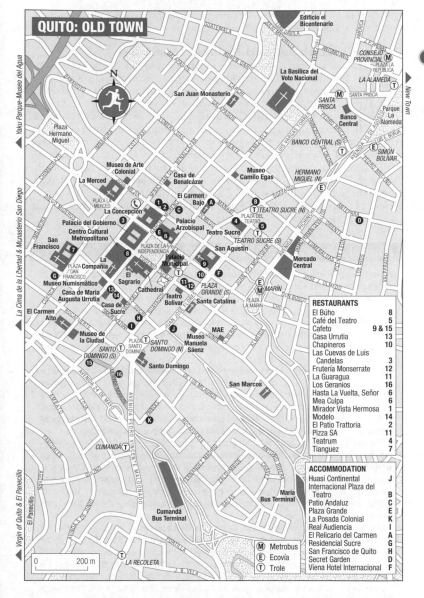

QUITO: OLD TOWN

RESTAURANTS

El Búho	8
Café del Teatro	5
Cafeto	9 & 15
Casa Urrutia	13
Chapineros	10
Las Cuevas de Luis Candelas	3
Frutería Monserrate	12
La Guaragua	11
Los Geranios	16
Hasta La Vuelta, Señor	6
Mea Culpa	6
Mirador Vista Hermosa	1
Modelo	14
El Patio Trattoria	2
Pizza SA	11
Teatrum	4
Tianguez	7

ACCOMMODATION

Huasi Continental	J
Internacional Plaza del Teatro	B
Patio Andaluz	C
Plaza Grande	E
La Posada Colonial	K
Real Audiencia	I
El Relicario del Carmen	A
Residencial Sucre	G
San Francisco de Quito	H
Secret Garden	D
Viena Hotel Internacional	F

Ⓜ Metrobus
Ⓔ Ecovía
Ⓣ Trole

0   200 m

Perpendicular to the cathedral on the west side of the plaza, the **Palacio de Gobierno** (Government Palace) was the site of another dramatic murder when, in 1875, President García Moreno was macheted to death in the outer corridor of the palace. (see "History", p.494). This white-stuccoed, perfectly symmetrical building – fronted by a long row of columns supporting an upper balcony – is both the seat of government and the presidential palace, and is guarded by a couple of ineffectual-looking soldiers decked out in antiquated gold-and-blue uniforms. Entry is not allowed, but they might let you take a peek inside the gate if you ask politely.

Palacio Arzobispal and Palacio Municipal

The grand and dazzlingly white **Palacio Arzobispal** (Archbishop's Palace), a two-storey Neoclassical building taking up most of the north side of the plaza, accommodates shops, restaurants and a tourist information office, which is the starting point for municipal walking tours (see box, p.85). Free events are sometimes staged in the **Patio Cultural**, one of its two covered courtyards inside. The taller, bright apricot-coloured building, embellished with fancy white pillars and plaster mouldings, to the left of the Palacio Arzobispal is the former **Hotel Majestic** (recently reopened as the *Hotel Plaza Grande*, see p.84), dating from the 1930s and one of the first buildings to break the two-storey level in the old town. The concrete **Palacio Municipal** (City Hall), built between 1968 and 1973, takes up the east side of the square, blending in surprisingly well with the neighbouring colonial buildings, thanks to its low, horizontal design and white-painted walls.

Colonial religious art and the Quito School

After the conquest, the Spanish Crown was faced with the task of colonizing its new territories and subsuming their indigenous population into its empire. From the beginning, conversion to Catholicism became one of the most powerful tools to consolidate power. Accordingly, **religious art and architecture** took on an enormous importance very early on: splendid monasteries and cathedrals dazzled and instilled awe in the natives, while paintings and sculpture were used both for visual religious instruction and to provide icons of worship that would replace their former idols.

In the early days, religious art was imported from Spain, but the need to disperse large quantities of it around the continent prompted the growth of home-grown **artists' workshops** and **guilds** in the colonial centres, where Spanish teachers trained *indígenas* and *mestizos*. This resulted in a unique blend of indigenous and European elements: carvings of biblical characters were frequently clothed in typical native dress, for instance, and sometimes given indigenous traits and colouring.

The main production centres of religious art were Quito, Bogotá and Cuzco, each developing its own style. Over time, Quito artists became known for their mastery of **polychromy** (decorative colouring), particularly in their carvings of Mary, Christ and numerous saints, made out of cedar or red oak. Characterized by bold colours and exuberant decoration, the style found its greatest expression between 1660 and 1765, when the proliferation of high-quality Quiteño artists gave rise to the **Quito School** of art.

Led by **Miguel de Santiago** and **Bernardo de Legarda** in the early eighteenth century, and later by Manuel Chili, known as **Caspicara**, the Quito School's most delicate and beautiful creations was its polychrome carvings, often of the Virgin, covered in sumptuous attire and exposing only the head, face, hands and feet. One of the most peculiar aspects of the style was an excessive take on **realism**, using human hair and false eyelashes, nails and glass eyes. The school's paintings were characterized by vivid shades of red against darker, duller tones.

The movement began to wane towards the end of the eighteenth century, when secular subjects such as landscapes, portraits and town scenes began to replace religious ones. It finally died out after Ecuador's independence from Spain in 1822, when the type of religious art the school produced was rejected for its associations with the old regime.

Centro Cultural Metropolitano and El Sagrario

The **Centro Cultural Metropolitano** (Tues–Sun 9am–5pm; ☎02/2584362, ⓦwww.centrocultural-quito.com), on the southwest corner overlooking the plaza, is the new focus of cultural life in the old town, housing gallery space for temporary exhibitions, lecture rooms, the municipal library and a museum, as well as elegant, glass-covered courtyards and a café.

The building occupies a site rich in **history**, supposedly the location of one of Atahualpa's palaces before becoming a Jesuit university in the early colonial period, then a military barracks, and once more a university – which in 1830 hosted the signing of the Act of Constitution of the Independent State. Its most infamous moment came in 1810, when a group of revolutionaries was executed in a cell inside the building. This gruesome incident and other milestones of Ecuador's journey to independence are commemorated in waxwork displays, which form part of the **Museo Alberto Mena Caamaño** (Tues–Sun 9am–5pm; $1.50), located within. The rest comprises a collection of colonial, republican and contemporary art.

Opposite the Centro Cultural Metropolitano, just off the plaza and adjoining the cathedral, is **El Sagrario**, a seventeenth-century church topped by a pale-blue dome, whose colourful interior features turquoise walls embellished with bright geometric designs and stone pillars painted dark coral. The underside of the main dome is covered with swirling multicoloured frescos, while the altar is often festooned with fresh white lilies.

La Concepción and the Iglesia de la Merced

Just off the northwest corner of the Plaza de la Independencia are the thick, impregnable-looking walls of **La Concepción**, Quito's oldest convent, dating from 1577 and off-limits to visitors. A couple of blocks west on Chile, the **Iglesia de La Merced**, built between 1701 and 1747, features a wonderfully over-the-top Baroque and Moorish interior that's one of the old town's highlights. Its ceilings and walls offer a confection of white, lace-like plaster relief against a sugary-pink background, looking like icing on a cake, with the side walls further adorned by dozens of oil paintings set in immense gilt frames. The main altar, carved by Bernardo de Legarda in 1751, and two side altars are resplendent with gold leaf, while the choir, on a raised gallery at the back of the church, is ablaze with yet more gilding. The clock tower contains a 5.7-tonne bronze bell, Quito's largest. You can also visit the adjoining **convent** (Mon–Sat 7am–noon & 1–6pm), built around a huge central patio enclosed within beautiful arched cloisters.

Museo Nacional de Arte Colonial and around

Directly behind La Merced, at Cuenca and José Mejía, is the **Museo Nacional de Arte Colonial** (currently closed for restoration; ☎02/2282297 for the latest), inside a restored sixteenth-century colonial house built around a colonnaded courtyard with a fountain. Its collection has been moved temporarily to the Casa de la Cultura (see p.97) until works are completed.

Dedicated almost exclusively to **religious art**, particularly oil paintings and carved, polychrome statuary, the museum contains some impressive work by Quito School artists (see box opposite). The first two rooms are devoted to the art of the sixteenth and seventeenth centuries, but the bulk of the collection, filling three rooms, is made up of eighteenth-century works.

For a bite-sized chunk of the same thing, head two blocks northeast to the **Casa de Benalcázar**, Sebastián de Benalcázar and Olmedo (Mon–Fri 9am–1pm & 2–5pm; free; ☎02/2288102). A splendid colonial mansion with a gorgeous courtyard, holding a small collection of religious paintings and statues in one room on the ground floor, the house is also the site of occasional free lunchtime concerts; call for programme details.

Iglesia San Agustín and around

Leading east downhill from the Plaza de la Independencia, the busy, pedestrianized stretch of **Chile** is worth a look for its beautifully renovated nineteenth- and early twentieth-century buildings, painted in rich colours set off by elaborate cornices and white-plaster window mouldings.

One block east of the plaza, at Chile and Guayaquil, the imposing **Iglesia San Agustín** dates from the sixteenth century but was substantially rebuilt in 1880 after an earthquake, and features a massive 37-metre bell tower crowned by a statue of St Augustine. Its dark, neo-Gothic interior contains a series of enormous paintings by the distinguished seventeenth-century artist, Miguel de Santiago, depicting the life of the church's namesake. The adjoining **Convento de San Agustín** has survived intact since its completion in 1627, and contains a fine cloister with two levels of thick stone columns. It was in the convent's chapter house (*sala capítular*) where fledgling patriots signed the Act of Independence on August 10, 1809, and the great hall also boasts an intricately painted, highly ornate ceiling and glittering gold-leaf altar. On the second floor of the convent, a **museum** (Mon–Fri 9am–12.30pm & 2–5pm, Sat 9am–1pm; $1) houses a large, dusty collection of religious paintings attributed to artists of the Quito School (see box, p.88).

Teatro Bolívar and Monasterio Santa Catalina

A block south of San Agustín, on Calle Eugenio Espejo, the flamboyant **Teatro Bolívar**, built in 1933, was lavishly refurbished in 1997 but gutted two years later by a fire which started in a neighbouring pizza place. The second restoration is ongoing and events are now regularly held (see p.112), but the theatre is still far from its original glory and funds are sorely lacking. The foundation in charge of its recovery offers night-time tours, combined with entertainment and dinner; for details and reservations contact the Fundación Teatro Bolívar (T02/2582486, W www.teatrobolivar.org).

Half a block down from the theatre, at Espejo and Juan José Flores, the **Monasterio Santa Catalina** is Quito's most colourful religious building, sporting bright, coral-coloured walls trimmed with white-plaster relief.

Plaza del Teatro, Teatro Sucre and Iglesia del Carmen Bajo

Two blocks north of San Agustín, on Flores, sits one of the most charming squares in the city, the intimate **Plaza del Teatro**. Often a venue for open-air jazz concerts (most Thursday evenings), it's surrounded by meticulously restored nineteenth-century buildings, including the white, temple-like **Teatro Sucre** (for theatre listings, see p.112). The theatre was built between 1879 and 1887 (symbolically on the site of the city slaughterhouse) and its glorious facade features six Corinthian columns and bas-reliefs of human figures representing music, drama and poetry. A block west, at Olmedo and Venezuela, stands the lovely stone **Iglesia del Carmen Bajo**, whose main entrance incorporates two enormous wooden doors, dating from 1745, elaborately carved with heraldic motifs.

Museo Camilo Egas

The **Museo Camilo Egas** (Tues–Fri 9am–5pm, Sat 10am–4pm; $0.50), in a handsome colonial house on the corner of Venezuela and Esmeraldas, exhibits an excellent overview of the paintings of Camilo Egas (1889–1962), one of Ecuador's most important twentieth-century artists. The early works from the mid-1920s are perhaps the most charming and accessible, romanticized depictions of native people in everyday life, which became instant classics in Ecuador and helped foster the *indigenismo* movement. His less optimistic later works traverse styles from social realism to surrealism, neo-Cubism and finally to abstract expressionism. It's a small museum but the quality of the paintings on show is high.

La Compañía and around

On the west side of the Plaza de la Independencia, García Moreno, known as the "Street of the Seven Crosses" after the large stone crucifixes lining its route, runs south towards El Panecillo, past a string of churches and other points of interest. About half a block from the plaza at García Moreno and Sucre is the most opulent of these, **La Compañía** (tourist schedule Mon–Fri 9.30am–5.30pm, Sat 9am–4pm & Sun 1–4pm, and night visits Wed–Fri 7.30–9.30pm; $2 with guide), built by Jesuits between 1605 and 1765 and completed just two years before Spain expelled the order from the continent. Boasting an extraordinary Baroque facade of carved volcanic stone, the church is piled high with twisted columns, sacred hearts, cherubs, angels and saints. Inside, any thoughts of restraint vanish amid the wild extravagance of gold leaf – there's a reputed seven tonnes of the stuff covering the altars, galleries, Moorish tracery and pulpit. Beautifully restored after a fire in 1996, the only testament to the damage is the smoke-blackened face of an angel, deliberately left uncleaned, peering down from the inner circle of the cupola.

Museo Numismático

In the old home of the Banco Central del Ecuador and across the street from La Compañía is the **Museo Numismático** (Tues–Fri 9am–5pm, Sat & Sun 10am–4pm; $1, free on Sun), which outlines the history of the country's various forms of currency. Starting off with spondylus shells, which were effectively

▲ La Compañía

used as money along the Pacific coast, the museum explores pre-Columbian commerce in salt, coca leaves, obsidian, axe heads, cloves and cinnamon, before passing on to the elegant gold and silver *reales* of the nascent Spanish colony. The post-independence section shows how the earliest examples of the *sucre*, Ecuador's first decimalized currency (created in 1868 and in use until 2000), turn out to have been minted in Birmingham, England.

Casa de María Augusta Urrutia and Casa de Sucre

Diagonally opposite the Museo Numismático is the **Casa de María Augusta Urrutia** (Tues–Sat 10am–6pm, Sun 9.30am–5pm; $2), a fine nineteenth-century mansion built around three inner patios. Guided **tours** are offered around the house where Doña María – widowed at an early age – lived alone with her 24 servants until her death in 1987. Many of the rooms have been left virtually untouched, and provide a fascinating glimpse of the tastes of Quito's upper classes in the twentieth century. The house is now owned by the charity Doña María founded in the 1930s (Fundación Mariana de Jesús), which aims to alleviate poverty in Quito by building low-price housing.

Further down the block to the east, at Venezuela and Sucre, the nineteenth-century **Casa de Sucre** (Tues–Fri 8am–4pm, Sat 8.30am–1pm; $1) was once the property of Ecuador's liberator, Field Marshal Sucre. Unless you're into military history, the battle plans, weapons, uniforms, standards and portraits of generals exhibited are not that exciting, though the building itself is a beautiful example of a late-period Spanish colonial house.

Museo de la Ciudad and Convento del Carmen Alto

Housed in a former hospital on García Moreno, the dynamic **Museo de la Ciudad** (Tues–Sun 9.30am–5.30pm; $3; ⓦwww.museociudadquito.gov.ec) uses replicas, scale models, mannequins, friezes and sound effects to illustrate the city's development. Exhibits include a scale model of the construction of the Iglesia San Francisco, with hundreds of miniature workers toiling away; a reconstruction of the inside of a sixteenth-century house and another of a workshop belonging to a Quito School artist. The old hospital's church is also worth a look, for its blazing red-and-gold interior and exuberant Baroque altarpieces.

Built as a rain shelter for the local Mass-goers, the eighteenth-century **Arco de la Reina** on the street outside, is a thick-walled arch spanning the street at the corner with Rocafuerte. Just beyond is the eighteenth-century **Convento del Carmen Alto**, where Carmelite nuns still live in complete isolation. They do manage to sell honey, herbs and wine through a revolving wooden contraption that allows them to remain hidden from view; to buy something, go through the iron gates, then through the small door next to the main entrance, and tap on the wooden screen in the wall (Mon–Fri 9–11am & 3–5pm; alternatively, the on-site shop is open Mon–Fri 9am–5pm).

Plaza San Francisco

Arguably Quito's most beautiful square, the vast, cobbled **Plaza San Francisco**, whose monochrome shades and sweeping proportions are accentuated by the absence of trees and benches, giving it an empty, slightly melancholy air, is quite a contrast to the cheerful leafiness of the Plaza de la Independencia.

Stretching across the plaza's western side is the monumental **Iglesia y Monasterio de San Francisco**, whose horizontal whitewashed walls are dominated by the twin bell towers and carved-stone portal of the church's entrance. Hidden behind this facade are the extensive buildings and seven courtyards that make San Francisco the largest religious complex in South America.

From the square, a broad flight of stone steps leads up to the front entrance of the **church**, whose construction began in 1536 shortly after the founding of Quito. Once your eyes become accustomed to the shadows you'll notice the walls, altars, pillars and pulpit are encrusted with gilt, almost rivalling the theatricality of La Compañía. The main altar fills a large, domed area and is adorned by Bernardo de Legarda's famous winged carving of the **Virgen de Quito**, which served as a model for the giant statue on El Panecillo (see p.94).

On each side are two lateral chapels, resplendent with gold leaf, and more gilt can be found in the adjoining **Capilla de Cantuña** (Cantuña Chapel), entered through a door to the left of the entrance to the Iglesia. Inside are a splendid altar and many paintings and carvings the Quito School produced (see box, p.89). According to legend, the chapel was built by an Indian named **Cantuña**, whom the Devil assisted to complete the work. When the time came to hand over his soul, however, Cantuña was saved on discovering that a single stone was missing from the structure.

On the other side of the church entrance is the door to the **Museo de San Francisco** (Mon–Fri 9am–1pm & 2–6pm, Sat 9am–6pm & Sun 9am–noon; $2), displaying an impressive collection of religious sculpture, paintings and furniture in a gallery off the monastery's main cloister. If you take advantage of the free guide service available at the entrance (small tip expected), you'll also be led to the otherwise locked **coro** (choir) of the church, housed in a raised gallery overlooking the central nave, which features a spectacular carved *mudéjar* (Moorish-style) ceiling and a row of 36 painted wooden carvings of Franciscan martyrs on the walls, above the choir stalls. Just outside there's a so-called **whispering corridor**, where two people speaking into diagonally opposite corners can hear each other's voices.

Plaza Santo Domingo and around

From the Plaza San Francisco, a three-block walk east along Simón Bolívar leads to Quito's third major square, the **Plaza Santo Domingo**, frequently used as a venue for outdoor concerts and festivals. Fronting its eastern side is the graceful **Iglesia Santo Domingo**, which Dominican friars built during the sixteenth century. Unfortunately, an ill-conceived interior remodelling took place in the nineteenth century, leaving the church with an altar that looks more like a miniature Gothic castle, surrounded by dozens of flickering candles. Still, you can't help but be impressed by the Moorish-influenced tracery on the ceilings. An adjoining monastery houses the **Museo Fray Pedro Bedón** (Mon–Sat 9am–4.30pm, Sun 9am–1pm; $2), which contains a large collection of Dominican religious art from the sixteenth to eighteenth centuries, including remarkable life-size sculptures of various saints with moving arms and hands, as well as gold and silver ornaments and beautiful furniture, delicately inlaid with bone and marble.

La Ronda

One block south from Plaza Domingo, Guayaquil crosses a narrow, pedestrianized section of Calle Morales still known by its original name of **La Ronda** (Ⓦ www.callelaronda.com). Lined with thick-walled, whitewashed buildings with wrought-iron balconies and billowing flags, this picturesque cobblestoned alley is one of Quito's oldest streets, and one of the few remaining stretches of eighteenth-century working-class and artisanal housing. In the early twentieth century it was the bohemian and artistic heart of the capital, but years of neglect left it a notorious haunt of thieves and lowlifes. A regeneration project has restored its charms, and many of the houses have been converted into galleries, cafés and shops, with the focus on Ecuadorian goods and traditional produce.

Museo Manuela Sáenz

A short walk northeast of Plaza Santo Domingo takes you to the **Museo Manuela Sáenz** (Mon–Fri 8.30am–noon & 2–4pm; $0.80) at Junín 709 and Montúfar, set in an imposing colonial house. The museum is primarily dedicated to the life of Manuela Sáenz (1797–1856), the lover of Simón Bolívar, and for a brief period one of the most influential women in Latin American history – the so-called Liberator's liberator – who died in exile, penniless. On display are their love letters, as well as many of their personal belongings, including Bolívar's silver dagger, revolver, sabre and, somewhat surprisingly, his chamber pot. Another key figure in Ecuador's struggle for independence, Field Marshal Sucre, is also well represented by his gem-encrusted spurs and dozens of portraits. Other rooms show coins, antique weaponry, religious art and carved ivory from Africa and China.

Museo Archivo de Arquitectura del Ecuador

A block east at the corner of Junín and Ortíz Bilbao in a charmingly renovated building is the **Museo Archivo de Arquitectura del Ecuador** or **MAE** (Tues–Sat 10am–5.30pm; $0.50), the best place to come if you want to get an understanding of Quito's architecture post-1880; descriptions are in Spanish only. Picking out key architects and buildings, it offers an overview of the capital's architectural development, mainly through text, photos and the occasional model. The various rooms are brought together on the ground floor, which shows a scale reconstruction of the historic centre and facsimile maps of Quito from 1573 to the present day.

El Panecillo and the Virgen de Quito

Rising over the southern edge of the old town is the hill known as **El Panecillo** ("the little bread loaf"), crowned by a magnificent, thirty-metre-high statue of the **Virgen de Quito**. The summit offers exhilarating views down to the city, spread out below like a blanket of pearl-white miniature houses enclosed by green hills. A long flight of steps leads here (a 40min walk) from the end of García Moreno, but violent muggings are common along the way so make sure you take a taxi instead (around $5 round trip with waiting time, around $7 from the new town). It's safe at the top, with teams of uniformed security guards patrolling the place (9am–7pm).

In contrast to the toy-town views, the winged Virgin is colossal up here, standing on an orb with a serpent curled around her feet, gazing serenely down to the city. You can climb the fifty-odd steps up the small tower on which she's standing to a **viewing platform** (daily 9am–6pm; $2). At weekends a **bus** service (45min; $0.75) runs every fifteen minutes between El Panecillo and the country's other famous landmark, La Mitad del Mundo (see p.121).

La Cima de la Libertad and Monasterio San Diego

The sweeping hilltop views are part of the pleasure of visiting **La Cima de la Libertad** (Tues–Thurs 8.30am–4.30pm, Fri 8.30am–1pm, Sat 9am–1pm; $1), a military museum on a neighbouring foothill of Volcán Pichincha, marking the site of the victorious **Battle of Pichincha** that sealed Ecuador's independence from Spain on May 24, 1822. The museum houses a large collection of nineteenth-century uniforms, weapons and other military paraphernalia, enlivened by some **murals** of key characters and events. Easily the most impressive is Eduardo Kingman's enormous 200-square-metre mural, which explores the nation's historical roots. You'll need to take a **taxi** up here (about $6–7) for the return ride from the old town, including waiting time at the top.

Between the two hills, just northwest of El Panecillo, the **Monasterio San Diego**, Calicuchima 117 and General Farfán (daily 9.30am–1pm & 2.30–5.30pm; $2), is a beautiful early-colonial Franciscan monastery of quiet, cloistered courtyards, a refectory with a painting of Christ sitting down to eat *cuy* (guinea pig) at the Last Supper, simple whitewashed walls and the fragments of some recently restored murals. Guided **tours** explore nearly the whole complex, offering a taste of both colonial and contemporary monastery life, disclosing secret doors and old pit tombs and reaching the top of the bell tower for views over the old town; only the modest living quarters of the monastery's current occupants remain off-limits. The church features an exquisite **pulpit** thought to be the second-oldest in South America – carved by an *indígena*, Juan Bautista Menacho – and a small **museum** offering a modest collection of colonial religious art.

Yaku, Parque-Museo del Agua

A kilometre or so north of El Panecillo near the El Placer neighbourhood, **Yaku, Parque-Museo del Agua** (Tues–Sun 9am–5pm, latest entry at 4pm; $3; Ⓦ www.yakumuseoagua.gov.ec) is set in Quito's old water treatment plant – a monolithic metal structure standing in the foothills of Volcán Pichincha. Guided tours take in the squares, fountains, vaults and exhibition rooms of the complex while the journey of Quito's water supply and the importance of water conservation is explained. The natural water sources in the mountainside here are said to have been the site of the Inca Athahualpa's ceremonial and purification baths. Whatever the truth of that legend, it's an impressive spot, commanding fine views down to the old town and across to neighbouring El Panecillo. To **get here** by public transport, take Metrobus Q to the Seminario Mayor stop on Avenida América (at Colón); from here, catch the "El Placer" bus, which will drop you outside the museum. A taxi from the old town will cost a couple of dollars.

Basílica del Voto Nacional

Perched on a small hill on Calle Venezuela, eight blocks north of the Plaza de la Independencia, the **Basílica del Voto Nacional** (towers daily 9am–5pm; $2; church Mon–Sat 7–8am & 6–7.30pm; free) is the tallest church in Ecuador, thanks to its two imposing, 115-metre towers plainly visible throughout the city. Built in a flamboyant, neo-Gothic style, it's a wild concoction of spires, flying buttresses, turrets, parapets, arches, gables and elaborate stained-glass windows. Despite construction beginning in 1892, the church – which is built largely in concrete – is still not entirely completed. The **gargoyles**, based on Ecuadorian fauna such as monkeys and jaguars, are a contemporary departure from the traditional representations of mythical creatures.

Don't miss the fantastic **views** from two vantage points accessed by lift and steep metal ladders: an unnerving buckling roof on the northern steeple, and a higher spot way up on the east tower, past the third-floor **café**, then on stairs and ladders past the clock machinery and belfry to an artificial floor made only

▲ View from the Basílica del Voto Nacional

of wide steel grille. From here, those with a head for heights can squeeze out onto tiny **ledges** on the spire's exterior for a genuine thrill.

Edificio El Bicentenario and Centro de Arte Contemporáneo

A few blocks north of the Basílica, on Luis Dávila and Montevideo, is the **Edificio El Bicentenario** (Tues–Sun 10am–8pm; $2), a triumphant rehabilitation of Quito's crumbling old Military Hospital into an impressive new exhibition and cultural centre – a bold project undertaken to commemorate the bicentenary of Quito's 1809 revolution (see p.493). For all its whitewashed colonnades, cobbled patios, tall windows and airy wards and corridors, the building (constructed between 1900 and 1929) seems uniquely well suited to house three large exhibition spaces, including the **Centro de Arte Contemporáneo**, dedicated to both visual and performing arts. Eventually the complex will also hold a library, auditorium, restaurant, café and shops, but till then it will present temporary exhibitions.

Parque Itchimbía

Looking directly southeast from the Basílica, you should make out on the hilltop opposite the glimmering outline of the **Itchimbía Centro Cultural** (Tues–Sun 9am–6pm; free), a stunning nineteenth-century market hall, reinvented as an art gallery and the centrepiece of the **Parque Itchimbía**, a green space commanding wonderful views over colonial Quito. The glass-and-metal structure, featuring an imposing octagonal cupola which looks particularly impressive when floodlit by night, was imported from Hamburg in 1889 and was originally located in the old town as the Santa Clara market hall, before its removal and re-inauguration as an exhibition space 115 years later. Contact the Centro Cultural Metropolitano for details of events and exhibitions (☎02/2584362, ⓦwww.centrocultural-quito.com). Once you're up here there's a charming place to refuel close by, *Mosaico* on Samaniego (see p.105).

The new town

The heart of Quito's **new town**, officially called **Mariscal Sucre** but known locally as **La Mariscal**, is roughly bound by avenidas Patria in the south, Orellana in the north, 12 de Octubre in the east and 10 de Agosto in the west. The main commercial artery, **Avenida Amazonas**, is lined with banks, tour operators and souvenir shops, but the social focus is the Plaza del Quinde (also called Plaza Foch), at the intersection of Reina Victoria and Foch, where bars, clubs, restaurants and cafés are often thronged with people in the evenings. The jumble of colonial-style town houses, Art Deco villas and functional 1970s blocks means La Mariscal isn't particularly attractive, but it is where the majority of visitors to Quito base themselves.

There are no really outstanding attractions in the new town proper, except for the first-rate **Museo del Banco Central**. Yet there is plenty of good stuff to do if you're willing to take a short taxi ride, most obviously the wonderful **TelefériQo**, a ski-lift-type gondola which swoops up to a lofty vantage point on the hills west of the capital. On the high ground east of town, the **Museo Fundación Guayasamín** and the associated **Capilla del Hombre** showcase the powerful art of Ecuador's most famous twentieth-century artist, while nearby **Guápulo** has the feel of a sleepy village far removed from the bustle and noise of the big city. Back in the centre, the new town does benefit from several precious green spaces, the **Parque La Alameda**, **Parque El Ejido**, and the extensive **Parque La Carolina**, where among the trees and cycle paths you'll find a botanical garden, a natural science museum and the **Vivarium**, exhibiting snakes and amphibians.

Parque La Alameda to Parque El Ejido

North of the old colonial centre lies a transitional area between the old and the new towns, the main landmark of which is the triangular **Parque La Alameda**, marked by a stately statue of Simón Bolívar at its southern end, a boating lake and the **Observatorio Astronómico** (Mon–Fri 9am–12.30pm & 2.30–5.30pm; $1) in the middle, built in 1873 and reputed to be the oldest observatory in South America. It houses a glorious brass telescope and an assortment of other astronomical devices collected during its long history.

Three blocks north of the park, on Juan Montalvo, stands the **Palacio Legislativo**, where the congress holds its sessions. There's a finely carved frieze on the front wall depicting key events of Ecuador's history, but the building's most interesting feature – Guayasamín's controversial mural, whose theme is the oppression of Latin America – is hidden from view inside. A short walk north takes you to the **Parque El Ejido**, a pleasant expanse of foliage and a favourite spot for impromptu football and volleyball games. It's also the site of a large weekend **art market**, where artists line the edge of the park along Patria with their paintings – most of them fairly mediocre, though you can sometimes find more unusual and accomplished works at a decent price.

Casa de la Cultura Ecuatoriana

Across from the Parque El Ejido, on 6 de Diciembre, the **Casa de la Cultura Ecuatoriana** (℡02/2223258, ⓦwww.cce.org.ec) is a complex of museums, theatres, auditoriums, exhibition spaces and a cinema, all housed in two buildings. The original, a distinguished neocolonial house built in 1946 and embellished inside with murals by Oswaldo Guayasamín and others, now contains the national archive, cinema and offices; it is somewhat overshadowed

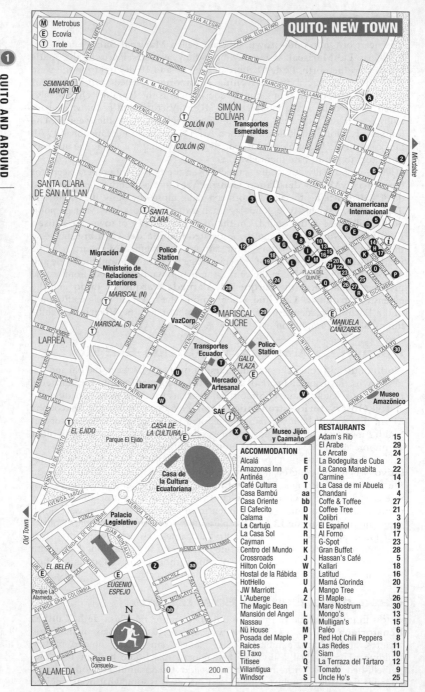

QUITO: NEW TOWN

Ⓜ Metrobus
Ⓔ Ecovía
Ⓣ Trole

Mindalae

ACCOMMODATION

Alcalá	E
Amazonas Inn	F
Antinéa	O
Café Cultura	T
Casa Bambú	aa
Casa Oriente	bb
El Cafecito	D
Calama	N
La Cartuja	X
La Casa Sol	R
Cayman	H
Centro del Mundo	J
Crossroads	K
Hilton Colón	W
Hostal de la Rábida	B
HotHello	U
JW Marriott	A
L'Auberge	Z
The Magic Bean	I
Mansión del Angel	L
Nassau	G
Nü House	M
Posada del Maple	P
Raices	V
El Taxo	C
Titisee	Q
Villantigua	Y
Windsor	S

RESTAURANTS

Adam's Rib	15
El Arabe	29
Le Arcate	24
La Bodeguita de Cuba	2
La Canoa Manabita	22
Carmine	14
La Casa de mi Abuela	1
Chandani	4
Coffe & Toffee	27
Coffee Tree	21
Colibri	3
El Español	19
Al Forno	17
G-Spot	23
Gran Buffet	28
Hassan's Café	5
Kallari	18
Latitud	16
Mamá Clorinda	20
Mango Tree	7
El Maple	26
Mare Nostrum	30
Mongo's	13
Mulligan's	15
Paléo	6
Red Hot Chili Peppers	8
Las Redes	11
Siam	10
La Terraza del Tártaro	12
Tomato	9
Uncle Ho's	25

by its huge and glittering mirror-clad replacement, designed in modernist style in the 1950s but not completed until 1992, primarily as the new home of the Museo del Banco Central.

Museo del Banco Central

Taking up the lion's share of this landmark oval building is the nation's premier museum, the **Museo Nacional del Banco Central del Ecuador** (Tues–Fri 9am–5pm, Sat & Sun 10am–4pm; $2), which houses an incomparable collection of pre-Columbian ceramics and gold artefacts, as well as colonial, republican and contemporary art.

Sala de Arqueología

The first hall off the central lobby is the huge **Sala de Arqueología**, where you'll find ceramic collections grouped according to the culture that produced them. Among the oldest pieces, near the entrance, are the simple female figurines crafted by the **Valdivia** culture (3500–1500 BC) – the first group in the Ecuador area to abandon a nomadic existence and form permanent settlements – which show different stages of female development, such as puberty, pregnancy and motherhood, in a touching, naturalistic style. Close by are many fine examples of **Chorrera** ceramics (900–300 BC), most famously the **whistle-bottles** in the form of various creatures, which mimic animal noises when water is poured into them.

Perhaps the most striking pieces in this room are the large, seated humans known as the **Gigantes de Bahía**, the work of the **Bahía** culture (500 BC to 650 AD), which range from 50–100cm in height and show men and women sitting with their legs crossed or outstretched, wearing many fine ornaments and elaborate headdresses. Also eye-catching are the pots and figurines of the northern coast's **La Tolita** culture (600 BC to 400 AD), comprising fantastical images including fanged felines with long, unfurling tongues, or realistic representations of decapitated "trophy heads".

Among the few non-ceramic works in the room are the **stone seats** supported by human figures on their hands and knees; these are the work of the **Manteño-Huancavilca** culture (500–1532 AD) and were probably thrones high-ranking authorities used during religious ceremonies.

Sala de Oro

At the far end of the Sala de Arqueología, a ramp leads down to the darkened **Sala de Oro**, where dozens of pieces of pre-Hispanic gold are displayed to stunning effect, their brilliance enhanced by black backgrounds and dramatic lighting.

Ecuadorian metallurgy goes back some two thousand years, when the emergence of large ceremonial centres spurred the production of decorative arts and crafts for votive offerings. The most finely crafted **ceremonial offerings** were produced by the La Tolita culture, whose work forms the bulk of the museum's gold collection and is characterized by beautiful filigrees and extremely fine detail worked on tiny objects. The masks, breastplates, headdresses, assorted jewellery and ceremonial bowls displayed here are both exquisite and exotic, with recurring motifs of cats, serpents and birds of prey. Highlights include the sun-like image of a mythical face sprouting dozens of twisted rays tipped by monkeys and snakes, and the feline mask adorned by an elaborate, removable headdress, from which two eyes hang suspended, their irises and pupils marked by green and black stones.

Sala de Arte Colonial

Back in the Sala de Arqueología, steps lead up to the **Sala de Arte Colonial**, where a massive, eighteenth-century Baroque altar greets you. Since religious themes were the only acceptable subjects for paintings and sculpture during much of the colonial period, this room is packed with numerous images of the Virgin, Christ, angels and saints. Among them are works by the most celebrated artists of the Quito School (see box, p.88), including Caspicara and Bernardo de Legarda. Although these **paintings** and **polychrome carvings** are brilliantly executed and wonderfully expressive, the most striking aspect is the gory and macabre nature of Hispanic colonial religious art: countless images of lacerated Christs dying in agony on the cross, a decapitated San Dionisio standing with his head in his hands and several paintings of Christ dragging his cross through the streets, showing blood spurting in thick jets from his wounds.

Other museum rooms

The adjacent **Sala de Arte de la República** shows how religious themes were gradually replaced by more humanist, secular ones during the nineteenth century, starting with portraits of revolutionary heroes and moving through landscapes and images of fruit-sellers, workers and festival dancers. The room's most appealing works are those produced in the 1930s and 1940s, when artists including Eduardo Kingman, Diógenes Paredes and Oswaldo Guayasamín turned their attention to *indígenas* and the need for social change.

This trend – known as *indigenismo* – continues in the **Sala de Arte Contemporáneo**, upstairs on the third floor, but quickly gives way to more diverse subjects and abstract styles. The quality in this room is rather uneven, but several exhibits really stand out, including Camilo Egas' *Subway*, and Guayasamín's *Angustia*. The museum's collection is topped off with the small **Sala del Mueble** on the third-floor landing, displaying a number of wooden chests exquisitely inlaid with shell, bone, ivory and ebony in geometric motifs.

Other collections at the Casa de la Cultura

The Casa de la Cultura is also home to several other permanent collections, including the **Museo de Artes Visuales e Instrumentos Musicales**, which holds a wide range of Ecuadorian art from the nineteenth century onwards, including paintings by Kingman, Guayasamín and Paredes, and more than a thousand **musical instruments**; and the *colección etnográfica*, displaying the **traditional costumes** of Ecuador's various indigenous communities.

TeléfériQo

Few attractions in Ecuador have made such a stir as the **TeléfériQo** (Mon–Thurs opens 10am, last tickets sold at 7pm, Fri 10am, last tickets 10pm, Sat 9am, last tickets 10pm, Sun 9am, last tickets 8pm; $4 or $7 for the express queue; ☎ 1800/835333), a modern cable-car system you'd commonly see in smart ski resorts, which transports six-person cabins from a base station at 3050m on the lower slopes of Volcán Pichincha, up to the antennae-barbed peak of Cruz Loma at around 4050m. It opened in 2005 to enormous excitement and fanfare, and instantly became Quito's most popular diversion for sunny days and clear evenings – hardly surprising considering there's nothing remotely comparable to this in Ecuador. The 2.5km ride glides by in around eight minutes, wafting noiselessly above the last treetops and over into the páramo moorlands of the high Andes to arrive at a series of lookouts (one of them indoors), which give grand views over a capital ringed by the ice-tipped volcanoes of Cayambe, Antisana and Cotopaxi.

This is the attraction's kernel of quality, smoothly operated, slickly organized and highly recommended. But there's an awful lot of flimflam to circumnavigate while you're here: souvenir stores, games arcades, artesanía shops, bars, cafés and food courts all seem to unfurl endlessly between the entrance and the cable car itself. There's even a dedicated amusement zone, **VulQano Park** (Mon–Thurs 11am–9pm, Fri 11am–11pm, Sat 10am–11pm, Sun 10am–9pm; $5 passport for five rides not including the best two or $10 for all rides), whose star turns are the *Montaña Rusa* (Russian Mountain) roller coaster and the "Ejection Seat", a two-seater sphere which is shot 60m into the air on elastic bands.

From the top of the cable car, short trails lead up to mountainside lookouts. Signs everywhere tell you to take it easy as you ascend and if you've arrived in Quito within a couple of days this is good advice, as you'll definitely feel the thin air; there is a medical centre up here in case of emergencies. Remember to bring warm clothing, because it can be bitingly cold up here, especially if there's no sun; there is an indoor area if you need it. Beyond the complex's damaged fences, the trail continues for about three hours (for the fit and acclimatized) along a grassy ridge to the summit of **Rucu Pichincha** (4627m). There have been a number of robberies and assaults around this peak, so you're strongly advised to give the hike a miss.

Practicalities

The simplest way of getting to the TelefériQo, west of the centre off avenidas Occidental and La Gasca, is to jump in a **taxi**, which will cost around $3–4 from La Mariscal but less from the old town. They can pass the barriers without having to pay the $2 parking fee applicable to private drivers. Alternatively, you can catch a designated white TelefériQo **minibus** (currently free, but a $1 charge has been normal in the past; ☎02/2252753 for group bookings) from the northern Ecovía terminal at Río Coca; the Iñaquito, Quicentro and El Jardín shopping malls, all next to Parque Carolina; and the Estación Norte, at the northern end of the Trole line. At weekends and peak times the minibuses leave every 20 minutes or so, but at other times it could be every hour or more.

At weekends and on sunny afternoons, the whole place can get very **crowded**, and waiting times for the cable car can be hours, when a system allocating journey times to tickets comes into operation and the express ticket is well worth the extra cost. It's quietest on weekday mornings.

Museo Jacinto Jijón y Caamaño and Museo Amazónico

A five-minute walk up Avenida 12 de Octubre from the Casa de la Cultura, on the corner with Roca, the **Museo Jacinto Jijón y Caamaño** (Mon–Fri 9am–4pm; $0.60) is located upstairs inside the library of the Universidad Católica. It's a smaller version of the Museo del Banco Central, with pre-Hispanic ceramics, seventeenth-century religious art and beautiful inlaid colonial furniture.

For something a little different, continue three blocks up 12 de Octubre to the Abya Yala building, whose first floor houses the **Museo Amazónico** (Mon–Fri 8.30am–12.30pm & 2–5pm; $2), dedicated to the indigenous peoples of the Oriente. It's not big-budget, but the exhibits – among them vibrantly coloured feather headdresses, a long dugout canoe and musical instruments – are absorbing. The downside is the lack of information on the different Amazonian groups, but you can find this in the excellent **bookshop** on the ground floor.

Mindalae

If you want a comprehensive picture of indigenous life and culture, head to **Mindalae** (Museo Etnohistórico de Artenasías del Ecuador), at the corner of Reina Victoria N26-166 and La Niña (Mon–Sat 9.30am–5.30pm, Sun 10.30am–4.30pm; $3), whose striking new building belies the timelessness of the crafts beautifully displayed over its five floors. Peoples from the coast, highlands and forest of Ecuador are represented in exhibits of clothing, weavings, ceramics, jewellery, musical instruments and tools of everyday life; other areas explain ancient solar astronomy, indigenous rituals and shamanism. A *mindala* (whence the museum's name) was a travelling merchant in pre-Inca times – fitting then that the museum includes a tempting handicrafts shop and fair-trade café.

Parque La Carolina

A kilometre north of La Mariscal is the southern tip of the large and leafy **Parque La Carolina**, the most popular green space in the city and always buzzing with football games, joggers, cyclists, hyperactive kids and strolling families, particularly on weekends. It's located in quite a swank part of town, flanked by a wealthy barrio full of smart condos to the east and brilliant views of the Pichinchas to the west, rising above the canopy of trees.

In the middle of the park, at Rumipamba 341 and Los Shyris, the **Museo Ecuatoriano de Ciencias Naturales** (Mon–Fri 8.30am–1pm & 1.45–4.45pm, Sat 9am–1pm; $2) suffers from a lack of cash, but does boast some fascinating bits and pieces, including the seven-metre skeleton of an anaconda, gigantic cranium of a blue whale and a chilling display of enormous spiders.

Next door to the museum on Rumipamba is the **Jardín Botánico de Quito** (Mon 9am–1pm, Tues–Sun 9am–5pm; $3.50), where you can see a good cross-section of native Andean plants on meandering paths through reconstructed habitats, from cloudforest to páramo to dry mountain scrub. The highlights are the "crystal palaces", two greenhouses devoted to Ecuadorian orchids and tropical plants – giving a taste of the country's extraordinary floral colour and diversity.

At the edge of Parque La Carolina at Amazonas 3008 and Rumipamba, is one of Quito's most unusual attractions, the **Vivarium** (Tues–Sun 9.30am–5.30pm; $2), part of a non-profit organization that promotes public education on Ecuador's native fauna and tries to improve conditions in the nation's zoos. On show in glass cabinets are 44 species of **reptiles** and **amphibians**, many of them **snakes**, accompanied by well-designed information panels explaining which are poisonous and where they're found in Ecuador – though it's unlikely you'll remember any of this when faced with one in the jungle. Showpieces here include an **Equis** (the Spanish for "x"), one of the country's deadliest snakes, and a five-metre king cobra; for a few dollars the staff will obligingly place a boa around your neck while you have your photo taken.

Museo Fundación Guayasamín

East of Parque La Carolina, in the hilltop barrio of Bellavista Alto at Bosmediano 543 (best reached by taxi), the **Museo Fundación Guayasamín** (Mon–Fri 10am–5.30pm; $3 or $2 if you have Capilla del Hombre ticket) houses one of Quito's most compelling collections of art. The museum's pre-Columbian pieces and colonial carvings and paintings are excellent, but the main attraction is the work of the late **Oswaldo Guayasamín**, Ecuador's most renowned contemporary artist.

Beginning with Guayasamín's early work from the 1940s, dealing mainly with "the struggle of the Indian", the collection moves through to his series *La Edad de la Ternura* (*The Age of Tenderness*), with his famous moon-faced, round-eyed women and children shown in close, tender embraces – a tribute to his and all mothers. Guayasamín's great triumph is his disturbing **Edad de la Ira** (*Age of Anger*) series, displayed in the final room, where massive canvases tower over you with repetitive images of giant clenched hands, faces screaming in agony, skeletal figures that look utterly defeated and bodies in positions of torture.

Capilla del Hombre

Overlooking the capital, the nearby **Capilla del Hombre** (Tues–Sun 10am–5.30pm; $3 or $2 if you already have Museo Guayasamín ticket), begun in 1995 but only completed in 2002 three years after Guayasamín's death, is a secular "chapel" dedicated not to any god, but to humanity itself. The two-storey gallery is therefore both a memorial to the suffering of the oppressed and victims of war and torture, and a celebration of Latin American identity and the positive aspects of human nature. The scope of the works is as ambitious as it is affecting, from the agonies of workers in the silver mines of **Potosí**, Bolivia, where eight million people perished over three centuries, to the poignancy of motherhood and the family, in the famous *La Ternura* (*Tenderness*), to the uncharacteristically light-hearted *Bull and the Condor*, representing the tensions between Andean traditions and Spanish influences. On the lower floor, an **eternal flame** flickers for the cause of human rights – though it was initially broken on the gallery's inaugural night when a child dropped a cola bottle on it. Above the chapel in the grounds of Guayasamín's house, are sculptures, a Mayan stela from Honduras and the memorial **Tree of Life**, where the artist's ashes were deposited.

The chapel is a ten-minute **walk** around the corner from the Museo Guayasamín at Mariano Calvache and Lorenzo Chávez; go a short distance uphill and turn right onto José Carbo and follow the road along to the chapel.

Guápulo

The outdoor terrace of the Fundación Guayasamín and the Capilla del Hombre afford views down to the picturesque village of **GUÁPULO**, perched on the steep slopes flanking the east side of town, whose narrow, cobbled streets and terracotta-roofed, whitewashed houses have the look of a Mediterranean village, and feel far removed from the hurly-burly of the capital. Still, Guápulo is less than two kilometres from the new town, a short taxi ride away.

Besides the quaint streets, charming houses and relaxed atmosphere, the principal attraction is the magnificent **Santuario de Guápulo**, a beautiful church and monastery built in the latter half of the seventeenth century, housing an impressive collection of colonial art and a masterful pulpit carved by Juan Bautista Menacho, one of the continent's finest sculptors. A fine museum inside, the **Museo Franciscano Fray Antonio Rodríguez** (Mon–Fri 8am–noon & 3–5pm; $1.50), named after the church's architect, displays some of the best pieces from the collection, such as Quito School paintings by Miguel de Santiago and elegantly carved ecclesiastical furniture. Guided tours (included in ticket price) are available in Spanish outside the hours of Mass.

Casa-Museo de Viteri

It's a rare privilege to be able to visit the home and studio of a celebrated painter, and thanks to the open invitation issued by **Oswaldo Viteri**, Ecuador's greatest living contemporary artist, you can do exactly that at the **Casa-Museo de Viteri**, in the wooded hills overlooking the northern fringes of the city at Juncal N64-196 and Ambrosi (appointments must be arranged in advance ☎02/2473114; ⓦwww.viteri.com.ec; $10; groups of ten or more preferred; a taxi there costs around $5–6). He or his wife, Marta, will guide you around their formidable **art collection**, surely one of the best and most interesting in the country. Spanning the centuries from pre-Columbian times to the present day, the works are ingeniously displayed to emphasize *mestizaje*, the mixing of races, cultures and traditions underpinning Ecuador's cultural identity. Among the many treasures are a model of the *Santa María*, one of Columbus's three ships, sailing on a sea of pre-Columbian axe-heads; an exquisite eighteenth-century representation of the Virgin of Quito with real hair and a silk dress; Amazonian-made Shuar violins, a striking example of Ecuadorian syncretism; and engravings by Goya and Picasso, mingling with ancient Jama ceramics.

The creative engine room of the house is Viteri's **studio**, filled with paints and brushes, works in progress, antique tomes and the sharp smell of oils and white spirit. Viteri's boldness and versatility with the brush are unmistakable in striking portraits such as *Autorretrato con Amigos* (*Self-portrait with Friends*). But he is perhaps best known for his **assemblages**, including the astounding *Ojo de Luz* (*Eye of Light*), mixed-media works combining colourful dolls made by Ecuador's indigenous communities with material such as sackcloth or ornate Catholic livery; again, these explore *mestizaje*, and the way modern "mixed" society is both born of and reacting against its colonial past.

Rumipamba

The Parque Arqueológico y Ecológico Rumipamba (Tues–Sun 10am–4pm; currently free, may charge soon), at avenidas Mariana de Jesús and Occidental on the western slopes of the city, is just a short hop by taxi from La Mariscal. The 32-hectare park shows vestiges of a prehistoric agriculturalist village, whose inhabitants eked life out of the volcanic soil from 3000 years ago, complete with irrigation channels and building foundations; the site wasn't continuously occupied, thanks to eruptions from Pululahua and Pichincha which destroyed parts of the village between 600 and 900 AD, but also surviving here are pre-Inca stone walls, thought to be the oldest in Quito. A small on-site museum exhibits some of the prodigious quantities of ceramics found in the park, which is crisscrossed with ancient trails or *culuncos*, which you are welcome to explore.

Restaurants and cafés

Quito boasts the best and most varied choice of **restaurants and cafés** in the country, from humble canteens to classy outfits offering a wide range of **world cuisines**, along with tasty **seafood** restaurants and typical **Ecuadorian and Latin American** restaurants. In Quito, *comidas típicas* generally comprise hearty food based around a fatty meat dish, such as roasted or fried pork (*hornado* or *fritada*), delicious cheesy potato cakes (*llapingachos*) and a range of soups (*caldos* or *locros*) and stews (*secos*); see Basics on p.42 for more details. Restaurants here are markedly more expensive than those outside the capital, but even the priciest are cheaper than their equivalents in Europe or North America. Set-menu meals, *almuerzos* at lunch and *meriendas* at dinner, are even better value, sometimes consisting of two or three courses for a dollar or two.

Many restaurants, particularly inexpensive and informal ones, have long opening hours (usually 8am–10pm), while more traditional establishments just serve lunch and dinner (often noon–3pm & 6–10pm); most places close on Sunday afternoons around 3pm. Otherwise, only unusual hours are noted in the listings, and phone numbers are included for those where advance **reservations** are advisable. Restaurants are marked on the maps on pp.80–81, p.87 (old town) and p.98 (new town).

The new town

The greatest concentration of restaurants is in the Mariscal area of the **new town**, and many of these specifically target foreigners. Some of the best restaurants, which cater to Quito's moneyed classes, are outside the main tourist zone, and well worth the taxi ride.

Cafés

El Cafecito Luis Cordero 1124, same location as the hotel (see p.82). Laid-back spot with a big open fire, smoke-stained walls, creaky wooden floors and a large choice of coffees and home-made cakes. Also offers inexpensive vegetarian lunches, light evening meals and breakfast specials that come with unlimited coffee.

Ceuce El Jardín mall, third floor. Classy café with enormous windows looking down to Parque La Carolina and the Quito skyline. Excellent national and international food and fairly reasonably priced.

Coffee Tree On the corner of Reina Victoria and Foch. Ecuadorian coffee, cakes, sandwiches, *empanadas* and full English breakfasts available at this popular café with outdoor seating and heaters. Open all hours, it's the place to come for a late snack.

Coffee & Toffee Calama E8-28 and Almagro. Buzzing open-fronted venue with outdoor seating and heaters, offering a wide menu of crowd-pleasers drawn from around the world, including smoked salmon, Thai rice and Wiener schnitzel. Vegetarian food, all-day breakfasts, cakes, coffee and cocktails also available. Usually features live music a couple of times a week. Open 24hr.

Colibrí Pinto E4-170 and Luis Cordero. Pleasant German-owned café, with a tree-shaded patio on a quiet street, offering good breakfasts, crêpes and sandwiches, as well as Central European specialities such as *rösti, leberknödelsuppe*, goulash and German sausages. Daily 8.30am–6.30pm.

Corfú Portugal and Los Shyris, east of Parque La Carolina, also in El Jardín Mall. According to locals, this café serves up the best lattes and cappuccinos in Quito. Mouthwatering ice cream and pastries, made at the associated bakery next door, *Cyrano*, make the perfect accompaniments.

Cultura Robles 21. Quiet, relaxed café on the ground floor of the eponymous hotel (see p.81), featuring the same arty decor and colourful frescos. Not cheap, but the breakfasts, cream teas, cakes, soups, crêpes and other snacks are

delicious, and it's one of the few places in town that serves Earl Grey tea. Closes 7pm.

El Español Juan León Mera and Wilson. Fantastic but pricey Spanish deli chain specializing in huge baguette sandwiches, crammed with imported serrano or parma ham. It's mainly takeout, but has a sit-down area as well.

HotHello Amazonas N20-20, in the eponymous hotel (see p.82). French-owned pavement café selling excellent, moderately priced pastries, cheesecakes, quiches, salads and sandwiches. Covered by transparent plastic screens when it rains and warmed by gas heaters.

Kallari Wilson E4-266 and Juan León Mera. Run by a cooperative of 21 Quichua communities of the Tena region, this café is the place to sample Oriente snacks like grilled plantain stuffed with cheese and yuca specialities, and sip organic home-grown coffee or organic Kallari (hot) chocolate, grown by their coop farmers. You can also buy rainforest handicrafts, fair-trade medicinal plants and soaps. Free wi-fi. Mon–Sat 9am–5.30pm, Sun 9am–1.30pm.

Magic Bean Foch E5-08, same location as the hotel (see p.82). Popular café-restaurant with a little garden warmed by hot coals, where you can sit out until late. Great for its moderately priced breakfasts, brownies, strudels, pancakes, toasted sandwiches, organically grown salads and other backpacker-friendly food.

Mango Tree Foch and Juan León Mera. Relaxed café in a pretty little covered patio draped with dangling green fronds, serving snacks, juices, coffee and good home-made bread. Closed Sun.

Mr Bagel Portugal and 6 de Diciembre, east of Parque La Carolina. American-owned café selling Quito's best bagels, as well as offering English-language newspapers and a book exchange. Good vegetarian lunches also available.

Mosaico Manuel Samaniego N8-95 and Antepara. From Parque Itchimbía, turn left at the gate and it's a short walk down the hill. ☏02/2542871. It may do delicious Greek food as well as some American classics, such as club sandwiches and New York cheesecake (reflecting its Greek–US ownership), but many well-to-do Quiteños come here to sit at elegant mosaic-topped tables with a cocktail and watch the sun set over the old town from the terrace balcony. Get here early for a seat.

Ecuadorian and Latin American cuisine

La Bodeguita de Cuba Reina Victoria N26-105 ☎02/2542476. Well-made mid-priced Cuban food, including delicious *ropa vieja* (shredded beef cooked in wine and tomato sauce), served in a rustic dining room covered in graffiti written by previous guests. Live Cuban music on Thursday nights (reservations essential), when it gets packed with locals eating, drinking and dancing until 2am.

La Casa de Mi Abuela Juan León Mera 1649 and La Niña. Really does feel like a granny's house, with its brown carpet and dark old chairs. A tiny menu – steak, chorizo, roast chicken and ravioli – but the quality is good and the service very friendly. Quite expensive. Mon–Sat 11am–3.30pm & 7–10pm, Sun 11am–3.30pm.

La Choza 12 de Octubre and Luis Cordero. Excellent, moderately priced *comida típica*, efficiently served in a space reminiscent of an elegant hacienda's dining room; where Ecuadorians go to eat top-shelf home cuisine. Closes 4pm Sat & Sun.

Mamá Clorinda Reina Victoria 1144. Friendly local restaurant serving tasty and good-value Ecuadorian dishes like *llapingacho* (mashed potato patties with fried egg and chorizo) and *caldo de gallina* (chicken soup). Regularly features live music. Closes Mon & Sun 5pm.

Mirador de Guápulo Behind *Hotel Quito*, Rafael León Larrea and Pasaje Stubel. A short taxi ride from the centre, this intimate and attractively decorated restaurant-bar, perched on the hill above Guápulo and commanding spectacular views over the church and eastern cordillera, serves delicious *comida típica*. It also features live Latin music Thurs–Sat nights.

🏃 **El Pobre Diablo** Isabela La Católica E12-06 and Galavis (daily menu online at ⓦ www.elpobrediablo.com). Best known as a hip night-time venue (see p.110), but in its daytime incarnation the restaurant should not be overlooked for its superb three-course *almuerzos* with juice ($4.60), diligent service and general good ambience. The à la carte choice is also very good. Mon–Fri lunch only.

La Querencia Eloy Alfaro N34-194 and Catalina Aldaz. Attractive but fairly pricey restaurant with pleasant views and colourful decor, serving some very good traditional cuisine, including *seco de chivo* and tasty *empanadas*. Closed Sun evening.

Red Hot Chili Peppers Foch 713 and Juan León Mera. Good TexMex restaurant with patrons' graffiti on its walls, serving generous portions of standards such as *enchiladas* smothered with cheese, accompanied by *frijoles*, sour cream and guacamole for $4–5. Closed Sun.

Los Troncos Av de Los Shyris 1280 and Portugal ☎02/2437377. Moderately priced Argentinian steakhouse with a huge charcoal grill sizzling up prime cuts of every type of meat. A popular place, so reservations are advised in the evenings. Closed Sun evening.

La Viña Isabel La Católica and Cordero ☎02/2566033. The large dining room can feel a bit impersonal, though the food is among the finest (and most expensive) in town; highlights are prawns cooked in wine with artichokes, and steak with wild mushrooms and asparagus. Closed Sat lunch & Sun.

🏃 **Zazu** Mariano Aguilera 331 and La Pradera ☎02/2543559. Modish, award-winning restaurant, whose virtuoso Peruvian chef brings great flair and international depth to traditional Latin American cuisine. Excellent in all areas, from wines and cocktails to desserts, but it's particularly strong on seafood; try the baked swordfish in pisco-soy consommé ($14). Mon–Fri 12.30pm–midnight, Sat 7pm–midnight.

Seafood and Japanese

La Canoa Manabita Calama 247 and Reina Victoria. Authentic, no-nonsense seafood restaurant like any on Ecuador's coast, serving inexpensive but good fish meals and set lunches, all accompanied with *chifles*. Closed Sun.

Mare Nostrum Mariscal Foch 172 and Tamayo ☎02/2528686. Excellent but expensive fish and seafood served up in a dark, Gothic interior complete with huge candlesticks, wooden chandeliers and windows painted with medieval tableaux.

La Paella Valenciana On the corner of Diego de Almagro N30-103 and República. Upscale Spanish restaurant specializing in wonderful seafood and its namesake paella. Closed Sun evening.

Las Redes Amazonas 845 and Veintimilla. This cosy little restaurant decked out with fishing nets on the ceiling serves moderate-to-expensive fish and seafood; a highlight is the excellent Gran Mariscada – mixed seafood pan-fried in butter, garlic and herbs. Closed Sun evening.

🏃 **Sake** Paul Rivet N30-166 and Whymper ☎02/2524818. Stylish and seriously good sushi restaurant on a par with anything outside of

Japan, boasting a massive (but pricey) menu with eel, octopus, sea urchin and Canadian conch. A short taxi ride from La Mariscal. Better to book Thurs–Sat.

Tanoshii At *Swissôtel*, 12 de Octubre 18-20 and Carrión ☎02/2566497. Expensive Japanese restaurant with first-rate *teppenyaki*, sushi and sashimi. The elegant white screens, black-lacquered tables and waiters in red-satin dressing gowns add to the exotic atmosphere. One of several excellent restaurants at this hotel.

Italian

Le Arcate Baquedano 358. Offers no fewer than 59 pizzas (the strangest, *alla russa*, is made with brie, bressaola, vodka and lemon) cooked in a huge wood-fired oven. Snappy service, smart decor and reasonable prices. Closed Sun from 4pm & Mon.

Carmine Baquerizo Moreno 533 and Diego de Almagro ☎02/2234785. Excellent but expensive Italian restaurant (formerly known as *Il Grillo*) with plenty of surprises on the menu beyond its delicious pizza, pasta and seafood, including tripe, rabbit's liver or snails. Attentive waiters and the steady flow of guests gives the place a good atmosphere. Closed Sun.

Al Forno Baquerizo Moreno E7-86 and Diego de Almagro. Warm atmosphere, thanks largely to the bonhomie of its Italian owners and to the wood-fired ovens that produce delicious pizzas. Vegetarian options and pasta also available. Closed Mon.

Tomato Juan León Mera and Calama. Relaxed place to nip in off the street, slink into a booth or a grab a stool for a quick pizza; also does breakfast, pasta and *almuerzos*. Informal, popular and busy in the evenings.

Eastern

El Arabe Reina Victoria 627 and Carrión. Inexpensive Middle Eastern restaurant serving delicious hummus, falafel, kebabs and shawarmas to take away or eat in.

Chandani Juan León Mera 1333 and Cordero. Small, simple and unfussy Indian restaurant doing great-value set-menus, or inexpensive vegetable, chicken or beef curry in a variety of different sauces. Closed Sun.

Hassan's Café Reina Victoria and Colón. Friendly, Lebanese restaurant offering inexpensive staples such as falafel and shawarma or grilled beef in a pitta with yogurt sauce and vegetables. Closed Sun.

Mongo's Calama E5-10 and Juan León Mera. Somewhat gimmicky themed "Mongolian" restaurant attracting a mainly gringo crowd. The big draw is a huge circular frying area where you take your food to be cooked after dousing it in your chosen sauces. Good value when the "eat as much as you like" deals go for half-price, which seems to be most of the time; cocktails are also just $1.

Siam Calama E5-10 and Juan León Mera, upstairs. Overlooking the heart of "gringolandia" from a glass-covered balcony and outside terrace, a colourful but fairly pricey spot with tasty, straight-forward Thai food. Closes Sun 4pm.

Uncle Ho's E8-29 Jose Calama and Almagro ☎09/0515067. Set between a curtain of bamboo fronds, this excellent Vietnamese restaurant offers generous portions and is authentic in execution of each dish, from summer rolls to noodle soups; fresh tofu also available. Closed Sun.

International

Adam's Rib Calama E6-15 and Reina Victoria. Busy, informal mid-range restaurant serving up huge portions of steak and ribs against a backdrop of American football on satellite TV. Predictably popular with US expats.

G-Spot Corner of Calama and Diego de Almagro. Inexpensive US–Ecuadorian-run burger bar with a reputation for serving addictive hamburgers with expertly cooked french fries. It's open late and popular with the post-party crowd.

Gran Buffet Carrión E4-157 and Amazonas. It's unlikely you'll leave this huge dining room hungry, thanks to its "whatever you want, as much as you want" policy. Pay $6 weekdays or $7 weekends and you have the run of the impressive buffet counter, brimming with meat, veg, seafood – cooked in a variety of styles – plus soups, salads, fruits, cheese and desserts. There's also a decent wine list. Closes Sun 5pm.

Latitud Corner of Reina Victoria and Foch. Swish tapas bar with a difference: pay a set price of $16 upwards and then you receive unlimited quantities of selected wines and tapas. Great if you fancy a tipple; Italian, French, Spanish, Chilean and Argentinean wines vie for your attention. Busy Thurs–Sat. Opens 4pm.

El Maple Corner of Foch and Diego de Almagro. Accomplished and popular vegetarian restaurant offering a broad menu of international dishes, from curries and pastas to burritos and stir-fries, with some Andean inventions thrown in for good measure. Does a filling *almuerzo* for under $3 and is also open for breakfast.

Mulligan's Calama and Juan León Mera. The familiar polished feel of a chain pub, serving hearty comfort food for the homesick, including buffalo wings and Key Lime pie, under the green glow of TVs tuned to the sports channel. Main courses $7–12.

Paléo Cordero and Reina Victoria. Cheerful Swiss–Italian restaurant with a strong alpine flavour in decor, thanks to its wooden bar, red tablecloths and timbered ceiling, as well as its *raclette-* and *rösti-*laden menu ($4–7). Good food and friendly service. Closed Sun.

La Terraza del Tártaro Penthouse floor of Edificio Amazonas, Veintimilla and Amazonas. Accessed by a glass elevator, a comfortable, moderately priced restaurant featuring wonderful views of the city. No great surprises on the international menu, but the food and service are good and the atmosphere very relaxed. Closed Sun.

The old town

Places to eat in the **old town** aren't as plentiful as those in the new and its few long-established restaurants are primarily geared to providing locals with tradi-tional Ecuadorian food. Yet with the area's ongoing regeneration, good new places are opening all the time. At one end of the spectrum you can sample classic, national home-cooking at several little places tucked away in La Ronda, or indulge yourself with some of the most becoming dining rooms and accom-plished menus in the capital, not least at the restaurants of the luxury hotels *Plaza Grande* and *Patio Andaluz*.

Cafés

El Búho On the corner of García Moreno and Espejo, inside the Centro Cultural Metropolitano. In the thick of things, so a good spot for a breather and a bite, whether it be a sandwich or full-on dish like breaded giant shrimp with whisky sauce. Moderate prices and good service.

Café del Teatro Plaza del Teatro. Definitely at the sophisticated end for Quito cafés, offering tradi-tional food with a spin, such as pork loin in *tomate de árbol* sauce. The heated outdoor seats make a good vantage point for enjoying live music and events in the plaza; the café puts on its own live music at weekends. Closes Sun 5pm.

Cafeto Chile 930 and Flores; and also Morales 983 in La Ronda. Great little coffee shop exclusively using organic Ecuadorian beans for their delicious espresso and flavoured brews. Indian chai, juices, beer, sandwiches and cakes are also available. Closed Sun.

Chapineros Chile 916 and Flores. This tiny old place has a handful of tables, leatherette booths and an old wooden counter. Serves tasty *humitas* and bargain sandwiches but little else. One for a quick pit stop rather than a lengthy feed.

Frutería Monserrate Corner of Espejo 0e2-12 and Flores. Trendy café-cum-fruit bar with exposed concrete pillars and an impressive double staircase flanking a covered courtyard. Racks in the kitchen groan with huge papayas, watermelons, pineapples and the like ready to be juiced on industrial scale. Snacks, Ecuadorian specialities, cakes and tarts are also available.

La Guaragua Espejo 0e2-31 and Guayaquil. Pleasant café with outdoor seating doing *humitas*, *tamales* and *empanadas*, as well as the usual snack food.

Mirador Vista Hermosa Mejía 0e4-51 and García Moreno. The main selling point is the panoramic view from the roof terrace, which is particularly enchanting after dark and best savoured with a hot tipple. Live music Thurs–Sat.

Modelo Sucre 391 and Moreno; also at Venezuela N6-19 and Mejía. In business since 1950, this little spot is the oldest café in Quito. Customers are shoehorned into the small room and tiny mezzanine to take their coffees, beers, sandwiches, *empanadas*, ice creams and pastries. Good for a cheap lunch or snack.

Tianguez West side of Plaza San Francisco. Lovely little café-restaurant under the stone platform on which the Iglesia de San Francisco stands, where you can have a taste of traditional Ecuadorian food, such as *fritada*, *mote* and *llapingachos*. It's aimed at tourists and is a bit pricey, but the outside tables and chairs on the plaza can't be beaten for atmos-phere. Also has an excellent crafts shop attached.

Restaurants

La Belle Epoque Corner of Chile and García Moreno, inside *Hotel Plaza Grande* ☎02/2510777. Stunning, flagship restaurant of the equally stunning hotel, featuring evocative turn-of-the-century-inspired decor, proficient service, mouth-watering – and expensive – international and French cuisine and breathtaking plaza views. Ring ahead for a table window.

Casa Urrutia García Moreno and Sucre, next to the Casa de María Urrutia museum ☎02/2584173. Decorated in the manner of the famous house next door, this classy restaurant offers excellent inter-national and French-leaning cuisine and features a wine and tapas bar in the vaulted cellar below. Closed Sat & Sun evenings and all day Mon.

Las Cuevas de Luis Candelas Benalcázar 713. Dark, cavernous restaurant owned by a friendly bullfighting fanatic, with pictures of famous toreadors on the walls and a stuffed bull's head in the corner of the room. The Spanish menu is quite appetizing, though the rather expensive food doesn't always live up to its promise.

Los Geranios La Ronda Oe1-134 and Guayaquil, upstairs. The modest exterior and homely courtyard dotted with potted geraniums disguise this little gem, specializing in *platos típicos* such as *yaguarlocro* (black-pudding soup) and *empanadas de viento* (sugar-topped cheese and onion pasties). Perfect for a nibble and to watch the goings-on in the street.

Hasta la Vuelta, Señor Third floor, Palacio Arzobispal, Chile and García Moreno. The menu is typical of countless corner cafés and diners across Quito, but rarely is traditional cuisine executed with such skill and attention to detail. The setting, a charming patio courtyard inside the Palacio Arzobispal, is also far from ordinary – as are the prices. Closed Sun evenings.

Mea Culpa Upstairs inside the Palacio Arzobispal, Chile and García Moreno ☎02/2951190. Beautiful restaurant overlooking the graceful porticoes of the Plaza Grande, summoning a colonial grandeur only fractionally undermined by the muzak. The food and wine, though expensive, is eclectic and delicious; ostrich fillet flambéed in brandy with apple and maple sauce, anyone? Book ahead for a window table. No shorts or sneakers. Mon–Fri 12.30–3.30pm & 7–11pm, Sat 7–11pm.

Pizza SA Espejo and Guayaquil. Clean and efficient pizzeria with wooden tables and benches, serving decent pasta, *calzone* and value set-meals in a polite and workmanlike manner.

Rincón de Cantuña García Moreno N6-52 and Olmedo, in the *Hotel Patio Andaluz* ☎02/2280830. Fancy and predictably expensive restaurant in an august, covered and colonnaded courtyard specializing in *comida típica* and Spanish cooking, with a few standard international numbers thrown in.

Theatrum In the Teatro Sucre, Manabí and Guayaquil ☎02/2289669. Suitably dramatic restaurant for its grand high ceilings, brass chandeliers, lush red padded screens, black chairs and crisp white tablecloths. The sophistication continues on its first-class "modern Mediterranean" menu, with dishes such as roast grouper with artichoke ragout. Main courses $9–20. Mon–Fri 12.30–3.30pm & 7–11pm, Sat 7–11pm, Sun 12.30–4pm.

Nightlife

The focus of Quito's **nightlife** is La Mariscal, particularly the streets north of Wilson between Juan León Mera and Diego de Almagro, which are crammed with small, steamy **disco-bars** and **clubs** pumping out high-decibel dance music. It's not all ear-shattering volumes and seething dancefloors, though; plenty of **bars** are geared more for drinking and chatting and others put on **live music**, often Cuban, rock, jazz and especially salsa, which is played almost exclusively in the ever-popular **salsotecas**, while **peñas** specialize in live *folklórica* (traditional folk music).

Most places tend to be fairly quiet through the week, totally packed Thursday to Saturday, and closed on Sundays. Bars are usually **open** from 8pm–3am, while clubs stay open from around 8 or 9pm until around 4am or longer, but often only from Thursday to Saturday. Although **cover charges** are usually minimal, some disco-bars and clubs have a small cover, which sometimes includes your first drink; others may have a *consumo mínimo*, meaning you have to spend a specified amount at the bar, usually the price of one or two drinks. Remember to take a **taxi** when travelling around Quito at night.

Bars

Bogarín Reina Victoria and Lizardo García. Stylish bar hosting excellent live music and serving drinks and snacks. Popular with a slightly older crowd. Closed Sun & Mon.

El Cafecito Luís Cordero 1124. Cosy café (see p. 000) that also serves as a relaxing place for an evening drink. Closes 10pm Mon–Thurs and midnight Fri & Sat.

Ghoz Bar La Niña 425 and Reina Victoria. A place to shoot some pool, throw some darts, play some games and tuck into some Swiss grub, while your eardrums are blasted by rock, pop and Latin.

King's Cross Underground Bar Reina Victoria 1781 and La Niña. Snug little bar, popular with expats, serving a decent range of imported beers, and with a large and smoky outdoor BBQ most nights.

El Pobre Diablo Isabel La Católica E12-06 and Galavis ⓦ www.elpobrediablo.com. One of Quito's most appealing bars and a favourite among young artists and writers. Expect good music (often live acts Thurs & Sat), a mellow atmosphere and tasty, reasonably priced food and drinks. Closed Sun.

La Reina Victoria Reina Victoria 530 and Roca. Surprisingly authentic British-style pub, with a roaring log fire, darts, decent pub food (fish and chips, shepherd's pie and BBQ nights on Sat) and good beers, including home-brewed bitter and stout. Closed Sun.

Sutra Lounge Juan León Mera and Calama, upstairs. Regularly features live music, usually rock or Latin, or failing that, favours playing live concerts on screen. Good cocktails.

Turtle's Head La Niña E4-57 and Juan León Mera. Bawdy, fun, Scottish-owned pub featuring its own microbrewery, which produces excellent draught beer, including bitters and Guinness-style creamy stout. Also serves British staples such as fish and chips and curry.

Disco-bars and clubs

La Bunga Francisco Salazar and Av 12 de Octubre. Popular 20-something dance venue, favouring rock rather than techno, particularly if it's Spanish-language. Vintage bands like the Cure sometimes also get airtime and there's occasional live music.

Cientochenta Japón E5-69 and Amazonas, behind CC Iñaquito. Very hip discoteca with a friendly vibe, playing a wide range of music where trendy young Quiteños go to be seen. Check ⓦ www.180.com.ec for information on special events.

Matrioshka Pinto 376 and Juan León Mera. The warm atmosphere and the welcome to people of all sexualities makes this, one of Quito's few openly gay and lesbian bars, a good place for a dance. Closed Sun–Tues.

No Bar José Calama 360 and Juan León Mera. Extremely popular with gringos and locals alike, with several dancefloors and loud pop and dance music. It's rammed on Thursdays and Saturdays, when dancing on the bar is a certainty.

Patatús Wilson 758 and Amazonas. With five bars, a "happy hour" lasting most of the day and plenty of space for dancing, this established favourite is often jumping. Fireplaces, pool, darts and table football are the attractions at quieter times. Popular with Brits and antipodeans.

Live music, peñas and salsotecas

La Bodeguita de Cuba Reina Victoria 1721 ☏02/2542476. Actually a restaurant (see p.106), but on Thursday nights it offers a spirited atmosphere, with people of all ages dancing to live Cuban music.

▲ Nightlife in Quito's new town

Fiestas in Quito

Aside from the national public holidays and mischief of Carnaval (see Basics, p.45), Quito features several of its own colourful **fiestas** that are worth a look if you're in town. The city's most prominent religious festival is **Good Friday**, when hundreds of barefooted penitents solemnly cross through the old town in mourning, many dressed in purple robes with pointed hoods, others dragging huge crucifixes and a few even wearing crowns of thorns. Another major event comes on **May 24**, honouring the day in 1822 that the colony finally threw off the Spanish yoke at the Battle of Pichincha, when Quito erupts in a spectacle of booming cannons and military parades. The biggest fiesta of the year kicks off at the beginning of December and lasts for a week until **December 6**, marking the city's foundation. Celebrations include street parties, music and dancing, processions, bullfights at the Plaza de Toros, the election of the *Reina de Quito* (beauty queen) and general high spirits. December is generally regarded by Quiteños as a party month, topped off on **New Year's Eve** with a street parade of *años viejos* – effigies, often of current political figures, which are burnt at midnight.

Cafelibro Carrión 243 between Leonidas Plaza and Tamayo Ⓦ www.cafelibro.com. Arty café with live jazz on Saturday nights, and on other evenings a variety of song and dance, music, poetry readings and sometimes even theatre. Check the website for programme details. Mon–Fri 5pm–1am, Sat 6pm–midnight.

La Casa de la Peña García Moreno 1713 and Galápagos Ⓣ 02/2284179. A popular *peña* in an old building with a timber-beamed roof near the Basílica, showcasing folk music. Performances usually start around 9.30pm or later on Saturdays. Call for details.

Mirador de Guápulo behind the *Hotel Quito* on Rafael León Larrea and Pasaje Stubel. Live Latin music from Thurs–Sat nights in this restaurant-bar boasting spectacular views (see also p.106). A short taxi ride from the centre.

Ñucanchi Peña Av Universitaria 496 and Armero Ⓣ 02/254096. A *folklórica* club featuring some of the best local acts, usually at the end of the week (Thurs–Sat).

Seseribó Edificio El Girón, Veintimilla and 12 de Octubre. A *salsoteca* that's a Quito institution on Thursday nights, but still busy Friday and Saturday, with a good mix of students and other gyrating devotees. Features occasional live acts.

Varadero Reina Victoria 1751 and La Pinta. Unpretentious bar-restaurant with live Cuban music (Wed, Fri & Sat), a great atmosphere and knockout *mojito cubano*, a potent cocktail of mint with rum and soda. Closed Sun.

Arts and entertainment

Culture in Quito is thriving and thanks to the recent regeneration, renovation or reinvention of some key institutions, including the Teatro Sucre and Edificio El Bicentenario, the artistic scene has been enlivened throughout the city. The best way to keep track of what's on in town is by checking the municipal events website Ⓦ www.quitocultura.com; the same body also produces a monthly information booklet. *El Comercio* newspaper also covers everything from cinema listings to theatre programmes.

The national centre for the arts, the **Casa de la Cultura**, 6 de Diciembre N16-224 and Patria (Ⓣ 02/2902272, Ⓦ www.cce.org.ec; see also p.97), is a leading venue for theatre, dance and classical music, showcasing international performers and home-grown talent, as well as frequent appearances from its own choral group and ballet company.

Theatre and folk ballet

The elegant, nineteenth-century **Teatro Sucre**, on the Plaza del Teatro (T02/2572823, Wwww.teatrosucre.com; see p.90), is a pleasure to visit regardless of what's playing. As Ecuador's national theatre, the shows are almost always of a very high standard and regularly feature international theatre, dance and music companies. The capital's other grand theatre, the Art Deco **Teatro Bolívar**, at Espejo 847 and Guayaquil (T02/2582486, Wwww.teatrobolivar .org; see p.90), badly damaged by fire just after an extensive restoration, is slowly rising from the ashes, and occasionally puts on events to raise funds for its recovery.

Other venues include the renowned **Teatro Malayerba**, Luis Sodiro E2-65 and 6 de Diciembre, near the Parque Alameda (T02/2235463), which puts on exciting new works in its small theatre, and **El Patio de Comedias**, 18 de Septiembre E4-26 and 9 de Octubre (performances Thurs–Sun 8pm; T02/2561902, Wwww .patiodecomedias.org), presenting new shows every month.

The **Ballet Andino Humanizarte**, based at the **Teatro Humanizarte** on Leonidas Plaza N24-226 and Lizardo García, entrance on the tiny street of Xaura off Lizardo García (Wed 7.30pm, T02/2226116), stages innovative contemporary theatre and dance productions, usually on Wednesday evenings. They also specialize in **folk ballets**, flamboyant traditional dance shows with colourful costumed dances from Ecuador's diverse cultural groups. The leading folk company is **Jacchigua** (T02/2952025, Wwww.jacchiguaesecuador.com), which performs at the Casa de la Cultura (Wed 7.30pm; $25). If this seems expensive, check out the Saruymanda troupe, who put on free performances (Fri 7.30pm) at the Patio Cultural inside the Palacio Arzobispal (see p.88).

Film

Cinema is very popular in Quito, with English-language **films** almost always shown in their original versions with Spanish subtitles. **Cinemark**, Plaza de las Américas at avenidas América and República (T02/2260301, Wwww .cinemark.com.ec), has huge screens, comfortable armchair-type seating and several adjacent restaurants; and **Multicines**, in the basement of the Iñaquito mall at Amazonas and Naciones Unidas, and at the CC El Recreo on Avenida Maldonado (T1800/352463, Wwww.multicines.com.ec), provides similar facilities. Both show American new releases, with the odd European or independent film thrown in. **Tickets** cost around $4, with discounts on weekdays before 6pm and all day Wednesday.

For world cinema and art-house productions, try **Ocho y Medio** (T02/2904720, Wwww.ochoymedio.net) at Valladolid N24-353 and Vizcaya in the suburbs of La Floresta, or the **Casa de la Cultura** (see p.97).

Classical music

The Casa de la Música at Valderrama and Avenida Mariana de Jesús (T02/2267093, Wwww.casadelamusica.com.ec), is a high-spec, purpose-built hall with superb acoustics, which attracts top-quality musicians and orchestras from across the globe. It's also the home of the Orquesta Filarmónica del Ecuador. The **Orquesta Sinfónica Nacional** gives regular concerts (usually Fri 8pm) at the Teatro Politécnico, at Ladrón de Guevara E11-253, and occasionally at the Teatro Sucre; call T02/2565733 for details.

Shopping

Quito can hardly be bettered for the range and quality of **handicrafts** on offer, so you can do all your **shopping** here rather than haul a bagful of souvenirs around the country. With the exception of a few expensive boutiques sourcing the very best from regional workshops, the prices aren't generally that much higher than at the point of production. For general goods, locals head to Quito's **shopping malls**, where the best supermarkets, electronic goods and brand-name clothes chains are, or its street **markets**, especially for cheap clothes, food and hardware. For cheap food and produce – including wonderful exotic fruits – try the bustling **Mercado Santa Clara** in the new town to the west of the Santa Clara Trole stop, at Versalles and Marchena, or the Mercado Central, at Olmedo and Pichincha, in the old town.

Handicrafts and leather goods

La Mariscal is well stocked with **artesanías** from across Ecuador, including brightly painted balsawood parrots and fish, shigra bags, Otavalo tapestries, chunky woollen sweaters, Panama hats, leather goods and tagua-nut carvings. A nucleus of shops for handicrafts, souvenirs and **leather goods** is along and around **Amazonas** and **Juan León Mera**. At the weekends there's an **art market** at **Parque El Ejido**.

La Bodega Exportadora Juan León Mera N22-24 and Carrión. Good range of attractive, quality handicrafts from many regions, most reasonably priced. Also has a nice selection of silver jewellery.
Camari Marchena Oe2-38 and Versalles Ⓦ www.camari.org. Fair-trade store providing an outlet for a number of small-scale producers. Lots on offer, from organic coffee and chocolate, to handicrafts, stationery and musical instruments.
Centro Artesanal Av 12 de Octubre N24-262 and Madrid. Plenty of stalls and choice, including an emphasis on indigenous paintings, as well as general handicraft exhibitions.
Folklore Olga Fisch Colón E10-53 and Caamaño; also at *Hotel Patio Andaluz* in the old town, and CC Quicentro Ⓦ www.olgafisch.com. Boutique of the late Olga Fisch, a renowned artesanía collector. The quality of the pieces on show is a notch above the rest, as are the prices.
Fundación Sinchi Sacha at *Café Tianguez* on the Plaza San Francisco, and the Mindalae museum (see p.102). Non-profit organization aimed at promoting fair trade and providing indigenous people, particularly from the Oriente, with a venue for their products. Stocks a wide variety of good-quality handicrafts at reasonable prices.

Galería Latina Juan León Mera N23-69 and Veintimilla Ⓦ www.galerialatina-quito.com. Upmarket and expensive, but stocks one of the best selections of handicrafts, jewellery and fine knitwear in Quito.
Hilana 6 de Diciembre N24-385 and Baquerizo Moreno. Sells wool and alpaca clothing and blankets woven with typical pre-Hispanic motifs – very attractive and not too expensive.
Homero Ortega & Hijos on the Plaza San Francisco and at Gil Ramirez Dávalos 3-86 Ⓦ www.homeroortega.com. Very good Panama-hat shop run by a Cuenca family that's been in the business for five generations.
Mercado Artesanal La Mariscal Jorge Washington and Juan León Mera. Huge artesanía market housing many of the vendors who used to clutter the streets of La Mariscal. Definitely worth a look for the sheer range, though the quality is not always of the highest level.
Tenería Cotacachi 18 de Septiembre 175 and Amazonas. Quito branch of a Cotacachi leather business, offering a comprehensive spread of leather items as well as a bespoke service.

Shopping malls

Most of Quito's **shopping malls** usually feature a supermarket and a food court. The **Feria de Ipiales**, once a seething and none-too-safe street bazaar engulfing much of Calle Chile in the old town, has been brushed away into eight new shopping centres nearby (and three more further afield), selling inexpensive clothes, household goods and electricals – possibly including your stolen camera. You may often see some of the following names preceded by "CC", for "Centro Comercial".

Iñaquito Amazonas N36-152 and Av Naciones Unidas ⓦ www.cci.com.ec. Often simply called CCI, this large mall is on the north side of the Parque La Carolina, with a multiplex cinema.

Ipiales Eight inexpensive malls in the old town replace the Ipiales street market: Granada, Plaza La Merced, also for handicrafts and leather goods; Ipiales Mires, Mejía and Mires; Hermano Miguel, Imbabura and Mejía; El Tejar, López and Hermano Miguel; Nuevo Amanecer, López and Hermano Miguel; La Merced, Cuenca 6-57 and Mejía, including beauty and photo services; Montúfar, Montúfar and Olmedo, including jewellery; and San

Martín, Av Pichincha near La Marín, including tattooing.

El Jardín Amazonas and República. This modern, high-end mall, conveniently located by Parque La Carolina, contains a huge food court.

Quicentro Av Naciones Unidas and 6 de Diciembre ⓦ www.quicentro.com. This smart mall, boasting lots of designer clothing stores, is a favourite of Quito's well-heeled fashionistas.

El Recreo Av Maldonado 14-205 ⓦ www .ccelrecreo.com. A large mall in the south of the city, by the El Recreo Trole stop, with shops at the more affordable end of the scale.

Books, magazines and music

English-language **books** and non-Ecuadorian **newspapers** and **magazines** are not particularly easy to get hold of outside La Mariscal and the big shopping malls. **Music** and films are widely available on CDs and **DVDs** costing only a dollar or so at countless shops and street stalls throughout the city. These are pirated copies – the real things cost up to ten times the price and are available at only a handful of upmarket outlets.

Confederate Books Calama 410 and Juan León Mera. Excellent "full-service" secondhand bookshop with a large and well-ordered English section.

The English Bookstore Corner of Calama and 6 de Diciembre. Introducing the modern bookstore feel to Quito, complete with on-site café, this shop offers a fine selection of secondhand books and a smattering of new titles.

Libri Mundi Juan León Mera N23-83 and Veintimilla, and at the Quicentro Mall ⓦ www.librimundi.com. Quito's best bookshop, with an excellent range of English books, novels and guidebooks, a much larger Spanish section,

and a good selection of books in other languages. The staff are very helpful and will go out of their way to get hold of a particular title for you.

Libroexpress Amazonas 816 and Veintimilla, and the Quicentro Mall. There's an impressive choice of English-language magazines here, including both mainstream and obscure titles.

Mr Books El Jardín Mall, third floor. Large bookshop with a good choice of both English- and Spanish-language books.

South American Explorers Jorge Washington 311. New and secondhand guidebooks in English available, and it also has a book exchange. See p.77.

Tours from Quito

There's no shortage of **tour operators** in Quito, with many of them located in La Mariscal, particularly along Amazonas, Juan León Mera and their adjoining streets. Almost all of them offer everything from half-day city tours to week-long trips into the jungle or cruises around the Galápagos Islands. While many dabble in whatever kind of tour is likely to keep the business going, some agencies are specifically geared to certain **adventure tours** such as **climbing**, **mountain biking**, **whitewater rafting** and **birdwatching**, which we list separately below.

For specialist Quito-based agencies offering **jungle trips** in the **Oriente**, please refer to our list on p.308; for those operating their own yachts in the **Galápagos**, see p.432.

Prices can vary wildly between operators, so it's worth shopping around; generally you'll get discounts the larger your group is, or if you have a packed lunch (*un boxlunch*) rather than a meal in a fancy restaurant. Cheapest are half-day trips to the Mitad del Mundo ($20–40), with day-trips to Cotopaxi, indigenous markets and nearby cloudforests ranging from $30–100, while biking, rafting and trekking tours come in around $45–70 per day, though entrance fees to national parks and reserves aren't often included. **Multi-day** trips vary in price by the type of accommodation offered, ranging from bare-bones camping to comfortable *hosterías*. When comparing prices, always make sure to check what is included, particularly equipment, food, accommodation and the availability of English-speaking **guides**. For multi-day trips, try to meet your guide beforehand – a good, personable leader can make a world of difference.

General operators

Standard day-trips from Quito offered by **general operators** include visits to the Mitad del Mundo monument (see p.121), indigenous markets of Otavalo (see p.136), Saquisilí (see p.186), Zumbahua (see p.190) and Parque Nacional Cotopaxi (see p.178). Many also offer birding tours to cloudforest reserves close to the capital, or combine tours based around accommodation in luxurious haciendas. The larger companies can put together complete **customized packages**, including hotel bookings and transfers, and almost all are agents for **Galápagos** cruise companies.

An increasing number of operators now also offer activity-focused **adventure tours**, such as **whitewater rafting** down the Toachi, Blanco or Upano rivers (grade III–IV rapids); **mountain biking** on nearby volcanoes such as Cotopaxi, with vehicle transport to the site; **horseriding** in the surrounding countryside; and **trekking** through the sierra or the subtropical cloudforests west of Quito.

Campus Trekking J. Vargas 99 and A. Calderón, Conocoto ☎02/2340601, ⓦwww.campustrekking.com. Dutch–Ecuadorian company particularly strong on trekking, using multilingual naturalist guides, good equipment and following original routes. Also for climbing, cultural, Galápagos and adventure tours.

CarpeDM Adventures Antepara E4-70 and Los Río ☎02/2954713, ⓦwww.carpedm.ca. Canadian-run agency with a conscience, offering tours of all types to all regions of Ecuador. Tours are carbon offset and a percentage of profits goes to local charities.

Ecuador Adventure Pasaje Cordova N23-26 and Wilson ☎02/2223720, ⓦwww.ecuadoradventure.ec. All-rounder offering culture tours of the big sights in and around Quito, and many adventure tours, including trekking, kayaking, mountain biking and whitewater rafting.

Ecuadorian Tours Amazonas 329 and Jorge Washington ☎02/2560488 ⓦwww.ecuadoriantours.com. Experienced and reliable operator providing the usual sierra tours, plus a wide choice of programmes in other parts of the country, including the southern coast.

Enchanted Expeditions De las Alondras N45-102 and De los Lirios, Floralp Building ☎02/3340525, ⓦwww.galapagosenchantedexpeditions.com. Professional outfit with an enormous number of touring options throughout Ecuador, including trekking, birding and archeological tours. Also offers customized packages and operates Galápagos yachts (see p.452).

Explorandes Wilson 537 and Diego de Almagro ☎02/2222699, ⓦwww.explorandes.com. Wide range of pricey tours out of Quito, Cuenca and Guayaquil, including many adventure-focused options such as cloudforest treks and whitewater rafting. Established over thirty years in Peru, fifteen in Ecuador.

Gulliver Juan León Mera N24-156 and Calama ☎02/2529297, ⓦwww.gulliver.com.ec. Youthful and friendly climbing, biking and hiking operator using a beautiful converted farm, Papayago (see p.180), near the Ilinizas as a base for its mountaineering trips.

Happy Gringo Travel Foch E6-12 and Reina Victoria ☎02/2220031, ⓦwww.happygringo.com. Anglo-Dutch tour operator offering everything from half-day city tours to themed 14-day adventures for "adrenaline junkies". Wide variety and helpful service.

Islazul Tours La Isla N26-46 and Mosquera Narváez ☎02/2224393, ⓦwww.ecuador-travel .net. Personalized and good-value trekking, horseriding and wildlife tours in the sierra and subtropical cloudforests. All tours guided by the Austro–Canadian owner.

Klein Tours Eloy Alfaro N34-151 and Catalina Aldaz ☎02/2267000, ⓦwww.kleintours.com. One of Quito's most established and polished operators offering something for everyone, from wildlife to cultural tours all over the country, Galápagos cruises, plus tailor-made packages.

Metropolitan Touring De las Palmeras N45-74 and De las Orquídeas ☎02/2988200, ⓦwww .metropolitan-touring.com. Huge travel agent and operator, with branches all over Ecuador and a wealth of resources, offering tours and packages throughout the country. It runs the "Chiva Express", a bus kitted with train wheels to tour parts of Ecuador's railways.

Nomadtrek Amazonas N22-29 and Carrión, second floor ☎02/2547275, ⓦwww .ecuadorstravelguide.com. German-run company offering a wide range of adventure tours, including trekking, biking, birding, climbing and cultural tours, plus kayaking courses and jungle journeys (see p.277).

Nuevo Mundo 18 de Septiembre E4-161 and Juan León Mera, Edif. Mutualista Pichincha ☎02/2509431, ⓦwww.nuevomundotravel.com. Wide choice of tours and tailor-made packages,

taking in horseriding, the Devil's Nose train ride, cloudforest treks and indigenous markets. Strong on the jungle, too (see p.277).

Positiv Turismo Jorge Juan N33-38 and Atahualpa ☎02/6009401, ⓦwww.positivturismo .com. Friendly Swiss–Austrian company providing excellent-value tours in the sierra. Tours are in small groups and some include light hiking.

Quasar Expeditions José Jussieu N41-28 and Alonso de Torres ☎02/2446996, ⓦwww .galapagosexpeditions.com. A top-end operator providing customized tours of the whole country, using luxury accommodation. Also an excellent cruise operator (see p.453).

Safari Tours Reina Victoria N25-33 and Colón, Banco de Guayaquil building 11th floor ☎02/2220426, ⓦwww.safari.com.ec. British–Ecuadorian-run operator with wide choice of tours, including custom trekking, climbing or jeep trips. Also offers women-only tours, with female drivers and guides. Also has information on many Galápagos boats.

Surtrek Amazonas 897 and Wilson ☎02/2231534, ⓦwww.surtrek.com. Offers various adventure tours, including light treks and expeditions, biking, mountain climbing, rafting, diving, jungle trips and cruises.

Tropic Ecological Adventures La Niña E7-46 and Reina Victoria ☎02/2225907, ⓦwww.tropiceco .com. Award-winning ecologically and culturally sensitive operator offering tours in the sierra and western cloudforests, and above all to the Oriente (see p.277).

Turismo Comunitario FEPTCE 9 de Octubre N27-27 and Orellana ⓦwww.turismocomunitario .ec. A federation acting as umbrella operator for dozens of community-run stays, tours and programmes across the country, many of them with indigenous groups.

Climbing and trekking operators

If you're looking to go **climbing** or **trekking**, you'll probably want to get a group together to reduce costs. With this in mind, you're best off checking out the specialist climbing operators, where not only are you more likely to find other willing participants, but also better qualified **guides** who know the popular mountains intimately, better **equipment** and a higher standard of safety. Don't cut costs when it comes to the latter – while many of the climbs near Quito are not technically difficult, the potential hazards are very serious. Check that your operator uses only guides qualified by ASEGUIM (Asociación Ecuatoriana de Guías de Montaña), and take a close look at its equipment before signing up. Ideally, the company should provide one guide for every two climbers. For more on climbing, see p.47; for a selection of Riobamba-based guides and operators, see p.216.

Andean Face Pasaje B/102, Jardines del Batán ⊤02/2438699, ⓦ www.andeanface.com. Socially responsible Dutch–Ecuadorian company specializing in high-altitude mountaineering and trekking. Offers glacier training and bespoke climbing expeditions. Compañía de Guías de Montaña Jorge Washington 425 and 6 de Diciembre ⊤02/2901551, ⓦ www.companiadeguias.com. Very reliable outfit run by a group of experienced and qualified Ecuadorian and Swiss mountain guides, taking climbers up all the main snow peaks, and on trekking trips across the sierra. Ecuadorian Alpine Institute Ramírez Dávalos 136 and Amazonas, office 102 ⊤02/2565465,

ⓦ www.volcanoclimbing.com. As well as guiding up all the main peaks and doing treks, offers a climbing school teaching basic mountaineering skills to beginners. Moggely Tours Calama E4-54 and Amazonas ⊤02/2906656, ⓦ www.moggely.com. Friendly, Swedish-run climbing and trekking operator that owns an acclimatization base, *Hostal Valhalla*, near Cotopaxi (see p.182). Sierra Nevada Joaquín Pinto E4-150 and Luis Cordero ⊤02/3884897, ⓦ www.sierranevada.ec. Small, dependable climbing operator offering rafting and biking, as well as accommodation in Quito.

Biking tours

Biking tours typically start from a high point (for example, the car park below the Cotopaxi refuge) and hurtle downhill on full-suspension **mountain** bikes to a pick-up point from where you are shuttled home. That's not to say it's all coasting; you'll get uphill stretches on many itineraries, even the day-trips, which make a satisfying challenge at altitude. Tours on **motorbikes** are also possible.

Arie's Bike Company Av Interoceánica Km22.5 vía Pifo, La Libertad, Calle de Los Hongos, LT5 ⊤02/2380802, ⓦ www.ariesbikecompany.com. Offering bike tours of one to fourteen days, which might include descents down volcanoes, into jungle from Papallacta or Baños and rides throughout the sierra. Biketours Ecuador Pinto E43-76 and Juan León Mera ⊤02/2474940, ⓦ www.biketoursecuador .com. Tours of one to six days on Marin mountain bikes, including one into the cloudforests of the Intag region.

Biking Dutchman Foch 714 and Juan León Mera ⊤02/2568323, ⓦ www.bikingdutchman.com. The original bike-tour operator in Ecuador – appropriately run by a pedalling Dutchman – with a wide range of mainly downhill biking tours from one to eight days, always with a support vehicle. Enduro Adventure Ecuador Pinto 356 and Juan León Mera, 2nd floor ⊤02/2549358, ⓦ www .enduroecuador.com. Not cycling, but endurance off-road motorcycling on dirt bikes, Honda XR 600s or 400s. Offers anything from day tours to fourteen-day 1900km odysseys.

Specialist operators

Below are some of the better niche operators, for birdwatching, honeymooning and whitewater rafting.

Neblina Forests Isla Floreana E8-129, El Sol Apartment Building, third floor, office 305 ⊤02/2267436 or 1800/5382149, ⓦ www.neblinaforest.com. Offers birdwatching tours in the cloudforests of the eastern and western flanks of the Andes, as well as the Amazon rainforest.

Tours Unlimited Julio Castro 379 and Valparaiso ⊤02/2222564, ⓦ www.tours -unlimited.com. Upper-end operator with a niche in arranging customized tours for newlyweds. Also does tours exploring the "power places and energy sites" of Ecuador.

Yacu Amu Foch 746 and Juan León Mera, second floor ⊤02/2904054, ⓦ www .yacuamu.com. Largest and longest-established whitewater rafting and kayaking specialist in Ecuador, offering runs on the best routes (grades II–V) in the Blanco, Quijos, Napo and Upano watersheds. Also does combination tours mixing rafting with caving, biking, hiking and the like, and runs a kayaking school.

Listings

Airlines Aerogal, Amazonas 7797 and Juan Holguín ☎02/2942800, ⓦwww.aerogal.com.ec; Air Comet, Checoslovaquia 640 and Suiza, Edif. Ana Capri ☎02/2251198, ⓦwww.aircomet.com; American, Amazonas 4080 and Unión Nacional de Periodistas ☎02/2995000, ⓦwww.aa.com; Avianca, Av Coruña 143 and Bello Horizonte ☎02/2237932, ⓦwww.avianca.com; Continental, World Trade Center, Tower B, 12 de Octubre and Luis Cordero ☎02/2557290, ⓦwww.continental .com; Copa, República de El Salvador 361 and Moscú ☎02/2273082, ⓦwww.copaair.com; Delta, corner of Av de los Shyris N35-174 and Suecia, Edif. Renazzo Plaza, ☎02/3301164, ⓦwww.delta .com; Iberia, Eloy Alfaro 939 and Amazonas, Edif. Finandes, 5th floor ☎02/2566009, ⓦwww.iberia .com; Icaro, Amazonas and Endara ☎02/2450928, ⓦwww.icaro.aero; KLM, 12 de Octubre N26-97 and Lincoln, Torre 1492 ☎02/2986859, ⓦwww .klm.com; LAN, Pasaje Río Guayas E3-131 and Amazonas ☎02/2992300, ⓦwww.lan.com; Santa Bárbara, República de El Salvador N354 and Moscú ☎02/3800082, ⓦwww.sbairlines.com; Saéreo, Indanza 121 and Amazonas ☎02/3301152, ⓦwww.saereo.com; Taca, Av República de El Salvador 1033 and Naciones Unidas ☎1800/008222, ⓦwww.taca.com; TAME, Amazonas N24-260 and Colón ☎02/3977100, ⓦwww.tame.com.ec; VIP, Amazonas N49-225 and Juan Holgín ☎02/3304621, ⓦwww.vipec.com.

American Express Represented by Ecuadorian Tours, Amazonas 329 and Jorge Washington (☎02/2560488); does not buy traveller's cheques but replaces lost cards and cheques, and sells cheques to Amex card users.

Banks and exchange Most facilities are in the new town and generally open Mon–Fri 8.30am–4pm or 5pm, and Sat mornings. Exchange and cash-advance facilities usually Mon–Fri 8.30am–2pm. Banco del Austro, Amazonas and Santa María, offers Visa and MasterCard ATM and Visa cash advance; Banco de Guayaquil, Reina Victoria and Colón, provides Visa and MasterCard cash advances (up to $1000), and ATMs for Visa, MasterCard, Cirrus, Maestro, Plus, also ATMs at the corner of Amazonas and Veintimilla; Banco del Pacífico, Amazonas N22-94 and Veintimilla, has MasterCard, Cirrus, Maestro ATM, with many other locations; Produbanco, Amazonas 3575 and Japón, MasterCard cash advance, and ATMs for Master-Card and Diners, also at Amazonas 350 and Robles, and at the airport. New-town shopping malls have ATMs. Most banks have stopped changing travel-ler's cheques, but this may be temporary; check ⓦwww.aetclocator.com for branches that change Amex. More convenient are the *casas de cambio*, such as VazCorp, Amazonas 21-169 and Roca (Mon–Fri 8.45am–5.45pm & Sat 9am–1pm), which changes cash and cheques; Euromoney, Amazonas N21-299 and Roca, changes Amex cheques (high commission) and cash; and Servicambios Money, Venezuela 913 and Chile, for Amex cheques and cash (not sterling).

Cameras Numerous film shops and processing labs on Amazonas, many of which print digital pictures or can put them on CD, such as International Color, corner of Amazonas N21-201 and Roca, repairs for analogue cameras; Foto Imagen, Av Mariana de Jesús E5-11 and Italia, for general repairs.

Car rental Major companies have offices just outside the airport, the best place to compare prices. Some also have downtown offices. For more on renting a vehicle in Ecuador, see p.36. Avis ☎02/3300979, Amazonas 4925 and Río Curaray ☎02/2255890; Budget ☎02/3300979, Colón E4-387 and Amazonas ☎02/2221814; Expo ☎02/2433127, Av América N21-66 and Bolivia ☎02/2228688; Hertz ☎02/2254257. You can rent minibuses with drivers with Trans Rabbit ☎02/23201388 or 02/3301496 (airport).

Climbing and outdoor gear Extensive climbing facilities are at the Rocódromo, Av Velasco Ibarra opposite the Coliseo Rumiñahui. MonoDedo has a climbing and mountaineering outlet there, as well as at Larrea N24-36 and Av Coruña, where they have an excellent climbing gym (Mon–Fri 11am–9pm, Sat 10am–1pm), and another store at Juan León Mera N23-84 and Wilson ⓦwww.monodedo.com. Climbing gear is also available at Los Alpes, Reina Victoria 2345 and Baquedano ☎02/2232362, sales and rentals; Antisana Sport, top floor CC El Bosque, Local 51 ☎02/2650670, climbing gear, good for boots in large sizes; Equipos Cotopaxi, 6 de Diciembre N20-36 and Jorge Washington, and elsewhere ☎02/2250038, ⓦwww.equiposcotopaxi .com.ec, camping, climbing gear, and Coleman fuel; white gas you can get at Kywi, 10 de Agosto 2273 and Cordero ☎02/2221832; both will fill your own containers. Kywi also stocks rubber boots, mosquito nets, machetes and ponchos. For kerosene ask at Moggely Tours, Calama E4-54 and Amazonas, and for methylated spirits try Farmacia Colón, 10 de Agosto and Colón. For more on stove fuels see p.41.

Cycling *ciclopaseos* are held every second Sunday (8am–2pm), when about 30km of key streets, including Amazonas, are closed off to traffic so cyclists can traverse the city north to south on empty roads; check ⓦ www.biciaccion.org for details. For rentals try the agencies listed on p.117 or the shops on Av de los Syris between Eloy Alfaro and Portugal.

Dancing lessons Around $5 an hour. Son Latino Dancing School, Reina Victoria 1225 and Lizardo García ☎02/2234340 for salsa; Ritmo Tropical, Amazonas N24-155 and Calama ☎02/2557094, salsa merengue and capoeira; and Tropical Dancing School, Foch E4-256 and Amazonas ☎02/2224713 for many Latin styles. For tango and *folklórica* try Auténtico Tango Argentino at Reina Victoria 1222 and Calama ☎02/2237977.

Dentists Dr Alfonso Arcos Baraona (English-speaking), Av República de El Salvador 525, Edif. Roasanía ☎02/2457268; and Dr Victor Peñaherrera, Amazonas 4430 and Villalengua ☎02/2255949

Doctors Dr John Rosenberg (English-speaking), Foch 476 and Diego de Almagro, first floor ☎02/2521104 or 09/9739734, doctor for the US Embassy; Alvaro Dávalos Pérez, La Colina 202 and San Ignacio ☎02/2500268, home ☎09/9739694.

Embassies and consulates Australians can get assistance at the Canadian embassy; Canada, Amazonas 4153 and Unión Nacional de Periodistas, Edif. Eurocenter, 3rd floor ☎02/2455499, ⓦwww.ecuador.gc.ca; Colombia, Colón 1133 and Amazonas, Edif. Arista ☎02/2221969; Ireland, Yanacocha N72-64 and Juan Procel ☎02/3570156; Peru, República de El Salvador 495 and Irlanda ☎02/2468410; UK, Naciones Unidas and República de El Salvador, Edif. Citiplaza, 14th floor ☎02/2970800, ⓦwww.ukinecuador.fco.gov.uk; US, Av Avigiras E12-170 and Eloy Alfaro ☎02/3985000, ⓦwww.ecuador.usembassy.gov.

Emergencies ☎911, police ☎101, fire ☎102, ambulance ☎131.

Hospitals Hospital Metropolitano, Av Mariana de Jesús and Nicolás Arteta (☎02/2261520, emergency and ambulance ☎02/2265020, ⓦwww.hospitalmetropolitano.org). Clínica Pichincha, Veintimilla E3-30 and Páez (☎02/2562408, emergency ☎02/2998777,

ⓦwww.hcp.com.ec). Hospital Voz Andes, Villalengua Oe2-37 and 10 de Agosto (☎02/2262142, ⓦwww.hospitalvozandes.org).

Ice skating Palacio de Hielo, at CC Iñaquito, Amazonas N36-152 and Av Naciones Unidas. There's an open ice hockey match on Sunday nights.

Internet Cheap (typically around $1 or less) and plentiful, especially around La Mariscal.

Laundry Best are in La Mariscal on Foch, Pinto and Wilson between Reina Victoria and Amazonas. Typical rates are around $0.80 per kg for wash; dried and folded clothes ready same or next day. Super Lavado, Pinto E6-32 and Reina Victoria (☎02/2502987), offers free pick-up and delivery.

Maps See Basics on p.61

Pharmacies Fybeca has 35 stores in Quito. Call ☎1800/392322 to find your nearest branch and for 24hr locations, one of which is at Amazonas N42-72 and Tomás de Berlanga. Farmacia Colón, corner of 10 de Agosto 2292 and Cordero also open 24hr.

Police ☎101. Policía Nacional Servicio de Seguridad Turística, Reina Victoria N21-208 and Roca ☎02/2543983, open daily 8am–7pm, is dedicated to tourist incidents; Dirección Nacional de la Policía Judicial, Roca 582 and Juan León Mera ☎02/2550770, open daily 24hr.

Post offices Main office at Japón N36-153 and Av Naciones Unidas, but there are 22 other branches. The most convenient for La Mariscal is at Reina Victoria and Colón, in Edif. Torres de Almagro; old-town branch is at Guayaquil 935 and Espejo (Mon–Fri 8am–7pm, Sat & Sun 8am–noon). Large packages are best sent from the office at Ulloa and Ramírez Dávalos. See also Basics p.60.

Travel agents IATA-accredited travel agents include Ecuadorian Tours, Amazonas 329 and Jorge Washington ☎02/2560488; Polimundo, Amazonas 2374 and Eloy Alfaro ☎02/2505244; and Metropolitan Touring, De las Palmeras N45-74 and De las Orquídeas ☎02/2988200.

Visas and extensions See Basics, p.59.

Moving on from Quito

Quito is a major transport hub, so it's quite common to return here periodically to pick up and drop off luggage between trips to the different regions of Ecuador or before **moving on** to another destination. Further transport details are listed at the end of the chapter on p.126.

By air

When you leave Ecuador by air from Quito, you must pay a $40.80 **departure tax** in cash at check-in; domestic flights are exempt. TAME provides the widest choice of destinations (☎02/3977100, ⓦwww.tame.com.ec), but Icaro (☎02/2450928, ⓦwww.icaro.aero) has a reputation for better service, and Aerogal (☎02/2942800, ⓦwww.aerogal.com.ec) has good Galápagos coverage among other destinations. Other domestic airlines include Saéreo (☎02/3301152, ⓦwww.saereo.com), at the time of writing only operating charter flights, but seeking schedules to Loja and Macas, and VIP (☎02/3304621, ⓦwww.vipec.com), which has good links to Lago Agrio and Coca. For details on Quito airport and transfers, see "Arrival" on p.75; for information on domestic air travel, see Basics on p.36; for contact details of domestic and international airlines, see "Listings" on p.118; for domestic flight destinations and frequencies, refer to "travel details" on p.126.

By bus

Most regional and long-distance journeys from Quito are likely to be by **bus**, almost all of which leave from the **Terminal Terrestre Cumandá**, a short distance south of the old town on Avenida Maldonado 3077, next to the Cumandá Trole stop. See also p.76 about the new Terminal Terrestre being built at Quitumbe in the south of the city.

If travelling with your luggage, take a **taxi** and insist on being taken to the main drop-off point *inside* the station complex. Drivers are often reluctant to do this as it costs them $0.50 to enter, so paying the fee for them should settle the argument. Ticket offices are downstairs and the buses are reached via a turnstile ($0.20), but once through, you can't re-enter the main hall. For **information** on bus schedules, refer to "travel details" on p.126 or call the station office (8.30am–5.30pm; ☎02/2571163).

A few bus companies also have offices in the **new town** (which can be a more convenient departure point than the Terminal Terrestre) where they also usually stop: Flota Imbabura, Manuel Larrea 1211 and Portoviejo (☎02/2236940), for Cuenca, Guayaquil, Manta, Ibarra and Tulcán; Flor del Valle, Manuel Larrea and Asunción (☎02/2527495), for Mindo and Cayambe, not stopping at the Terminal Terrestre; Panamericana Internacional, Colón 852 and Reina Victoria (☎02/2505099), for Huaquillas, Machala, Loja, Guayaquil, Manta and Esmeraldas; Transportes Ecuador, Juan León Mera 330 and Jorge Washington (☎02/2581977), for Guayaquil; Transportes Esmeraldas, Santa María 870 and 9 de Octubre (☎02/2505099) for Esmeraldas, Musine, Lago Agrio, Coca.

International buses to other South American countries are operated by Panamericana Internacional (see p.120) for Caracas (its only direct service), Pasto, Cali, Bogotá, Medellín, Lima, Arica, Santiago, La Paz and Buenos Aires; Expreso Internacional Ormeño, Av Los Shyris 11-68 (☎02/2460027), for Lima (its only direct line), Cali, Bogotá, Caracas, La Paz, Santiago and Buenos Aires; and Transportes Rutas de América Internacional, Selva Alegre Oe1-70 and 10 de Agosto (☎02/2503611), for Lima, La Paz, Buenos Aires and Caracas; there can be considerable waiting times and layovers between connections on all these services. It's less expensive to take regular **interprovincial buses** to the border and change on the other side, allowing you to cover large distances at your own pace.

By train

A huge investment is underway to revitalize parts of Ecuador's long-moribund train network, so that the service from Quito will eventually reach Riobamba and the Devil's Nose (check ⓦwww.efe.gov.ec or ☎02/2585710 for the latest). In the meantime, you'll have to make do with the tourist train to Latacunga (Sat & Sun 8am; $10 return) running to Latacunga, and calling at Tambillo, Machachi, and the

Area Nacional de Recreación El Boliche adjoining the Parque Nacional Cotopaxi (see p.178). The train leaves from the beautifully restored Estación de Ferrocarril Chimbacalle, just off Avenida Maldonado 2km south of the old town. It's a beautiful ride (4hr; return leg leaves 2.30pm, arriving around 6.30pm), taking you through sweeping agricultural landscapes around Volcán Cotopaxi, which on clear days can be seen even as you pull out of Quito. Buy tickets beforehand from the office at Bolívar 443, between García Moreno and Benalcázar (Mon–Fri 8am–4.30pm ☎02/2582930), and bring along your passport (or a copy).

Metropolitan Touring (Ⓦwww.metropolitan-touring.com) operates the Chiva Express, a converted truck on rails with seats inside and on the roof, which does several rail itineraries from Quito.

Around Quito

The most dramatic attraction **around Quito** may be the looming outline of the potentially explosive **Volcán Pichincha**, but the most famous, busiest and most developed is **La Mitad del Mundo**. Almost directly north of the city, it's a complex celebrating, and positioned (almost) on, the equator, with a monument, museum, exhibition spaces and the famous line itself, marked in the ground. On high ground overlooking the monument is a prehistoric site, **Catequilla**, which, it was discovered only recently, *is* exactly on the equator. Also nearby, and often included on trips to La Mitad del Mundo, is the huge volcanic crater **Pululahua**, whose foothills are home to thousands of acres of rich, cultivated farmland.

Northeast of Quito are **Calderón**, production centre for dough figurines, **Guayllabamba**, home of the capital's zoo, and **El Quinche**, an important religious centre with an impressive church.

Southeast of the capital are the market town **Sangolquí**, **San Rafael**, with its excellent museum on artist **Eduardo Kingman**, and the **Refugio de Vida Silvestre Pasochoa**, a woodland refuge surrounding a volcanic crater where trails pass through abundant native forests rich in birdlife.

Other excursions and attractions within a short distance of the capital, but discussed in other chapters, include the birdwatching mecca of **Mindo** (see p.342), the **cloudforest reserves** a few hours northwest of the capital, such as Bellavista, Tandayapa, Maquipucuna and Santa Lucía (pp.338–341), the fabulous hot springs at **Papallacta** (p.283), the huge artesanía market at **Otavalo** (p.135), the ruined pyramids of **Cochasquí** (p.133) and the **Cotopaxi** national park, dominated by its famous volcano (p.178).

La Mitad del Mundo and around

Twenty kilometres north of Quito, at 2483m on the fringes of the dusty town of San Antonio de Pichincha, lies the colonial-styled complex of whitewashed buildings, gift shops, snack bars and museums known as **LA MITAD DEL MUNDO** (The Middle of the World), straddling the line that divides the earth's northern and southern hemispheres and gives the country its name – the **equator** (latitude of 0° 0' 0"). **Charles–Marie de La Condamine** and his geodesic mission first ascertained its exact demarcation in 1736–44, and a monument to this achievement was raised across the line in 1936. Deemed not grand enough, it was replaced in 1979 with the current one. Modern GPS readings have revealed that even the new monument is seven seconds of a degree south of the true equator, roughly 240m adrift, but the finding has done little to dent the popularity of the attraction – local crowds flock to the site, particularly on Sundays and holidays, when music and dance performances are held in the afternoons.

The complex

From the entrance to the site (Mon–Thurs 9am–6pm, Fri–Sun 9am–7pm; $2, plus $1.50 if using car park), a cobbled street, lined with busts of La Condamine's expedition members, leads up to the thirty-metre-tall **La Mitad del Mundo monument**, a giant concrete monolith replete with large metal globe. From its base, a line representing the equator extends outwards – even running down the middle of the aisle (and altar) of the church within the complex. Inside the monument is the **Ethnographic Museum** ($3), accessed via a lift. Once at the top, you descend by stairs through the museum, which displays region-by-region exhibits on Ecuador's indigenous populations and their customs, with fine exhibits of native dress and artefacts.

Among the other sites in the complex are various **national pavilions**, representing the countries that took part in the expedition, each with its own little museum. A **planetarium** (40min; $1.50) on site offers rather unimpressive hourly shows, but the more stimulating **Fundación Quito Colonial** (daily 10am–5pm; $1.50), contains richly detailed miniature models of Guayaquil, Cuenca and Quito – featuring their own artificial sunrise and sunset. Also within the complex is a **post office**, gift shops, an ATM, restaurants and snack bars. Pig out – and then try the weighing scales here, knowing you've actually lost a little weight while on the equator. Thanks to the earth's own bulging waistline, gravity is weaker here, so you weigh less; unfortunately, your mass will be the same.

Practicalities

To get to the complex from Quito, take the Metrobus northwards to the Ofelia stop and catch a "feeder" bus marked Mitad del Mundo. At weekends a special bus service (45min; $0.75) runs every fifteen to thirty minutes between the complex and El Panecillo in the old town (see p.94). A **taxi** from the new town will cost around $12–15 one-way, or $20–25 return including waiting time. Most **tour** operators in Quito arrange trips here, to Pululahua and to the various archeological sites around the area.

Museo Inti Ñan

If you find the Mitad del Mundo complex a little dry, try the enjoyable **Museo Inti Ñan** (daily 9.30am–5.30pm; $3), which houses an idiosyncratic collection of equator-related experiments and curios and exhibits on indigenous cultures and their beliefs. The tone is light-hearted: having shot a blow dart into a pumpkin, you can try to win a certificate for balancing an egg on a nail on the equator, which they claim really *does* go through their property. The museum is a bit fiddly to find; turn left after leaving the complex and walk a few hundred metres uphill, then follow signs left again down a short driveway.

Catequilla, Pambamarca and Rumicucho

Long before La Condamine came to Ecuador, it was known the equator passed through this region and, some might say, with far greater accuracy than the Enlightenment explorer. On a dusty hill overlooking town 3km to the east, the extraordinary **Catequilla** (also called Kati-Killa), a huge and ancient circular

platform bisected by the equator pays testament to the astronomical sophistication of the pre-Columbian Quitu-Cara culture, who built it around 800 AD.
Along with **Pambamarca**, a large undeveloped ceremonial site connected to
the December solstice, and the impressive **Rumicucho** ($0.50 charged by the
local community), a terraced ruin on a dramatic ridge-top, both nearby, this trio
of ancestral ruins sounds a refreshing note of gravitas to counter the enjoyable,
but rather hollow tackiness of the modern Mitad del Mundo complex. You can
visit them with Calimatours (☎02/2394796, ⓦwww.calimaecuador.com),
office inside the Mitad del Mundo complex.

Pululahua

A visit to the Mitad del Mundo is commonly combined with a trip up to the
rim of the extinct volcano of **Pululahua**, whose 34-square-kilometre **crater**
– one of the continent's largest – has been protected since 1966 as a **geobo-
tanical reserve**. Its unusual topography and associated microclimates not only
support rich, cultivated land on the valley floor, but also lush cloudforests, 260
types of plants and a large variety of orchids. Outlooks on the rim afford **views**
over bucolic scenery within the crater, beautiful networks of fields and small
settlements squeezed around the two volcanic cones of Pondoña and Chivo, all
cradled by the thickly forested and deeply gullied crater walls. It's best to get up
here early in the morning as thick clouds engulf the crater later in the day.

Practicalities

The first is 4km from the equator monument, heading north on the Calacalí
highway (1hr walk), and turning right on a paved road that climbs to a car park
(30min walk) at the **Ventanillas** viewpoint, from where a steep **trail** leads
down to the crater settlements below (30min down, 1hr back up; horses
sometimes available). **Buses** heading to Calacalí pass the Ventanillas turn-off,
though at weekends you've a good chance of getting a lift or a *camioneta*. A **taxi**
will take you from the Mitad del Mundo to the viewpoint and back for about
$5. Calimatours (☎02/2394796, ⓦwww.calimaecuador.com), office inside the
Mitad del Mundo complex, and Colibritours (☎02/2395972 or 09/9923358,
ⓦwww.colibritoursecuador.com) by the *Equinoccio* restaurant, just north of the
complex, arrange trips to the crater for around $8. Just before the viewpoint is
a turn-off to an exclusive restaurant and hotel *El Cráter* (☎02/2439254,
ⓦwww.elcrater.com; ❾ including breakfast).

The second access is more suitable for independent motorists; turn right near
the filling station about 3km further along the Calacalí highway onto a track
leading up to the **Moraspungo** guard post, where you may be asked to pay the
$5 reserve **entrance fee** if you plan to continue into the reserve on the eight-
kilometre dirt track that winds down to the crater floor. Near the guard post
are cheap, basic **cabins** and camping facilities.

It's 15km from Moraspungo or 2.5km from Ventanillas to *La Rinconada*
(☎02/02498880 or 09/1733486, ⓦwww.crateraventura.com), a **restaurant**
retreat tucked away in the northern corner of the crater, the retirement bolt
hole of Ecuador's most famous long-distance runner, Rolando Vera. As well as
getting a good square meal here, you can **camp** ($3; equipment provided) or
stay in the hacienda (❺) and hire **horses** to explore the crater. Make contact
first, and they will pick you up from the bottom of the Ventanillas descent.

Calderón

Just 9km northeast of the capital's outskirts sits **CALDERÓN**, a small town
renowned for its brightly coloured figurines made of bread **dough** (*masapán*).

The tradition is to take these to the cemetery on All Saints' Day and the Day of the Dead (Nov 1 and 2) and place them on graves as an offering to departed souls. You can't eat most of these painted and varnished figurines, but you wouldn't want to chew off the intricate details, such as extravagant mock-filigree ruffs and fibrous hair. You can tuck into *guaguas de pán* (**bread babies**), with *colada morada*, the sweet, hot and purple, seasonal drink made with fruit, herbs and purple cornflour.

In town on Carapungo, the main street, there are a number of good **artesanía shops** (Mon–Fri & occasionally Sat). To get here by bus, take the Metrobus to the Ofelia stop and a "feeder" for Calderón.

Guayllabamba and El Quinche

Beyond Calderón, the Panamericana sweeps 700m down into the dry Guayllabamba gorge and plain. Stalls laden with jumbo avocados and exotic fruits line the main road into **GUAYLLABAMBA**, 32km from the capital and home to Quito's zoo, the largest and best designed in the country. A few kilometres outside town, the **Zoológico Guayllabamba** (Tues–Fri 9am–5pm, Sat & Sun 9.30am–5pm; $3.50, guides free, English spoken) puts the emphasis on crowd-pleasing native fauna, such as the Andean spectacled bear, pumas and condors.

Buses bound for Cayambe, such as Flor del Valle, which leave from Manuel Larrea and Asunción in the new town, usually stop at or just outside Guayllabamba (45min–1hr). It's a 30-minute walk up a cobblestone road to the zoo; at weekends there's a free bus, otherwise a **camioneta** will take you for a small fee.

About 7km southeast of Guayllabamba lies the village of **El Quinche**, famous for its outsized **church**. For pilgrims, its most important feature is the wooden image of **El Virgen del Quinche**, carved at the end of the sixteenth century by artist and architect **Diego de Robles**, who was saved from tumbling hundreds of feet into the Río Oyacachi by a thorn snagging on his clothes.

Since Robles cheated death, the Virgin has been credited with countless other miracles, depicted by paintings inside the church and plaques on the walls. Visitors make their way from across the country to venerate her, especially during the **festival** in the third week of November, climaxing on November 21, and throngs of people receive blessings all year round. There are regular **buses** to El Quinche via Pifo from the Río Coca stop on the Ecovía system in Quito and others from Guayllabamba.

Sangolquí

The most important town in this region, **SANGOLQUÍ**, 15km southeast of the capital, has an impressive **church** with an imposing facade and grand bell tower. Yet it's much better known for its **market**, which runs all week, but on Sundays (and to a lesser extent, Thursdays) expands from its three dedicated market squares to fill much of the town. It's a hard-edged and busy affair, perhaps lacking the charm of a highland-village market, but the energy of the local commerce is compelling, and being so close to Quito it makes an easy day-trip for those with limited time. **Buses** leave regularly from Plaza Marín in the old town (25min). For places to stay, see "Outskirts of Quito" on p.85.

San Rafael and the Museo de la Casa de Kingman

Twenty minutes from Quito or five minutes by bus from Sangolquí, and easily combined with a trip to the latter's market, **SAN RAFAEL** has little of inherent interest, except for the excellent **Museo de la Casa de Kingman** (Thurs–Fri 10am–4pm, Sat & Sun 10am–5pm; $2; ☎02/2861065, ⓦwww .fundacionkingman.com), a block from the park at Portoviejo and Dávila. Occupying a peaceful spot high on the banks of the Río San Pedro, this was the house of **Eduardo Kingman**, one of Ecuador's greatest twentieth-century artists. Kingman is best known for depicting the privation of Ecuador's indigenous peoples, often capturing their plight in the expressiveness of their hands – a technique he later taught Oswaldo Guayasamín. There are some wonderful pieces exhibited here that support Kingman's considerable reputation, as well as some colonial and republican art.

Buses to Sangolquí pass right by San Rafael's park, from where the museum is just a short walk away. A **taxi** from Quito costs around $10.

Refugio de Vida Silvestre Pasochoa

Thirty kilometres southeast of Quito, the luxuriant **Refugio de Vida Silvestre Pasochoa** ($10) is a dense forest spread over **Cerro Pasochoa** (4200m), an extinct volcano whose western side collapsed in an eruption more than 100,000 years ago. The inaccessibility of the terrain, hemmed in by the crater's remaining walls, has left the forest largely undisturbed, despite its proximity to Quito.

The **reserve** is managed by the Quito-based Fundación Natura, at Av República 481 and Diego de Almagro (☎02/2272863, ⓦwww.fnatura.org), which has installed visitor facilities, including private en-suite rooms ($10), basic refuge ($6), **campsite** ($5) and a kitchen; bring a sleeping bag and food. A variety of trails lead through the forest, rich in beautiful native **trees** and **plants** – including Andean cedars, orchids and podocarpus (Ecuador's only native conifer), as well as 126 species of **birds** (a guide for sale at the entrance lists them all). One trail rises out of the forest and heads up across the páramo, following the outer slopes of the crater rim. It's a six- to eight-hour hike up to the **summit** of Cerro Pasochoa; **guides** can be booked in advance ($10–40 depending on hike).

Practicalities

By prior arrangement, the reserve staff can pick you up in a *camioneta* ($5) from Highway 35, the main road running nearby; they will supply details. Otherwise, from Plaza La Marín in Quito's old town, take one of the frequent **buses** to the small town of Amaguaña (25min), also on Highway 35, then take a **camioneta** ($6; arrange pick-up for the return journey, or take a Movistar card for the mobile phone at the refuge) from the plaza to the reserve entrance, reached along a seven-kilometre cobbled access road leading south

Volcanic activity

Although Rucu (meaning "old" in Quichua) is extinct, Guagua ("baby") has experienced renewed **volcanic activity** in the last few years, after more than three centuries of near silence. It has long been on **yellow alert**, warning of ongoing seismic activity and the possibility of an eruption. Should that occur, Quito would more than likely escape the lava flow, but not the dispersion of ash. The volcano's last notable eruption, on October 5, 1999, produced an eighteen-kilometre-high column of ash and vapour that leered over the city in a giant mushroom cloud. Despite this display, experts don't consider Quito to be in imminent danger. For more on volcanoes, see p.34.

from town. You can walk from Amaguaña in less than two hours, though you will have to keep asking for directions as it's badly signposted.

Volcán Pichincha

Rising over the west side of Quito, the broad-based, emerald-sloped **Volcán Pichincha** has two main peaks: the slightly lower, serene-looking **Rucu Pichincha** (4675m) lies just beyond the hilltops, looming over the new town; **Guagua Pichincha** (4794m), 10km west of the city centre, is a highly active volcano, which erupted spectacularly in 1999, covering Quito in ash and dust.

Rucu Pichincha

Rucu Pichincha has been virtually out of bounds to climbers in recent years because the access routes to it from Cruz Loma and La Loma de las Antenas (the aerial-topped peaks clearly visible from the city) were extremely dangerous, due to the frequent assaults and robberies. The TelefériQo (see p.100) takes hundreds of people up to Cruz Loma each day, but we recommend not attempting the three-hour hike to the summit beyond the perimeter fences. Check with SAE (see p.77) for the latest security conditions.

Guagua Pichincha

Guagua Pichincha is best reached from the village of Lloa, southwest of Quito, from where a signposted dirt track leads up to a **refuge** just below the summit (about 5–6hr walk). The refuge is basic; bring your own food and sleeping bag if spending the night ($5), during which it gets very cold.

Most **climbing operators** in Quito (see p.116) offer the Guagua climb as a day tour, including four-wheel-drive transport to or near the refuge.

Travel details

Trains

Quito to: El Boliche, Parque Nacional Cotopaxi (1 Sat & Sun; 2hr 30min); Latacunga (1 daily Sat & Sun; 4hr).

Buses

Quito to: Alausí (3 daily; 5hr); Ambato (every 5min; 2hr 30min); Atacames (8 daily; 6hr 30min); Baeza (28 daily; 3hr); Bahía de Caráquez (3 daily; 8hr); Baños (every 15–30min; 3hr 15min); Coca (20 daily; 10hr); Cotacachi (4 daily; 2hr 20min); Cuenca (every 15–30min; 11–12hr); El Ángel (20 daily; 4hr); Esmeraldas (every 20–30min; 6hr); Guaranda (every 30min; 4hr 30min); Guayaquil (every 10–20min; 8hr); Huaquillas (16 daily; 12hr); Ibarra (every 15–20min; 2hr 30min); Lago Agrio (28 daily; 8hr); Latacunga (every 10min; 2hr); Loja (20 daily; 14hr sierra route, 16hr coast route); Macará (3 daily; 15hr); Macas (4–8 daily; 10hr); Machala (21 daily; 10hr); Manta (31 daily; 8hr 30min); Mindo (1–2 daily; 1hr 30min); Nanegalito (10 daily; 1hr 45min); Otavalo (every 10min; 2hr); Papallacta (28 daily; 1hr 30min); Pedernales (15 daily; 5hr); Pujilí (every 30min; 2hr); Puyo (25 daily; 5hr); Quevedo (23 daily; 4hr 30min); Riobamba (every 15min; 4hr); Salinas (7 daily; 10hr); San Gabriel (17 daily; 4hr 15min); San Lorenzo (9 daily; 7hr); San Vicente (4 daily; 9hr); Santo Domingo (every 10–15min; 3hr); Saquisilí (12 daily, Thurs every 30min; 1hr 30min); Sigchos (2 daily; 5hr); Tena (21 daily; 5hr); Tulcán (every 10–20min; 5hr).

Flights

Quito to: Baltra (3–4 daily; 3hr 15min); Coca (12 daily Mon–Fri, 3 Sat & Sun; 30min); Cuenca (8 daily Mon–Fri, 4 Sat, 5 Sun; 45min); Esmeraldas (1–2 daily, not Sat; 30min); Guayaquil (27 daily Mon–Fri, 12 Sat, 14 Sun; 45min); Lago Agrio (8 weekly; 30min); Loja (2 daily Sun–Fri, 1 Sat; 50min–1hr); Macas (1 Mon–Fri; 30min); Manta (5–6 daily; 45min); San Cristóbal (1–2 daily; 3hr 15min).

2

The northern sierra

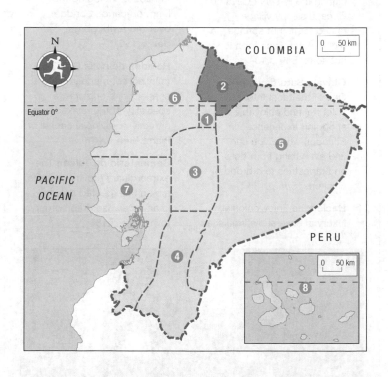

CHAPTER 2

Highlights

* **Quitsato** Ecuador's most engaging equator monument, thanks to its enormous sundial, which makes full use of the special properties at the centre of the earth. See p.132

* **Oyacachi** Amid forested hills high in the Reserva Cayambe-Coca, a sleepy village famed for its hot springs – a picturesque place for a long, hot soak. See p.134

* **Otavalo Saturday market** One of the most intense, colourful and enjoyable shopping experiences in Ecuador, where you can find everything from dolls and tapestries to a brood of chickens. See p.135

* **Haciendas** Enjoy colonial luxury at several distinguished estates around Otavalo and Cayambe, some of which are still working farms. See p.140

* **Autoferro de Ibarra** A curious bus on rails clattering over the old rail line towards the coast, including the long, precarious bridge over the Ambi gorge. See p.156

* **Helados de paila** Delicious fruity sorbet made in huge copper pans or *pailas*, a speciality of the relaxed and attractive provincial capital of Ibarra. See p.157

* **Cementerio de Tulcán** The extraordinary topiary gardens are an unexpected delight in an otherwise drab border town. See p.168

▲ Hacienda Pinsaquí

The northern sierra

A magnificent sequence of volcanoes, sparkling crater lakes and patchwork scenery, the **NORTHERN SIERRA** extends northeast from Quito for 140 kilometres to the Colombian border. Down on the ground along the Panamericana, the main transport artery, this translates as 250km of highway snaking between cloud-piercing mountain peaks, windblown hilltop passes, warm valleys bursting with fruit orchards and flower plantations and a couple of major ecological reserves. For many visitors, the prime lure has long been the region's vibrant markets, and although many key destinations are within easy reach of Quito, wandering from the bus-laden Panamericana will quickly take you into seldom-visited countryside.

Leaving the capital, the first town of any significant size is **Cayambe**, set at the foot of **Volcán Cayambe** – the highest point in the world on the equator. Close by are the pre-Inca ruins of **Cochasquí**, the **Quitsato equator monument** and the bone-warming hot springs of **Oyacachi**, an idyllic village nestled in the high forests of the vast **Reserva Ecológica Cayambe-Coca**. The main attraction of the region, however, just forty minutes from Cayambe and two hours from the capital, is **Otavalo**'s irresistible artesanía market. One of the continent's most famous markets, it's at its biggest on Saturday but good throughout the week, bursting with an irresistible array of weavings, garments, carvings, ceramics, jewellery and many assorted knick-knacks. The weaving tradition in the Otavalo valley predates even the Incas, and virtually all of its towns specialize in a particular area of craftwork, from embroidery and woven belts to bulky knitted socks; furthermore, the nearby towns of **Cotacachi** and **San Antonio de Ibarra**, are the respective national centres of leather goods and woodcarving. An easy excursion to **Laguna Cuicocha**, tucked in the southernmost corner of the striking **Cotacachi-Cayapas reserve**, gives a taster of the wildernesses unfurling westward, not least the teeming cloudforests of the **Intag region** beyond.

The largest city in the northern sierra, **Ibarra**, 30km north of Otavalo, charms with elegant, whitewashed buildings and its relaxed atmosphere. Once the point of departure for a famously hair-raising **train** ride to the coast at San Lorenzo, Ibarra now sits at the head of a new road providing the country's fastest highway link between the sierra and the sea, descending through dramatic scenery from highlands to cloudforests to coast. A few kilometres north of Ibarra, the old road to the Colombian border branches off from the Panamericana and climbs to **El Ángel**, the 3000-metre-high access point to the remote **Reserva Ecológica El Ángel**, where undulating páramo grasslands are speckled with rare *frailejones* flowers. Meanwhile, the Panamericana ascends the dry and dusty **Chota valley**, one of the few places where African and Andean traditions have blended, on its

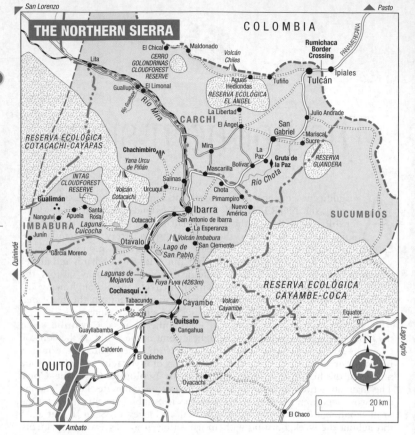

THE NORTHERN SIERRA

San Lorenzo · Pasto

COLOMBIA

El Chical · Maldonado
Lita
CERRO
GOLONDRINAS
CLOUDFOREST
RESERVE
Guallupé · El Limonal
Volcán
Chiles
Rumichaca
Border
Crossing
Ipiales
Tulcán
Aguas
Hediondas
Tufiño
RESERVA ECOLÓGICA
EL ÁNGEL
Julio Andrade
La Libertad
CARCHI
El Ángel
San
Gabriel
Mariscal
Sucre
RESERVA ECOLÓGICA
COTACACHI-CAYAPAS
Chachimbiro
Yana Urcu
de Piñán
Mira
La
Paz
Gruta de
la Paz
RESERVA
GUANDERA
Salinas
Mascarilla
Río Chota
INTAG
CLOUDFOREST
RESERVE
Gualimán
Volcán
Cotacachi
Urcuquí
Chota
Pimampiro
SUCUMBÍOS
Nangulví
Santa
Rosa
Apuela
Laguna
Cuicocha
Cotacachi
Ibarra
San Antonio de Ibarra
Nuevo
América
IMBABURA
Junín
La Esperanza
García Moreno
Otavalo
Volcán Imbabura
San Clemente
Lago de
San Pablo
Lagunas de
Mojanda
Fuya Fuya (4263m)
RESERVA ECOLÓGICA
CAYAMBE-COCA
Cochasquí
Tabacundo
Volcán
Cayambe
Equator
0°
N
Tocachi
Cayambe
Quitsato
Guayllabamba
Cangahua
Calderón
El Quinche
QUITO
Oyacachi
0   20 km
El Chaco

Ambato

Quinindé · Lago Agrio

way to **Tulcán**, a frontier town close to Colombia that plays unlikely host to some remarkable topiary gardens.

Cayambe and around

Overshadowed by the eponymous volcano, **CAYAMBE** (2850m) is worth a quick visit for its renowned home-made **cheese** and **bizcochos** – buttery biscuits locals carry around by the bagful. It's also a regional centre for Ecuador's **flower industry** (its fourth-largest export), evident in the shimmer of plastic-sheeted greenhouses gleaming across the valley. For much of the year it's a quiet provincial town most travellers skip on their way from Quito to Otavalo, but during the **fiestas** of late June, things really get busy when *indígenas* descend from the surrounding villages for singing, dancing, parades and bullfights. The celebration kicks off with **Inti Raymi** (Quichua for "sun festival"), which heralds the summer solstice and continues for several days until it merges with the **fiesta of San Pedro** on June 29, honouring the town's patron saint.

Apart from this, there are few things to see in Cayambe other than the archeological site of **Puntiazil** and the local museum with corresponding finds. Still, the town makes a good base for exploring the area, as does the splendid **Hacienda Guachalá**, a short distance away.

Arrival and information

Buses between Quito and Otavalo (every 5–10min; 40min from Otavalo, 1hr 20min from Quito) **arriving** in Cayambe stop at the two roundabouts next to the bullring. Flor del Valle, at Manuel Larrea and Asunción in Quito's new town (☎02/2527495), also run regular direct buses, saving you a trip to the Terminal Terrestre. For **transport** around the region, **taxis** wait in Cayambe's main plaza and charge about $45 for a full day, enough to take you to most of the local sights, including Oyacachi and Cochasquí, while **camionetas** for the Cayambe refuge can be hired from the marketplace. Buses to Tabacundo head west out of town on Bolívar near the bullring and pass the turn-off for the Cochasquí ruins. The Banco del Pacífico, Jarrín and Junín, has a MasterCard **ATM**.

Accommodation

During the June fiestas it can be hard to find a **place to stay** in Cayambe, so make sure to reserve well in advance.

Cayambe Bolívar 107 and Montalvo ☎02/2360400. The cheapest centrally located hotel in town offers rooms with sparkling, white-tiled floors and TV. ❷

La Gran Colombia Av Natalia Jarrín and Calderón ☎02/2361238. More business-oriented than the other hotels listed here, this rather smart spot also has a popular on-site restaurant. ❷

Mitad del Mundo Av Natalia Jarrín and Argentina ☎02/2360226. Adequate, inexpensive rooms, with or without bath, plus an indoor, heated pool, sauna and steam room (Sat & Sun). ❶–❷

Shungu Huasi Camino a Granobles, off the Panamericana 1km back from *Café Cayambe* ☎02/2361847, ⓦwww.shunguhuasi.com. Spacious grounds, a good Italian restaurant and horseriding tours make this place the best of a cluster of self-contained hotel complexes to the north of the town. ❺

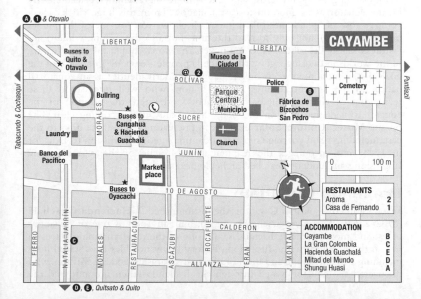

The Town

The centre of Caymbe is the leafy **Parque Central**, at the northern end of which is the town's grandest building, which houses the **Centro Cultural Espinosa Jarrín** and **Museo de la Ciudad** (Wed–Sun 8am–5pm; free), exhibiting pieces recovered from the nearby **Puntiazil**, an important ceremonial site of the ancient **Cayambi** people. The site itself, located down a grassy track by the town cemetery, has not borne well the passage of time, though the remnants of a large pyramid are discernible. At the centre of the site once stood a large **cylinder** (destroyed in 1834) made of packed earth, which measured celestial movements; a similar device has been reconstructed at the Quitsato monument just outside town.

For local **shopping**, several little **biscuit factories** are dotted around town – the Fábrica de Bizcochos San Pedro, opposite the cemetery, is one of the best – and many stores sell the speciality *queso de hoja*, a salty, white cheese boiled and wrapped in *achira* leaves. **Market** day is Sunday, when the town streets and marketplace on Junín and Restauración are filled with stalls selling many kinds of locally grown fruit and vegetables.

Eating and drinking

For **places to eat** besides simple pizzerias and fast-food chicken outlets try *Aroma* (closes 8pm, Sun 6pm & all day Wed), Bolívar and Rocafuerte, a popular spot serving traditional dishes, plus vegetarian meals on request; you could also take a taxi 2km north up the Panamericana to *Casa de Fernando* or *Shungu Huasi*, regarded as the best local restaurants.

Quitsato equator monument

Seven kilometres south of Cayambe, just before the turning to Cangahua and *Hacienda Guachalá*, at Km70 on the Panamericana, is the **Quitsato** equator monument (Ⓦ www.quitsato.org), taking the form of a **giant sundial** (*reloj solar*), spanning 54 metres across with a ten-metre-high cylinder, placed exactly on the equator, as its gnomon to cast a shadow. From this huge clock face, a compass rose of light stones inlaid into dark allows you (or one of the guides on hand, at least), not only to read the time, but also the month, while other features indicate the solstices and equinoxes. The words "quitsa to" mean "centre of the world" in the language of the Tsáchila people (see p.488), and one of the goals of the monument is to link Ecuador's modern identity as an equatorial nation to the ancient cultures of the region, who well understood these techniques of charting celestial movements and knew the position of the equator to a degree (pardon the pun) that is only just becoming clear. The on-site **Museo Cultura Solar** explains in fascinating detail these links to the past, including good coverage of La Condamine's geodesic mission to Ecuador in 1743, and encourages the reappraisal and rescue of the region's many languishing and under-researched archeological sites

Hacienda Guachalá

Seven kilometres south of Cayambe, the distinguished 🏛 **Hacienda Guachalá** (☏02/2363042, Ⓦ www.guachala.com; ⑦), built in 1580, is one of Ecuador's oldest and most affordable haciendas, and one of the most charming places to stay in the northern sierra. In its long history many notables have stayed here, including La Condamine and the 1743 French–Spanish Geodesic Mission, who discovered the equator passed through the hacienda's then grounds, and the

English explorer and mountaineer Edward Whymper, who in 1882 found eleven new species of bugs and beetles in its gardens "before breakfast".

The main building has comfortable, unpretentiously ageing rooms with fireplaces, private bathrooms and hot showers around a large cloistered and cobbled courtyard. The grounds are dotted with agapanthus and alpacas, horses graze the fields and can be hired for $5 per hour, and other attractions include a covered pool, games room, lounge, library and small photograph museum in one of the two chapels. The **restaurant** serves hearty meals ($15) all day to both guests and visitors, including delicious *locro*, cheese and potato soup topped with avocado.

Buses from Cayambe to the hacienda leave from the corner of Restauración and Sucre every twenty minutes (15–20min trip; last bus 7.30pm), and a taxi ride costs just a few dollars. If coming from Quito on a bus to Cayambe, ask to be dropped at the unmarked turn-off to Cangahua, then wait for the bus there or walk for about a kilometre up the tree-lined road towards Cangahua. The hacienda organizes horseriding in the surrounding countryside and *camioneta* or taxi **tours** to Oyacachi, local archeological sites and other points of interest (around $30).

Cochasquí

About 24km west of Cayambe and 70km north of Quito are the ruins of **Cochasquí** (daily 8.30am–4.30pm; $3), one of the country's most significant pre-Inca archeological sites. Built at 3100m by the Cara or Cayambi people around 900 AD, the site's fifteen flat-topped pyramids were constructed from blocks of compressed volcanic soil (*cangahua*), now coated in grass, at the base of Mount Fuya Fuya. Long ramps lead up to most of the pyramids, which were levelled off to accommodate wooden structures that have long since rotted away.

One theory posits Cochasquí was a **fortress**, and the pyramids do occupy an important strategic position, with Quito and the volcanoes Cotopaxi and the Pichinchas visible in the distance. Perhaps more compelling, though, is the idea that the site was a kind of **observatory** – excavations have revealed the remnants of circular platforms, thought to be calendars of the sun and moon. Holes drilled nearby probably held pillars that would have cast shadows over sundials, and the site is also aligned with the summit of Cayambe volcano, over 30km away, and the Puntiazil site (see p.132), another ancient monument used for gauging celestial movements; shamans still congregate at the site around the solstices and equinoxes to perform spiritual rites. Although many of the pyramids are little more than large overgrown mounds, the eerie atmosphere and striking **views** alone merit a visit.

Tucked away behind the ruins are two reconstructions of ancient **Cara houses** (circular structures with thatched-grass roofs built around a living tree), a **medicinal plant garden**, plus a small **museum** exhibiting artefacts recovered from the site. Local Spanish-speaking **guides**, one of whom also speaks English, will meet you at the entrance and show you around the site for free (though tips are always appreciated).

There are no direct **buses** to Cochasquí. Instead, take a bus servicing the Tabacundo road, and get off at one of the turnings for Cochasquí. From here, you're faced with an 8km uphill **walk** (3hr), so take adequate water and food. A **taxi** from Tabacundo or Cayambe costs around $8–10 per hour, or go with one of the many **tour operators** in Quito (see p.116) that include Cochasquí in day-trips through the region.

Reserva Ecológica Cayambe-Coca

Heading southeast of Guachalá, the dirt road climbs through onion fields and páramo grasslands for an hour's drive until it passes the Las Puntas hills, site of the entrance checkpoint to the vast **Reserva Ecológica Cayambe-Coca** (daily, 7am–6pm; $10, though this is often overlooked; ID required). Founded in 1970 the reserve protects over 4000 square kilometres of land, from 5790m to just 600m above sea level. This huge range in altitude spans ten ecological zones that harbour a staggering number of plant and animal species, including nine hundred birds (among them the condor, mountain toucan and Andean cock-of-the-rock), and rare mammals, such as the spectacled bear and dwarf deer. Also living within the reserve are **Quichua**-language speakers at **Oyacachi**, a village renowned for its hot springs, and the **Cofán** people, in the far northeast of the reserve at **Sinangoé**, who offer family-based **accommodation** for $30–40 per person per day (arrange through the Fundación Sobrevivencia Cofán; ⓦ www.cofan.org).

The reserve's highest point is the summit of **Volcán Cayambe** (5790m), Ecuador's third-highest mountain; just south of the summit is the **highest point** on the equator, reputed to be the only place on the planet where the latitude and average temperature are both zero degrees. The volcano has a **refuge** ($17) at about 4700m, reached by a 25-kilometre dirt track leading southeast from Cayambe, with bunks, kitchen facilities, electricity and running water; bring a sleeping bag. The **climb** from the refuge to the summit (6–7hr) is regarded as more dangerous than either Cotopaxi or Cayambe for its many crevasses, risk of icefall, strong winds and frequent bouts of poor weather, though many agencies in Quito (see p.116) can arrange guides, equipment and transport. Nearer the refuge is an area of crevasses and ice walls often used by climbing schools and agencies for technical training.

There are several other points of **access** to the Cayambe-Coca reserve, mostly in the Oriente. The road from Papallacta to Baeza and Lago Agrio borders the easily accessed southern and eastern edges of the reserve, and the most common points of entry along this road are from Papallacta (see p.283), El Chaco (see p.286) and Lumbaquí, 70km west of Lago Agrio.

Oyacachi

Not far beyond Las Puntas checkpoint, the entry road descends into soft cloud-forest and ends at **OYACACHI**, nestled at 3200m in the crook of a valley. The village lies at the high end of one of the oldest routes into the Oriente, very likely the one Gonzalo Pizarro used during his ill-fated search east for El Dorado (see p.275). One legend maintains two families met here to establish the community, one from the highlands (the Parión family), the other from the rainforests in Oriente (the Aigaje family); it might be a quaint story, but almost every one of the village's Quichua-speaking residents has one of these names. They live by the reserve's environmental regulations, which prevent them from developing or cultivating the surrounding terrain, but do grant them generous plots of communal and individual land nearby. Self-imposed rules prohibit the sale of cigarettes and liquor in the village. A hydroelectric dam provides energy, and trout farming, cheese production and **woodcarving** bolster the local economy. On the main street opposite the school is a **communal store** many local families supply, where you can buy anything from a simple *batea* (tray) to elaborate animal carvings.

The main attraction for visitors though, apart from the starting point for a **hike** to the Oriente (see opposite), are the thermal springs, **Fuentes Termales** (daily 8am–4pm; $2), where you can wallow in the warmth of several steaming pools while admiring the wooded hills around you. Apart from weekends, when there's a woodcarving **market** at the entrance, you'll have the place to yourself.

Oyacachi receives few tourists, but there is a **bus** service from Cayambe (Mon, Wed & Fri leaves Oyacachi at 4am, returns from Cayambe 3.30pm; Sat leaves 4am, returns 2pm; Sun leaves 4am, returns around 7.30am, leaves Oyacachi again at 2pm; journey 1hr 45min), meaning unless you come on Sunday you'll probably have to stay the night here. The **hotel** (no name, ask for it or the owner, Elgar Parión; ☎02/2288968 is the shared number for the whole village; ❷) has a few perfectly comfortable yet simple rooms with a shared bathroom. **Campers** can pitch their tents near the springs for a few dollars. You can get **meals** up the street from the hotel at *La Oyacacheña* (no sign), run by María Zoila Aigaje, who cooks up a mean fresh trout. Other locals would also be happy to cook for you; just ask around. A **taxi** or **camioneta** from Cayambe costs around $20–30 one-way (1hr 15min), or around $40 for a full day.

Trails from Oyacachi

An ancient **trail** from Oyacachi follows the Río Oyacachi down to El Chaco in the Oriente (see p.286), a stunning two- to three-day hike traversing the cloudforest of the Cayambe-Coca Reserve. The first section of 10km or so takes you down a dirt road past the various settlements of Oyacachi, including its older centres. Before it was devastated by an earthquake in 1974, the village was located 45 minutes downhill at **Muacallacta**, where you'll now find ruins as well as a reconstructed traditional house; local guides can show you around. The oldest known parts of Oyacachi, probably pre-Columbian, are at Cedropamba about 8km down the road, where there's a grotto shrine, probably sacred long before the arrival of Christianity.

Beyond here, the road peters out and the going is more difficult. At the time of writing all the bridges were in good repair, but when they are washed out locals cross the river on pulleys and wires. **Guides** are recommended and are readily available in Oyacachi. They can provide horses, though you may need to bring your own **tent**. Ask around for Héctor Parión, who organizes a half-day hike from Oyacachi that includes a thrilling **rappel** down a thirty-metre rock face.

Another good **hike** crosses the highland parts of the reserve through páramo and past glittering lakes southwards to **Papallacta** (see p.283). The track begins at Las Puntas checkpoint, but you may need to get permission to use it from the Ministerio del Ambiente office in Cayambe (☎02/2110370), at H. Once and Rocafuerte, opposite the CAMAL building at the south end of town. On foot it'll take two days, but the route is passable by 4WD vehicles, taking less than an hour.

Otavalo

Only two hours' bus ride from Quito, **OTAVALO** (2535m) is one of Ecuador's top attractions, thanks largely to its world-renowned **Saturday market**. For hundreds of years, *indígenas* from at least seventy surrounding villages have brought their crafts and produce down from the hills for a day of frenzied barter and sale here. Nowadays, it draws producers from across Ecuador and Colombia as well, along with hundreds of overseas travellers who flood the town's streets every weekend and fill its disproportionate number of hotels. Although much of the business is still local – including an animal market that's as authentic as they come – substantial sections of the market are devoted to tourists, with a boggling range of carvings, clothing, craftwork, musical instruments, ceramics and souvenirs. It's most famous, though, for its **weavings**, sold mainly at the **Plaza de Ponchos** in the heart of the tourist zone, a dizzying labyrinth of colourful hanging tapestries and garments. During the week, Otavalo has a quiet provincial air, but **walks** to the nearby lakes, mountains or weaving villages are more than enough to keep you busy here for days.

Some history

Otavaleños have been accomplished weavers since pre-colonial times, when they traded textiles for *achiote* (a red dye) and cotton with peoples from the Oriente. The **Incas** finally took control of the region in 1495, beginning almost five hundred years of exploitation of the Otavaleños' skills. The Incas brought llamas and alpacas with them for wool, which was easier to weave and dye than cotton, and extracted tribute from the weavers. The locals, meanwhile, adopted Inca clothing, a form of which can still be seen in the traditional dress of native women; it reputedly resembles Inca dress more closely than that of any other indigenous people of the Andes.

The Incas only ruled for forty years before the **Spanish** swept in, soon establishing infamous **obrajes**, forced-labour sweatshops in which men, women and children were put to work for endless hours in atrocious conditions. With the introduction of silk, the spinning wheel and the treadle loom, Otavaleños began producing large quantities of quality textiles, supplying Spanish aristocrats all over the colonies. Not much improved for the *indígenas* after independence under the equally pernicious **huasipungo** system

---

Tour operators in Otavalo

Otavalo's **tour operators** offer similar tours out of town; typically, these are day-trips to weaving villages and the homes of artisans in the area (around $20), to the nearby lakes Cuicocha and Mojanda ($20–30) and trekking or horseriding ($25–50 per day). Taxi tours from the Parque Central to the lakes and villages are about $15 for two or three people, though the "guiding" won't be as proficient.

Diceny Viajes Sucre 10-14 and Colón ☎&℻06/2921217. Friendly outfit operated by *indígenas*, offering information and tours of weaving villages in English, French, Spanish and Quichua, plus hiking, horseriding and longer visits to a remote jungle community in the Oriente.

Fundación Cordillera Colón 4-12 and Sucre ☎06/2923633, ⓦwww.all-about -ecuador.com and www.chachimbiro.com. The All About EQ agency offers a wide range of tours and activities, from riding to rafting as well as community stays. Chachimbiro Tours organizes one- or multi-day trips to Chachimbiro hot springs and spa (see p.160).

Runa Tupari Sucre and Quiroga on the Plaza de Ponchos ☎&℻06/2925985, ⓦwww .runatupari.com. Intercultural exchanges with local indigenous communities, with accommodation in "rural lodges" ($23 including breakfast and dinner), as well as standard tours of the area and one- to four-day treks led by an indigenous guide.

La Tierra Salinas 5-03 and Sucre ☎06/2923611. Has mountain bikes for rent, and offers biking and horseriding tours to Mojanda, Cuicocha, local villages and other sites of interest.

Zulaytur Corner of Colón and Sucre, upstairs ☎&℻06/2922791, ⓦwww.geocities .com/zulaytur. Organizes "social and anthropological" village tours in easy Spanish, horseriding trips and visits to nearby mountains and lakes.

Traditional clothing in Otavalo

With business acumen as honed as their weaving skills, many Otavalo weavers have been able to afford travel abroad thanks to the popularity of their craft; and while thousands of Otavaleños have set up outlets across the world, their prosperity on the international market hasn't tainted their cultural identity. For the most part, Otavaleños still wear **traditional garments** even as they own gleaming pick-up trucks, electric looms and modern hotel blocks. Women can often be seen in embroidered white blouses (*camisas*), shawls (*rebozos*), black-wrap skirts (*anakus*), gold-coloured bead necklaces (*walkas*) and red-bead bracelets (*maki watana*), with their hair wrapped up in strips of woven cloth (*cintas*). Men sport dapper blue ponchos (*ruwanas*) and mid-calf-length white trousers (*calzones*), with their hair braided (*shimba*) beneath felt hats (*sombreros*). Both wear *alpargatas*, sandals made from the fibre of the *penko* cactus.

(see p.492), but in the middle of the nineteenth century, the Industrial Revolution in Europe allowed the mass production of textiles, sending the *obrajes* into decline. The Otavalo weavers continued to work on a small scale in the traditional styles – often using old techniques, such as the backstrap loom – to satisfy local demand. This changed in 1917 with the adaptation of techniques used to make Scottish tweeds. The new fabrics, known as *casimires*, proved hugely popular in Ecuador and rekindled the industry, but it wasn't until the **Agrarian Reform Law** of 1964 that the oppressive *huasipungo* system was finally made illegal, breaking up the great estates and giving *indígenas* their own five-hectare plots of land. More importantly, the weavers could at last profit from their talents by setting up their own home businesses, and the rise of regional tourism opened up the Otavalo valley to the outside world and spread the word of its marvellous textiles. Thanks to the success of the weaving industry, the Otavaleños are now one of the most prosperous indigenous groups in South America, as well as being at the political and cultural forefront of the country's under-represented peoples.

Arrival and information

The **bus** terminal, on Atahualpa and Neptali Ordoñez at the northeastern edge of the town, is serviced by Trans Otavalo and Trans Los Lagos from Quito (passing by the Avenida Occidental). If riding on other interprovincial bus lines, you'll probably be dropped off at the Panamericana, at the far southern end of Atahualpa, from where it's at least a six-block walk north to the nearest accommodation – an unsafe journey at night.

Taxis are available around the terminal and at the Parque Central, and charge $1 for a local trip (or around $50 to go to Quito). Still, Otavalo is easy to navigate on foot and **walking** across the town centre (Plaza de Ponchos to the Parque Central) only takes five minutes. Mountain **bikes** are available from La Tierra, Salinas 5-03 and Sucre ($10 per day; ☎06/2923611), which also offers maps and "emergency kits" for basic repairs; and at *Valle del Amanecer* hotel. Always check your bicycles to make sure they are in good working order before you leave. There is currently no train service to Otavalo.

For **information** and **maps**, try the municipal office at Bolívar 8-38 and Calderón (Mon–Fri 8am–12.30pm & 2–5.30pm, Sat 9am–4pm; ☎06/2920460, ⓦwww.otavalo.gov.ec) or the Cámara de Turismo, at Sucre 7-12 and García Moreno (☎06/2921994, ⓦwww.otavaloturismo.com).

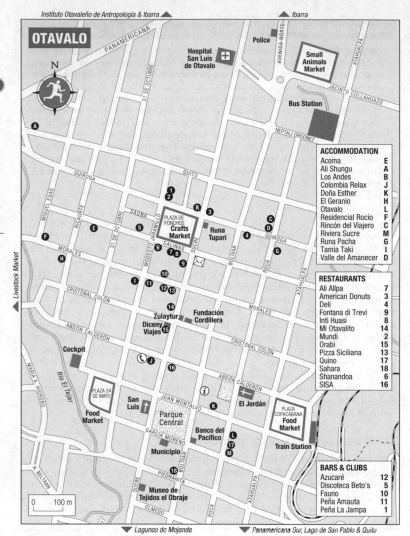

Accommodation

Otavalo seems to have more than its fair share of **hotels**, considering most of them are virtually empty during the week. Even so, things can get busy on Friday nights, so reserve in advance during high season if you have your heart set on something. **Campers** should contact *Rincón del Viajero* (see listings below), which runs a campsite ($5 per person; group discounts) by its farm about 1km out of town, or *La Luna* ($2.50), 4km on the way to the Lagunas de Mojanda (see p.145). If it's peace you're after, there's almost as much choice in the countryside around town; see box, p.140 for more details.

Acoma Salinas 07-57 and Ricaurte ☎06/2922966, ⓦwww.hotelacoma.com. Striking hotel of "highland-colonial" design with plenty of wood, natural light and whitewashed walls, built and owned by a family of local musicians. Commodious rooms with cable TV, optional en-suite bathrooms and handsome suites available. Breakfast included. ⑤–⑥

Ali Shungu Quito and Quiroga ☎06/2920750, ⓦwww.alishungu.com. The best place to stay in Otavalo, run by a hospitable American couple and dedicated local staff. Lavishly decorated with plants and fine weavings, it features comfortable, heated rooms overlooking a colourful garden towards Volcán Imbabura, powerful hot showers, a superb restaurant (see p.143), and free wi-fi. Two family apartments also available (⑧). No check-out time. ⑦

Los Andes Sucre and Quiroga ☎06/2921057. Though a little noisy, there are great views of the market from the top floor, where the rooms have balconies. All come with cable TV, but avoid the musty internal rooms on the other floors. ❷

Colombia Relax Abdón Calderón 5-05 and Sucre ☎09/2926827. Nondescript modern hotel whose inexpensive rooms have private baths and cable TVs. ❸

Doña Esther Juan Montalvo 4-44 and Roca ☎06/2920739, ⓦwww.otavalohotel.com. Convincing colonial reproduction offering attractive, well-lit and fragrant rooms with private baths and cable TV, set around a pretty courtyard. Good restaurant (closed Mon) with fireplace and giant pizza oven. ⑥

El Geranio Ricaurte 1-01 and Morales ☎06/2920185, ⓔhgeranio@hotmail.com. Quiet, popular, out-of-the-way budget choice in two parts: slightly more expensive units in a modern concrete pile, and cheaper rooms in a rickety but endearing wooden addition at the back, overlooking a breezy courtyard. Use of a kitchen included. ❷

Otavalo Roca 5-04 and Juan Montalvo ☎06/2920416. Distinguished, renovated hotel in an old colonial building, with two bright, leafy, covered courtyards surrounded by high-ceilinged rooms warmed by gas heaters. Polished floorboards and a smart restaurant and café add to the feel of a grand hotel. Breakfast included. ⑥

Rincón del Viajero Roca 10-17 and Quiroga ☎&ⓕ06/2921741. Clean, safe and quiet rooms with optional en-suite baths and complimentary breakfast, plus sitting room with fireplace and a roof terrace with games area, pool table and hammocks. Run by a hospitable American–Ecuadorian family. There's a good restaurant and breakfast is included. ❹

Riviera Sucre García Moreno 3-80 and Roca ☎06/2920241, ⓦwww.rivierasucre.com. Charming old hotel featuring greenery cascading down from balustrades and an abundant garden, offering simple rooms with TVs, optional baths, plus a games room, book exchange and small café warmed by a fire on chilly nights. ❷–❹

Residencial Rocío Morales and Miguel Egas ☎06/2920584, ⓕ2921806. Inexpensive hotel on the edge of town, whose helpful owners keep clean, simple rooms (a few of them en suite), with smarter, pricier cabins a few blocks away on the Panamericana. ❷

Runa Pacha Roca and Quiroga ☎06/2925566. Modern hotel with choice of shared or completely tiled private baths, cable TVs and balconies – though rooms with the latter tend to be noisier. Parking is also available. ❷

Tamia Taki Modesto Jaramillo 5-69 and Morales ☎&ⓕ06/2920684. No-frills, budget option close to the Plaza de Ponchos, with a friendly staff and cosy little covered patio. Rooms with shared bath are even cheaper. ❶

Valle del Amanecer Corner of Quiroga and Roca ☎&ⓕ06/2920990. Popular backpackers' hotel with bamboo-thatched rooms around a cobbled courtyard shaded by palms and hammocks. On-site laundry, book exchange, board games, bike rentals, hot water and restaurant. Breakfast included. ❸

The Town

Positioned between the peaks of Cotacachi and Imbabura, Otavalo's environs are far prettier than the town itself, whose new hotels, craft shops, restaurants, internet cafés, textile outlets and cargo exporters now swamp the last remaining scraps of older architecture.

Apart from market days and boisterous fiestas (see box, p.142), this is a quiet provincial town with only a few landmarks and attractions. Starting at the **Parque Central**, you'll find a statue of **Rumiñahui**, the valiant Inca general who led a fierce resistance against the Spanish, the elegant **municipio** building and the main church of **San Luis**, on the park's western side, perhaps less striking than Otavalo's other major church, **El Jordán**, two blocks east at Calderón and Roca.

There are several fine **haciendas** in the Otavalo region, originally built to oversee local *obrajes*, which generally cost more than accommodation in town, but are well worth it for their character, colonial architecture and beautiful grounds. Anything newer **country hotels** lack in historical charm, they often make up for in comfort and location. Most places listed offer horseriding or hiking expeditions.

As well as those listed below, there are many other good upmarket places to stay around Otavalo, in the nearby weaving village of **Peguche** (see p.145), around **Cotacachi** (see p.148) and near the **Lagunas de Mojanda** (see p.145), all close enough for you to get an early start at the Saturday market.

Ali Shungu Mountaintop Lodge 5km west of Otavalo near the community of Yambiro ☎06/2920750, ⓦwww.alishungumountaintoplodge.com. The ever-changing play of light and shade across Imbabura and Lago San Pablo is experienced nowhere better than at this peaceful lodge, perched on a hilltop and backed by the forests of its own 40-acre private reserve. The four cosy and fully equipped guest-houses, each self-contained with wood-burning stove, kitchenette and garden, have huge windows which make the most of the extraordinary views. Price includes breakfast and dinner, two hours horseriding, wi-fi access, unlimited bottled water, tea and coffee; there's also no check-out time. A range of activities is offered, including talks by a local *yachac* (healer) on the rich archeological history of the reserve and region. ❾

Hacienda Cusín 9km southeast of Otavalo, on the edge of San Pablo del Lago ☎06/2918013, ⓦwww.haciendacusin.com. Beautiful, early seventeenth-century hacienda, set amid peaceful gardens with little cobbled courtyards connected together and bursting with flowers. Rooms feature en-suite baths and striking views of the estate and its environs, and some have fireplaces and beamed ceilings. The complex includes a converted monastery, garden cottage, library, games room and an excellent restaurant. Many activities offered, including horseriding. Reservations required. ❾

Hacienda Pinsaquí Panamericana Norte, Km5 ☎06/2946116, ⓦwww .haciendapinsaqui.com. Historic hacienda built in 1790, which hosted Simón Bolívar and signatories of the 1863 Treaty of Pinsaquí between Colombia and Ecuador. Stately drawing and dining rooms with huge fireplaces, courtyards with trickling fountains, and luxurious but simple rooms pervaded by the faint aroma of furniture polish and wood-smoke evoke a bygone age. Equine-related trappings and trophies abound, particularly in the snug bar, hung with stirrups and show-jumping memorabilia. All rooms cost the same, though some are far larger than others, and breakfast is included. Guided horse rides $30 for three hours. ❾

Hacienda Zuleta 12km east of Lago de San Pablo ☎02/2662182, ⓦwww.zuleta .com. A working dairy farm and hacienda dating from 1690 and former home of Ecuadorian president Galo Plaza Lasso, set in bucolic countryside near the village of Zuleta, famed for its embroidery. Nine comfortable guestrooms with garden views accommodate visitors, who are treated as guests of the family. The farm produces delicious organic fruit, vegetables, trout and dairy products, and activities include horseriding (multi-day programmes available), embroidery trips and visits to condor repopulation projects. Reservations and minimum two-night stay required. ❾

Las Palmeras Inn Just south of Quichinche ☎06/2922607, ⓦwww.laspalmerasinn .com. A 150-year-old hacienda in a countryside setting with great views of Cotacachi and Imbabura, offering accommodation in garden cottages with fireplaces, family suites, rooms within the main house, and dorm beds ($15) including breakfast. Plenty of activities are offered and the main lodge includes a games room, restaurant, two lounges, internet café and reference library. ❼

A block and a half south of the park is the wonderful **Museo de Tejidos el Obraje**, Sucre 6-08 and Piedrahita (Mon–Sat 9am–noon & 3–6pm; $2), where lifelong weavers Don Luis Maldonado and his wife, Luzmaría, demonstrate traditional methods of local textile production, from cleaning and carding wool to spinning, drying and weaving it on pedal and backstrap looms. The town's other museum, the **Instituto Otavaleño de Antropología** (Mon–Fri 8.30am–12.30pm & 2.30–5.30pm; free) across on the northern edge of town just off the Panamericana, has exhibits on archeology, ethnography, musical instruments, scale models of the town's fiestas and a small academic library.

If you're around on a Sunday afternoon (about 3–4pm) head to the north side of the Plaza de Ponchos to view a brisk game of **pelota de mano**, in which two opposing teams hit a tiny, hard black leather ball high into the air across the square with their bare hands.

Town markets

Every Friday afternoon, Otavalo comes to life as pick-up trucks laden with merchandise and vendors bent double under great blocks of textiles stream into town from the surrounding countryside, preparing for the fabulous **Saturday market**, which includes one of the largest and most colourful artesanía markets on the continent. If you can't make it to town on a Saturday, it's worth noting this crafts market has become such big business that most of the town's weaving and artesanía shops stay open throughout the week; you'll find stalls on the Plaza de Ponchos every day, and on **Wednesdays** it's almost as busy as the real thing.

The **Plaza de Ponchos** is the centre of the **artesanía** activity, where *indígenas* dressed in all their finery offer a staggering choice of clothes, textiles, hammocks and weavings, as well as jewellery, ceramics, dolls and many other craftworks. The stalls spill off the square in all directions, especially up Sucre, all the way to the Parque Central. By 7am on Saturday morning, the market is already abuzz, even though the tour groups from Quito don't roll in until around 9 or 10am.

Although the sales patter is not at all aggressive, you will be expected to **haggle**, which should result in significant discounts, often by 25 percent or more. If you want to take a **photo** of someone, always ask first, or better still, buy something then ask. Also, take heed that Otavalo's markets can get very crowded, providing perfect cover for **pickpockets** and **bag slashers**, so protect your belongings.

One of the joys of the Saturday market is that large sections of it have nothing to do with souvenir knick-knacks and tourist dollars at all. Even on the Plaza de Ponchos (north side), you'll find **vegetable** and **grain sellers** and a row of street restaurants with huge pans and cauldrons supplying food to local shoppers. Pick your way through the crowds south up Modesto Jaramillo via hardware and everyday-clothing sections to the town's main **food market**, at and around the Plaza 24 de Mayo (there's more at the Plaza Copacabana too). This covered square has all the bustle of an eastern bazaar, charged with the smells of whole hogs roasting on spits, steaming vats of crab soup and the sizzle of meat and potatoes. You can't help wondering if some of the victuals have come straight from the **livestock market** (5–10am), a packed field of herd animals bellowing through the early morning mists, tugging hard on their busily negotiating owners. To get there, go to the west end of Calderón, cross the bridge, and then follow the crowds going up S. J. Castro to the Panamericana and the market ground on the other side. A second **animal market** by the bus station deals with fowl, *cuyes* (guinea pigs), puppies and kittens – and other small creatures, thankfully not all destined for the kitchen.

Festivals in Otavalo

Otavalo hosts several major **festivals**, including **San Juan** on June 24, which is celebrated with bonfires and fireworks as *indígenas* from the surrounding villages parade in costumes and masks, dancing and singing their way to the Church of San Juan, west of town. The festivities last for several days, blending with the **Inti Raymi** celebration of the solstice on June 21 and those for **San Pedro** on June 29, and together are known as "Los San Juanes", providing a Christianized gloss to what was doubtless a pre-Columbian celebration. The San Juan fiesta once involved a kind of ritual fighting (*tinku*) between rival villages, but today the ceremonies are largely confined to ritual bathing in the Peguche waterfall, followed by shindigs in the outlying communities; foreigners should only attend these events if they have an invitation to do so from a local, and should show sensitivity at all times.

Another big event, the **Fiesta del Yamor**, during the first two weeks of September, is a twentieth-century and primarily *mestizo* celebration, seeing bullfights, music, dancing and traditional food and drink, including *yamor* itself, a *chicha* made from seven types of corn and prepared over twelve hours. Among the smaller events are **Mojanda Arriba** (Oct 30–31), a two-day walk from Quito to Otavalo, stopping at Malchinguí over the Mojanda hills, marking the foundation of the town, and **Diciembre Mágico**, a minor arts festival in the weeks leading up to Christmas.

After the traders have packed up their stalls and the smell of discarded mangoes has turned from sweetness to decay, locals head to the **cockpit** (*gallera municipal*), on 31 de Octubre behind the produce market, for a flutter (Sat 9pm–2am). It will set you back $1 to sit around a blood-smeared circle watching two cocks try to peck each other to death.

Eating and drinking

Otavalo's **restaurants** cater to a broad clientele and feature a wide choice of cuisines, with pizza parlours in particular abundance. Most establishments are open daily from breakfast to 9 or 10pm, often later if there are enough customers. **Prices** are a bit higher than at other provincial restaurants, but are still very affordable, at $3–7 for the typical main course. The best place to stock up on cheap fresh fruit and vegetables is naturally the Saturday produce market, where the vendors also offer high-cholesterol meals of *chicharrón* and *llapingachos* for not much more than a dollar or two. As with most things in Otavalo, restaurants become more colourful at the end of the week, when many put on live Andean **folk music** (*folklórica*), often of a high standard.

Cafés

American Donuts Corner of Sucre and Quiroga. One of the town's best bakeries, offering breakfasts, coffee, croissants, rolls, loaves, cakes and doughnuts. Open daily till 10pm.

Deli Quiroga and Bolívar. Friendly little place offering good and inexpensive international food, especially TexMex *fajitas* and *burritos*, as well as pizza and pasta. Breakfasts available on Saturdays too. Closed Mon & Tues.

Mundi Quiroga and Modesto Jaramillo. Well-sited café on the Plaza de Ponchos, great for taking a break and a bite to eat in comfortable low-slung chairs on market days. Crêpes, salads, sandwiches and snacks for $2–3.

Oraibi Sucre and Colón. Serves good vegetarian food, including quinoa soup and quiche, and stages live music on Saturday nights in its pleasant little courtyard. Closed Mon & Tues.

Sahara Corner of Bolívar and Piedrahita, upstairs. Lounge on cushions on the floor and enjoy Middle Eastern food served on low tables – or order a hookah pipe filled with fruit-flavoured tobacco.

Shanandoa Salinas and Modesto Jaramillo. Also known as *The Pie Shop*, a choice spot for juices, milkshakes, sandwiches and, above all, tasty home-baked pies with several fruity fillings. A Plaza de Ponchos stalwart, in business for almost thirty years.

Restaurants

Ali Shungu Quito and Quiroga ☎06/2920750. Otavalo's best restaurant, in the eponymous hotel, using as much local organic produce as possible; the tomatoes burst with flavour in the lasagne. Great range and plenty of vegetarian dishes – and justifiably pricier than local rivals. Live music Friday evenings. Last orders Sat–Thurs 8.30pm, Fri 9.30–10pm.

Árbol de Montalvo Juan Montalvo 4-44, at *Doña Esther*. Attractive restaurant serving quality Mediterranean cuisine with organic vegetables, but the speciality is pizza cooked up in a large wood-burning oven dominating the dining room.

Buena Vista Salinas 5-09. Reliable restaurant on the Plaza de Ponchos with a predictable, if inexpensive, menu of meat, fish, chicken, pasta and a few vegetarian options thrown in.

Fontana di Trevi Sucre 12-05 and Salinas, second floor. Reasonably priced pizzas and pasta in a clean upstairs dining room overlooking a busy shopping street.

Inti Huasi Salinas and Sucre. Nicely presented restaurant with tablecloths and napkins, doing the standard *platos típicos* well, in big portions, with efficient service and at a good price. Popular with locals and foreigners alike. *Almuerzos* for $2–3.50.

Mi Otavalito Sucre 11-13 and Morales. Reasonably priced traditional food, including inexpensive set-menu options, such as $3 for a hearty four-course menu *del día*, and tasty à la carte fried fish. Closes Sun–Thurs 4pm.

Pizza Siciliana Morales and Sucre. The town's most popular pizzeria, notable for its excellent live music on Fridays and Saturdays and occasionally during the week, too. Pizzas from $4–14, depending on size and toppings, which include vegetarian options.

Quino Roca and García Moreno. Colourful restaurant specializing in seafood dishes, including fish stew, trout and shrimp. Closed Mon lunch.

SISA Abdón Calderón 4-09 and Sucre, upstairs. Classy but moderately priced restaurant serving tasty meals of trout and large salads. Live music Friday and Saturday. Part of an arts complex that includes a bookshop, gallery, café and art workshop. Under renovation at the time of writing.

Nightlife

The energy and excitement the market generates finds an outlet on Friday and Saturday nights at Otavalo's **discos** and **peñas**, many of which feature **live music** at some point in the evening. At the *peñas*, this is likely to be **folklórica**, traditional Andean folk songs accompanied by *rondador* (small panpipes), *quena* (wooden flute), *charango* (a lute, sometimes made from armadillo shell) and guitars, though salsa and tropical music are also performed on occasion.

Azucaré Morales and Sucre. Usually features live music on Saturdays, but seems more popular with local youngsters when the DJ is in control. Diverse musical tastes. Fri–Sun 9pm–2am; $1.50.

Discoteca Beto's Salinas and 31 de Octubre. Conventional club experience in a dark, three-floor venue strafed by ultraviolet lights and laser beams, pumping out hot merengue, salsa, techno and rock hits into the small hours. Fri & Sat 9pm–3am; $1.50, one drink included.

Fauno Morales and Jaramillo. This disco-bar usually features live music on Fridays and Saturdays, when the cover charge is a little more, but includes a free cocktail. Tues–Sun 4pm–2am; $1–2.

Peña Amauta Jaramillo and Morales. Friendly, long-established *peña* consistently popular with visitors, showcasing good, established *folklórica* groups, sometimes followed by less-expert new bands. Try the guayusa cocktails, hot infusions of the eponymous leaves from the Oriente, topped off with a healthy slug of sugar-cane spirit. Food also available at the upstairs restaurant, *Mi Viejo Café*, Fri & Sat 8pm–3am, live music from 10pm; $2.

Peña La Jampa Jaramillo 5-69 and Quiroga. The most popular venue of the moment, featuring live *folklórica*, a large dancefloor overlooked by two galleries and a good mixed crowd. Thurs–Sat 8pm–3am; $2.50.

Listings

Banks and exchange Banco del Pacífico, corner of Moreno and Bolívar on the Parque Central, has a MasterCard ATM; Banco del Austro, Quiroga and Sucre on the Plaza de Ponchos, has Visa and MasterCard ATM. To change traveller's cheques try Fax Cambios, Salinas and Sucre (closed Sun), three percent commission; or VazCorp, Sucre and Colón (Mon–Fri 8.30am–5pm, Sat 8.30am–2pm).

Language schools Instituto Superior de Español, Sucre 11-10 and Morales ☏06/2922414, ⓦwww.instituto-superior.net; Mundo Andino, Salinas 4-04 and Bolívar ☏06/2921864, ⓦwww .mandinospanishschool.com; Otavalo Spanish Institute, 31 de Octubre and Salinas, third floor ☏06/2921404, for Quichua too.

Medical services Centro Medico Quirurgico "El Jordan", Quiroga and Roca (daily 8am–7pm, ☏06/2921159), has 24hr emergency service; doctors Patricio and Rubén Buitron speak some English. Hospital San Luis de Otavalo is on Sucre, 500m north of Plaza de Ponchos (☏06/2920444). Police station Av Norte, north of Bolívar ☏06/2920101.

Around Otavalo

A trip to Otavalo doesn't have to end when the market vendors pack up shop; there's plenty to do outside of town, not least explore the many nearby **weaving villages**, which often each specialize in certain crafts. Local tour agencies (see box, p.136) combine visits to several villages, giving you a cross-section of the different techniques and traditions employed by each. **Peguche**, within walking distance northeast of Otavalo, has a cooperative that features weaving demonstrations and a secluded waterfall nearby, while the villages huddled around the reed shores of **Lago de San Pablo**, 3km southeast of Peguche, are also home to many weavers. The villages celebrate colourful **fiestas**, including the banner-waving processions of Los Pendoneros, held in San Rafael and San Roque on October 15. **San Rafael** hosts the costume

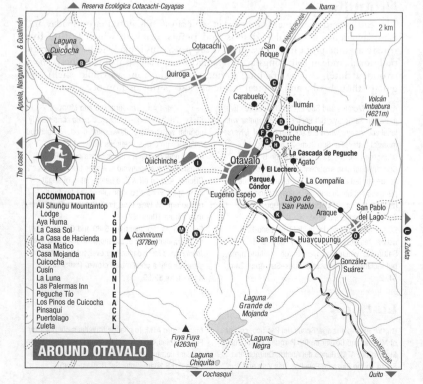

ACCOMMODATION
All Shungu Mountaintop Lodge	J
Aya Huma	G
La Casa Sol	H
La Casa de Hacienda	D
Casa Matico	F
Casa Mojanda	M
Cuicocha	B
Cusín	O
La Luna	N
Las Palermas Inn	I
Peguche Tío	E
Los Pinos de Cuicocha	A
Pinsaquí	C
Puertolago	K
Zuleta	L

AROUND OTAVALO

ritual of El Coraza on August 19, in which one of the village's wealthiest men appears in a feathered hat hung with so much gold chain and jewellery that his face is concealed. If you turn up at any of these fiestas, try to be discreet (or better yet, invited), as they can be rather private affairs. The festival of Pawkar Raimi held in Peguche and Agato (Feb & March), usually includes plenty of music-making and concerts open to all.

The **Lagunas de Mojanda**, three lakes surrounded by brooding, cloud-hung peaks south of town, are set in ideal country for hiking and horseriding, while another popular excursion is to **Laguna Cuicocha**, on the edge of the huge **Cotacachi-Cayapas reserve**, extending from the páramo down to tropical forests in the coastal Esmeraldas province. The lake is best reached from **Cotacachi**, 11km north of Otavalo, a smart little town famous for its market, leather goods and boutiques. Your best bet for leaving the crowds behind, though, is by taking a bus west to the remote **Intag region**, where small villages such as **Apuela** and **Junín** nestle in richly forested hills, and where you can soak in thermal springs at **Nangulví** and visit nearby pre-Inca ruins at **Gualimán**.

Otavalo, as of late 2010, will be the jumping-off point for a **new road down to the coast**, skirting the edge of previously very remote communities near the southern fringes of the Cotacachi-Cayapas reserve before joining the main highway to Esmeraldas at Quinindé. This will cut many hours off the journey for anyone heading to Atacames and neighbouring beach resorts, as well as several northwestern cloudforest reserves, including Los Cedros (see p.339).

Peguche

Three kilometres northeast of town, **PEGUCHE** is one of the nearest weaving villages to Otavalo, a quiet community comprising a central square and a few unmarked streets lined with simple, whitewashed houses, and a surprising number of peaceful country hotels – testament to its popularity as alternative base to the bustling town next door. Almost all the families here are involved with the textile business, though many of them now use electric looms rather than traditional means. The best places to see high-quality **weavings** are at the galleries of **José Cotacachi**, one of which is in the main square, and the other just behind the church. The village is also known for producing **musical instruments**, including the *rondador* (Ecuadorian panpipe), and for the talented *folklórica* musicians who play them, regularly performing in Otavalo *peñas* on weekend nights.

Set in a eucalyptus grove about a kilometre southeast of the village, the sacred waterfall of **La Cascada de Peguche** is the site of ceremonial bathing during Inti Raymi and the San Juanes fiestas (see box, p.142), but for the rest of the year it's a popular picnic spot, particularly at weekends. To get here from Peguche, head south along the main street for about fifteen minutes until you reach some whitewashed arches and a low, barn-shaped building marking the entrance. You can also walk there in 45 minutes from Otavalo by heading east out of town towards the railway tracks, then turning left onto a cobbled road running parallel to them. Keep with the road where it leaves the tracks to go up the hill, and follow it around to the south to the entrance. From the main terminal in Otavalo, Co-op Imbaburapac and Transportes 8 de Septiembre **buses** make the short hop to Peguche every twenty to thirty minutes, while **taxis** from Plaza de Ponchos take five to ten minutes and cost a couple of dollars.

▲ La Cascada de Peguche

Accommodation

Aya Huma By the railway tracks up from the waterfall ☎06/2690333, ⓦwww.ayahuma.com. A charming old house providing pleasant, simple rooms with hot water in shared or private baths next to a garden with hammocks. Has a book exchange, small library and a good restaurant with live music on Saturdays. ❹

La Casa de Hacienda On the road to Ilumán, turn-off at Panamericana Km3 ☎06/2946336, ⓦwww.casadehacienda.com. Swiss-owned establishment featuring mini chalet-style cabañas at the foot of Imbabura, each with rocking chairs on the porch and views of Otavalo. ❻

Casa Matico Peguche ☎06/2690289, ⓦwww.casamatico.com. Local indigenous family providing affordable bed-and-breakfast accommodation as a window onto traditional life. They offer lessons in cooking corn *humitas* and fire-roasted tortillas, give guided hikes around Imbabura as well as assistance in haggling at the Otavalo market, though

they sell crafts from their own women's cooperative, Huarmi Maqui. ❺

La Casa Sol North of the Cascada de Peguche ☎06/2690500, ⓦwww.lacasasol.com. Tile-roofed, wood-and-adobe houses clustered on the hillside like a little village with winding passageways and archways. Rooms come with private bath, fireplace, balcony and access to the pretty gardens, though guests can also relax in a lounge, reading room, games and television area or dining room. Breakfast included and discounts for students and Rough Guide readers (say at check-in) staying for more than three days. ❼

Peguche Tío Just off the Panamericana at the north end of the village ☎06/2690179, ⓦwww.geocities.com/peguchetio. Distinctive, circular wooden building with a lookout tower, offering modest rooms with private baths and fireplaces, plus a stage and dancefloor for monthly live music, and a library and craft shop. ❸–❹

Lago de San Pablo and Parque Cóndor

You can continue a walk from the top of the Cascada de Peguche up over the hill to the south and down the other side towards **Lago de San Pablo**, a large cobalt-blue lake mirroring the green skirts of Volcán Imbabura. It's also easy to reach from Otavalo (1hr 30min–2hr) on a number of tracks and trails crisscrossing the hillside in between. One pleasant route is via **El Lechero**, a sacred tree standing solitary on a hilltop, with panoramic views of Otavalo and

Lago de San Pablo. To get there, take Piedrahita southeast out of town, and follow the cobblestone road uphill, bearing left as you ascend. It's always best to hike in a group for **safety**; assaults have been reported particularly in the area of El Lechero.

The lake itself has been a popular destination for well-off Ecuadorians, who like to sail, windsurf and water-ski there. Several upmarket **resorts** sit on its shores, the best of which is *Puertolago*, on the Panamericana 5.5km from Otavalo (☎06/2920920, ⓦwww.puertolago.com; ➐), a purpose-built hotel offering chalets equipped with cable TVs and fireplaces, plus use of sailboats, windsurfing boards, pedalos and a hotel ferry for lake cruises.

More interesting are the weaving villages, **La Compañía**, on the northern shore, which produces sashes (*fajas*) and hair wraps (*cintas*), and **Huaycupungu**, at its southern shore, 7km south of Otavalo, where the *totora* reeds which grow in abundance at the water's edge are woven into floor mats (*esteras*), hats and fans.

On the top of a high hill between Otavalo and the lake, by the community of Pucará Alto not far from El Lechero, the excellent Dutch-managed **Parque Cóndor** (Tues–Sun 9.30am–5pm; $3.25), a rehabilitation centre for **birds of prey**, is worth a visit for a chance to see a selection of Ecuador's most elegant avian hunters. Among fifteen or so species, including barred hawks, black-chested buzzard-eagles and king vultures, is an "owl ruin", where spectacled and other owls rule the roost in a mock tumbledown temple. The thrill of seeing the park's namesake condors up close is only bettered by watching their wild counterparts occasionally circling above the park. Trained Harris's hawks and an American kestrel perform flight demonstrations (11.30am & 4.30pm) against a scenic backdrop stretching to Volcán Chiles and Colombia on clear days.

It's about an hour's **walk** up here from Otavalo or from La Cascada. Buses from town will run (via Eugenio Espejo) when the road has been improved, but till then a **taxi** will cost about $3.

Agato, Ilumán and Carabuela

Besides Peguche, there are dozens of indigenous **weaving villages** in the Otavalo valley, each with their own niche specialisms, such as tapestries (*tapices*) or embroidery (*bordado*), but Agato, Ilumán and Carabuela are the ones to visit as they maintain textile workshops you can drop into during the day.

Miguel Andrango, perhaps Ecuador's most famous weaver, is based in **Agato**, 1km east of Peguche, where you can see demonstrations of the backstrap loom at his family's **Tahuantinsuyo Weaving Workshop**. Just east of the Panamericana in **Ilumán**, 6km north of Otavalo, similar demonstrations are given at the **Inti Chumbi Co-op** on the plaza, though hat-making is also an important local industry. However, the village is better known in Ecuador for its *curanderos* (**healers**) and *brujos* (witchdoctors); there are around thirty of them practising their art, involving a curious mixture of pagan and Christian rituals and herbal medicine to drive out illnesses or evil spirits. If you visit one, be prepared to walk away coated in spit; it's all part of the cure.

Further along, **Carabuela** has a few open workshops, the most interesting of which is that of Don José Carlos de la Torre, who demonstrates his production technique in all its stages, from the sheep to the loom, including a double-ended spinning wheel. Each of his exquisite **ponchos** takes about three months to create, making the $200 price tag good value.

Buses to most villages cost about $0.20 and leave the main terminal regularly during the day, or your could take a **tour** from Otavalo, which may combine visits to several workshops and ensure that the weavers are expecting you.

Lagunas de Mojanda

The three dark lakes of the **Lagunas de Mojanda** are clutched by grassy hills 16km south of and 1200m above Otavalo, and the dramatic scenery has made the area a favourite for hikers, horseriders and other visitors, who normally visit on tours from Otavalo (see box, p.136), or from one of the nearby hotels that arrange excursions. A cobblestone road winds up from Otavalo to the **Laguna Grande de Mojanda**, by far the largest of the three lakes, more than 2km wide. On the other side of the lake, a clear trail corners eastwards to **Laguna Negra**, while a less-used path continues 1km south to **Laguna Chiquita**. Beyond the ring of ragged peaks encircling the lakes, topped by Fuya Fuya (4263m) and Yanaurcu (4090m), is a trail to Cochasquí and a cobblestone track down to Tabacundo.

You can take a **taxi** from Otavalo to the lakes ($10 one-way, $6 per hour waiting time for return trip), and then walk back down to town (3hr 30min) to enjoy the spectacular views. Be aware, though, that the Mojanda area has had an unfortunate history of **robberies** and **violent assaults**, so make sure to ask about safety before heading off; going with a group on a tour is safer than making an independent visit.

Accommodation

The best **accommodation** near the lakes – and one of the most peaceful hotels in the region – is 🌿 *Casa Mojanda*, 3.5km up Mojanda road from Otavalo (☎09/9731737, ⓦwww.casamojanda.com; ⑨), a collection of beautiful whitewashed cottages poised on a hillside, with stunning views of the Imbabura, Cotacachi and the Cushnimuri mountains. Run by an American–Ecuadorian couple, the hotel features an organic garden that supplies delicious produce for its largely vegetarian restaurant, and a portion of the profits goes to the Mojanda Foundation, supporting progressive educational and environmental initiatives. Many of the cottages have their own fireplaces and the price ($200 a double, with tax), includes breakfast, afternoon tea and dinner. Among the other perks are an outdoor Japanese-style hot tub, games room, piano and library, plus guided horseriding tours ($25 per two hours) and hiking expeditions. There's a cheaper "dormitory" for large families, and discounts for children and nationals too.

A little further up towards the lakes on a side road, *La Luna* (☎09/93156082, ⓦwww.hostallaluna.com; ❸–❹) is a good choice if you're on a budget but desire a relaxed and attractive hotel outside Otavalo. It features comfortable rooms with or without private baths and fireplaces, as well as dorm beds ($6), and a **campsite** ($3). Buses for *La Luna* leave Otavalo (Mon–Fri 1pm & 6pm) from Piedrahita and Jaramillo, or a taxi costs $3.

Cotacachi

A grandiose, flag-lined boulevard welcomes you to **COTACACHI**, west of the Panamericana and 11km from Otavalo, signalling that you've arrived somewhere special. As well as being a self-proclaimed "eco-city" which has successfully cut down waste and pollution, Cotacachi is a prosperous community thanks to its flourishing **leather industry**.

Arrival and information

Buses for Cotacachi leave from the Otavalo terminal every ten to fifteen minutes (5.30am–7.30pm), and return to Otavalo from the station at 10 de Agosto and Salinas, at the north end of Cotacachi (you can also hail them on

Peñaherrera as they leave town). The town is also good for accessing Laguna Cuicocha in the Cotacachi-Cayapas reserve (see p.148); pick up a **taxi** or **camioneta** from around the bus station ($7–10 return trip, including 1hr waiting time).

Information is available at the Casa de las Culturas (see below), at the corner of Bolívar and 9 de Octubre, and the Banco del Pichincha has a Cirrus **ATM**, on Parque Olmedo at the south end of town. The **post office** is at 9 de Octubre and Sucre and the **phone office** is Peñaherrera and Sucre.

Accommodation

Bachita Sucre 16-74 and Modesto Peñaherrera ☎06/2915063. Cheap hotel providing decent rooms, but no hot water in those with shared bathrooms. Breakfast available for $1.50. ❷

El Mesón de Flores García Moreno 13-67 and Sucre ☎06/2916009. A charming colonial house with creaky floorboards and en-suite rooms set around a pretty courtyard decked in flowers. It also has a good restaurant. ❼

La Mirage 500m north of town on 10 de Agosto ☎06/2915237, in North America ☎1-800/327-3573, ⓦwww.mirage.com.ec. A "contemporary hacienda" and one of the most expensive hotels in the country (upwards of $430 a double), featuring peacock-filled gardens, palatial rooms with fireplaces, four-poster beds with a scattering of fresh rose petals, Graeco–Roman-styled swimming pool, tennis court and excellent restaurant. On-site spa offers such luxurious treatments as "Cleopatra's Bath", a thirty-minute soak in a milk-and-oil bath, followed by a wrap in a thermal blanket and a massage in the special "Egyptian Room". Price includes breakfast and dinner. ❾

Sumac Huasi Juan Montalvo 10-09 and Pedro Moncayo ☎&ⓕ06/2915873. Clean, modern and comfortable hotel featuring rooms with cable TVs, private baths and hot water. Breakfast is served in a third-floor conservatory with good views. ❺

Tierra Mia Bolívar and 10 de Agosto ☎&ⓕ06/2915755. Friendly budget choice with clean simple rooms (mostly en suite), hot water, and free parking. ❸

The Town

Dozens of smart boutiques selling every conceivable form of leatherware line 10 de Agosto, the main street running north–south up to the Parque San Francisco, the focus of the **Sunday leather market**, and the best place to pick up a bargain on a bag, belt or jacket.

To escape the smell of tanned hides, head to **Casa de las Culturas**, at the corner of Bolívar and 9 de Octubre (Mon–Fri 9am–1pm & 3–7pm, Sat & Sun 9am–4pm; free), a handsome old building ingeniously reinvented after a fire, housing a small collection of paintings by Guayasamín and some pre-Columbian ceramics, as well as temporary exhibitions, internet access, a library and **tourist information** (☎06/2915140, ⓦwww.cotacachi.gov.ec). You could also stop in at the nearby **Museo de las Culturas**, García Moreno 13-41 and Bolívar (Mon–Fri 9am–noon & 2–5pm, Sat 2–5pm, Sun 10am–1pm; $1, including guided tour in Spanish), set in a cloistered colonial building and showcasing Cotacachi traditions through costumed mannequins and exhibits on craftwork and fiestas. It lies in the shadow of the white-domed **La Matriz** church, which stands on the grand and leafy **Parque Abdón Calderón**.

Eating and drinking

Apart from the fancier hotels, good choices for **dining** include the slightly touristy *El Leñador*, Sucre 10-12 and Juan Montalvo, which offers varied menus and good trout dishes, and *La Marquesa*, 10 de Agosto 12-65 and Bolívar, offers the standards and inexpensive set meals.

Reserva Ecológica Cotacachi-Cayapas

Covering more than two thousand square miles of the western Andes, the **Reserva Ecológica Cotacachi-Cayapas** ($5 or $1 if visiting Laguna Cuicocha only) was established in 1968 and spans from the summit of Volcán Cotacachi (4944m) down to the coastal lowlands (300m), protecting ecological habitats from the páramo grasslands in the east to the dense rainforests of Esmeraldas province. The reserve is part of the **Chocó** bioregion, which extends into southern Colombia, where high levels of rainfall support one of the earth's most diverse ecosystems. Twenty percent of Ecuador's endemic plants are found here, as well as thousands of mammals, birds and insects, including Andean spectacled bears, ocelots, jaguars and river otters.

From Cotacachi and Otavalo, it's easy to get to the centre of the highland section, **Laguna Cuicocha** ("Guinea Pig Lake" in Quichua), a spectacular crater lake at 3060m, located at the foot of the dormant Volcán Cotacachi in the southeastern tip of the reserve. The two islands in the middle of the lake, **Isla Wolf** and **Isla Yerovi**, are a pair of old volcanic cones that grew up from the floor of a collapsed crater 200m below, and according to legend were used by the Incas as a prison. They're off-limits due to on-site research, but you can jaunt across the lake on a **motorboat** ($2 per person), or learn more about it in the **visitor centre** (9am–4pm, with lunch break). Better still, you can walk around the rim of the crater on a well-kept, circular **trail**. The ten-kilometre hike (best walked counterclockwise) takes about five hours to complete, though your effort is rewarded by wonderful views of Cayambe and Cotacachi on clear days, not to mention orchids and giant hummingbirds, and even condors if you're lucky. The trailhead is behind the guard post at the reserve entrance; check here about safety conditions before setting off as there have been sporadic **robberies**.

The access to **climb** the snow-dusted peak of Volcán Cotacachi begins at some antennas to its east, at the end of the dirt road heading north from the guard post. It's not a technical climb, but there is some scrambling near the top as well as risk of rock fall. A **guide** is recommended, not least because fog often makes finding routes difficult; ask at *El Mirador* restaurant (see opposite) or tour agencies in Otavalo.

Practicalities

To get to Laguna Cuicocha, take a **bus** (every 10–15min) from the Otavalo terminal to Cotacachi or Quiroga, a village about five minutes from Cotacachi. From either, go by **taxi** or **camioneta** to the lake ($3–4 one-way, $7–10 return trip with waiting time); from Otavalo a taxi is about $8–10 one-way. If you fancy **walking** back from the lake through beautiful scenery on the old road to Quiroga (9km, 3–4hr), turn left off the main road at the junction with the old road, and continue east where the new road turns west, about 2km below the guard post.

The lowland **forests** of the reserve are best accessed by boat from Borbón, up the ríos Cayapas and Santiago (see p.150), but such a journey is best attempted outside the dry season (July–Dec), when water levels can be too low to go very far. You can also reach **cloudforest** areas from the Los Cedros reserve (see p.339), which borders Cotacachi-Cayapas to the south.

You can stay at the smart new-built **hotel** by the dock, *Cuicocha* (T06/2648040, Wwww.cuicocha.org; ➐ including breakfast and dinner), which has comfortable cabins by the shore, two of which have simply stunning views. About 4km beyond the guard post, *Los Pinos de Cuicocha* (T09/9001516, Wwww.lospinosdecuicocha.com; ➏ includes breakfast) sits on the ridge above the lake and has the feel of a farmstead. Horses are available for hire and riding lessons are offered. *El Mirador* (☎08/6821699, ✉miradordecuicocha@yahoo .com; ❷–❸), on the hill directly behind the dock, offers simple cabins and great views. All of these hotels have competent **restaurants**.

The Intag region

West of Laguna Cuicocha, the dirt road climbs to 3300m before descending into the remote and subtropical **Intag region**, where only a few isolated settlements sit amid richly forested hills. The area has become a focus of conservation efforts and several private reserves are guardians of these precious portions of **Chocó bioregion cloudforest**, one of the world's ten biodiversity "hotspots".

You can visit two reserves near the village of **Santa Rosa** about 34km from Cuicocha. The **Intag Cloud Forest Reserve** (☎06/2648509, ⓦwww .intagcloudforest.com; $44 per person in groups of eight or more, including meals and guided walks; reservations essential), which protects five square kilometres of primary and secondary forest ranging from 1800 to 2800m in altitude. High rainfall (2500mm annually) and humidity nurture an incredible array of flora and fauna, including more than twenty types of hummingbird, which you can expect to see zipping around. Visitors can stay at a simple **lodge**, equipped with solar-heated showers and composting latrines, and get to enjoy delicious vegetarian food. The owners helped found DECOIN (see contact details below), a local environmental organization that works on regional ecotourism projects and provides information on all the latest developments.

Santa Rosa is also the base for the nearby **Reserva Alto Chocó**, a 2500-hectare cloudforest concern run by the Quito-based Fundación Zoobreviven, 6 de Diciembre N32-36 and Whymper (☎02/2522916, ⓦwww.zoobreviven.org), which welcomes volunteers to work on reforestation projects, trail maintenance, environmental education programmes and patrolling the reserve against illegal loggers.

Apuela

Thickly forested hills enclose the small village of **APUELA**, located at the confluence of ríos Apuela and Azabi. The town has two simple streets, shops selling little more than biscuits, cola and tuna, a battered church and lethargic men sitting around the volleyball court on the main square. While there's not much of interest here in the village, hiking **trails** festoon the surrounding hills, and the villages of **Nangulví** and **Gualimán** provide worthwhile nearby excursions. Two environmental NGOs have offices in the Apuela: the local coffee-producing association AACRI (☎06/2648489, ✉aacri@andinanet.net), whose agro-tourism projects involve trips to or volunteer placements at nearby coffee farms and the like; and DECOIN (☎06/2648953, ⓦwww.decoin.org), which will have information on visiting and volunteering at local reserves.

Transportes Otavalo **buses** leave for Apuela from the Otavalo terminal (8am, 10am & 2pm; buy your ticket early). Apuela's few **hotels** are simple and inexpensive, the best option being the *Pradera Tropical* (☎06/2468557; ❷), not far from the school, for its en-suite cabins boasting hot water.

Nangulví

Less a village than a sparse group of homesteads strung along the road west of Apuela, **NANGULVÍ** has better accommodation than its neighbour and features the appealing **Piscinas de Nangulví** (daily 6am–9pm; $1), a hot springs complex set in a gorgeous location in a steep-walled valley. Its five thermal pools (and a larger plunge pool of cold diverted river water), are busy at weekends, but during the week you'll be able to enjoy the scenery from the steaming waters in peace.

Buses from Otavalo to García Moreno (leaving 8am, 10am & 2pm) pass through Nangulví; otherwise, it's an hour's **walk** if you follow the road down from Apuela and, at the second bridge, turn left and keep going till you reach Nangulví. **Accommodation** is available just before the pools at *Cabañas Río Grande* (T06/2648296; ④), a collection of clean, flower-draped wooden cabins with private bathrooms and electric showers, set in pleasant riverside gardens, and at the newer *Hostería Tierra Sol* (T06/2920168; ③), which offers similar, but is 1km uphill from the baths. You can also stay at the *Complejo Nangulví*, the pools complex itself (T06/2648291; ④), in comfortable en-suite rooms (no hot water); use mosquito repellent at night. For **restaurants**, the complex does inexpensive *almuerzos*, but *Río Grande* provides better food and a more varied menu.

Gualimán

In the hills above Nangulví, on a spectacular three-kilometre-long **plateau**, stands **GUALIMÁN**, a complex of more than seventy overgrown pre-Columbian ruins, most obviously a few large pyramid mounds with ramps. Despite the plateau's apparent isolation, tucked away at its far end is a basic **hotel** (T06/2641863 in Ibarra; ② including breakfast; reserve in advance), offering simple rooms with shared baths, and whose friendly owners keep a little **museum** displaying ancient ceramics found at the site. Accommodation includes a guided tour of the plateau and the ruins.

A Transportes Otavalo Buses for **Peñaherrera** leave the Otavalo terminal at 1pm (Transportes Otavalo) and 3pm (Co-op 6 de Julio), passing Apuela after 2 hours 30 minutes, and the Gualimán trailhead around 45 minutes later (ask the driver to drop you off). Walking from Apuela and Nangulví takes two to three hours.

Junín

From Nangulví it's a 30-minute drive southwest to **García Moreno**, where there are a couple of basic hotels and restaurants, but no reason to stay. Northwest of García Moreno, a bumpy dirt track leads up to the remote community of **JUNÍN**, the site of a dramatic 1997 demonstration which saw hundreds of villagers burn a Mitsubishi-owned mining camp to the ground – due largely to the company and government officials ignoring local concerns that contaminated mining waste and camp latrines were discharging straight into the Río Junín, the only water supply for hundreds of families. The village then set up its own **lodge** and thirty-square-kilometre **cloudforest reserve** in a bid to make an alternative income based on ecotourism. The community has also launched a successful organic coffee-growing cooperative.

Nevertheless, the mining threat is still present, albeit from a different company, and Junín's ecotourism venture needs as much support as possible if the miners are to be kept out. Staying at the community **lodge** in the forest 20 minutes from the village costs $30 per person, including three good meals. There's enormous scope for **hiking** in the surrounding forests, which are streaked with waterfalls, and guides are on hand to help you explore. **Volunteers** are also welcomed for teaching English, reforestation, trail maintenance and work on other projects in the community ($15 a day or $450 per month). Junín has one phone (T02/2863864) or, better, try local activist Rosario Piedra on T08/8871860. DECOIN (see p.151) can also put you in touch.

Buses for Chaguayacu Alto (beyond García Moreno) leave Otavalo at 8am and 2pm, from where it's a 45-minute walk to Junín, although you can arrange to be picked up in the community's truck. In the wet season the road beyond García Moreno can be impassable to vehicles (4hr by horse), so always ring ahead. You can also take a bus from the Ofelia terminal in Quito (on the Metrobus line) direct to García Moreno (leaves 3pm). A new road from Otavalo to the coast via Quinindé is due to open in late 2010 and is likely to affect transport arrangements; call ahead to check the latest.

Ibarra and around

Some 115km north of Quito, the Panamericana passes around the base of Volcán Imbabura to reveal **IBARRA** (2225m), basking in a broad, sunny valley. Known as the *ciudad blanca* (white city), its low blocks of whitewashed and tiled buildings gleam with stately confidence, interrupted only by the occasional church spire. It was founded in 1606 to oversee the region's textile workshops, but only a few of Ibarra's original colonial buildings survived the great earthquake of 1868, from which the town eventually recovered to become the commercial and transport hub of Imbabura province. Ibarra's population of more than 100,000 people, an unusual blend of *mestizos*, *indígenas* and Afro-Ecuadorians from the nearby Chota valley, makes it by far the largest highland city north of Quito, but despite this, it still enjoys a relaxed pace of life and an easy-going charm.

Ibarra's a great place to unwind, with good hotels, cafés and bars, a pleasant climate and friendly residents. It's also not nearly as touristy as Otavalo, while being close to the craft villages of **La Esperanza** and **San Antonio de Ibarra**, a good base for **hikes** in the surrounding countryside and for visiting the excellent hot springs at **Chachimbiro**. It's also a jumping-off point for the **coast**, by way of lush subtropical valleys filled with fruit farms and forests.

Among the most important local **festivals** are the **Fiesta del Retorno**, on April 28, commemorating the return of the town's citizens after the 1868 earthquake; **independence day**, on July 17, marking Simón Bolívar's triumph over the Spanish at the Battle of Ibarra in 1823; and the biggest of all, the **Fiesta de los Lagos**, on the last weekend in September, celebrating the city's foundation (Sept 28) with parades and decorated floats rolling through town and motorcar races held at **Laguna Yahuarcocha**.

Arrival and information

Buses use the terminal on Avenida Gómez and Espejo, southwest of the centre, with the exception of a couple of local destinations serviced from points nearby. Use taxis to get around downtown after dark.

The well-staffed Ministerio de Turismo **tourist office**, García Moreno 376 and Rocafuerte (Mon–Fri 8am–1pm & 2–5.30pm; ☎06/2955711, ⓦwww .imbabura.gov.ec), and the municipal I-Tur office at Oviedo and Sucre (Mon–Fri 8am–12.30pm & 2–5.30pm; ☎06/2608489, ⓦwww.ibarraturismo.com) should both be able to provide **maps** and general **information**.

Local city buses ply the main thoroughfares, and **taxis** can be found around the main parks, bus stations and downtown streets, costing $1 for a local ride.

Accommodation

Ibarra has a wide selection of good-value **hotels** and just about all of them have hot water. Several rock-bottom budget joints are located in the rougher

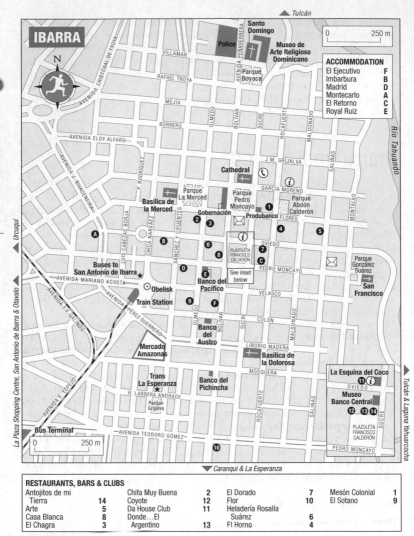

RESTAURANTS, BARS & CLUBS

Antojitos de mi		Chifa Muy Buena	2	El Dorado	7	Mesón Colonial	1
Tierra	14	Coyote	12	Flor	10	El Sotano	9
Arte	5	Da House Club	11	Heladería Rosalía			
Casa Blanca	8	Donde...El		Suárez	6		
El Chagra	3	Argentino	13	El Horno	4		

downtown areas around the train station, but these are pretty grim and aren't worth the few saved cents.

Ajaví Av Mariano Acosta 16-38, 200m southwest of town ⌕06/2955221, ⌕2955640. Smart hotel aimed at business clients, with ample rooms, phones and cable TVs, plus pool, gym and spa facilities as well as weekend live music. ❼

Chorlaví Panamericana Sur Km4.5, outside town ⌕06/2932222, ⓦwww.haciendachorlavi.com. Converted colonial hacienda with whitewashed buildings and an old monastery – now a cocktail

bar – set in palm-fringed gardens with pool, spa, tennis courts and a cockfighting arena. Rooms are comfortable with period furnishings, phones, cable TVs and private baths. The restaurant is locally renowned but price, and weekend live music draws swarms of tour groups. Reservations advised. ❻

El Ejecutivo Bolívar 9-69 and Colón ⌕06/2956575. Has an on-site internet café, and rooms come with everything a budget traveller could desire: private bath, hot water and cable TV; some even have balconies. ❷

Imbabura Oviedo 9-33 and Chica Narváez ☎06/2950155, ⓕ92958877, ⓔhotel_imbabura @hotmail.com. The most charming of the budget choices (if you don't mind shared bathrooms; good hot showers) for its large, high-ceilinged rooms around a pretty courtyard. Breakfast available in the patio café, and there's left-luggage and laundry service. Don't miss the owner's fascinating archeological museum and miniature bottle collection. ❷

Madrid Pedro Moncayo 7-41 and Sánchez y Cifuentes ☎06/2956177, ⓕ2955301. Comfortable rooms with private bath, phone and cable TV – but avoid those without windows. Internet service and parking also available. ❸

Montecarlo Av J. Rivadeneira 5-63 and Oviedo ☎06/2958266, ⓕ2958182. A business-oriented hotel, offering an indoor heated pool, sauna, steam room and jacuzzi (open Sat, Sun & holidays). Rooms are carpeted and have phones, private baths and cable TVs. Parking also available. ❻

El Retorno Pedro Moncayo 4-32 and Rocafuerte ☎06/2957722. Nice clean rooms and a restaurant serving meals until 4pm. Private baths and TVs available. ❸

Royal Ruiz Olmedo 9-40 and P. Moncayo ☎&ⓕ06/2641999. Smarter than average hotel with clean, comfortable and carpeted rooms with private baths, phones and cable TVs. Extras include a sauna, steam room and parking. ❺

The Town

The best place to start exploring is Ibarra's focal point, the **Parque Pedro Moncayo**, featuring a statue of the eponymous nineteenth-century journalist, politician and local. The neatly clipped lawns and lofty palms of this grand square are flanked to the north by the **cathedral**, adorned with a golden altar and displaying portraits of the disciples by **Rafael Troya**, born here in 1845 and one of Ecuador's greatest artists. Along the west side of the park, the seat of the province's government, the **gobernación**, is a colonial-style building painted in white and butterscotch, which looks ravishing under evening floodlights.

A block to the west, tall flowering trees fill the quieter Parque Victor M. Peñaherrera, better known as the **Parque la Merced** after the **Basílica de la Merced**, an imposing grey-stone church crowned with a weighty statue of the Virgin and housing a towering red-and-gold altarpiece. Opposite the basilica, on the eastern side of the park, the old **infantry barracks** give the square a distinctly Mediterranean flavour with its impressive Moorish castellations and arches, under which **street vendors** in their sunshaded stalls sell the sweet Ibarra specialities, *nogadas* and *arrope de mora* (see p.157).

A block south of the Parque Pedro Moncayo, the **Plazoleta Francisco Calderón** was the city marketplace until the 1960s, but is now its cultural focus with occasional shows, concerts, dance performances and readings held on the corner stage. Along its northern side a new development – with a bar, artesanía, *heladería* and several restaurants – provides a good spot to sit in the sun and enjoy a beer, an inexpensive meal or ice cream. Nearby on the little *plazoleta* at Sucre and Oviedo, a lonely coconut tree, known as **La Esquina del Coco**, is a rather unlikely emblem of city pride, supposedly the reference point used by President García Moreno for the layout of the new city after the destruction of the 1868 earthquake.

Four blocks south is the modern **Basílica de la Dolorosa**, Sucre and Avenida Pérez Guerrero, which suffered earthquake damage in 1987, but despite its later reconstruction offers little to see beyond its fresh white-and-cyan interior. Heading west down Avenida Pérez Guerrero, the teeming **Mercado Amazonas** is open daily and supplies clothes and produce in the heart of downtown.

At the northern end of Bolívar, the **Museo de Arte Religioso Dominicano** (daily 8am–noon & 2–6pm; $0.50) holds a small collection of interesting eighteenth- and nineteenth-century canvases by fine Ecuadorian artists, including Troya, Reyes and Salas, along with Quito School carvings, church silver, an old harmonium and assorted stuffed animals. Next to the museum is the **Iglesia Santo Domingo**, which itself features some flamboyant paintings inside.

Museo Banco Central

Just off the Plazoleta Calderón, the engaging **Museo Banco Central**, Sucre and Oviedo (Mon–Fri 8.30am–1.30pm & 2–5pm; $1), concentrates on Ecuadorian archeology from prehistory to the Inca era, particularly in the northern sierra; items include a **gold funeral mask** from the nearby Pimampiro area and a grisly diorama of the bloody war between the Incas and the Caranqui at Laguna Yahuarcocha (see p.159). Don't miss the superb ceramics, including the mythological beast of the **Jama-Coaque** culture (350 BC to 1540 AD), with its penetrating eyes, tusked teeth and fish mouth. There's also a temporary exhibition space, **library** and small bookshop selling subsidized books in Spanish.

The train from Ibarra

Once extending to San Lorenzo down on the coast, Ibarra's railway now runs from the **train** station only as far as Primer Paso, a 45-kilometre journey serviced, actually, by an *autoferro*, a converted bus on rails (Sat–Sun 9am, returning 4pm; 1hr 40min trip; $3.80 one-way, $7.60 return; ticket office open daily 8am–noon & 2–6pm, but it's best to pitch up about 30min before departure to buy your ticket ☎06/2950390, ⓦ www.efe.gov.ec). The train only departs if there are at least twelve passengers or $60 worth of ticket sales – though you can always pay the difference if there aren't enough people. The ride itself is fun; you can sit on the roof while the train skirts vertiginous drops, clatters over the rickety 120-metre **Ambi bridge** and disappears into the gloom of at least a dozen tunnels, one with its own waterfall. At the end of the route in the Tulquizán sector, the train pulls in near the faded *Hostería Tulquizán*,

▲ Parque Pedro Moncayo, Ibarra

Paragliding around Ibarra

FlyEcuador, at the corner of Oviedo 9-13 and Sánchez y Cifuentes (☎06/2953297, ⓦwww.flyecuador.com.ec), offers **paragliding** (*parapente*) courses and tandem flights from the hills around Ibarra. You can launch yourself off Yuracrucito, a hill to the east of town, from where you drift 620 metres back to earth suspended on a paraglider, or even try El Bestial, a 1000-metre jump.

across the river by cable swing, where you can get lunch, swim in the pool for a few dollars and sleep in rustic cabins, although most visitors just while away a few hours here rather than stay the night. You are at the hotel's mercy once you cross because they seldom take people back over the river until the train is about to depart. The tracks cross the road a little before the final stop (ask the driver to be let off), from where you can take a **bus** back to Ibarra (30min) or to San Lorenzo on the coast (3hr).

Eating, drinking and nightlife

Most of Ibarra's **restaurants** are south of the main squares up to Calle Velasco, though there are countless budget options where you can get perfectly good *almuerzos* and *meriendas* for a dollar or two, or cheap Chinese food from the cluster of **chifas** (Chinese restaurants) along Olmedo between Flores and Velasco. All visitors to Ibarra should try the wonderfully smooth and flavoursome **helados de paila**, a sorbet prepared in great copper pans (*pailas*) kept cool on a bed of straw and salted ice, into which fruit, sugar and water are stirred – found at a number of excellent *heladerías* throughout town. Other local specialities are sold at the stalls around the Parque La Merced, namely **nogadas** – nougat-style treats made from sugar, milk, egg whites and walnuts, sometimes flavoured with cinnamon, aniseed or vanilla – and **arrope de mora**, a sticky blackberry syrup, usually diluted with water or spirits.

Cafés

Arte Salinas 5-43 and Oviedo. Artist-owned café-cum-art gallery with a classy wooden interior and outside sculpture garden. Intellectual flourishes abound, from the mock triptych menu to the Frida Kahlo cocktail. Mon–Sat from 4pm. Concerts Fri or Sat.

🏃 **Flor** Av T. Gómez 6-44 and Atahualpa. Smart Swiss-owned operation that runs its own dairy and offers fantastic cheeses, yogurts, milkshakes and ice creams – plus great crêpes, fondue and raclette. A little more expensive than other cafés, but worth it. Mon–Sat 8am–10pm, Sun 5–8pm.

🏃 **Heladería Rosalía Suárez** Oviedo 7-79 and Olmedo. In business since 1897, this is the oldest and most famous place to devour tasty *helados de paila* (sorbets), and also watch them being made; many delicious flavours to choose.

Restaurants

Antojitos de mi Tierra Plazoleta Calderón. Excellent, friendly little place specializing in Ecuadorian dishes, such as delicious *humitas*, *bonitísimas* and *quimbolitos*, which make the perfect accompaniment to a coffee served alfresco. Good set-lunches for about $2. Irregular hours.

Casa Blanca Bolívar 7-83 and Moncayo A popular restaurant serving *platos típicos* in an attractive old house set around a courtyard and fountain. If you like *empanadas* the time to come is 4–8pm, when they cook them up fresh right in front of you at the entrance. Closed Sun.

El Chagra Olmedo 7-48 and Flores. Intimate eatery doling out inexpensive *platos típicos* and trout under the not-so-romantic glow of a large-screen TV.

Chifa Muy Bueno Olmedo 7-25 and Flores. Cheap Chinese food, served in massive portions and available 24hr.

Donde...El Argentino Plazoleta Calderón. Friendly Argentinian steak-and-grill house with outdoor seating, offering affordable meals that are best devoured with a jar of Argentinian wine. Closed Mon.

El Dorado Oviedo 5-47 and Rocafuerte. Smart restaurant in the eponymous hotel, staffed by waiters in bow ties and offering good *platos típicos*, including *carne colorada, empanadas, bonitísimas* and chicken in cider, for $4–8 per main course.
El Horno Rocafuerte and Flores. Tasty pizzas (from $2.50) cooked in a big clay oven that dominates the restaurant. Vegetarian options and wine available. Occasional live music. Tues–Sun 6pm–midnight.

Mesón Colonial Rocafuerte 5-53 and García Moreno. Expansive dining rooms in a grand old house with a chequered floor, somewhat bizarrely decorated with big animals printed on blankets. Snappy service, floral tablecloths, good *platos típicos* and fine *almuerzos* for only $2. Lunches only, closed Sun.

Bars and clubs

The presence of a large university on the outskirts of Ibarra means that at weekends hundreds of students are out on the prowl, looking for noisy fun at the town's various **bars** and **discos**. The younger crowd often ensures a fizzing atmosphere, even if the town's size makes the action feel more dispersed than in, say, Otavalo.

Coyote on Plazoleta Calderón, Pedro Moncayo and Sucre. Easy-going bar and restaurant (open at night only) with comfortable seating.
Da House Club Oviedo and Sucre. Plays a mix of pumping techno, hip-hop and Latin dance music. Closed Sun.

El Sotano Olmedo and Colón. Friendly and popular bar for students and Ibarreños alike, with a mellow atmosphere and occasional live music. Daily 5pm–2am.

Listings

Banks and exchange Banco del Austro, Colón and Bolívar, has a Visa ATM and offers cash advances; Banco del Pacífico, P. Moncayo and Olmedo, has a MasterCard ATM; Banco del Pichincha, Mosquera and Bolívar, has an ATM for Visa, MasterCard and Diners Club; Produbanco, Sucre and Flores, has a MasterCard ATM.
Laundry Rocafuerte 8-39 and Moncayo.
Medical services Instituto Médico de Especialidades, Jacinto Egas 1-83 and T. Gómez (☎06/2955612) and Clinica Médica del Norte,

Oviedo and Olmedo (☎06/2955099) both have 24hr emergency service; Hospital San Vicente de Paúl, Vargas Torres 11-56 (☎06/2957272), is also open 24hr.
Police and immigration Av J. Roldos and Av V.M. Peñaherrera, at the north end of town ☎06/2950444 (immigration ☎06/2951712).
Swimming Olympic-sized pool at Rafael Troya and Chica Narváez.
Tour agencies Recotur, Olmedo 5-79 and García Moreno ☎06/2957795.

San Antonio de Ibarra

Just off the Panamericana, 6km west of Ibarra, **SAN ANTONIO DE IBARRA** is not much more than a handful of streets and a little square, but has nevertheless chiselled its way to fame as a major centre for **woodcarving**. Its plentiful shops and galleries are crammed with a huge array of subjects and styles, mostly carved in cedar, from saints and angels to chess sets and life-size carvings of Don Quixote. San Antonio's best-known artist is **Luís Potosí**, whose gallery is on the main square, and who seems to have a predilection for nude mothers nursing their newborns. There are many other artists' **showrooms** located on the main square and Avenida 27 de Noviembre; **prices** range from $1500 for large pieces down to $1 for a keyring.

Buses to San Antonio leave the obelisk in Ibarra every twenty minutes (10min); a **taxi** is a couple of dollars.

La Esperanza and around

At the foot of Volcán Imbabura, 8km south of Ibarra on a cobblestone road, sits **LA ESPERANZA**, a tranquil village where Simón Bolívar planned the defeat of General Agualongo and his Spanish forces. On July 17, 1823, Bolívar's troops swept down from this hillside into Ibarra, winning its independence by trapping the Spanish in a time-honoured pincer movement. Forty-five years later, when it was flattened by the 1868 earthquake, Ibarra again looked to La Esperanza for assistance, its survivors taking refuge here for four years while the city was rebuilt. A century on, La Esperanza briefly became a hippie enclave as its soil nurtured fields of magic mushrooms, but these days most visitors come for the restful atmosphere, the excellent mountain walks, and the village's discreet but flourishing artesanía scene, including a leather workshop, and several others specializing in marquetry (*taracea*) for guitar inlays and embroidery (*bordado*). For fine embroidered tablecloths (*manteles*) and napkins, Guadalupe (Lupita) Gómez de Arroyo (☎06/2641951) will stitch custom designs.

Volcán Imbabura and Cubilche

La Esperanza makes an excellent base for climbing **Volcán Imbabura** and **Cubilche** to the west, and trails for both begin to the right by the bridge up from the *Casa Aída* hotel. The IGM (see p.61) San Pablo del Lago **map** (1:50,000 scale) is a good resource, but both of the town's *hostales* provide information as well, and can also provide a **guide** ($7–10 per day). Hiking to the summit of Volcán **Imbabura** (4621m) is straightforward, except for some loose rock at the top, and takes about ten hours round trip. Get an early start and don't forget food, water and warm clothing. Other options include taking a **camioneta** up as far as the water tank, about three hours' walk from the summit (around $5, ask at *Casa Aída*), or just spending a day walking through the pastureland around the mountain's base.

Compared with Imbabura, the summit of **Cubilche** (3826m) is an easier proposition (3hr trip), offering great views of the lake and Ibarra.

Practicalities

Buses to La Esperanza (every 20min, 30min trip; last bus 7.30pm) leave Ibarra from the Parque Grijalva, a few blocks south of the obelisk. Tell the driver you want a **hotel**, otherwise you'll be taken to the end of the village about fifteen minutes away. *Casa Aída* (☎06/2660221; ❷) is the best, with a restaurant, simple and pleasant rooms, a two-floor thatched cabin, and clean, shared bathrooms and hot showers. Another option is to stay at the nearby indigenous village of **SAN CLEMENTE**, which runs its own community ecotourism project, called Pukyu Pamba (☎09/9161095, ⓦwww.sclemente.com; $22 or $35 per person per day depending on comfort of the house, including three meals and activities, except for horse rides $10 and trips using 4WD vehicles $15). Visitors can stay with families, learn about embroidery, hear local musicians and join in dances, go on hikes or a four-day trek to Nueva América (see p.165), horseriding with local guides, learn Quichua and generally get to know about the community. Buses leave from the same Parque Grijalva in Ibarra about every two hours (40min).

Laguna Yahuarcocha

On the northern outskirts of Ibarra and flanked to the east by misty hills, **LAGUNA YAHUARCOCHA** ("lake of blood" in Quichua) was the site of the decisive 1495 defeat of the indigenous Cara people by the Incas under

Huayna Capac. Their victory was the gory climax of a seventeen-year campaign, a massacre of twenty to fifty thousand Cara, whose bleeding bodies turned the waters crimson. The survivors became so respected for their fighting skills that Inca royalty subsequently employed them as bodyguards in Cusco. Nowadays, herons swoop in and out of the dense reedbanks here, while *campesinos* gather bundles of the *totora* reeds and dry them on the shore to make mats – a picturesque setting marred by the strangling tarmac of a race track around its perimeter, the venue for competitions during Ibarra's September fiestas.

To visit, take a **bus** (every 15min; 10min) in Ibarra from the obelisk, or on Oviedo at the corner of Sánchez y Cifuentes; you can **walk** back to Ibarra on quiet paths and backstreets (1–2hr).

Urcuquí and Chachimbiro

URCUQUÍ, 22km by winding road northwest of Ibarra, is little more than a pretty rural village with a pleasant tree-filled square, brilliant-white church and simple hotel. Few people stop here, save hikers for the beautiful four-day trek to the remote **Piñán lakes** around Yana Urcu de Piñán mountain (4535m) inside the Cotacachi-Cayapas reserve, an outing best arranged through a Quito- or Otavalo-based operator (for example, Campus Trekking ☎02/2340601, ⓦ www.campustrekking.com.ec).

Sixteen bumpy kilometres beyond Urcuquí, along a flower-lined cobbled road that weaves through charming countryside, lies **CHACHIMBIRO** tight in a valley in the foothills of Yana Urcu de Piñán, a popular **thermal springs** complex (daily 7am–10pm, $3.50 for the recreational area and $3 for the medicinal; ☎06/2923633, ⓦ www.chachimbiro.com), a selection of hot mineral baths and swimming pools managed by the Fundación Cordillera. The recreational zone includes a large pool with water slides, children's pools and a games room, but the real fun is to be had in the medicinal area, where you can loll about in hot pools, one scorchingly so (55°C), a sauna, steam room, "natural" jacuzzi and get a mud massage. The volcanic waters are rich in sulphur, chlorides, iron, copper and manganese – widely believed to provide relief from neuralgia, arthritis and rheumatism.

Practicalities

Buses to Urcuquí (every 30min, 30min trip) and Chachimbiro (7.30am and noon, returning at noon and 3pm; 1hr 15min trip) leave Ibarra from the terminal; for buses to the latter, arrive early on weekends when it gets very crowded. You can also book a **tour** with the Fundación Cordillera in Otavalo (see box, p.136) and take their *ranchera* to the site. A range of **rooms** and family cabins are available inside the spa complex (⑥ ⑦), or you can rent a mattress and sleeping bag in *la choza* ("the hut") for $9–10 at the site. More distinguished accommodation can be found at two haciendas nearby: *Hacienda San Francisco* (☎06/2934161, ⓦ www.hosteriasanfrancisco.com; ⑦), on the Vía Chachimbiro Km19, is an attractive, isolated hacienda with its own heated pool, set amid rolling countryside; and *Hacienda Pantaví* (☎02/2347476, ⓦ www.hosteriapantavi.com; ⑥ including breakfast), the other side of Tumambiro at Km6 on the Vía Salinas, offering similar amenities.

From Ibarra to the coast

It wasn't long ago that the train to San Lorenzo from Ibarra was the only way to get to the remote northern coast, but today, a paved **road** speeds from Ibarra down the parched Chota and Mira valleys, slicing through crumbling hillsides prone to falling rocks as it descends into the warmer, moister climes of the lush lowlands and the Pacific coast in just three and a half hours. As for the **train**, all that remains is a truncated 45-kilometre **tourist service** from Ibarra to Primer Paso in an old bus bolted onto a set of bogeys (see p.156 for details). It's still worth the ride, even if it is just a fraction of the original 200-kilometre journey.

Buses from Ibarra regularly service the highway to San Lorenzo (every 50min between 9am & 6pm), with a few going on to Esmeraldas (four daily). At **Lita**, roughly the halfway point, you may need to show your passport at a **police checkpoint**. The road meets the coastal highway to Esmeraldas about 8km from San Lorenzo, the final destination.

El Limonal and Bospas Fruit Forest Farm

Some 39km beyond the junction at Salinas, a small settlement where the San Lorenzo road leaves the Panamericana, **EL LIMONAL** sits on the east side of the Río Guallupe, a tributary of the Río Mira rising to the south. You may also hear it referred to as Guallupe, which is actually to the river's west, and on some maps both are confusingly marked as **La Carolina** – the name of the administrative district.

At 900m the climate is warm enough for fruit farming, and nowhere is this better illustrated than at the *Bospas Fruit Forest Farm and Lodge*, 800m uphill from the main square (T06/2648692, W www.bospas.org; $17 per person including breakfast; meals available for $5, farm produce is free; dorm beds for $13), an organic **forest farm**, where a wide range of different trees and bushes have been planted close together to improve diversity of produce, sustainability, wildlife habitat and water usage. Among the abundance on the farm, you'll find more than 20 kinds of fruit and 110 tree species. The **lodge** has three attractive en-suite rooms commanding splendid views over the valley and a small pool for taking the sting out of the midday sun. The hospitable Belgian environmentalist owner organizes treks and horse rides in the area and encourages visits to local farms, and his Ecuadorian wife gives salsa lessons. **Volunteers** are welcome to work on the farm ($225 contribution for four weeks or $17 a day).

A couple of **hotels** in the village cater for local *serranos* fleeing the highland chill each weekend, the best of which is the friendly *El Limonal* (T06/2648688; ❸), with simple rooms and swimming pools.

Cerro Golondrinas Cloudforest Reserve

A sleepy village just downhill from El Limonal, **Guallupe** is the access point for the **Cerro Golondrinas Cloudforest Reserve** 15km to the northeast (T06/2648662, W www.fgolondrinas.org). This 14-square-kilometre reserve around Cerro Golondrinas peak (3120m) makes a fine spot for birdwatching, with more than two hundred recorded species, including tanagers, toucans, hummingbirds and even condors. The foundation offers a variety of walking tours in the reserve, between subtropical, cloudforest and páramo zones, including one starting from the neighbouring El Ángel reserve (see p.163). There's accommodation at different elevations in the reserve at two rustic **lodges** ($25 per person including meals), another lodge at 3000m in the páramo, operated by the community of Morán ($10 with meals, plus $2 access fee), or in Guallupe village ($15 with meals). **Volunteering** opportunities are available for a $280 per month contribution.

Reserva Privada Las Siete Cascadas

About 11km beyond **Lita**, a small town that's home to some Awa *indígenas*, at Km111 on the road to San Lorenzo is **Las Siete Cascadas** private reserve and lodge (T09/4307434, W www.lassietecascadas.com; packages including meals, guided hikes and lodging from $40 per person), a 207-hectare tract of protected forest, where paths lead to seven waterfalls glittering among the greenery; all of them can be visited in the course of a five-hour walk. Accommodation is in rooms with or without bathroom in the lodge, or in tents with mattresses on a platform with views over the forests. Day visitors are also welcome to explore the forest (prices on group size; $21 per person in a pair with guide and two meals), go tubing, rappelling and swimming.

The old road to Colombia

Some 33km north of Ibarra, the Panamericana forks at the village of **Mascarilla**, a black community with an impressive sideline in clay masks and figurines; there's a **checkpoint here** (have your passport ready). To the left is the **old road** to Colombia via **Mira**, which is paved as far as **El Ángel**, but for the final 48km to Tulcán is in poor shape and rarely used; to the right, the busy Panamericana ascends the sun-baked Chota valley before turning to Bolívar, La Paz and San Gabriel on its way up to Tulcán and the Colombian border.

Mira

The old road climbs sharply out of the dusty Chota valley after Mascarilla, and then up the fifteen-kilometre ascent to **MIRA** (2400m; ⓦ www.mira.ec), a hillside town whose striking views of the countryside have earned it the title "balcony of the Andes" – according to its signposts, at least. The town is also known for its excellent **woollens**, sold both in Otavalo and locally at places like **Artesanías Ana Guerrero** (opposite the bus stop on the main road) and **Co-operativa Artesanía Mira**, further up the hill.

Buses run every 30 minutes from Ibarra to Mira until 6pm (1hr), and the last returning bus departs at 3pm; buses leave every 30 minutes from Mira to El Ángel (20min). The only **place to stay** is *Residencial Mira*, off the main square at González Suárez 8-01 and Chonta Huasi (☎06/2280228; ❷), with simple rooms and a shared electric shower.

El Ángel and around

From Mira the road continues its climb for the next 25km to **EL ÁNGEL** at 3000m. It's a friendly highland town whose most famous resident was topiarist **José Franco Guerrero**, responsible for the fantastic gardens in Tulcán (see p.168); the **Parque Libertad**, at the top of the town was his herbal sketchpad for the more advanced creations to come. A peaceful place, El Ángel only gets busy during its **Monday market**, held on the streets running downhill from the Parque Libertad, where you'll find clothes, produce and fresh fish caught from the nearby mountain lakes.

Most people come here to access the nearby Reserva Ecológica El Ángel, but another possibility is spending a few pleasant hours at **La Calera hot springs** (daily 7am–6pm; $1), 11km southwest of town, at the bottom of a winding cobbled road in the crook of a forested valley. The site is pretty well deserted during the week, when you'll have its naturally heated pool and cooler, larger swimming pool all to yourself – though the latter is emptied three times a week for cleaning (Mon, Wed & Fri after 1pm). At weekends, **jeeps** leave for the springs when full from the Parque Libertad ($1), but at other times you'll have to rent a **camioneta** (25min; $6 one-way, $9 return).

Practicalities

Transportes Espejo **buses** from Quito (15 daily, 4hr) travel via Mira (45min) and Ibarra (1hr 30min) to the Parque Libertad. When leaving El Ángel, Transportes Mira buses depart from the larger Parque Calderón in front of the church and go hourly to Mira, Ibarra and Tulcán (last bus to Tulcán at 1.30pm; 1hr 15min). **Taxis** ply the scenic route between El Ángel and Bolívar, on the Panamericana, usually leaving when full from around the Parque Libertad. The **phone office** is on the Parque Calderón, the **post office** is on Grijalva between the two parks.

El Ángel has only a few **places to stay**, the best of which is *Hostería El Ángel*, Panamericana Norte and Av Espejo 1302, by the roundabout on the south edge of town (T&F06/2977584, Wwww.ecuador-sommergarten.net; ❻ including breakfast), which has clean, comfortable rooms with baths and hot water. The hotel offers **tours** of the reserve on foot or on horseback and stays at its *Cotinga Lodge*, a rustic cloudforest cabin near the community of Morán. *Paisajes Andinos*, Ríofrio and Segunda Transversal (T06/2977557; ❷), has en-suite rooms with TVs, and the *Los Faroles* restaurant, on the corner of Parque Libertad (T06/2977144; ❷), has a few simple rooms in a family home, mostly with bunks and a shared shower.

Reserva Ecológica El Ángel

Established in 1992, the **Reserva Ecológica El Ángel** ($10), 15km north of the town of El Ángel, is home to some of Ecuador's most interesting páramo landscapes, a windblown rain-soaked wilderness of rolling grassland hills and lakes, ranging in altitude from 3644m to 4768m. It's most famous for its **frailejones**, peculiar furry-leaved plants endemic to the northern Andes, which grow on dark stems up to seven metres in height and cover 85 percent of the reserve's 160 square kilometres, covering the hillsides like a ghostly vegetal army. The reserve's **wildlife** includes foxes, deer and condors, and streams teem with rainbow trout. In a few of its sheltered pockets, forest supplants the soggy

▲ Páramo of the Reserva Ecológica El Ángel

moorland, and dense thickets of trees such as the **polylepis** – draped with mosses, orchids and bromeliads – make the best places to spot hummingbirds and armadillos.

Practicalities

There are three **routes** to the reserve. The **first** and most convenient follows the old road from El Ángel to Tulcán for 15km until a guard post, from where a one-kilometre trail leads to the two **Lagunas El Voladero**, and then to Laguna de Potrerillos, a two-hour walk away. The **second route** heads northwest from El Ángel through La Libertad to the reserve guard post at **El Salado**, from where a dirt road leads up past the Cañón El Colorado to a viewpoint on Cerro Socabones. Beyond that, the road descends to the hamlet of **Morán**, where there's simple lodging (☎08/6416936) and guides. The **third route** runs along the road heading west out of Tufiño, skirting the northern part of the reserve and the Colombian border; enquire before travelling in these remote border areas as they can be unsafe.

The Ministerio del Ambiente office in El Ángel, at Salinas and Esmeraldas, second floor of the Sindicato de Choferes building (☎06/2977597), can provide **information** about visiting the reserve and put you in touch with local **guides** ($10–15 per day).

From El Ángel town you can take a **camioneta** or **taxi** to the reserve ($12 one-way, $25–30 return with waiting), or get a ride on the **milk truck** which leaves the Parque Libertad around 8am for **Morán** and returns around 10–11am.

The charm – and penetrating chill – of the páramo can be experienced first-hand by **staying** at *Polylepis Lodge* (☎06/2954009, ⓦwww.polylepislodge .com; ❽), 14km from El Ángel and about a kilometre beyond El Salado check-point, in a private reserve buffering the national one, in rustic stone cottages with beds or capacious bunks, fireplaces and private bathrooms; the two-person cottages also come with jacuzzi. Activities available here include a night-time stroll through *polylepis* forest while being regaled with myths and stories from a native guide.

The Panamericana to Tulcán

At the Mascarilla junction, the busy Panamericana continues east up the sere and dusty **Chota valley**, where the only greenery clings tightly to the banks of the Río Chota. This and the Mira valley are home to a number of Afro-Ecuadorian communities, the principal highland settlement being the slightly ramshackle town of **Chota**. The communities have developed a unique culture, an exotic mix of African and Andean traditions best experienced at a cultural performance (check the local press or ask at the tourist office in Ibarra). Their distinctive **Bomba music** features percussion, guitars and impromptu instruments, such as those made from leaves, while local **dances** involve such feats as balancing a bottle on the head, thought to represent the traditional African way of carrying objects. The valley is also home to many of Ecuador's best professional footballers, despite a lack of grass pitches or stadiums.

A few kilometres further on, in the dry **Quebrada de Ambuquí** (Ambuquí Gorge), local **resort-hotels** draw weekend crowds of affluent Colombians and Ecuadorians, but few gringos. The best of these is *Oasis*, at Km39 (☎&Ⓕ06/2941200; ❽), which hosts a live Afro-Ecuadorian music show at weekends and features "mini cabañas" set around three pools, one with a wave machine (weekends only).

Pimampiro and around

Several kilometres away, **El Juncal**, a small settlement famed for its prodigious number of international footballers, marks the turn-off 8km southeast to the dusty hillside town of **PIMAMPIRO**, best used as a jumping-off point for treks in the páramo and cloudforests of the Reserva Cayambe-Coca, 20km to the south (see p.134). One possibility is a community-stay at **Nueva América**, an indigenous village close to the Cayambe-Coca reserve, where you can learn about medicinal plants and explore high-altitude forests (you're up at 3200m) or hike across the páramo to the Laguna Puruhanta. Prior reservations are essential; ask for details at the Municipio, at Flores and Imbabura in Pimampiro (☏06/2937118, ⓦ www.pimampiro.gov.ec). **Buses** to Pimampiro leave from the bus terminal in Ibarra every 20 minutes (1hr 15min).

Gruta de la Paz

About 26km north of El Juncal, and 6km beyond **Bolívar**, a tidy little hillside town of pastoral views and pastel houses, is the similarly well-tended village of **La Paz**. From here, a cobblestone road leads 6km down into a gorge threaded with waterfalls to the major shrine of **GRUTA DE LA PAZ**, an important pilgrimage centre with its own "village" including basilica, telephone office, souvenir shop, restaurants and hotels. Water from the heart of the 40-metre deep **grotto**, which has its own stalactite-strewn chapel, is channelled down to tepid **thermal pools** (Tues–Sun) in a picturesque setting nearby.

The grotto gets very crowded at weekends, holidays and on the first weekend of July, during the **festival** for the Virgen de La Paz. At weekends, **jeeps** (*patroles*) ferry visitors to the grotto from the main squares in Bolívar and San Gabriel ($0.50), and on Saturdays a **bus** leaves the cathedral in Tulcán at 8am, returning about 3pm ($2 each way). During the week the grotto is much quieter but you'll have to **rent a jeep** to get there (around $3 from La Paz, $5 from Bolívar, $8 from San Gabriel). Lodging here is mostly intended for pilgrims, and is basic and very cheap.

San Gabriel and around

The farming centre of **SAN GABRIEL**, 22km north of Bolívar, is the busiest town between Ibarra and Tulcán – it even has traffic lights – and features a thriving **Saturday market** and narrow streets cluttered with advertising slogans and shop signs. About 4km outside town is the impressive 30-metre-high **Cascada de Paluz**, which makes for a pleasant hour's walk. At 7km west of town, the **Bosque de los Arrayanes**, a lush 16-hectare myrtle forest, is also a popular spot for a picnic. If you need a **place to stay** in town, the pick of a basic bunch is *Residencial Montúfar*, on the Parque Principal (☏06/2290163; ❶–❸), which has a few en-suite rooms. **Buses** between Quito and Tulcán stop at San Gabriel on request.

About 18km from San Gabriel – halfway to Tulcán – a dirt road branches east at **Julio Andrade** making the descent down to Lumbaquí on the Baeza–Lago Agrio road in the Oriente. Enquire about **safety** before travelling this way – Colombian guerrilla activity has destabilized the area.

Reserva Guandera

Ten kilometres east of San Gabriel, the hamlet of **Mariscal Sucre** is the point of access for the **RESERVA GUANDERA**, protecting more than ten square kilometres of rare high-altitude cloudforest and páramo grassland along the ridge of Loma del Corazón. The **cloudforest** (3100–3600m) is the last significant tract of its type in northern Ecuador and, considering its altitude, is extraordinarily diverse in plants and wildlife, with more than 150 recorded **bird** species (a world record for this altitude), including the newly discovered chestnut-bellied cotinga and the swallow-tailed nightjar. Andean spectacled bears can occasionally be seen around the páramo, pumas roam the entire reserve and occasionally come close to the research station, and the dominant tree, the **Guandera**, towers up to 30m and casts out its roots from the top, creating a thick forest canopy rich in mosses, bromeliads and orchids. The Fundación Jatún Sacha manages the reserve and works closely with the community in Mariscal Sucre to encourage sustainable agriculture practices.

Access to the reserve is through Mariscal Sucre, easily reached from San Gabriel. The reserve's adobe research station is a 90-minute walk from the village, at 3330m on the edge of the forest (❼, including board), has several cosy dorms with shared baths, hot water and 24hr electricity, and **volunteers** are also welcome. You should give notice of your arrival in advance to Fundación Jatún Sacha in Quito, Eugenio de Santillán N34-248 and Maurián, Urbanización Rumipamba Casilla 17-12-867 (☏02/2432240, ⓦwww.jatunsacha.org).

Tulcán and around

TULCÁN (2950m), the provincial capital of Carchi, is a skittish frontier town, shifting people with ruthless efficiency across the Ecuadorian–Colombian border, 7km away. The main bus terminal has dozens of services primed for Quito, and every other car seems to be a taxi or *camioneta* shuttling to and from the frontier. Commerce thrives here, with **markets** on Thursdays and Sundays, and shops crammed with merchandise crowd the narrow streets. Since dollarization, however, and the resulting rise in domestic prices, business has not been so brisk. Where Colombians used to trawl the town looking for bargains, Ecuadorians are now the ones making the quick trip over the border in search of cheaper goods.

Most travellers don't linger in Tulcán, but if you've got time between buses, make sure you see the splendid **topiary gardens** in the town cemetery, or for longer layovers, you could visit the isolated **thermal springs**, set high in beautiful páramo near **Tufiño** to the west (depending on the security situation; see box below). The town's two spirited **fiestas** occur on April 11, for the cantonization of Tulcán, and November 19, to mark the day Carchi became a province.

Arrival and information

Buses from within Ecuador deposit you at the large terminal on Bolívar, from where it's 1.5km uphill northeast to the city centre and most of the hotels; a taxi will take you for $1. Regular **vans** travelling from the Colombian border usually drop people off at the Parque Ayora, though you can ask the driver to

---

Travel warning

Drug trafficking and Colombian **guerrilla activity** have destabilized areas around Tulcán. Always enquire with your embassy before travelling through border areas off the Panamericana. In Tulcán itself, you should always carry your **passport** and documents with you and resist exploring the streets at night. More than in most places in the country, the police here are encouraged to arrest and detain anyone who does not have their papers in order.

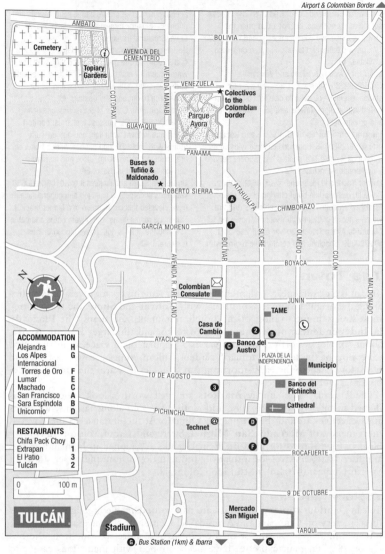

ACCOMMODATION

Alejandra	H
Los Alpes	G
Internacional
Torres de Oro	F
Lumar	E
Machado	C
San Francisco	A
Sara Espindola	B
Unicornio	D

RESTAURANTS

Chifa Pack Choy	D
Extrapan	1
El Patio	3
Tulcán	2

0   100 m

TULCÁN

Stadium

Ⓖ, Bus Station (1km) & Ibarra ▼   ▼ Ⓗ

take you on to the bus terminal for a little extra. The **airport** is a few kilometres east of the centre, but there is no bus service there and **taxis** cost about $3 each way. The cost of a trip to most destinations is $1, or $3.50 to the border. You can get basic tourist **information** at the municipal office at the cemetery (Mon–Fri 8am–1pm 2–5pm; ⓦ www.carchi.gov.ec), and there's another office at the Rumichaca border.

Accommodation

The fairly buoyant hotel industry in Tulcán makes for good-value rooms, many of which have cable TV, private bath and hot water as standard.

Alejandra Sucre and Quito ☎06/2981784. Not as spruce as it once was, but not a bad price for private parking and tidy rooms equipped with cable TVs, private baths and towels. Single rooms also available. ❷

Los Alpes Av J.R. Arellano and Veintimilla ☎06/2982235. Satisfactory hotel by the bus station, useful if you need to dive into a room on arrival late at night. Towels and soap, cable TVs and private baths. ❷

Internacional Torres de Oro Sucre and Rocafuerte ☎06/2980296. Upgraded cheapie with all the trimmings – cable TVs, phones and laundry service – and breakfast included. ❺

Lumar Sucre and Pichincha ☎&℉06/2980402. Reliable, businesslike hotel offering clean, well-furnished en-suite rooms with cable TVs and hot water – not all of them with windows, however. ❺

Machado Ayacucho and Bolívar ☎06/2984221, ℉2980099. Spacious and comfortable rooms with accoutrements like private baths, soap, towels and phones – plus the largest (cable) televisions in town. Breakfast included. ❻

San Francisco Bolívar and Atahualpa ☎06/2980760. Adequate budget option with hot water, cable TV and the choice of shared or private bath. Avoid the stale interior rooms and go for something bright and airy upstairs. ❷

Sara Espindola Corner of Sucre and Ayacucho ☎&℉06/2985925. The smartest, most comfortable place in town, with light and airy en-suite rooms with cable TVs and phones. Added bonuses are its sauna, steam room, disco and laundry service. Breakfast included. ❼

Unicornio Sucre and Pichincha ☎&℉06/2980638. Wall-to-wall carpets, a paint job and general facelift have elevated this old standard to a higher bracket. Fair-value rooms come with private baths and cable TVs, and the hotel is right above a good Chinese restaurant. ❸

The Town

Tulcán is a classic linear settlement strung out lengthways for several kilometres along the original route to Colombia, with **Bolívar** and **Sucre**, the two centre-most streets, home to most of the hotels, restaurants and shops. The **Plaza de la Independencia** marks the centre of town, and the larger **Parque Ayora**, about six blocks north down Bolívar, is a popular open space. With the great exception of the fabulous topiary gardens, Tulcán comes across as a cold and bleak town, where the early-morning sun struggles to warm the grey-concrete buildings and dusty streets.

The Thursday and Sunday **markets** are well worth a look, when Sucre is draped in billowy white textiles, and clothes are sold along Tarqui, with fruits and vegetables around the corner on Olmedo. At the entrance to the covered meat market of **Mercado San Miguel**, Sucre and Tarqui, you can find huge blocks of ice – used for cold medicinal drinks – wrapped in highland grasses and furry *frailejón* leaves for insulation, brought down from the upper slopes of Volcán Cumbal (4764m), just inside Colombia.

Topiary gardens

Tulcán's glorious **topiary gardens** are its one undeniable highlight, located at the cemetery on Cotopaxi and Avenida del Cementerio (daily 8am–5.30pm) a fifteen-minute walk northeast of the centre, or a short taxi ride from the bus station ($1). Fragrant cypresses have been snipped with meticulous care into more than a hundred different figures and patterns, including Arabian palms, Egyptian columns, Inca trapezoids and formal French lines.

Eating and drinking

Hearty **Colombian food** is making inroads – and not just for homesick nationals. Try a *bandeja paisa*, which comes in big portions piled high with vegetables, or the tasty *pollo sudado*, a flavoursome chicken stew less appetizingly translated on one menu as "sweaty chicken".

Chifa Pack Choy Sucre and Pichincha, ground floor of *Unicornio Hotel*, ☎06/2982713 or 2980638. Very popular Chinese place with big portions at low prices. Open late.

Extrapan Bolívar and Boyaca. The best bakery in town, boasting a tempting range of inexpensive buns and pastries, but also with full meals like chicken and rice at its restaurant and bar. Open until midnight and a good choice for a late-night bite.

Mamá Rosita Sucre and Chimborazo. Specializes in inexpensive *comida típica*, including *secos* and the many various permutations of pork.

El Patio Bolívar 5-47 and Pichincha. Excellent Colombian food in a restaurant with an identity crisis – interior thatched awning and bamboo-and-reed walls versus gaucho saddlebags, wagon wheels and swinging doors. Main courses for $2–5.

Tulcán Sucre 52-029 and Ayacucho. Unremarkable café, but a possibility if you're stuck for breakfast, with a $1 cheese roll, juice, coffee and eggs combo.

Listings

Airlines TAME, Sucre and Junín (☎06/2980675), or at the airport (☎06/2982850), has flights to Cali (12.30pm Mon, Wed & Fri) and Quito (3.30pm Fri & Sun); the office staff move to the airport branch around flight-departure times.

Banks and exchange Banco del Austro, Ayacucho and Bolívar, has a Visa and MasterCard ATM; Banco del Pichincha, on Plaza de la Independencia, has an ATM for Visa and Diners Club; and Casa de Cambio, Ayacucho and Bolívar, provides fair rates for changing Colombian pesos. Official money-changers

carry IDs and hang around the Plaza de la Independencia, dealing in dollars and pesos.

Consulate Colombia, Bolívar and Junín (Mon–Fri 8am–1pm & 2–3pm; ☎06/2980559).

Medical services Clínica del Volante, Bolívar 48-056 and Rocafuerte (☎06/2981889, ⓕ2980361), has 24hr emergency service, and Dr Winston Revelo there speaks a little English; the town hospital is at 10 de Agosto 9-17 (☎06/2980315).

Police Av Manabí and Guatemala ☎06/2980622.

West of Tulcán

The road west of Tulcán traverses remote and haunting páramo grasslands bordering the Reserva El Ángel (see p.163), before descending into subtropical forests around **Maldonado** and **El Chical**.

Geothermal activity deep below **Volcán Chiles** heats numerous thermal springs that bubble along the Colombian border around the village of **Tufiño**, 18km west of Tulcán; some are over the border and you may pass for the day to visit them, but formal crossings into Colombia must be made at Rumichaca (see p.170). This is a sensitive and potentially dangerous border area (see also the travel warning, p.166) and you should not travel here without prior enquiries with your embassy about the safety situation.

Buses to Tufiño (11 daily, 45min trip; last bus back 5pm), Maldonado and El Chical (daily at noon, plus Mon, Thurs & Sun at 1pm; 5hr and 5hr 15min respectively; bus returns early next morning) leave Tulcán from opposite the Instituto Tecnico Superior, R. Sierra and Avenida R. Arellana, near the Parque Ayora.

Aguas Hediondas

The best hot springs are **Aguas Hediondas** ("stinking waters"; $1), set at 3500m in an isolated valley split between Ecuador and Colombia, 6km west of Tufiño (1hr 30min walking). The sulphur-rich waters are thought to be highly curative – you'll leave from a long soak feeling fresh, revitalized but egg-scented.

At 8am every Sunday, a **bus** departs from Tulcán cathedral on Sucre and goes direct to the springs, returning in the afternoon. The Maldonado buses also pass the turn-off for the springs 2km beyond Tufiño.

Volcán Chiles and around

Fifteen kilometres west of Tufiño, just beyond the murky green waters of the **Lagunas Verdes** inside the Reserva El Ángel, the road rises above 4000m at **El Azuay**, its highest point, as it skirts **VOLCÁN CHILES** (4723m), which straddles the Colombian border to the north. El Azuay is 3km south of the summit (3hr up, 3hr down, 3hr back to Tufiño), a technically straightforward, but possibly foggy or snowy climb. Dress for the worst, hire a **guide** in Tufiño ($10–15), and take the 1:50,000 IGM **map** of Tufiño.

The Colombian border

Seven kilometres east of Tulcán, the international Rumichaca bridge marks the Colombian border; upstream, you can see the old, stone bridge crossing, fronted by two buildings, one of which is now a tourist information office (Mon–Fri 9am–5pm; ☎06/2984184). The modern customs controls on both sides (6am–10pm) are quite efficient and have a **telephone office** and **restaurant**.

To cross the border, you'll need an **exit stamp** from Ecuadorian customs, in the building marked *Migración*, and an **entry stamp** from the Colombians on the other side of the bridge (both stamps free); stamps are always required, even if only visiting Ipiales for the day. If you're arriving from Colombia, see Basics, p.59 for more on Ecuadorian entry requirements.

Colectivos to the border leave when full from the corner of Venezuela and Bolívar, on the Parque Ayora (10min; $0.80), while a **taxi** costs $3–4. On the other side of the bridge, Colombian *colectivos* make the 3km journey to **Ipiales**, a town with plenty of hotels and transport links, for $0.50, while taxis are around $3. *Colectivos* to **Tulcán** are $0.80 and stop at the Parque Ayora; a taxi from the border to anywhere in town should be $3–4, or from the park $1. Official **moneychangers** on both sides, offer acceptable rates for cash dollars and pesos, but always check the calculations and money you receive before handing anything over.

Travel details

Buses

Cayambe to: Ibarra (change in Otavalo); Otavalo (every 10–15min; 45min); Oyacachi (1 daily Mon, Wed, Fri–Sun; 1hr 45min); Quito, (every 5–10min; 1hr 20min).

Ibarra to: Baños (2 daily; 5hr 30min); Chachimbiro (2 daily; 1hr 15min); Cotacachi (every 30min; 30min); El Ángel (hourly; 1hr 30min); Esmeraldas (4 daily; 8hr 30min); Guayaquil (10 daily; 10hr); Guallupe (every 50min; 1hr 30min); La Esperanza (every 20min; 30min); Lita (every 50min; 2hr); Mira (hourly; 1hr); Otavalo (every 5min; 30min); Pimampiro (every 15min; 1hr 15min); Quito (every 10min; 2hr 30min); San Antonio de Ibarra (every 20min; 10min); San Lorenzo (every 50min; 3hr 30min); San Miguel de Yahuarcocha (every 20min; 15min); Santo Domingo (every 30min; 5hr 30min);

Tulcán (hourly; 2hr 30min); Urcuquí (every 30min; 30min); Zuleta (hourly; 50min).

Otavalo to: Apuela (5 daily; 2hr 30min); Cayambe (every 10min; 45min); Cotacachi (every 10min; 20min); García Moreno (3 daily; 4hr); Ibarra (every 5min; 30min); Peguche (every 20min; 15min); Peñaherrera (2 daily; 3hr 30min); Quito (every 10min; 2hr); San Pablo del Lago (every 15min; 20min).

Tulcán to: El Chical (1–2 daily; 5hr 15min); Huaquillas (1 daily; 18hr); Ibarra (every 5–10min; 2hr 30min); Maldonado (1–2 daily; 5hr); Quito (every 5–10min; 4hr 30min–5hr); Tufiño (11 daily; 45min).

Flights

Tulcán to: Cali, Colombia (3 weekly; 45min); Quito (2 weekly; 30min).

The central sierra

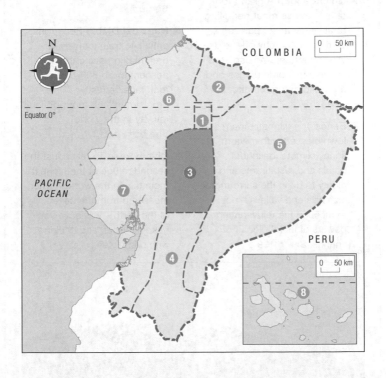

CHAPTER 3 # Highlights

* **Parque Nacional Cotopaxi**
The flawless cone of
Cotopaxi, one of the highest
active volcanoes in the world,
is an enticing prospect for
climbers and dominates the
country's favourite highland
park. **See p.178**

* **Quilotoa loop** A grand tour
of the sierra's most beguiling
rural landscapes, passing
vertiginous patchwork fields,
windswept páramo, isolated
indigenous communities and
the Quilotoa crater lake.
See p.187

* **Baños** The ultimate spa resort
town blessed with a warm,
sunny climate, delightful
hotels and restaurants and
plenty to do in the surrounding
lush hills and valleys – not
to mention the rejuvenating
powers of its fabulous hot
springs. **See p.199**

* **Salinas** High in the bucolic
hills above Guaranda,
this small indigenous
village is the very model of
coordinated community life,
with every soul employed
in its many cooperatives,
producing everything from
cheese to chocolate.
See p.211

* **Nariz del Diablo** Ecuador's
definitive train journey, a
breathtaking switchback
descent of an 800-metre
rock face, is justly
proclaimed "the most difficult
railway in the world".
See box, p.213

* **Chimborazo** To reach just the
second refuge of the highest
mountain in the world – when
measured from the centre
of the Earth – will leave you
gasping for air and choking
with pride. **See p.219**

▲ Cotopaxi

The central sierra

S outh of Quito, the two parallel chains of the Andes running the length of Ecuador rise to their most dramatic and spectacular heights in the **central sierra**, forming a double row of snowcapped peaks the nineteenth-century German explorer, Alexander von Humboldt, memorably christened "the avenue of the volcanoes". Eight of the country's ten highest summits are found here, including **Chimborazo** (6268m), **Cotopaxi** (5897m) and **El Altar** (5320m), towering over a series of inter-montane basins separating the two ranges. Sitting in these basins, at an altitude of around 2800m, are the region's principal towns – **Latacunga**, **Ambato** and **Riobamba** – strung north to south along the Panamericana. On a very clear day, the drive south from Quito through this parade of mountains facing each other across the highway ranks among the world's great road journeys. Frustratingly, the highest peaks are often lost in the low, grey clouds so typical of the region, and it's quite possible to travel right through the central sierra without spotting a single summit.

Yet even with these pinnacles hidden from view the landscape is stunning. Almost every mountain is covered by a dense patchwork of fields stretching up the slopes to extraordinary heights. Alternating strips of maize, barley, potatoes and *quinoa* (a cereal grown only in the Andes) form streaks of intense greens and muted yellows, oranges and limes, splashed with the occasional scarlet poncho of the *indígenas* tending the crops. This deeply rural region is the **indigenous heartland** of Ecuador, a place still brimming with Quichua-speaking communities whose lifestyles and work patterns have remained virtually unchanged for centuries. The economic and social focus of these communities – and the best place to get a feel for traditional Andean life – are the weekly **markets** held throughout the region. One of the largest and most exciting is at the small town of **Saquisilí**, near Latacunga, where hundreds of red- and pink-shawled *indígenas* fill the streets, examining mountains of fresh produce or stalls selling anything from rope to soap. Other notable markets include those at the village of **Zumbahua**, also near Latacunga, and the town of **Guamote**, south of Riobamba.

Most visitors stick to the more obvious destinations like **Parque Nacional Cotopaxi**, dominated by the perfect cone of the eponymous volcano, and the little town of **Baños**, whose warm climate, spectacular setting and thermal springs have made it a magnet for Ecuadorians and foreigners alike – despite the renewed activity of nearby Volcán Tungurahua. Another favourite with gringos is the famous **train ride from Riobamba**: it no longer runs all the way to Guayaquil, on the coast, but the hundred-kilometre stretch as far as the dramatic incline known as the **Nariz del**

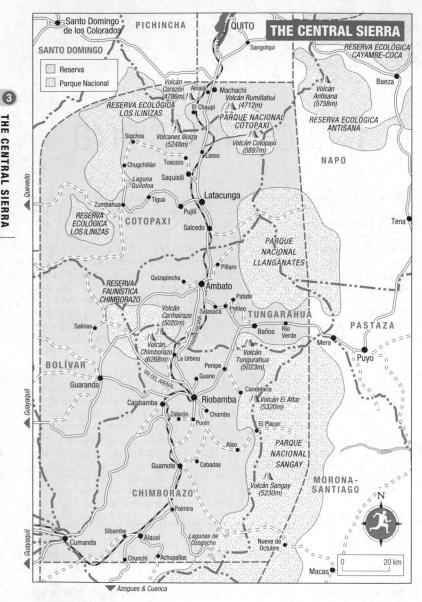

THE CENTRAL SIERRA

Diablo ("**Devil's Nose**") is maintained as a tourist service, offering fanatastic views and a thrilling ride.

To get the most out of the central sierra it's worth straying off the beaten track, into the more remote areas east and west of the Panamericana. Rewarding outings include a trip to the stunning crater lake of **Quilotoa**, approached from Latacunga via some of the most gorgeous scenery in Ecuador; a trip from Ambato to the isolated town of **Guaranda**, then on to the lovely, lost-in-the-hills village of **Salinas**; or an exploration of the valleys, lakes and peaks of **Parque Nacional Sangay**, a sprawling wilderness area east of Riobamba, approached from various access points scattered around the western cordillera.

Most of the region's highlights can be reached by local **buses**, which make their way along the most potholed and precarious dirt roads to dozens of highland villages. Otherwise, many towns on the Panamericana have *camioneta* cooperatives which you can hire to take you to and from outlying points. In addition, the ninety-kilometre stretch of **railway** between Quito and Latacunga has been recently overhauled, and now operates as a weekend tourist service (see p.120 for details). For **weather**, expect regular afternoon rainfall and plenty of cloud cover from September to May, with June to September significantly sunnier and drier. At this altitude it can be bitterly cold at any time of year, though when the sun comes out for long spells it's often warm enough for just a t-shirt.

Machachi, the Ilinizas and around

Heading south from Quito, the jolting, potholed Panamericana winds its way past a trail of dusty satellite towns, soon emerging into open, cultivated pastures flanked by the eastern and western cordilleras. If you're lucky with the weather, you'll be treated to superb views of Volcán Cotopaxi, its fat, white cone dominating the region. A handful of lesser peaks punctuate the surrounding landscape, including Volcán Corazón, opposite the small town of **Machachi**, and, a little further south, the two **Ilinizas**, popular with climbers wanting to acclimatize before tackling Cotopaxi.

Machachi

About 35km south of Quito along the Panamericana, a side road shoots east for a kilometre or so to **MACHACHI** (2950m). There's nothing special about the town itself, but its setting – within a ring of hills and volcanoes – is magnificent and makes it a good base for climbers eyeing up the Ilinizas, Corazón, Rumiñahui and Cotopaxi.

Arrival and information

Arriving in Machachi on one of the frequent Transporte Mejía **buses** from near the Villaflora trolley stop in Quito, you'll be dropped on the main street, Avenida Amazonas, leading down towards the square. **Internet** facilities in Machachi can be found on Colón, just off the main square.

Accommodation

The best **place to stay** is the friendly *Hospedería Refugio Chiguac* (☎02/2310396, ⓔgermanimor@punto.net.ec; ❹ including breakfast, other meals $6), at Los Caras and Colón, complete with beamed ceilings, a stag's head on the wall and a blazing fire. The rooms have shared bathrooms with hot water, and those on a budget can sleep in the dorm for $5 or **camp** in the garden for $3. *La Estancia Real* (☎02/2315760; ❷), two blocks south of Amazonas at Luis Cordero and Panzaleo, just off the market, has clean and spacious rooms with private bathrooms, but the service is variable. Northwest of town at Km415 on the railway, you'll find greater comfort and character at the **hacienda** *La Alegría* (☎02/2462310 or 09/9802526, ⓦwww.haciendalaalegria.com; ❼ including breakfast, **⑨** full board), an organic farm run by a family with a strong tradition of equestrianism. Guests can stay in the farmhouse or extension with en-suite rooms; activities on offer include horseriding.

The Town

Except for immersing yourself in the sprawling Sunday **market**, there's not a lot to do here, but you may as well wander around its **central square**, dominated by the handsome old **Teatro Municipal** and the white-walled **church**, whose interior is embellished by swirling, brightly coloured Baroque designs, and a gilded altar proclaiming "Fear of God". You could also visit the nearby **Güitig plant**, where Ecuador's most famous mineral water is bottled; it's 4km northeast of the town (head downhill along Pareja, the street one block west of the square; $2 there by *camioneta* from main square), and has a couple of swimming pools (daily 7.30am–3.30pm; $0.50) filled with cold, crystal-clear mineral water. On or around July 23, the town celebrates "**El Chagra**", the Andean version of the cowboy, with rodeos and parades.

Eating and drinking

For **restaurants**, try *El Pedregal* on Colón and Pareja, serving bargain staples including fried chicken, or the two *chifas* on the same street not far from the square. The best dining is at *Café de la Vaca* (☎02/2315012; daily 8am–5.30pm), on the Panamericana Km41, 4km south of Machachi, which serves excellent food ($5–10), especially beef, using produce from their dairy farm; it's busy at weekends.

Aloasí and El Chaupi

There are frequent bus connections from Avenida Amazonas in Machachi to the nearby villages of **Aloasí** and **El Chaupi**, as well as to Quito and Latacunga. Several **camioneta** cooperatives provide a faster alternative; pick one up on Amazonas, or call Cooperativa Luis Cordero (☎02/2314625) to collect you from an outlying base.

Just south of the turn-off to Machachi another side road branches west to the village of **ALOASÍ**, about 1km back from the highway. Apart from its beautiful rural setting, Aloasí's main interest is as a base for climbing **El Corazón**, an extinct volcano sitting immediately west of the village. Its 4788-metre summit can be reached in about five hours on a strenuous but straightforward hike by acclimatized and fully prepared walkers, following the track branching west from the **train station**, 1.5km west of the village square. A very appealing place to **stay** here is the delightful ⚹ *La Estación* (☎02/2309246; **⑤**), a nineteenth-century farmhouse right next door to the train station, with comfortable rooms, polished wooden balconies, open fires and great views of El Corazón, plus a newer annexe with individual fireplaces. You can practically step off the Quito–Latacunga train service (the "Machachi" stop; see p.175) into the *hostal*; otherwise, take a **camioneta** direct from Machachi ($2–3), or a **bus** to Aloasí's central square from Machachi (every 30min) followed by a half-hour walk up the cobbled road leading to the train station.

Continuing south down the Panamericana, you come to the signposted turning to the village of **EL CHAUPI**, sitting at the end of a seven-kilometre cobbled road, a thirty-minute **bus** ride from Machachi (every 30min). This rural, isolated village enjoys a privileged setting, with stunning views onto the Ilinizas to the west and Cerro Rumiñahui to the east. As the closest community to the Ilinizas, it's a popular base for climbers and there are a few simple **places to stay**. *Nina Rumy* (☎02/2864688; **❷**, half board **❸**), at the entrance to the village, features no-frills wooden rooms with bunks and beds, kitchen and shared bath. About 50m back from the church, *Hostal Llovizna* (☎09/9699068; ❸ including breakfast) provides simple rooms with bunks around a large seating area heated by two central fires, with a kitchen plus ping pong and billiards. The owner keeps the key for the Ilinizas mountain refuge, *Neuvos Horizontes*, and can provide information on weather and conditions. Another option is *Hacienda San José* (☎09/9737985; ❸ including breakfast), a working dairy farm about 3km along the road heading south from the main square, a 45-minute walk from the village (or take a *camioneta* for $2–3), where you can also go horseriding ($10 per half day).

Reserva Ecológica Los Ilinizas

Looming over the west side of the Panamericana is the sharp, jagged outline of the twin-peaked **Ilinizas**, two massive pyramids of rock about a kilometre apart joined by a wide saddle, which are the namesakes of an **ecological reserve** (entrance $5) set up in 1996 to protect just under 1500 square kilometres of rugged hilly terrain, páramo, lakes and cloudforest of the western cordillera.

The horseshoe-shaped reserve curves from the Ilinizas and El Corazón around the northern half of the Quilotoa loop to Zumbahua and beyond (see p.190). In its eastern region, the reserve is most easily **accessed** from El Chaupi on the road beyond *Hostal Llovizna* (see p.177), from where expeditions to climb the two Ilinizas most commonly depart. The larger **Iliniza Sur** (5248m) dominates the view from the Panamericana; it's an exciting technical climb only experienced mountaineers should attempt. Strong, confident hill walkers can manage **Iliniza Norte** (5126m), though there is a demanding scramble near the summit and the altitude can be really debilitating if you're not sufficiently acclimatized. The basics of climbing the Ilinizas are outlined below; the route on both peaks is difficult to follow in bad weather, so use of a guide is strongly advised (for recommended **climbing guides** in Quito see p.116).

Both Norte and Sur are approached from the *Neuvos Horizontes* **refuge** ($10; see above) at 4765m, just below the saddle between the two peaks. It has bunks for 25 people (bring a sleeping bag), cooking facilities, gas lighting and running water.

Climbing the Ilinizas

The easiest way of getting to the refuge is to take a 4WD **camioneta** (about $15 from El Chaupi; arrange through your *hostal*) to the car park lot known as **La Virgen**, marked by a shrine to the Virgin Mary, near the base of the Ilinizas, 9km from El Chaupi. From La Virgen, you continue on foot along a clearly marked trail to the refuge (2–3hr). To get to the refuge entirely **on foot** takes around five to seven hours from El Chaupi, or about four to six hours from *Hacienda San José*. Coming back, allow about three to four hours to get from the refuge down to El Chaupi.

From the refuge count on needing two to three hours to reach the summit of **Iliniza Norte**. The route is easy to follow, though very steep in parts. The bulk of it involves crossing a rocky ridge – via the unnervingly named Paso de Muerte ("Death Pass"), which requires great care in high winds and snow. The final climb to the summit, marked by an iron cross, involves some scrambling and a head for heights. Coming down is quite fast if you follow the scree slopes below the ridge (1hr 30min).

Climbing **Iliniza Sur** involves a steep ice climb and crossing crevasses, something that is becoming increasingly complicated with the rapidly changing state of the glaciers. You'll need plenty of experience and full mountaineering equipment. You should also wear a helmet to provide protection from falling rocks. It takes three to five hours to reach the summit depending on conditions, after an early start from the refuge.

Parque Nacional Cotopaxi

Cotopaxi's shape is the most beautiful and regular of all the colossal peaks in the high Andes. It is a perfect cone covered by a thick blanket of snow which shines so brilliantly at sunset it seems detached from the azure of the sky.

Alexander von Humboldt, 1802

Almost opposite the Ilinizas, the snowcapped, perfectly symmetrical **Volcán Cotopaxi** (5897m) forms the centrepiece of Ecuador's most-visited mainland national park, **Parque Nacional Cotopaxi** (daily 8am–5pm, last entrance 3pm; $10), covering 330 square kilometres of the eastern cordillera. With its broad, green base and graceful slopes tapering to the lip of its crater, Cotopaxi is the most photogenic of the country's thirty or so volcanoes, and on a clear day makes a dizzying backdrop to the stretch of highway between Quito and Latacunga. One of the highest active volcanoes in the world, it's also one of Ecuador's most destructive, with at least ten major eruptions since 1742 responsible for repeatedly destroying the nearby town of Latacunga. It's been fairly quiet since its last burst of activity in 1904, and today Cotopaxi is the most popular climb in Ecuador. Although the volcano dominates everything around it, and the aim of most visitors is simply to get a close-up view before turning home, a number of other attractions make a visit to the park very rewarding – namely the starkly beautiful **páramo**, all rolling moorland streaked by wispy clouds and pockets of mist. At an altitude of some 3500–4500m, the air here is thin and crisp, and the tundra-like vegetation is made up principally of cropped *pajonales* (straw-like grass) and shrubs, lichens and flowers adapted to harsh climates. Over ninety species of **birds** inhabit the park, including the tury hummingbird, Andean hillstar and Andean lapwing, while **mammals** include white-tailed deer, rabbits, Andean foxes and pumas.

Less inspiring are the stuffed animals on display at the **Museo Mariscal Sucre** (daily 8am–noon & 1–4pm), 10km from the main entrance checkpoint and often the first stop on a Cotopaxi tour. Outside the museum there's a short self-guided **trail** to introduce you to the páramo, but a more satisfying way to explore this habitat is on the one-hour footpath around the **Lago Limpiopungo** around 5km further up the road – a long, shallow lake lying at 3800m, surrounded by boggy reeds that provide a habitat for numerous birds. When the clouds part, its waters present a striking reflection of the 4712-metre peak of **Cerro Rumiñahui**, looming over it to the northwest, whose lower slopes can be reached by a path branching off the north shore of the lake. Most visitors continue a further 13km from here as far as the **parking area**, known as the Parqueador del Refugio, sitting at 4600m on the slopes of Cotopaxi. From here, a footpath leads steeply up a scree slope to the **José F. Ribas refuge** (4800m), a popular target for day visitors. It looks tantalizingly close, but if you're not acclimatized it can be a real struggle; count on taking 45 minutes to an hour to reach it. Once there, you can warm yourself with hot tea and snacks.

From a junction near the lake, one track goes to the northern park control, and another skirts northeast around Cotopaxi passing by several archeological sites, most notably **El Salitre**, the remains of an Inca *pucará*, or fortress, used to control access down to the Amazon basin. Apart from the atmospheric scenery,

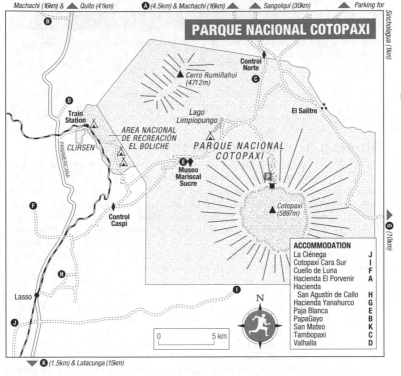

there's not a great deal to see here, though you can see some of the pieces recovered from the sites at the Museo.

Visiting the park

The park's most commonly used **entry point** is off the Panamericana, about 25km south of Machachi and 7km before the little village of Lasso. Here, a signposted turn heads east for 6km to the **Control Caspi** guard post, situated 3km before the park boundary proper. Unless you're on a **guided tour** (provided by many of the Quito operators listed on p.117, and outfits in Latacunga listed on p.185) you'll have to sort out your own **transport**. The easiest way to get here is to take a **bus** down the Panamericana to the main signposted entrance, from where you should be able to get a Cooperative Zona Verde **camioneta** (☎03/2719875) into the park (around $35 to the refuge car park, $60 return with waiting). Alternatively, you can hire *camionetas* from outside the train station in the nearby village of **Lasso** (Cooperativa de Camionetas de Lasso ☎03/2719493; $40 to the parking area, and $60 for the round trip, including waiting time), or from Machachi for around $55 (you'll probably be taken via the northern Pedregal access road). *Camionetas* can also be booked to pick you up from nearby hotels, or to collect you from the parking area at a prearranged time. If staying in a hotel near the park (see p.180), the staff should be able to arrange transport for you, but if you want to go all the way up to the refuge parking area make sure they've got a 4WD vehicle; it takes about 40 minutes to get from the Panamericana to Laguna Limpiopungo, and a little over an hour to get to the parking area below the refuge.

Camionetas

Note that unless otherwise stated, all prices quoted for **camioneta** rides are per group and not per person.

There's a second access point at the **Control Norte** at the north end of the park, reached by an eighteen-kilometre track (mostly cobbled) from Machachi via Pedregal (or a 30km dirt road from Sangolquí).

Staying in and around the park

There are a few **accommodation** options for those looking to **stay inside the park**. The Cotopaxi **refuge** (reserve beforehand in high season on ☏09/9902346; $17 per person) has bunks and mattresses, cold running water, electricity and basic cooking facilities; it's mainly used by climbers the night before they ascend. A much better choice for park visitors and those wishing to acclimatize is ⚵ *Tambopaxi* (☏09/9448223 or 02/2220241 in Quito, ⓦwww.tambopaxi.com; $23 for a dorm mattress; there's one en-suite four-person room ❽). At an altitude of 3750m some 2km from the Control Norte, it offers stunning views of Cotopaxi, well-insulated rooms with sheets and warm duvets and a good restaurant (lunch and dinner are around $10 each, and breakfast is $6.50). Staff here can also arrange guided hikes, horse and bike rides, transport to and from the park and offer **camping** facilities ($6 per person) that are far better than the park's own two official camping areas. The first of the park-run campsites (the only one with running water) is midway between the information centre and Laguna Limpiopungo; take the first left after the information centre and head for the concrete outbuilding. The second (with no facilities) is another 2–3km up the road towards Cotopaxi, this time signed to the right of the road. *Paja Blanca* (☏09/3971760 or 02/2314234; ❸ with breakfast), next to the Museo, offers basic cabins sleeping around a dozen with kitchenettes, mattresses and quilts, but no hot water; you can get meals at their restaurant. El Boliche also offers a few rudimentary places to stay (see p.182).

There's a far greater choice of hotels and haciendas just **outside** the park, most of which can be reached by *camioneta* from Lasso for a few dollars.

Cotopaxi Cara Sur At the end of the Ticatilín road (turn left/east, just south of Lasso) at the southern borders of the park; reservations with Agama Expediciones, Jorge Washington 425 and 6 de Diciembre in Quito ☏02/2903164 or 09/8002681, ⓦwww.cotopaxi-carasur.com. Simple adobe cabins built at 4000m on the southern slopes of Cotopaxi, with bunks and fireplace, another with kitchen and lounge, and outbuildings with hot-water showers. Also has a fixed camp at 4780m. Horses, treks and climbing packages available. ❸

Cuello de Luna ☏09/9700330 or 02/2905939, ⓦwww.cuellodeluna.com. Just south of the sign on the Panamericana announcing the main turn-off to the park, a signed 2km track leads west to this comfortable hotel with a choice of spacious cabins with private bathrooms and open fireplaces, or

semi-private mattresses in the loft ($16 per person). Breakfast included. ❻

Hacienda El Porvenir (also known as *Volcanoland*) 4.5km northwest of the Control Norte on the Pedregal road ☏/℗02/2231806, ⓦwww.volcanoland.com. An adobe lodge on the flanks of Rumiñahui with Cotopaxi's summit poking into sight beyond. Comfortable accommodation, cheaper with shared bath, good traditional food and plenty of activities including biking, hiking, riding, fishing and excursions to a nearby hacienda. Breakfast included. ❻

Hacienda San Agustín de Callo 5km south of the park's main entrance ☏03/2719160 or ☏/℗02/2906157, ⓦwww.incahacienda.com. This glorious colonial hacienda is built on the site of Inca ruins and incorporates some of the stonework into its structure, including the "Inca

Chapel" complete with original trapezoidal windows and walls of carved volcanic rock. The accommodation is luxurious and beautifully designed, with fireplaces in all the rooms and even in some bathrooms. Biking, trekking, horseriding and market visits are offered. Rates include some meals and a day tour. ➒

Hacienda Yanahurco 10km east of the park ☎02/2445248, ⓦwww.haciendayanahurco.com. A huge, working cattle ranch in an isolated valley location offering twelve guest rooms, all with private bath, hot water and fireplace or heater; range of riding, fishing and hiking packages also available. ➎

Hostería La Ciénega ☎03/2719093, reservations in Quito ☎02/2541337, ⓦwww.hosterialacienega .com. Just south of Lasso, reached along a 1km side road branching west from the highway, this seventeeth-century hacienda boasts an exquisite private chapel and beautiful gardens. The rooms in the main building have lots of character but are a little faded; those in the modern annexe are enlivened by cosy log fires. ➑

🏃 **PapaGayo** 500m up a turning on the right (west), 15km past the toll south of Machachi ☎02/231002 or 09/99462268, ⓦwww.hosteria -papagayo.com. Charming old farmhouse on attractive grounds, reinvented as a relaxed and funky countryside hangout. Popular and a good meeting place, with a stove-heated sitting room and restaurant, tasty food, internet, barn bar, farm animals and numerous activities arranged by the friendly managers. Camping costs $4, dorm beds are $8, and then a choice of rooms according to budget. ➌–➏

San Mateo A few kilometres south of Lasso at Km 75 on the Panamericana ☎03/2719015, ⓦwww.hosteriasanmateo.com. An attractive and compact country hotel offering rooms or four-person cabañas with mountain views, private baths and hot water, and a restaurant serving organic home-grown produce. Activities on offer include

Climbing Cotopaxi

It's possible to **climb Cotopaxi** with little or no technical mountaineering experience, but high altitude, crevasses and steep sections of snow and ice mean it's something not to be taken lightly. You'll need to be fit, strong, fully acclimatized and have a good, reliable and experienced **guide**, preferably certified by ASEGUIM (Asociación Ecuatoriana de Guías de Montaña), particularly now that rapid deglaciation is changing routes and conditions. Many climbing and tour companies in Quito offer guided climbs up Cotopaxi, and can rent out equipment – see p.117 for a list of recommended companies. Typical **costs** are around $180 to $250 per person depending on group size, with properly qualified guides ($150 upwards otherwise), including all equipment, transport and food.

Usually, you arrive at the **refuge** on Cotopaxi the afternoon before climbing (see opposite), and will probably be taken to practise crampon and ice-axe techniques at a nearby glacier if you're inexperienced. Then you'll try to catch a few hours' sleep before being woken at around midnight for a 1am start, the idea being to summit at sunrise and descend before the heat of the day makes the snow and ice unstable and unsafe. The ascent takes, on average, six to eight strenuous hours, and involves negotiating several crevasses and climbing on snow and ice, including a couple of short sections where you'll be front pointing (climbing steep ice with the front spikes of your crampons). The effort is rewarded by exhilarating views from the top onto all of Ecuador's major peaks and down to the wide crater, steaming with sulphurous fumes. The descent normally takes three to four hours.

If you plan to do this climb, the importance of **acclimatizing** properly beforehand cannot be stressed enough; staying in and around the park for a few days, going for plenty of hikes in the area, and climbing a couple of smaller peaks will greatly aid your summit attempt while reducing the risk of developing altitude sickness. Note that if you're walking up to the refuge from the Panamericana it's a 30km-plus muscle-sapping slog that will tire you out before the climb proper; break the hike into manageable pieces over a few days, rest and acclimatize. Cotopaxi can be climbed all year round, but December and January are regarded as the **best months**, with February to April a close second. The late summer (Aug–Sept) can also be good, but is likely to be windy.

riding, climbing, hiking and milking cows on a neighbouring farm. **⑦**
Valhalla 19km south of Machachi, shortly before the CLIRSEN turning, 1km up signposted drive (gate closed to vehicles 6pm–8am unless by arrangement) ☎09/3998391 or 02/2554984 in Quito, ⓦwww.hostelvalhalla.com. Bright-orange hostel on a hillside at 3500m, commanding fantastic views of 16 nearby peaks from the rooftop

terrace, including Cotopaxi rising behind. Good acclimatization base with rooms available for a range of budgets, depending on extras like private bath or wood-burning stove, while dorm bunks cost $9 and camping $5. Run by Moggely Climbing, so plenty of scope for arranging activities. Meals available and discounts for children and SAE members. **④–⑦**

Area Nacional de Recreación El Boliche

Adjoining the northwest border of Parque Nacional Cotopaxi, the small 200-hectare **Area Nacional de Recreación El Boliche** (daily 7am–4.30pm; $10 ticket interchangeable with Cotopaxi's) mainly caters to family groups and Quito weekenders. There are picnic tables, restaurants, barbecue spots and short self-guided **hiking trails** up towards Cerro Rumiñahui (see p.178) or through its forests. El Boliche also has a **train station**, the penultimate stop on the weekend Quito–Latacunga tourist service (see p.120), and two **interpretation centres**, one by the entrance covering the history of the recreation area, and another a five-minute walk up the hill past a field of llamas and alpacas, having more captivating displays on Ecuador's protected areas and habitats.

The **access** to El Boliche is on the Panamericana some 17km south of Machachi, marked by a huge sign for "CLIRSEN", a satellite-tracking station set up by NASA in 1960. From the turning it's 3km or a 30-minute walk to the Boliche entrance post. You can **stay the night** at El Boliche at some simple cabañas (**②**) that have showers but no bedding (bring a sleeping bag), or at various campsites, two of which have hot showers ($5 per tent).

Latacunga and around

Some 20km south of the turn-off to Cotopaxi, **LATACUNGA** (2800m) is a charming, mid-sized market town huddled on the east bank of the Río Cutuchi. With its handsome, colonial-style buildings and bustling streets, it makes an agreeable base from which to organize forays into this part of the sierra, in particular to the not-to-miss crater lake at Quilotoa (see p.191), or to the hectic indigenous market in nearby **Saquisilí** (see p.186). It also makes an alternative launchpad for trips to Cotopaxi, well catered for by the town's tour operators. If your visit coincides with either of the town's two famous and colourful **Mama Negra** fiestas, one on September 24 and the other on the weekend before November 11 (see box, p.184), you'll be treated to a riotous display of parades and street dancing. Otherwise, Latacunga's charms are a good deal more sedate, and can be enjoyed in an afternoon's wander around town.

Arrival and information

Buses coming into town will drop you at or near the large **bus station** on the Panamericana – on the opposite side of the river from the town – from where you can catch a **taxi** to the centre ($1–2), or walk there in about ten minutes over the 5 de Junio bridge. The recently restored **train station**, where you'll arrive if you take the weekend train from Quito (see p.120), is three blocks north of here, just west of the Panamericana.

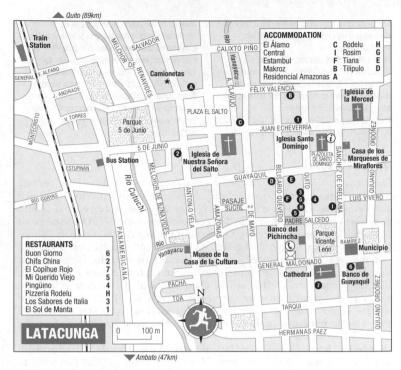

Information is available at the Captur office by the Iglesia Santo Domingo at Sánchez de Orellana and Guayaquil (Mon–Fri 8am–noon & 2–5pm; ☎03/2814968), and a small office upstairs at the bus station, both of which keep brochures, maps and leaflets in Spanish. **Internet** cafés are on the pedestrianized strip of Padre Salcedo and on Quito near Rodelu.

Accommodation

There's a cluster of **hotels** on the Panamericana, around the intersection of 5 de Junio, but you're better off continuing into the centre, where you'll find a choice of decent budget and mid-range places, but no real upmarket options.

El Álamo 2 de Mayo and Echeverría ☎03/2812043. Offers light, comfortable rooms with flowery curtains, TVs and decent en-suite bathrooms and has a restaurant open all day from breakfast. ❸

Residencial Amazonas Félix Valencia 4-67, Plaza El Salto ☎03/2812673. Best of a grubby bunch of bottom-dollar hotels around the noisy market square. ❶

Central Sánchez de Orellana and Padre Salcedo ☎03/2802912. Established hotel with clean, spacious, carpeted rooms with private bath and TV, run by a friendly owner. For those with a car, the hotel also has its own parking – something of a rarity in Ecuador. ❸

Estambul Belisario Quevedo 6-44 ☎03/2800354. Spotless little hotel with wooden floors, good hot showers (private or shared) and quiet rooms around a courtyard. Laundry facilities and cafeteria also available. ❸

Makroz Félix Valencia 8-56 and Quito ☎03/2800907, ⓔhotelmakroz@latinmail.com. Currently the most comfortable in town, this modern hotel is equipped with cable TV, carpets, laundry service, games room, parking and restaurant. Breakfast included. ❻

Rodelu Quito 16-31 ☎03/2800956, ⓔrodelu @uio.telconet.net. Comfortable, well-run hotel with neatly kept rooms, good bed linen and curtains, en-suite bathrooms, phone and TV in rooms and private parking. The rooms on the upper floors are cheaper and less well appointed. Breakfast included. ❸–❺

Rosim Quito 16-49 and Padre Salcedo ☎03/2802172, ⓕ800853. Spacious, clean rooms with firm, comfortable beds and large en-suite bathrooms. Those at the back of the hotel are very quiet. Discounts for YHI members. ❸

Tiana Guayaquil 5-32 and Quito, ☎03/2810147 or 08/5737829, ⓦwww.hostaltiana.com. Friendly,

well-run hostel in a handsome old building offering comfortable dorm beds ($8) and private doubles, all with shared bath. Also comes with free wi-fi and a café serving good coffee and light meals. ❸

Tilipulo Guayaquil and Belisario Quevedo ☎03/2810611. Bright, tidy rooms with wooden floors, warm bedding and tiny bathrooms. Friendly management, but avoid the corner rooms, which get the worst of the noise from the busy inter-section below. ❸

The Town

Despite its colonial look, most of Latacunga's architecture dates from the late nineteenth or early twentieth century – a fact owed to Cotopaxi's repeated and devastating eruptions, which have seen the town destroyed and rebuilt five times since its foundaiton in 1534, most recently in 1877. The focal point of town is the **Parque Vicente León**, a leafy square enclosed by iron railings that is locked after dark. A **cathedral**, with whitewashed walls both inside and out, dominates the south side, while the austere **municipio** flanks the east side. A couple of blocks north the twin-towered **Iglesia Santo Domingo** is the most impressive of the town's churches, with its Grecian pillars and extravagantly painted interior covered with swirling blue, green and gold designs. Right in front of it, on the little Plazoleta de Santo Domingo, you'll find a small **artesanía market** selling knitwear, *shigras* and other souvenirs (closed Thurs & Sun).

Opposite the *plazoleta* is the **Casa de los Marquesas de Miraflores** on Sánchez de Orellana and Guayaquil (Mon–Fri 8am–noon & 2–6pm; free), an elegant colonial building and museum with an "archeological-industrial" exhibition displaying pieces recovered from a local textile mill (including the bones of a small boy), which the 1877 Cotopaxi eruption destroyed. The town's daily **main market** is a huge, outdoor affair spreading over Plaza El

---

Mama Negra fiestas

A highlight of the Latacunga year is its renowned **Mama Negra fiestas**, commemo-rated twice in religious and secular festivals within a few weeks of each other. The fiesta is thought to have derived from the expulsion of the Moors from Spain or the astonish-ment of the local *indígenas* on seeing black people (the slaves that the Spanish had brought here to work in nearby mines) for the first time. The colourful **religious celebration** (also called the *Santísima Tragedia*) is held on September 24, with brightly costumed paraders and various mischief-making characters: the white-robed *huacos*, the whip-wielding *camisonas*, and the belle of the ball, a blacked-up man gaudily dressed as a woman – the Mama Negra. In the midst of this, the focus is supposedly the Virgin of the **Iglesia de la Merced** (known as Our Lady of the Volcano because she is believed to have saved the city many times from Cotopaxi's eruptions), who is paraded through the town and up to **El Calvario**, the concrete monument on the hill to the east of town. The flamboyant **secular Mama Negra festival** usually begins on the Saturday before November 11 (though the big parades have been scheduled for the Friday in recent years to discourage excessive drinking) and features the same cheerful costumes and characters, marching bands and street dancing. The festive mood continues with cultural events and bullfights until November 11, the day of Latacunga's **independence**.

Crafts and markets

The market in Ecuador is far more than just a place to do the shopping: it's the great weekly gathering that binds together diverse communities. People flock from outlying villages to meet, catch up on news, share stories, and if there's time left, buy and sell wares and produce. You won't be filling your bags at most – the real thrill is to be present at the week's most important social occasion and succumb to an all-out sensory blitz – but some specialist markets do provide the perfect opportunity to stock up on a boggling range of artesanía (handicrafts), including sumptuous weavings, elaborate carvings and much more.

Weavings on display, Otavalo market ▲

Panama-hat shop, Montecristi ▼

Weaving

Ecuador's best-known craft is **weaving**. The most famous examples come from Otavalo, where **textiles** have long been one of the principal attractions at its market. The highest quality weavings are still made by traditional means using backstrap looms by the master-craftsmen of the Otavalo valley. Although you'll also see plenty of tourist-oriented chunky woollen hats, gloves and sweaters bulk woven on electric looms, the home-woven belts, blouses, hair wraps, shawls, ponchos and hats are as much a part of indigenous traditional dress as ever.

Further down the sierra, Salasaca is famous for its colourful **tapestries**, and villages in Cotopaxi province produce **shigras**, bags made from woven Cabuya fibres. Further south, around Cuenca, you'll find beautiful **ikat ponchos**, made by the time-consuming process of weaving tie-dyed threads.

The country's most famous woven export is the **Panama hat** – an unfortunate misnomer, as the *toquilla* fibres used to make the hats uniquely grow to the right condition only in Guayas and Manabí provinces in coastal Ecuador. Weavers toil in dimly lit workshops in and around Montecristi and in the Cuenca area to produce exquisite *superfinos* for the world's rich and famous – as well as more affordable hats for the rest of us.

Woodcarving

There's a strong tradition of **woodcarving** in San Antonio de Ibarra in the northern sierra, which enjoys a reputation for some of the best work on the continent. Far removed from the graceful lines and intricate chiselling of San Antonio's figures and furniture, you'll find unfussy, hand-carved utilitarian forms such as trays and spoons at many other places like Oyacachi or the Plaza Rotary market in Cuenca.

Heading eastwards to the Andean foothills of the **Oriente**, brightly coloured balsa parrots and toucans are made in all sizes, from the smallest keyrings to mammoth carvings you'd have trouble hauling through the front door. Further into the Oriente, blowpipes, bows and arrows and knitted fibre bags are as much tools of the trade as handicrafts, though necklaces and ceremonial headdresses are often available too (avoid those made from bird feathers; it's illegal to export them). **Tagua nuts**, also known as vegetable ivory, are the sustainable alternative to the real thing, and are carved throughout Ecuador into animal miniatures.

▲ Woodcarver at work, Oyacachi

▼ Tagua-nut hand-carved chess set

Other crafts

Cotacachi, near Otavalo, and Quizapincha, outside Ambato, are national centres for **leather goods**, both brimming with belts, bags and jackets. In other highland towns such as La Esperanza, outside Ibarra, you can order bespoke riding gear, or buy made-to-measure **embroidered** textiles, tablecloths and blouses.

Other towns have their own specialities. Chordeleg, not far from Cuenca, is famous for its jewellery and precious metals, while in Calderón, north of Quito, **bread dough** is used for making colourful figurines, originally baked as edible offerings to place on graves during the Day of the Dead, but now varnished, painted and used as decorations year round. The charming naïve **paintings** of sierra life and legends can be bought in all the tourist centres, but the style developed in the remote community of Tigua in Cotopaxi province, where there is a dedicated gallery.

▼ Bread-dough figurines

Agreeing a price, Otavalo market ▲

Saquisilí market ▼

Sealing the deal

Haggling is an art that's second nature to local stall holders – they can make you think you're walking away with a bargain no matter how much you've paid. What's more, prices in Ecuador are generally such that, relative to home, you'll get a great deal even if you're hopeless at negotiating. In craft markets, you should find lower prices than in most of the Quito boutiques, but you'll still be expected to haggle.

It's best to treat the process as a good-natured conversation rather than an argument, a kind of circling courtship dance that eventually leads to a marriage of opposing prices. Badgering endlessly over a few cents definitely kills the fun; both parties should end the transaction smiling.

Market Days

In Ecuador, a market is never very far away, and you can visit one any day of the week.

For crafts, Otavalo's artesanía market is superb and open every day, but at its best on Saturdays. If you're less keen on shopping but still want to soak up some ambience, try Saquisilí's enormous market; it takes up nearly every plaza, street and pavement in town and is jam-packed with poncho-clad customers.

Sunday Cotacachi, Salasaca (crafts); Sangolquí, Machachi, Santo Domingo (general); Cañar, Saraguro (indigenous markets); Parque El Ejido, Quito (fine art)

Monday Ambato, El Ángel (general)

Tuesday Latacunga (general)

Wednesday Pujilí (indigenous market); Otavalo (crafts)

Thursday Saquisilí, Guamote (indigenous markets); Tulcán (general)

Friday Zalarón (indigenous market)

Saturday Otavalo (crafts & general); Zumbahua (indigenous market); Latacunga, Riobamba (general)

Salto (also known as Plaza Chile), off Avenida Amazonas, and is at its liveliest on Saturdays. Just off the market, on the corner of Vela and Padre Salcedo, is the **Museo de la Casa de la Cultura** (Tues–Fri 8am–noon & 2–6pm, Sat 8am–3pm; $0.50), incorporating the ruins of an eighteenth-century watermill, the Molinos de Montserrat, built by Jesuits but destroyed by a succession of natural disasters. It now houses an ethnographic museum covering popular art, archeology and local folklore.

Eating and drinking

For **drinking and nightlife**, try the bars on the Padre Salcedo pedestrian walkway or head to *Galaxy* (Fri & Sat), Latacunga's best club, on a hill at the fringes of the town at Barrio El Mirador, with music pumping out over several dancefloors.

Buon Giorno Corner of Sánchez de Orellana and General Maldonado, Parque Vicente León. Long-established pizzeria in a good location; pleasant enough dining room and large portions. Opens 1pm.
Chifa China Antonio Vela and 5 de Junio 76-85. Clean and cheap Chinese restaurant, serving a mixture of Ecuadorian and Asian dishes. Usually open when everywhere else has closed for the night.
El Copihue Rojo Quito and Tarqui. Superior Chilean-owned restaurant with colourful weavings and dramatic landscapes on the wall, mainly serving steaks, chops and mixed grills. Closed Sun.
Mi Querido Viejo Salcedo and Quito. Laid-back reastaurant with great antique decor set around an old furnace. Specializes in ribs and shrimp, and has set *almuerzos* at $2.50.

Pingüino Quito 73-102 and Guayaquil. A good stop for snacks, coffee, milkshakes and ice creams.
Pizzería Rodelu Quito 16-31, in the *Hotel Rodelu*. Tasty pizzas cooked in a wood-fired oven in the hotel dining room. Also a good place for breakfast. Closed Sun.
Los Sabores de Italia Quito and Guayaquil. Simple restaurant serving the best pizzas in Latacunga, as well as delicious, hot sandwiches made of pizza dough with locally produced cheese, olive oil and black pepper.
El Sol de Manta Corner of Echeverría and Quito. Fast and efficient *cevichería* mainly doing inexpensive *almuerzos*, seafood and *encebollados*, but also specialities such as *guatita* (tripe). Often busy at lunch, and closes at 3.30pm.

Listings

Banks Banco del Austro (Visa and MasterCard), on the corner of Quito and Guayaquil; Banco de Guayaquil (Visa and MasterCard), on General Maldonado and Sánchez de Orellana; Banco Pichincha on the *parque* (MasterCard). Laundry Su Lavandería on Hermanas Paez and Lavatex on Gallindo and Amazonas.
Post office Corner of Belisario Quevedo and General Maldonado; the Andinatel office is next door.
Tour operators Expediciones Volcanroute on Guayaquil and Quevedo (☎03/2812452, ✉volcanroute@hotmail.com) for treks around Cotopaxi, Quilotoa and the Ilinizas; Neiges, at Guayaquil 5-19 and Belisario Quevedo (☎03/2811199, ⓦwww.neigestour.com.ec), for climbing and walking trips to Cotopaxi and the

Ilinizas, horseback trekking, fishing trips and day-trips to Laguna Quilotoa; Selvanieve (☎03/2802529 or 2812895), at Padre Salcedo and Quito, a Scottish–Ecuadorian company offering various climbing and trekking tours; Tovar Expeditions, on Guayaquil and Quito (☎03/2811333, ⓦwww.expeditionstovar.com), specializes in climbing and is run by an ASEGUIM guide; and TribuTrek, at *Hostal Tiana*, Guayaquil 5-32 and Quito (☎03/2810147, ⓦwww.tributrek.com), a Dutch–Ecuadorian company offering hiking tours around Quilotoa, Cotopaxi and Chimborazo. Several hotels offer guided day-trips up to Cotopaxi (around $45 per person depending on group size, including lunch) and to Laguna Quilotoa ($45), including the *Estambul* and the *Central*.

Moving on from Latacunga

The bus station, on the other side of the river over the 5 de Junio bridge, is well connected for most local and many interprovincial locations. A few

▲ Saquisilí market

major destinations such as Riobamba and Cuenca do not have services that stop at the terminal; you can hail these buses as they pass on the Panamericana nearby. Alternatively, you could take one of the regular buses to Ambato and change there. On Thursdays, the day of the Saquisilí market, many local destinations are diverted to that town and leave from there rather than Latacunga. For details about transport around the Quilotoa loop see the box on p.188.

Saquisilí

A twenty-minute bus ride northwest of Latacunga, **SAQUISILÍ** is a quiet, slightly ramshackle little town that explodes into life with its **market** – one of the biggest in the highlands – every Thursday morning. It fills seven plazas, each one specializing in different types of goods. There's an extraordinary breadth of merchandise for sale, supplying just about every consumer need of the hundreds of *indígenas* who journey here from all over the central sierra. Lining the pavements are mountains of vegetables balanced on wooden crates, sacks full of grain, mounds of fluorescent yarns used for weaving shawls, kitchen utensils, finely woven baskets and curiosities, including stuffed animals from the Oriente. Also on Thursday, about a ten-minute walk north of the centre, dozens of sheep, cows, pigs and the odd llama exchange hands in the **animal market** (before dawn to around 10am), dotted with women clutching tangled cords attached to squealing piglets.

Away from the market, the **church** on the main square is worth a look. Its original facade has been preserved, but everything behind it was replaced in the 1970s – the interior is quite striking, with its brightly painted windows, blue-and-white metal roof and minimalist altar. Otherwise, there's little else to do in Saquisilí, and nothing to draw you here outside market day.

Practicalities

It's easy to come in for the morning from Latacunga, with **buses** leaving every five minutes on market day (every 10min other days) from the bus station. Still, checking into a **place to stay** on Wednesday night allows you to catch the action and the animal market early. On the attractive *parque central* (about the only square not part of the market), the *San Carlos* on Simón Bolívar and Sucre (☎03/2721057; ❺) offers bright, clean rooms with private bath, electric shower and attractive views of the church and hills behind. A couple of blocks south at the corner of Simón Bolívar and Pichincha, *Salón Pichincha* (☎03/2721247; ❷) is small and very basic, and also has an an inexpensive restaurant. Among the very few other restaurants in town is *Cevichería Paty*, next to the bakery a few doors down from the *San Carlos*, which only irregularly has seafood despite its name. Otherwise, try your luck at the unnamed corner canteens or countless pavement food stalls.

The Quilotoa loop

Some 90km west of Latacunga and the Panamericana, in one of the most beautiful parts of the Andes, the isolated **Laguna Quilotoa** is a spectacular emerald-coloured crater lake. It's most directly approached along the road from Latacunga to Quevedo (see p.351), via the villages of **Pujilí**, **Tigua** and **Zumbahua**. Once there, you can take a different route back, heading north to the villages of **Chugchilán** and **Sigchos**, then southeast to rejoin the Panamericana near the market village of Saquisilí. This route – totalling around 200km – often referred to

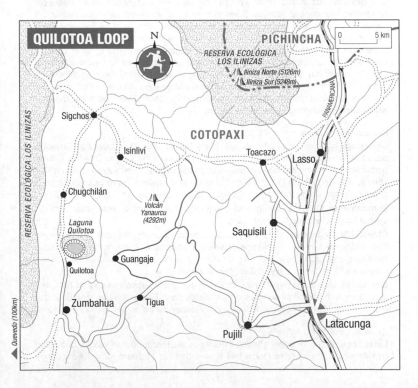

as **the Quilotoa loop** or the Quilotoa circuit, can just as easily be done in the opposite direction to that described below. If you can, try to time your stay in Zumbahua with the Saturday-morning **market**, one of the most fascinating in the sierra, or one of the major Catholic festivals like Epiphany or Corpus Christi (see opposite for dates); both are wonderful spectacles.

You'll find **accommodation** in Tigua, Zumbahua, Quilotoa, Chugchilán and Sigchos, but most of it is pretty basic, with the main exceptions of Tigua and Chugchilán. If you want to sleep in the simpler places, particularly at Quilotoa at 3850m, a warm **sleeping bag** is a welcome bonus as it gets very cold at night. Count on spending a minimum of two days to do this route; it's much better to take three or more nights if you want to do it at a more relaxing pace, which will also give you time to explore the magnificent countryside with hikes or horse rides. If you are driving around the loop in your own vehicle, there are **filling stations** in Sigchos and Zumbahua stocking extra and diesel.

Pujilí

Heading west from Latacunga for 12km leads to the pretty little market town of **PUJILÍ**, whose centre is marked by a beautifully tended **plaza**, presided over by a handsome church with an intricately carved wooden door. Pujilí has a large

---

Travelling around the Quilotoa loop

When planning **bus** transport around the loop, it's the section between Zumbahua and Sigchos that is the most infrequently serviced and needs most attention; timetables change and journey times can vary, so make enquiries beforehand if travelling on a tight itinerary. Buses on the loop are often very full, especially on market days; get there early and be prepared for a squeeze. An alternative is to take a **camioneta** to your first overnight stop from Latacunga, and lifts to other parts of the loop with local pick-up owners in Zumbahua, Chugchilán and Sigchos (this will be very dusty if you're travelling in the back); there's also an early-morning **milk truck** running between Sigchos and Chugchilán you can ride on. If time's short, consider renting a vehicle or going with a Quito- or Latacunga-based **tour company**, many of which offer two-day trips around the circuit.

Buses: clockwise

Latacunga to: Zumbahua (1hr 45min). Every 30min (until 7pm) buses to Quevedo pass the turn-off to Zumbahua, a five-minute walk from the village. One bus (Transportes Illiniza) leaving at noon passes through the village on its way to Quilotoa (2hr 15min), and Chugchilán (3hr 45min). There are also several Vivero buses that pass through Zumbahua on their way to Quilotoa, leaving at 10am, 11.30am and 12.30pm.
Zumbahua to: Quilotoa (30min) and Chugchilán (1hr 30min). Several daily from the central square; last one leaves 1–2pm.
Chugchilán to: Sigchos (1hr). Daily at 3am, except Sunday. Besides this, there are two additional buses on Thursday (between noon and 2pm), one on Saturday (between noon and 2pm) and four on Sunday (4am, 4.30am, 5.30am and noon). Latacunga (3hr 45min): daily at 3am, Sun at noon.
Sigchos to: Latacunga (2hr 15min). Daily, leaving hourly between 3am and 7am, and at 2.30pm, with additional services on Wednesday and Friday (1.30pm) and Saturday (10.15am, 12,30pm, 1.30pm & 2.30pm) and Sunday (same as Sat, plus one at 4pm).

Buses: counterclockwise

Latacunga to: Sigchos (2hr 15min). Regular buses throughout the day. Chugchilán (3hr 45min). A Transportes Iliniza bus leaves daily at 11.30am (buy tickets early),

Sunday **market** and a smaller one on Wednesday, held on Plaza Sucre, two or three blocks from the main square. You'll find everything from vast quantities of plastic containers to the characteristic mountains of fresh produce laid out in front of indigenous and *mestizo* women sitting cross-legged on the ground. While you're here, try a bit of *panela*, enormous "loaves" of coarse brown sugar, sold at several stalls. If you're in the area around Corpus Christi (a moveable feast in June, on the first Thursday after Trinity Sunday), don't miss the town's celebrations of this **festival**, involving fabulous costumes and masked dancers, as well as competitions to climb up wavering poles many metres high to retrieve prizes tied to their tops.

If you want to **stay**, you'll find basic but adequate rooms at *Residencial Pujilí* at Vicente Rocafuerte 5-17 (☎03/2723649; ❷), a couple of blocks from the plaza, towards the market. It's above a roast-chicken **restaurant**, one of a number of basic places serving food around town. There are **buses** between Pujilí and Latacunga every ten minutes, plus regular services to Quevedo to get to Zumbahua.

Tigua

From Pujilí, the road climbs higher and higher, giving stunning views down to the valley floor. As you ascend, the temperature begins to drop noticeably and

with additional Saturday services (10.30am & 2.30pm). On Thursday this bus leaves from Saquisilí at 11.30am (buses leave every 5–10min from Latacunga to Saquisilí). Isinliví (around 3hr). Daily except Thursday and Saturday at 12.15pm and 1pm; Saturday at 11am and 12.15pm. On Thursdays buses leave Saquisilí at 11am and 11.30am.

Sigchos to: Chugchilán (1hr), Quilotoa (2hr) and Zumbahua (2hr 45min). Daily at 1.30pm and 2.30pm, with additional services on Wednesday (4am) and Friday (5am).

Chugchilán to: Quilotoa (1hr), Zumbahua (1hr 45min), Latacunga (3hr 45min). Daily buses at 4am, except Sunday at 6am and 10am. Also buses towards Quevedo, passing only Quilotoa and Zumbahua leave on Wednesdays at 5am, Fridays at 6am, Saturdays at 4am, and Sundays at 9am and 9.30am.

Zumbahua to: Latacunga (1hr 45min). Hourly buses from the main Quevedo–Latacunga road, plus buses from Chugchilán, via Quilotoa, which leave Zumbahua's plaza at 5.30am daily, except Sundays at around 7.30–8am and 11.30am–noon.

Milk truck

Ask about the *lechero* ($1) at local hotels in these villages.

Sigchos to: Chugchilán (1hr). Daily at 7am.

Chugchilán to: Sigchos (1hr). Returns to Sigchos anytime between 8am and 10am.

Camionetas

Latacunga to: Laguna Quilotoa (around $40), Chugchilán (around $60) and Isinliví ($40), from the corner of Valencia and Antonio Vela, Plaza El Salto.

Zumbahua to: Laguna Quilotoa ($5) and Chugchilán ($20–30), from the main square, or ask in any of the hotels around the square.

Chugchilán to: Laguna Quilotoa ($20–25), Zumbahua ($25–30), Sigchos ($20–25) and Isinliví ($35) from the main square.

Sigchos to: Chugchilán ($20–25), Laguna Quilotoa ($30–40) and Isinliví ($10) from the main square.

soon you're in starkly beautiful countryside. After crossing a pass, the road levels out on the páramo, dotted with igloo-shaped thatched shelters known as *chozas*, a dwelling hut characteristic of the rural sierra.

About 53km west of Latacunga is the village of **TIGUA** (3600m; more accurately Tigua Chimbacucho, as Tigua is the catch-all name for thirteen local communities), whose modern, tiled-roof houses contrast sharply with the rough thatched huts elsewhere. The most impressive of the village's buildings, perched on the hillside above the road, is an **art gallery** cooperative, devoted to the naive art, painted on sheep hide, for which Tigua is famous throughout Ecuador. The gallery sells the works of around thirty-five local artists, painted in the characteristic Tigua style, showing scenes of daily life, legends and village fiestas against a background of brightly coloured peaks and fields. Decorated festival masks, representing characters that feature in local folklore, including wolves, lions, dogs, monkeys and tigers, as well as basketwork and painted boxes, are also available. The prices are higher than what vendors next to Laguna Quilotoa charge but reflect the quality of the paintings: expect to pay around $30-plus for a mid-size painting by the more established artists like Alfredo Toaquiza, whose father was the first person to begin painting in this style in 1973.

The best place to **stay** around here is the charming *La Posada de Tigua* (by reservation in Latacunga on ☎03/2814870 or 09/1612391, ⓦwww.laposadadetigua .com; ❺ including breakfast and dinner), a working dairy farm at 3450m, tucked nearer the valley floor 3km before Tigua village, down a winding signposted 800-metre track. The small farmhouse, warmed on cold nights by an old wood stove by the front door, has rustic rooms, two shared bathrooms (one of which has an antique alcohol-heated shower) and serves delicious meals. You can also hire horses here to ride to Quilotoa in a couple of hours, or hike there in twice the time. Bus drivers know the farm and can drop you at the turning.

Zumbahua

About 11km beyond Tigua, a side road leads downhill to **ZUMBAHUA** (3500m), a small village set about half a kilometre north of the Latacunga–Quevedo road; if your bus is continuing to Quevedo, get off here and walk for five minutes or so down to the village. It's a poor place, with muddy, potholed streets, tin-roofed houses and dust blowing about, but the setting is spectacular thanks to the backdrop of sharp peaks covered with chequered fields. Zumbahua's large **central square** looks desolate and empty through the week, but on Saturdays is crammed with traders, buyers and produce to make it one of the most enjoyable and colourful **markets** in the sierra. Among the piles of potatoes and beans, you may see freshly chopped sheep's heads (along with various other parts of their anatomy), used to make soup that's often prepared at the makeshift stalls. Other curiosities include a row of barbers and a cluster of tailors who mend clothes on old-fashioned sewing machines.

The best of a selection of cheap and basic **hotels** is the *Cóndor Matzi* (☎03/2814611; ❶) on the square. It's got a hot-water shower and small, tidy rooms with bunks and clean linen, and kitchen facilities, but has a slightly abandoned feel to it. If no one's there to let you in, ask around in the village for the key. Just round the corner, *Oro Verde* (❶) has simple rooms with no-frills en-suite bathrooms (with unreliable hot water) and a simple restaurant. A few doors along, *Richard* (❶) has basic dorm rooms and one double with concrete floors, and decent hot showers inside and out back. Apart from the hotels mentioned above, there are a couple of very basic **restaurants** just off the square. The Andinatel **phone office** is near the church.

There are several daily **buses** to Quilotoa (last one leaves 1–2pm), or locals will take you there by **camioneta** for about $5 – just ask around on the square, or in your hotel. The four-hour, ten-kilometre **hike** to the lake became less attractive after the road was paved, but **guides** are available from *Cóndor Matzi* for more interesting páramo hikes.

Laguna Quilotoa

Laguna Quilotoa is a breathtaking glass-green lake lying in the crater of an extinct volcano, surrounded by steep slopes and jagged cliffs. From the main road where through-buses will drop you, it's a straightforward five-minute walk up to the lake, which remains hidden from view until you're practically on top of it. On the way up you'll pass an **entrance kiosk** where you pay a $1 visitor's fee, used to aid the local community of **Quilotoa** (3850m), whose meagre shacks huddle by the side of the track up to the lake. Local artists gather around the crater, near the parking area, trying to sell their Tigua-style paintings, while children flock around, hoping to prise a sweet or a few cents out of you. It's possible to **walk down to the lake** from the crater's edge in about thirty to forty minutes, following the path that starts at a muddy chasm just left of the parking area. It's steep, and not to be undertaken lightly, but the solitude and views at the bottom are highly rewarding. Getting back up involves either a stiff one-hour climb, or a 45-minute **mule ride** ($5), which you can organize at the top. The **walk around the rim** (5–6hr; an hour less with mules) is much more challenging and, in places where the path has worn away, rather precarious; you may benefit from the services of a guide ($10) or mules ($15). **Guides** and **muleteers** are available for many other hikes, too, including to the Chichucaucho hot(-ish) springs ($18), the Cueva de los Incas in local cloudforest (5hr; $12), and Chugchilán ($15).

Many of the simple **hotels** in Quilotoa are really just family homes with a few beds for tourists jammed in, with minimal privacy and heating; at this altitude a warm sleeping bag is recommended. The best and most patronized are *Cabañas Quilotoa* at the entrance to the community, a large building and a newer annexe (with shared electric showers), which are both chilly despite woollen blankets, a fireplace and the occasional wood-burning stove; *Princesa Toa*, opposite the lake viewpoint, which has the benefit of being a new building and better insulated than most, and features a restaurant upstairs as well as cabañas down on the shore; and *Pachamama* next door, with simple rooms stuffed full of bunks and beds with shared hot showers. All charge the same **rates** at $3 per person for lodging or $8 with breakfast and dinner. A genuine slice of comfort is outside the community, at the *Quilotoa Crater Lake Lodge* (T09/1571274 or 08/5023559 in Quito; ⑦ including breakfast), the orange timber-framed building above the main road opposite the village; it has pleasant rooms, private baths, gas-heated showers, electric blankets and satellite TV in the restaurant. Each of these hotels can provide **meals**.

Chugchilán

North of Quilotoa, a hair-raising 22-kilometre drive along a narrow dirt road skirting a cliff edge takes you through dramatically beautiful scenery to **CHUGCHILÁN** (3180m), a tiny settlement in a remote rural setting. It's home to little more than a dozen families and a women's **knitting cooperative** selling woollens. Although one of the poorest villages in the region, it's the location of some of the most comfortable places to stay on the whole loop as well as an excellent base for hiking, mountain biking and horseriding.

One of the most popular trips involves catching the early-morning bus to Laguna Quilotoa and **hiking** back from the crater via the village of Guayama and the scenic **Toachi canyon** (3–5hr; quite hard going for the last hour); you can hire a guide in Chugchilán or Quilotoa. Other good excursions are to a nearby carpentry workshop, the **Centro Artístico Don Bosco**, in Chinalo a couple of kilometres down the road to Sigchos, and to a **cheese factory** (closes around 11.30am) two hours' walk north of the village; a Swiss NGO built it in 1978 but it's now run by locals, from whom you can buy a variety of cheeses (only sold whole). Your hotel will be able to help you out with directions, guides, horses or *camionetas* as required for these and countless other local hikes, or contact Humberto Ortega, who leads guided horse rides (his house is just uphill of *Mama Hilda's*).

For **accommodation**, try the ground-breaking ✈ *Black Sheep Inn* (☎03/2814587, ⓦ www.blacksheepinn.com; ❽, including all meals, with discounts for students, seniors and SAE members), up a steep path on the road towards Sigchos, about half a kilometre east of Chugchilán's main square. This lovely guesthouse has rooms in thatched adobe huts, most with wood-burning stoves, or a funky, bunkhouse dorm for those on a tighter budget ($20 per person). Run by a couple of North Americans committed to sustainable, eco-friendly agriculture, the *Inn* offers tasty vegetarian cooking, home-made brownies with free tea and coffee, a lounge with plenty of books and fantastic views, internet access, hand-outs with maps and extensive notes on hikes and local sights, a 100-metre zip-line cable ride down the hillside, a yoga studio, a massage room and a sauna to keep the highland chill at bay. It's very popular so reservations are advised.Alternatively,there's friendly *Mama Hilda's* (☎03/2814814, Ⓔͤmama_hilda@hotmail.com; ❻ including breakfast and dinner), on the main road nearer the village centre, which offers clean and tidy rooms – the newer and dearer ones have split-levels and fireplaces – and shared bathrooms with hot-water showers. Next door, downhill, the *Hostal Cloudforest* (☎03/2814808, ⓦwww.cloudforeshostal.com; ❸ including breakfast and dinner, or $7 per person in a dorm) has pleasant, good-value rooms with shared or private hot-water bathrooms, internet access and a **restaurant**. They also sell knitwear from the cooperative. Horseriding and hikes can be arranged from all three hotels.

Sigchos

Twenty-four kilometres north of Chugchilán, the road passes through the busy little town of **SIGCHOS** (2850m). With its paved streets, modern school and conspicuous absence of ponchos, you get the distinct impression you've left the rural sierra behind. It's more of a place to pass through than to base yourself, but if you get stuck you'll find decent en-suite **rooms** at the orange-painted *La Posada* (☎03/2714224; ❶) on the Plaza 24 de Mayo (the square with the covered basketball court), which also has the town's best **restaurant**, serving the standard menu of chicken, meat or fish and rice. Continuing east, you're quickly in wild countryside again, winding down countless hairpins into a spectacular canyon. Coming out of this, the landscape becomes tamer and less striking as you head back towards the Panamericana by way of Toacazo.

Isinliví

A worthwhile detour from the traditional Quilotoa loop is to the small and largely *mestizo* village of **ISINLIVÍ** (3000m), about 12km southeast of Sigchos (take the road heading downhill from the southeast corner of town). The village is a small centre of woodcarving proficiency, the relatively recent influence of an Italian mission, but the main attraction is the beautiful setting and the excellent hiking and horseriding trips. A great place to **stay** here is *Llullu Llama* (☎03/2814790,

Ⓦwww.llullullama.com; Ⓖ including dinner and breakfast), a cosy, relaxing and environmentally friendly *hostal*, with a range of rooms from bunks ($18, including dinner and breakfast) to private doubles, whose friendly Dutch–Ecuadorian owners can supply you with hiking information and can find guides and horses. **Buses** (around 3hr) via Sigchos leave Latacunga daily except Thursday at 12.15pm and 1pm (Sat 10.30am and 12.15pm); on Thursdays, they leave from Saquisií at 11am and 11.30am. Check the hotel website for the latest transport details.

Salcedo

Back on the Panamericana, some 10km south of Latacunga, is the little town of **SALCEDO** (officially San Miguel de Salcedo), famous around these parts for its fruity ice cream, widely available around town. Otherwise, there's nothing particularly exciting about the town, though it does boast a very beautiful **central square**, with tall palms and immaculately tended lawns. Overlooking the square is a gorgeous whitewashed, colonial **church** (usually locked) and a rather grand **Palacio Municipal** of pink-hued stone. Wrapping up the town's attractions is the lively and unpretentious **Sunday market**, held round the corner from the square.

With plenty of **buses** whizzing up and down the Panamericana, getting stuck here is unlikely to be a problem. If you do need a **place to stay** for the night, try *La Casona* (Ⓣ03/2728224; Ⓒ) at Bolívar 6-34, a stately hotel on the main square with fresh en-suite rooms set around a pleasant courtyard. The best **restaurant** is *La Casa del Marquez*, on García Moreno and Quito at the north exit of the town, which offers good, inexpensive food in a plush dining room.

Ambato and around

Sitting in a fertile agricultural zone some 47km south of Latacunga, **Ambato** is an important commercial centre with a bustling downtown core; there's little here to hold your interest for more than an afternoon, and many travellers choose to pass straight through on their way to Baños or Riobamba. Still, it's handy as a jumping-off point for a couple of neighbouring low-key attractions, including **Quizapincha**, a major producer of leather goods, **Salasaca**, famous for its weavings, **Patate**, a small village set in a fruit-growing valley, and, for the more adventurous, the **Parque Nacional Llanganates**, one of Ecuador's least-explored wildernesses.

Ambato

San Juan de Ambato – known simply as **AMBATO** (2580m) – was founded in 1570, but very little remains of its colonial character due to a catastrophic **earthquake** that virtually razed the city to the ground in 1949. The modern buildings that sprang up in its wake are for the most part bland and unattractive, making Ambato a less appealing place for a stopover than Latacunga or Riobamba, the two other main central sierra towns on the Panamericana. The town does have a couple of enjoyable museums, plenty of banks and some great-value hotels and decent restaurants. If you're passing around Carnaval time (just before Lent, in February or early March), don't miss the **Fiesta de las Flores y las Frutas**, held over several days, with big parades, beauty pageants, bullfights, music and plenty of fruit and flowers; you'll need to book a room in advance when it's on. Unlike the rest of the country, water fights are banned in Ambato during Carnaval.

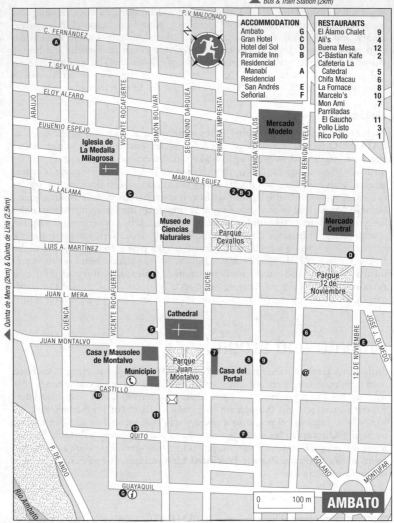

Bus & Train Station (2km)

Quinta de Mera (2km) & Quinta de Liria (2.5km)

ACCOMMODATION	
Ambato	G
Gran Hotel	C
Hotel del Sol	D
Piramide Inn	B
Residencial Manabí	A
Residencial San Andrés	E
Señorial	F

RESTAURANTS	
El Álamo Chalet	9
Ali's	4
Buena Mesa	12
C-Bástian Kafe	2
Cafeteria La Catedral	5
Chifa Macau	6
La Fornace	8
Marcelo's	10
Mon Ami	7
Parrilladas El Gaucho	11
Pollo Listo	3
Rico Pollo	1

AMBATO

Arrival and information

Ambato's **bus terminal** and **train station** (currently disused) are right next to each other a couple of kilometres northeast of the centre; taxis to the centre ($1) line up outside, or you can walk up to Avenida de las Americas, directly behind the bus terminal (turn right and right again after exiting the bus station) and catch a local bus to the downtown Parque Cevallos. (Those heading directly to Baños should note that Baños buses don't leave from the terminal; instead, take a taxi to the "Mayorista" bus stop.) **Taxis** in town rank around Parque Cevallos and the central Parque Montalvo; to book, call Cooperativa de Taxis 12 de Noviembre (☎03/2410833).

Information is available at the Ministerio de Turismo office (Mon–Fri 8.30am–1pm & 2.30–6pm; ☎03/2821800) at Guayaquil and Rocafuerte, next door to the *Ambato* hotel. The Ministerio del Ambiente (☎03/2848452), a short taxi ride ($1) from the town centre at Alfredo Baquerizo 603 and Pasaje Tamayo, has information on Parque Nacional Llanganates (see p.197).

Accommodation

While mid-range **accommodation** is spread about town, Ambato's cheapest hotels are on or near the Parque 12 de Noviembre. It's a slightly run-down area, but it is central, busy and reasonably safe during the day. With the exception of the cheaper places, most rates include breakfast.

Ambato Guayaquil 01-08 ☎03/2421791, ⓦwww .hotelambato.com. Ambato's top hotel, offering quiet, spacious rooms with quality though slightly dated furnishings and decor, and big picture windows looking down to the Ambato river valley. Also has private parking, a decent restaurant and a pleasant outdoor terrace. **❼**

Hotel del Sol Corner of Luis A. Martínez and 12 de Noviembre ☎03/2825258. Modest, but clean and cheerful rooms with private bath in a bright-green building on the corner of Parque 12 de Noviembre. Good for the price, but can be noisy. **❸**

Gran Hotel Rocafuerte 11-33 and Lalama ☎&Ⓕ03/2824235. Friendly hotel overlooking a pretty church, with a café and private garage. Most rooms are large, with en-suite bath, carpets and cable TV, though some are looking a little worn. **❺**

Residencial Manabí Cuenca and Fernandez ☎03/2826693. Quiet, family-owned *residencial* a

few blocks from the centre with basic but adequate little rooms with shared bath. A couple of rooms at the front have balconies. **❷**

Piramide Inn Mariano Egüez and Cevallos ☎03/2421920. Well-run hotel offering comfortable rooms with spotless en-suite bathrooms and cable TV, and windows that seem to do a better job at keeping out the noise than most places. **❹**

Residencial San Andrés 12 de Noviembre and Montalvo ☎03/2821604. Spotless budget rooms with tiled floors, green or salmon-pink painted walls and private bathrooms. They all face on to a small internal patio and so are a bit dark. **❷**

Señorial Corner of Cevallos and Quito ☎03/2825124, Ⓕ2829536. Bright, cared-for rooms (ignore the awful plastic headboards), gleaming en-suite bathrooms, good showers and cable TV. A few are on the small side, so ask to see a room first. **❼**

The Town

Ambato's focal point is the leafy central square, the **Parque Juan Montalvo**, overlooked by the city's brash, modern **cathedral**, monolithic **Municipio** and the **Casa del Portal** – a handsome survivor of the 1949 earthquake, sporting a row of graceful stone arches spanning the width of the square. The square is named after the locally born nineteenth-century writer (see Contexts pp.495 & 507), the most distinguished of the trio of former residents that gives Ambato its nickname, "the city of the three Juans"; the other two are the novelist **Juan León Mera**, and lawyer and polemicist **Juan Benigno Vela**. Sitting on the north corner of the square, the humble, whitewashed **Casa de Montalvo** (Mon–Fri 9am–noon & 2–6pm, Sat 10am–1pm; $1) was Montalvo's birthplace and former home, and displays a moderately interesting collection of photos, manuscripts, clothes and other personal effects. Adjoining it is the **Mausoleo de Montalvo** (same hours and ticket), an elaborate Grecian-style temple in which the writer's carved wooden coffin is displayed on a platform, forming a kind of morbid altar.

Three blocks northeast is the city's second major square, **Parque Cevallos**. On Calle Sucre, lining its northwest side, the Instituto Técnico Superior Bolívar houses Ambato's most compelling attraction, the **Museo de Ciencias Naturales** (Mon–Fri 8.30am–12.30pm & 2.30–6.30pm, Sat 9am–5pm; $1), an old-fashioned natural history museum spread over five halls of a nineteenth-century building. The displays kick off with some evocative early twentieth-century photos of the region's volcanoes, including one showing fumaroles spouting dramatically out of Cotopaxi's crater in 1911. The bulk of the collection is formed by stuffed animals, including a jaguar, puma, elephant, boa, spectacled bears, iguanas, monkeys and condors. These are later followed by a stomach-churning display of preserved "freak animals", including a two-headed calf, a three-legged hen and a lamb with one head and two bodies.

Also downtown is the handsome **Iglesia de la Medalla Milagrosa**, a French Romanesque-style church built of lovely golden stone, at the corner of Rocafuerte and Egüez. If you're around on a Monday, check out the sprawling **market** spread over several sites, including the Mercado Central, next to the Parque 12 de Noviembre, and the Mercado Modelo, a couple of blocks further north. Otherwise, jump in a taxi or a bus from Parque Cevallos and head out to the **Quinta de Mera** (Wed–Sun 9am–4.30pm; $1), a couple of kilometres north of the centre in the suburb of Atocha. The former home of Juan León Mera, it's a grand nineteenth-century adobe house with an overhanging clay-tiled roof supported by thick wooden pillars. There are some original furniture and paintings inside, but what makes a trip here worthwhile are the lush gardens and woods that fill the extensive grounds. Paths lead through at least 200 species of plants (seven endemic) down to the river, and half a kilometre east to the neighbouring **Quinta de Liria**, once the fine house of Dr Nicolás Martínez, head of an influential local family at the turn of the last century, which has been recently restored and is open to visitors. Across the main road from the Quinta de Liria, the **Centro Cultural La Liria** (same hours and ticket as Quinta de Mera) displays changing exhibitions of photography, sculpture and paintings.

Eating, drinking and nightlife

Ambato offers a very respectable choice of places to **eat**, from budget to fine dining, except on Sundays when many are closed. It's particularly strong on cheap **spit-roasted-chicken** places such as *Rico Pollo* and *Pollo Listo*, opposite each other on the corner of Cevallos and Egüez. **Nightlife** is very quiet through the week, but livens up on Fridays and Saturdays; popular **bar-nightclubs** include *Ilusiones*, at Quisquis 1717 and Madrid, which has a restaurant on the ground floor and a disco upstairs, and *Imperio Club*, at Pacha and Saraguro. The *Coyote Club* at Bolívar and Guayaquil is a good place for a beer and TexMex nibbles and often has live music at the weekends.

El Álamo Chalet Cevallos and Montalvo. Classic, mid-priced *comida típica*, including *humitas*, *quimbolitos* and *seco de chivo* (goat stew), as well as international food in a comfortable atmosphere.

Ali's Bolívar and Mera. Grill house with booths and cowheads on the wall specializing in meat, particularly big T-bone steaks which you can watch sizzling away in the kitchen.

Buena Mesa Quito 924. Smart, modern exterior and an expensive but appealing French-based menu – including seafood crêpe, coq au vin and trout *meunier* – which arrives well prepared. Closed Sun.

C-Bástian Kafe Egüez and Cevallos. Shi-shi café with glass tables and bustling waiters in white shirts and black aprons, serving steak, chicken, burgers, sandwiches, salads, cocktails and drinks to an appreciative clientele. Closed Sun.

Cafeteria La Catedral Bolívar 17-50 in the CC La Catedral. A presentable café offering snacks, drinks and inexpensive *almuerzos*. Closed Sun.

Chifa Macau Vela and Montalvo. Clean and well-lit restaurant serving a mixture of Ecuadorian and Chinese dishes. Good choice for a budget meal.

La Fornace Av Cevallos 17-28. Intimate, relaxed and very popular place, serving delicious, inexpensive Italian food; pizzas are cooked in a large clay oven in the dining room.

Marcelo's Castillo and Rocafuerte. Spick-and-span, cheerful café serving snacks, sandwiches, burgers, hot dogs and the great Chilean classic *el Barros Luco* (griddle-fried beef with melted cheese), as well as 24 flavours of ice cream.

Mon Ami Corner of Sucre and Montalvo, upstairs. Low lighting, plush fabrics and a position above the *parque* lend a vaguely Gallic romantic feel to this restaurant – even if the French influence doesn't stretch much beyond crêpes on the menu. Closed Sun evening.

Parrilladas El Gaucho Bolívar and Quinto. Tasty, charcoal-grilled *parrilladas* served in a dimly lit basement dining room with neon lights on the wall. Popular with local families and good value. Closed Sun.

Listings

Banks and exchange Banco del Pacífico (Master-Card and Cirrus ATM), Lalama and Cevallos and at corner of Bolívar and Montalvo (MasterCard and Visa ATM); Banco de Guayaquil (Visa, MasterCard and Cirrus ATM), corner of Sucre and Juan Léon Mera; Produbanco, Montalvo 5-30 and Sucre, and corner of 5 de Junio and Cevallos (MasterCard and Cirrus ATM); Banco del Austro, corner of Castillo and Sucre (Visa ATM).
Car rental Localiza, Atahulalbay and Victor Hugo ☎03/2844524.

Laundry Magic's, Rocafuerte between Castillo and Montalvo.
Medical Services Hospital Regional de Ambato, Av Pasteur and Unidad Nacional ☎03/2420533.
Police Atahualpa 568 ☎03/2843656.
Post office Parque Juan Montalvo, at the corner of Castillo and Bolívar.
Telephone office Andinatel, Castillo and Rocafuerte.
Travel agents Clantour, Cevallos 1857 and Quito ☎03/2421814; Ecuadorian Tours, Sucre 960 and Quito ☎03/2428392; Metropolitan Touring, CC Caracol, Loc 59-62 ☎03/2820211.

Quizapincha

QUIZAPINCHA, a small, otherwise unprepossessing village up in the hills, just 10km west of Ambato, is something of a surprise: it's crammed full of family-run "factories" and shops selling **leather goods**, most of which are bulk-bought by wholesalers and distributed around the country. The quality is generally high and the prices low; you can pick up a fitted leather jacket for around $30 and a well-stitched shoulder bag for around $12. As it's less well known than Cotacachi (see p.148), the leather-manufacturing town near Otavalo, it attracts fewer tourists, keeping prices down.

Buses to Quizapincha leave every half-hour from Ambato's Plaza Rodó, six blocks north up Martínez from Plaza Cevallos. It's a lovely ride, crossing the river and climbing high onto the opposite wall of the valley, giving striking views down to Ambato. Ask to be dropped at the *tiendas de cuero* (leather shops), most of which are clustered near the entrance to the village. If you come back to Ambato at nightfall, you'll be treated to dazzling views of the city lights spread out below you on the valley floor.

Píllaro and Parque Nacional Llanganates

Just north of Ambato, a side road shoots east from the Panamericana for 20km to **Píllaro**, an agricultural village known for its **bullfights** and fine hand-crafted guitars. The time to be here is August 10, during the **festival** of San Lorenzo, when bulls are released to charge through the streets and chased on foot by exuberant crowds.

Otherwise, Píllaro's main interest is as a gateway to the **Parque Nacional Llanganates**, created in 1996 to protect the Llanganates mountain range, a spur of the eastern Andes. A wild, little-visited territory of forbidding mountains, bleak páramo, unnamed lakes and impenetrable forest, the mountains have gone down in Ecuadorian mythology as the hiding place of vast quantities of **gold** that was on its way to Peru to pay for Atahualpa's ransom (see p.490), buried here by the general Rumiñahui on hearing the conquistadors had murdered the Inca leader. The legend gained greater currency in the late sixteenth century when a Spanish soldier named Valverde dictated a map to the treasure on his deathbed, known as *el Derrotero de Valverde*. Since then, countless expeditions have set off to unearth the mythical stash of gold; none has found it.

Most tourists skip the Llanganates, probably deterred by the area's notoriously bad weather (heavy rain and thick fog) and by the fact the park has no real infrastructure or marked trails. If you're keen to visit, your best bet is with one of the **tour operators** in Baños (see p.206) who offer treks in the park; you could also ask around in Píllaro for a local **guide** and **mules** a couple of days before you want to set off. You'll need to come fully equipped and self-sufficient (you will also need to provide shelter for the guide). The driest time of year here is December and January.

Salasaca and Pelileo

About 14km southwest of Ambato down the road to Baños, **SALASACA** is a small strip of a village, named after the Salasaca *indígenas* who live here and in the surrounding area. Originally from Bolivia, the Salasacas were relocated to this region by the Incas as part of the *mitimae* system, a practice intended to help colonize new areas and undermine local resistance. The Salasacas still have a very distinct identity, and in some places still buy and sell land according to the original divisions, or *mitmakuna*, granted to their ancestors when they settled here. They are famous for their custom of dressing in black – in mourning, it is said, for the Inca Atahualpa – and for their elaborate woollen **weavings**, mostly rugs or wall hangings showing images of stylized human forms or geometric animal motifs. The best time to come and buy is on Sundays, when the town square, right by the main road, hosts a busy **handicrafts market**; on other days, the workshops dotted on and around the square, including the Cooperativa Artesenal near the church, are worth a visit. You can **stay** at *Runa Huasi* (T09/9840125, or ask locally for Alonso Pilla; ❸), a simple rural hostel with shared baths and valley views about ten minutes' walk from the main road; the owners can give tours of the surroundings.

A further 5km down the road, **PELILEO** is to jeans what Quizapincha is to leather, with dozens of small shops selling nothing but. They look a bit tacky but the quality isn't bad and it's a cheap place to stock up on a pair or two. There's little else going on in this town, which was erected from scratch after the dreadful 1949 earthquake completely demolished the original Pelileo, 2km from its present site. **Buses** from Ambato to Baños pass through Salasaca and Pelileo.

Patate

The little farming village of **PATATE**, reached by climbing into the hills 5km east of Pelileo, and then making a breathtaking descent into a lush cultivated valley, is styled as the "Valley of Eternal Spring". Patate's warm and sunny climate is its main appeal, and a smattering of comfortable and secluded **country hotels** dot the valley, great places to recharge the batteries and go on the odd walk in the hills. The village itself is pleasant enough, with its central square filled with bright flowering trees, and features a tourist complex ($1), popular with weekenders from Ambato; it offers two outdoor pools with great views, a sauna, steam room and restaurant. Patate has also become a launchpad for **excursions** to a nearby hilltop aerial station known as Las Antenas, used as an observation point for watching the frequent displays of fireworks produced by **Volcán Tungurahua** (see box, p.199), when the sky's clear. *Camionetas* will take you there from Patate for about $5, including an hour's wait at the top. Transportes Patate **buses** serve the town, and leave every twenty minutes from Plaza La Dolorosa in Ambato and Transportes Valle from the main terminal.

Between the square and the pools, the *Jardin del Valle Hospedaje* (T03/2870205; ❸) is the **place to stay** in town, with pleasing rooms and good prices. For something a little classier, take a *camioneta* from the square ($3; call T03/2870042) to one of two lovely **haciendas** in the hills to the north, up a scenic cobbled road leading to Baños: at 8km, *Hacienda Leito* (T03/2859329, Wwww.haciendaleito.com; ❼ including breakfast and dinner), founded by Jesuits almost four hundred years ago, is now a luxury hotel with a spa and swimming pool; another 3km up the road is the impeccably managed ⚔ *Hacienda Manteles* (T09/8715632, or Quito 02/2233484, Wwww.haciendamanteles.com; ❻), a rustic farmhouse hideaway offering fabulous views down the valley. Both haciendas offer a range of activities, including horseriding treks through the valley and hikes up to nearby cloudforest.

Baños and around

Continuing east from Salasaca and Pelileo, the Ambato–Puyo road threads its way down the narrow Río Pastaza gorge before arriving at the small resort town of **Baños**, 44km southeast of Ambato. A good 1000m lower than most sierra towns, at 1820m above sea level, Baños enjoys a warm, subtropical climate

Volcán Tungurahua

In October 1999, **Volcán Tungurahua** – the 5023-metre volcano whose smoking cone lies just 8km south of Baños – resumed activity after almost eighty years of dormancy. Baños and neighbouring villages were forcibly evacuated and roads were sealed off, leaving some 20,000 people homeless. By January 2000, no big eruption had materialized and 5000 locals (anxious that rogue soldiers were looting their homes) fought their way through military blockades, armed with shovels and rocks. The authorities subsequently agreed to reopen the town, which quickly recovered as a popular resort and, as far as tourism was concerned, it was as if nothing had happened.

Tungurahua (meaning "throat of fire" in Quichua) did not go back to sleep but continued regularly to belch gas and lava. Then, in August 2006, activity increased dramatically with a violent, explosive eruption that wiped out three hamlets on the volcano's western slopes (Chilibu, Choglontuz and Palitagua), accompanied by a ten-kilometre-high ash cloud. Most residents had been evacuated prior to the explosion, but some refused to leave and seven people were killed.

At the time of writing, volcanic activity continues on a low to medium level. It's business as usual in Baños, which was unaffected by the 2006 explosion – but be aware the **risk** is ongoing. Most hotels have evacuation instructions stuck on the walls, and large yellow arrows and dotted lines on the streets point the way to a designated **safety zone** on the eastern side of town, in the Santa Ana area. Before you decide to visit Baños, you should get **news** on Tungurahua's state from the daily reports in all the national newspapers, from the SAE in Quito (see p.77), from the Instituto Geofísico's (Spanish) website Wwww.igepn.edu.ec or from your embassy.

and a spectacular location, nestled among soaring green hills streaked with waterfalls. With the **thermal baths** that give the town its name, a great choice of good-value hotels and restaurants and excellent opportunities for **outdoor activities** such as hiking, cycling, horseriding and rafting (see p.206), it's easy to see why both nationals and foreigners make Baños one of the most visited destinations in the country – despite the unpredictable condition of the **Tungurahua volcano** towering above the town to the south (see box, p.199). Tungurahua's unpredictability is something of a draw in itself, with tourists flocking to high vantage points on cloudless nights to watch it spit lava and igneous rocks into the sky like fireworks. A *chiva* (wooden bus) leaves town for the Bellavista **observation point** every night at 9pm, returning around 11pm; tickets cost $3 from Córdova Tours at the corner of Maldonado and Espejo. Tungurahua can also be viewed from several other points, including near the village of Patate (see p.198).

East of Baños, **the road to Puyo**, in the Oriente, offers one of Ecuador's most scenic approaches to the Amazon basin, taking you past a string of diaphanous waterfalls along the way. Some hang right over the road, while others are approached along short trails, including the thundering **Pailón del Diablo** close to the village of **Río Verde**, about 20km down the road. Another road links Baños to Riobamba, skirting the slopes of Tungurahua and providing access to **Parque Nacional Sangay** via Penipe and Candelaria (see p.223); the road is subject to frequent landslides outside Baños. The **best months** to

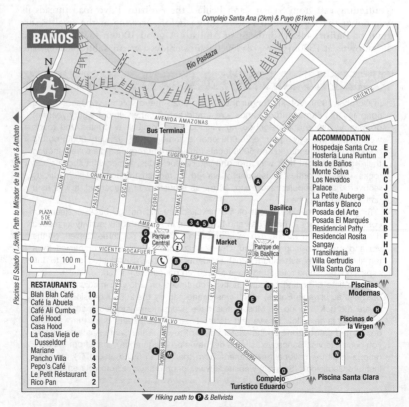

visit Baños are between September and April; from May to August it can be cloudy and rainy.

Arrival and information

Buses drop passengers inside or right next to the **bus terminal**, three blocks north of Parque Central, just off the main road. The helpful **tourist office** (daily 8am–12.30pm & 2–5.30pm; ℡03/2740483, ⓦwww.banios.com) is a short walk away at Thomas Halflants and Rocafuerte, and you can pick up maps and leaflets here. It's not far from the terminal or the *parque* to most hotels, but if you want to take a **taxi** you'll find them ranked at both locations. **Town buses** run every fifteen minutes during daylight hours between Agoyán east of town to El Salado to the west, stopping in the centre behind the market on Rocafuerte.

Accommodation

Baños has a huge choice of **places to stay**, especially at the middle and lower end of the scale, usually offering comfortable accommodation at a very reasonable price. Availability is unlikely to be a problem during the week, but if you've got somewhere particular in mind, it's worth booking ahead for weekends and during holidays such as Carnaval and Semana Santa, when you'll probably be charged a little extra.

Hospedaje Santa Cruz 16 de Diciembre and Montalvo ℡03/2740648. Great-value French-run hostel with clean and tidy en-suite rooms around patios. Large range of DVDs for hire. ❸

Hostería Luna Runtun On a hill east of town, 8km by road, turning 2km east of Baños ℡03/2740882, ⓦwww.lunaruntun.com. Swiss-run luxury retreat perched on a spur affording spectacular views of Baños and of Tungurahua, with landscaped gardens and a spa centre offering massages, mud baths, facials, steam baths and sauna. A fantastic place to unwind. Includes breakfast and dinner. Taxi from Baños is $6. ❾

Isla de Baños Thomas Halflants 1-31 ℡&℉03/2740609, ⓦwww.hosteriaisladebanos .com. Appealing German-run hostel, set in an attractive landscaped garden with riotous greenery around a pond, offering comfortable rooms with scrubbed wooden floors and spotless en-suite bathrooms. Also has a spa with steam boxes and whirlpool, café, library and can arrange horse and jeep tours. Breakfast included. ❹

Monte Selva Thomas Halflants and Montalvo ℡/℉03/2740566, ⓦwww.monteselvaecuador. com. Pleasant cabins with sofas and cable TV, dotted around pretty gardens on a hillside. Facilities include spa ($5), sauna, swimming pool and billiards room. Breakfast included. ❼

Los Nevados Ambato and Pasaje Hermano Enrique Mideros ℡03/2740673. Modern, functional and spotlessly clean budget *hostal* with a covered rooftop bar-café. All rooms (one to four beds) have private bath and cable TV. ❸

Palace Montalvo 20-03 ℡03/2740470, ⓦwww .hotelpalace.com.ec. A favourite with tour groups, this old-time upper-end hotel offers well-furnished en-suite rooms with cable TV, as well as indoor and outdoor pools, sauna, steam bath and jacuzzi and a games room ($5 entry for non-residents). Buffet breakfast included. ❼

La Petite Auberge 16 de Diciembre and Montalvo ℡03/2740936, ⓦwww.lepetit.banos.com. Delightful French-run hotel set back from the road in its own peaceful garden, with a pleasant open-sided sitting area, a spa centre and a choice of en-suite rooms and split-level suites, all attractively furnished, many with fireplaces and patios. Breakfast included at its good restaurant, *Le Petit Restaurant*. Discounts in low season. ❸–❺

Plantas y Blanco Martínez and 12 de Noviembre ℡03/2740044. Charming, French-owned *hostal* offering clean rooms with private or shared bath and lots of services, including laundry, free internet, luggage storage and movie rental. Added highlights are the great breakfasts served on the rooftop terrace, the morning steam bath, and its excellent little bakery next door. ❸

Posada del Arte Pasaje Velasco Ibarra and Montalvo ℡/℉03/2740083, ⓦwww.posadade larte.com. A lovely house in a pretty spot on the edge of town, with a comfy sitting room and huge TV showing films in English. The en-suite rooms feature polished wooden floors and firm mattresses and the pricier ones (⑥) have open fires, bathtubs and views of the waterfall. A great restaurant is attached. Breakfast included. ⑤

Posada El Marqués Pasaje Velasco Ibarra and Montalvo ☎03/740053, ⓦwww.marques.banios .com. Good-value, comfortable hotel in a gorgeous spot, right by a waterfall splashing down the mountain. Splendid views from the upstairs rooms (all en suite) and the balcony, and use of the kitchen is included. ④

Residencial Patty Eloy Alfaro 556 and Oriente ☎03/2740202. Bargain rooms with shared bath on three floors around a courtyard, and use of kitchen facilities. Pretty basic, but it's kept clean and is a backpackers' institution. ②

Residencial Rosita 16 de Diciembre and Luis A. Martínez ☎03/2740396. Reasonable lower-end option, offering rooms with one to three beds with shared bath, and four two-bed apartments with a kitchen. All a bit basic and worn, but airy and clean enough. ②

Sangay Plaza Ayora and Montalvo ☎03/2740490, ⓦwww.sangayspahotel.com. Long-established hotel offering suites, cabañas, and rooms in the older "colonial" building which has the feel of a faded Central European spa resort. Good service, though, and plenty of facilities ($6 for non-guests), such as pool, spa, tennis and squash courts and a masseur. Breakfast included. ⑥–⑦

Transilvania 16 de Diciembre and Oriente ☎03/2742281, ⓦwww.hostal-transilvania.com. Plain rooms and building, but a real gem for value, as you'll get private bath, cable TV and breakfast, plus there's internet access, a room to watch DVDs and a great little Israeli restaurant. ②

Villa Gertrudis Montalvo and Eloy Alfaro ☎03/2740441, ⓦwww.villagertrudis.com. An elegant old house with a pretty garden offering simple yet comfortable rooms that haven't changed much in the three decades or so the place has been open; some have bathtubs and feather duvets. ⑤

Villa Santa Clara 12 de Noviembre and Velasco Ibarra ☎03/2740349, ⓦwww.hotelvillasantaclara .com. Quite smart for the money if you plump for the en-suite rooms set around a little garden, though rooms with shared bath in the main building are simpler. Cafeteria offers seven different types of breakfast. ②–③

The Town

Founded by the Dominicans in 1553 as a staging post between the sierra and the Oriente, and a base from which to evangelize the Amazonian *indígenas*, Baños has evolved into a tidy, prosperous little town built around the luxuriantly landscaped Parque Central. Enclosed as it is by such dramatic, verdant scenery, there's little to catch your eye in the town itself, with the exception of the massive **Basílica de Nuestra Señora del Rosario de Agua Santa** on Calle Ambato, dominated by a pair of 58-metre spires. This "moderated Gothic" basilica is the latest incarnation of the town's church, which lava has threatened or earthquakes have razed at least half-a-dozen times in its history. It attracts thousands of pilgrims each year, who come to worship **Nuestra Señora de Agua Santa**, a supposedly miraculous icon credited with rescuing Baños and its citizens from countless calamities over the years, many of them – including volcanic eruptions, fires and collapsing bridges – vividly depicted in a series of paintings inside the church. Faith in the Virgin's powers to intervene in the face of disaster still runs very strong in the community, as was demonstrated in September 1999, when the icon was paraded through the town in a procession attended by thousands of people in an attempt to invoke protection from Tungurahua. Upstairs from the cloisters, a **museum** (daily 8am–5pm; $0.50) houses a fascinating and quite bizarre assortment of objects including a shrunken head from the Oriente, pickled snakes in jars, priests' robes, the processional wardrobe of the Nuestra Señora and a collection of stuffed Ecuadorian wildlife put together by someone with a very poor grasp of anatomy.

The baths

Usually top of the agenda for any visitor to Baños is taking a plunge in one of the town's six **thermal baths**, four of which are in the centre and two on the

▲ Baños

outskirts. They're all a little institutional-looking, fashioned into rectangular concrete, open-air pools with no-frills changing facilities, but wallowing in yellow-brown waters heated by Tungurahua makes for an irresistible treat. The best time for a soak is an hour or so before sunrise – few gringos manage to drag themselves out of bed at this time, and you'll be sharing the waters with local Ecuadorian families. It's all very friendly and atmospheric, especially in the thin dawn drizzle.

The most appealing set of thermal baths is the **Piscinas de la Virgen** at the eastern extreme of Avenida Martínez, sitting at the foot of a waterfall that tumbles down a rocky cliff; at night it's floodlit to spectacular effect. There are three daytime pools (4.30am–5pm; $1.60), plus a couple of separate pools downstairs only open at night (6–10pm; $2), all of which are touted as being good for stomach and liver ailments; the biggest pool is closed at night. About half a block north, the **Piscinas Modernas** (Fri–Sun 8am–5pm; $2) consist of a large serpentine-shaped pool filled with cold mineral water and a smaller, warmer one (26°C). A couple of blocks southwest on Rafael Vieira, the **Piscina Santa Clara**, also known as the Piscina del Cangrejo (Sat–Sun 8am–5pm; $1.50), is more of a classic swimming pool for doing lengths, and is filled with 23°C mineral water. You can also swim lengths to loud music in the three-lane pool next door at **Complejo Turístico Eduardo** (daily 9am–6pm; $3) or wallow in their sauna and spa complex. About 2km east of town (a 30min walk, or take any bus to Puyo) off the right-hand side of the road, the **Complejo Santa Ana** (Fri–Sun 8am–5pm; $1.50) has a big cold pool, and a couple of smaller, warmer ones – they're a bit shabby but in a nice enough spot, set back from the road with a backdrop of green hills. In the opposite direction, 1.5km west of the centre, the popular **Piscinas El Salado** (daily 4.30am–5pm; $1.50) offers five small pools at various temperatures, each heavily mineralized and reputedly highly curative, plus an ice-cold river for a cool dip. Unfortunately, the baths lie in a danger zone right in the crook of a ravine leading up to the volcano – a gorgeous spot, but, if the volcano is looking active, one of the last places you want to be. Because of its precarious location, by law no public money can be allocated for its improvement, of which it is in increasing need; a few of its most secluded pools have been washed away and cannot now be restored. Local **buses** leave for El Salado every fifteen minutes (6am–5pm) from Vicente Rocafuerte and Eloy Alfaro, behind the market; alternatively, get there on foot in about 25 minutes (turn left up a prominently signed fork off the road to Ambato).

In addition to the baths, a sub-industry of **spa** treatments and **massage** therapies has sprung up in town. Many of the smarter hotels have their own spas, featuring any or all of the saunas, steam rooms (*turcos*), steam boxes (*baños de cajón*), whirlpools (*hidromasaje*), therapeutic and relaxing massages, facials, aromatherapy, medicinal mud baths, and a range of other alternative treatments, which non-residents are generally welcome to use for a fee; see the accommodation listings for more details. El Refugio (daily 6.30am–8pm; $6 for the basics; ⓦwww.spaecuador.info), 1km east of town in the Barrio San Vicente, is a dedicated spa complex offering most of the above treatments and more. Back in town, you can also get massages (from around $25 per hour) at Stay in Touch Therapeutic Massage, at Martínez and Alfaro, or Chakra, nearby on the corner of Martínez and Alfaro, which specializes in Thai and Swedish massage.

Zoológico San Martín and around

A couple of hundred metres beyond the turn-off to El Salado, another turning heads north across the San Martín bridge to the **Zoológico San Martín** (daily 8am–6pm; $1.50), located in a narrow valley. It's a well-managed zoo, with fairly spacious enclosures for its occupants, including fenced-off natural areas for the larger mammals. Opposite is the **Acuario, Serpentario y Aves Exóticas San Martín** (same hours; $1) housing a decent representation of reptiles and fish from the coastal and eastern rainforests, including the highly poisonous *equis* (fer-de-lance), plus a few colourful birds. A further 50m down the road on the right is a signed path leading to the **Cascada Inés María** – not the most striking waterfall in the area, but still attractive. The zoo is 3km from the centre of Baños and can be reached by **buses** (every 15min weekends, 30min Mon–Fri) from the market at Vicente Rocafuerte and Eloy Alfaro; alternatively, it's about a 40-minute walk.

Eating, drinking and nightlife

Baños boasts a great spread of international **restaurants** offering everything from crêpes to curries, as well as traditional Ecuadorian food and the ubiquitous pizza. Most places are inexpensive (main courses $2–5) and tend to open around 8am for breakfast and close around 10pm; you'll find a cluster of decent restaurants on Ambato between Thomas Halflants and Eloy Alfaro. Baños' most famous **speciality** is a type of toffee made from sugar cane, called *melcocha*, which is hung from the wall and stretched into long, pale-gold strips before being sold in small plastic packets on the street. For **nightlife**, head to the stretch of Eloy Alfaro between Ambato and Espejo, where there's a cluster of bars and clubs serving cheap cocktails and beers, occasionally to live music (when a small cover charge might apply). Most venues open daily around 8pm, but usually only the ones that have pulled in a crowd will still be open in the small hours.

Restaurants and cafés

Café La Abuela Eloy Alfaro and Ambato. Cosy café with warm lighting, lots of natural wood and an agreeable choice of breakfasts, salads, snacks, pancakes and ice cream. Also has a well-stocked bar, with decent cocktails and five types of rum.
Café Ali Cumba Maldonado and Rocafuerte, on the square. Excellent ground coffee, breakfasts,

smoothies, cakes, muffins, sandwiches and home-made bread served up by a chatty Danish owner.

Blah Blah Café Corner of Martinez and Halflants. Small, cheap and cheerful café serving good breakfasts, salads, sandwiches, omelettes, pancakes and fruit juices, among other snacks and light meals. Closed Wed.

Café Hood Maldonado and Ambato. Good food and a menu oriented towards TexMex are on offer at this little restaurant enjoying a nice location overlooking the square. Closed Wed.

🏃 **Casa Hood** Martínez and Thomas Halflants. Very popular restaurant with huge range of international (mostly vegetarian) cuisine, including Indian, Chinese, Indonesian, Thai and Mexican. Also has a big book exchange and a choice of videos to play ($1) before 5pm, with a film screening at 4.30pm. Open from 3–10pm; closed Tues.

La Casa Vieja de Düsseldorf Ambato and Eloy Alfaro. Good service, a friendly atmosphere and a decent choice of fish and seafood. They also offer the "*oreja de elefante*" (elephant's ear), a massive but thin piece of steak that will fill much of your plate.

🏃 **Restaurante Mariane** Rocafuerte and Halflants. Wonderfully indulgent French food, including *steak à la crème*, *poivre et cognac* (peppered steak in a brandy cream sauce) and *crêpe au chocolat* in a dining room featuring a huge old gramophone, among other oddities.

Pancho Villa Ambato and Alfaro. Cheerful Mexican restaurant serving delicious, inexpensive food in a room covered in postcards from around the world, largely sent by satisfied customers. Good margaritas, too. Closed Sun.

Pepo's Café Ambato and Eloy Alfaro. Quiet place on a busy thoroughfare, offering a range of inexpensive Ecuadorian and international dishes.

Le Petit Réstaurant Attached to *La Petite Auberge* hotel on 16 de Diciembre and Montalvo. Warm, cosy French-run bistro serving excellent crêpes, steaks and trout, as well as their speciality meat and cheese fondues.

Rico Pan Corner of Ambato and Maldonado. Popular bakery and café, serving sandwiches in delicious wholemeal bread and a range of snacks, salads and light meals. Plenty of newspapers to read and a book exchange. Closed Sun pm.

Bars and discos

Buenavista Eloy Alfaro and Espejo. Identifiable by the large mural of Buddha spinning discs, mainly Latin numbers judging from the dancefloor, which is often among the most packed on the street. $1–2 cover.

Leprechaun Bar Eloy Alfaro and Espejo. Often crammed with happy, gyrating *salseros* spinning across an ample dancefloor, while the upstairs area is more suited to less energetic pursuits.

Peña Ananitay 16 de Diciembre and Espejo. This popular spot is one of the best places to hear live *folklórica*; intimate and atmospheric, with great music and a small dancefloor. Opens at 9.30pm.

Peña Bar Mocambo Eloy Alfaro, just north of Ambato. Three-floor venue with a small bar downstairs and space for dancing, plus a pool table upstairs, where there are also balconies well sited for people-watching.

Pipas Bar 16 de Diciembre between Ambato and Oriente. Colourful bar, decorated with surreal murals on the walls and a pool table downstairs. Excellent *piña coladas*.

Son Cubano Eloy Alfaro and Oriente. This lively place, popular with the local youths, plays a mixture of salsa and dance music.

Volcán Eloy Alfaro and Espejo. Friendly, rustic little bar with a band which plays Andean folk music most nights. Try their *volcán* cocktail, a concoction of hard spirits that goes down like molten lava.

Listings

Banks and exchange Banco del Pacífico, corner of Halflants and Rocafuerte (Visa, MasterCard, Cirrus ATM); Banco MM Jaramillo Arteaga, Ambato and Halflants; Comercial Torres, Halflants and Martínez, changes traveller's cheques; Le Petit Breton, 16 de Diciembre between Montalvo and Martínez, changes traveller's cheques and euros.

Camping equipment Varoxi, at Maldonado and Oriente, repairs rucksacks and sells others of reasonable quality, many of which are made on site.

Language schools Baños Spanish Center, Oriente 8-20 and Julio Cañar ⊕03/2740632, ⓦwww.spanishcenter.banios.com; Ciudad de Baños Languages School, Ambato 5-22 and Eloy Alfaro ⊕03/2740317, ⓦwww.escueladeidiomas .banios.com; Mayra's Spanish School, at Efren Reyes 3-30 and Martínez ⊕03/2742850, ⓦwww .mayraspanishschool.com; International Spanish School, 16 de Diciembre and Espejo ⊕03/2740612; Instituto de Español Alternativo (IdEA), corner of Alfaro and Montalvo ⊕03/2741315; Raices Spanish School, 16 de Diciembre and Pablo A Suárez ⊕/ⓕ 03/740090, ⓦwww.spanishlessons.org.

Laundry La Vieja Molienda, Thomas Halflants and Martínez; Le Petit Breton, Oriente and Eloy Alfaro;

Lavandería La Herradura, Luis A. Martínez and Eloy Alfaro.

Police and immigration Casa de Gobierno, Thomas Halflants between Ambato and Vicente Rocafuerte ☎03/2740122.

Post office Thomas Halflants, between Ambato and Vicente Rocafuerte.

Telephone Andinatel office on the corner of Vicente Rocafuerte and Thomas Halflants.

Activities and tours around Baños

Few visitors come to Baños without wanting to strike out into the surrounding countryside to explore its hills, ravines, rivers and waterfalls. There are a number of highly rewarding **hikes**, many of them giving superb views onto town or Volcán Tungurahua when the weather's clear. **Cycling** is another great way to explore independently, especially along the descending road to Puyo. In addition, several **tour operators** offer a wide range of guided excursions, including: **horseriding** in the hills around Baños; **whitewater rafting** on the Río Pastaza (class III rapids), or other rivers such as the Patate (II–III), Palora (III–IV) and Anzu (III); **canyoning**, which involves rappelling down river ravines; **hikes** and treks in the nearby Llanganates and Sangay national parks; and **jungle trips**, which usually mean a bus or jeep ride to Puyo, followed by an hour or two's drive to a base in the rainforest. Several companies also offer **climbing tours** – they traditionally focused on Tungurahua, but since it became active, attention has moved to other peaks such as Cotopaxi and Iliniza. The road up to the mountain refuge is closed, and the volcano supposedly out of bounds to climbers, though a few operators have been ill-advisedly approaching the summit by a reverse route. If you're considering booking a climbing tour, Baños (1820m above sea level), is not the ideal base from which to embark on a high-altitude trek or climb. A few agents also offer **bridge jumps** (also called *puenting*) from the Río Blanco bridge, 8km east of town; it's a risky activity at best, which is least hazardous and stressful to the rope if you swing off gently rather than leap headfirst.

Do not underestimate the risks involved in sports such as rafting, canyoning, *puenting* and climbing, which can be **dangerous activities** when led by untrained people using substandard equipment. Standards of safety are not as high as often taken for granted at home. Make sure your guide is properly qualified where possible (AGAR for rafting; ASEGUIM for climbing), and your gear is in good condition. Beware of bottom-dollar operators who may be cutting corners on safety.

Hiking

There are several interconnecting **footpaths** leading up the mountainside over the south side of town, all clearly marked on the large colour map of Baños available at the tourist office and many local shops. Starting at the south end of Maldonado, a path heads up for around 45 minutes to a large white cross marking a spot called **Bellavista**; the views at the top are breathtaking. From here, you can continue uphill for another kilometre or so to the *Hostería Luna Runtun*, where you can loop west on a downhill path that takes you to the **Mirador del Virgen**, from where it's an easy downhill walk back to Baños (the round trip takes around four hours). The *mirador*, marked by a statue of the Virgin, can be reached directly from Baños in about thirty minutes on the path starting at the south end of Juan León Mera. On the opposite side of the town, follow the path starting at the corner of Reyes and Amazonas, behind the bus terminal, for about ten minutes down to the **San Francisco bridge** spanning the beautiful Río Pastaza gorge. Across the river, several paths lead steeply up the hillside, as well as east and west along the bank of the gorge, linking up with several other bridges across the river.

Another enjoyable walk west is to the **zoo** and waterfall nearby; continuing on from both leads up to the village of Lligua, from where a trail leads to hilltops with fine views. The paths around Baños are generally safe, but a few **robberies** and **assaults** have been reported on them.

Canyoning

Canyoning is a sport that beginners with a good head for heights can have a go at – provided they have an experienced guide with good equipment who knows the route well. The best canyoning area is around the Río Negro (27km east of town), though the San Jorge waterfall (11km east) is a popular, if less spectacular, alternative. Although several agencies offer canyoning trips, **Franco de Antoni**, the owner of Pequeño Paraíso at Río Verde (see p.208), is the best person to speak to; he introduced the sport to the region and leads trips for $40 per person.

Cycling

Countless establishments in Baños rent **mountain bikes** for around $5 per day; the quality is improving and most bikes now come with front suspension. You should shop around for the best bikes and test the brakes, gears and tyres before committing yourself; consider also asking for a helmet, pump and basic toolkit. The most popular **cycling route** is east along the road to Puyo (for more details) – paved and mostly downhill, but with uphill stretches appearing fairly often – returning to Baños on one of the half-hourly buses that trundle along the road (you can store your bike on the roof; last bus around 6pm). Most people are happy to limit themselves to the first fifteen kilometres to the village of Río Verde, near the Paillón del Diablo falls, reached in one or two hours from Baños; the scenery is stunning, but beware of narrow sections, sheer drops and the pitch-black 100m tunnel at Km7, which should be cycled with care and a light if you have one; you can bypass other tunnels on the old road to the side. Some people complete the whole 61km to Puyo, a challenging ride (5–6hr) with some stiff uphill stretches along the second half of the journey. Several agencies rent out **motorbikes**, scooters and buggies for around $10 per hour, and quad-bikes for around $8 per hour; wear a helmet and ride defensively.

Tour operators

Adventurandes Eloy Alfaro 554 and Oriente ☎03/2740202. Offers two- to four-day jungle trips, as well as a range of trekking programmes around the central sierra volcanoes. Most tours are around $35 per day.

Caballos Con Christián At *Hostal Isla de Baños*, Juan Montalvo and Thomas Halflants 1-31 ☎&℻03/2740609. Offers one-day horse treks for experienced and novice riders at around $30 in the foothills of Tungurahua or outside the Baños area, including jeep transport, lunch and horses in good health.

Córdova Tours Corner of Maldonado and Espejo ☎03/2740923, ⓦwww.cordovatours.banios.com. Runs a *chiva* (wooden, open-sided bus) to the waterfalls on the road to Puyo including the Pailón del Diablo waterfall (10.30am & 3.30pm); and to watch the volcano by night (9–11pm).

Expediciones Amazónicas Oriente 11-62 and Thomas Halflants ☎03/2740506, ⓦwww .expedicionesamazonicas.com. Long-established outfit offering a wide range of activities including bridge jumps, canyoning, hiking and a three-day jungle "shaman tour", which includes participation in a shaman ritual, and a go at using a *cervátana* (blowgun).

Geotours Ambato and Halflants ☎03/2741344, ⓦwww.geotoursbanios.com. Offers a range of half- to two-day rafting trips on the ríos Patate, Pastaza, Palora and Jatun Yacu for around $60 for 3hr on the river.

Jose and 2 Dogs Maldonado and Martínez ☎03/2742438 or 09/2205211, ⓔjosbalu_99 @yahoo.com. Small, dependable company with friendly guides and access to some of the most beautiful canyoning routes other places rarely use.

Rain Forestur Ambato 800 and Maldonado ☎/⑤03/2740743, ⓦ www.rainforestur.com.ec. Jungle-tour specialist with experienced guides and a good reputation. Most tours (around $35 per day) are around Puyupungo, an hour's drive south of Puyo.

Ringo Horses At *Pizzería El Napolitano*, corner of Martínez and 12 de Noviembre ☎03/2740262. Horseriding treks to suit all levels of ability, with a good choice of well-cared-for horses.

East to Puyo

East of Baños, the road to Puyo begins its descent towards the Oriente, carving its way through the Pastaza Valley, high above the river. It's been dubbed the *Ruta de las Cascadas* for the many **waterfalls** that stripe the green valley walls, some of them falling right overhead from overhanging rocks. The vegetation is exuberant and exotic, with numerous wild orchids peppering the hillsides. It's 61km to Puyo, but the star attractions, namely the waterfalls and **cable cars** (*tarabitas*), and most spectacular scenery is in the upper section, making convenient targets for visits by bike.

The first stop is 7km from town just before the first tunnel, from where the **Tarabita Guamag** makes a 430m run across the gorge to the impressive **Agoyán waterfall** on the other side. You may want to push on 3km to the longest and most popular of the three *tarabitas*, which scuds 500m along a wire to the gorgeous **Manto de la Novia** waterfall; 1km further, another cable ride runs 400m across the valley to the **San Pedro falls**. All rides cost $1 and there are trails to the falls on the other side.

Río Verde

About 3km beyond Tarabita San Pedro and 15km from Baños is **Río Verde**, a village of modest houses, stores and truckers' stops, which is gradually reinventing itself as a recreation spot with its new boating pond and the pleasing **San Miguel** falls, reached by path from the old bridge. The real reason to pause here is to see the thundering **Pailón del Diablo** ("Devil's Cauldron"), a brute of a waterfall where the Río Verde judders down the gorge below town into the Río Pastaza. A well-maintained path leads 1km down from the car park by the church to the *Pailón* restaurant, where you'll be asked for $0.50 to see the falls from a series of viewing platforms amid swirls of fine spray.

A short walk beyond the restaurant, a wobbly bridge leads across the river to **accommodation** at *El Otro Lado* (☎03/2884193 or 09/2614798; ❹ including breakfast and dinner), three romantic and secluded cabañas (book in advance as this is a long way to come with your luggage to be disappointed) with private baths, hot water and electricity surrounded by 80 hectares of explorable forest and a restaurant nearby with great views of the waterfall. Other options in and around Río Verde include *Miramelindo* (☎03/2884194 or 02/2907131, ⓦ www .miramelindo.banios.com; ❹), the prominent building with the multicoloured roof tiles across the main road, which has pleasant en-suite rooms, hot water, swimming pool, spa treatments and a good restaurant. A couple of kilometres east of Río Verde, the Swiss-run *Pequeño Paraíso* (☎09/9819756, ⓦ www.hostel -banos-pequenoparaiso.com; ❻ including breakfast and dinner) is a peaceful place to stay, offering comfortable en-suite cabins with hot water, kitchen facilities, a natural 45-metre basalt climbing wall (with bolts and anchor), a pool, volleyball court and access to hikes through bird-filled forests (home to the Andean cock-of-the-rock). The friendly owner also leads canyoning and climbing expeditions in the area and can provide equipment. **Camping** is also possible here for $5 per person.

Río Negro to Puyo

About 2.5km east of Río Verde is the little village of **MACHAY**, from where a short trail leads through the forest to a series of pretty **waterfalls**. A further 10km east is the little hamlet of **RÍO NEGRO**. There's a turn here that leads 3km south to the *Vrindavan Jardín Ecológico* (☎09/3968555, office in Baños at the corner of Maldonado and Martínez ☎02/2235369 or 08/6016152, ⓦwww .fincavrindavan.com; ❸ including yoga lesson), a spiritual retreat offering "alternative relaxation" through yoga, African drumming, meditation and ayurveda classes, as well as walks into the forests and horseriding. The simple cabins have a shared bath with hot water and inexpensive vegetarian meals ($3 for three courses) are available in the dining room. Campers can stay for $5 and there are volunteer opportunities for $25 per week.

Heading east from Río Negro and entering Pastaza province, the scenery opens out, revealing broad views of the valley, now hot and humid with Oriente air. **MERA** (17km further and 44km from Baños) has a church, a phone office, a basic hotel, and a **police checkpoint** at which you will probably be asked to show your passport. Some 7km down the road, there's a greater military presence at **SHELL**, more hotels (but no reason to stop) and an airstrip which several light-aircraft charter companies use to service remote communities in the Oriente, most of which you'd need permission to visit. A couple also fly to cities including Quito, Lago Agrio and Coca, but these are not generally regarded as tourist services. Beyond Shell is the *Ecoparque Monte Selva* (☎03/2886821; ❺, camping $10 per person including tent, entrance and breakfast), an animal rehabilitation centre of sorts ($2), combined with swimming pools ($3) and guided woodland trails. Ten kilometres to the east lies **Puyo**, the capital of Pastaza provinces, from where roads head north to Tena and south to Macas. **Buses** run from Baños to Puyo every 30 minutes.

Guaranda and Salinas

From Ambato, most tourists head either east to Baños or south to Riobamba, with few opting for the route west to Guayaquil. This is a shame, as the road provides one of the most scenic bus rides in the sierra – especially the first 99km to **Guaranda** through low, round, intensively cultivated hills, with some dizzying views onto Chimborazo. Guaranda has a beautiful location and some handsome colonial-style architecture, but there's little to keep you interested for more than a couple of hours. Nearby, **Salinas** is one of the prettiest and most rewarding villages in the whole sierra.

Guaranda

About two hours after leaving Ambato, you wind your way down to **GUARANDA** (2670m), which sits in a shallow basin surrounded by hills. It's hard to believe this is the provincial capital of Bolívar, what with its physical isolation and sleepy, small-town air. The centre of town is marked by the charming **Parque Bolívar**, lined with old adobe houses with painted wooden balconies and sloping, red-tiled roofs flecked with lichen. The square also houses a grand, twin-towered **church**, a striking mixture of bare stone and white stucco, and the gleaming, white-walled **Municipio**, looming over the mature palms that give this place a more tropical look than its climate warrants.

Arrival and information

The **bus station**, on the outskirts of the town centre about ten blocks east of Parque Bolívar, is served by a few taxis. In town, you'll find **taxis** hanging around Plaza Roja, where **local buses** pull in and out. **Information** is available at the municipal tourist office inside the E-Mapa building on Moreno and 7 de Mayo (Mon–Fri 8am–noon & 2–4pm; ☎03/2980327). **Internet** facilities are available at Compumás on 10 de Agosto and 7 de Mayo, and around the corner on 7 de Mayo at Technisoft. Banco Pichincha, Azuay and 7 de Mayo, has an **ATM** for Visa, MasterCard and Diners.

Accommodation

The fanciest **place to stay** is *La Colina* (☎03/2980666, ℱ2981954; ❼), Av Guayaquil 117 and Guaranda, perched up on a hill overlooking the town with fantastic views. There's also a reasonable restaurant and a small indoor pool, gym and sauna. In the centre, the best choice is *Hostal de las Flores* (☎03/2984396; ❹), Pichincha 402 and Rocafuerte, a charming old house with wooden floorboards and artfully decorated en-suite rooms. Stand-bys include *Ejecutivo*, García Moreno 803 (☎/ℱ03/2982044; ❸), with clean white walls, firm beds and parquet flooring, and the large, echoing *Cochabamba*, at García Moreno and 7 de Mayo (☎03/2981958; ❹), whose en-suite rooms are fairly comfortable though showing their age.

The Town

The town's narrow, cobbled streets see relatively little traffic, and it's not unusual to spot someone leading his horse down the road, or a couple of hens clucking around the pavement. After you've nosed around the square, and checked out the **Museo Escuela Cultura Andina** (Mon–Fri 8am–noon & 2–4pm; free) in an old hospital on 7 de Mayo and Rocafuerte – a building at least as interesting as its displays on archeology, local culture and medicine – the only real "sight" to head for is the towering stone statue of "**El Indio Guaranga**", the sixteenth-century indigenous chief after whom the town is said to have been named. It's up on one of the nearby hills ($1 by taxi; 45min walk), with sweeping views down to the town and across to Chimborazo, and a modest museum of history (variable hours; free) alongside it. Otherwise, there's a colourful Friday or (bigger) Saturday **market** on the Plaza 15 de Mayo, where you'll see *campesinos* from local villages trading wheat, barley and maize for fruit brought up from the coast.

Eating and drinking

For **restaurants**, try *La Estancia* (closed Mon evening), García Moreno and Sucre, decorated in wood like a country estate with a bull's head and saddles, or similar *La Bohemia* (closed Sun), on the park. For a **drink** and a bite, you can't beat *Los 7 Santos* (closed Sun), on Convención de 1884 and 10 de Agosto, a wonderful arty café abundant with flowers and plants.

Salinas

The final bend in the dirt road branching north from Guaranda for 30km suddenly reveals a dramatic view of **SALINAS** (3550m), a collection of white houses huddled together near the foot of a vertical wall of rock, surrounded by rolling fields and plains. This isolated village, also called "Salinas de Guaranda" to distinguish it from the coastal resort, is named after the abundant supplies of salt that have been exploited here since pre-Hispanic times.

The village is today best known for its flourishing cooperatives, which were established with the help of a Salesian missionary, Father Antonio Polo, in 1971. The **FUNORSAL** foundation (Fundación de Organizaciones de Salinas) he founded provided locals with training, materials, technical support, bank loans and accounting assistance. It transformed villagers' lives: sheep owners who had previously sold raw wool to middlemen for a pittance began to spin their own yarn and supply directly to manufacturers for a decent profit; and dairy farmers set up highly productive milk and cheese factories, supplying retailers at a national level.

Visiting the village's cooperatives ($1 per person), particularly the **cheese factory**, **wool workshop** and **chocolate workshop**, makes for an enjoyable and enlightening few hours, especially if you take a local guide to show you around ($10), which you can arrange at the community tourist **information** office on the *parque central* (Mon–Sat 8am–5/6pm, Sat & Sun 10am–1pm; ☎03/2390024 or 2390020, ⓦwww.salinerito.com). They also offer numerous **tours**, horse rides, bike trips and local hikes and can help with visits to the **Subtrópico**, the warmer subtropical part of the province in the west, such as **Piedra Blanca**, a community ecotourism venture (☎03/2608544 or 09/3044290, ⓦwww.piedrablanca.org; ❹) with a simple lodge and plenty of opportunities to explore its surrounding forests.

Practicalities

Six local **buses** a day (five on Sat & Sun; 1hr) run in each direction between Salinas and Guaranda's Plaza Roja. The last bus from Salinas leaves at 3pm, and from Guaranda at 4pm. For **accommodation**, try *El Refugio* (☎03/2390022 or 2210044; ❷–❸), a pleasant, rustic hotel run by a cooperative and offering private en-suite rooms and cheaper ones with shared bath. The hotel also has an inexpensive **restaurant**, offers Spanish lessons and has a small archeology museum on the ground floor. Another nice option is the smaller *Samilagua* (❷) opposite, with good mattresses and a medicinal plant garden.

Riobamba and around

From Guaranda, a serpentine dirt road leads 61km east to **Riobamba**, the liveliest and most attractive city in the central sierra, sitting on the Panamericana 52km south of Ambato. With an appealing blend of fast-paced buzz and old colonial charm, Riobamba easily merits a visit in its own right, but can also be combined with worthwhile excursions. Most famously, it's the start of the **Devil's Nose train ride** and is also a popular base for visiting **Volcán Chimborazo**; nearby **Guano**, a rug-manufacturing centre, and **Zalarón**, with its authentic highland market, are somewhat less demanding targets. East of Riobamba, the northern stretch of **Parque Nacional Sangay** offers some great trekking opportunities, in particular to the volcanic crater of **El Altar**, approached from the community of **Candelaria**, and to **El Placer hot springs** and **Volcán Sangay**, both reached from the village of **Alao**.

Riobamba

The self-proclaimed "Sultan of the Andes", **RIOBAMBA** (2735m) is a handsome city made up of stately squares, flaking pastel-coloured buildings, cobbled streets and sprawling markets. An important centre since the early days of the colony, the place was dealt an abrupt and catastrophic blow in 1797 when a massive earthquake left it in ruins, though it was quickly rebuilt where it stands today, 20km north of its original site. Located in the centre of the Ecuadorian sierra, Riobamba is a major trading nucleus, with part of its appeal stemming from the lively mix of suited city dwellers and large numbers of indigenous traders from the countryside. The main **market day** is Saturday, when the city overflows with energy and colour. Another draw is the wonderful view (if the weather cooperates) across the city to Volcán Chimborazo; most hotels have flat roofs, so if you wake up on a clear morning – the earlier the clearer, usually – ask to go up to the roof patio.

Arrival and information

Riobamba's main **bus terminal** is the Terminal Terrestre (☎03/2962005), a couple of kilometres from the centre, at the intersection of avenidas Daniel León Borja and De La Prensa, cabs into the centre cost $1, or you can take a bus down Daniel León Borja as far as the train station. If you're arriving from Baños or the Oriente, you'll pull in at the smaller **Terminal Oriental** (☎03/2960766) on the corner of Espejo and Luz Elisa Borja, about 1km northeast of the centre and served by plenty of taxis and city buses. Other bus stations are dotted around the periphery of downtown, servicing outlying communities – details are given in the relevant accounts in this chapter. The **train station** (☎03/2961909) is very central at Avenida Daniel León Borja and Carabobo. In town, you'll find plenty of **taxis** hanging around Parque Maldonado, Parque Sucre and Parque Libertad. If you need to call one, try one of the cooperatives (☎03/2960088, 2961646 or 2966011).

The very helpful **Ministerio de Turismo** (Mon–Fri 8am–1pm & 2–6pm; ☎/⒡03/2941213) is in the Centro de Arte y Cultura on Avenida Daniel

The Devil's Nose train ride

In 1899, after 25 years of frustrated plans and abortive attempts, work finally started on Ecuador's first **railway**, which would link the coastal city of Guayaquil with the capital, Quito, in the highlands. The first hundred-kilometre stretch was laid without too much difficulty, but as the tracks advanced eastwards towards the mighty barrier of the Andes it was obvious a serious challenge lay ahead. The greatest obstacle, which prompted the line to be dubbed "the most difficult railway in the world", was met 130km east of Guayaquil when the tracks reached a near-vertical wall of rock, known as **El Nariz del Diablo (The Devil's Nose)**. The ingenious engineering solution was to carve a series of tight zigzags out of the rock, which allowed the train to climb at a gradient of 1-in-18, from 1806m to 2607m, by going forwards then backwards up the tracks. Once past Alausí in 1902, progress sped up and the tracks reached Riobamba in 1905 and Quito in 1908. The line went on to face many financial difficulties and soon acquired a reputation for poor equipment and administration and frequent delays and derailments.

The service from Guayaquil to Riobamba and Quito continued to run, with interruptions, until 1997, when El Niño-related weather devastated the tracks. The hundred-kilometre stretch from Riobamba to Sibambe, at the end of the Devil's Nose descent, has since been restored and is now operated as a **tourist service**, offering spectacular views of Chimborazo and Carihuairazo and a thrilling descent down the Devil's Nose itself. The most popular way to travel is on the roof of the train – much to the amusement of locals who watch it trundle by, piled high with its cargo of gringos.

Taking the train

The train leaves Riobamba on Wednesdays, Fridays and Sundays at 7am, taking three to four hours to get to the town of **Alausí**, from where it's another hour to the little station of **Sibambe**, at the bottom of the Nariz del Diablo (though delays sometimes make the journey much longer). After a twenty-minute pause, the train heads back up the Nariz del Diablo and stops at Alausí at around 1.30pm (for more on Alausí, see p.227), where it pauses again for over an hour, prompting many passengers to travel the last stretch by bus (2hr), cutting several hours off the return journey. The train finally gets back to Riobamba at about 6–7pm. **Tickets** cost $11 for the standard Riobamba–Sibambe–Alausí route, and a further $3.50 for the slow haul back from Alausí to Riobamba (when you can often have the train to yourself). You can buy them at the city's train station (Tues, Thurs & Sat 10am–6pm, also in the morning before departure from 6am; ☎03/2961909). An alternative is to join the train at Alausí (arrive by 10am to be on the safe side) for the Nariz del Diablo alone (Alausí–Sibambe–Alausí), a ticket for which costs $7.80 and can be bought in Riobamba or at the station in Alausí.

If you plan to **ride on the roof**, dress in layers – the weather is freezing at the beginning of the journey but warms up considerably after a couple of hours. It's a good idea to take your sleeping bag to sit on, if you've got one, or to buy one of the inexpensive cushions on sale by the tracks, as the tin roof offers little comfort. Vendors climb onto the roof at various stops along the way to sell refreshments – but it's still a good idea to take your own water and food. The traditional train is regularly replaced by two smaller and less nostalgic **autoferros** (a bus chassis attached to rail undercarriages), especially during the week when there aren't so many passengers. The service is subject to unpredictable changes, so call the station office ahead for all the latest news.

León Borja and Brasil; there's also a small information office at the bus terminal. For basic information on Volcán Chimborazo or Parque Nacional Sangay, take a taxi to the **Ministerio del Ambiente** (Mon–Fri 8.30am–4.30pm; ☎03/2963779) at 9 de Octubre, near Calle Duchicela, or to the

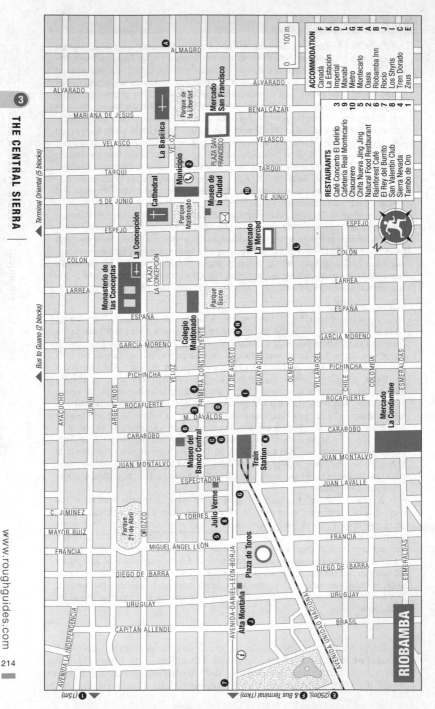

RIOBAMBA

ACCOMMODATION
Canadá	F
La Estación	K
Imperial	D
Manabí	L
Metro	G
Montecarlo	H
Oasis	A
Riobamba Inn	B
Rocío	J
Los Shyris	I
Tren Dorado	C
Zeus	E

RESTAURANTS
Café Concerto El Delirio	3
Cafetería Real Montecarlo	9
Chacarero	10
Chifa Nueva Jing Jing	5
Natural Food Restaurant	2
Rainforest Café	6
El Rey del Burrito	7
San Valentín Club	8
Sierra Nevada	4
Tambo de Oro	1

ALMAGRO
ALVARADO
MARIANA DE JESÚS
VELASCO
TARQUI
5 DE JUNIO
ESPEJO
COLÓN
LARREA
ESPAÑA
GARCÍA MORENO
PICHINCHA
ROCAFUERTE
M. DÁVALOS
CARABOBO
JUAN MONTALVO
ESPECTADOR
V. TORRES
MIGUEL ÁNGEL LEÓN
DIEGO DE IBARRA
URUGUAY
CAPITÁN ALLENDE

ALVARADO
BENALCÁZAR
VELASCO
TARQUI
5 DE JUNIO
ESPEJO
COLÓN
LARREA
ESPAÑA
GARCÍA MORENO
PICHINCHA
ROCAFUERTE
CARABOBO
JUAN MONTALVO
JUAN LAVALLE
FRANCIA
DIEGO DE IBARRA
URUGUAY
BRASIL

VELOZ
PRIMERA CONSTITUYENTE
10 DE AGOSTO
GUAYAQUIL
OLMEDO
VILLARROEL
CHILE
COLOMBIA
ESMERALDAS

AYACUCHO
JUNÍN
ARGENTINOS
VELOZ

C. JIMÉNEZ
MAYOR RUIZ
FRANCIA
OROZCO

Parque de la Libertad
Mercado San Francisco
La Basílica
Municipio
Cathedral
PLAZA SAN FRANCISCO
Museo de la Ciudad
La Concepción
Parque Maldonado
Monasterio de las Conceptas
PLAZA LA CONCEPCIÓN
Parque Sucre
Colegio Maldonado
Mercado La Merced
Museo del Banco Central
Parque 21 de Abril
Train Station
Julio Verne
Plaza de Toros
Alta Montaña
Mercado La Condamine

AVENIDA DANIEL LEÓN BORJA
AVENIDA UNIDAD NACIONAL
AVENIDA LA INDEPENDENCIA

▲ Terminal Oriental (5 blocks)
▲ Bus to Guano (2 blocks)
▲ ❶ (15m)
▲ ❸ (250m), ❺ ❼ & Bus Terminal (1km)

0 100 m

Fundación Natura office, at Segundo Rosero and Saint Amound Montriu in the Barrio Los Álamos.

Accommodation

There are some good budget to mid-priced **accommodation** options in Riobamba, but nowhere really smart in the town centre. If you're after luxury, you'll need to take a bus or taxi to one of the **out-of-town options**, which also tend to be much quieter. If arriving in Riobamba the night before the "Devil's Nose" train departs in the high season, it's worth phoning ahead to book a room, as the most popular places fill very quickly. Most of the very cheap hotels are clustered around the train station.

Canadá Av de la Prensa 23-31 ⓣ/ⓕ03/2946676. Modern hotel (with English-speaking owners) diagonally opposite the bus terminal, offering simple, spotless rooms with private bath and cable TV. ❹

La Estación Av Unidad Nacional 29-15 and Carabobo ⓣ03/2955226, ⓕ2951541. Well-presented hotel by the train station, offering tidy rooms with private bath and cable TV. The more comfortable suites cost the same, but are on the noisier street side of the building. Early breakfast served for those making the train ride. ❹

Imperial Rocafuerte 22-15 ⓣ03/2960429. A notch above the real cheapies, with spacious, reasonably comfortable rooms with and without private bath; popular and good value, though the TV in the central living room can be noisy. Also organizes day-trips to Chimborazo. ❷

Manabí Colón 19-28 ⓣ03/2967967. Old-fashioned, rather dated hotel offering light, tidy rooms with wooden floors, cable TV and en-suite bathrooms, or cheaper ones with shared bath (❷). There's also an on-site garage. ❸

Metro Av Daniel León Borja and Lavalle ⓣ03/2961714. Simple, clean rooms in a distinctive older hotel with lots of light, en-suite bathrooms and cable TV (in most rooms). Has its own parking. ❷

Montecarlo 10 de Agosto 25-41 ⓣ03/2960557. Very colonial-looking place with comfortable, carpeted rooms with private bathrooms and cable TV, arranged around a lovely two-storey courtyard festooned with hanging plants. Breakfast included. ❺

Oasis Veloz and Almagro ⓣ03/2961210. Friendly family hotel at the quieter end of town, with pleasant outdoor space and en-suite rooms with cable TV. The mattresses could be a little plumper. ❸

Riobamba Inn Carabobo 23-20 ⓣ03/2961696, ⓕ2940974. Well-run hotel with pleasant, cared-for rooms, some with attractive new bedding and curtains, others more dated. All have private bathroom and most have cable TV. Has private parking and breakfast is included. ❹

Rocío Brasil 21-68 ⓣ03/2961848. Pleasant, tidy, good-value *residencial* on a quiet side street, run by an elderly couple. Rooms are spacious and come with private bath and cable TV. Breakfast not available. ❸

Los Shyris Corner of 10 de Agosto and Rocafuerte ⓣ03/2960323. A hotel with low ceilings and dowdy wallpaper, kept clean and tidy by the friendly staff. It's popular with backpackers for its central location, internet access and huge cable TV in a cosy lounge area; most rooms have private bath. ❸

Tren Dorado Carabobo 22-35 ⓣ/ⓕ03/2964890. Popular hotel with a choice of newer, quiet rooms at the back (no TV), or slightly older ones at the front (with cable TV), all with private bath. Also offers outside washtubs and clothes lines, early-morning breakfasts before the train ride and tours to Chimborazo. ❹

Zeus Av Daniel León Borja 41-29 ⓣ03/9680360 or 2968036, ⓦwww.hotelzeuscom.ec. Large hotel that's a bit more flashy than the competition, but has a lovely restaurant. Standard rooms have cable TV and private bath, but are slightly drab, while executive suites have more ostentatious furnishings and bathtubs. ❻

Out-of-town

Abraspungo Km3.5 along the road to Guano ⓣ03/2944299, ⓦwww.abraspungo.com.ec. Upmarket, tastefully designed lodge, offering a rustic, hacienda-style look with plenty of modern comforts. Includes a buffet breakfast. Can be reached by taxi ($3) or the bus to Guano. ❽

La Andaluza 16km north of Riobamba on the Panamericana ⓣ03/2949370, ⓦwww.hosteria-andaluza.com. A converted hacienda keeping a degree of its historic charm with antique furnishings and fireplaces, complemented with mod cons such as cable TV. The restaurant is good and popular with tour groups. ❽

El Troje Km45 along the road to Chambo ⓣ03/2622200, ⓦwww.eltroje.com. Modern, country hotel in a secluded spot featuring chintzy comfort and frilly valances, as well as an indoor pool and spa. ❼

A number of outfits and independent guides offer a range of **tours around Riobamba**. For day visitors, the most popular target is the refuge at 4800m on the slopes of Volcán Chimborazo, from where you can take a strenuous half-hour hour walk up to the second refuge (5000m); see p.220 for details. Several hotels in Riobamba offer good-value **day-trips** here, including the *Tren Dorado* (see p.215) and the *Imperial* (see p.215), though these aren't recommended for any serious mountaineering. Dedicated **climbing companies and guides** (see below) concentrate on guided ascents of Chimborazo (6268m), the highest peak in Ecuador and the most popular volcano climb after Cotopaxi; most also offer climbs up neighbouring Carihuairazo (see p.221) and other central sierra volcanoes. Some also do multi-day **hiking** programmes around the sierra, providing tents, sleeping bags, food and transport. All prices quoted below are per person for a group of two people, including a guide and equipment rental.

Riobamba is also a great place to arrange **mountain-bike tours**, ranging from riding down the slopes of Chimborazo to outings around rural villages along backroads or multi-day tours of the Atillo or Ozogoche lakes. There are two excellent dedicated operators, who use good bikes, protective equipment and a support vehicle: **Biking Spirit**, at Alta Montaña (see below), offers rides for all levels; and **Probici**, Primera Constituyente 23-51 and Larrea (T 03/2941880 or 2961759, W www .probici.com; if there's no one there, ask in the fabric shop opposite).

If you're interested in supporting **community tourism** initiatives in Chimborazo, get in touch with the Corporación de Desarrollo Comunitario y Turismo de Chimborazo, Veloz 22-28 between Colón and Espejo, CC High Fashion, Office 106 (T 03/2951996, W www.cordtuch.org.ec), which coordinates fifteen local projects, mostly in remote indigenous villages. Generally, for a modest charge, you'll have the pleasure of being the guests of these communities, experiencing rural highland life first hand and get the chance to be taken on hikes, horse rides, mountain-bike trips or climbing expeditions by people who have spent all their lives in these hills.

Climbing companies and guides

Alta Montaña Av Daniel León Borja 35-17 and Diego Ibarra T 03/2942215, E aventurag @ch.pro.ec. Well-respected company offering ascents up Chimborazo (they manage

The City

The best place to start exploring Riobamba is the **Parque Maldonado**. This wide square is lined by the city's most impressive nineteenth-century architecture, including the colonnaded, peach-and-white **Municipio** (where Ecuador's first constitution was signed in 1830) and other flamboyant colonial buildings. On the northwest side of the square is the relatively new **Museo de la Ciudad** (Mon–Fri 8am–12.30pm & 2.30–6pm, Sat 8am–4pm; free) in a stately and elegantly restored building, with displays on Sangay national park, some stuffed animals and temporary art exhibitions. Across the square, the delicately carved stone facade of the **cathedral** is Riobamba's only survivor of the 1797 earthquake, painstakingly transported and reassembled here when the town was rebuilt. The city's two other major churches are the Neoclassical, pink-domed **Basílica**, three blocks southeast on Parque La Libertad, and the red-brick, neo-Gothic **Iglesia de la Concepción**, a couple of blocks northeast of Parque Maldonado.

Adjoining the Iglesia de la Concepción, the **Monasterio de las Conceptas** houses one of the best museums of religious art outside Quito (entrance on Argentinos, Tues–Sat 9am–noon & 3–6pm; $3). A series of small rooms around both refuges), Cotopaxi, El Altar and many other peaks (around $180), as well as being specialists for logistically difficult climbs, such as Sangay. There are many trekking options, including a five-day hike around Chimborazo ($90–350 depending on length), and the Inca trail with the chance to get there from the beautiful Atillo lakes, plus horse-riding and mountain biking. Recommended.

Andes Trek Colón 22-25 and 10 de Agosto ☎03/2940964, ⓦwww.andes-trek.com. Run by established guide Marcelo Puruncajas and his sons, who've been climbing Chimborazo for decades. Offers guided ascents up all the sierra peaks, including Chimborazo ($180), and hiking programmes around Cotopaxi, Chimborazo and Sangay protected areas from $70 per day.

Expediciones Andinas Urb. Las Abras, 3km along the road to Guano, opposite *Abraspungo* ☎03/2964915, ⓦwww.expediciones-andinas.com. A polished full-service outfit run by respected mountaineer Marco Cruz, offering everything from treks (with or without llamas to carry bags), horse rides, single ascents up Chimborazo (four-day programme costing $490 per person for a group of 4–6) to multi-climb packages and treks ($1760 each for 4–6 people for a sixteen-day tour including five peaks). Uses its own mountain lodge, the comfortable and heated *Estrella del Chimborazo* at 4000m, as base camp for Chimborazo. Best to book in advance.

Julio Verne Travel 22-25 and Av Daniel León Borja ☎/03/2963436, ⓦwww.julioverne -travel.com. Reputable Dutch–Ecuadorian operator specializing in adventure tours, including mountaineering, cycling (full-suspension mountain bikes), whitewater rafting, jungle trips and multi-day treks; the latter includes the Inca trail from Alausí to Ingapirca, five days in the páramo around the El Placer hot springs, or around the spectacular El Altar peak. Good equipment.

Veloz Coronado Expediciones Chile 33-21 and Francia ☎03/2960916, ⓔivoveloz @yahoo.com. Run by Ivo Veloz, an ASEGUIM qualified guide, who comes from a strong mountaineering family (his father has climbed Chimborazo 230 times in forty years). Chimborazo ascents start at $200 per person.

a leafy patio is devoted to various themes, with most pieces dating from the eighteenth century. The bulk of the collection is made up of carvings and paintings, but the museum's most prized possession is a gold, jewel-encrusted monstrance used to display the consecrated wafer of the Eucharist during Mass, believed to be one of the most valuable in South America.

Other museums inlcude the **Museo del Banco Central**, Veloz and Carabobo (Mon–Fri 9am–5pm, Sat 10am–4pm; $1), which features illuminating pre-Columbian artefacts, with detailed descriptions in English of the development of local and national cultures from 10,000 BC onwards, finishing off with a section on colonial religious art. The imposing **Colegio Maldonado** (Mon–Fri 8am–1pm; $0.25), on **Parque Sucre**, has a modest natural history collection; even if the museum is closed, it's worth taking a look inside the college building to admire its marble staircases and arcaded courtyard. If you're in town on a very clear day, wander out to the **Parque 21 de Abril**, a small, landscaped hill about eight blocks north of Parque Sucre, which has fine views over the town and across to Chimborazo.

If you're around on a Saturday you can't fail to be impressed by the immense **market** bulging out of the streets bounded by calles España, 5 de Junio,

Guayaquil and Argentinos. The range of products for sale is staggering, from squawking chickens to rubber boots; for **artesanías** head to the Plaza La Concepción, in front of the church, where you'll find many *shigra* bags, ponchos, shawls and jewellery. If you're not in town on Saturday you can still catch the smaller-scale Wednesday version, as well as the daily covered **fruit and vegetable market** at La Condamine, or the smaller **flower and fruit market** at La Merced, off Colón, between Guayaquil and Olmedo. Something else to look out for is **tagua nuts** (see *Crafts and markets* colour section) carved into items ranging from massage contraptions to jewellery; there are a handful of tagua carving shops on Daniel León Borja between Lavalle and Francia.

Eating, drinking and nightlife

Riobamba offers a decent choice of **restaurants**, but very little in the way of **nightlife**. What exists is usually only open from Thursday to Saturday; the city's favourites – *La Vieja Guardia*, on Manuel E. Flor and Zambrano, and *Romeo & Juliet Bar*, on Vargas Torres and Avenida Daniel León Borja – are both fairly small disco-bars playing a mixture of salsa and dance music.

Café Concerto El Delirio Primera Constituyente 28-16. Beautiful colonial house, once the home of Simón Bolívar, with a flower-filled patio and a cosy indoor dining room with a crackling log fire. Its elaborate meat and fish dishes (often swimming in sauces) are pricier than average ($5–9 a main course), and it can feel a bit touristy, but it's pleasant enough when there's live *folklórica* music.
Cafetería Real Montecarlo 10 de Agosto 25-41. Good-value snacks, sandwiches and some main meals served in intimate wooden booths; soft lighting and soothing music make it more of an evening place.
Chacarero 5 de Junio 21-46. Small, popular, family-run restaurant serving the best pizzas in Riobamba; a typical small one goes for around $4. Mon–Sat 3–10pm, Sun 4–9pm.
Chifa Nueva Jing Jing Miguel Ángel León and 10 de Agosto. Noodle and rice dishes like any other *chifa*, but this one's particularly popular because of the gargantuan portions.
Natural Food Restaurant Tarqui and Veloz. Inexpensive vegetarian meals along with standard meat dishes. The two-course veggie *almuerzo* is only $1.50 and filling. Closed evenings and all Sun.
Rainforest Café next to *Tren Dorado* on Carabobo and 10 de Agosto. An option for early breakfasts

before train departures, this jungly café done up with tiger-print tablecloths also serves up crêpes, hot drinks and snacks. Closed Mon.
El Rey del Burrito Av Daniel León Borja and Costales. Inexpensive Mexican restaurant on the ground floor of a large old house decorated with sombreros and textiles, serving reasonable *enchiladas*, *burritos* and all the other standards.
San Valentín Club Av Daniel León Borja 22-19. Lively, diner-style café-bar that's best for evening meals, cooking up pizzas, burgers, tacos and *burritos*, best washed down with plenty of beer. Fills with a young and cheerful local crowd. Tues–Sat 5pm–midnight.
Sierra Nevada Primera Constituyente and Rocafuerte. This comfortable, colourful converted home has a wide-ranging menu, including breakfasts, steaks, pasta and prawns in coconut; they also do a good value *almuerzo* and vegetarian numbers, if you ask.
Tambo de Oro Carlos Zambrano and Junín, five blocks west of the Parque 21 de Abril ☎03/2962668. Not very central, but the delicious home-made soups, such as the prawn bisque, and well-prepared meat and fish dishes make the 5 min taxi ride worthwhile. Closed evenings.

Listings

Banks Banco del Pacífico, corner of Av Borja and Zambrano has a MasterCard and Visa ATM; and Banco de Guayaquil on Primera Constituyente, between Moreno and Pichincha, has a Visa, MasterCard and Cirrus ATM; Banco Pichincha, corner of Moreno and Primera Constituyente, has Cirrus and Plus ATM.

Buses Local city buses regularly go to the Terminal Terrestre along Orozco, returning down Av Daniel León Borja; for the Terminal Oriental, they leave from the train station.
Festivals The biggest are Las Fiestas Abrileñas, leading up to April 21, which commemorates the victory over the Spanish at the Battle of Tapi in

1822, and November 11 for the Independence of Riobamba.

Health Private hospitals Clínica Metropolitana, Junín 25-28 and García Moreno (☎03/2941930), and Clínica San Juan, Veloz and Los Alamos (☎03/2944636).

Laundry Blue Fountain, Carababo 22-35 and 10 de Agosto.

Police Calle Policía ☎03/2969300.

Post office 10 de Agosto 21-72 and Espejo.

Telephone office Andinatel at Tarqui and Veloz.

Travel agents Most general travel agents are strung along the main artery formed by Daniel León Borja and 10 de Agosto. For climbing, trekking and biking tour operators and guides, refer to the box on pp.216–217.

Guano and Santa Teresita

The sleepy little village of **Guano**, 8km north of Riobamba, is set in a picturesque valley (now strung with a rickety *tarabita* cable car) and boasts a lovely, flower-filled square, where there's a small **museum** showing pre-Columbian ceramics and the mummy of a monk, and a couple of handsome old churches. Guano is best known as a **rug-manufacturing** centre; there are lots of small workshops dotted about the square making and selling rugs of questionable taste – though you can ask for your own designs. Most are made from sisal, which is grown and cut down in the fields surrounding the village. You'll also find leather products, particularly cushions, and other assorted *artesanía*. Guano is quick and easy to reach from Riobamba, with **buses** leaving every ten minutes from the Mercado Dávalos at Rocafuerte and Nueva York, three blocks north of Ayacucho.

From Guano, frequent buses shuttle to the neighbouring village of **Santa Teresita**. From the village's church, where they drop and pick up passengers, it's a twenty- to thirty-minute downhill walk to the **Balneario Los Elenes** (buses go all the way on Sunday, when it gets busy), a rather dog-eared bathing complex with four cold spring-fed pools (daily 6am–6pm; $0.25). The setting is outstanding though, with fabulous views onto Tungurahua, and thanks to a local microclimate the weather is often warm and sunny.

Punín and Zalarón

Ten kilometres south of Riobamba is **PUNÍN**, an otherwise unremarkable place – were it not for the large number of prehistoric animal **fossils** discovered there in 1923. These included a fossilized human skull dating to about 8000 BC, which became known as Puninoid Man, the oldest human remains uncovered in Ecuador; there's a small **museum** in the village displaying some of the specimens.

Eleven kilometres along a looping road west of Punín is **ZALARÓN**, an indigenous village and home to a wonderful local **Friday market**, filled with red-ponchoed shoppers doing a day's trade. **Buses** to both villages leave from the stop on Avenida Juan Félix Proaño and Olmedo outside the public hospital at the southern end of Riobamba. Regular buses depart for Punín taking twenty minutes; for Zalarón (45min), they leave weekdays at 6.30am, returning 12.30pm, or take a *camioneta* from Punín.

Volcán Chimborazo and around

At 6268m, **Volcán Chimborazo** is the highest peak in Ecuador. A giant of a volcano thought to have last erupted some 10,000 years ago, its base spans approximately 20km and its upper elevations are permanently covered in snow and ice. The summit was once imagined to be the highest in the world and still enjoys the distinction of being the furthest point from the centre of the earth and the closest to the sun – thanks to the bulge around the equator.

Facing Chimborazo to the northeast, **Carihuairazo** (5020m), a jagged trio of craggy spires that contrasts with the snowy bulk of its more famous neighbour, is a very respectable mountain in its own right and a popular preparation climb for a later attempt on Chimborazo.

Both mountains form the topographical centrepieces of the 58,560-hectare **Reserva Faunística Chimborazo** ($10 entrance fee, irregularly collected from the guard post on the road up to Chimborazo's refuges), created in 1987 as a haven for alpacas, llamas and especially **wild vicuñas**, which disappeared from Ecuador around the time of the Conquest. Following a very successful reintroduction programme, there are now more than 2500 vicuñas eking life from the thin air and marginal terrain high up around Chimborazo.

Visiting the Chimborazo refuges

The two mountain **refuges** perched on Chimborazo's slopes make obvious targets for **day-trips** from Riobamba. The lower **Hermanos Carrel refuge** can by reached by car in about ninety minutes from Riobamba; the easiest way to get there is to take a *camioneta* from near the train station (about $25) or arrange transport with your hotel or a tour operator.

A fair challenge for most day-trippers is the walk from the first refuge up to the second **Whymper refuge** (45min–1hr), named after Edward Whymper, the British climber who made the first ascent of Chimborazo in 1880 with the Carrel brothers. At an altitude of 5000m, there's only 200m vertical height between the refuges, but it can be totally exhausting if you're not acclimatized. With any luck, the views will more than repay the effort, but it's possible everything will be hidden by clouds; self-guided trails are in construction to give visitors something to do while up here; take plenty of sunscreen, water and very warm gear. This is the larger and more comfortable of the two refuges, but both have fireplaces, cooking facilities, running water, electricity and cost $10 for the night. Hot drinks, soup and snacks are available at both. If you're sleeping at either, bring a warm sleeping bag; there are lockers to store your gear while you're climbing, but you'll need to bring a lock. For information on either refuge contact Alta Montaña which manages them (see box, pp.216–217 for details).

Climbing Chimborazo

Although not Ecuador's most technically difficult ascent, the **climb** to the summit of Chimborazo from the Whymper refuge requires large reserves of strength and stamina, previous climbing experience and confidence with full mountaineering equipment. Full **acclimatization** is essential, and climbing several other peaks in advance, such as Iliniza Norte, Carihuairazo and even Cotopaxi, is common preparation.

There are several **routes to the summit**, though following rapid deglaciation, the one known as the **Normal Route** is currently considered the safest and is the most commonly used. Fast-changing conditions and the vagaries of the local climate make it imperative to go with a **guide** who knows the mountain well (see box, pp.216–217). Most climbers set off around midnight or earlier, taking seven to ten hours to reach the summit from the Whymper refuge and about three to four to descend. The way up is relentlessly steep, and a long, hard slog, first over unstable rocky terrain, where route-finding is difficult, and then on snow and ice. Along with all the standard mountaineering equipment, you should wear a helmet because of the risk of rock fall in a section known as **El Corredor** (the corridor). The route tops out at the **Veintimilla summit** (6267m), from where it is a leg-sapping haul across a bowl of snow to the main **Whymper summit** (6268m), which can take anything from twenty minutes to an hour each way, depending on snow depth. The mountain has three other summits – trying to conquer them all in one go (called *La Integral*) is a rarely achieved feat of bravura carried off by only the most accomplished mountaineers. The **best months** for climbing Chimborazo are January and December; between June and October it can be windy, but it can be climbed, weather permitting, year-round.

Climbing Carihuairazo

Carihuairazo (5020m) can be approached on a rough track 14km northeast of the crossroads known as the *Cruce del Arenal* on the Ambato–Guaranda road. The track passes through **Mechahuasca**, the area used for rearing vicuñas as part of the reintroduction programme. From here it is about four hours' walk to good camping areas below the rocky slopes beneath the glacier; other scenic camping spots (at around 4300m) can be approached from **La Urbina** in the south (see below), after a beautiful day's walk up the Mocha valley. Climbers typically leave around 3am and take about seven hours to get up and down. There's some ice climbing with a messy, mixed terrain scramble towards the top; crampons, ice axe and rope are essential. The true summit, a seemingly inaccessible tower of rock at the end of a precarious ridge, will be out of reach to all but the most experienced climbers. Hiring a **guide** is strongly recommended and most of the climbing outfits listed on pp.216–217 offer trips to Carihuairazo.

Staying around the Chimborazo reserve

There are a few lovely places to base yourself around the Chimborazo reserve. One of the most charming is in **LA URBINA**, 26km north of Riobamba on the Panamericana, from where signs lead 800m west to ⚓ *Posada La Estación*

▲ Memorial, Volcán Chimborazo

(☎03/2944415; ❹), a former railway station sitting on high moorland. Now an attractive walkers' hostel, at 3620m this is the highest point on Ecuador's train line and a perfect base for acclimatization; the legendary Reinhold Messner, the first man to climb all of the world's 8000-metre peaks, stayed here before his ascent of Chimborazo. It's very chilly at night but there's a roaring fire in the dining room, hearty, warming meals ($4 breakfast, $6 lunch and dinners each), hot water bottles in the beds and a simple shared bathroom with piping hot showers. The owners, Alta Montaña in Riobamba (see box, pp.216–217), whose manager, Rodrigo Donoso, is an excellent English-speaking climber and guide, can arrange hikes, bike rides and horse treks, as well as mountaineering expeditions and walks to the glaciers of Chimborazo to see the dying trade of the *hieleros*, local men who cut blocks from these rivers of ice, wrap them in straw and carry them down to sell at the Riobamba markets.

Over on the west side of the mountain, there are a couple of places you can stay on the Vía del Arenal. About 32km from Riobamba are the indigenous Puruháe communities of **PILINGUÍ SAN PABLO** and **CHORRERA** (3860m), which are working together in an ecotourism initiative to offer guiding services, mountain climbing, bike rides, equipment rental, treks and hikes and camping in community grounds. They also have a simple lodging in the *Casa Cóndor* (☎09/7580033 or 03/2606774, ⓦwww.cordtuch.org.ec; packages from two to ten days, ❹), a building in vague avian form with shared bath, a dorm and a couple of private rooms. About 1km further up in the peaceful **Totorillas valley** is the comparatively luxurious *Estrella del Chimborazo* mountain lodge (☎03/2964915, ⓦwww.expediciones-andinas.com, reservations essential; ❽ half board), with traditional thatched roofs and timber beams, heating, hot water and bathrooms shared between two rooms. It's managed by Marco Cruz, one of Ecuador's most celebrated mountaineers, who leads expeditions through his tour company in Riobamba, Expediciones Andinas (see box, pp.216–217).

Parque Nacional Sangay

The **Parque Nacional Sangay** (ⓦwww.parquesangay.org.ec) is Ecuador's largest highland reserve, a sprawling wilderness – and a UNESCO World Heritage Site – covering more than 5000 square kilometres of the eastern Andean cordillera, spilling down into the Amazon basin (see also p.329). The park's stunning sierra scenery takes in three volcanoes (Tungurahua, El Altar and Sangay), over three hundred lakes, pristine páramo and native cloudforest, providing a habitat for spectacled bears, Andean condors, pumas and deer, among other mammals, while jaguars, monkeys and ocelots inhabit the lower, tropical areas. There's very little infrastructure for tourists and no marked trail system. Apart from the **Guamote–Macas road**, slicing through the park from the sierra to the Oriente, access to Parque Nacional Sangay is via a number of remote, potholed dirt roads leading to the various *guarderías*, or **ranger stations**, serving the different areas of the park, often situated near local communities that can be reached by bus. The **entrance fee** for foreigners is $10; the ticket is valid for two weeks in all the park's various sectors.

Starting at the northern end of the park, the main attractions begin with **Volcán Tungurahua** (5023m), a snowcapped volcano normally approached via the Guardería Pondoa, south of Baños, but currently off-limits due to renewed volcanic activity (see box, p.199). To the south, **El Altar** is the highest point in the park and the fifth-highest mountain in Ecuador. Once a volcano, an ancient eruption blew it asunder, leaving a jagged skeleton of rock, now a spectacular semicircle of nine summits teetering over a dazzling crater lake and a popular target for trekkers. Irascible **Volcán Sangay** (5230m), one of the world's most active volcanoes, is the third great peak in the park, a difficult-to-reach and hazardous climbing proposition. Both it and **El Placer hot springs** are approached from the Guardería Alao, in the village of Alao, reachable by bus from Riobamba. Further south, there's wonderful trekking around the **Lagunas de Atillo** and the **Lagunas de Ozogoche**, clutches of beautiful páramo lakes set in rugged scenery (see p.227).

The **best months** to hike in these highland areas of Sangay are November to February, when the weather is at its driest and sunniest, though downpours can occur at any moment, so come prepared. Outside these months the area is prone to cold, wet, windy and sometimes foggy conditions.

El Altar

Twenty-five kilometres east of Riobamba, **EL ALTAR** (5320m) is an extinct, heavily eroded volcano rising to the south of Volcán Tungurahua. Named Cupac Urcu, or "sublime mountain", in Quichua, El Altar boasts a breathtaking crater set within an amphitheatre of jagged, ice-capped peaks studded with hanging glaciers that are constantly rumbling and cracking. The principal of the volcano's nine craggy summits is **El Obispo**, a difficult technical climb not conquered until 1963 and best left to experienced mountaineers. Lying in the bottom of the crater is **Laguna Amarilla** (4300m), whose yellow-green waters are dotted with blocks of ice that have calved off the glaciers above. A wide gap in the west side of the crater opens onto a flat plain known as the **Valle de Collanes**, providing easy access down to the lake.

Hiking to El Altar

El Altar can be reached on a highly rewarding two- to three-day round-trip **hike**, starting from the tiny village of **Candelaria**, a fifteen-kilometre drive down a dirt track southeast from the village of **Penipe**, which sits 22km northeast of Riobamba on the road to Baños. There are three to four weekday **buses** to Candelaria (two on Sat, none Sun; 1hr 30min) from the Terminal Oriental in Riobamba; alternatively, you can get to Penipe on any of the frequent Riobamba–Baños buses, and once there hire a truck from the square (about $10, ask around).

A popular option is to spend the first night at the *Hacienda Releche* (T 03/2949761; ❹), a fifteen-minute walk from Candelaria, where you can get good meals or use the kitchen yourself (extra charge). From here, you can hire **horses** and a guide for the five- to six-hour haul up to the Collanes plain ($8 each way), at the foot of the volcano, where the hacienda keeps a simple **refuge** with cooking facilities (same prices) and running water (you'll need a sleeping bag). You'll pass the park ranger station en route and will have to pay the $10 entrance fee. From the plain it's only a couple of hours up to the gap in the crater rim, from where you can scramble down to the edge of the lake in about thirty minutes. Heading back, count on taking about an hour to get back up to the plain and another three to four hours back to Candelaria; some stretches of the path get extremely muddy after rainfall, so consider taking gaiters or rubber boots.

An alternative to doing it independently is to join a **guided hike** here, offered by Julio Verne Travel and Marco Cruz Expeditions in Riobamba (see p.217).

Alao, El Placer and Volcán Sangay

Southeast of Riobamba, a spectacular rough dirt road with bird's-eye views follows the Alao valley down to the small community of **ALAO**, gateway to **El Placer hot springs** and **Volcán Sangay**. The park ranger station at the end of the road running through the village is where you pay the $10 park **entrance fee**. They also have a few **beds** with use of a kitchen and bathroom, available for a few dollars. If there's no one in the station when you get there, chances are they'll be back within a few hours; if no one turns up, ask around in the village.

There are a few small stores in Alao where you can buy basic foodstuffs but you should bring all fresh **food** in from Riobamba. It takes about two and a half hours to get to Alao from Riobamba: **buses** leave from the Terminal La Dolorosa on Puruhá and 10 de Agosto, eight blocks east of the Mercado San Francisco, according to an irregular timetable (Mon–Fri 6.25am; Mon, Wed, Fri & Sat noon & 6pm; Tues & Thurs 2pm, 4pm & 6pm); it may also be possible to arrange a lift in with the park staff from the Ministerio del Ambiente office. As well as returning buses, a daily milk truck sets off from the centre of Alao every day at 7–8am for Riobamba.

El Placer

About 25km east of Alao, **El Placer** (which appropriately translates as "pleasure") is a fabulous natural pool filled with thermal water. There's a small changing area near the pool and a timber **refuge** with bunks, cooking facilities and a toilet. It's inaccessible by vehicle, so you'll almost certainly have it to yourself – it's hard to imagine a more rewarding and exotic end to your hike than here.

The well-marked **trail** (an abandoned road) to El Placer heads east from Alao and takes in some glorious scenery, including wild páramo, alpine forest and humid cloudforest. If you have your own transport or have come in from Riobamba by *camioneta*, it's possible to do the first 15km in a sturdy **4WD**, bringing you to within 4km of pretty **Laguna Negra** from where it's about a four-hour hike to El Placer. Another alternative is to hire **horses or mules** for about $10 (ask in the village the day before), which can take you to within a two-hour hike of the springs.

If you intend to do it all **on foot**, expect the hike to take approximately nine to eleven hours in total – it's possible to cram these into a single day if you set off early, but it's more comfortable to camp en route and spread it over two days. The terrain is not too difficult, with only a couple of hours' steep uphill walking there, though it's a bit tougher coming back. This hike is definitely best done in dry, warm weather; you might still want to carry rubber boots with you to negotiate a few extremely muddy areas.

Volcán Sangay

Exquisitely symmetrical **Volcán Sangay** (5230m) is one of the most active volcanoes in the world, being in a state of continuous eruption since 1934. This makes any attempt to climb it a seriously risky undertaking due to frequent rock and ash explosions out of its three craters. Add to this the sheer inaccessibility of the mountain and it becomes clear why it's one of the lesser-climbed peaks in Ecuador. Yet significant numbers of undeterred, adrenaline-hungry climbers pass through determined to have a go – enough to have prompted locals in access communities to organize **guide** associations: in Alao, the Asociación de Portea-dores y Guías de Turistas; and in Guarguallá, the Asociación de Guías Indígenas de Guarguallá, part of a community ecotourism project. You can also arrange trips through the climbing agencies in Quito and Riobamba (see p.117 & pp.216–217). Due to tricky logistics and route finding, this is not an expedition to be undertaken without a guide.

Guarguallá is currently considered to have better access to Sangay than Alao, being a little closer and having better-equipped guides (if you are hiring locally). You should contact Rafael Ushca in Licto, who is the coordinator of the Guarguallá guides and can be reached on ☎09/1661563; he charges $180 per person for the basic five-day expedition, including food, horses, guide, equipment and lodging and he can pick you up from Riobamba or Licto. In Alao, the best-known guides are Roberto and Carlos Cas, Casimiro Leme and Casimiro Quirray; ask the park rangers in Alao to put you in touch with them or ask around in the village. The hike in typically takes two days, with overnight stops at Plazapamba and La Playa, both of which have basic **shelters** – but bring a tent in case they are occupied. Another route from Alao goes via Culebrillas and Yanayacu to La Playa. The ascent (around 3–5hr up, 2hr down) is not strictly a technical climb but can be made difficult if there is a lot of snow and ice near the top, so you will need crampons and an ice axe. It's usually climbed in the dark when it tends to be less cloudy and there's less risk of rock fall.

As well as your mountaineering equipment, consider bringing rubber boots for the atrocious mud on the way to base camp and a **helmet** to guard against falling rocks – though guides joke this will just be to show rescuers where your head once went. They have a point: a helmet can only protect you so much against the bullet-speed stones firing out of the cone. Sulphur gas emissions can badly irritate the lungs and throat before you realize it, so don't hang around on the summit plateau. Do not underestimate the risks involved in doing this climb. You can get more advice from the SAE in Quito (see p.77) and the Ministerio del Ambiente office in Riobamba (see p.195) before embarking on the trip.

South to Alausí

Almost 20km southwest of Riobamba, the Panamericana trails past the dusty, unremarkable town of **Cajabamba**, standing on the site occupied by Riobamba until it was destroyed by an earthquake in 1797. A little further south, sitting right by the highway, is the **Iglesia de Balbanera**, said to be the first chapel the conquistadors raised in Ecuador and founded on September 15, 1534. Though considerably altered since then, it still preserves an early-colonial stone facade around the entrance, embellished with gargoyles and carvings of angels and topped by a traditional Andean bell tower. On a cloud-free day, the chapel presents an impressive photo opportunity, standing right in front of the dramatic, snowcapped cone of Chimborazo. South of the church, both the highway and the rail tracks skirt the wide **Laguna de Colta**, its grey waters backed by pale-green hills dotted with fields. Its shores are lined by tall reeds, which local *indígenas* gather to be woven into mats and other articles; you'll find many for sale in Cajabamba's Sunday-morning market, lining each side of the highway.

South of the lake, the Panamericana carves its way through increasingly wild and less cultivated country as it approaches the small town of **Guamote**, the site of one of the most enjoyable indigenous markets in the sierra. Rewarding side roads off this stretch of the highway head east to **Laguna Atillo** and **Laguna Ozogoche**, high on the páramo in **Parque Nacional Sangay**. The Panamericana heads down to **Alausí**, the final town on the central sierra.

Guamote

Fifty kilometres south of Riobamba, **GUAMOTE** (3050m) is an attractive town, if slightly down-at-heel, sporting a few handsome timber buildings from the railway era in the early twentieth century, with their characteristic balconies leaning on thick wooden pillars. Although the train from Riobamba still chugs through the middle of town it's no longer a vital commercial artery – these days Guamote's *raison d'être* is its massive Thursday-morning **market** that almost rivals that of Saquisilí with its size and vigour. Hundreds of *campesinos* inch their way through the streets, with the largest swell of crowds between 10am and noon. Don't miss the chaotic **animal market** up in the field behind the Iglesia de San Vicente, where ducks, chickens, sheep, piglets and guinea pigs (ranked among the most delicious in the country) change hands, while, all around, loudspeakers compete in volume to advertise the latest miracle cures.

Practicalities

Buses to Guamote leave Riobamba every ten minutes on Thursdays from Avenida Unidad Nacional and Avenida de la Prensa close to the Terminal Terrestre. **Trains** from Riobamba pass through town on Wednesdays, Fridays and Sundays at around 10am (see box, p.213); the train station is in the middle of town, on the Calle Principal. For a **place to stay**, try *Inti Sisa* (T03/2916529, W www.intisisa.org; ❷) run by a non-profit organization working for community development. They offer en-suite rooms (❺) or dorm beds ($10 per person), meals, mountain biking, horseriding and local tours, including to Chimborazo. Other options are the *Ramada* on Vela and Riobamba (T03/2916442; ❸), with neat parquet floors and tiled bathrooms, and the simple *Residencial Turismo* (T03/2916173; ❶) with modest but clean little rooms in an old wooden building directly opposite the railway station; ask in the pharmacy next door if no one's in.

Lagunas de Atillo and the road to Macas

About 500m south of the turn-off to Guamote on the Panamericana, a couple of large signs point east to Macas and the Lagunas de Atillo, marking the start of the controversial new **Guamote–Macas road** slicing through the **Parque Nacional Sangay** to the Oriente – one of the most scenic routes in the country, as it traverses raw páramo, mountain lakes, tumbling waterfalls and descends into virgin forest.

About 48km southeast of Guamote, the road passes a network of lakes known as the **Lagunas de Atillo**, in whose icy waters the Puruháe people are said to have drowned their most reviled criminals in pre-Hispanic times. The most beautiful is **Laguna Magdalena**, dramatically framed by jagged, spiky peaks – bus drivers are usually happy to stop for a couple of minutes at the **mirador** looking down to it. Just beyond, the road climbs to a pass through the eastern cordillera, flanked by a small lake filled with sinister-looking water. A few kilometres east is the **Guardería Atillo** park ranger station, where you pay your entry fee ($10) for Sangay park. The little settlement of **Atillo** is a good base for exploration, with (basic) **accommodation** at *Los Saskines* (T09/4811161; ❶) and owners who can cook you up a fresh trout.

East of here the road gradually leaves the windswept páramo behind as it descends towards the Amazon basin, flanked by steep slopes covered by dense cloudforest. As you get lower, the climate gradually becomes warmer and moister, feeling almost tropical by the time you reach the tiny community of **Zuñac**, 15km on from the ranger station. Five kilometres east of here is the park's second ranger station, the Guardería Purshi, followed a further 5km east by the hamlet of **San Vicente de Playas**. About 20km further is another park entrance sign and a car park, giving onto a trail that follows the **Río Cugusha** upstream (3–4hr one way) to a sensational 80-metre **waterfall** crashing through forest where you can often see capuchin monkeys. The next proper village is **Nueve de Octubre**, about 28km east of San Vicente de Playas, also home to another ranger station, the Guardería Nueve de Octubre. Some 20km short of Macas, just before you descend the drop known as the Loma del Tigrillo, there's a dramatic bend in the road from where a short trail leads to a **viewpoint**; the turbulent confluence of the Upano and Abanico rivers, with ashen Volcán Sangay brooding in the distance, is visible from here. The road ends its descent at **Macas** (see p.226).

Buses run on simultaneous schedules leaving Macas and Guamote at 7am, noon and 4pm (5hr). In addition, there are two to three daily buses to Atillo from Riobamba's **Mercado San Francisco**, 10 de Agosto and Benalcázar.

Lagunas de Ozogoche

Back on the Panamericana, 20km south of Guamote, a rough 36-kilometre dirt road branches east from the village of Palmira to the **Lagunas de Ozogoche**, a cluster of beautiful lakes sitting high on the páramo. The lakes are best known as the site of a curious phenomenon no one has been able to explain: periodically, usually in September, hundreds of migratory plovers (locally called *cuvivi*) quite suddenly plunge deep into the icy waters of the lakes and kill themselves. Each year the Ozogoche community pays tribute to this little-understood event in a festival of traditional music and dancing, which visitors are welcome to attend; contact the Fundación Cultural Flores Franco for more details (☎03/2943168 or 09/3395005, ✉hfloresf@ecuanet.net.ec). Interestingly, the spur of mountain overlooking the lakes is known as Ayapungo – Quichua for "door of death". If you're happy to overlook these morbid details, the area makes for great wild **camping**, though you'll need either your own transport or a *camioneta* from Guamote to get here (around $15–20).

Alausí

Some 43km south of Guamote, lying far below the highway in a round valley enclosed by hills, **ALAUSÍ** (2350m) is an atmospheric little railway town made up of crumbling adobe houses. Every Wednesday, Friday and Sunday, crowds gather around the rail tracks from 10–11am to watch the train from Riobamba glide right through the middle of town, where it pauses for a short stop while vendors clamber onto the roof to sell refreshments. About two and a half hours later, the train reappears on the way back from the Devil's Nose ascent (see box, p.213 for details on times and ticket prices), at which point most people get off to take a bus (saving a few hours), before it trundles along the track on to Riobamba.

Practicalities

It's very easy to catch a **bus** straight out of town to Riobamba (2hr trip), Quito (5hr) or Cuenca (4hr), from the corner of the main street, 5 de Junio, and 9 de Octubre, a few blocks from the **train station** (☎03/2930126), at the north end of 5 de Junio. If you want to stay, you'll find plenty of **hotels**, including the *Europa* (☎03/2930200; ➌) on 5 de Junio and Esteban Orozo, the *Panamericano* (**restaurant** attached), at the corner of 5 de Junio and 9 de Octubre (☎03/2930156; ➌) and the *Americano*, García Moreno 151 (☎03/2930159; ➌), all with private bath and cable TV. The Banco de Guayaquil at 5 de Junio 143 and Ricaurte near the station has a Visa and MasterCard ATM.

All buses from Alausí to Cuenca pass **Chunchi**, 35km to the south – which is the access to the mysterious Cañari ruins of **Puñay**, laid out in the shape of a macaw and said to have strange magnetic properties – and **El Tambo**, 93km from Alausí, an otherwise unremarkable village that is an access point to the **Ingapirca** ruins, Ecuador's most important Inca archeological site (see p.233).

Travel details

Buses

Alausí to: Cuenca (7 daily; 4hr); Quito (7 daily; 5hr); Riobamba (every 30min; 2hr).

Ambato to: Baños (every 10min; 50min); Cuenca (2 daily; 8hr); Guaranda (12 daily; 2hr); Guayaquil (every hour; 6hr 30min); Latacunga (every 15min; 1hr); Loja (2 daily; 12hr); Patate (every 20min; 45min); Pelileo (every 30min; 30min); Píllaro (every 30min; 35min); Puyo (every hour; 3hr); Quito (every 5min; 2hr 20min); Quizapincha (every 30min; 20min); Riobamba (every 30min; 1hr); Salasaca (every 30min; 20min); Tena (2 daily; 6hr).

Baños to: Ambato (every 10min; 50min); Coca (2 daily; 10hr); Guayaquil (2 daily; 6hr) Puyo (every 30min; 2hr); Quito (every 30min; 3hr 30min); Riobamba (every 30min; 1hr); Río Verde (every 30min; 30min); Tena (hourly; 4hr 30min).

Guaranda to: Ambato (every 30min; 2hr); Guayaquil (hourly; 4hr 30min); Latacunga (hourly; 3hr); Quito (every 30min; 4hr 30min); Riobamba (10 daily; 2hr); Salinas (5–6 daily; 1hr).

Latacunga to: Ambato (every 15min; 1hr); Baños (every 15min; 2hr); Chugchilán (2–3 daily; 3hr 45min); Isinliví (2 daily; 3–4hr); Pujilí (every 10min;

20min); Quevedo (every 30min; 4hr); Quilotoa (1 daily; 3hr); Quito (every 10min; 2hr); Salcedo (every 10–15min; 15min); Saquisilí (every 10min; 20min); Sigchos (7 daily; 2hr 15min); Zumbahua (every hour; 2hr).

Machachi to: Aloasí (every 30min; 10min); El Chaupí (every 30min; 30min); Quito (hourly; 1hr).

Riobamba to: Alao (3–4 daily Mon–Fri, 2 daily Sat; 2hr 30min); Alausí (every 30min; 2hr); Ambato (every 15min; 1hr); Baños (hourly; 2hr); Candelaria (3 daily Mon–Fri, 2 daily Sat; 1hr 30min); Cuenca (7 daily; 6hr); Guano (every 10min; 15min); Guaranda (6 daily; 2hr); Guayaquil (every 30min; 4hr 30min); Huaquillas (2 daily; 10hr); Latacunga (every 15min; 2hr); Puyo (hourly; 4hr); Quito (every 15min; 3hr 30min); Santo Domingo (hourly; 5hr); Tena (6 daily; 7hr).

Trains

The train ride from **Riobamba to Sibambe**, via the **Nariz del Diablo** (Devil's Nose) descent, leaves Riobamba on Wednesdays, Fridays and Sundays at 7am and costs $11 (Riobamba–Sibambe–Alausí). For more information on this service, see box, p.213.

The southern sierra

CHAPTER 4   # Highlights

* **Ingapirca** On a striking hillside perch overlooking idyllic scenery, the best-preserved Inca ruin in the country displays exquisite trademark stonemasonry. See p.233

* **Cuenca** Ecuador's third-largest city is regarded as its most beautiful for its dignified architecture, flower-draped courtyards, cobbled streets and leafy plazas. See p.236

* **Museo del Banco Central, Cuenca** Without a doubt the region's best museum, holding the remains of Tomebamba, the great city of the Inca's northern empire, and other exhibits. See p.242

* **Cajas** A stunning and easily accessed wilderness of sweeping páramo views, sparkling lakes and exposed crags caressed by whirling mists. See p.248

* **Podocarpus** This beautiful national park descends from austere páramo into lush cloudforests, a memorable landscape teeming with wildlife and streaked with waterfalls and glinting rivers. See p.262

* **Vilcabamba** The slow pace of this peaceful village – and the great hiking nearby – has rightly made it a fixture for many travelling between Ecuador and Peru. See p.265

▲ Catedral Nueva, Cuenca

The southern sierra

As you head south down the **Panamericana** from the central highlands, the snowcapped peaks and rumbling volcanoes give way to a softer, gentler landscape of lower elevations and warmer, drier climates. Ecuador's **southern sierra** – made up of the provinces of Cañar, Azuay and Loja – was until recently a very isolated part of the country, left without proper roads to the capital and Guayaquil until the 1960s. The region still has a lonely, faraway feel to it, reinforced by its sparse population, scarcity of large towns and long stretches of wild, uninhabited countryside. Its charms, however, are considerable, with some of the most rewarding and beautiful pockets of Ecuador tucked away here.

The main urban centre – and only large city – of the southern sierra is **Cuenca**, famed for its stunning colonial architecture and graceful churches and monasteries. Easily the country's most captivating city, it was raised on the site of the ruined city of Tomebamba, built by the **Incas** in the late fifteenth century following their conquest of the region, which had been occupied by the **Cañari** people for almost a thousand years (see p.489). Virtually nothing remains of Tomebamba, but you can get an idea of the remarkable stonework the Incas were famous for – executed without iron to carve it or wheels to transport it – at the ruins of **Ingapirca**, Ecuador's only major Inca ruins, within easy striking distance of Cuenca. On Cuenca's doorstep is an attraction of a very different nature: the starkly beautiful wilderness of **Parque Nacional Cajas**, which provides some of the best backcountry hiking and trout fishing in the country, if you're willing to put up with a bit of rain and mist.

South of Cuenca, the sense of remoteness and abandonment increases as you pass mile after mile of largely uncultivated hills and pastures. The few villages and one-horse towns staggered down the highway seem scarcely to have entered the twentieth century, let alone the twenty-first, with their steep cobbled streets, ageing stuccoed houses and grand old churches. The town of **Saraguro**, in particular, feels like a real step back in time, with an indigenous population that maintains a centuries-old tradition of dressing in black. Further south, the small provincial capital of **Loja** is an island of comparative motion and activity, hemmed in by jagged, deep-green hills that soar over the town. It serves as a good jumping-off point for a couple of highly worthwhile excursions: east to **Parque Nacional Podocarpus**, stretching down from the sierra to the tropical cloudforests of the Oriente, close to the old gold-mining town of **Zamora**; and south to the laid-back gringo hangout of **Vilcabamba**, nestled in a peaceful mountain valley. Loja is also the starting point of the only direct bus service to Peru; for more details see p.269.

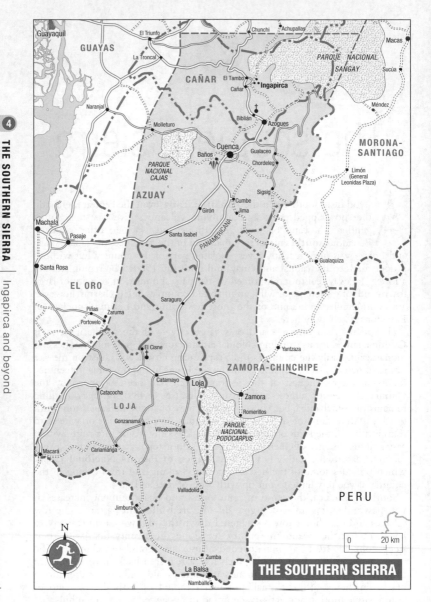

Ingapirca and beyond

Leaving the central sierra behind at Alausí (see p.227), continue 93km south on the Panamericana and you'll reach **El Tambo**. From here, a side road branches 8km east from the highway to the southern sierra's first important attraction, **Ingapirca**. Though not as dramatic or well preserved as the Inca remains of

Peru, Ingapirca is nonetheless an impressive site that certainly deserves a visit, if only to witness the extraordinary mortarless stonework for which the Incas are renowned. South of here, only a few low-key attractions dot the 79km separating El Tambo from Cuenca: namely the small market town of **Cañar**, the hilltop sanctuary of **Biblián** and the sleepy provincial capital of **Azogues**.

Ingapirca

Perched on a breezy hill commanding fine views over the surrounding countryside, **INGAPIRCA** (daily 8am–6pm; $6 including guide), which roughly translates as "Inca wall", was built during the Inca expansion into Ecuador towards the end of the fifteenth century, on a site that had been occupied by the Cañari people for over five hundred years. The Incas destroyed most of the Cañari structures (though a burial site remains), replacing them with their own elaborate complex that probably functioned as a place of worship, a fortress and a *tambo*, or way-station, on the Inca Royal Road connecting Cuzco to Quito.

Since then, many of the Inca buildings have been dismantled, their large stone blocks hauled away by Spanish colonists to be used as foundations for churches and other buildings; however, the complex's central structure – known as the **Temple of the Sun**, or the Adoratorio – remains substantially intact and dominates the whole site. It's composed of an immense oval-shaped platform whose slightly inward-tapering walls are made of exquisitely carved blocks of stone, fitted together with incredible precision. Steps lead up to a trapezoidal doorway – a classic feature of Inca architecture – that gives onto the remains of a rectangular building within the platform. It is the superior quality of the platform's stonework, usually reserved for high-status buildings, that suggests this was a ceremonial temple.

The rest of the site consists mainly of low foundation walls, possibly the remains of storehouses, dwellings and a great plaza, among other things. There's not a great deal left, but the **guides** stationed near the site entrance can explain various theories about what once stood where (some speak a little English). They'll also take you on a looping one-kilometre path in and out of the ravine behind the ruins, to the nearby **Cara del Inca** ("Inca's Face"), a huge rock face resembling a human profile with a hooked nose, as well as several other rock-hewn curiosities, including the **Casa del Sol** with its circular, supposedly astronomical, carvings, or the **Silla del Inca**, a large boulder with a chair cut into it, actually a broken piece of a small Inca bath from the hill above. Count on a guided tour of the site taking two hours. There's also a small **museum** (with an attached book and craft shop) just inside the entrance displaying Cañari and Inca pots, tools, jewellery and a skeleton found on site.

Baño del Inca

There's another obscure but interesting ruin 8km from Ingapirca on the road towards El Tambo, near the little village of **Coyoctor**. The **Baño del Inca** is an Inca bathing complex chiselled out of an enormous rock with channels and receptacles eventually leading out onto the adjacent field for irrigation. The site hasn't been fully excavated and there's no control or entry fee, though occasionally a guide will be hanging about to show you around for a tip. It's a thirty- to forty-minute walk to Coyoctor from the turn-off on the road to El Tambo. 6km from Ingapirca, followed by a right turn at the crossroads in the village; or a thirty-minute walk along a disused railway heading southwest from El Tambo (a *camioneta* from here costs $3).

Practicalities

The two **access roads** for Ingapirca leave the Panamericana at El Tambo and Cañar (7km south), and meet in the middle at the small village – also known as Ingapirca – overlooking the archeological site, a five-minute walk away. **Getting there** is easy on the buses running between El Tambo and Cañar every twenty minutes, passing through Ingapirca village. In addition, from Monday to Friday two daily Transportes Cañar buses come directly to the site entrance from Cuenca (a 2hr trip; $2), leaving Cuenca's bus terminal at 9am and 12.20pm and returning from Ingapirca at 1pm and 3.45pm; on weekends there is only one bus in each direction, leaving Cuenca at 9am, and leaving Ingapirca at 1pm. If you're coming in from Cuenca and miss the direct bus, it's easy enough to catch one of the regular buses to Cañar and then a connection to Ingapirca.

If you want to **stay** overnight, the best place for miles around is the peaceful, comfortable *Posada Ingapirca* (☎07/2827401, ⓦwww.grupo-santaana.net; ❻), a lovely 120-year-old farmhouse with splendid views and a good restaurant, just uphill from the ruins. In Ingapirca village, you'll find basic but reasonably clean rooms with or without private bath at *Intihuasi* (☎07/290018; ❷) and *El Huasipungo* (no phone; ❷), a few doors away. Both hotels have simple restaurants, and there's another between them; the hotels and restaurants are all easily located. Alternatively, just south of El Tambo, *Cuna del Sol* (☎07/2233264; ❻) is a tourist complex on an old farm with pool, steam room and games fields. In addition to the **restaurants** mentioned above,

---

The Inca Trail to Ingapirca

The **Inca Trail to Ingapirca** is a three-day hike following a forty-kilometre stretch of the route – and in some parts the original path – of the Inca Royal Road that once linked Cuzco, the Inca capital, with Tomebamba (where Cuenca now stands) and Quito. The hike begins in the tiny village of **Achupallas**, which is an hour's drive along a vertiginous road from the small railway town of **Alausí** (see p.227). *Colectivo* trucks leave Alausí for Achupallas between 11am and noon daily except Saturdays, and there's one daily bus at around 1–2pm. Your surest bet is to hire a *camioneta* to take you there from opposite the *Panamericano* hotel in Alausí, at the corner of 5 de Junio and 9 de Octubre; if there's none there, just ask around and someone will offer to take you.

Most hikers set off from Alausí between 5–6am. Alternatively, you could turn up in Achupallas the day before you want to start walking – there's a simple little hostel here called *Ingañán* (☎03/2930652; ❷), where you can also get meals. If you're hiking it independently, it's essential to take the IGM **maps** of Alausí, Juncal and Cañar, as well as full **camping equipment** and warm, waterproof clothing. Rubber boots or gaiters will also come in handy, as there are some extremely boggy spots to negotiate. Try to take as light a pack as possible, though, as you'll be hiking between 3100m and 4400m, which can be quite hard going. The **terrain** you'll cover is mainly wild, open páramo, with some beautiful ridge walks giving fantastic views. Most of it is uninhabited, but the final 8km or so is quite populated with *campesinos*, and you'll probably get a lot of attention from kids asking for sweets, pencils or money.

The hike is commonly divided as follows: day one takes you from Achupallas up the Tres Cruces valley to the Laguna Las Tres Cruces (6–8hr), though you may want to cut this hard day short and pitch your tent in the páramo a couple of hours short of the lakes; day two takes you from Laguna Las Tres Cruces to a small collection of Inca ruins known as Paredones, by the shore of Laguna Culebrillas (6–7hr); and day three goes from the Paredones ruins to the Ingapirca ruins (4–5hr).

there's a simple canteen at the Ingapirca site itself, and plenty of truckers' stops on the main road through El Tambo.

Cañar

Seven kilometres south of El Tambo, **CAÑAR** is a small town with narrow, twisting streets lined by attractive, colonial-style architecture. It's normally very quiet, but bursts into life on Sunday mornings with its weekly **market** – a good place to admire the beautifully embroidered skirts and blouses the local women are famous for, as well as the finely woven belts the men wear, embellished with intricate motifs on both sides; you might also see men wearing traditional *samarros*, sheepskin trousers used for horseriding. While Cañar is a more appealing place than El Tambo, which is just a ten-minute bus ride away, the **accommodation** here is not particularly inspiring: on the plaza, at the corner of Pichincha and Bolívar, the ageing *Residencial Mónica* (☎07/2235486; ❷) has small but relatively clean rooms, while those at *Ingapirca*, at Sucre and 5 de Junio (☎07/2235201; ❸), are faded and musty but have TVs and private bath (none too clean by some reports). A basic bunch of **restaurants**, all offering simple *menus del día*, include *Los Maderos* on Calle Pichincha, or the *Reino Cañari* or the *Florida International*, both on 5 de Junio.

Biblián

Some 26km south of Cañar, the extravagantly turreted and spired **Santuario de la Virgen del Rocío** sits on a hillside high above the Panamericana, overlooking the little village of **BIBLIÁN**. The origins of this neo-Gothic temple date to 1894, when a terrible drought occurred. The villagers carried an image of the Virgin Mary up the hillside, where they prayed she would intervene and save them from starvation. The rains miraculously arrived, and a **church** was built on the site where the image had been placed; it was completed in 1908. You can walk up to it in about twenty minutes from the Panamericana, following a clearly signed flight of steps – it's worth it for the fine views down to the valley in which Biblián sits, and to see the church's interior, set against the bare rock of the hill. The Virgin's feast day is celebrated on September 8, when huge crowds come to venerate the image. Three kilometres south of Biblián, just off the Panamericana, the great-value *Hostería El Camping* (☎07/2240445; ❹) offers spacious, comfortable **rooms** with private bath, a pleasant restaurant and an indoor swimming pool with steam baths.

Azogues

Continuing down the Panamericana, around 7km south of Biblián you'll reach **AZOGUES** (2560m), a charming town made up of steep, narrow streets and handsome nineteenth-century houses. Many of the buildings in the centre have painted wooden balconies, and a few have the undersides of their eaves painted in intricate designs, as was traditional during colonial times. The chief appeal here is just strolling around for an hour or two, admiring the architecture and soaking up the atmosphere. Worth visiting is the monumental, twin-towered **Iglesia San Francisco**, which houses the Virgen de la Nube ("Virgin of the Cloud"), wrapped in a white cloak and perched on a gold-leaf altar. Standing on a small hill to the southeast of the centre, the church is visible from most parts of town, most strikingly when it's illuminated at night; you can walk there in about thirty minutes or take a taxi for $1.50. There's also the rather fun **Museo Regional** (Mon–Fri 8am–noon & 2–6pm; free) at the back of the Casa de la Cultura, five blocks south of the *parque central* on Bolívar and General Enríquez, with mannequins and dioramas showcasing the region's crafts and traditions. One of the most important local crafts is weaving Panama hats – most are bundled off to Cuenca to be exported, but you can normally spot a few at the Saturday-morning **market** a couple of blocks south of the *parque central*.

Practicalities

Azogues' **bus terminal** is just off the Panamericana – called Avenida 24 de Mayo as it runs through the town – a couple of blocks northwest of the *parque central*. You'll find smart, modern **accommodation** with private bath and cable TV at the *Rivera* (✆07/2248113; ❺), south down Avenida 24 de Mayo at its corner with 10 de Agosto. For more character, head up to *Hostal Peleusi* (✆07/2245445; ❸), on the corner of Matovelle and Serrano, overlooking the very pleasant *parque central*; the hotel is above a good **restaurant**, *La Fornace*, a *gelatería* and pizza parlour. Other places to eat include *El Padrino*, on Bolívar 6-09 and 10 de Agosto, which serves decent chicken dishes in a pleasant old dining room, while *La Fogata*, at 3 de Noviembre and Avenida 24 de Mayo, specializes in fish and seafood. A few blocks south of the park, at the corner of Bolívar and Tenemaza, *El Che* isn't a bad place to grab a juice, coffee, taco and a snack. The Pacífictel **phone office** is on the north side of the *parque central*.

Cuenca

Santa Ana de los Cuatro Ríos de Cuenca, otherwise known simply as **CUENCA** (2530m), is Ecuador's most seductive – and possibly its most beautiful – colonial city. A classic example of a planned Renaissance town in the Americas, Cuenca is a UNESCO World Heritage Site and shares many architectural features with Old Quito: narrow, cobbled streets, harmonious, balconied houses with interior courtyards and an abundance of flashing white churches and monasteries – all presented without the pollution, noise and overbearing crowds of the capital.

Founded by the Spaniards on April 12, 1557, Cuenca was not the first dazzling city to be erected here: the Inca Tupac Yupanqui founded the city of **Tomebamba** here around 1470, which was said to have rivalled Peru's Cuzco with its splendour. Its glory was short-lived, however, as the city was destroyed during the Inca civil war that broke out during the second decade of the sixteenth century, prompted by rival claims to the throne by the brothers Atahualpa and Huáscar. By the time Cieza de León (one of the chroniclers of the Spanish conquest) saw it in 1547, Tomebamba was in ruins, but enough remained to evoke its former grandeur: "These famous lodgings of Tumibamba were among the finest and richest to be found in all Peru...The fronts of many of the buildings are beautiful and highly decorative, some of them set with precious stones and emeralds...Today, all is cast down and in ruins, but it can still be seen how great they were." These days, Cuenca's Inca legacy has all but vanished, hinted at only by the foundation stones of some of its buildings, and some modest ruins excavated in the twentieth century.

Arrival, information and getting around

A popular destination to fly to from Quito (around $85 each way), Cuenca is served by TAME (Ⓦwww.tame.com.ec) and Aerogal (Ⓦwww.aerogal.com.ec) flights. The airport, (information on ✆07/2862203), Aeropuerto Mariscal

RESTAURANTS & CAFÉS

Amerindia Café	17	Govindas	12	New York Pizza	1
Café Austria	11	Heladería Holanda	6	El Paraíso	9
La Barraca	7	El Jardín	U	El Pedregal Azteca	3
Cacao y Canela	13	El Jordán	15	Los Pibes	4
El Cafecito	S	El Maíz	18	Raymipampa	8
Los Capuliés	10	El Mirador	P	Villa Rosa	2
Café Eucalyptus	5	Moliendo	14	Wunderbar	16

0   200 m

ACCOMMODATION

Alli Tiana	P
El Cafecito	S
Casa Naranja	B
La Casona	W
Chordeleg	F
Cofradía del Monje	Q
Colonial	I
Crespo	T
Cuenca	H
El Dorado	K
Inca Real	N
Macondo	A
Mansión Alcázar	J
Milán	R
Norte	E
La Orquidea	M
Paredes	C
Pichincha	L
Posada del Ángel	G
Posada Todos Santos	V
San Andrés	D
Santa Lucía	O
Victoria	U

Lamar, is only 5km east of the centre along Avenida España. The easiest way to get into town is by taxi (about $2–3), or you can catch a Transportes Ricuarte bus on Avenida España (about every 10min) that will take you up Calle Vega Muñoz, on the northern edge of the city centre. The **bus terminal** is also on Avenida España, close to the airport; again, the easiest way to get into the centre is by taxi, or you can catch a bus from Avenida España, as detailed above.

The iTur office, on the main square at Sucre and Benigno Malo (Mon–Fri 8am–8pm, Sat 8.30am–1.30pm; ☎&℉07/2821035), has **information**, maps, numerous leaflets, the helpful booklet *Estar en Cuenca* and *agendas culturales*, listings of the month's cultural events. The information office at the bus terminal (Mon–Sat 8.30am–noon & 2.30-6pm; ☎07/2868482) is also good for travel advice and maps.

The **city centre** is confined to a fairly compact grid on the northern bank of the Río Tomebamba. It's easy enough to get to most sights on foot, but if you're tired you'll be able to flag down a yellow **taxi** on any main street; rides within the city have a fixed tariff of $1.50. For details of radio taxis, see "Listings", p.247.

Accommodation

Cuenca boasts a wide choice of mid-priced and upmarket hotels, many of them in restored colonial-style houses built around little courtyards. Good budget accommodation is thinner on the ground, though there are a few decent options. Wherever you plan to stay, it's best to book ahead if arriving on a Friday – or any kind of fiesta (see "Listings", p.247) – as Cuenca is a popular weekend destination with Ecuadorians and accommodation can fill quite quickly. Most places include breakfast in the nightly rate.

Alli Tiana Corner of Presidente Córdova and Padre Aguirre ☎07/2831844, ⓕ2821788. A modern hotel offering thirty carpeted rooms with firm beds, private bath, cable TV and phone – not luxurious but perfectly fine. The view over the city from the restaurant is one of the best in town. ⑤

El Cafecito Honorato Vásquez 7-36 ☎07/2832337, ⓦwww.cafecito.net. Popular budget rooms, both shared and private and with or without private bath, set around an attractive courtyard filled with wooden tables and potted plants. It's also a café-restaurant-bar and can be noisy on Thursday, Friday and Saturday nights; the quietest rooms face the back. Free luggage storage. Dorm beds are $6. ④

Casa Naranja Mariscal Lamar 10-38 and Padre Aguirre ☎07/2883820 or 2825415, ⓦwww .casanaranja.galeon.com. Quiet *hostal* in a restored colonial house with two inner courtyards and minimalist, white-walled rooms. Internet and kitchen facilities are available and the owners make and sell jewellery and woollens. ⑤

La Casona Miguel Cordero 2-134 and Alfonso Cordero ☎07/2811131, ⓦwww.lacasonahotel .com.ec. Comfortable, spacious rooms, many with high ceilings and large windows, in a restored nineteenth-century mansion in a quiet residential district south of the river, three blocks south of the Parque de la Madre. Also comes with restaurant, free internet access and laundry service. ⑥

Chordeleg Gran Colombia 11-15 and General Torres ☎07/2824611, ⓕ2822536. Lovely old *hostal* featuring lots of highly polished wood and pleasant, if unexceptional, en-suite rooms around a glass-covered courtyard – though some suffer from the noise of the busy street outside. ⑤

La Cofradía del Monje Presidente Córdova 10-33 and Padre Aguirre ☎07/2831251, ⓦwww .cofradiadelmonje.com. Smart timber-floored rooms, some with balconies overlooking Plaza San Francisco and the domes of the new cathedral beyond. Also has a cafetería. ⑥

Colonial Gran Colombia 10-13 ☎07/282379, ⓔhcolonia@cue.satnet.net. Colonial-style building with a pretty, central courtyard (used as the dining area), festooned with plants. Rooms are simple but comfortable, with private bath and cable TV; those at the front look onto the Iglesia Santo Domingo. ⑤

Crespo Calle Larga 7-93 ☎07/2842571, ⓦwww .hotelcrespo.com. Cuenca's most distinguished hotel, operating since 1942 in a handsome, 140-year-old building overlooking the river. Lots of dark wood and old-fashioned elegance, along with modern comforts like soundproofed windows, an hour's free internet each day and central heating. Specify a room with a river view. ⑧

Cuenca Presidente Borrero 10-69 ☎07/2833711, ⓕ2833819. Housed in a distinctive old building with a recently remodelled interior, *Hotel Cuenca* features smart, carpeted rooms with high ceilings, brightly painted walls, cable TV and private bath. ⑥

El Dorado Gran Colombia 7-87 ☎07/2831390, ⓕ2831663. Smart, modern, international-style hotel with a gym, sauna, steam baths and good-quality rooms with large cable TVs; those in the new block ("*de lujo*") are fractionally more expensive than the older rooms, but are immaculately furnished. ⑨

Inca Real General Torres 8-40 ☎07/2823636, ⓔincareal@cue.satnet.net. The rooms (all en suite) are simple and quite small for the price, but the blue-and-white timber building is splendid, arranged around three glass-covered courtyards. ⑦

Macondo Tarqui 11-64 ☎07/2840697, ⓕ2830836. Quiet, beautiful old house with waxed wooden floors, high ceilings, spotless rooms (shared and private bath) and a delightful garden with chairs and a hammock. Guests can use the kitchen in the afternoon. ④–⑤

Mansión Alcázar Bolívar 12-55 and Tarqui ☎07/2823918, ⓦwww.mansionalcazar.com. Exquisitely renovated colonial building housing one of Cuenca's most luxurious hotels, boasting a grand courtyard converted into a stately drawing room replete with chandelier and fountain. The rooms are equally sumptuous, fragrant from the freshly scattered petals on the beds, some of which are four-posters. Free internet access and wi-fi round out the amenities. ⑨

Milán Presidente Córdova 9-89 ☎/ⓕ07/2831104. Friendly, well-run *hostal* offering small rooms with shared and private bath, balconies and cable TV. Rooms can be noisy from the traffic, but some have lovely views of the Iglesia San Francisco. Also offers laundry facilities and free films each night. Breakfast included on a covered rooftop patio with great views. ④

Norte Mariano Cueva 11-63 ☎07/2827881. Tidy, budget rooms with freshly painted walls, swept floors, decent bedding and firm mattresses, but few rooms in the hotel have outside windows and those near the TV area are noisy. At night this is not the most salubrious of areas. ❷

La Orquidea Presidente Borrero 9-31 and Bolívar ☎07/2824511, ⓕ2835844. Attractive hotel in a renovated old building, offering twelve simply furnished but stylish rooms with lots of natural wood, pale walls and good-quality en-suite bathrooms. A good choice in this price range. ❺

Paredes Luis Cordero 11-29 ☎07/2835674, ⓕ2834910. Large, light, mostly en-suite rooms in an extravagantly decorated old mansion with brightly painted pillars and cornices. Old oil paintings, gramophones and lots of bric-a-brac lying around, as well as a resident parrot. A little run-down but full of character. ❷

Pichincha General Torres 8-82 ☎07/2823868. Large, budget hotel with friendly owners, offering anonymous but clean and spacious rooms (one to four beds) with high ceilings, bare wooden floors and shared bath, kitchen and internet access. It can get noisy in the communal lounge and there have been reports of unreliable hot water. ❷

Posada del Ángel Bolívar 14-11 and Estévez de Toral ☎07/2840695, ⓦwww.hostalposadadelangel .com. An old building remodelled with two brightly painted covered courtyards, with comfortable rooms boasting plenty of storage space, cable TV

and private bath. Thirty minutes' free internet included. ❼

Posada Todos Santos Calle Larga 3-42 and Tomás Ordóñez ☎07/2824247. Well-maintained hostel with nice, carpeted rooms and good en-suite showers. The friendly owners are knowledgeable about sites and activities in the region and offer a welcome *canelazo* on arrival. ❺

San Andrés Gran Colombia 11-66 and Tarqui ☎07/2841497, ⓦwww.hotelsanandres.net. An attractive colonial building with courtyard and patio, comfy en-suite rooms with cable TV and "air purifiers" and brisk, friendly service. ❼

Santa Lucía Presidente Borrero 8-44 ☎07/2828000, ⓦwww.santaluciahotel.com. Beautiful hotel in a fine old house, built in 1859 and now tastefully restored with generously furnished en-suite rooms, most equipped with bathtubs, as well as strongbox, cable TV and minibar. There's also parking, a restaurant and café, along with a drawing room complete with grand fireplace. ❽

Victoria Calle Larga 6-93 ☎07/2827401, ⓦwww .grupo-santaana.net. Smart new conversion of an old building backed with smoked glass to give stunning views over the river (rooms 207 and 205 being particularly good). The hotel's restaurant, *El Jardín* (see p.244), is highly regarded. ❽

The City

Despite being Ecuador's third-largest city, Cuenca's **downtown** core is a very manageable size. If you're short of time, it's possible to get a feel for the town's charms and take in the best of its architecture in a leisurely afternoon stroll. That said, if you want to go inside the churches, visit a couple of museums and save some time for shopping, you'll need two or three days here. If possible, try to make your stay coincide with a Friday or Saturday evening, when the town's churches are illuminated to stunning effect, or Sundays during the day, when traffic is kept out of the main square. Most churches are open 7am–noon and 6–8pm.

The Parque Calderón and around

Perhaps the most distinctive feature of Cuenca, clearly visible from most parts of town, are the large, sky-blue domes of the nineteenth-century **Catedral Nueva** (officially called La Catedral de la Inmaculada Concepción), which flanks the west side of the town's central square, the flowery **Parque Calderón**. The domes sit towards the back of the building over a jumble of outsized turrets, arches and buttresses, while the immense twin-towered facade looming over the square dominates the front. Inside, the large central nave features some gorgeous stained-glass windows and a very ornate high altar, made up of a gold-leaf canopy supported by four gilded columns, resembling some kind of over-the-top bandstand. The cathedral's grand scale and self-confidence contrast with the modest **Catedral Vieja** (or El Sagrario) facing it across the square. Occupying the site of a mud-and-straw chapel built immediately after the city was founded, and then expanded in 1567 using the stones of the destroyed city of Tomebamba, the present building largely dates from the late eighteenth

▲ Good Friday celebrations, Parque Calderón

century (it became a cathedral in 1787), and is characterized by its low, horizontal outline, simple, whitewashed walls, clay-tiled roof and central bell tower, used by La Condamine's geodesic mission as reference point to measure the shape of the Earth (see p.493). During a recent six-year restoration, original frescoes dating back to the late sixteenth century were uncovered on the walls; most of the other murals are from the early twentieth century.

Just off the Parque Calderón, on Calle Sucre, the Plazoleta del Carmen – a tiny square more commonly known as the **Plaza de las Flores** – is home to a daily **flower market**, presided over by *chola* women wearing blue- or pink-checked aprons, long black plaits and Panama hats. Right behind it stands the **Iglesia El Carmen de la Asunción**, a white-walled, eighteenth-century church with a beautiful carved stone portico. One block south of the flower market, on Córdova and Padre Aguirre, you'll find another market square, the **Plaza San Francisco**, this one selling a diverse mix of chunky knitwear, wall hangings and cheap clothes and shoes. It's overlooked by the peach-and-white **Iglesia San Francisco**, rebuilt in the early twentieth century in a Neocolonial style, sporting smooth, stuccoed walls embellished with lots of plaster relief. Inside, the only survivors of the original church, built in the eighteenth century, are the high altar adorned by a carving of the Virgin de la Inmaculada by Bernardo de Legarda (the famous Quito School sculptor; see box, p.88) and the gold-leaf pulpit. Three blocks north, on Gran Colombia and Padre Aguirre, the grey-blue, twin-towered **Iglesia Santo Domingo** is another early twentieth-century church built in the colonial style. It's worth popping inside to admire the intricate geometric motifs covering every inch of the arches and ceilings, and the series of eighteenth-century paintings on the walls, depicting the Mysteries of the Rosary.

Iglesia San Sebastián and Museo de Arte Moderno

Six blocks west of the Parque Calderón, past the brilliant-white walls of the nineteenth-century **Iglesia del Cenáculo**, the **Iglesia San Sebastián** marks the western limit of Cuenca's *centro histórico*. Built in the seventeenth century, this is one of the city's oldest churches and features a single bell tower over the right-hand side of the entrance, giving the church a slightly lopsided appearance. The quiet little square in front of it was the scene of Cuenca's most scandalous crime of the eighteenth century, when the surgeon of the French geodesic mission was murdered over his love affair with a Creole woman.

The single-storey whitewashed building with blue windows spanning the southern side of the square was built in 1876 and has served as a temperance house, a prison, an asylum for beggars and an old people's home, and currently houses the municipal **Museo de Arte Moderno** (Mon–Fri 8.30am–1pm & 3–6.30pm, Sat & Sun 9am–1pm; free). The museum puts on high-quality temporary exhibitions of national and Latin American artists.

Museo de las Conceptas and the Museo de Esqueletología

A couple of blocks southeast of the Parque Calderón, the **Monasterio de las Conceptas**, founded in 1599, hides behind the thick, white walls separating its occupants from the outside world. Part of the convent is open to the public as the **Museo de las Conceptas** (Mon–Fri 9am–5.30pm, Sat 10am–1pm; $2.50), with its entrance at Hermano Miguel 6-33. The museum houses a large collection of predominantly religious paintings and sculpture from the seventeenth to nineteenth centuries, as well as a roomful of nineteenth-century toys in room 12, including some small wooden dolls and music boxes, brought here by young novices entering the convent. While you're here, take a look at the attached **Iglesia de las Conceptas**, giving onto Presidente Córdova, which features a flamboyant steeple, some finely carved wooden doors and an impressive gold-leaf altar inside.

For a change of pace, walk two blocks north to Bolívar 6-57 and Presidente Borrero to the little **Museo de Esqueletología** (Mon–Fri 10.30am–1pm & 3–6.30pm, Sat 10am–2pm, Sun 10am–7pm; $1.50). The collection inside houses an unusual array of skeletons, from the tiny frames of a hummingbird and foetus skulls to the rather larger condor, llama and elephant calf; don't miss the sawfish skeleton, a species now on the verge of extinction due to aggressive fishing.

Calle Larga

The southern limit of old Cuenca is marked by **Calle Larga**, which runs parallel with and backs on to the Río Tomebamba. You can't see the river from the street – just a continuous stretch of handsome old houses, including, at no. 10-04, the Panama hat workshop (and store) of Rafael Paredes & Hijos, which incorporates the **Museo del Sombrero** (Mon–Fri 9am–6pm, Sat 9.30am–5pm, Sun 9.30am–1.30pm; free), where you'll be shown a selection of antique hat-making implements, including a nineteenth-century contraption used for measuring the shape of the head, and coached through the various stages of hat creation. A few blocks downhill, few houses on the street are more impressive than no. 7-07, the beautifully restored former home of Dr Remigio Crespo Toral, a nineteenth-century intellectual and diplomat. In 1946 it was turned into Cuenca's first museum: the **Museo Remigio Crespo Toral** (Mon–Fri 9am–1pm & 3–6.30pm, Sat–Sun 9am–1pm; free), housing a small but noteworthy collection of pre-Hispanic ceramics and tools, documents dating from the city's foundation, religious paintings and sculpture and a *salón* furnished as it was left by Dr Crespo.

Continuing a block and a half east brings you to the **Museo de las Culturas Aborígenes** at Calle Larga 5-24 and Mariano Cueva (Mon–Fri 8.30am–6pm, Sat

8.30am–1pm; $2.50 including guide in Spanish, English or French), which exhibits an excellent, wide-ranging and well-presented collection of pre-Columbian ceramics and artefacts, beginning with Stone Age tools, flints and dinosaur teeth and ending with accomplished Inca earthenware. With over five thousand pieces, this is one of the best private collections in the country. You can stock up on books, postcards, crafts and replicas in the museum shop, and sip a home-roasted coffee in the *Amerindia Café* inside (see opposite).

Along the Río Tomebamba

Between the Museo Remigio Crespo Toral and the Museo de las Culturas Aborígenes, opposite Hermano Miguel, a set of **stone steps** (*escalinata*) leads down to the **riverside**, giving wonderful views onto the back parts of Calle Larga's grand houses, hanging precipitously over the steep riverbank. At the bottom of the steps, the excellent Centro Interamericano de Artesanías y Artes Populares (CIDAP) has a small but highly enjoyable **Museo de Artes Populares** (Mon–Fri 9am–1pm & 2–5pm, Sat 10am–1pm; free), bringing together arts and crafts from all over Latin America in exhibitions that change every six months. In addition, every month it exhibits and sells the work of a different Ecuadorian artist or artisan, making the museum a fine place to pick up something original. There's also a shop selling a range of local crafts.

From here you could walk along the river west, then regain higher ground for the **Zoológico Amaru** at Benigno Malo (Mon–Fri 9am–1pm & 3–6pm, Sat & Sun 10am–5pm; $2). The centre displays a selection of native reptiles, fish and amphibians, including the feared piranha, bushmaster and fer-de-lance, all kept safely behind glass and often hidden from view among leaves and branches. Crystallized venom is produced here for antidotes.

Heading east from the steps along the riverbank (or a block from the Museo de las Culturas Aborígenes) you'll come to the white **Iglesia Todos los Santos**, which rises impressively over the Río Tomebamba. A church has stood on this site since the earliest days of the colony, and it's thought the first Catholic Mass in Cuenca took place here. The current building dates from the late nineteenth century. Half a block east of the church is the **Puente Roto** (Broken Bridge), the remains of an old stone bridge, used now as a viewpoint onto the river.

Museo del Banco Central and around

About half a kilometre east of the Iglesia Todos los Santos, at the eastern end of Calle Larga, the **Museo del Banco Central** (Mon–Fri 9am–6pm, Sat 9am–1pm, last entry an hour before closing; $3) is Cuenca's most polished and absorbing museum. The ground floor contains a room devoted to the Inca city of Tomebamba, displaying some beautiful **Inca artefacts** including jewellery, fertility symbols and ritualistic objects. Also on the ground floor is a collection of **nineteenth-century art**, dominated by religious paintings and sombre portraits, but with some wonderful *costumbrista* (folk art) pieces showing indigenous people dancing, playing the fiddle or roasting a hog. The highlight of the museum is the **Sala Etnografía Nacional** on the first floor, which illustrates the diversity of Ecuador's indigenous cultures using day-to-day objects and reconstructions. Displays include an extraordinary exhibition of Shuar *tsantsas* (shrunken heads) from the southern Oriente; a model of a masked dancer from the southern sierra; a collection of festival costumes; and many musical instruments. At the bottom of the building is the **Museo Numismático**, holding coins and notes of the republican and colonial epochs, dating back to the mid-seventeenth century.

Entrance to the Museo del Banco Central includes access to the **Pumapungo archeological park** (same hours), right behind the museum, which is where most of the artefacts displayed in the museum's archeological *sala* were found. Excavations have revealed this is where the most important religious buildings of Tomebamba were located, though all that's left to see are the foundation walls. The site also features the so-called **Jardines del Inca**, combining the ruins with botanical displays of important Andean plants and a bird-rescue centre.

About 300m west along Calle Larga, the **Museo Manuel Agustín Landivar** (Mon–Fri 8am–1pm & 3–6pm; free) has pieces from the Cañari, Inca and colonial periods and gives access to the **Ruinas de Todos los Santos**, where you'll see an Inca wall with several trapezoidal niches and an old colonial water mill built with Inca stones; it's worth looking into if you're walking along the river, but not sufficiently impressive to merit a special visit.

Mirador de Turi

The best spot for a panoramic view of the whole city is the **Mirador de Turi**, a lookout point in front of the Iglesia de Turi, perched high on a hill some 4km south of the centre. The **views** are particularly theatrical on Friday and Saturday evenings when the city could almost be mistaken for a lavish Hollywood film set, with all its church steeples floodlit. A taxi costs about $3 each way; during the daytime there's a bus marked "Turi" (every hour) from the corner of 12 de Abril and Avenida Fray Vicente Solano, on the southern bank of the Río Tomebamba, which will drop you at the bottom of the hill from where it's a half-hour walk up to the *mirador*. Not far from the top, the **Galería Eduardo Vega** (Mon–Fri 9am–6pm, Sat 9.30am–1.30pm; ⓦwww.eduardovega.com) is well worth a stop for its gorgeous glazed ceramics made on site by Ecuador's leading ceramicist – a good place to pick up a gift or two.

Eating, drinking and nightlife

Cuenca offers the best choice of **restaurants** south of Quito, with the usual staple of cheap lunches supplemented by gringo-oriented snacks like crêpes and burritos, as well as fine international cuisines and high-quality *comida típica*. There are a handful of places where you can go for a quiet **drink** through the week, but Cuenca's **nightlife** only really takes off on Thursday, Friday and Saturday nights, when the city's disco-bars and *salsotecas* fill with teenagers and 20- somethings; bars tend to close around 1am, with disco-bars and nightclubs staying open until 3am.

Restaurants and cafés

Amerindia Café Museo de las Culturas Aborígenes, Calle Larga 5-24. Quiet café perfect for a breather between museums, most notable for its Ecuadorian coffee, roasted on site. They also make their own chocolate. Same hours as the *museo* (see p.241).

Café Austria Corner of Benigno Malo 5-95 and Juan Jaramillo ☏07/2840899. Good cakes, ice creams and specialities such as *Guglhupf* and *Apfel-strudel* in this delightful café, no longer Austrian-run, but with the recipe book in safe hands.

La Barraca Presidente Borrero 9-68 and Gran Colombia ☏07/2825094. Large and prominent café, serving pleasing breakfasts, snacks, baguette sandwiches and a small range of standard dinners.

Cacao y Canela Corner Presidente Borrero 597 and Juan Jaramillo ☏07/2820945. Great little café-bar that's a haven for anyone with a sweet tooth, for the soul-cheering hot chocolate, irresistible cakes, pastries and other goodies. Savouries available too. Mon–Sat 4–11pm.

El Cafecito At the eponymous hotel, Honorato Vásquez 7-36. Laid-back café offering reasonably priced cakes, sandwiches, pastas, salads, *quesadillas* and other light meals, inside a covered courtyard. An ever-popular travellers' hangout.

Los Capulíes Presidente Borrero 7-26 ☏07/2845887. Expensive *comida típica* aimed squarely at tourists, served in an attractive courtyard dining room with a gurgling fountain. Has live Andean music at lunchtimes and on Thursday,

Friday and Saturday nights; the service and quality can be uneven. Closed Sun.

Café Eucalyptus Gran Colombia and Benigno Malo ☎07/2849157. Excellent US-run restaurant in a distinguished building with a wide-ranging international menu offering everything from Vietnamese *chaotom* to Jamaican jerk chicken skewers to English Bakewell tart, all served in tapas-size portions (most are $1.50–4). The bar serves good wines and beers, which are free to women during ladies' night (Wed 6–10pm). Live music on Sat. Thriving place, so call to book a table. Closed Sun.

Govindas Juan Jaramillo 7-27 and Presidente Borrero ☎07/2450531. Good, economical vegetarian restaurant plucking a selection of meat-free favourites from the global crop of cuisines: pizza, pasta, curry, tacos plus salads and cheap *almuerzos*. Closed Sun.

Heladería Holanda Benigno Malo 9-55. Scrubbed pine benches, clogs hanging on the wall and posters of windmills and tulips set the scene for the tasty ice cream, yogurts, cakes and sandwiches served in this Dutch-run café.

El Jardín *Hotel Victoria*, Calle Larga 6-93 ☎07/2827401. Well-to-do restaurant with huge smoked-glass windows giving pretty views over the river. The fairly expensive continental cuisine is delicious and particularly strong on seafood.

El Jordán Calle Larga 6-111 and Presidente Borrero ☎07/2850517. Upmarket Middle Eastern and international cuisine served in an impressive three-salon dining room, one in Louis XV style, the middle in "European" and the riverside tranche in Arabic. You may need to reserve at weekends when there are often belly-dancing shows. Closed Sun.

El Maíz Calle Larga 1-279 and Los Molinos. The best place to sample traditional Cuenca cooking, such as *troncha* (beef marinated in vinegar), *seco de chivo* and *cuy* ($15), plus Andean dishes with a modern twist. Fresh, colourful interior as well as outdoor seating with river views. Closed Sun.

El Mirador *Hotel Alli Tiana*, corner of Presidente Córdova and Padre Aguirre ☎07/2821955. Worth putting up with the bland decor and uninspired menu of fried chicken and steak for the superb views over the city, especially when it's illuminated on Friday and Saturday nights. Phone to book a window seat to make the most of it. Open daily from 7am–9.30pm.

Moliendo Honorato Vásquez 6-24 and Hermano Miguel ☎07/2828710. Fantastic little Colombian restaurant offering inexpensive, authentic cuisine including *arepas* (corn pancakes) with a variety of delicious toppings. Wash it down

with a *refajo*, a lager shandy turbo powered by a hit of *aguardiente*. The owner is thinking about retiring, so call ahead. Closed Sun.

New York Pizza Takqui 10-43 and Lamar ☎07/2842792. Plastic-looking pizzeria, but the pizzas and *calzones* are good and inexpensive, and it's open late on Friday and Saturday nights. It does free local deliveries too.

El Paraíso Tomás Ordóñez 5-84. Modest little canteen with bare cement floors and rickety wooden tables, serving delicious freshly squeezed fruit juices and cheap vegetarian lunches, usually involving noodles or grains.

El Pedregal Azteca Gran Colombia 10-29. Large, lively, mid-priced restaurant in a beautifully restored old house, serving excellent Mexican (explicitly not TexMex) food, including *enchiladas*, tacos and *quesadillas*. The atmosphere is especially good on Friday and Saturday nights, when there are live *mariachis*. Closed Sun.

Los Pibes Gran Colombia and Luis Cordero. Quick service and appetizing pizzas and lasagnes are the hallmarks of this rustic-style restaurant, which sports a bamboo roof, log walls and red-checked tablecloths. Attracts a young crowd.

Raymipampa Benigno Malo and Bolívar, Parque Calderón ☎07/2834159. *The* classic eating place in Cuenca, both for its unbeatable location under the colonnaded arcade of the Catedral Nueva and for a devoted local following which ensures the place is always packed. Inexpensive crêpes, pastas, stir-fries, meats and much more are served at a brisk pace.

Villa Rosa Gran Colombia 12-22 ☎07/2837944. Upmarket restaurant favoured by Cuenca's bourgeoisie, set in an attractive covered patio. Offers well-executed but somewhat pricey international dishes like *riñones al jerez* and wild trout, with some Ecuadorian specialities. Closed Sat & Sun.

Wunderbar *Escalinata*, off Calle Larga. This German-run café-bar is a great place for lunch on a sunny day, when you can eat in the little garden among the trees and flowers. Serves gringo-pleasing snacks and light meals, including aubergine and mozzarella sandwiches and Caesar salads. Mon–Fri 11–1am, Sat 3pm–1am.

Bars and discos

El Cafecito Honorato Vásquez 7-36. This arty café-bar makes a good place for a quiet drink through the week but gets packed with locals and gringos at weekends when the music is turned up a few notches.

Hotel El Dorado Gran Colombia 7-87. There's a small piano bar on the sixth floor of this upmarket hotel, with great views over the city. A quiet spot for a wind-down cocktail.

La Mesa Gran Colombia 3-55 and Tomás Ordóñez. Funky *salsoteca* with a bright, fun decor, a small dancefloor and a great atmosphere – especially lively on Wednesdays.

Prohibido Centro Cultural Cruz del Vado, Condamine 12-102 ☎07/2840703. If your musical tastes include gothic, heavy metal and "doom", then you'll find like-minded folk at this bar-cum-gallery, copiously decorated in depictions of skulls, writhing succubi and reproductive organs. Not to everyone's taste, but undeniably different. Mon–Sat 9am–10pm.

La Siembra Honorato Vásquez 7-22 and Presidente Borrero. Mellow café-bar taking up several small rooms, with soft lighting, flickering candles, wicker chairs and bluesy music. A good place to hang out and chat over a few beers.

Tal-Cual Calle Larga 7-57 and Paseo 3 de Noviembre. Relaxed café-bar with pleasing riverside views and a prominent stage for live music, usually salsa or other Latin. Some Thursdays there are jams and music solos, more to listen to than dance to. Snacks available. Open Fri & Sat.

Tinku Calle Larga 4-68 and Jervés. Large, attractive venue in a rambling old house with plenty of dance space under a covered courtyard, plus plenty of seating and a pool table upstairs. Either live music or DJs each night, but Friday is the best evening to go. Wed 6pm–midnight, Thurs–Sat 6pm–2am.

Bar del Tranquilo Presidente Borrero and Presidente Córdova. Buzzing bar open Wednesdays to Saturdays, usually with live music from Thursday onwards.

Wunderbar *Escalinata*, off Calle Larga. A café during the day (see opposite) that turns into a popular bar at night attracting a good mix of foreigners and locals alike with its stylish interior, international bottled beers and occasional live *folklórica* music.

Shopping

With its strong tradition of artesanía, Cuenca offers great scope for **shopping**. In particular, it's one of the most important export centres of the **Panama hat** industry (see box, p.385), with some of the finest-quality hats in Ecuador produced here. The best-known factory open to the public is Homero Ortega & Hijos, directly behind the bus terminal at Av Gil Ramírez Dávalos 3-86 (Ⓦwww.homeroortega.com); visitors are shown the various stages of the hat-making process before ending up at the salesroom – prices aren't cheap, with basic Panamas going from around $10 and *superfinos* from $50 upwards, but they still cost a good deal less than they're sold for abroad. Another quality producer is K. Dorfzaun, Av Gil Ramírez Dávalos 4-04 with similar prices. These are both out towards the bus terminal; for somewhere downtown, try Rafael Paredes & Hijos at Calle Larga 10-41, home of the Museo del Sombrero (see p.241).

The best place for local **artesanía** is the outdoor market at **Plaza Rótary**, some four blocks northeast of the Parque Calderón. Thursday is the main market day, but you'll find stalls here every day of the week, selling vast quantities of ceramic pots and lots of basketwork and carved wooden kitchen utensils. A block to the west, the **Mercado 9 de Octubre** on and around the Plaza Cívica is a lively produce market that's worth a look, more for the atmosphere than to fill your bags, though it rather pales in comparison with the enormous **Feria Libre** on the western periphery of the city at Avenida de las Américas and Avenida Remigio Crespo, a general market which is at its busiest on Wednesdays and Saturdays. A good variety of local artesanía is also sold on the **Plaza San Francisco**, and in the covered stalls inside the **Casa de la Mujer**, General Torres 7-33, on the west side of the same square. If you like **ceramics**, be sure to visit Artesa on the corner of Gran Colombia and Luis Cordero – it's one of the country's top manufacturers of fine ceramics, and sells a wide range of bowls, vases, plates and other items, hand-painted in beautiful colours and designs; you should also have a look at the Galería Eduardo Vega up near the Turi *mirador* (see p.243). Finally, you'll find a number of **antique**-cum-bric-a-brac shops on Presidente Córdova, near the Museo de las

Cuenca's **tour operator** scene is still pretty low-key, with relatively few companies competing for your business, and most offering fairly similar trips to Parque Nacional Cajas, Ingapirca, the craft villages of Gualaceo, Chordeleg and Sigsig, and to the scenic Yunguilla valley and Giron waterfall. Most operators are closed on Sunday.

Club de Andinismo Sangay Contact through the climbing and outdoor supplies shop Explorador Andino, Borrero 7-52 and Sucre. Staff welcome visitors to come with them on hikes and treks around Cuenca (often to Cajas), and occasionally further afield. They usually have an expedition two or three Sundays each month. You pay a fee, but it's a not-for-profit organization, so it's good value.

Expediciones Apullacta Gran Colombia 11-02 and General Torres ☎07/2837815, ⓦwww.apullacta.com. Offers tours to all the popular destinations, including hikes in Cajas national park (around $40 per person with guide, more for multi-day treks) and a "crafts tour" to workshops in local villages where you can see weavings being dyed, Panama hats being woven and talk to the artisans (around $45 per person). Camping gear available for rent.

Mama Kinua Centro Cultural General Torres 7-45 and Sucre on the northeast corner of Plaza San Francisco (☎07/2840610 or 2878377). Not a tour operator as such but a cultural centre with library and restaurant promoting the traditional Andean way of life. Staff can arrange visits to the "Kushiwaira" ethnotourism project – a chance to visit local indigenous communities around Cuenca, learn about farming, craftwork, cheese making, cooking and general highland daily life, and go for walks or horse rides in the surrounding hills.

The Travel Center Hermano Miguel 5-42 and Honorato Vásquez ☎07/2823782, ⓕ2820085, ⓦwww.terradiversa.com. The leading tour operator in Cuenca, a great place to get tour information, brochures, maps, use storage lockers and a copying service and talk to multilingual assistants about the widest range of tours. As well as the usuals, it offers horse treks in the countryside around Cuenca (from $50 per person) and mountain-bike rides around Cajas, to Ingapirca or descents towards the lowlands and rainforest.

Conceptas, selling curiosities like old crucifixes, saints, stirrups, coins, watches and pots.

Listings

Airlines Aerogal, Av Aurelio Aguilar and Solano ☎07/2815250, and at airport ☎07/2804444, ⓦwww.aerogal.com.ec; Copa, Mariscal Lamar 989 and Padre Aguirre ☎07/2842970, ⓦwww.copaair .com; Tame, Av Florencio Astudillo 2-22 ☎07/2889097 and at airport ☎07/2868437 or 2805876, ⓦwww.tame.com.ec.

Banks and exchange Banco de Guayaquil (Visa/ MasterCard/Cirrus ATM), on Sucre, between Hermano Miguel and Presidente Borrero; Banco del Austro (Visa/MasterCard ATM), corner of Sucre and Presidente Borrero; Banco del Pacífico (Visa/ MasterCard/Cirrus ATM, changes traveller's cheques), Benigno Malo and Gran Colombia, and at Museo del Banco Central; Vazcambios, at Gran Colombia and Luis Cordero, changes traveller's cheques and currency.

Camping and fishing equipment Tatoo Adventure Gear, Av Solano 4-31 and Florencia Astudillo (ⓦwww.tatooo.ws), wide range of gear. Bermeo Hermanos, Presidente Borrero 8-35 between Sucre and Bolívar (☎07/2831722). Explorador Andino, corner of Calle Larga and Benigno Malo (☎07/2847320), manufactures hiking and camping equipment. Marathon Sports, Bolívar between Cordero and Borrero (☎07/2885223).

Car rental Several inside the airport or nearby on Av España and Elias Liut, including: Austral ☎07/809286; Avis ☎07/2863902; Bombuscaro ☎07/2828949; and Localiza ☎02/3963800.

Cinemas Casa de la Cultura on Sucre just off the main square; Teatro Cuenca, Padre Aguirre and Mariscal Lamar; Multicines, 5-screen multiplex on Plaza Milenio at Cornelio Marchán and José

Peralta, and also at the Mall del Río; Cine 9 de Octubre, Mariscal Lamar and Mariano Cueva.

Festivals April 12 for the city's foundation and November 3 for its independence; these are big events spread over several days. Religious festivals such as Corpus Christi are important, but the "Pase del Niño" festival on Christmas Eve is the biggest, a huge colourful procession of children and families, floats and dancers, and biblical tableaux.

Health Private: Hospital Santa Inés, Av Daniel Córdova Toral 2-113 ☎07/2817888; Hospital Monte Sinai, Miguel Cordero 6-111 and Av Solana ☎07/2885595. State-run: Hospital Vicente Corral Moscoso, Av El Paraíso ☎07/2822100; Clínica Santa Ana, Av Manuel J Calle ☎07/2814068.

Immigration Av Ordóñez Lazo and Cipreses, CC Astudillo.

Internet facilities Cheap and plentiful, with several on Benigno Malo south of the main square to Calle Larga; others on Honorato Vásquez between Presidente Borrero and Hermano Miguel.

Language schools CEDEI, Tarqui 13-45 and Pío Bravo (☎07/2834353, ⓦwww.cedei.org), has good Spanish and Quichua courses, and TEFL certificates; Sí Centro, Juan Jaramillo 7-27 and Presidente Borrero (☎07/2820429, ⓦwww .sicentrospanishschool.com), also offers homestays and activities; Amauta Fundación, Presidente Córdova 5-58 and Hermano Miguel

(☎07/2846206, ⓦwww.amauta.edu.ec); Simón Bolívar, Cordero and Gran Colombia (☎07/2839959, ⓦwww.bolivar2.com), activities offered; Sampere, Calle Larga and Hermano Miguel (☎/ⓕ07/2841986).

Laundry Zona Limpia, Calle Larga 9-49 and Benigno Malo; Lavandería, Juan Jaramillo and Cordero; Lavahora, Honorato Vásquez 7-72 and Luis Cordero, close to *El Cafecito*; Fast Klin, Hermano Miguel and Calle Larga.

Police Luis Cordero, between Presidente Córdova and Juan Jaramillo (☎07/2822856). Emergency ☎911, police ☎101, fire ☎102.

Post office Main post office at Presidente Borrero and Gran Colombia.

Taxis Radio taxis include: Atenas ☎07/2826464; Latinamericano ☎07/2837173; and Transvista ☎07/2886885.

Telephone office Etapa, at Benigno Malo and Presidente Córdova; Pacífictel is more or less opposite.

Travel agents For tour operators offering trips around Cuenca, see box opposite. For booking or changing flights: Austrotur, Luis Cordero 5-14 and Vásquez ☎07/2831927; Delgado Travel, Gran Colombia 5-21 ☎07/2835667; Metropolitan Touring, Sucre 6-62 ☎07/2837340; The Travel Center, Hermano Miguel 5-42 and Honorato Vásquez ☎07/2823782.

Around Cuenca

There are a number of very rewarding excursions you can make in the area around Cuenca, using the city as a base for day-trips. Fifteen minutes away, the thermal baths of **Baños** are supremely relaxing, particularly after a spot of hiking or fishing in **Parque Nacional Cajas**, forty minutes west of the city, packed with trout-filled lakes, brooding mountains and swirling mists. Heading east, you can visit the rural communities of **Gualaceo**, **Chordeleg** and **Sigsig** on a scenic bus ride through the hills, and find out more about the crafts produced there. Southwest of Cuenca, on the road to Machala, the small town of **Girón** makes a worthwhile excursion for its nearby waterfall surrounded by lush vegetation.

Baños

Eight kilometres west of Cuenca, **BAÑOS** – not to be confused with the major spa town of the same name in the central sierra (see p.199) – is a pretty village perched on the side of a hill, dominated by a beautiful twin-towered church, often illuminated at night. The place is famous for its volcanic **thermal springs**, whose 75°C waters have been channelled into three commercial bath complexes; they can get very crowded on sunny weekends, but are usually quiet and blissfully relaxing through the week. By far the most attractive is the **Balneario Durán** (daily from 5am/6am; $5.50; ⓦwww.hosteriaduran.com), made up of whitewashed, Spanish-looking buildings with terracotta roofs under which you'll find four thermal pools and two sets of Turkish baths; it's on Avenida Ricardo Durán, just off the main road as it enters the village. The **Balneario Rodas** (daily; $4.50; Ⓦ www.hosteriarodas.com) has a less appealing concrete outdoor pool, but its "*termas exclusivas*" ($6.50) – a small, very hot indoor pool (45°C) with a cold-water pool for cooling off – are deliciously invigorating. The third, **Agapantos** (daily; $2.25; Ⓦ www.agapantos.com), has two warm pools and one cold, and also offers treatments, massage, steam boxes and jacuzzi in its spa (Thurs–Sun). Baños is small enough that you'll be able to find each of the facilities easily.

Once you're done soaking yourself, there's little else to do other than wander up to the church, from where you get bird's-eye views down to the valley below. Another pleasant route follows the stream just up from the church for a gentle half-hour stroll through a fragrant eucalyptus grove.

Baños is a fifteen-minute **bus ride** from Cuenca – catch one (every 10min) from Calle Vega Muñoz or the bus terminal. The best **place to eat** in Baños is at the *Hostería Durán*, which has a reasonably priced café for snacks, a restaurant serving *comida típica* and a more expensive restaurant serving international food.

Parque Nacional Cajas

Only 35km northwest of Cuenca, **PARQUE NACIONAL CAJAS** is one of the most beautiful wilderness areas in Ecuador: a wild, primeval landscape of craggy hills and glacier-scoured valleys studded with a breathtaking quantity of lakes (235 at last count), glinting like jewels against the mottled earth and rock surrounding them. Spread over 290 square kilometres of high páramo (3000–4500m), the park offers superb **hiking** and **trout fishing** opportunities and – despite sitting on the doorstep of a major city – a tremendous sense of solitude, with visitors kept at bay by the rain and fog that so frequently plague the area. This inhospitable environment harbours more **flora** and **fauna** than first impressions might suggest: native *quinua* trees, with their gnarled and twisted branches, grow alongside the rivers that thread through the park, and many species of shrubs and flowers adapted to harsh climates – such as the orange-flowered *chuqiragua* – survive on the moorland. There's also a tract of dense, humid cloudforest, peppered with orchids and bromeliads, on the eastern edge of the park. The park is also home to wildcats, pumas, deer and some spectacled bears, though you're far more likely to see ducks, rabbits and perhaps some recently reintroduced llamas. Cajas is also rich in birdlife, including woodpeckers, hummingbirds, mountain toucans and Andean condors. Human relics include a scattering of pre-Hispanic **ruins**, probably of former shelters for those travelling between the sierra and the coast, as well as a four-kilometre restored section of the Ingañán, an old **Inca road**, conserving much of its original paving.

The best place to start exploring Parque Nacional Cajas is at the **Information Centre** (daily 8am–5pm) on the edge of the shimmering **Laguna Toreadora**, easily reached from Cuenca along the paved highway running through the park on its way to the coast (see "Practicalities", p.250, for details and alternative access points). This is where you register your visit, pay your $10 **entrance fee** (if you have not already done so at the Quinuas road control 8km closer to Cuenca) and pick up a free 1:70,000 colour **map** of the park.

Hiking in Parque Nacional Cajas

The official map details ten **hiking routes** across the park, ranging from short hops of an hour or two to end-to-end treks of two or three days. You can

▲ Parque Nacional Cajas

supplement this map with 1:50,000 IGM maps covering the area (Cuenca, Chaucha, San Felipe de Molleturo and Chiquintad), but the black-and-white copies can be hard to read.

The most popular **day-hike** (a combination of route 2 and part of route 1; 5–6hr) starts at the Information Centre, taking you northeast past Laguna Toreadora, through a *quinua* forest and down southeast past **Laguna Totoras** and **Laguna Patoquinuas**. The hike ends back at the highway, some 8km east of the Information Centre, at the Quinuas checkpoint, where you can catch the bus back to Cuenca; ask the warden to show you the path, which is straightforward to follow and quite easy-going.

Alternatively, there's a good hike (also 5–6hr), which starts 4km further west along the highway from the Information Centre, at the **Tres Cruces** hill on the left-hand (south) side of the road. At 4160m, the hill straddles the continental divide between waters draining west into the Pacific and east into the Amazon basin – you can scramble up it in about fifteen minutes, for great views over the park. The trail (route 5 on the map) takes you down past a string of three lakes – Negra, Larga and Tagllacocha – bringing you to the Ingañán (paved Inca road) by Laguna Luspa, before heading right (west) back towards the highway.

There are numerous possibilities for **multi-day hikes** too – consult the park map and IGM maps and ask the warden for guidance. It's essential to come well prepared: with the possibility of thick fog obscuring visibility, and a tendency for paths to peter out into nowhere, you should bring emergency food and ideally a survival blanket even on short day-hikes, in case you get lost. Although it's often hot enough to hike in a t-shirt when the sun's out (usually in the morning), the temperature can quickly drop below freezing in bad weather, and is perishing at night, so take plenty of layers and warm gear, including a hat and gloves. You'll also need waterproof clothing and sturdy, waterproof boots, preferably with gaiters; if you're camping make sure your tent is well sealed or you'll have a wet and miserable time. It's driest between June and August, but it might rain, hail or snow at any time of the year.

Practicalities

Parque Nacional Cajas is located near the paved highway between Cuenca and Guayaquil via Molleturo. Regular **buses** ply this route either from Cuenca's Terminal Terrestre, or from the Occidental bus company terminal at Mariscal Lamar and Miguel Heredia (hourly 7am–5pm). Ask to be dropped either at the turning (Km15) for the **Laguna Llaviuco** control (3km walk) or at the Information Centre (Centro de Informaciones) at **Laguna Toreadora**, about a forty-minute drive from Cuenca (Km33.5). A second unpaved road runs along the southern boundary of the park past the communities of **Soldados** (where there is a control) and Angas; a bus leaves the Puente del Vado area in Cuenca at 6am, returning by the checkpoint at around 4pm (ask for the latest as this is irregular). The park's head office (managed by ETAPA) is also in Cuenca in the Edificio Morejón, Presidente Córdova 7-56 and Luis Cordero (☎07/2829853, Ⓦwww.etapa.com.ec).

There are basic **refuges** ($4) at both the Toreadora Information Centre (bunks, cooking facilities and a fireplace but no wood) and at Laguna Llaviucu (advance reservation to stay here ☎07/2841929), for which you'll need to bring a warm sleeping bag, as well as many campsites in the park, which are marked on the map. Both Toreadora and Llaviucu also have simple **restaurants** but these are often only open during busy weekends. You'll get better food and lodging 1km east of the Llaviucu turning, just off the highway, at the beautifully located *Hostería Dos Chorreras* (☎07/2853154 reservations open in the afternoon after 3pm, Ⓦwww.hosteriadoschorreras.com; ❻), which has an upmarket (but still reasonably priced) restaurant with a blazing log fire and a daily changing menu. It also has comfortable, heated **rooms** and offers **horse treks** and fishing trips in the park. For details of Cuenca-based operators offering **tours** to Cajas, see the box on p.246.

Gualaceo, Chordeleg and Sigsig

In contrast to the forbidding, rugged scenery of Cajas, the landscape east of Cuenca is gentle and pastoral, characterized by rippling hills and fertile orchards and fields. From Cuenca, a very scenic paved road leads through these hills to the small market town of **Gualaceo**, continuing to the villages of **Chordeleg** and **Sigsig**, known for their handicrafts. Gualaceo and Chordeleg both have enjoyable Sunday-morning **markets**, while Sigsig – which also has a small Sunday market – is best visited during the week when its Panama hat factory-shop is open. This area is also a little-used jumping-off point for the southern **Oriente**, with rough but scenic roads snaking down from Gualaceo to Limón, and from Sigsig to Gualaquiza (see p.332). **Buses** to Gualaceo (a 1hr trip), Chordeleg (1hr 15min) and Sigsig (1hr 40min) leave every half-hour from Cuenca's bus terminal.

Gualaceo

On the banks of the Río Gualaceo 36km east of Cuenca sits **GUALACEO** (2330m), known as the Jardín del Azuay (Garden of Azuay) for its rich agricultural land and mild climate. It's one of the most important fruit-growing centres in the region, and every March celebrates the Fiesta del Durazno (Peach Festival) with street parties and peach-tastings. The town's **central plaza** is the site of a lively **Sunday-morning market**, packed with stalls piled with fresh produce; there are also a few craft items and souvenirs available on Avenida Roldós, near the bus terminal (a couple of blocks southeast of the plaza, towards the river). The **Museo Artesanal del CIDAP** (Wed–Sun 9am–6pm; free), on Loja and Sucre at the entrance to the *Parador*

Turísitico (see opposite), has displays about weaving with *paja toquilla* (the fibre used for Panama hats) and the production of **Ikat shawls** (called *macanas* or *chales*), woven on backstrap looms. Just outside town 2km to the west on the road to Cuenca is Ecuagenera (Mon–Fri 9am–3pm, Sat 9am–noon; $3, ☎07/2255237, ⓦwww.ecuagenera.com), Ecuador's largest **orchid** exporter; there are more than 2500 species here, at least 500 of which are in bloom at any one time. Tours to see orchids in regional cloudforest reserves are available.

Information is available at the Ministry of Tourism office in the *municipio* on the central plaza, or at the iTur office on the other side of the bridge at Ignacio Jaramillo and Vásquez (Mon–Fri 8am–1pm & 2–5pm, Sat & Sun 9am–noon & 2–5pm; ☎07/2256608). Most people are happy to make a passing visit to Gualaceo, but if you want to **stay** try *Residencial Gualaceo* (☎07/2255006; ❷) at Gran Colombia 3-02 (a couple of blocks northwest of the plaza) for reasonable budget rooms, or the *Parador Turístico* (☎07/2255110; ❺), about 1km south of the centre on Gran Colombia, for upmarket rooms with a pool, sauna and good restaurant. The best **place to eat** in the centre is *Don Q*, a few doors down from *Residencial Gualaceo*, where basic but well-prepared staples are served.

Chordeleg

From Gualaceo, the road from Cuenca continues 6km east to **CHORDELEG**. Smaller and quainter than Gualaceo, Chordeleg presents a very pretty picture as you approach it along the main road, Calle Juan Bautista Cobos, lined by lovely old terraced houses with sloping terracotta roofs. Look right as you head up the road and you'll see a number of shops selling **ceramics**, which the village is noted for; the largest selection is available at the **Centro de Artesanías**, about halfway up. Chordeleg is also famous as a centre of gold and metalwork, particularly delicately worked filigree **jewellery**, an art that's been practised here since pre-Hispanic times. Numerous shops keep the tradition alive in the village, but a lot of it is made from low-grade gold, so beware of parting with large sums of money. These and other local crafts, including embroidery and hat production, are highlighted in the **Museo Municipal** (Tues–Fri 9am–5pm, Sat & Sun 10am–4pm; free) in the *municipio* on the plaza, along with some pre-Columbian artefacts of the area. You'll also find lots of Panama hats and colourful textiles at the village's Sunday-morning **market**. For **information** head to the iTur office (Tues–Sun 8am–5pm) on the corner of Alfaro and Cobos, a block downhill from the plaza. You can stay at the *Viguz* (☎07/2223313; ❷) on Guayaquil north behind the plaza and pick up a filling *campesino* meal at a number of simple **restaurants** across from the church.

Sigsig

A further 18km along the road, **SIGSIG** is a remote agricultural village sitting in gorgeous, hilly countryside near the banks of the Río Santa Bárbara, from whose swaying reeds (*sigses*) it takes its name. Surprisingly – for such a small, out-of-the-way place – it's one of the most important centres of **Panama hat** production in the province. A good place to buy one at a reasonable price is the **Asociación de Toquilleras María Auxiliadora**, a women's weaving cooperative in the old hospital next to the river, a ten-minute walk from the centre on the road to Gualaquiza. The building often appears locked up, but shout or ring the bell, because there's pretty well always someone about. Back in town on the Parque 3 de Noviembre, the upper square with the striking modern church, is the **Museo Municipal** (Mon–Fri 8am–1pm & 2–4.30pm; free), showing pieces from the local Tacalshapa culture (500–1470 AD) and the prehistoric Chobsi culture (8000–5500 BC).

Few tourists make it to Sigsig let alone **stay** here, but if you need a bed for the night you'll find basic, airy rooms at *Residencial Lupita* (no phone; ❷) on the main road running through the centre of the village. *Restaurant Turismo*, opposite the covered market building, serves cheap soups, fried meats and other staples.

Girón and El Chorro

Forty-five kilometres southwest of Cuenca on the highway to Machala, the small hill town of **GIRÓN** is built around a pretty central square overlooked by once-grand old houses with clay-tiled roofs and wooden balconies, and a rather avant-garde concrete church with an enormous blue cross towering over the entrance. Girón's single claim to fame is that an important treaty was signed here in 1829 by generals of Gran Colombia and Peru, after the Battle of Tarqui in which the Peruvians were defeated (see p.494). The colonial mansion where the treaty was signed has been splendidly restored by the army and turned into the **Museo Casa de los Tratados** (daily 8am–6pm; $1.25), displaying military memorabilia, including a reconstruction of the table where the signing took place.

If this isn't your thing, head out of town to **El Chorro**, a long, slender waterfall tumbling down a steep cliff between a tangle of lush vegetation. It's a two-hour uphill hike from Girón along 5km of dirt road: ask for directions from the traffic lights on the main road running through town. There's a dollar charge to visit the **mirador** overlooking the fall, or you can hike up the stiff, two-hour trail to a viewpoint onto a second, higher waterfall, out of sight from below; the walk is tough in parts, and involves clinging onto some cords attached to the rock. There's a pleasant **refuge**, *El Chorro de Girón* (☎07/2275783 or 2883711, ❶), right next to the waterfall, offering hearty, inexpensive **meals** and beds, or you can **camp** for $4; it's not always open during weekdays, so phone in advance. Note that the owners can also organize transport here from Cuenca. This is a lovely, remote spot, and makes a great base for off-the-beaten-track hiking through the hills and nearby cloudforest.

Jima

Southeast of Cuenca, about fifteen minutes beyond Cumbe on the Panamericana is the turning for **JIMA**, a small village set in a clutch of idyllic green hills, where a **community-based ecotourism** project (no contact details) is in full swing. You can stay with families and make the most of the beautiful surroundings on guided hikes and horse rides, fish in the Río Moya and explore the **Bosque Tambillo**, a cloudforest, which can be traversed on a trek from the highlands down to La Florida, a short bus ride from Gualauquiza in the Oriente. The first weekend of October is the **Fiesta de Chicha de Jora**, a celebration of the ancient Andean alcoholic fermented corn tipple, which includes dances, live music, beauty pageants, an agricultural fair and, most importantly, a competition to judge the best chicha from dozens of entrants. Head to the **Information Centre**, whose staff can make logistical arrangements for all activities, provide equipment and guides and put you up with local families. There's more formal **accommodation** at the *Centro de Capacitación* (☎07/2418398; ❶) at the high school, with shared bathrooms and electric showers, or at the *Hostal Chacapampa* (☎07/2418046; ❷), where you can use the kitchen. Transportes Jima **buses** leave from Cuenca's Feria Libre, Avenida de la Américas (5 daily, 6 Sat; 1hr 30min).

South of Cuenca: Saraguro

South of Cuenca, the Panamericana winds its way through increasingly remote and isolated countryside, passing only a handful of villages on its way to the city of Loja. The most interesting stop en route is the small agricultural town of **SARAGURO** ("land of corn" in Quichua), 140km south of Cuenca and 64km north of Loja, the site of a lively and atmospheric Sunday-morning market. As you approach from the north, a large sign proudly announces your arrival in "*Saraguro, Tierra de Maíz, centro indígena más importante de América*" – the centre of one of the most distinct highland groups of Ecuador, the **Saraguro indígenas**. Their forebears, originally from the altiplano region of Lake Titicaca in Bolivia, were relocated here by the Incas during their expansion into Ecuador, as part of the *mitimae* system used to consolidate colonization. More than 500 years on, the Saraguros are still set apart by their particularly pure form of Quichua and very distinctive clothing. The men wear black ponchos and black knee-length shorts, often over black wellington boots used for their farm work, while the women wear pleated black skirts and hand-woven black shawls, fastened by elaborate silver or nickel brooches called *tupus*. Saraguros have also maintained very traditional forms of celebrating religious **festivals**. Their Easter celebrations, in particular, follow a strict pattern of processions, re-enactments and symbolic rituals, all marked by their great solemnity. Other important Saraguro festivals include Tres Reyes (January 6), Corpus Christi (early or mid-June) and Christmas.

Most Saraguro *indígenas* live as cattle herders in rural farming communities, but just about all of them come into town for the Sunday-morning **market** for

▲ Saraguro local

fresh produce, cattle and household goods, and Sunday Mass, held in the handsome, honey-stone church on the main plaza.

Practicalities

There's little to do here other than soak up the atmosphere, and most visitors are happy to pass through for a couple of hours or so. If you want to stay, you'll find simple budget **accommodation** with shared bath at the friendly *Residencial Saraguro* (T07/2200286; ❷) on Calle Loja and Antonio Castro, and more comfortable rooms, with or without private bath and TV, at the *Samana Wasi* (T07/2200315; ❸), near the Panamericana on 10 de Marzo; the interior rooms here aren't so nice. The best **place to eat** is *Mama Cuchara* on the plaza, which serves uncomplicated but tasty Ecuadorian food at reasonable prices. **Buses** from Cuenca and Loja pass through town at least every hour.

Loja and around

Marooned at the bottom of the country and several hours' drive from any other major town, **LOJA** is a remote but thriving little provincial capital. Thanks to its isolation, it has long been good at taking care of its own affairs, even dabbling with self-government in 1857 – not to mention its distinction of being the first city in the country to generate electricity, in 1897. With a progressive emphasis on learning and culture, the city boasts two universities, a law school and a major music conservatory, which give the place a youthful, vibrant atmosphere. Spread over a fertile valley at 2100m above sea level, Loja is about 500m lower than most sierra cities, and noticeably warmer (usually 16–21°C).

Loja's most exciting **fiesta** kicks off on August 20 when the icon of the Virgen del Cisne arrives in the cathedral for a two-month "visit", having been carried on foot from El Cisne (see p.259), accompanied by hundreds of pilgrims. The festivities which follow culminate on September 8 with the Feria de Integración Fronteriza, a huge craft and trade fair Simón Bolívar established in 1824, in an effort to promote cross-border relations; the fair is still attended by many Peruvians today.

The town sits on the doorstep of the western edge of **Parque Nacional Podocarpus** (see p.262), a pristine tract of páramo and cloudforest, and is the best place to get information on the park or arrange a visit. The eastern part of the park, over the sierra and down towards the Oriente, is approached from **Zamora**, easily reached by bus from Loja. Loja is also the gateway to **Peru** via two border crossings (see the box on p.269 for full details), one of which is a short hop from **Vilcabamba**, an easy-going village that has become an obligatory stop for many backpackers before leaving the country.

Arrival and information

TAME flights from Quito ($82 each way) and Guayaquil ($72 each way) land at the **Aeropuerto La Toma** (T07/2677140), just outside the small town of **Catamayo**, 33km west of Loja (30min drive). Shared taxis to the centre charge around $5 per person; otherwise a private taxi costs $15. Loja's **bus terminal** is 2km north of the centre on Avenida Cuxibamba; from here you can pick up any local bus heading south towards the centre, or one of the taxis that hang around the terminal. **Taxis** charge $1 for journeys within the city, and can usually be flagged down on the main avenues or around the *parque central*.

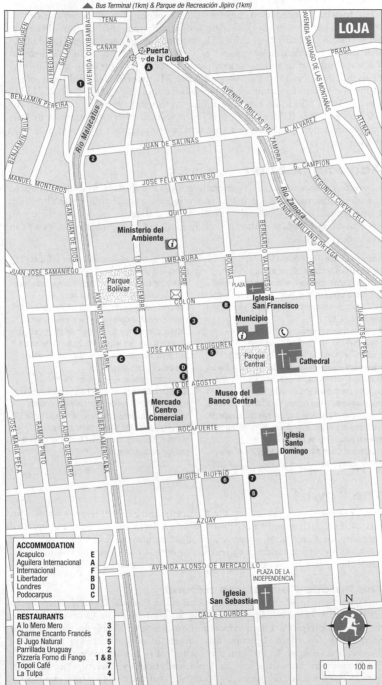

Bus Terminal (1km) & Parque de Recreación Jipiro (1km)

LOJA

TENA

CAÑAR

Puerta
de la Ciudad
A

F. EGUIGUREN
ALFREDO MORA
GALLARDO
AVENIDA CUXIBAMBA

AVENIDA SANTIAGO DE LAS MONTAÑAS

PRAGA

BENJAMÍN PEREIRA

AVENIDA ORILLAS DE ZAMORA

D. ÁLVAREZ

ATENAS

BENJAMÍN RUIZ

Río Malacatus

JUAN DE SALINAS

G. CAMPIÓN

MANUEL MONTEROS

JOSÉ FÉLIX VALDIVIESO

Río Zamora

SEGUNDO CUEVA CELI

SAN JUAN DE DIOS

QUITO

AVENIDA EMILIANO ORTEGA

JUAN JOSÉ SAMANIEGO

Ministerio del
Ambiente

IMBABURA

BOLÍVAR

BERNARDO VALDIVIESO

OLMEDO

Parque
Bolívar

18 DE NOVIEMBRE

SUCRE

PLAZA

Iglesia
San Francisco

AVENIDA UNIVERSITARIA

COLÓN

B

Municipio

JUAN JOSÉ PEÑA

JUAN JOSÉ SAMANIEGO

3

5

Parque
Central

Cathedral

JOSÉ ANTONIO EGUIGUREN

C

D
E
F

10 DE AGOSTO

Museo del
Banco Central

AVENIDA LAURO GUERRERO
AVENIDA IBEROAMERICANA

Mercado
Centro
Comercial

JOSÉ MARÍA PEÑA
RAMÓN PINTO

ROCAFUERTE

Iglesia
Santo
Domingo

La Virgen (800m)

MIGUEL RIOFRÍO

6

7

8

AZUAY

ACCOMMODATION
Acapulco   E
Aguilera Internacional A
Internacional   F
Libertador   B
Londres   D
Podocarpus   C

AVENIDA ALONSO DE MERCADILLO

PLAZA DE LA
INDEPENDENCIA

Iglesia
San Sebastián

N

RESTAURANTS
A lo Mero Mero   3
Charme Encanto Francés   6
El Jugo Natural   5
Parrillada Uruguay   2
Pizzería Forno di Fango 1 & 8
Topoli Café   7
La Tulpa   4

CALLE LOURDES

0   100 m

Parque La Argelia (4km) & Jardín Botánico (4km)

For **tourist information**, head to the excellent iTur office on the central square, at the corner of José Antonio Eguiguren and Bolívar (Mon–Fri 8am–1pm & 3–6pm; ☎07/2581251, Ⓦwww.loja.gov.ec), where the helpful staff should be able to answer most of your questions about Loja, Vilcabamba, Zamora, Podocarpus and its surroundings. You can pick up maps and information on Parque Nacional Podocarpus at the **Ministerio del Ambiente** office, in the INDA building, at Sucre between Imbabura and Quito (☎07/2571534), though if you plan to do extensive hiking in the park, you'll probably need the relevant 1:50,000 IGM maps from Quito. Several other organizations in Loja have information on Podocarpus; for details of these refer to "Practicalities" in the park account on p.264.

Accommodation

Loja offers a decent spread of generally good-value **hotels**, from the budget to the very comfortable. Unless you're arriving during the festival of the Virgen del Cisne (Aug 20–Sept 8), there's unlikely to be a shortage of beds, so there's no need to book ahead. Breakfast is usually included in the room rate, except in the budget options.

Acapulco Sucre 07-61 ☎07/2570651, Ⓕ2571103. Clean and tidy rooms, mostly looking onto an internal courtyard, with nylon bedspreads and dated furnishings, with private bath and cable TV. There's parking, restaurant, laundry service and free internet. ❺

Aguilera Internacional Sucre 01-08 ☎07/2572892, Ⓕ2572894. Quiet rooms (nicer upstairs) with antique furniture, cable TV and private bath, a short walk from the centre. A place to unwind, with its sauna, gym, and steam baths, perfumed with eucalyptus leaves. ❻

Internacional 10 de Agosto 15-30 ☎07/2578486. Old-fashioned house with nicely painted woodwork and adequate rooms with private bath around an internal patio. Fine for the price. ❷

Libertador Colón 14-30 ☎07/2560779, Ⓦwww .hotellibertador.com.ec. Downtown Loja's best hotel, offering smart, well-furnished rooms with cable TV, direct-dial phone and good bathrooms. Also has a decent restaurant, a small pool, a sauna and steam bath. Ask for a room in the new block. ❼

Londres Sucre 07-51 ☎07/2561936. Well-maintained old house owned by a friendly young couple, offering spacious rooms with high ceilings, wooden floors and bare white walls. Clean, shared bathrooms and lots of plants and flowers around. The best of the cheapies. ❷

Podocarpus José A. Eguiguren 16-50 ☎/Ⓕ07/2581428, Ⓦwww.hotelpodocarpus.com. ec. Comfortable, modern rooms with spotless en-suite bath, good-quality bedding and cable TV in every room. The hotel's back rooms are quietest. Laundry service, wi-fi, restaurant and parking all available. ❻

The Town

Loja's **centre** – wedged between the Malacatos and Zamora rivers – is a curious mix of the concrete and the colonial. While it lacks the uniform architectural harmony of Cuenca, it preserves enough handsome, old eighteenth- and nineteenth-century buildings to lend its *centro histórico* a graceful colonial look, while the town's well-cared-for parks and open spaces further add to its appeal.

The Parque Central and around

Loja's centre is marked by the large, palm-filled **Parque Central**, lined by an eclectic collection of buildings competing for your attention. On the north side, the new **municipio** is a huge concrete monstrosity, saved only by the exuberant murals in its courtyard depicting folk images of *indígenas* playing instruments, dancing and cooking. To the east, the **cathedral** boasts a towering white facade flamboyantly trimmed in yellow and gold, with brightly painted pillars and a tall spire. Its interior is equally ornate, especially the coffered ceiling, whose every detail is picked out in vivid colours. In subdued contrast, the former **Casa de Justicia**, on the south side of the square, is a traditional early eighteenth-century mansion with whitewashed adobe walls, a clay-tiled roof and an overhanging upper floor leaning on thick wooden posts. Inside, the **Museo del Banco Central** (Mon–Fri 9am–1pm & 2–5pm; $0.40) displays a modest collection of pre-Columbian ceramics and religious sculptures in rooms off a creaking wooden veranda.

A couple of streets leading off the square are dotted with elegant nineteenth-century houses sporting painted balconies, shutters and eaves, particularly on **Bolívar**, from the Parque Central towards Calle Lourdes, and **10 de Agosto**, between Bolívar and 18 de Noviembre. Nearby, the busy **Mercado Centro Comercial** is on 18 de Noviembre and 10 de Agosto, considered by many to be the model city market – well managed, clean and run with unfussy competence.

A couple of blocks east of the market along Bolívar sits the imposing **Iglesia Santo Domingo**, whose immense twin bell towers Lojanos cherish as a symbol of their city. Inside, the church is crammed with over a hundred biblical-themed oil paintings hanging amid swirling floral motifs covering the walls and ceilings.

The Plaza de la Independencia and around

A few blocks south down Bolívar from the Iglesia Santo Domingo you'll reach the **Plaza de la Independencia**, so called because it was here that Loja's citizens gathered on November 18, 1820, to proclaim publicly their independence from the Spanish Crown. It is undoubtedly the city's most beautiful square, enclosed by colonial-style buildings that look like outsized dolls' houses with their brightly painted walls, balconies, shutters and doors, and the cheerful, blue-and-white **Iglesia San Sebastián**. Gorgeous hills rising steeply over the rooftops frame the east side of the square, providing a beautiful backdrop as they catch the rays of the late-afternoon sun.

Head south past the church for a block, and then turn right into the restored **Calle Lourdes**, locally regarded as the jewel of all the town's thoroughfares. Between Bolívar and Sucre, the entire street, which boasts some particularly well-preserved buildings, has been given an extensive facelift, the woodwork repaired, and the houses spruced up in bright colours to show off the architecture.

Loja's outskirts

Loja has several worthwhile sights on the outskirts of town. The **Puerta de la Ciudad** (daily 8am–9.30pm; free), a mock early-colonial gatehouse complete with tower, crenellations and portcullis, marks the northern entrance to town at the confluence of the two rivers and contains temporary art exhibitions, tourist information, and a pleasant café on the second floor. You can climb up the tower for attractive views of the town and its environs. About 1km north of this, the **Plaza de El Valle** is a paved square surrounded by pretty, rustic-style buildings and a lovely old colonnaded church. Continue three blocks north to reach the **Parque de Recreación Jipiro** (☏07/2583357), a large, landscaped park with an ornamental lake and a novelty children's playground featuring models of buildings from around the world, such as the Eiffel Tower, an Arabic mosque and a truly bizarre replica of Moscow's St Basil's Cathedral, replete with slides. Jipiro is a very popular open space for Lojanos, who also come to enjoy the heated **swimming pool** here (daily 8am–6pm; $1), equipped with retractable glass roof, or the little **planetarium** in the dome of the "mosque" which has regular 30-minute shows at weekends ($0.25). The plaza and the park can be reached on foot in about twenty minutes, or on buses marked "El Valle" or "Jipiro" from the centre.

At the opposite end of town, about 4.5km south along Avenida de los Conquistadores, the **Parque La Argelia** (daily 8am–6pm; $0.50) is a mini slice of wilderness on the edge of the city, with excellent trails running through hills, forests and streams. A part of the park (with a separate entrance, across the highway) is the four-hectare **Jardín Botánico Reynaldo Espinosa** (Mon–Fri 8am–6pm, Sat & Sun 1–6pm; $1), home to a great variety of native and introduced plant species, including many orchids. Parque La Argelia is on the road to Vilcabamba, so can be reached on any bus from Loja to Vilcabamba from the terminal; alternatively, take a taxi there for about $1.50.

The whole of Loja can be taken in with sweeping, panoramic **views** from a lookout point at the foot of the statue of the **Virgen de Fátima** (El Churo), perched on a hillside east of the city. To get there, walk east up Riofrío, cross the river, and follow the path up the hillside.

Eating, drinking and nightlife

Loja offers some inviting, affordable **restaurants** that tend to be packed at lunchtime and very quiet later on, with most winding down around 9pm. If you're after **nightlife** (which tends to be tranquil through the week and liveliest on Fridays and Saturdays) head for *Fiesta Disco Club*, Loja's most popular dance spot at 10 de Agosto and J.J. Peña. The smart but relaxed *D'Class*, Avenida Orillas del Zamora and Zarzas, is a good spot for a drink and a chat. For **live acts** – Loja is renowned for producing some of the country's finest musicians – try the vibrant *Casa Tinku* (Wed–Sat), Lourdes and Sucre, which usually has good live music on Friday and Saturday nights. Good backups are *El Viejo Minero* on Sucre 10-76 and Riofrío, a small and cosy bar, filled with mining memorabilia, which regularly features impromptu live music at weekends, and *La Leyenda* (Thurs–Sat; $2), corner of Carrión and Avenida Rodríguez, which features acoustic acts and solo guitarists among the less gifted karaoke-style wannabes.

Restaurants and cafés

A lo Mero Mero Sucre and Colón. Simple little restaurant giving onto a busy street, with wooden benches and tables and sombreros on the wall, serving inexpensive Mexican food. Closed Sun.

Charme Encanto Francés Miguel Riofrío between Bolívar and Sucre. Fancy restaurant focusing on French cuisine, but also serving a versatile international menu in well-to-do surroundings. Pricier than most but the food is good. Closed Sun.

El Jugo Natural J.A. Eguiguren and Bolívar. Good place to pick up a freshly squeezed juice, some breakfast and a traditional snack, such as *quimbolitos*.

Parrillada Uruguay Juan de Salinas and Av Universitaria ☎07/2570260. Friendly, family-run

restaurant serving delicious, succulent meat cooked over charcoal on a traditional cast-iron *parrilla* (grill). If you're not up to their huge portions, try the steak baguette for a light meal. Closes Sun 5pm.

Pizzería Forno di Fango Bolívar and Riofrío ☎07/2586883. Full Italian menu and, most importantly, enjoyable pizzas cooked up in a wood-fire oven. Take away and delivery service available.

Topoli Café Riofrío and Bolívar. Great for coffee, snacks, sandwiches, yogurt and breakfasts.

La Tulpa 18 de Noviembre and Colón. Popular for its good-value traditional food, such as *humitas*, *fritada* and *cesinas*, and cheap set breakfasts, lunches and dinners. Good on Sunday evenings when it's hard to find somewhere open.

Listings

Airlines TAME, at airport ☎07/2677306. ⓦwww .tame.com.ec.

Banks and exchange Banco del Austro (Visa ATM and cash advance), corner of J.A. Eguiguren and Bolívar; Banco de Guayaquil, J.A. Eguiguren and

Valdivieso (Visa, MasterCard ATM, changes Amex traveller's cheques, cash advance); Banco de Loja, corner of Bolívar and Rocafuerte (Visa ATM).

Car rental Arricar at the *Hotel Libertador* ☎07/25588014, ⓔvilcatour@impsat.net.ec;

Bombuscaro, 10 de Agosto and Av Universitaria ☎ 07/2577021; Localiza ☎ 07/2581729, Av Neva Loja and Av Isidro Ayora.

Consulate Peru, Sucre 10-56 and Azuay ☎ 07/2571668.

Hospitals Hospital Militar, Colón and Bernardo Valdivieso (☎ 07/2578332); Clínica San Agustín, 18 de Noviembre and Azuay (☎ 07/2570314); Clínica Santa María, Cuxibamba and Latacunga (☎ 07/2581077).

Internet facilities Cheap and plentiful. Try World Net, at Colón 14-69 and Sucre; Cybertren at the Parque Jipiro; Ciber Crispin, at Sucre and Colón.

Laundry Maxilim Lavandería on the corner of 10 de Agosto and 24 de Mayo.

Police and immigration Av Argentina, Tebaida Alta ☎ 07/2573600.

Post office Sucre 05-85 and Colón.

Telephone office Pacífictel on José A. Eguiguren and Bernardo Valdivieso.

Tour operators Exploraves Birdwatchers, at Lourdes 14-80 and Sucre (☎ 07/2582434, http://exploraves .com) offers birdwatching tours to Podocarpus led by an English-speaking ornithologist ($70 a day with food, binoculars and transport); Sisacuna Tours, Bernardo Valdivieso 11-71 and Mercadillo (☎ 07/2570334, ✉ sisacunatours@gmail.com) goes to Podcarpus, Puyango, Vilcabamba, Zaruma, Yamana and El Cisne among others, plus rock climbing to Ahuaca and other hikes ($35–135 depending on trip). Ask any of these operators or tourist offices about the state of the recently completed *ruta ecológica*, a hiking and riding route between Loja and Vilcabamba.

Travel agents Reliable travel agents for booking or changing flights include Vilcatur at the *Hotel Libertador*, Colón 14-30 (☎ 07/2588014).

Moving on from Loja

Loja is the hub of Ecuador's deep south, from where you can get direct buses to three **border crossings** into Peru: Huaquillas (see p.413), **Macará** (see p.269) and Zumba (see p.270) – the one at Macará being the most popular and convenient. Roads down to **the coast** go via **Piñas** (near **Zaruma**, worth a stop if you're passing; see p.411), **Balsas** and **Alamor**, the latter a launchpad for the Puyango petrified forest north on the Arenillas road, as well as south to **Zapotillo**, another seldom-used crossing into Peru. North from Loja, the Panamericana links the town to **Cuenca** and the rest of the sierra, while to the east another paved road leads to **Zamora** and into the Oriente.

Many southbound visitors to Loja, however, are looking to pick up connecting transport to **Vilcabamba**, which they can do easily. Buses leave every 15 to 30 minutes from the terminal until 8.45pm (1hr 30min) as do faster Vilcabambaturis minibuses (every 30min; 1–1hr 15min; $1). Another option is taking the less comfortable taxi *ruta* (shared taxi; $1) from the southern end of Avenida Iberoamérica. For more details on destinations and frequencies see "Travel details" on p.270.

West to El Cisne

West of Loja, the road to Machala meanders through parched, rippling hills on its way down to the coast. Some 43km out of town, at the small community of **San Pedro**, a paved road branches north and climbs steeply uphill for 22km. A striking sight awaits you at the top, as the road twists around the hill and dips down to reveal a carpet of rustic, terracotta roofs clustered around a huge, white, neo-Gothic basilica, whose pinnacles and spires dwarf everything around it. This is the tiny village of **EL CISNE** and its famous **Santuario**, home to a sixteenth-century painted cedar effigy of the Virgin Mary, carved by Diego de Robles. This icon, known as the **Virgen del Cisne**, is the subject of a fervent cult of devotion, attracting pilgrims year-round from southern Ecuador and northern Peru. This devotion reaches its apogee during the **Fiesta de la Virgen**, which begins on August 15. The following day, thousands of pilgrims begin a seventy-kilometre trek to Loja, carrying the Virgin on their shoulders. The image arrives on August 20, where she is deposited in Loja's cathedral, while the partying continues in the city.

You begin to get an idea of the faith invested in this icon at the **museum** attached to the basilica (daily 8am–6pm; $1; if closed, ask in the bookshop at the base of the clock tower, opposite), crammed with hundreds of gifts brought to thank the Virgin for her favours, from exam certificates and medals to jewellery and vases. There's also a large collection of tiny model buses and trucks, left by drivers in return for her protection. Tucked away in a hushed, softly lit side room next door, you'll find a collection of eighteenth-century religious paintings and carvings, along with some richly embroidered garments and silver lecterns. Other than getting a glimpse of all this, there's not much else to do in El Cisne, but if you get stuck here you'll find clean, budget **rooms** at *Hostal Medina* (no phone; ❷) on Calle Machachi, the road leading down to the church. There are a couple of basic **places to eat** on the plaza in front of the basilica. There are three daily **buses** to El Cisne from Loja (2hr).

East to Zamora

A paved road heading east connects Loja with the small town of **ZAMORA**, sitting 64km away in foothills on the edge of the Oriente, the other side of the Sabanilla Pass which, at 2700m, is one of the lowest crossing points in the Andes. For most visitors Zamora's main use is as a base for visiting the lower section of **Parque Nacional Podocarpus** (see p.262), but the bus ride here is itself worthwhile, with the road snaking down from the sierra past numerous waterfalls, giving occasional views onto miles of densely forested hills. As you get lower, the air becomes warmer and moister, and the vegetation becomes increasingly lush, with giant ferns hanging over the road. At 970m above sea level, Zamora has a subtropical climate, with an average temperature of 21°C – a stark contrast to the coolness of the sierra.

Arrival and information

Daily **buses** make the two-hour journey from Loja to Zamora, arriving at the terminal at the eastern end of town, which is within easy walking distance of all **hotels**. **Taxis** – part of the Cooperativa Río Zamora (☎07/2605065) – are stationed behind the bus terminal from 5am until 10pm.

General tourist information is available from iTur, Diego de Vaca in the shopping mall by the market (daily 8am–12.30pm & 2–5pm; ☎07/2607526). You can get a map of the Parque Nacional Podocarpus as well as **information** about it at the Ministerio del Ambiente office (☎07/2606606), just out of town on the road to Loja. Local **banks** do not have any money-changing, cash advance facilities nor ATMs, so bring everything you need.

Accommodation

Zamora does not offer an enormous choice of accommodation, but what there is covers a decent range, from bottom-dollar to fairly smart. The downtown hotels are supplemented by a couple of attractive out-of-town options, easily reached by taxi.

Betania Francisco de Orellana and Diego de Vaca ☎07/2607030. One of the best in town, with very clean, tiled floors and smart en-suite rooms with hot water and cable TV. Breakfast is included. ❺

Chonta Dorada Pió Jaramillo and Diego de Vaca ☎07/2606384. The spacious en-suite rooms with cable TV make this spot a good-value pick. ❷
Copalinga 3km east of town on the road to Podocarpus ☎09/3477013, ⊛www.copalinga.com.

For more peaceful surroundings you can stay in the wooden cabañas, set amid the forested hills of this private reserve. Most have private bath, hot showers and a balcony, but there are budget "rustic" cabins with bunks and shared facilities; advance reservations required for all. ❸–❻

Hostería El Arenal 12.5km east of Zamora on the road to Gualaquiza ☎07/2606971, ⓦwww .hosteriaelarenal.com.ec. This is the place to go for a splurge, with fancy rooms, swimming pool, jacuzzi, sauna, steam room and a great

restaurant. Peacocks strut the attractive grounds and fish ponds bubble with tilapia, while a frog-raising paddock provides the frogs advertised on the menu. A zip line and a 4WD course are the final eccentric touches. ❺

Seyma 24 de Mayo and Amazonas ☎07/2605583. Just a short jaunt from the river, this place is bottom-dollar and although it's basic and spartan, it is fairly clean and well swept; showers are shared and cold-water only. ❶

The Town

Sitting at the confluence of the Zamora and Bombuscaro rivers with a backdrop of steep, emerald-green hills rising over its rooftops, the town's setting is lovely, yet the town itself is unattractive, with sprawling grid-laid streets and functional, cement-built houses. Despite having been founded by the Spaniards in 1549 it's still, at heart, a modern, rough-and-ready pioneer town, its main function being to service the local gold-mining industry – which it's being doing on and off for four hundred years.

Although visitors to Zamora mainly use it as a base from which to visit Podocarpus, there are a couple of other sights to take in while you're here, including a 1600-square-metre **clock** – apparently the largest clock face in the world – in the hillside above the market, where it glitters like a fairground at night. A block from the *parque central* is the **Refugio Ecológico Tzanka** (daily; $2), on Tamayo and Mosquera, once the town rubbish dump, but now a small zoo and orchid garden.

Eating, drinking and nightlife

For **restaurants**, *King Ice Fast Food*, on the north side of the square, does surprisingly tasty burgers and grilled-chicken sandwiches, as well as traditional favourites (*arroz con pollo*, *cecinas*) and ice cream, while *La Choza*, on Sevilla de Oro opposite the hospital, does a mean tilapia and grilled chicken. *Chifa Zhang's*, also on Sevilla de Oro, is open daily and supplies reliable noodle- and rice-based

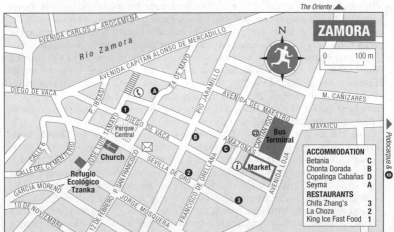

The Oriente ▲

ZAMORA

N

0   100 m

Río Zamora

AVENIDA CARLOS J. AROCEMENA

AVENIDA CAPITÁN ALONSO DE MERCADILLO

DIEGO DE VACA

P. IBSASI

24 DE MAYO

PÍO JARAMILLO

AVENIDA DEL MAESTRO

M. CAÑIZARES

MAYAICU

DIEGO DE VACA

Parque Central

AMAZONAS

Bus Terminal

JOSÉ LUIS TAMAYO

CALLE 6

CALLE DEL CEMENTERIO

Church

Refugio Ecológico Tzanka

SAN FRANCISCO

SEVILLA DE ORO

FRANCISCO DE ORELLANA

Market

AVENIDA LOJA

GARCÍA MORENO

10 DE NOVIEMBRE

12 DE FEBRERO

JORGE MOSQUERA

Loja ▼

ACCOMMODATION
Betania   C
Chonta Dorada   B
Copalinga Cabañas   D
Seyma   A
RESTAURANTS
Chifa Zhang's   3
La Choza   2
King Ice Fast Food   1

Podocarpus & ❶ ▶

staples, while the restaurant of the *Chonta Dorada* hotel does hearty, inexpensive breakfasts, *almuerzos* and *meriendas*.

If you're looking for **nightlife**, *Macharos*, Avenida Loja and Mayaicu, is Zamora's most popular bar and *Toto*, Avenida del Maestro and Pasaje Tamayo, is the most happening disco.

Parque Nacional Podocarpus

Spilling down the eastern flanks of the Andes towards the tropical valleys of the Oriente, **PARQUE NACIONAL PODOCARPUS** presents a spectacular landscape of high páramo, dense, dripping cloudforest, rushing waterfalls and crystalline rivers. Its wide-ranging altitudes (900–3600m), climates and habitats harbour a staggering diversity of flora and fauna, including an estimated 3000 to 4000 plant species, over 500 recorded bird species – hummingbirds, toucans, tanagers and parrots among them – and important populations of mammals such as mountain tapirs, giant armadillos, *pudu* (dwarf deer), spectacled bears, monkeys and pumas. The park was created in 1982, partly to protect some of the country's last major stands of podocarpus trees (Ecuador's only native conifer, also known as *romerillo*), whose numbers commercial logging had drastically reduced. Other notable trees here include the cinchona (known locally as *cascarilla*), whose bark is the source of **quinine**, first discovered in this very region.

There are two **main entrances** to the park, corresponding to its geographical divisions: one is the **Sector Cajanuma** in the Zona Alta (upper section), near Loja; the other is the **Sector Bombuscaro** in the Zona Baja (lower section), reached from Zamora. Also in the Zona Baja is a third, little-visited entry post at **Sector Romerillos**, the gateway to a very rugged, long-distance hike down to an even less frequented entrance to the **Sector Valladolid** in the far south. The southwestern reaches of the park are often visited on guided hikes and horse treks from the small village of Vilcabamba (for more details see p.265), though there's no formal entry post here. **Tickets**, available at the entrance posts, cost $10 and are valid in all sectors for up to five days.

Sector Cajanuma

Spread over the northern part of the Zona Alta, steep ridges covered with cloudforest and high, lake-studded páramo characterize the **Sector Cajanuma**. With average elevations of over 3000m, daytime temperatures usually hover around 12°C, though it can get much colder when the wind whips up and the rains start to fall. Rain is very common between February and April, leaving the park's trails very muddy; the driest months are usually July to September. The Cajanuma **entrance post** is 15km south of Loja, on the road to Vilcabamba. Any bus to Vilcabamba will drop you here, but you're left with an eight-kilometre uphill slog (2–3hr) to the main **ranger station** and park entrance proper, at an altitude of 2750m. The only way to get there directly is by taxi from Loja (about $14 each way; arrange to be picked up for the return), or with a tour operator from Loja (see p.259).

From the ranger station – which offers floor space and a few **bunk beds** (bring a sleeping bag; $5) for overnight visitors, plus kitchen facilities – there are some well-defined **trails** striking into the park. The **Sendero al Mirador** (3.5km) leads steeply uphill through lush, temperate forest to a lookout point, high on a ridge, giving stunning views across the deep-green mountainsides poking up through the clouds. This makes a very rewarding half-day hike, and is good for spotting **birds**, including the bearded guan, grey-breasted mountain toucan, rainbow starfrontlet, chestnut-bearded coronet and red-hooded tanager (all these can also be seen around the access road close to the ranger station).

▲ Parque Nacional Podocarpus

Sendero Las Lagunas is a much more demanding hike, leading for 14km through cloudforest and high páramo to the eerily beautiful **Lagunas del Compadre**, a network of fourteen lakes at 3200m above sea level, surrounded by bare granite and sharp, rocky peaks. It takes around six to eight hours to reach the lakes from the ranger station, with some strenuous uphill hiking along the way. There are good **camping** spots around the lakes, which have been stocked with rainbow trout, so if you bring a fishing rod you may be able to catch your supper. With luck, you may also be able to spot mountain tapirs, which are quite common in this area.

Sector Bombuscaro

Down in the Zona Baja, at the foot of the Cordillera Oriental, **Sector Bombuscaro** is a sensory extravaganza of riotous vegetation, moss-scented air, squawking birds, fluorescent butterflies, gurgling waterfalls and ice-cold rivers. At just under 1000m above sea level, it rarely sees daytime temperatures fall below a very pleasant 18°C, and even during the rainy season (generally March–July) the weather is unlikely to spoil your fun so long as you have waterproofs and a few layers; the driest months are usually from October to December.

The **entrance** is easily reached from the town of Zamora, either on foot (a 1hr 30min walk) along the road branching south for 6km from behind the bus terminal, following the Río Bombuscaro, or by taxi for around $5. From the parking area at the end of the road, marked by a park entrance sign and a usually empty wooden kiosk, it's a further twenty minutes on foot up to the **ranger station**. Close by, there are a couple of short, signed paths to **waterfalls**, the most impressive being the ninety-metre **La Poderosa** on the Río León (30min walk). You can take a refreshing dip in the *balneario* (bathing area) – a gorgeous bit of river with hundreds of butterflies hovering around the rocks on the banks.

There are several **trails** through the park, and one of the best is the **Sendero Higuerones**, which follows the Río Bombuscaro for about 3km through secondary and primary forest, taking an hour or so each way without stops; to stay on this path, ignore the footbridge over the river after 1km. As you walk, you're likely to see an extraordinary number of birds such as Andean cock-of-the-rocks, green jays, white-breasted parakeets, copper-chested jacamars, paradise tanagers and orange-eared tanagers, among many others. There are also many biting insects, so be sure to take plenty of **insect repellent** with you. If you plan to stay overnight in the park, you can **camp** by the ranger station or sleep in one of the basic wooden huts nearby (bring a sleeping bag), and use the cooking facilities in the station.

Sector Romerillos

Twenty-five kilometres south of Zamora, the tiny village of Romerillos has a third **entrance** to the park, which is the starting point for an adventurous but demanding three- to four-day circular hike through lush, dense cloudforest, with a fair amount of uphill climbing into páramo. After the first 38km stretch of the loop, however, the hike becomes extremely difficult, with thigh-deep mud in parts, and an increasingly indistinct trail. If you plan to do this hike, be sure to get a good local guide, the necessary 1:50,000 IGM maps, and to talk to the ranger at Romerillos before you set off, partly for **information** about the route, partly so someone can start looking for you if you're unlucky enough to get lost. You can get to Romerillos on a twice-daily **bus** (6.30am & 2pm) from Zamora's terminal, or by **taxi** for about $25; the journey takes around ninety minutes.

Sector Valladolid

The fourth and remotest formal entrance to the park is accessed from **Valladolid**, a town 105km south of Loja and 67km south of Vilcabamba (several daily buses here from both places), where there is a Ministerio del Ambiente office and a basic hotel. Few people make it here but if you're keen to explore the area, ask the park rangers to put you in touch with a good local guide, and bring full equipment and detailed IGM maps.

Park practicalities

You can pick up a rudimentary **map** of the park at the Ministerio del Ambiente offices in Loja (see p.256) and Zamora (see p.260). In Loja, the conservationist group Fundación Arco Iris, at Segundo Cueva Celi 03-15 and Clodoveo Carrión (℡07/2577449, ℗www.arcoiris.org.ec), is an excellent source of **information** on Podocarpus, with useful **field guides** to the park's birds and trees. They manage the northern area of the park accessed at San Francisco, east of Loja on the Zamora road, where there are some hiking trails, and operate an interpretation centre and a **hostel** with a kitchen, two furnished private rooms ($10 per person), or dorm bunks ($8; bring sleeping bag). Also in Loja, Nature and Culture International (℡07/2573691, ℗www.natureandculture.org), at Mercadillo 18-10 and J.M. Peña, runs a research station (the Estación Scientífica San Francisco, about fifteen minutes east of the Arco Iris turning) in a private cloudforest reserve adjacent to the park, which is geared more to researchers than informal visitors, though their office can provide general information. Fundación Arco Iris and the Ministerio del Ambiente should be able to find a **guide** for you costing around $10–15 per day. Another option is to visit the park with Loja-based **tour** operators (see "Listings", p.259) or birding specialists based in Quito.

Reserva Tapichalaca

The **Reserva Tapichalaca**, signposted on the road north of Valladolid, lies contiguous with Parque Nacional Podocarpus, and encompasses the same habitats, ranging from high páramo down to subtropical forests. It's an extraordinarily biologically sensitive area, and is the only known habitat of the **Jocotoco Antipitta**, a rare species of bird discovered here a decade ago. Other rarities include mountain tapirs, spectacled bears, imperial snipe and neblina metaltails, which you might be lucky enough to catch a glimpse of along the trails which weave between páramo and forest. They can also be spotted in the renowned birding and botanical area of Quebrada Honda. The reserve is managed by the Fundación Jocotoco (contact Javier Roballo ☏09/7101536 or the office ☏02/2272013, ⓦwww.fjocotoco.org), which offers **accommodation** at a simple cabin sleeping six to eight ($10 per person; bring sleeping bag and food). Transport and guiding can be arranged through Javier.

Vilcabamba

Just over 40km south of Loja, sitting in a beautiful valley enfolded by crumpled, sunburnt hills, **VILCABAMBA** is a small agricultural village that's become something of a tourist magnet over the last couple of decades. It first caught the attention of the outside world back in 1955, when *Reader's Digest* published an article claiming Vilcabambans enjoyed a considerably higher than average life expectancy, with a very low incidence of cardiovascular health problems. Soon Vilcabamba was being touted as "the valley of eternal youth" and the "valley of longevity", as international investigators unearthed a string of sprightly old people claiming to be up to 120 or 130 years old. More rigorous studies revealed these claims to be wildly exaggerated, and to date no hard evidence has been produced to support theories of an abnormally long-living population in Vilcabamba – though scientists acknowledge villagers in their 70s and 80s tend to be extremely fit and healthy for their age.

These days Vilcabamba feels like a place not quite grounded in reality – partly because of the myths associated with it, partly because of the high proportion of resident gringos who've come here in search of the simple life (and, inevitably, have ended up competing vigorously with each other for business), and partly because of the conspicuous presence of foreign tourists. People head here for a variety of reasons. Some come for the hallucinogenic cactus juice, **San Pedro**, the village has become famous for, even though this is illegal and heavily frowned on by locals. Others come for the hiking and birding in the nearby hills of **Parque Nacional Podocarpus**, but most come just to relax, enjoy the warm climate and nice views, or maybe take a horse ride or indulge in a massage or steam bath. The **best months** to be here are June to September, while October to May can often be rainy. Daytime temperatures usually fluctuate between 18°C and 28°C.

Arrival and information

Buses and minibuses (every 15–30min) from Loja's bus terminal drop passengers off at Vilcabamba's **bus terminal** on the main road running into town, the Avenida de la Eterna Juventud, a couple of blocks from the central square. Many of the hotels are an easy walk from here, but some are a good fifteen- or twenty-minute walk away – if carrying a heavy pack you might want to hop in one of the pick-up trucks hanging around the bus terminal that act as **taxis**, charging about $1.50–2 per ride.

The municipal **tourist office** (daily 8am–noon & 3–6pm; ☏07/2640090) is opposite the church on the Parque Central; staff hand out **maps** and booklets (which enthusiastically promote the longevity theory, with many black-and-white photos of centenarians as evidence) and can give advice on accommodation, restaurants, transport and tour operators. Limited pre-trip information can be found on the English-language **website** ⓦwww.vilcabamba.org. Tourist information and a wide range of **books** (to buy or exchange) in English and fourteen other languages are available at Craig's Bookstore, 1km out of town on the road

to Yamburara. Ask about **Spanish lessons** here, at your hotel, or try La Cumbre
Spanish school on Juan Montalvo 07-36 (☎07/2640283).

Accommodation

There's an enormous amount of **accommodation** to choose from for such a
small place, most of it very reasonably priced. Where you stay can make a big
difference to your experience of Vilcabamba, so consider whether you want to
mingle with lots of other travellers or if you want somewhere quiet with a local
feel to it, or just somewhere private, where you can enjoy the countryside.
Traditionally, travellers have never been hassled when they arrive at the bus
terminal. Lately, however, one or two places have started doing just that, using
taxi drivers to assist them. Don't feel pressured – check out a few places for
yourself before making any decisions.

Hosteria El Agua de Hierro Across the bridge on
the road to Yamburara ☎/℗07/2640314, ⓦwww
.hosteriaelaguadehierro.com. Slick operation, offering
a choice of shared rooms (from $7.50 per person) or

private rooms, all with cable TV and shared or private
hot shower. Facilities include an attractive pool with
slide, steam baths, seven hot tubs, volleyball court,
table tennis, pool table and evening movies on a

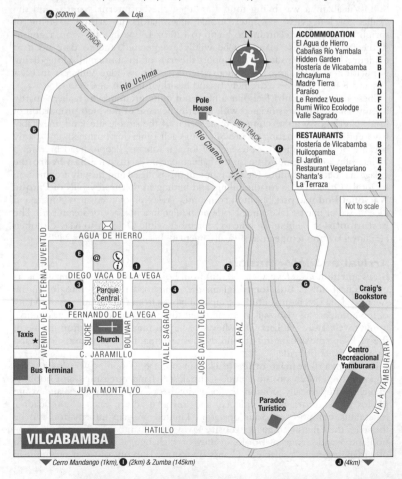

ACCOMMODATION

El Agua de Hierro	G
Cabañas Río Yambala	J
Hidden Garden	E
Hostería de Vilcabamba	B
Izhcayluma	I
Madre Tierra	A
Paraíso	D
Le Rendez Vous	F
Rumi Wilco Ecolodge	C
Valle Sagrado	H

RESTAURANTS

Hostería de Vilcabamba	B
Huilcopamba	3
El Jardín	E
Restaurant Vegetariano	4
Shanta's	2
La Terraza	1

Not to scale

giant TV. Great value but feels rather like a college campus. Ask to be put in the new building. Recently opened a spa. Has wi-fi; breakfast included. ❺

🏃 **Cabañas Río Yambala (aka Charlie's Cabins)** 5km east along the road to Yamburara ☎09/1062762, ⓦwww.vilcabamba -hotel.com. Five thatched wooden cabañas (with shared or private bath) in a scenic, secluded location overlooking the Río Yambala, with a sauna nearby. Cabaña #2 has the best views and its own kitchen; meals are also available in a rustic (but pricey) all-day restaurant. There are marked trails to cloud-forest and waterfalls, and up to a refuge, *Las Palmas* (see p.269), on the edge of Parque Nacional Podocarpus, which you can reach on foot or by horse. Taxis between cabañas and village cost about $4. ❸

Hidden Garden Sucre, just north of Parque Central ☎07/2640281, ⓦwww.vilcabamba.org /jardinescondido.html. Gaily painted rooms with en-suite bathroom, around a beautiful walled garden with a pool, jacuzzi and hammocks. Dorms for $10 also available. It has an excellent Mexican restaurant, *El Jardín* (see p.268), plus kitchen and laundry facili-ties. A little overpriced, but breakfast included. ❺

Hostería de Vilcabamba Av Eterna Juventud, as it enters the village ☎07/2640272. Well-furnished rooms with cool marble floors, mirror wardrobes and comfortable beds. Has a pool, sauna, steam baths, whirlpool and an attractive restaurant and bar. Upmarket, but bordering on snooty. Breakfast included. ❻

🏃 **Izhcayluma** 2km south of the centre on the road to Zumba ☎07/2640095, ⓦwww .izhcayluma.com. Popular, friendly German-owned hostel set in pretty gardens overlooking the Vilcabamba valley. The rooms and cheaper dorms ($10 per person) come with porch, hammock and private bath and there's a gorgeous pool and a good restaurant (breakfast included in room rate) with specialities including goulash and *käsespatzen* (home-made pasta oven-baked with onions and cheese). Includes free use of mountain bikes to coast to town down a steep hill. The taxi ride is $1.50. ❺

🏃 **Madre Tierra** 2km before town, a short uphill walk west of the main road from Loja; ask your bus driver to drop you off at the turning; ☎07/2640269, ⓦwww.madretierra1.com. A choice of shared budget rooms ($12 per person), comfortable mid-price rooms (some with private bath) and very stylish suites with fabulous views in a picturesque spot on the edge of the village.

Serves tasty, international organic cuisine, always with a vegetarian option, in its patio restaurant and has a small, pretty pool and a spa centre offering a range of treatments that are half-price for guests. Always popular, so book ahead if you're set on staying here. ❺–❽

Paraíso Av Eterna Juventud ☎07/2640266. Comfortable, tiled cabañas in a pretty garden with a wonderful pool and an outdoor whirlpool, sauna, and steam room (facilities only open on weekends). Also offers a rustic bamboo-covered restaurant and a peculiar pyramid for meditating in. Relaxing and welcoming, with a more local crowd. For the price, best deal in town on a weekend. Breakfast included. ❸

Le Rendez Vous Diego Vaca de Vega 06-43 and La Paz ☎09/2191180, ⓦwww.rendezvousecuador .com. Friendly, French-owned hotel offering rooms with terraces, hammocks and private bath with hot water, facing a pretty, central garden (plus 3- or 4-bed dorms at $12 per person). Price includes a good breakfast, featuring home-made bread, plenty of fresh fruit and proper coffee, brought to your room. Also has wi-fi and bikes available to rent. ❺

🏃 **Rumi Wilco Ecolodge** 15min walk northeast of the centre ☎07/2640186, ⓦwww.rumiwilco.com. Set in the private, 100-acre Rumi-Wilco Nature Reserve, this eco-lodge offers several accommodation options, all quiet, secluded and with cooking facilities: Pole House, a wooden cabin on stilts by the Río Chambo sleeping up to 4 people (❺); similar, recently built, River Cabin (❹); and the Adobe Shared Houses, three simple adobe buildings with double rooms (❷), fireplaces and herb garden. In addition, there is a camping area ($3.50 per person) with kitchen and bathroom facilities. Check availability and directions in the Primavera craft shop on the Parque Central, opposite the church; do not attempt to go at night or without directions from the shop. Best for those staying more than one day; be sure to bring food. Discounts available for long stays, or credits for volunteer work reforesting or teaching English.

Valle Sagrado Fernando de la Vega, Parque Central ☎07/2640386, ⓦwww.vilcabamba.org /ValleSagrado.html. Slightly worn – this was the village's original hotel – but fine budget rooms offering use of kitchen facilities and a pretty garden with hammocks and table tennis. Laundry service, book exchange and baggage storage available, plus horseriding tours. ❸

The village and around

There's not a great deal to do in the village itself. The focal point is the leafy **Parque Central**, surrounded by the main cornerstones of village life: the church, the *municipio* and the telephone office. The **church** is quite a grand affair, with its large, white Neoclassical facade sporting a row of apricot-coloured pillars. It's worth wandering down to the square around 6 or 7am – you'll catch a beautiful dawn chorus, and the early-morning light is gorgeous. A short walk southeast of town down Calle Diego de la Vega for 1.5km will bring you to the **Centro Recreacional Yamburara** (daily 8am–6pm; $0.30), the site of a swimming pool ($0.50), a small zoo and an impressive orchid garden (closed at lunchtime).

Striking a little further afield, you could hike up **Cerro Mandango** for fabulous, panoramic views over the valley. The hill resembles a person lying down – with the forehead, nose and chin quite distinct from certain angles – and rises over the village's southeastern side. The tourist office can give you a map with instructions on finding the path, which can be tricky. It's best to set out before 7am to avoid walking during the hottest part of the day; take plenty of sunscreen and water with you. For other hikes and excursions to Parque Nacional Podocarpus and bordering reserves, see "Tours and hikes around Vilcabamba" below.

Spa treatments

A number of people in the village offer **massages** and **spa treatments**. At the *Madre Tierra* hotel you can experience full-blown spa treatments from facials and "hot clay baths", to Swedish reflexology and colonic irrigation; for a selection, try the "Special Well-Being" package, which lasts for almost four hours. It's also possible just to pop in and use the steam baths or hot tub. The *Izhcayluma* hotel is another good bet for massages, facials and other treatments.

Eating and drinking

Most hotels offer food as well as rooms, sometimes as a package with the room rate. Vilcabamba offers an appealing choice of good-value Western-style dishes alongside the more usual *comida típica*. Most places are very quiet in the evening, and wind down by 9pm. There are several other simple places around the square.

Hostería de Vilcabamba Av Eterna Juventud, as it enters the village. Tasty and reasonably priced Ecuadorian food served in an attractive dining room flooded with sunlight from a glass atrium. The starched linen tablecloths give this place an upmarket feel.

Huilcopamba Corner of Diego Vaca de la Vega and Sucre, on Parque Central. Hearty and appetizing meats, pastas, noodles and home-made soups in a nice location on the corner of the square, with outside tables and chairs.

El Jardin *The Hidden Garden*, Sucre. Very good Mexican restaurant in the garden of the hotel, serving authentic, home-made cooking using plenty of organic and home-grown produce, including yogurt and cheese. Good vegetarian dishes.

Shanta's Over the bridge heading east on Diego Vaca de la Vega. Good and inexpensive restaurant with items ranging from fish and pasta to pizzas and crêpes in chocolate sauce. It also has a late bar fronted by saddle-topped stools, and an impressive cocktail list.

La Terraza Corner of Diego Vaca de la Vega and Bolívar, on Parque Central. Very popular restaurant with colourful decor and a nice atmosphere, serving well-prepared Mexican, Thai and Italian dishes (always with vegetarian choices). Does a good cup of coffee too.

Restaurant Vegetariano Diego Vaca de la Vega and Valle Sagrado, no sign. Well-presented and imaginative salads, soups, pastas and crêpes are served in this vegetarian restaurant. Set menu.

Tours and hikes around Vilcabamba

Vilcabamba offers great hiking and birding opportunities up to the cloudforests around Parque Nacional Podocarpus (see p.262), and several outfits and guides offer **tours** of the area. If you're keen to go hiking **independently**, go up to *Cabañas Río Yambala* and take advantage of the colour-coded trail system heading up to their private reserve, 8km up the valley, contiguous with the Parque Nacional Podocarpus. The trails lead to swimming holes on the river and viewpoints, while the "red route", especially rewarding, involves a five-hour trek up to their refuge on the edge of a cloudforest. You can also hike independently in the Rumi Wilco reserve ($2 entrance fee, or free to guests at the *Rumi Wilco Ecolodge*), where well-signposted paths lead across the mountainside.

Avetur In the *Valle Sagrado* hotel. An association of local people involved in tourism, but dedicated to bettering the social and environmental condition of the area. They offer guided day-treks and horse rides towards Podocarpus (from $20), including staying overnight in their refuge, which they've equipped with solar power, or three-day camping trips up to Laguna Rabadilla de Vaca or Laguna Margarita.

Caballos Gavilán Sucre and Diego Vaca de la Vega, or at the *Restaurant Huilcopamba* on Parque Central ☎07/2640158 or 08/9883051, ✉gavilanhorse@yahoo.com. Run by New Zealander Gavin Moore, who offers excellent combined hiking and horse-riding tours up to the cloudforest from $80 per person, including food and a night in a cabin on the edge of the park, or day rides from $16 for two hours up to $35 (including lunch) for a full day.

José María Arboleda ☎08/9790555. Experienced and knowledgeable birdwatching guide, offering trips to Podocarpus from $30 per day.

Orlando Falco Contact him at the Primavera craft shop on the plaza, opposite the church ☎07/2640186, ⓦwww.rumiwilco.com. Orlando is an outstanding naturalist guide who speaks English and offers full-day tours ($25–35) into the tropical cloudforests of Parque Nacional Podocarpus. You're taken to the trailheads in an ancient Land Rover before setting off on foot on your chosen route, pausing frequently while he points out features of the flora and fauna.

Las Palmas Eco-tours At *Cabañas Río Yambala* ☎091062762, ⓦwww.vilcabamba-hotel.com. Take tours 8km up the valley to their private Las Palmas Cloudforest Reserve and into neighbouring Podocarpus. They lead one- to three-day hikes and horse treks (from $39 to $164 per person), and are the only people to offer canopy-walkway tours through the treetops accessed by a zip line. Within their reserve, the wattle-and-daub *Las Palmas* refuge, which has a fireplace, private rooms, kitchen and hot-water shower, can be used as a base for longer treks.

South to Peru

The most convenient **border crossing into Peru** from the southern sierra is via a paved road from Loja to the frontier town of **Macará**, 190km to the southwest, a much more pleasant and efficient alternative to the frenetic **Huaquillas** crossing on the coast (see p.413), though those based in Vilcabamba or looking for an interesting route into the thick of the Peruvian highlands might consider the remote and adventurous frontier passage at **Zumba**, due south.

Via Macará

Regular buses make the five-hour journey from the terminal in Loja to **MACARÁ** along the Panamericana via the town of Catacocha, with a slower service on subsidiary roads via Cariamanga. Three daily **direct buses** also go all the way from Loja to **Piura** in Peru (7am, 1pm & 11pm; 8hr journey; $8, best bought a day before travel), operated by Cooperativa Loja Internacional (☎07/2579014), which has offices in Loja at the bus terminal and at 10 de Agosto and Avenida Lauro Guerrero. In Vilcabamba, there's an office near the bus terminal or you can buy tickets from one of the *hostales* in Vilcabamba that act as agents, including *Madre Tierra* and *Las Ruinas de Quinará*; note this bus does not go through Vilcabamba.

There isn't much to do in Macará, but if you stay the night there's decent accommodation. The best places are *Terra Verde*, on Calle Lazaro Vacao a couple of blocks west of the Coop Loja Internacional terminus (☎07/2694540; ❸), the smartest hotel in town, with clean a/c rooms; *El Conquistador* on Bolívar and Calderón (☎07/2694057; ❸) with fans, cable TVs and private bathroom; and *Espiga de Oro*, on Antonio Ante and 10 de Agosto by the market (☎07/2694405; ❷), which is a little cheaper for only having cold water, but has en-suite facilities and a choice of air conditioning or fan. Nearby *D'Marcos's*, Veintimilla and Calderón, offers standard, inexpensive **food**. The **banks** do not change currency or traveller's cheques, but you can find moneychangers with Peruvian *soles* at the border and around the park where taxis to the border are ranked.

The crossing

If you're on the through bus to Piura it will simply wait while passengers have their passports checked and stamped. If you've taken the bus to Macará, you'll need to get to the **international bridge** between Ecuador and Peru, a little over 2km southwest of town, which you can walk to in about forty minutes, or take a taxi ($1) or *colectivo* ($0.25) from 10 de Agosto at the park near the market. Either side of the bridge, the Ecuadorian and Peruvian **immigration offices**, where you get your exit and entry **stamps**, are open 24hr. In **La Tina**, the little settlement on the Peruvian side, you'll be whisked away by *colectivo* to **Sullana** (2hr), from where there is easy transport to the larger city of **Piura** (40min further). You could also hop on the international buses direct to Piura as they pass through Macará.

Via Zumba

There's a less-used border crossing near **ZUMBA** over 145km due south of Vilcabamba, on a rough, slow road through remote and beautiful country, which is serviced by eight daily buses from Loja (6–7hr) via Vilcabamba (5–6hr). From Zumba, where there are a few simple hotels, catch a *ranchera* (Mon–Fri 8am & 2.30pm, Sat–Sun 8am, 10am & 2pm) or hire a private *camioneta* to **La Balsa**, about 1 hour 30 minutes away on a potholed road, which is prone to landslides and closures in the rainy season. The Ecuadorian immigration office, not far from the **international bridge** over the Río Canchis, is open 24hr, though you may have to search around for an official at quiet times. Once in Peru, *busetas* ferry you to Namballe (20min), from where there is transport to San Ignacio (around 2hr), a nice enough place to spend the night, then Jaén (3–4hr), a city of reasonable size with hotels, money-changing facilities and transport connections to major centres.

Travel details

Buses

Cuenca to: Ambato (every 30–60min; 7hr); Azogues (every 5min; 30min); Cañar (every 30min; 1hr 30min); Chordeleg (every 30min; 1hr 15min); El Tambo (every 15min; 1hr 40min); Girón (served by buses to Machala every 15min; 40min); Gualaceo (every 15min; 45min); Guayaquil (every 10–30min; 4–5hr); Huaquillas (18 daily; 5hr); Ingapirca (2 daily Mon–Fri, 1 Sat; 2hr); Loja (every 30–60min; 5hr); Macas (7 daily; 8–10hr); Machala (every 15–30min; 4hr); Quito (every 30–60min; 9hr); Riobamba (every 40min; 6hr); Santo Domingo (5 daily; 10hr); Sigsig (every 30min; 1hr 40min). **Loja** to: Alamor (4 daily; 6hr); Cariamanga (13 daily; 3hr); Catamayo (every 30min; 50min); Cuenca (every 30–60min; 5hr); El Cisne (3 daily; 2hr); Gonzanamá (8 daily; 2hr 30min); Gualaquiza (10 daily; 6hr);

Guayaquil (11 daily; 8–10hr); Huaquillas (6 daily; 5hr); Macará (14 daily, plus 6 daily via Cariamanga; 5hr); Machala (13 daily; 6hr); Piñas (2 daily; 4hr 15min); Piura, Peru (3 daily; 8hr); Quito (12 daily; 14–16hr); Saraguro (hourly; 2hr); Vilcabamba (every 15–30min; 1hr–1hr 30min); Yantzaza (20 daily; 3hr 30min); Zamora (24 daily; 2hr); Zaruma (1 daily; 4hr 30min); Zumba (8 daily; 6–7hr). **Zamora** to: Cuenca (3 daily; 7hr); Gualaquiza (8 daily; 4hr); Guayaquil (2 daily; 10hr); Loja (27 daily; 2hr); Romerillos (2 daily; 1hr 30min).

Flights

Cuenca to: Guayaquil (3–4 daily; 30min); Quito (5–6 daily; 45min). **Loja** to: Guayaquil (Tues, Thurs & Sat 1 daily; 30min); Quito (2–3 daily; 50min–1hr).

5

The Oriente

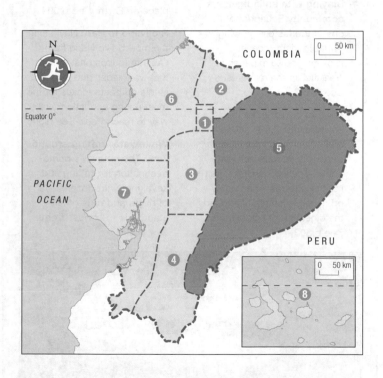

CHAPTER 5

Highlights

✳ **Jungle lodges** Immerse yourself in the sights and sounds of the rainforest from the relative comfort of one of the Oriente's many jungle lodges, most of which are accessed by boat. See p.277

✳ **Staying with an indigenous community** Ecuador has one of the fastest-growing "ethnotourism" scenes, allowing you to experience "real life" in the rainforest. See p.278

✳ **Añangu parrot licks** It's an extravaganza of sound and colour when hundreds of parrots descend on clay banks – called clay licks, salt licks or *salados* – and chew off mineral-rich chunks to aid the digestion of acidic fruits. See p.303

✳ **Parque Nacional Yasuní** A World Biosphere Reserve and the country's largest national park, harbouring the majority of Ecuador's mammals, over a third of all Amazonian bird species and more tree species for its size than any place on Earth. See p.304

✳ **Río Napo to Peru** Navigating the muddy Río Napo from Coca to Iquitos past remote Kichwa villages and isolated jungle outposts makes for the most daring and little-travelled way to reach Peru. See p.306

✳ **Whitewater rafting around Tena** The country's prime destination for rafting and kayaking, with dozens of rivers and runs of all standards to choose from. See p.309

▲ Kayakers enjoy a stretch of white water in Tena

5

The Oriente

N o other Ecuadorian habitat overwhelms the senses like the tropical rainforest, with its cacophonous soundtrack of birds and insects, the rich smell of steaming foliage and teeming soil, the glimmer of fluorescent birds and butterflies in the understorey, or the startling clamour of a troop of monkeys clattering through the canopy above. This is the Oriente's star attraction, and what most visitors are here for – though the region, which occupies a massive area covering almost half the country, contains a good deal more besides. The *alto* (high) Oriente starts on the eastern Andean flank, where the high, windswept páramo steadily gives way to dripping montane forests, swathed in mist and draped with mosses and epiphytes, as the elevation decreases. Waterfalls plunge into broadening valleys, and temperatures rise the further you descend. Down in the foothills, poised between the sierra and the lowlands, lies a beguiling landscape of rippling hills and verdant, subtropical forests, home to a startling diversity of birds. Continuing east, the mountain ridges eventually taper away into the *bajo* (low) Oriente like talons sinking into the deep velvet of a vast emerald wilderness: Ecuador's Amazonian jungle, one of the country's most thrilling destinations.

The only practical way of getting into the rainforest – which in places stretches for more than 250km to the borders of Colombia and Peru – is to go on one of the numerous **jungle tours** on offer. These range from simple day-trips into pockets of forest close to a town, through staying with a rainforest community or at a jungle lodge, to rugged multi-day camping treks into the remotest tracts of primary jungle in the far eastern reserves. Nearly every tour will involve hiking through lush forests and navigating coiling rivers and lagoons in dugout canoes, often done at night to see the red eyes of caiman and hear the deafening chorus of nocturnal creatures. The most pristine areas, namely the **Reserva Faunística Cuyabeno** and the **Parque Nacional Yasuní**, are best reached from the pioneer oil towns **Lago Agrio** and **Coca** respectively, and demand at least four or five days to enjoy properly. Closer to Quito, and favoured by those with limited time on their hands, **Tena**, **Puyo** and **Misahuallí** are near smaller, more accessible patches of forest. Visits to or stays with **indigenous communities** are also likely to figure in tours from Tena and Puyo. Tourism is much less developed in the far southern Oriente, though **Macas** is home to a handful of operators and projects.

The **climate** in the low Oriente is what you'd expect from a rainforest – hot, humid and plenty of rain. The wettest months are April to July, but expect cloudbursts most days year round, usually in the early afternoon. Average daytime temperatures are around 25°C, though daily highs can be over 32°C. With such consistent conditions, the Oriente doesn't have a high tourist season;

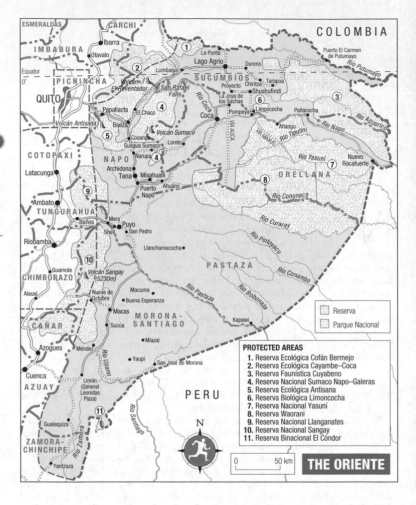

at slow times of year, when there are few tourists in the country as a whole (Feb to mid-June & Sept–Nov), it's worth asking for discounts.

Routes into the Oriente

The oil **infrastructure** has made the Ecuadorian Amazon one of the most easily accessed rainforest areas in the continent, with its centres of jungle tourism all within a day's bus journey of Quito. There are two main **routes to the Oriente**. The first leaves the capital and descends into the Amazon basin from the Papallacta pass, splitting at Baeza, north to Lago Agrio (and then Coca), and south to Tena and the faster way to Coca. The second drops from Ambato through Baños to Puyo, where it meets the road between Tena and Macas. A new gravel road runs from Guamote (south of Riobamba) directly to Macas, slicing through Parque Nacional Sangay, and other poorer roads descend from Tulcán to Lumbaqui (on the Baeza–Lago Agrio road) and from Cuenca and Loja into the southern Oriente.

The region is militarily sensitive and you'll be required to produce your **passport** at regular checkpoints. More so than at other places in the country, it's important you have original documents rather than copies. As far as **security** is concerned, the areas adjacent to the Colombian border are currently unsafe due to infiltration of guerrilla and paramilitary units and should be avoided (see box, p.293).

Some history

The **jungle** – *la selva* – has held a curious place in the national psyche since the time of the **conquistadors**. Rumours of the jungle being *el pais de canela* ("the land of cinnamon"), a place of abundant fruits and spices, and the legend of El Dorado, the "Golden Man", drew the early explorers here, suggesting to them a land of staggering natural riches. But the first Europeans to venture here soon found this fabled earthly paradise had a nightmarish underside; their parties were plunged into an impenetrable green hell (*"el infierno verde"*), teeming with poisonous snakes and biting insects. A string of catastrophic expeditions in the early colonial period quickly discouraged the Spanish from colonizing the Oriente at all. Even until the 1960s, most people, save for a sprinkling of missionaries and pioneers, kept away, leaving the forests and its inhabitants well alone.

This all changed in the late 1960s following the discovery of large **oil and gas reserves** (see box, p.289), now the country's most important source of wealth. The Oriente was divided into 200-square-kilometre *bloques* (blocks) and distributed between the companies, who proceeded to drill and blast in search of black gold. Roads were laid, towns sprouted virtually overnight and large areas of rainforest were cleared. The Oriente was transformed into a "productive" region and colonists streamed in on the new roads, looking for jobs and levelling still more land for farms. The speed of the destruction was dramatic and the Ecuadorian government, under widespread international pressure, began setting aside large tracts of forest as **national parks and reserves**; the largest three – **Sangay** (mainly in the Oriente, but most easily accessed from the highlands; see p.222), **Cuyabeno** and **Yasuní**, a UNESCO World Biosphere Reserve – were created in 1979; another three medium-sized parks – **Antisana**, **Sumaco** and **Llanganates** – were formed in the mid-1990s.

The issues today

Even though there are more than 25,000 square kilometres of protected land in the Oriente – well over half of which is pristine Amazonian rainforest – conservationists are worried the cash-strapped Ecuadorian government is unable (or unwilling) to make sure it stays that way. The task of balancing the needs of a faltering economy against the obligation to protect some of the most important forests on the planet has been among Ecuador's central problems for the past few decades. Meanwhile, oil activity is ongoing in several crucial protected areas, including Yasuní.

While most people would concede the oil industry has been very much a mixed blessing for the country, the **indigenous peoples** of the region – which include the Siona, Waorani, Secoya, Achuar, Shuar, Kichwa (who have rejected the Spanish spelling of their name "Quichua"), Cofán and Záparo – have had the most to lose. Many groups, rejecting the Western way of life, have been driven into ever smaller, remoter territories where it becomes increasingly hard to support themselves by traditional means. Their rivers and soil already polluted from industrial waste, most of the communities are under mounting pressure to

There are dozens of **jungle tour operators** in Ecuador competing for your attention, including many local agencies working directly out of the main centres of the Oriente: Lago Agrio, Coca, Tena, Misahuallí, Puyo and Macas. The greatest concentration of jungle tour operators, however, is found in the Mariscal area of **Quito**, giving you the luxury of having your tour fully organized before you set out for the Oriente. A selection of recommended Quito-based operators is listed below, but shop around to find the price, guide and itinerary that suits you. Transport to the starting point of the tour (usually an Oriente town, easily reached on public transport) and any applicable national park entrance fees are rarely included in the price. All prices quoted below are per person.

Amazing Ecuador Juan de Dios Martinez Mera N34-399 and Portugal ☎02/2468267 or 2278559, ⓦ www.amazingecuador.com. In the Cuyabeno reserve, with four-, five- or eight-day trips that include bilingual guides. Around $40 per day.

Cuyabeno River Lodge Pinto E4-360 and Amazonas ☎02/2903629, or 2527151, ⓦ www.cuyabenoriver.com. Economical tours of the Cuyabeno reserve, exploring its various black- and whitewater river systems by canoe, visiting local communities, with a mixture of camping and nights in cabins. Offers tours of four ($241), five ($407), or eight days ($990).

Dracaena Pinto 446 and Amazonas ☎02/2546590 or 08/0537066, ⓦ www.theamazon dracaena.com. Friendly, family-run outfit offering four- and five-day tours ($200–250) to the Cuyabeno, staying at their established campsites within the reserve.

Fundación Sobrevivencia Cofán Mariano Cardenal N74-153 and Joaquín Mancheno, Carcelén Alto ☎02/2470946, ⓦ www.cofan.org. The Cofán community of Zábalo offers programmes of four days minimum ($95 per day) in comfortable cabañas, with options for trekking, camping and canoeing. It can also put you in touch with other Cofán ecotourism projects, including those at the Comuna Dureno east of Lago Agrio (see p.288) and Sinangoé in the Cayambe-Coca reserve (see p.134).

Kem Pery Tours Ramírez Dávalos 117 and Amazonas, Edificio Turismundia, 1st floor ☎02/2226583, ⓦ www.kempery.com. Offers trips to the Waorani reserve where they operate the *Bataburo Lodge* under a special agreement with the Waorani (see box, p.305).

Magic River Tours of Lago Agrio represented in Quito by Positiv Turismo, Voz Andes N41-81 and Mariano Echeverría ☎02/2629303 or 09/7360670, ⓦ www.magicrivertours .com. Specializes in non-motorized canoeing trips down the quiet tributaries of the

sell out to the oil industry, both culturally and territorially. In recent years, **ecotourism** has emerged as a great hope for some groups seeking to adapt to a life in which external influences are inevitable, bringing in badly needed income, strengthening the case for the conservation of the forests within an economic framework and reasserting cultural identities.

Visiting the jungle

There are three ways to visit the jungle: on a **guided tour**; by staying at a **jungle lodge**; or by staying with an **indigenous community**. Getting into the wilderness and being immersed in the sights and sounds of the rainforest is the whole point of a tour, and modern luxuries, such as 24–hour electricity, (hot) running water and completely insect-free buildings are absent in all but the most comfortable jungle lodges. Ecuadorian authorities, conservation groups and indigenous communities frown upon **unguided travel** in the lower Oriente, which is not recommended for your own safety anyway. Off the main

Cuyabeno reserve; a five-day package to the Cuyabeno lakes runs at $320, while an eight-day package to the remote Lagartococha lakes costs $800. Accommodation is either in tents or at their rustic lodge.

Neotropic Turis Pinto E4-360 and Amazonas ☎02/2521212, ⓦwww.neotropicturis .com. Operators of the *Cuyabeno Lodge*, on the Laguna Grande, which is constructed from hardwoods brought into the reserve. It's still rather simple, but has hot showers, a small library and research facilities. They use bilingual nature specialists accompanied by Siona guides. A five-day tour costs around $407, with an English-speaking naturalist guide.

Nomadtrek Amazonas N22-29 and Carrión, 2nd floor ☎02/2547275, ⓕ2546376, ⓦwww.nomadtrek.com. Nomadtrek, in partnership with some Siona, built the *Tapir Lodge* (ⓦwww.tapirlodge.com) in the Cuyabeno lakes area. It's generally considered the most comfortable lodge in the reserve and consists of a bungalow with shared and private bathrooms and a fifteen-metre tower housing suites. Multilingual naturalist guides lead the rainforest walks on offer. A five-day trip costs around $450.

Nuevo Mundo 18 de Septiembre E4-161 and J.L. Mera, Edificio Mutualista Pichincha ☎02/2509432, ⓦwww.nuevomundotravel.com. Operates the *Manatee Amazon Explorer*, a luxurious air-conditioned river cruiser that navigates the lower Napo on regular four- or five-day excursions; visits include the Yasuní reserve ($20 entrance fee), an observation tower and a parrot lick ($25). From $794 per person in a double cabin.

Tropic Ecological Adventures La Niña between Reina Victoria and D. Almagro ☎02/2225907 or 2234594, ⓦwww.tropiceco.com. Award-winning ecologically minded agency that works alongside community-based ecotourism projects throughout the Oriente, as well as liaising with established lodges such as *Kapawi* (see p.331). They work particularly closely with a Waorani community, offering four-day ($850), five-day ($950), or six-day ($1150) tours, including floating downstream in dugout canoes on the Shiripuno River.

Tropical Birding El Condor Oe4-145 and Brasil ☎02/2447520, ⓦwww.tropicalbirding .com. This upmarket, specialist birding operator offers two-week tours of the Oriente ($3690 all-inclusive), guided by English-speaking ornithologists. Accommodation sites include *Wildsumaco Lodge* (see p.299), *Gareno Lodge* (see p.321), *Sacha Lodge* (see p.302) and the *Napo Wildlife Center* (see p.303). Most clients prebook from abroad, so contact well in advance if you're interested.

rivers, trails are few and difficult to follow, and it's all too easy to get lost in a potentially dangerous environment. Furthermore, stumbling on indigenous groups, such as the Tagaeri, a branch of the Waorani who don't take kindly to intruding strangers, could get you into serious trouble, as could an encounter with Colombian guerrilla groups around the Colombian border in northern Sucumbíos province.

Jungle lodges

Staying in a **jungle lodge** offers the most comfortable (and expensive) way to experience the rainforest. Stays usually last from three to five days and all logistical problems are taken care of for you, including river transport, food and any necessary permits and guides. Most lodges consist of cabañas and a communal dining and relaxing area, constructed in wood and thatch, close to primary forest and often a lengthy ride by motor canoe from the nearest town. The cabañas themselves range from a bed and four plank walls to handsomely adorned rooms with ceiling fans, private bath, hot water and electricity –

Jungle essentials

Many organized tours will supply essential items such as mosquito nets, rubber boots, toilet paper, bedding, food and clean water – but always check before you go so you'll know what you need to bring. Check an operator's camping and water purification equipment to see if they work, if appropriate, and make sure tents and nets provide adequate protection from bugs and insects. Put all your belongings in **waterproof bags**, especially valuables and important documents, and carry a rain jacket or poncho. **Banking facilities** are poor in the Oriente, particularly for traveller's cheques, and you should take as much cash as you need for the whole excursion. You will also need:

Binoculars Your guide should carry a pair, but you'll enjoy the scenery more with a pair of your own.

Camera see p.64 for details.

Clothing A long-sleeved shirt and lightweight trousers for protection against insects and swimwear for cooling off in rivers. Bring a hat to block the sun on boat trips. Spare insoles can make a pair of rubber boots much more comfortable.

Emergency supplies A first-aid kit, compass and whistle.

Insect repellent Lots of it – keeping covered up is a priority. DEET is very effective but it's potent and melts synthetic materials, so store and apply it safely. Sand flies can be more bothersome than mosquitoes, but respond to any kind of repellent.

Light sources Bring a flashlight and extra batteries; electricity is not always available and you'll need one for getting about the lodge or campsite (or spotting caiman) at night. Candles and waterproof matches or a gas lighter, for evenings in a lodge or cabaña without power, are also a good idea.

Malaria pills A course of which should be started in advance as prescribed by your doctor. You should also have had an inoculation against **yellow fever**, particularly if you plan to enter Cuyabeno or Yasuní or intend to travel onwards overland to Colombia or Peru. For more vaccination advice see "Health", p.30.

Passport You'll need one to enter the Oriente; it must be the original, not a copy.

Sun cream Particularly needed during river journeys.

Water purifier and bottles For camping and basic tours.

though the nature of their location means even the most well-appointed lodge falls short of luxury. Days are clearly structured, with guided hikes or canoe trips, and guides are generally of a high standard; in the most expensive places, they'll be English-speaking naturalists and ornithologists working with a local guide who'll know the forest intimately.

Most lodges have contact offices in Quito, and visits must be booked prior to arrival, though generally only the higher end lodges, such as *Sacha, Kapawi* and *La Selva*, recommend reservations be made weeks or even months in advance. Meals, guided forest walks and activities, and river transport to the lodge (where appropriate) are generally included in the price of a stay, but travel to the nearest Oriente town is usually separate; most lodges can help you arrange this if necessary.

Indigenous-community stays

A growing number of **indigenous communities** in the Oriente have started ecotourism projects, giving visitors a glimpse of village life in the rainforest by staying with a family or in simple cabañas just next to a community. The income raised from guests is intended to provide a sustainable alternative to more destructive means of subsistence, such as logging or farming the poor rainforest soil. The economic success of a project also demonstrates the value of conserving the surrounding forests – the other big attraction of a stay – to government agencies under strong pressure from commercial interests to make forest areas more financially productive, as opposed to "unproductive" community territory.

A few projects run slick operations, often in tandem with an outside partner, but the majority are starting out and remain pretty unsophisticated, so you may have to bring your own equipment (rubber boots, mosquito nets and so on – see the box opposite). Most use simple wooden cabañas with beds and mattresses, clean sheets and sometimes mosquito netting, while bathrooms range from basic latrines to flushing toilets, with most having facilities shared between guests. **Forest walks** are a particular highlight, as your hosts often make excellent guides, and the majority are qualified "native" guides, though you'll need to speak some Spanish to get the most from their extensive knowledge. A common emphasis is on **intercultural understanding**, and you're likely to be treated to singing, dancing and folkloric presentations – you may even be asked to perform something yourself in return.

The main centres for organizing visits to an indigenous community are **Tena**, **Puyo**, **Lago Agrio** and **Macas**. Allow several days to organize a stay, as the communities need time to make arrangements, and it can be difficult to establish contact in the first place. A good book, combining a discussion of the virtues of indigenous ecotourism with a guide to some of the projects on offer, is *Defending our Rainforest: A Guide to Community-Based Ecotourism in the Ecuadorian Amazon* by Rolf Wesche and Andy Drumm. You should be able to find it in Quito's better bookshops or at the SAE. Another good source of information is the Quito-based Federación Plurinacional de Turismo Comunitario, 9 de Octubre N27-27 and Orellana (Ⓦwww.turismocomunitario.ec).

Jungle lodges of the Oriente

The following is a list of all the **jungle lodges** covered in this chapter, with a page reference to the relevant account in the guide text.

Bataburo Lodge See p.305.

Cabañas Aliñahui See p.320.

Cabañas Lodge El Albergue Español See p.319.

Cabañas San Isidro See p.316.

Cabañas Shiripuno See p.320.

La Casa del Suizo See p.320.

La Casa Sinchi Sacha See p.320.

Cotocacha Amazon Lodge See p.320.

Cuyabeno Lodge See "Neotropic Turis" p.277.

Gareno Lodge See p.320.

Huaorani Ecolodge See p.305.

Jungle Lodge el Jardín Alemán See p.320.

Kapawi Ecolodge See p.331.

Liana Lodge See p.320.

Misahuallí Jungle Lodge See p.319.

Napo Wildlife Center See p.303.

Pañacocha Lodge See p.302.

Sacha Lodge See p.302.

Sani Lodge See p.302.

La Selva Jungle Lodge See p.303.

Shiripuno Lodge See p.305.

Tapir Lodge See "Nomadtrek" p.277.

Tiputini Biodiversity Station See p.306.

Yachana Lodge See p.320.

Yacuma Lodge See p.320.

Yarina Lodge See p.303.

Yuturi Lodge See p.303.

Wildsumaco Lodge. See p.299.

Guided tours

Taking a **guided tour** is the cheapest way to visit the jungle, usually costing from $35–60 per person per day. The more people there are, the cheaper the tour will be, but the optimum number is between four and six so that everyone has a chance of hearing the guide and of having the wildlife pointed out to them individually before it disappears. **Discounts** are best negotiated in the low season, from February to mid-June and September to November. The best places to meet people looking to share a jungle tour, in roughly descending order, are Quito, Baños, Tena, Misahuallí, Puyo and Macas. Lago Agrio and Coca are home to a growing number of guides and agencies, but groups heading into the jungle from these towns are often formed in Quito, making it hard for independent travellers to find people to form their own group; still, you may be able to supplant yourself onto a trip.

All tours should provide **accommodation** – anything from modest cabañas to *campamentos* (open-sided camping platforms) to *carpas* (standard tents) – and adequate **food and equipment**, including water, rubber boots and mosquito nets if necessary. Always check what you're getting before you hand over money. It's also crucial to get a **guide** who has the knowledge and enthusiasm to illustrate the jungle as a vivid living world; meeting them yourself in advance is the best way to find out if they're any good and check the standard of their English (where necessary). All guides should be able to produce a licence from the Ministry of Tourism, though this is no guarantee of quality. You can report guides to the ministry or SAE if they behave inappropriately, by hunting for food, leaving litter, or visiting indigenous communities without making a contribution or seeking permission. While some agencies use an accredited guide alongside a "native guide" for the same group – combining biological and scientific information with indigenous myths and local plantlore – the term

▲ Oriente jungle lodge

"native" may not be synonymous with "indigenous", often referring to anyone that lives in the Oriente.

If your tour includes a visit to an indigenous community, it's crucial your guide or operator has their **permission** – ask to see the written *convenio* (agreement) between the community and the operator when booking, which helps emphasize this is a priority with tourists, and encourages the operator to follow good practices.

The northern Oriente

The **northern Oriente**'s wealth of natural beauty and wildlife, its indigenous communities and a hard-boiled frontier spirit have all helped make it one of the country's most exciting destinations. Within the provinces of Sucumbíos, Napo and Orellana that make up the region, six major nature reserves and a proliferation of private reserves and protected areas provide excellent opportunities to experience the Amazonian jungle. The two most important are the **Reserva Faunística Cuyabeno** and the **Parque Nacional Yasuní**, in the east, defending over 15,000 square kilometres of pristine rainforest stretching to the Peruvian border. The reserves are reached by bus or canoe from **Lago Agrio** and **Coca**, the administrative and infrastructural centres of the oil industry. **Tena**, the third main town of the northern Oriente, isn't as close to such extensive forest areas and wildlife populations are likely to be lower, but it's the most pleasant of the three for its fresher climate, friendly atmosphere and proximity to a host of Kichwa communities offering ecotourism programmes. Tena is also rapidly becoming a centre for **whitewater rafting**, and at only five hours by bus from Quito is growing into the Oriente's most popular tourist destination. The jungle traveller's traditional favourite, **Misahuallí**, a river port close to Tena, provides access to the many cabañas and lodges of the upper Río Napo and boasts a number of local jungle-tour agencies and guides.

In the northwestern Oriente, three more ample reserves, **Reserva Ecológica Cayambe–Coca** (covered in Chapter Two), **Reserva Ecológica Antisana** and **Parque Nacional Sumaco Napo–Galeras** hold dense cloudforests and montane forests, sometimes impenetrably thick, where hiking is a serious challenge. The little colonial town of **Baeza** sits between the three reserves, making it the most convenient base for such expeditions. In the valleys below Baeza, most notably the **Quijos valley**, waterfalls streak the landscape and **Volcán El Reventador**, a smouldering green–black cone, watches over the **San Rafael falls**, Ecuador's biggest at 145m. On the uppermost reaches of the Amazon basin, **Papallacta** is a quiet, highland town perched in the hilly fringes of the Cayambe-Coca reserve, and its hot springs provide a good antidote to the crisp mountain air.

Catching a plane from Quito to Lago Agrio or Coca distils a lengthy bus journey into a thirty-minute hop.

The road to Baeza

East of Quito, the road heads steeply up to the **Papallacta Pass**, at 4064m the highest paved road in Ecuador. Giant oil and supply trucks shudder up and down this eastern flank of the Andes on their way to Lago Agrio and Tena via Baeza, but despite the traffic it's an attractive route, traversing a range of habitats as it plunges over 2km in vertical height across 40km.

At its highest point, named La Virgen after the simple shrine on the roadside, a track heads north up to some radio masts, the access point for the beautiful **Páramo de Papallacta** grasslands at the southwestern corner of the Reserva Ecológica Cayambe-Coca. Nearby, on the banks of a páramo lake is *Campucocha* (☎02/3801134, ⓦ www.campucocha.com; ❾), an upmarket country hotel in a private reserve bordering the larger national one, which offers birdwatching trips, horse rides and excellent guided trout-fishing expeditions.

Crossing the Papallacta Pass takes you over the continental divide, past bare, lake-studded hills eclipsed by the four glacier-streaked peaks of **Volcán Antisana** (5758m) looming through the clouds to the south (see p.316). As the highway descends beyond Papallacta, the temperature and humidity rise and the páramo grasses transform into dripping fronds and broad, waxy leaves. Nearing **Baeza**, rolling pastoral landscapes take over, banked by steep hillsides coated in the thick, green mantle of cloudforest.

Walks around Papallacta

There are plenty of good **hikes** in the hills around Papallacta, but take a **compass** and the IGM 1:50,000 **map** for Papallacta; it's notoriously easy to get lost in the featureless páramo, which is often wet, cold and, between June and August, snowy. The best time to come is from October to February, but you'll need warm clothes and waterproofs year round. The **Fundación Terra** at the head of the valley above *Las Termas de Papallacta* manages three short and easy trails nearby (1–4hr), including their self-guided Sendero de la Isla ($2) along the Río Papallacta, and offers horse rides depending on the weather ($6 per hour). For more serious hikes and treks in the Reserva Ecológica Cayambe-Coca to the north of town, talk to someone at the **Fundación Ecológica Rumicocha** (ⓦ www.rumicocha.org.ec), which has an office on Papallacta's Calle Principal and is responsible for managing this part of the reserve. It offers **hiking tours** using either tents or its two refuges, which are small but comfortable and heated by open fires, and can provide guides for $15 a day, plus $13 per person for the reserve entrance fee and support for the foundation.

One of the longer walks begins by heading up the main road toward Quito for 2km to the slender **Laguna Papallacta**, disfigured at its eastern end by a promontory of lava. This is the northern tip of a six-kilometre **lava flow** running all the way up the Río Tumiguina valley, the remnants of Volcán Antisana's eruption of 1773. A moderate to strenuous trail traverses the flow, passing some small lakes before ending at the larger Laguna Tuminguina, a full day's hike from town. Another day-walk is over the waterlogged **páramo** of the Reserva Ecológica Cayambe-Coca from the antennas above the Papallacta Pass down to the thermal springs, giving you the best of this bleak landscape: undulating hills, windswept grasses and silent, mist-laden lakes, with perhaps the occasional glimpse of such creatures as the South American fox, the white-tailed deer, the carunculated caracara, the plumbeous sierra finch and the Ecuadorian hillstar, a high-altitude hummingbird.

Papallacta

About 60km from Quito, **PAPALLACTA** (3120m) is most famous for its steaming **hot springs** – highly ferrous pools reputed to relieve numerous ailments, from kidney trouble to ganglions. The town itself, a string of buildings huddling the road, isn't of much interest, but lying in a steep, green valley, its location and surrounding scenery are stunning.

Arrival and information

Buses from Quito to Lago Agrio and Tena via Baeza pass Papallacta every forty minutes; the journey takes 1hr 30min. Some buses will drop you on the paved main road bypassing the town, from where *camionetas* (6am–6pm) will take you into town or up to the thermal baths for $2 per load (up to four people). Other buses take the unpaved road to the town itself, and can drop you (on request) at the junction know as "La Y", from where you can walk up to the Termas (1.5km; signposted) or take a *camioneta* ($1.50 for four). Taxis (same price) can also be booked with José Quizahuano on ☎08/4790698. Establish with your bus driver in advance where he will drop you off.

Accommodation

The best **accommodation** is at ⚵ *Las Termas de Papallacta* (☎06/2320620, Quito office at Foch E7-38 and Reina Victoria ☎02/2568989, ⓦwww .termaspapallacta.com; ❾), which offers comfortable rooms or heated, spacious cabins for up to six people, some fitted with sunken bath and a private outdoor hot tub ($152). There are several other hotels dotted along the road between the Termas de Papallacta and the village, including the friendly *Hostería Pampa Llacta* (☎06/2320624, Ⓔpampallactatermales@hotmail.com; ❻), halfway down; it has a nice indoor pool, two outdoor pools and a restaurant, and offers a variety of lodging from compact singles with fireplaces to spacious family cabins sleeping four ($61) or seven ($135). Down in the village, *El Viajero* (☎08/7042389; ❷) is a simple budget hotel on the Calle Principal while *Coturpa* (☎06/2320640; ❺), opposite the Complejo Santa Catalina, offers en-suite rooms and has a private thermal pool, sauna and steam room for guests at weekends. **Camping** is possible at the *Termas de Papallacta* for $6 per person.

The Town

Papallacta's best hot spring – perhaps the best in Ecuador – is **Las Termas de Papallacta** (ⓦwww.termaspapallacta.com), a one-kilometre, twenty-minute uphill slog from town in the crook of the valley. There are two beautifully deisgned, well-managed **bathing complexes** here, both with on-site restaurants (lunch menu $14). On the left, the **Balniario** (daily 6am–9pm; $7) has nine thermal pools, ranging in temperature between 36°C and 42°C, and three cold pools built in gentle terracotta curves and natural rock, while the heart-stoppingly cold Río Papallacta itself offers a serious cool-off. Don't miss the three secluded little pools up the hill to the left of the restaurant: the top one is over 40°C and is perfect for supine gazing at the mountain ridges. On the other side of the road, the **Spa** (9am–6pm; $18) has six large pools with water jets and bubble massagers for the exclusive use of guests staying in the complex's accommodation, as well as a "Thermal Club" offering a range of spa treatments.

At the lower end of the town proper, the slightly dilapidated community-run **Complejo Santa Catalina** (daily 6am–6pm; $3; ☎06/2320640) has four hot pools and one cold one, including a proper swimming pool, which get very crowded at weekends.

Eating and drinking

Eating in Papallacta is bound to involve fresh trout from the nearby fish farms and lakes. The best and most expensive **restaurant** is at the *Termas de Papallacta*, which has a dining room in the bathing complex and in the main hotel, and serves excellent food, with much of the fresh produce grown in their organic vegetable garden. For a cheaper feed, try the *Hostería Pampa Llacta*, whose trout is fresh out of its own pond, or the popular *Choza de Don Wilson* at La Y de Papallacta, where the well-prepared trout and chicken staples come with good views of the valley and a lively atmosphere.

Baeza

From Papallacta the road follows the steep descent of the Papallacta and Quijos rivers for 37km before reaching **BAEZA** (1920m), the largest town between Quito and Lago Agrio. There's not a lot to do in town, but its location in attractive pastoral hills between three large, richly forested reserves – Cayambe-Coca directly to the north, Sumaco Napo-Galeras to the east (see p.299), and Antisana to the southwest (see p.316) – makes it a convenient base for local hikes as well as expeditions into the remoter depths of these protected areas.

Arrival and information

Baeza is split into three small and distinct parts. **La Y de Baeza** is the junction where the road from Quito splits, with one branch heading northeast to Lago Agrio and the other south to Tena. **Buses** to Tena pass all three parts of town, while those to Lago Agrio can drop you at La Y, from where **colectivos** ferry people every fifteen minutes up to Baeza Colonial and Andalucía.

For **information** on all three reserves, call in at the Centro de Comunicación Ambiental (☎06/2320605, 06/2320240) on the corner of Ramírez Dávalos and Rey Felipe II in Baeza Colonial.

Accommodation

There are a handful of **places to stay**, but when the pipelines need servicing oil workers can take up all the rooms in town. In the Baeza Colonial

---

Hikes around Baeza

There are several relatively straightforward half-day **hikes around Baeza** – all with good birding potential – that let you make the most of its hillside location. The IGM 1:50,000 Baeza **map** is a good resource; you may also need rubber boots if it's been raining, as trails can get very muddy. To access the best local trails, start from the right-hand side of the church in the old town and take the road heading up through the pastureland. About 700m on, you'll reach a bridge at a fork in the path. If you continue right without crossing the bridge, you follow the **Río Machángara** up an increasingly thickly forested hill to the southwest. The left fork over the bridge takes you up to the mountain ridge overlooking Baeza. Roughly 1km later, this latter track splits again. The steep, muddy branch to the right leads up through lush forest to some **antennas** on top of the hill, affording spectacular views of Baeza and the Quijos valley. The other branch continues along the **mountain ridge**, also with great views, but further along the forest gets very dense and the trail hard to find, so if you attempt this route it's worthwhile seeking out a **guide**, which will cost around $20 a day; try Rodrigo Morales (☎06/2320467) or ask at **Gina's** restaurant in Baeza. You can loop down from the mountain ridge round on a trail leading back to Nueva Andalucía.

neighbourhood, *La Casa de Rodrigo* (T06/2320467; ❸) offers rooms with private bath and has kayaks for rent. Next door, above the restaurant, *La Casa de Gina* (T06/2320471; ❷) has a choice of simple rooms with shared or private bath. In the Nueva Andalucía's neighbourhood, on Avenida de los Quijos, *Samay* (T06/2320170; ❷) has basic but sprightly wooden rooms with TV, while further down the hill, the slightly dearer *Dido's* (T06/2320114; ❷) has comfortable rooms with private baths and large TVs; it's also a good source for information on local walks. There are also a couple of good places to stay in the lush hills south of Baeza on the road to Tena, excellent bases for hiking and birdwatching (see p.316).

The Town

From La Y, you can see the rusting corrugated-tin roofs of **Baeza Colonial** about 1500m up the hill on the Tena road; the original village still shows the trappings of its history, with little wooden houses lining a pair of steep, cobbled streets up to a church. There's a small museum (Mon–Fri 9am–5pm; free) in the Centro de Comunicación Ambiental, on the corner of Ramírez Dávalos and Rey Felipe II, showing ceramics and displays on history and tourism in the region. Across the Río Machángara, about 800m further along this road, the new town, **Nueva Andalucía**, has grown steadily since it was founded in 1987 after an earthquake hit the area. Built along the quiet road to Tena, it is now substantially larger than its older neighbour and has all of the town's services, the hospital, post office and Andinatel office.

Eating and drinking

The best **restaurant** is *Gina's*, on the east side of the square in the old village; tour groups often stop here for its ample trout, meat or vegetarian dishes costing around $3. If you're looking for a local guide, this is a good place to start enquiries. Their sister restaurant *El Viejo*, next to *Dido's* in Andalucía, is similarly good.

The Quijos valley

Passing only a handful of settlements on the way, the road heading north from Baeza to Lago Agrio courses through the broad **Quijos valley** for almost 70km. The route may be a principal artery of the oil business, with the Trans-Ecuadorian Oil Pipeline hedging the road like a hard shoulder much of the way to Lago Agrio, but in recent years much work has been done to develop the region's potential for tourism. To the left, the vast Cayambe-Coca reserve stretches off high into the northern sierra; on the right, beyond the rocky shores of the Río Quijos, banked by grazing land and fruit farms, the wilds of the Parque Nacional Sumaco-Napo Galeras disappear in knots of cloud-cloaked ridges – a stunning area for hiking, biking, horseriding, kayaking, rafting and a host of other activities. The two main settlements of the Quijos valley, **Borja** and **El Chaco**, make the obvious bases for exploration. Beyond El Chaco, the two biggest natural attractions of the area, **La Cascada de San Rafael** and **Volcán El Reventador**, stand either side of the road.

Borja

Eight kilometres down the road from Baeza, the twin heating towers of the Sardinas oil-pumping station (where crude is heated to 80°C to make it viscous enough to pump over the Andes) signal the town of **BORJA.** This oil industry landmark may break the horizon for miles around, but Borja holds the most comfortable **places to stay** in the valley and is close to the starting point of rafting trips (usually organized from Quito). *La Campiña de Quijos* (☎06/2856231, ⓦ www.campquijos.com; ➏), at the end of a private drive 100m west of the main street, is a converted farm offering cabins with private baths, along with a pool, pleasant gardens and plenty of farmyard animals. Staff can arrange horse rides, hiking trips and rappelling, among other things, and will cook in their restaurant whatever you can catch in their trout ponds. A couple of kilometres west of town is *Hacienda Cumandá* (☎06/2320406 or 02/2244862; ➎), a handsome old house in pastureland near forests and the river, which also offers rafting, horseriding and hiking and has a good restaurant. On the other side of Borja, on the main road, *Quijos* (☎06/2320046; ➌) isn't a bad choice for the money, offering cabins with spacious en-suite rooms and cable TV. The best **restaurant** is *Doña Cleo* (daily 6.30am–9pm), 100m west of the main street, serving up a full menu of trout, shrimp, steak, chicken and pasta dishes.

El Chaco

After 10km, **EL CHACO**, the largest town before Lago Agrio and a local centre of cheese and naranjilla production, is one of the accesses to the lowland section of the **Cayambe–Coca reserve**. From town, a dirt road and path follows the Río Oyacachi, (reputed to be rich in gold, though panning will give you no more than a few specks of fine gold dust), passing viewpoints and cutting through dense forest, before eventually coming out at the highland village of Oyacachi. This three-day uphill **hike** is usually attempted with a guide coming downstream – and downhill – from Oyacachi (see p.134). The Centro de Información Ambiental, by the police station at the entrance to El Chaco, is a great place to get **information** about the valley's attractions, pick up maps and brochures, find guides for hikes and get the latest on hiking conditions at Volcán El Reventador. It also has a high-speed satellite **internet** connection ($1 per hour).

El Chaco's best **hotel** is the quiet *La Guarida del Coyote* (☎06/2329421; ➌) in Barrio Los Guayabos on the hill overlooking the town (from the Centro de Información Ambiental go four blocks north and turn left to the top of the hill; a taxi is $1), for its cosy cabañas with fireplaces and en-suite rooms with TV, hot water, pool and nice views of the valley. In town, *Kathryn* (☎06/2329146; ➋), on Chaco and Quito by the vegetable market, is reasonable, with a choice of rooms with private bath, TV and hot water. The town has long been a truck stop and offers plenty of cheap and basic street **comedores**, *La Fogata* being the best of them.

For the next 60km or so beyond El Chaco, the road traverses increasingly remote territory. Colonization here came to an abrupt end in March 1987, when a powerful **earthquake** rocked the area, sending cascades of mud and debris down the hillsides, killing over a thousand people.

La Cascada de San Rafael

Some 48km from El Chaco, the Río Quijos incises a gash between some tree-fringed cliffs before crashing down 145m – **La Cascada de San Rafael** – sending great clouds of spray wafting upwards. A concrete bus shelter on the right of the road marks the **entrance** to the falls (ask the bus driver for the stop). Behind the shelter take the dirt road a few hundred metres down to the guardhouse; if anyone's around (usually weekends and holidays), they'll charge you $1 for entrance, plus, somewhat controversially, a $10 park entrance fee, since it was ruled the falls were part of the Reserva Ecológica Cayambe-Coca. Beyond the guardhouse you'll see

▲ La Cascada de San Rafael

some simple prefab cabins built by the state electricity company, but now available as basic **accommodation** (❶; bring your own bedding), or you can **camp** for $2. You'll also have to bring all your own **food** and water, though there are proper facilities and lodging at *Hostería Reventador* (see p.288), a short way east of the turning for the falls.

There are two **trails** to the falls giving you quite different views. The easy **first trail** leads to a fine viewpoint opposite the falls (1hr 30min to the viewpoint and back), and begins at the arrows to the left behind the cabins. The **second** (2hr 15min there and back), leading to breathtaking views from the top of the falls, involves a bit of scrambling over rock at the end, which can be tricky in the wet. Ask the guards for directions and about the state of the river (sometimes prohibitively high); they will **guide** you for a few dollars if they have time.

Volcán El Reventador

On the rare occasions when the cloud lifts you can see **Volcán El Reventador** (3562m) poke its triangular mass through the greenery, 9km to the west of the San Rafael falls. El Reventador means "the burster", an apt name as the volcano's been popping away since the first record of its activity was made in 1541. Its 3.5-kilometre crater is evidence a colossal eruption once took place, ripping the volcano apart and leaving it a fraction of its former size.

Its last major outburst was in November 2002, when it spewed more than 200 million cubic tons of ash and rock – the country's largest **eruption** since Tungurahua's in 1886 – over 15km into the sky. The cloud drifted westwards, smothering the highway and nearby villages, and quickly reached Quito 90km away, where inches of ash fell, closing schools and the airport for days. Lava flows spilled down from the breached crater, burning wide streaks through its forested slopes, and a new cone was formed on the eastern slopes of the volcano, 600m below the summit. The eruption also moved the oil pipeline twenty metres in places, thankfully without breaking it.

Hiking to the summit is a strenuous (but non-technical) two- to four-day proposition, complicated by the fact that the traditional route up was obliterated by the eruption, which also changed the terrain significantly from what's recorded on the IGM 1:50,000 *Volcán El Reventador* map – making a knowledgeable guide essential. If you're considering this climb, check **the current condition** of the volcano in advance, consult the Instituto Geofísico website (Ⓦwww.igepn.edu.ec) and make local enquiries. If you go, you'll need a machete, along with the other usual hiking supplies.

The nearest **accommodation** is at *Hostería Reventador* (☎06/2818221, 09/4989098; ❺), Km100 Vía Quito–Lago Agrio, east of the turning for the San Rafael falls, which has simple rooms, a pool, waterslide, optional tours and rather lacklustre service. Victor Cansino, who works here and knows the area well, can be hired as a **guide**.

Lago Agrio and the Reserva Faunística Cuyabeno

LAGO AGRIO, once a marginal outpost on the frontiers of the jungle and the country, has become the black, pumping heart of Ecuador's oil industry; it's a city so important that in 1989 it was made the capital of the new province of Sucumbíos. Lojanos looking for a new life in the Oriente founded the settlement (whose official name is Nueva Loja) only a few decades ago, but in the late 1960s it was used by Texaco as a base for oil exploration, and soon after took its nickname from Sour Lake in Texas, the company's original headquarters.

Oil remains Lago Agrio's *raison d'être*, although the basic infrastructure of hotels, paved roads and transport links the industry brought have given tourism a foothold – largely in the form of an access point for visits to the vast, forested expanse of the **Reserva Faunística Cuyabeno**, one of the Oriente's most beautiful and diverse.

Arrival and information

The town's centre runs along **Avenida Quito**, the main road connecting Coca and Quito to Lago Agrio, which is also where you'll find most of the hotels and restaurants. **Buses** will usually drop you on or within a block of this road. If you need to catch a Baeza- or Quito-bound bus, you must board at the **bus station** 2km northwest of the centre on Calle del Chofer; for more on buses see "Listings", p.291. Lago's **airport**, served by TAME and VIP flights from Quito (around $65–70 each way) is 4km east of the centre; a taxi into town costs a few dollars.

Tourist **information** is available at the Cámara de Turismo, second floor of the *Hotel Ecuador* on avenidas Quito and Colombia (☎06/2832502), while the Ministerio del Ambiente office, Eloy Alfaro and Avenida Colombia (Mon–Fri 8am–12.30pm & 1.30–5pm; ☎06/2830139), has basic information on the Cuyabeno reserve and some ecotourism projects. **Internet** facilities are at the *Araza Hotel*, Av Quito 619 and Narváez. **Taxis** – white and yellow pick-up trucks – cost $1.25 minimum in daytime and $1.50 at night; try Cooperativo Terminal Terrestre (☎06/2831043) if you need to call one. Otherwise, there are plenty of them on Avenida Quito, particularly around the market area. For general **safety**, always take a cab at night.

Ecuador's oil industry

Oil has been mined in Ecuador since 1917, but it wasn't until Texaco struck rich with sites around Lago Agrio sixty years later that the Oriente really figured in the industry. Oil currently accounts for over forty percent of Ecuador's export income, dominating the economy but making it vulnerable to global price fluctuations. When its value fell in the 1980s, the government signed away increasingly larger areas of the Oriente to oil production to make up for the lost revenue; today, virtually all of the Ecuadorian Amazon is available for oil extraction, even indigenous territories and protected areas. The law states that whatever the land's designation, the oil and minerals below belong to the state, which can grant concessions for their extraction as it sees fit. The economy's thirst for oil has been satisfied at considerable cost to the environment.

The damage begins with **prospecting**; in a typical search, over a thousand helicopter sites are cleared and hundreds of seismic tests destroy thousands of acres of forest. During **drilling**, waste oil products are collected in filthy pits laced with toxic metals that contaminate surrounding river systems; when work is finished they're covered under a thin layer of earth and left to continue polluting. **Roads** are built, unlocking the forest to colonizers who deforest large areas of unsuitable land for farming which quickly becomes degraded. Oil **transportation** is also hazardous; breaks in Ecuador's pipelines have resulted in around seventeen million gallons of oil pouring into the environment – a fraction of the amount dumped as **waste**, thought to be many billions of gallons.

The toll on **local populations** has been horrific. In the north, the Cofán, Siona and Secoya have been languishing since their rivers were polluted beyond use, forcing them to overhunt the forests and move to the cities to find work in unskilled and poorly paid jobs, sometimes, ironically, in dangerous oil clean-up work. Other indigenous groups have been victims of aggressive and divisive corporate tactics: leaders are bought off or villages are bribed with cash and promises to build schools and medical centres (while neighbouring and similarly affected settlements are offered nothing) to obtain permission for oil exploration. When these tactics fail, strong-arm methods – intimidation, restriction of movement, paramilitary activity – have sometimes been used. **Toxic discharges** have also been linked to dramatic increases in rates of cancer, miscarriages, skin complaints and birth defects. A Harvard medical team found unusually high incidences of eight types of **cancer** in areas affected by oil activity.

Indigenous opposition to the oil companies has become better organized. In 1993 and 2003, a lawsuit was filed against Texaco on behalf of 30,000 indigenous people, who claim their land or health has been affected by the company allegedly dumping toxic waste-water into Oriente river systems between 1964 and 1992. It's estimated it will cost $6 billion to clean up the 18 billion gallons of toxic waste the company is alleged to have dumped – thirty times greater than the amount of crude spilled in the *Exxon Valdez* disaster. At the time of writing, the case was ongoing. Some indigenous groups are opting for **direct action**. In 2005 protestors forced Petroecuador, the state-owned oil company, to cease crude oil production for a week, and in 2006 to shut down the Trans-Ecuadorian Oil pipeline for several days. The concerted efforts of the Kichwa community of Sarayaku in Pastaza have so far successfully thwarted the attempts of an oil company to drill on its territory. Other communities of the Shuar, Achuar and Záparo have also managed to organize resistance.

It's an uphill battle for indigenous peoples to protect their land. Ecuador is thought to be losing as much as 2000 square kilometres of forest per year, proportionally the continent's highest rate. According to US and government figures, Ecuador's oil reserves will be exhausted in just a few years; if the destruction continues at the current rate conservationists predict the Ecuadorian Amazon will be completely deforested within thirty years.

5

In recent years, the **conflict in Colombia** has affected the town and armed units are believed to have infiltrated the region (the border is just 21 km away). Although this has so far had little impact on tourists, shootings have occurred in the town and there have been kidnappings in the border areas. You should make enquiries with the authorities before travelling here, and check postings on your embassy websites.

Accommodation

A little extra cash goes a long way with **accommodation** in Lago Agrio. The plentiful rock-bottom choices are mostly unattractive and noisy, while for a few dollars more you can have a bright, clean room with air conditioning, cable TV and fridge. Only the more expensive rooms will have hot water.

Araza Hotel Av Quito 610 and Narváez ⓉFax06/2830223, Ⓕ2831247. The most comfortable place in town, featuring big, soulless rooms with all the accoutrements, such as a/c, cable TV, private baths and hot water, plus an outdoor pool and wi-fi. ⓿

D'Mario Av Quito Ⓣ06/2830172, Ⓦwww.hotel dmario.com. While the downstairs rooms of this popular hotel are a bit musty, those on the middle floor (❺) are fresher and cleaner with a/c, cable TV,

fridge and phone; the top-floor suites (❻) have all of those, with bigger rooms and hot water. Also has a pool, sauna, weights room and free wi-fi. ❹

Ecuador Av Quito and Pasaje Gonzanamá Ⓣ06/2830183. This decent budget hotel is popular with Ecuadorians, and has fans, TV and private baths. There's also a restaurant and parking. ❷

Gran Colombia Av Quito Ⓣ06/2831032. Sprightly hotel with gleaming, flower-decked frontage and a range of brightly painted rooms with fan or a/c,

fridge and cable TV (with hot water and DVD player in the dearer rooms (**6**)). Sadly, caged birds and a roaming monkey blot the record. **4**

Gran Hostal del Lago Av Quito, 1km west of the centre ☎&Ⓕ06/2832415. The comfortable concrete cabins here come with a/c, cable TV and wi-fi, and there's also a pool, sauna and steam room, all surrounded by pleasant gardens. **7**

Los Guacamayos Av Quito ☎06/2830601. One of the better budget hotels, offering small rooms strung down long open-sided corridors; facilities can include private bath, cold water, fan, a/c and TV (**3**), with prices dropping the more you forgo. **2**

Lago Imperial Av Colombia and Av Quito ☎06/2830453. Pleasant rooms equipped with fan, private bath, hot water and cable TV as standard; a/c and wi-fi cost slightly more. **4**

The Town

Lago Agrio has a hot and bustling centre along its main street, **Avenida Quito**, where its high-fronted buildings seem a little grandiose for a hard-edged frontier town. A couple of blocks to the north, Lago's central park, fronted by a simple church, is about the only gesture to greenery you'll find. Outside Lago, the signs of rapid colonization and oil exploitation are all too clear – oil pipelines crisscross a bulldozed landscape, where only a few sad scraps of forest remain from the sea of vegetation that once surrounded the town.

Around 15,000 **Cofán** lived in this area when Texaco arrived, but disease and displacement made them among the worst-hit by the industry; they now number only a few hundred, squeezed into five small communities, three of which are in the forests on the Río Aguarico. At Lago's Sunday **market**, between avenidas Quito and Amazonas, some Cofán come wearing traditional dress – a long tunic and sometimes a headdress for the men, and colourful blouses, skirts and jewellery for the women – to trade their produce and craftwork, including hammocks, bags and occasionally necklaces made from animal teeth, iridescent insects or birds' beaks. **Artesanías Huarmi Huankurina** ("United Women"), 12 de Febrero 267 and 10 de Agosto (Tues–Sun, but irregular hours), and Artesanías Cofán (irregular hours), Jorge Añasco and Vicente Narváez, also sell crafts from the region's indigenous communities, including hammocks, bags, ceramics and blowpipes.

Eating and drinking

Two of the most popular **restaurants** in town are next-door rivals owned by the *D'Mario* and *Gran Colombia* hotels, offering fairly standard menus as well as pizza. Both have low cane chairs with giant cushions, and tables spilling out on to the pavement, oddly evoking the air of a Paris bistro in the heart of the Oriente. Across the road, *Pedacito de Colombia* dishes up good, cheap Colombian specialities and *almuerzos*, while the *Chifa Estrella China* nearby on Avenida Quito is the place for reliable Chinese food. There's no shortage of **bars** and **clubs** in town, mostly catering to legions of macho oil workers. Some places can be a bit rough, so exercise caution and discretion.

Listings

Airlines TAME, Francisco de Orellana and 9 de Octubre ☎06/2830113, and at the airport ☎06/2832365, ⓦ www.tame.com.ec; VIP, at airport ☎06/2830333, ⓦ www.vipec.com.
Banks and exchange Banco de Guayaquil, 12 de Febrero and Av Quito (Visa, MasterCard ATM); Banco Pichincha and Banco Internacional, both on 12 de Febrero and Av Quito, have Visa ATMs.

Buses Buses to the Colombian border depart from Av Colombia and Añasco. *Rancheras* and scrappy oil-company buses for Coca, Shushufindi and other more local destinations leave from around the market and from the stadium a block to the west on Av Amazonas. Other destinations are serviced from the bus terminal 2km northeast of the centre. See "Travel details" on p.332 for further information.

Consulate Colombia, avs Quito and Colombia
☎06/2830114. Look for the flag in an upstairs
window.

Police and immigration Av Quito and Manabí
☎06/2830101. Daily 8am–noon & 1–6pm.
Post office Vicente Rocafuerte and 12 de Febrero.

East of Lago Agrio: the Reserva Faunística Cuyabeno

The **Reserva Faunística Cuyabeno**, one of Ecuador's largest reserves, encompasses over six thousand square kilometres of rainforest, holding the Río Cuyabeno basin and much of the watershed of the lower Río Aguarico as far as the Peruvian border. Protecting areas with species that survived the last ice age, Cuyabeno harbours abundant birdlife with 494 recorded species (a number that continues to grow) and a staggering 228 tree species per hectare. The reserve also contains a huge network of lakes and lagoons, including fourteen major interconnected bodies of water and large areas of inundated forest. Among them are two main black-water lake systems: the **Cuyabeno Lakes**, which include the Laguna Cuyabeno and Laguna Grande, and **Lagartococha**, at the eastern end of the reserve bordering Peru. In contrast to the nutrient-rich whitewater rivers originating in the Andes, black-water rivers typically form where there is little soil sediment and generally originate in the Amazon basin

Community stays and jungle tours from Lago Agrio

From Lago Agrio, most jungle excursions go to the beautiful forests of the Reserva Faunística Cuyabeno (see p.292). There are several possibilities for people wishing to arrange **indigenous-community stays** in or near the reserve, with the Cofán, Siona or Secoya people. A good place to go for further information is **La Dirección Bilingüe de Sucumbíos** on Avenida Quito and 20 de Junio (☎06/2832681), near the *Gran Hostal de Lago*. It's an institution responsible for the bilingual education of indigenous people and can put you in touch with the contacts for communities offering tourism programmes; the current contacts are listed below. You can also visit the reserve with a couple of more conventional **tour operators** based in Lago.

Indigenous-community stays
Cofán communties Contact FEINCE (Federación Indígena de la Nacionalidad Cofán del Eucador), Km3.5, Vía a Quito, Lago Agrio ☎06/2831200.
Secoya communties Contact Javier Piaguaje, President of the community of San Pablo ☎09/9389984, or the community of Sehuayá ☎09/1077578, ⓦwww.secoyas.com.
Siona communities Contact Venancio Criollo, President of the Organización de la Nacionalidad Siona del Ecuador ☎09/1324171.

Lago Agrio tour operators
Magic River Tours Primera and Paca Yacu, next to the chocolate factory ☎02/2629303 or 09/7360670, ⓦwww.magicrivertours.com. A German-owned company specializing in non-motorized canoe trips, paddling or drifting down small tributaries in the Cuyabeno reserve (5 days $320), accompanied by an English or German speaker and an expert indigenous guide.
Pioneer Tours No address, but on a dirt road off Avenida Amazonas to the south in Barrio Colinas Petroleras ☎06/2831845 or 09/7532159, ⓔpioneertourscialtda @yahoo.es. Run by Galo Sevilla, who has more than twenty years' guiding experience; tours typically head to a basic campsite by the Laguna de Cuyabeno with local Siona and Secoya guides and cost $40 per person per day.

itself; the water takes on a dark tea-like colour from the vegetable humus that falls into it, which also makes it very acidic and rich in tannins. Some people come to the reserve specifically to see its **aquatic wildlife**, such as pink freshwater dolphins, turtles, black caiman, anaconda, manatee, giant otters, countless colourful frogs and toads and 450 species of fish.

The boundaries of the reserve have changed since its creation in 1979, particularly following major incursions by oil companies and settlers into the western areas around Tarapoa. The governments of the time largely ignored this destruction, but in 1991, after considerable pressure from international agencies and CONAIE (Confederation of Indigenous Nationalities of Ecuador), a vast tract of land on the eastern side was added, almost tripling the size of the reserve. While the reserve is now less accessible to colonizers and far better protected by politically active indigenous communities (including Kichwa, Cofán, Secoya, Siona and Shuar), who are struggling to defend their cultures and territory against oil company encroachment, oil extraction is still causing problems through toxic waste and spills that have drained into the Cuyabeno basin; for more on the effects of the oil industry in the Oriente see the box on pp.289.

Visiting the reserve

The main road east of Lago Agrio is the most straightforward way of reaching the reserve. It follows the Río Aguarico to the settler village of **Dureno**, skirting Cofán territory before reaching **Chiritza**, about 50km east of Lago Agrio; some tour agencies take canoes into the southern section of the reserve from here. There are two main **access points** to the reserve. The first is where the road crosses the Río Cuyabeno, beyond the oil town of Tarapoa, from where the river can be navigated down to the Laguna Cuyabeno and the other main lakes. The second is by canoe on the Río Aguarico, which can be navigated from Lago Agrio to the lowest parts of the reserve, but is more commonly joined at Chiritza,

Visiting the reserve independently is not recommended, but agencies in Quito and Lago Agrio offer a range of **guided tours** (see pp.116–117 & p.292 for details). Shorter tours are usually based around the lakes, while longer ones tend to go to the eastern reaches around the Río Aguarico or Río Lagartococha. **Indigenous-community stays** are also becoming a growing force in the region (see box, p.292). **Transport** to Lago Agrio from Quito, and the reserve **entrance fee** ($20), aren't generally included in the price of a tour.

South of Lago Agrio: the road to Coca

The 93-kilometre road running between Lago Agrio and Coca was built to facilitate access between the burgeoning oil towns in the late 1970s. It opened up the area to a flood of colonists to whom the government promised all the land they could clear, in an effort to bring economic productivity to the

Travel warning: the Colombian border

Despite the **Colombian** border being only 21km north of Lago Agrio, the Oriente is **not a safe place** from which to enter Colombia. The US-led "Plan Colombia" has encouraged the displacement of Colombian **guerrilla** and **paramilitary** units – who are making their presence felt – into Ecuadorian territory. You should **avoid all border areas** in Sucumbíos; if you're heading to Colombia, cross at Tulcán in the northern sierra (see p.166).

Oriente. The rainforest was speedily hacked down for farming, and the soil, too poor to support long-term agriculture, became degraded pastureland within a few years. Meanwhile, oil companies scoured the region, and a giant latticework of **pipelines** now spreads out from the road; at night the flicker of the refinery fires dyes the sky an unearthly orange. The landscape is not totally unappealing,

Francisco de Orellana and the discovery of the Amazon

In February 1541, when a band of 200 Spaniards, 4000 *indígenas* and thousands of assorted horses, dogs and pigs set out from Quito to explore new lands to the east, few of them could have expected that some of their party would end up making the first recorded descent of the Amazon – a journey of over 6000km down part of the largest river system in the world.

They were led by Gonzalo Pizarro, younger brother of the ruthless Francisco (the conqueror of the Incas), and soon joined by Captain **Francisco de Orellana**. He had won honour as a young man – and lost an eye – in the battles of Lima and Cusco, and at thirty years old was still hungry for adventure.

Even before the expedition had left the mountains, hundreds of *indígenas* had died in the freezing passes, and as they descended into the uncharted forests, they were running desperately low on food. By Christmas, the group had travelled around 400km from Quito, when they stumbled across the Río Coca. Having eaten all their pigs and most of their dogs, they decided their only choice was to build a boat and send a vanguard led by Orellana downstream in search of food. Orellana never made it back to his leader and the waiting men – a failure which saw him branded a traitor for centuries afterwards.

The captain had a group of sixty men, some weapons and a few supplies, but within a couple of weeks they were "eating hides, straps and the soles of their shoes cooked with certain herbs" and forest roots which poisoned them "to the point of death". Worse still, the river (they'd now entered the Napo) had become so fast-moving they knew they wouldn't be able to go back upstream, and they were carried down into territory where war drums raged on either side of the river. Yet Orellana was a great diplomat as well as soldier, and unlike most conquistadors, he was well versed in indigenous languages and picked new ones up with prodigious speed, an ability that saved his life many times on his journey. Here, instead of fighting, he embraced a local chief and gave him European clothes, receiving an abundance of partridges, turkeys and fish in return.

Before long, over 1000km from Pizarro's camp, their only concern was to stay alive. By June 1542, they reached the Río Negro (near what is now Manaus), naming it after its deep-black waters. News of their presence spread before them, and they came across empty villages with decapitated heads nailed to posts in warning.

A fierce tribe of warrior-women – whom they named **Amazons**, after the female warriors of Greek mytholody – then attacked them. The chronicler of the journey, Friar Gaspar de Carvajal, described how the Spanish boats looked like "porcupines" after their shots rained down; the friar himself lost an eye in the exchange. Although these women were never spotted again, it has been hypothesized they were male warriors from the Yagua tribe, who sport pale yellow, grass-style skirts and headgear. On August 26, 1542, the expedition finally came to the mouth of the world's greatest river and named it Orellana, though it soon became known as Amazonas, after the tribe.

Orellana returned to Spain in May 1543 but set out for the river again in December 1545. The ill-equipped expedition lost a ship and more than 220 men before reaching South America. As they entered the Amazon estuary, they'd already run out of food and the remaining ships became separated on the rough tidal waters. Orellana died from illness and grief in November 1546, finally defeated by the river that had brought him fame.

but feels miserably squandered, with livestock and white-trunked trees dotting tired fields backed by the odd patch of forest in the distance. Simple homesteads lie at the roadside, and some of the successful ones guard defiant gardens and orchards from the surrounding grassland. Also along this road is evidence of the new commercial interests in the Oriente – vast plantations filled with sterile rows of African oil palms.

About halfway to Coca, an army of fruit, sweet and juice sellers ambushes buses pausing in **Proyecto**, where an eastbound road leaves the main Coca highway. This road is the only land access for **Limoncocha** and **Pompeya** (see p.301 for details on both towns), and is serviced by regular buses as far as **Shushufindi**, an unsightly town of refineries, compounds and gas-storage tanks, 25km away. Beyond it, the dirt road turns south, accompanied by several smaller pipelines, which shoot off to suck oil from two-thousand-square-kilometre *bloques* of land and pump it back to Lago Agrio. A further hour's drive will take you to Limoncocha and then Pompeya on the Río Napo some thirty minutes later.

From Proyecto, the Coca road reaches **La Joya de los Sachas**, where there are a couple of simple hotels, but no reason to stop unless you want to catch a bus to Shushufindi. Some 39km later, just outside Coca, you'll have to disembark and show your passport at the checkpoint at Payamino. Keep an eye on your bus – they are sometimes impatient to leave and not always aware that you aren't on board.

Coca

The booming oil town of **COCA**, capital of **Orellana** province (and officially named Puerto Fransico de Orellana), remained a forgotten outpost in the midst of virgin jungle, cut off from the rest of the world except by boat or plane, until the 1970s. It was the discovery of black gold that led to a speedy influx of oilers and colonists, and the sleepy village soon mutated into an urban nightmare.

It's improved a little since then, but with fewer tourist facilities than Lago Agrio or Tena and with nothing to see or do, Coca is still a town you'll not want to linger in. It's best use is as a gateway to the primary forest downstream on the **Río Napo** or south along the **Vía Auca**, a newly colonized oil road tearing south through the jungle to the ríos Tiputini and Shiripuno. Access to the rainforest is easiest on one of the many guided tours offered by operators in Quito (see p.114) or Coca (see p.298), ranging from short hops down the Napo to adventurous multi-day trips, deep into the jungle, including to the vast **Parque Nacional Yasuní** (see p.304) and the neighbouring **Waorani Reserve** (see p.305). Some of Ecuador's best **jungle lodges** (see box, p.305) are also found on this stretch of the Río Napo; if you're planning on staying in one, book before arriving in Coca.

Coca is also a departure point for Iquitos in the Peruvian Amazon via the newly opened border crossing at **Nuevo Rocafuerte**. For more information on getting to Peru see "Boats" in "Listings" on p.298 and refer to Nuevo Rocafuerte on p.306.

Arrival and information

Coca's **bus terminal** is on Napo and Sergio Saenz, twelve blocks north of the waterfront, but the major bus companies also arrive and depart from offices on or near Napo, a few blocks from the river (see "Listings" on p.299 for details).

COCA

JUAN MONTALVO

Trans
Esmeraldas ★

Ⓑ
BOLÍVAR

Trans Zacaray ★   ★ Trans Baños
                    Ministerio ⓘ
                    del Ambiente

CUENCA

Transportes Loja ★

ROCAFUERTE

TAME
❷   Ⓖ
Flota Pelileo ★

GARCÍA MORENO   GARCÍA MORENO

ELOY ALFARO   ❸

❶

ⓒ

Ⓓ   ESPEJO
                    ❹
                    ❺

FCUNAE

Capitanía   PADRE CAMILO TORRANO Ⓔ

Ⓕ

ⓘ Centro de
Interpretación

Río Napo   Dock

▼ Vía Auca

RESTAURANTS & DRINKING

Casa del Maito	5
Emerald Forest Blues Bar	4
Medianoche	2
Ocaso	3
Parrilladas Argentinas	1

0   100 m

ACCOMMODATION

El Auca	C
Hostería Amazonas Coca	D
La Misión	E
Oasis	F
Puerto Orellana	A
San Fermín	B

The main road from Lago Agrio comes in from the northeast, passing the airport, and some buses may drop you on this road at the fringes of the town centre. You can walk in, but white pick-up trucks – the town's **taxis** – usually patrol the main routes and can take you to any destination in town for $1. This main road continues south to a large metal bridge over the river, the start of the Vía Auca. The entrance to the **airport** is about 1km down the Lago Agrio road from the town centre; flights from Quito are operated by TAME and VIP, and cost around $60–65 each way. **Boat** arrivals come in at the municipal dock between Napo and Amazonas, but some of the smarter tour companies use the dock at *La Misión* hotel.

The **Centro de Informacion Turística** on the waterfront, opposite the Capitanía (Mon–Fri 8am–noon & 2–4pm, Sat 8am–1pm), is the first place to come for **information** about the town and Parque Nacional Yasuní. You might also get a few answers from the **Ministerio del Ambiente** on Amazonas and Bolívar (Mon–Fri 8am–12.30pm & 1.30–5pm; ☎06/2881850) about nearby reserves and any new ecotourism initiatives, or the **Ministerio de Turismo**, Avenida 9 de Octubre and Chimborazo (☎06/2881583) about local attractions. Online information is available at Ⓦ www.orellanaturistica .gov.ec.

Accommodation

Coca has numerous very cheap and barely adequate **places to stay**, geared to oil workers, but if you're willing to fork out a little extra you'll be well catered to.

Hostería Amazonas Coca Espejo and 12 de Febrero ☎06/2880444. A good option for its bright, fresh rooms (some with river views) with fans (❹) or a/c (up to ❺), all with private bath, hot water and cable TV. The hotel also has a bar, restaurant and internet service and accepts traveller's cheques (you have to stay until they clear). ❹

El Auca Napo and García Moreno ☎06/2880127, Ⓕ2880600. A popular choice, with a large, peaceful garden, fronted by wooden cabins that are clean and compact, with fans, private bath and electric showers. More expensive rooms (❼) come with a/c and cable TV, while cheaper, smaller rooms without hot water are also offered. Accepts and changes traveller's cheques for guests. ❻

La Misión Padre Camilo Torrano ☎06/2880544, Ⓦwww.hotelamision.com. One of Coca's better long-established hotels, offering slightly dated but comfortable rooms, furnished with mocha carpets, cable TV, phone, wi-fi, fridge and a/c for a little extra. It's in a quiet location overlooking the Río Napo and guests can cool off in the pool. ❻

Oasis Padre Camilo Toranno, east of the bridge ☎06/2880206. The town's cheapest passable place, the *Oasis*' scraggy exterior is compensated for with decent rooms that have private bathrooms and battered fans. For a few dollars extra, rooms with hot water, a/c and a TV are also available. ❷

Puerto Orellana 2km from the centre on the Lago Agrio road, near the Texaco station ☎06/2880970. Coca's plushest and most modern hotel features comfortable rooms, all with a/c, private bath, hot water, cable TV, phones and wi-fi. ❻

San Fermín Bolívar and Quito ☎06/2880802, Ⓦwww.wildlifeamazon.com. Comfortable, well-priced hotel featuring lots of natural wood, cool white tiles and abundant potted plants. Offers a range of budget rooms with fans and shared or private bath, or en-suite doubles with a/c. Also has an on-site tour operator. ❷–❺

The Town

Until recently, its chaotic and filthy, potholed streets lined with ramshackle houses ensured visitors left Coca in a hurry, taking canoes to lodges further down the **Río Napo**. Yet concerted efforts by its authorities have succeeded in neatening up sections of the waterfront and in paving some of its main roads. There's no *parque central* in town (a symptom of its explosive growth, as if no one had time to plan one), which sprawls outwards from the north bank of the Río Napo. Its central streets, Napo and Amazonas, run north–south and are busiest in the few blocks around the river, though the town's produce **market**, *municipio* and bus station are a dozen blocks to the north. Napo even looks quite respectable now, but you only have to peek down the parallel roads to the east to see the town's shabbier side. Most hotels and restaurants are along the southern end of Napo or around the waterfront.

Eating and drinking

There are many cheap and unattractive **restaurants** dishing up fried chicken and beer to oil-workers in Coca, but few to be excited about. *El Auca* hotel has a good air-conditioned restaurant tourists and better-off locals patronize, and a jar of their delicious lemonade is a good antidote to the heat; next door, on the other side of reception, you can buy ice cream. Late-night meals (6pm–2am) are available from *Medianoche* on Napo, opposite *El Auca*. *La Misión*'s restaurant is pricier than its rivals, but the food and service are good. *Ocaso*, on Eloy Alfaro and Napo, is very popular with locals and serves up hearty portions at a decent price. *Parrilladas Argentinas*, on Cuenca and Inés, is best for char-grilled steaks, chicken and chops, while *Casa del Maito*, along the waterfront, specializes in *maitos*, a delicious traditional fish dish, usually tilapia, which is wrapped up in a leaf with a palm heart and char-grilled.

The *Emerald Forest Blues Bar*, on Espejo and Quito, is a good place to meet travellers and have a **drink**.

Listings

Airlines Tame, on corner of Napo and Rocafuerte ☎06/2881078, ⓦwww.tame.com.ec; VIP, Av Alejandro Labaka, next to the airport ☎06/2881453, ⓦwww.vipec.com. Flights are busy, so book well in advance and reconfirm regularly. For frequencies see "Travel details" p.332.

Boats Boats (motorized canoes) to jungle lodges are always prearranged for travellers as part of their tour. A regular public service downstream to Nuevo Rocafuerte ($15; a 10–12hr trip) leaves by 8am (be there early for a good seat) Tuesday and Thursday, returning early on Thursday and Sunday

Tours from Coca

Most tours from Coca are organized in advance from Quito (see p.114), though a small number of local **guides** and **tour agencies** operate out of town; some of these offer only a middling standard of guiding and very few speak English. Always make it clear what you expect from your tour and whether essential equipment (see box, p.278) and transport is included. Touring out of Coca without a guide is not recommended. A few operators offer the 800km trip down the Río Napo from **Coca to Iquitos** in Peru, including Wildlife Amazon and Luis Duarte, listed below; refer also to the Nuevo Rocafuerte account on p.306 for further details.

Tour operators and guides

Emerald Forest Expeditions Quito and Espejo ☎06/2882309 or 09/9594604, ⓔluisemerald@gmail.com. Luis García, the leading guide of this outfit, speaks excellent English and is very experienced. He runs four- and five-day trips ($240 and $300 per person, respectively) to the very rustic *Pañacocha Lodge* (no electricity and basic latrines) on the Río Pañayacu, five hours downstream off the Río Napo.

Luis Duarte Ask at *La Casa del Maito* restaurant ☎06/2882285, ⓔcocaselva @hotmail.com. Luis runs two-day trips to Iquitos in a high-speed twin-engine boat ($500 per person, minimum ten passesngers). Trips can also be extended to more gentle seven-day tours and he can help arrange transport for smaller groups.

River Dolphin Expeditions Guayaquil and Amazonas ☎06/2882336 or 09/4603087, ⓦwww.amazon-green-magician.com. Tours led by Ramiro Viteri, a Kichwa from the Pastaza forests, who is also a professional chef. Be crystal clear on what the tour includes – some travellers have reported ending up with something very different from what they were expecting. Prices typically range from $50–70 per day, increasing for more exotic itineraries.

Wildlife Amazon *Hotel San Fermín*, Bolívar and Quito ☎06/2880802, ⓦwww .wildlifeamazon.com. Reliable, professionally run outfit offering a wide range of jungle tours (around $550 for 5 nights), including a Coca–Iquitos (Peru) trip (7 nights, $800).

Wimper Torres ☎06/2880336 or 2880017. Enthusiastic guide offering adventurous tours of three to eight days to the ríos Shiripuno, Nushiño, Cononaco and Curaray south of Coca, the Pañacocha area off the Río Napo and Jatuncocha, near Peru. Torres speaks Spanish but can contract an English-speaking translator for an extra fee. At least a week's notice is required to organize a tour, which costs around $60 per person per day (minimum of four people).

Indigenous-community stays

FCUNAE Federación de Comunas Unión de Nativos de la Amazonia Ecuatoriana opposite *La Misión* hotel; contact Sergio Shigunago (☎06/2881033). Offers community-based tours to San José de Payamino (Kichwa) on the Río Payamino, Zancudo (Cofán) on the Aguarico, and Verde Sumaco (Kichwa). There is an emphasis on the cultural dimension, with traditional dances and shamanic ceremonies, as well as the more typical jungle hikes, waterfalls, caves, dugout canoes, birdwatching and wildlife walks. Itineraries are of two to four days and cost $50–60 per person per day.

(12hr). It stops at requested villages on the way. There's not much regular public traffic apart from this, but ask at the Capitanía (☎06/2880231) for boat departure schedules, as you can often negotiate a ride; Peruvian cargo boats returning to Peru (usually in the third week of the month) are generally willing to take passengers. There is no regular service upstream to Misahuallí, as most people now go there by the Coca–Tena road. You must register at the Capitanía before you leave Coca by boat; if going to Peru, you must also get your passport stamped at the Policía Nacional office in Nuevo Rocafuerte.

Buses Trans Esmeraldas and Trans Baños run the best services to Quito; buy tickets in advance. It's faster to go via Loreto than Lago Agrio, a route also regarded as safer at night. Trans Baños has four buses daily to Quito via Lago Agrio and three nightly via Loreto, and other buses to Ambato, Tena, Baños and Puyo; Trans Esmeraldas has two nightly buses for Quito; Transportes Loja runs a nightly bus to Quito and one evening bus to Santo Domingo, Machala and Loja; Flota Pelileo has a bus to Ambato, Tena, Baños, Guayaquil and Puyo; Trans Jumandy, at the terminal, has a regular service to Tena and Puyo. Buses and *rancheras* to local destinations, including Lago Agrio and south down the oil road to the ríos Tiputini and Shiripuno, leave from the bus terminal.

Exchange Banco Pichincha, at Quito and Bolívar, has a Visa and MasterCard ATM; Banco de Internacional, Cuenca and 9 de Octubre has a Visa ATM. No banks in Coca exchange currency or traveller's cheques, but *El Auca* changes traveller's cheques for guests.

Migration police Upstairs on Napo and Rocafuerte, over the street from *El Auca* ☎06/2881594.

Telephone office Andinatel, on the corner of Eloy Alfaro and 6 de Diciembre.

Coca to Tena by road

If you've come into Coca from Lago Agrio in the north, there are two other ways you can leave town: by **river to the east** (see p.300), or by **road to the west**, all the way to Tena. With a new bridge over the Río Payamino and a freshly surfaced road, the six-hour bus ride to Tena is more comfortable than it once was, but on hot days bus drivers seek what little shade there is – even if it means driving on the wrong side for miles on end. The only town of any importance on the road is **LORETO**, about 57km from Coca, where you'll find a couple of basic hotels and restaurants, a police station and little else. Shortly afterwards the road begins coiling up into the foothills of the Andes, passing the verdant wilds of the **Parque Nacional Sumaco Napo-Galeras** to the north, gaining height to give astounding views of the plush carpet of the Napo basin unfurling to the horizon. Some 135km from Coca, you reach **Narupa** (also known as "Km 24"), a tiny hamlet that marks the junction with the Baeza–Tena highway. From here, it's 34km south to Tena, or 40km north to Baeza.

Parque Nacional Sumaco Napo-Galeras

Bounded by the Loreto road to the south and the Tena–Baeza road to the west, the **Parque Nacional Sumaco Napo-Galeras** ($5) harbours over 2000 square kilometres of pristine Pleistocene areas, where there are incredible amounts of undiscovered life; the few scientific forays into its reaches have revealed a staggering forty percent of the plant samples taken to be new species. On clear days you'll see the cleft peak of Volcán Sumaco (3732m) soaring upwards from the wooded hills, marking the centre of the park. Dense forests and vertiginous ravines have so far kept human influence at bay and access is difficult, though not impossible. One of the main **entrances** is at the tiny village of **Guagua Sumaco**, about 30km west of Loreto. Just west of the village, a dirt road shoots 8km north from the main road up to the smaller village of **Pacto Sumaco**. On the way, 200m or so up the road, you'll pass a Ministerio del Ambiente park office (bunks available; ➊), a good place to start organizing a guide for climbing the volcano (see p.300). Contuing up the road, 1km short of Pacto Sumaco, you'll pass the entrance to Swedish–US-run **Wildsumaco Lodge** (Ⓦwww .wildsumaco.com; ➒ including all meals). It sits in its own wildlife sanctuary, where trails provide outstanding **birding** opportunities, with recorded sightings of over four hundred species. The lodge itself offers very comfortable accommodation, or you can access its trails as a day visitor ($20).

Heading into the park proper, a poor trail from Pacto Sumaco leads past the glassy **Laguna de Pacto Sumaco**, eventually to arrive at the summit of the mist-shrouded **Volcán Sumaco**; if you plan to climb it (three days minimum round-trip) or explore any part of the park, be sure to get advance information and hire a guide at the Ministerio del Ambiente park office (see p.299). *Wildsumaco Lodge* (see p.299) can also help organize a guide, if you contact them in advance; alternatively, guided ascents and hikes (using local guides) are also organized from Tena by RICANCIE, the community tourism coordinator (see box, p.312).

Pacto Sumaco is served by a very slow daily **bus** (Transportes Expreso Napo) from Tena, leaving Pista de Avionetas in Tena at 4pm and arriving in Pacto Sumaco around 8pm. The return journey leaves Pacto Sumaco at 5am. Alternatively you can get to Guagua Sumaco on frequent buses from Coca or from the village of Narupa (passed by Quito–Tena buses; see p.299). If you prefer to avoid the eight-kilometre uphill hike from here (2.5–3hr), you can arrange a free pick-up with *Wildsumaco Lodge* if you're staying there. Failing that, a **taxi** from Loreto will get you here for around $20.

East of Coca

From Coca, the muddy waters of the lower Río Napo flow in broad curves for over 200km to **Nuevo Rocafuerte** on the Peruvian border. Long, motorized canoes ply the shallow river, searching for the deepest channels between large and slowly shifting sandbanks, while half-submerged logs wag vigorously in the currents. The region is only sparsely populated, and you'll pass just the odd Kichwa homestead linked to the riverbank by steep dirt footpaths. The Río Napo is the region's motorway, and its network of tributaries and backwaters forms the basic infrastructure to remote indigenous communities deep within the remaining tracts of pristine rainforest. In the forests to the south, between the ríos Napo and Curaray, lies the **Waorani Reserve**, home to about two

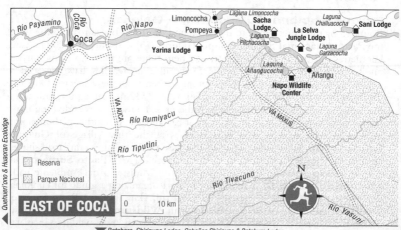

▼ *Bataboro, Shiripuno Lodge, Cabañas Shiripuno & Bataburo Lodge*

thousand people. Their territory acts as a buffer zone to the **Parque Nacional Yasuní**, Ecuador's largest national park, protecting a number of habitats and an extraordinary wealth of flora and fauna.

Since Coca became more accessible in the 1970s, this wild part of the eastern Oriente has been one of the country's top natural attractions, and also the location of several of the best **jungle lodges** (see box, pp.302–303), which provide the most comfortable way of experiencing the rainforest here. Many of them have an observation tower – a high vantage point to see life in the jungle canopy that's all but invisible from the ground – and own private reserves close to much larger national parks. A number of less expensive **jungle-tour operators** (see boxes on pp.276–277 & p.298) also run trips down the Río Napo from Coca, some using their own basic accommodation, others making do with tents and campsites. **Añangu**, three hours' drive east from Coca, on the edge of the Parque Nacional Yasuní, is one of the few indigenous communities along the lower Napo that has developed its own ecotourism programme.

Pompeya and Limoncocha

Taking a motorized canoe 33km (1hr 30min) downstream from Coca will bring you to the tiny settlement of **Pompeya**, barely visible from the river – unlike the heap of unsightly, rusting containers dumped by the oil industry. At the eastern edge of the settlement are the sparkling whitewashed buildings of the Misión Capuchina, where there's a good collection of ceramics and pre-Columbian objects from the Oriente in their **Museo de Cicame**. It doesn't get many visitors, so if you want to see it ask your tour guide for a quick stop there on the way to or from your destination. Walking west from the mission brings you to Pompeya's **market** area, active on Saturday mornings, when communities from along the Napo bring their home produce and jungle meat up for sale while other stalls sell clothes, gas and beer.

About a thirty-minute drive north on the bumpy road from Pompeya is the pleasant village of **LIMONCOCHA**, where neat cabins are set at regular intervals, some bordered by trimmed hedges and carefully tended lawns. Just a short walk from the village is the **Reserva Biológica Limoncocha**, conserving 46 square kilometres of rainforest and swamps around the light-green waters of **Laguna Limoncocha**. The lake used to be a good place for

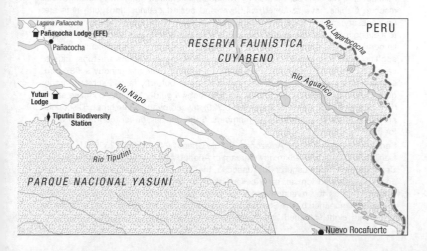

spotting caiman, but when Occidental Petroleum developed five oil fields near here in 1992, the blasting and drilling badly disturbed wildlife populations. Pressure from local groups, particularly the Secoya, has tempered oil exploitation here, allowing a formidable diversity of bird species to re-establish themselves; more than 460 species have been recorded, including several endemics such as the Martín kingfisher. The reserve's other lake, the black-water **Laguna Yanacocha**, lying to the east and enveloped in vegetation, is steeped in local myth and is rumoured to be home to especially large anacondas.

Practicalities

Many local families happily accept visitors into their homes and there are some old community-owned tourist cabañas in the reserve that may soon be rehabilitated; either way, for a **place to stay**, drop-ins should be accommodated.

Several **buses** and *rancheras* service Limoncocha from the town of Shushufindi, about 1 hour 30 minutes away (see p.295), itself easily accessible from either Lago Agrio or Coca. Of these, only three *rancheras* continue on to Pompeya, returning immediately, roughly corresponding to the working day at 6am, noon and 4pm. From Coca it's much faster to get to Pompeya by motorized canoe, but availability can be a problem.

Lodges on the lower Río Napo

These **lodges on the lower Río Napo** are reached by a motor-canoe ride from **Coca** (included in the price), and are usually visited in stays of four or five days, by prior reservation from home or Quito, where most have an office; prices quoted do not include bus or air transport to and from Coca. The lodges listed below are marked on the map on pp.300–301. All prices listed are per person.

Napo Wildlife Center see "Añangu" opposite.

Pañacocha Lodge No-frills, rustic lodge (no electricity and basic latrines) on the Río Pañayacu five hours downstream from Coca off the Río Napo. Bookings and tours with Emerald Forest Expeditions in Coca (see p.298).

Sacha Lodge Julio Zaldumbide 397 and Valladolid, Quito ☎02/2509504, 2508872 or US toll-free ☎1-800/706-2215, ⓦwww.sachalodge.com. One of Ecuador's most luxurious jungle lodges, 80km from Coca on the marshy fringes of Pilchacocha, *Sacha* is surrounded by 13 square kilometres of its own primary forest reserve. Cabins have screened windows and sealed ceilings (mosquito nets are unnecessary), private bath, ceiling fans, verandas with hammocks and are connected to a dining room and observation deck. There's 24-hour hot water and electricity, plus laundry facilities. Activities include well-marked trails of varying difficulty, wildlife spotting from a stunning 275-metre canopy walkway above the treetops, plus a canoe trip to a 43-metre observation tower soaring over the canopy – 587 bird species have been seen. There are also tours of its butterfly farm. Each tour group gets its own English-speaking naturalist and Kichwa guide. You can combine stays here with trips to *La Casa del Suizo* (see p.320), owned by the same group. Discounts are available for children and SAE members. $690 per person for four days or $870 for five days.

Sani Lodge Roca 736 and Amazonas, Pasaje Chantilly, Quito ☎02/2558881, ⓦwww.sanilodge.com. About 48km downstream of Añangu and four hours' canoe ride from Coca, on the remote Laguna Challuacocha, the *Sani Lodge* is set in 40,000 acres of community-owned forests, an excellent place to spot some 550 bird species and wildlife such as the manatee and large black caiman that inhabit the lake. Built, owned and managed by the Sani Isla Kichwa community, it's a small and comfortable lodge with eight screened and thatched cabins, each with private bathroom and

Añangu

The Kichwa community of **AÑANGU**, on the south shore of the Napo, about 66km downstream of Coca, has access to two stunning natural resources. Inside the northern reaches of the Parque Nacional Yasuní and only an hour's walk west from the community, **Laguna Añangucocha** is one of the largest lakes in the region. It's bordered by dense forest, where peccaries and pumas forage and the waters twitch with caimans, piranhas and *paiche*, a fish that reputedly nudges the 200-pund mark (though there are rumours some weigh twice as much). The area is also excellent for birdwatchers, holding 560 species and two **parrot licks** (an exposed clay bank) near the community. The licks provide an extraordinary spectacle as thousands of parrots squabble over the best perches to peck at and gulp down the clay, the mineral-rich content of which helps them digest the harsh acidic fruits they usually eat.

The community has its own **lodge**, the ⚘ *Napo Wildlife Center* (reservations in advance in Quito on ☎02/2528261, ⓦwww.napowildlifecenter.com), composed of ten beautiful and spacious cabins on Añangucocha, with private bathrooms, hot water, electric lights and hammocks on porches overlooking the lake. Next to the dining room, a 36-metre observation tower allows you to scan

solar-power hot showers, and a bar and dining room overlooking Challuacocha. A thirty-metre observation tower provides a fantastic view of the canopy and there are a number of trails accessing to different lacustrine ecosystems, which you can visit with a local expert as well as a multilingual naturalist. Rates are $510 per person for four days and $680 for five days. Profits are reinvested in community projects.

La Selva Jungle Lodge Mariana de Jesus 211 and Prada, Quito ☎02/2550995 or 2232730, ⓦwww.laselvajunglelodge.com. Award-winning lodge about 100km downstream from Coca and 10km past *Sacha Lodge*, offfering simple cabins with kerosene lamps, mosquito nets, private bath with cold water and excellent food. It's a good area for wildlife and birding; excursions include night walks, caiman-watching, kayak journeys (unaccompanied is also possible), trips to a 45-metre observation tower and many possible hikes, one of which goes to a specially prepared campsite with tents, mattresses and sheets. Its butterfly farm produces specimens for export, plus the Neotropical Field Biology Institute here means there are working scientists *in situ*. $717 per person for four days, $852 for five days.

Yarina Lodge Amazonas N24-240 and Colón, Quito ☎02/2503223 or 2545179, ⓦwww.yarinalodge.com. Only an hour from Coca, so you're less likely to spot the variety of wildlife here other remoter lodges boast. Still, there is *tierra firme* (forest on well-drained soil) nearby and they do have a seasonally flooded and some primary forest with a range of trails to explore with Kichwa guides, as well as opportunities for canoe trips along the Río Manduro to Laguna Sapococha, where monkeys are often seen. Rooms include private bath and hot water, and the price is more affordable than most; four days for $320 per person.

Yuturi Lodge Amazonas N24-240 and Colón, Quito ☎02/2504037 or 09/9935322, ⓦwww.yuturilodge.com. At 180km (5hr) from Coca, these simple cabins (mosquito nets are a necessity) are on a small hill surrounded by a lake on one of the Napo's tributaries. The surrounding forest is on loan from local Kichwa, who help with guiding. German and English-speaking guides are available, but knowing some Spanish makes tours more rewarding. Possible excursions include trips to Huarmi Yuturi, canoe expeditions to Manduro Lagoon and visits to Kichwa families. Four days cost around $360 per person, while five days cost $460 per person.

the forest canopy with binoculars for monkeys and bird species. Highlights of a stay here include possible sightings of giant otters; walks down the "manakin trail" where six species of manakin can be spotted; and visits to the parrot licks, where hides (blinds) have been built for better observation of the blue-headed and orange-cheeked parrots, cobalt-winged parakeets, scarlet-fronted parrotlets and scarlet macaws that feed there in a frenzy of sound and colour. Extremely knowledgeable local guides (who also work as Yasuní park rangers) backed up by bilingual naturalists, lead jungle walks and canoe rides. A three-night package costs $720, while four nights is $920 per person in a double, including boat transport from Coca and park entrance fees.

Pañacocha

Travelling roughly 100km, or five hours, downstream of Coca and then doubling back for a few more kilometres northwest and upstream along the Río Pañayacu, brings you to the brooding waters of **PAÑACOCHA** ("piranha lake" in Kichwa), the centrepiece of a 560-square-kilometre protected forest created in 1994, connecting the enormous Yasuní and Cuyabeno reserves on either side. From the lake, several coiling waterways retreat into thick primary rainforest, where ocelots, jaguars, nine species of monkey and over five hundred bird species can be seen. As well as the eponymous **piranha** – which are unnervingly easy to catch in the murky waters – the rivers are home to beautiful, rosy-pink freshwater dolphins. Although the area has remained relatively untouched, the new protected forest has no government resources or management plan, leaving it vulnerable to exploitation and damage; there are reports an oil company has built illegal seismic exploration lines within the protected area.

Emerald Forest Expeditions run tours to their rustic **lodge** on the Pañayacu, a little downstream of Pañacocha, see box, p.298 for details.

Parque Nacional Yasuní

Parque Nacional Yasuní ($10, plus $3 per day for camping) encompasses just under 10,000 square kilometres of tropical rainforest around the basins of the ríos Tiputini, Yasuní, Nashiño and Curaray. The gap at the western end, in the shape of a giant horseshoe, was made into **Reserva Waorani** in 1990 for the 21 Waorani communities living here; it is effectively a 6000-square-kilometre buffer zone preventing colonization and oil exploitation from the west.

Yasuní is part of the "Napo Pleistocene refuge", an area of rainforest thought to have survived the ravages of the ice age, allowing species here to thrive and diversify, generating scores of endemic species. It's theorized that this long period of development is why the Amazon rainforest is much more biodiverse than its African and Asian counterparts, which the ice age affected. Yasuní claims almost sixty percent of Ecuador's **mammal species**, including 81 species of bat, larger animals such as jaguars, ocelots, tapirs, twelve primate species and aquatic mammals including pink freshwater dolphins, manatee and giant otters. Over 520 **bird species** have been recorded, including harpy eagles and sunbitterns, and one recent botanical study found 473 **tree species** in only one hectare, which is thought to be a world record. Most of the park consists of forest on well-drained soil (*tierra firme*), but other life zones include **seasonally flooded forest** (*várzea*) and permanently flooded **swamp forest** (*igapó*). Scientists today believe they've only scratched the surface of identifying all life here.

UNESCO was quick to declare Yasuní an International Biosphere Reserve in 1979 – two months prior to the park's official creation – to strengthen its protected status before **oil companies** could start prospecting. Despite this, the park is under attack from several of them and roads have already been built into protected areas. At Pompeya (see p.301), barges ferry oil vehicles across the Río Napo to a gravel road, known as the **Vía Maxus** after the oil company that built it, which cuts right through the northern arm of the park for 150km. Entrance to the park here is monitored to allow access only to oil workers and members of the three small **Waorani communities** who live inside Yasuní, preventing settlers from colonizing the forest. Even so, environmentalists complain the road destroyed fifty saltpans, disturbed centres of animal activity and was built of contaminated waste materials. Nor is this the only concern: as many as five oil companies are operating inside the park, and the threat of new roads, waste dumping, destruction and contamination is never very far away. The **damage** hasn't only been environmental; Waorani living in and around the reserve have persistently suffered from malicious interference, as some oil companies continue to exploit community divisions, bribe leaders, spoil hunting grounds and pollute water supplies.

Visiting the park

Although a national park, Yasuní is an inaccessible tract of rainforest that remains relatively unexplored. Visiting independently is not recommended, as it's costly, potentially damaging and dangerous. Three Waorani groups, the **Tagaeri**, **Taromenane** and **Oñamenane**, have rejected all contact with the outside world and are understandably hostile to the uninvited. Several operators arrange adventure tours into the park (see boxes on pp.276–277 & p.298); if your tour is going into Waorani territory, it's important the operator has **full permission** from the community concerned to do so and is making a satisfactory contribution to it. Day-trips are sometimes offered from nearby *Sacha* or *La Selva* jungle lodges (see box, pp.302–303), and it is also possible to **stay inside the park** at

---

Lodges in the Reserva Waorani

Note that an additional $20 community donation (to the Waorani) must be paid to stay in the following lodges. The following prices are per person.

Bataburo Lodge Operated by Kem Pery Tours in partnership with the Waorani (see p.305). Wood-and-thatch cabins on the Río Tigüino with mosquito nets, shared bathrooms (private bathrooms available at extra cost), limited electricity and an observation tower. Reached by a bus ride from Coca (3–4hr) followed by a motorized canoe ride (3–4hr) down the Río Tigüino. Four days costs $310.

Huaorani Ecolodge 2nd floor, La Niña E7-46 and Reina Victoria, Quito ☎02/2234594, ⓦ www.huaorani.com. Small, Huaorani-run lodge consisting of five comfortable, screened palm-thatched cabins with porches and private bathrooms on the Río Shiripuno, reached on a five-seater chartered plane from Shell. Learn about the Huaorani culture while hiking through the forest searching for peccaries, learning to use a blowgun or paddling down rivers in a dugout canoe. Offers four- to six-day programmes at $150 per day, including accommodation and full board. Return transport from Quito an extra $250 per person.

Shiripuno Lodge Baron de Carondelet OE3-126 and Veracruz ☎02/2271094, ⓦ www.shiripunolodge.com. Eight simple, thatched cabins with private bathrooms on the Río Shiripuno, reached by bus (3hr) then motor canoe (4hr) from Coca. Hikes, piranha-fishing, butterfly-watching, trips to a salt lick and Huaorani community visits are all on offer, as well as outstanding birding opportunities. There's no electricity on site, with all lighting provided by candles. Tours cost $90–130 per day, including accommodation, meals and transport from Coca. Adjacent, and managed by the same outfit, is the Shiripuno Research Station (ⓦ www.shiripunoresearch.org), which coordinates research on local wildlife projects and welcomes volunteers.

the *Napo Wildlife Center* near Añangu (see p.303), in its northwestern reaches. Alternatively, there are several options (see box, p.305) for staying in the Reserva Waorani, outside the park proper but sharing the same biodiversity.

You might also try the **Tiputini Biodiversity Station** (through the Universidad San Francisco de Quito in the capital ☏02/2971961, ⓦhttp://192.188.53.69/tiputini), built primarily for research, education and conservation, but open to visitors with plenty of advance notice. Located in primary forest on the Río Tiputini at the northern fringes of the park, it is reputed to be one of the best places in the Oriente to see wildlife (especially monkeys), as the area has largely escaped interference. See their website (in English) for more information.

Nuevo Rocafuerte and crossing to Peru

Around ten hours downstream of Coca, **NUEVO ROCAFUERTE** is about as far as you can go along the Río Napo before the Peruvian border. It's a small town of limited resources with a clear police and military presence. It has a couple of cheap, basic **hotels**, back from the river a few blocks past the military checkpoint, with unreliable electricity and water, and a couple of uninspiring restaurants. The only reason you're likely to come here is if you're travelling between Ecuador and **Peru**, a crossing made possible by the improved relations between the countries. A couple of **agencies** and guides (see p.298) offer the trip from Coca to Iquitos, in Peru, among their itineraries, which helps take the pain and uncertainty out of what can be a difficult and time-consuming journey. Otherwise, you can take the **riverboat** from Coca to Nuevo Rocafuerte (Tues & Thurs; 10–12hr; $12), and then arrange onward travel yourself (see p.306). The river journey takes at least five relatively uncomfortable – but exciting – days, and at the moment is not particularly well established for tourists. Before you attempt this route, you must check border conditions and requirements with the Jefetura Provincial de Migración in Coca (on Napo opposite *El Auca*). For more information on the boat from Coca, see "Listings", p.298.

Practicalities of the crossing

You'll need to get your **passport stamped** at the Policía Nacional in Nuevo Rocafuerte before heading into Peru.

From Nuevo Rocafuerte, you'll need to charter a **boat** across the border to **Pantoja** in Peru (2hr–2hr 30min; around $70 flat rate for the boat), where you get an **entry stamp** and find a cheap **place to stay** (basically, spare rooms in people's homes). From Pantoja, boats leave for Iquitos, sometimes regularly, but sometimes up to ten days apart; since there are no fixed schedules, you should allow for plenty of time in your itinerary. Deck space is cramped and often shared with animals; you'll be sleeping in a hammock that you may need to purchase beforehand. It's not a bad idea to bring spare food, means to purify water, eating utensils, toilet paper and plenty of insect repellent. It's a four-day journey (around $40) if you get off at **Mazán** and take a motor-taxi short-cut across a huge river bend, followed by another two-hour boat trip (around $5) to **Iquitos**; staying on the Pantoja boat and navigating the bend will add thirteen hours (effectively another day) to your journey. Iquitos is a major Amazon town – and the largest city in the world that cannot be reached by road – with plenty of hotels, restaurants and tourist facilities, as well as onward transport by boat or air. Those coming **into Ecuador** at Nuevo Rocafuerte can pick up the boat returning to **Coca** on Thursday and Sunday mornings (departs around 5am, 12hr; contact the Capitanía in Nuevo Rocafuerte on ☏06/2382169 for information).

Tena

TENA (500m), the Oriente's largest and most important town for the best part of the last hundred years, is also by far the most agreeable of the region's three big towns, with plenty for visitors to see and do.

This is one of the best centres for **community ecotourism** in the Oriente, where you can easily arrange a stay with local Kichwa families, mostly in nearby villages easily reached by road or river. Tena sits at the head of the Napo basin, where a huge number of tributaries converge to produce a cluster of river rapids, waterfalls, mountain streams, and sand and pebble beaches, allowing for a host of

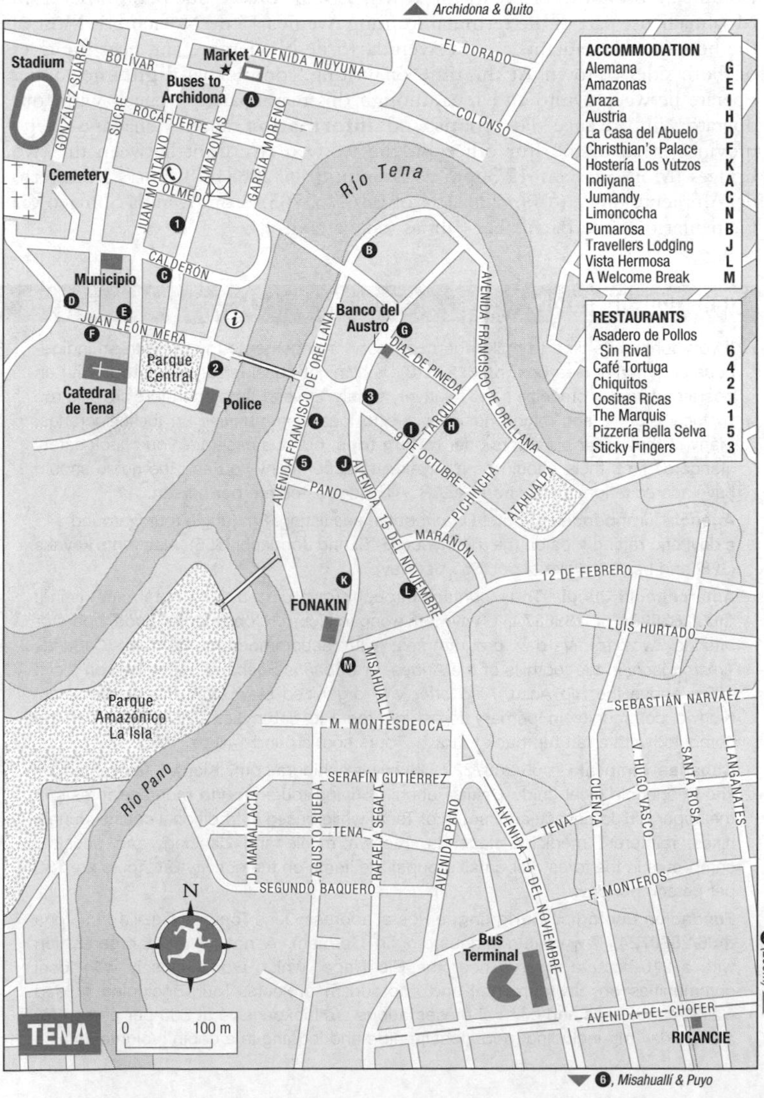

Archidona & Quito
ACCOMMODATION
Alemana G
Amazonas E
Araza I
Austria H
La Casa del Abuelo D
Christhian's Palace F
Hostería Los Yutzos K
Indiyana A
Jumandy C
Limoncocha N
Pumarosa B
Travellers Lodging J
Vista Hermosa L
A Welcome Break M
RESTAURANTS
Asadero de Pollos Sin Rival 6
Café Tortuga 4
Chiquitos 2
Cositas Ricas J
The Marquis 1
Pizzería Bella Selva 5
Sticky Fingers 3
Stadium
Market
Buses to Archidona
Cemetery
Municipio
Parque Central
Catedral de Tena
Police
Banco del Austro
FONAKIN
Parque Amazónico La Isla
Bus Terminal
RICANCIE
Río Tena
Río Pano
Bolívar
Avenida Muyuna
El Dorado
Colonso
Gonzalez Suarez
Sucre
Rocafuerte
Amazonas
García Moreno
Juan Montalvo
Olmedo
Calderón
Juan León Mera
Avenida Francisco de Orellana
Díaz de Pineda
Tarqui
9 de Octubre
Pichincha
Atahualpa
Pano
Avenida 15 del Noviembre
Marañón
12 de Febrero
Luis Hurtado
Misahuallí
Sebastián Narváez
M. Montesdeoca
Serafín Gutiérrez
D. Mamallacta
Agusto Rueda
Rafaela Segala
Tena
Avenida Pano
Cuenca
V. Hugo Vasco
Santa Rosa
Llanganates
Segundo Baquero
F. Monteros
Avenida del Chofer
N
TENA
0 100 m
N (200m)
6, Misahuallí & Puyo

aquatic activities. A tour from Tena is bound to involve at least one of swimming, climbing up brooks, bathing in waterfalls or tubing, not to mention **whitewater rafting** and **kayaking**, for which the town is rapidly becoming internationally famous, thanks to the scores of runs, from Class I to Class V, all within easy striking distance. A sizeable kayaking contingent already comes to Tena during the northern hemisphere's off season in December and January.

Arrival and information

The bus terminal, 1km south of the centre, is where all **long-distance buses** stop except those from Archidona, which arrive at the corner of Amazonas and Bolívar in the northern part of town. **Local buses**, such as those from Misahuallí, use part of the terminal fronting Avenida 15 de Noviembre. Most of the hotels and restaurants are on Avenida 15 de Noviembre and near the river on both sides of town. At the time of writing, commercial **flights** no longer operate between Quito and Tena, though this may change – check with tour operators in advance. For **maps** and **information** about Tena and Napo province, head to the Itur office on the western riverfront between the two bridges (Mon–Fri 8am–12.30pm & 2–5pm; ☎06/2888100). Tena's Ministerio del Ambiente office (☎06/2887154 or 08/4763765) is on Avenida Sumaco Vía Cementario in the Barrio Las Palmas (take a taxi).

Tena tour operators

If you don't have time to make the necessary arrangements to stay with an indigenous community (see box, pp.312–313), you might consider a **jungle tour** with an operator who can organize a trip relatively swiftly. Several Tena operators are also run by local Kichwa and might include visits to local communities on their itineraries. Many of these tour operators offer **rafting trips**, but it is essential you check safety standards first; there should be a kayaker to accompany you and the guide should have accreditation, ideally from AGAR. All prices listed are per person.

Agencia Limoncocha at hotel *Limoncocha*, see listing. For jungle tours (around $45 a day) and rafting trips on the Jatunyacu ($40) and Jondachi ($55). Also rents kayaks ($28) and has a kayak school ($55 per day).

Amarongachi Jungle Trips contact through *Travellers Lodging* hotel, see listing; ☎06/2888204 or 2886372, ⑩www.amarongachi.com. Consistently good operator offering two- to five-day programmes, with accommodation at their *Cabañas Amarongachi* in the foothills of the Andes, or *Cabañas Shangri La*, perched on a cliff 100m above the Río Anzu. Also offer well-organized stays with the Amarongachi Kichwa community in primary forest on the Río Jatunyacu. Visits here can be combined with a raft trip back to town. Tours cost around $40 per day.

Cabañas Pimpilala ☎06/2887322, ⑩www.sinchipura.com. Kichwa family, led by knowledgeable local guide Delfín Pauchi, running tours around montane forests in the upper Río Jatunyacu area south of Tena, while based in traditional cabins. Jungle hikes, rainforest medicine, legends, Kichwa music and dancing, and possible camp-outs in the forest (for small groups) are items on the activity list. Tours are $35 per person per day.

Fundación Ecológica Curiquingue Postal address: Jens Töniges, Casilla 111, Tena ☎06/2870724, ⑩www.curiquingue.org (in German). A not-for-profit organization with a 210-hectare reserve near the Río Napo, which works closely with local communities on environmental and ecotourism projects. Tours including guided walks, canoe trips and cultural presentations are inexpensive at $60 per person for a three-day trip including food, (local) guide and lodging in a cabin. Volunteers also

Tena isn't a large town and it's easy enough to get around on foot; walking from the central park in the north to the bus terminal in the far south shouldn't take more than twenty minutes. White pick-up trucks operate as the town's **taxis** and will take you to any in-town destination for a fixed price of $1.

Accommodation

Tena offers a far greater choice of decent **places to stay** than any other town in the northern Oriente, with a number of good-value hotels offering such luxuries as hot water, cable TV and air conditioning. With the exception of the budget hotels, most places include breakfast.

Alemana Av 15 de Noviembre 210 and Diaz de Pineda ☎06/8286409. Deckchairs and chirping insects line a plant-filled courtyard, and although rooms are on the dark side each has private bath and are regularly sprayed for bugs; those with electric showers, cable TV and fan cost double but are still inexpensive. Go for a room away from the road. ❸
Amazonas Juan Montalvo and Juan León Mera ☎06/2886439. A place to consider if you're watching the pennies; unlike most of its

bottom-dollar rivals it's reasonably quiet, adequately clean and has fair-sized rooms. ❶
Araza 9 de Octubre 277 ☎06/2886447, ⓦwww .hostal-araza.com. A little sterile, but the rooms are comfortable and come with cable TV, private bath, good hot water and a/c, while more expensive suites (❹) come with desk and fridge. Also boasts a car park and laundry service. ❸
Austria Tarqui and Diaz de Pineda ☎06/2887205. Convenient yet quiet location with clean and

welcome for ecological and environmental work, minimum three weeks ($280 contribution per month).
Runa Ñambi Juan León Mera 628 and Calderón ☎06/2888926 or 2886318, ⓕ06/2888926. Very flexible jungle, rafting and kayaking trips, and jungle tours to the Runa Huasi community or one of several lodges. Costs $12–40 per person depending on itinerary and group size.
Sacharicsina Tour Montesdeoca 110 and 15 de Noviembre ☎06/2886839, ⓦhttp:// mitglied.lycos.de/sacharicsina. Run by a Kichwa family who have some rustic cabañas on the Río Illoculín, southwest of Tena, and other lodging near Misahuallí on the Río Puni. Horseriding, waterfalls and jungle walks are on the agenda for $30–40 per day.

Whitewater rafting specialists
AquaXtreme Avenida Francisco de Orellana, near the entrance to the Parque Amazónico La Isla ☎06/2888746 or 09/3115246, ⓦwww.axtours.com. Whitewater trips offered on the rivers Anzu ($50), Jatunyacu ($55), Misahuallí ($70), Pastaza ($60) and Upano ($320 for 4 days), and canyoning trips from $40 that include transport, lunch, and equipment.
Ríos Ecuador Tarqui 230 y Diaz de Pinera ☎06/2886727, ⓦwww.riosecuador .com. Part of the well-established Yacu Amu Rafting stable, offering rafting and kayaking trips on the Jatunyacu, Misahuallí, Jondachi, and Anzu rivers. Expect to pay $60–85 per day.
River People Avenida 15 de Noviembre and 9 Octubre, opposite the footbridge ☎06/2887887 or 2888349, ⓦwww.riverpeopleraftingecuador.com. Professional English-run outfit with good guides, offering a range of river-based tours including 1- to 14-day kayak trips; rafting on the Jatunyacu, Blanco, Toachi, Hollín, Misahuallí and Quijos rivers ($50–70 including good picnic lunch); kayaking schools; and a combined rafting and jungle tour to their cabins at the confluence of the Jatunyacu and Illoculín rivers near the Parque Nacional Llanganates.

spacious rooms with cable TV, private bath and hot water, set around a pleasant courtyard. ❹

La Casa del Abuelo Juan León Mera and Olmedo ☎06/2888926, ⓦwww.tomas-lodge.com. Well-designed rooms with cable TV, private bath, hot water, comfortable beds, wi-fi and patio, in a mock-rustic building of stone and wood; some rooms have a/c. Also runs an attractive cabaña complex (*Establo de Tomás*) 4km outside Tena on the Río Lupi, by a forest and lagoon that are good for birdwatching. ❹

Cristhian's Place Juan León Mera and Sucre ☎06/2886047. Mammoth five-storey hotel kitted out in gaudy granite tiles, with functional rooms equipped with cable TV, private bath, hot water and a/c. The main attraction is the spa with jacuzzi, pool, gym, sauna and steam room (visitors can use for $4). Cheaper interior rooms (❺) are available which do not include breakfast or access to the spa. ❼

Indiyana Bolívar and Amazonas ☎06/2886334. A friendly and well-presented, family-run hotel offering a handful of big, light rooms with polished wooden floors, cable TV, private bath, hot water, laundry service and garage. Breakfast costs extra. ❹

Jumandy Calderón 309 and Amazonas, no phone. Very cheap *residencial* featuring a pretty communal balcony and potted plants that go some way to make up for the noisy location, grubby walls, cramped rooms and thin mattresses. ❶

Limoncocha Sangay 533, about 300m east of the bus terminal, off Av del Chofer ☎06/2887583, ⓦhttp://limoncocha.tripod.com. Inexpensive German–Ecuadorian family hostel on a hillrise, with a pleasant view over town. The best rooms have fan, cable TV and electric shower. Amenities include kitchen and internet facilities, while jungle and rafting tours are also on offer. ❷

Hostería Los Yutzos Agusto Rueda 190 and Av 15 de Noviembre ☎06/2886717 or 2886769, ⓦwww .geocities.com/losyutzos. Tena's best hotel, with a pretty, peaceful little garden overlooking the river. The rooms are smart and comfortable with hot water, cable TV, minibar, fans or a/c. Get a balcony if you can. ❻

Pumarosa Francisco de Orellana ☎06/2886320. A complex on the river with a volleyball court, bar, restaurant, gardens, games room and disco (can be noisy Fri & Sat). The rooms vary in size and some have a/c (❺). Accepts traveller's cheques. ❹

Travellers Lodging Av 15 de Noviembre 438 and 9 de Octubre ☎06/2886372. A good meeting place, complete with tour agency, a pizzeria, laundry service and rooms with cable TV and private bath. The top floors are best (and more expensive), not least for their reinforced anti-earthquake joists, hot water, fridges and city views. ❸

Vista Hermosa Av 15 de Noviembre 622 and 12 de Febrero ☎06/2886521. As the name suggests, this *hostal* has fine views over the river from each of its open-air patios. All rooms come with fans and cable TV, but the best to be had are at the top. ❸

A Welcome Break Agusto Rueda and 12 de Febrero ☎06/2886301. Ten simple, lime-green rooms with little cane lamps and desks and shared bath, plus a dormitory with bunks. Cheap, considering use of a kitchen is thrown in. There's also a good little restaurant next door. ❷

The Town

Within sight of the Andean foothills and cooled off by its two rivers, Tena enjoys a slightly fresher climate than its oil-town rivals, Coca and Lago Agrio, and its longer, calmer history lends it a more established and civilized atmosphere. The **northern half** of Tena is the oldest part, with narrow streets, a modest cathedral fronting the central park, and the post and phone offices. It's also the quieter half, as most of the traffic is routed around it and over a bridge to the main thoroughfare, **Avenida 15 de Noviembre**, that divides the more sprawling southern half of the town. The bus terminal stands at the less attractive southern fringes of town, so don't be put off by first impressions.

Locals, a mixture of *mestizos* and Kichwas, often relax on the city's **river beaches** – strips of sand or pebbles at the water's edge – or amble around the pleasant **Parque Amazónico La Isla** (Mon–Sat 8.30am–5pm, Sun 8am–1pm; $2), reached by a wooden thatched-roofed footbridge over the Río Pano about 200m south of the main pedestrian bridge. It's not actually an island but the wooded tip of a patch of land at the confluence of the rivers. A high observation tower overlooks the treetops and town, and self-guided paths meander through botanical greenery past caged animals recovering from injury and abuse, to swimming spots along the river.

Eating, drinking and nightlife

Inexpensive **restaurants** abound in Tena, serving up the usual fried chicken or fish dishes for $2–4 a main course; if this is what you're after, try the popular *El Son Costeño*, inside a shopping arcade on Amazonas and Juan León Mera. In addition to the places listed below, the more expensive hotels are where you should look for anything more exciting. Most restaurants are open every day from breakfast to 9 or 10pm at night. Tena's favourite **disco** is *La Gallera* at *Hotel Pumarosa* (Fri & Sat), which blasts out Latin dance hits into the small hours on its dry-iced dancefloors. Alternatively, head down to the waterfront, where a string of little bars sometimes feature music and dancing.

Asadero de Pollos Sin Rival Av 15 de Noviembre and Sanmiguel, a block and a half south of the bus terminal. Straightforward restaurant where you'll find the best barbecued rotisserie chicken in town – *sin rival*.

Chuquitos García Moreno, near the footbridge. A popular choice for its excellent riverside position and good, reasonably priced food including steaks, tilapia, shrimp, chicken and vegetable dishes, plus less common numbers such as *guatita*, frogs' legs and kidneys.

Cositas Ricas Av 15 de Noviembre and 9 de Octubre. Part of *Travellers Lodging*, so it caters to a mainly international crowd, with hamburgers, pizzas and vegetarian dishes, plus the usual beef, chicken, pasta and fish *platos*. Weekday set menus are cheap.

The Marquis Amazonas and Olmedo. The classiest restaurant in town by some margin, for its wine glasses and starched table linen and napkins. It's run by a professional Colombian chef specializing in Latin American food, particularly steaks and *parrilladas*

(typical main courses go for $6–10), though vegetarian dishes can be cooked on request. French and Chilean wines are also available. Closed Sun.

Pizzería Bella Selva Av Francisco de Orellana ☎06/2887964. A good pizza parlour on the waterfront. Try the family-size pizza packed with ham, bacon, salami, mushrooms and a fried egg, or a more exotic one, topped with bananas. Takeaway service and free delivery within town.

Sticky Fingers Av 15 de Noviembre and 9 de Octubre. Coffee shop in the River People agency office, offering real coffee, cakes, muesli and yogurt breakfasts, along with crumbles, meat pies and other treats not normally found in jungle towns. Usually open Mon–Sat mornings when raft trips are in process.

Café Tortuga Av Francisco de Orellana. Attractive, Swiss-run riverside café doing the best breakfasts in Tena, real coffee, great deli sandwiches, salads, fresh juices and desserts. Closed Sun lunch and Mon after 11am.

Listings

Banks and exchange Banco del Austro, corner of Av 15 de Noviembre and Dias de Pineda, has a 24hr Visa ATM; Banco Pichincha, Amazonas 117 and Juan León Mera has an ATM. Amazon Money, Av 15 de Noviembre 422 and 9 de Octubre, 2nd floor above ice cream shop, cash traveller's cheques and change currency.

Festivals February 12 for provincialization and November 15 for the town's foundation, both of which involve drinking, dancing, the odd parade

and partying. Second weekend after New Year's Day is the Napo River Festival, a new event held to raise awareness of the importance of Ecuador's great river.

Internet Cheap, and at several places including CucupaNet on García Moreno by the footbridge and Compunet, Amazonas and Olmedo.

Post office Olmedo and García Moreno.

Telephone office Andinatel, on the corner of Olmedo and Juan Montalvo. Closed Sun.

Around Tena

Although Tena is most commonly used as a launching pad for jungle tours in the upper Napo region, there are a few places nearby you can visit independently. To the north of Tena, a trip to the colonial town of **Archidona** can be combined with a visit to the **Cavernas de Jumandy**, the most developed and easily accessed of many caves in the area, or one of the two local forest reserves, the Reserva Ecológica Monteverde or the

Indigenous-community stays around Tena

In addition to the conventional operators (see box, pp.308–309), Tena has a burgeoning number of **community ecotourism projects**, coordinated by RICANCIE (Red Indígena de Comunidades del Alto Napo para la Convencia Intercultural y el Ecoturismo) and driven largely by the region's politically active and environmentally aware Kichwa population. In most cases, the whole community is involved, from the building of simple tourist cabañas near the villages to the training of their guides. Tours typically include guided forest hikes, cultural exchanges through music, dance and narration, participation in a *minga* (shared community work), blowpipe competitions, swimming, tubing and canoeing, discussions on the use of medicinal plants and craftwork demonstrations.

RICANCIE programmes

Ricancie Avenida del Chofer and Hugo Vasco, Tena (☎06/2888479, ⓦwww.ricancie .nativeweb.org) This organization coordinates several community-based ecotourism enterprises based in the upper Napo region around Misahuallí and Ahuano. Accommodation is in fairly rustic cabañas usually equipped with shared showers and occasionally flushing toilets, but a few are still without running water. Circuits are available whereby you visit a series of neighbouring communities as part of one package, and prices are around $45 per person per day including food, lodging, transport from office in Tena, guides and excursions; shamanic ceremonies and an English translator cost around $30–35 extra, per group (make requests at least a week beforehand). Drop-ins usually cannot be accommodated and arrangements should be made a few days in advance.

Alukus A one-hour drive west from Tena, towards Parque Nacional Llanganates. The community offers hikes through the foothills of the Andes, where you can see numerous waterfalls, swim in pools and clamber over the massive boulders of the Río Jatun Yaku, amongst myriad butterflies.

Capirona On the Río Puni about 3km south of Misahuallí. One of the world's first community-based ecotourism projects, with well-marked trails through colourful *capirona* trees to a salt-lick cavern that is great for seeing nocturnal creatures. Every tour is treated to excellent cultural presentations of song, dance and the making of

Reserva El Parra. Beyond here, the scenery en route to Baeza (see p.284) concertinas into a range of forested gullies and ridges as you pass between two remote protected areas, the **Parque Nacional Sumaco Napo-Galeras** and the **Reserva Ecológica Antisana**.

Heading 7km south of Tena brings you to **Puerto Napo**, where there's a road bridge over the eponymous river. Two roads branch off the main highway to the east at this point, servicing either side of the upper Río Napo. Along the northern bank, one runs for 17km as far as the port of **Misahuallí**, the long-established embarkation point for tours of this region. On the southern shore, and joined by a bridge from Misahuallí, the other road passes several tourist cabañas, the **Estación Biológica Jatún Sacha** and, 28km down the line, the crossing point by boat over the river at **La Punta**, from where the road dribbles on for a couple of kilometres as far as **Ahuano**. Meanwhile, the southbound main road from Tena and Puerto Napo continues to Yuralpa where a French oil company has its operational base. A bridge and 7km of road are the only things missing to make the link from Puerto Napo to Coca, but the inevitable rise of the oil and lumber industries in the area means they won't be long in coming.

traditional crafts. Reservations are essential and should be made well in advance during high season.

Chuva Urcu South of Ahuano on the Río Gusano, reached by a drive from Tena, canoe trip and 3-hour hike. The community has built pleasant cabañas overlooking the river, and lead strenuous two-day hikes (bring a water purifier) to the top of the Chuva Urcu mountain ridge, where fantastic views make the trek worthwhile. Other activities include gold panning, basket weaving and spear fishing for catfish.

Huasila Talag About 12km southwest of Tena on the Río Talag. Located in the Andean foothills, this community offers mountain hikes in the nearby Cordillera de Huasila, excellent for birdwatching, butterflies, orchids, walks along the Jatunyacu and waterfalls. Explanations of medicinal plants are given.

Machacuyacu 15km east of Tena, north of the Río Napo. Machacuyacu community members lead hikes through this landscape of elevated ground dotted with viewpoints over the Napo valley, as well as to caves steeped in myth. Demonstrations include the use of a blowgun, hunting and fishing techniques and typical dance and song.

Río Blanco North of the Río Napo and Ahuano, reached by a two-hour uphill hike. Well-established enterprise offering attractive cabañas in a peaceful setting twenty minutes' walk from the community. The typical four-day programme here includes guided hikes in the beautiful Cordillera Galeras and cultural presentations, but a highlight is the medicinal plant garden tended by an expert shaman, who can explain the uses of over four hundred species.

Runa Huasi On the Río Arajuno, near Ahuano. Easily reached from Tena, this community has prettily decorated cabañas a ten-minute walk from AmaZOOnico (see p.321), an excellent animal rehabilitation centre, which is visited during a stay. Hikes are also offered in local primary forest to a fossil lake, and lessons are given on medicinal plants.

Pacto Sumaco A 3 hour 30 minutes drive northeasat from Tena takes you to the little community of Pacto Sumaco (see p.299), where local guides will take you hiking through Parque Nacional Sumaco Napo-Galeras (see p.299), with its abundant birdlife. You can also arrange to hike to the summit of Volcán Sumaco, camping in refuges.

Archidona and around

ARCHIDONA, a well-kept town that sits in cultivated fields in the hills 10km north of Tena, was the first capital of the Oriente until 1920, when control shifted to Tena with the formation of the new (and now defunct) Napo–Pastaza province. Since its foundation in 1560, missionaries have ensured the place has stayed shipshape and the **church** is a case in point, its rude concrete blocks painted layer by layer in brown, white and yellow like a Lego building. Apart from gawping at the church and wandering around the pleasant central square, Archidona won't keep you occupied for very long. Not far from the town are a number of caves and petroglyphs including the Cavernas de Jumandy and dozens of carved boulders in the fields around Cotundo (see box, p.314 for more details). Down a dirt track at the southern end of Archidona, you can also see a huge sacred stone carved with over eighty petroglyphs, thought to be over two thousand years old.

Cavernas de Jumandy

About 4km north of Archidona are the **Cavernas de Jumandy** (daily 9am–5pm; $2), the region's best-known system of caves. Named after the indigenous general who was supposed to have hidden here before leading an uprising against the Spanish in 1578, the caves have long been venerated by local Kichwa communities. Today, they're part of a gaudy tourist complex with swimming pool, garish plastic waterslides, a few caged animals, a restaurant and **cabins** (T06/2889185; ❷), making it altogether less of a spiritual experience. Still, the caves themselves are worth a look, as their dripping bat-clung passages extend for several kilometres underground. The main cave near the entrance is lit, but guides from reception can lead you on longer tours into the dark recesses, across pools of chilly water (for which you'll need your swimming gear) to deep plunge holes. The guide will have a torch, though it's a good idea to take your own, so long as you can master swimming and holding it at the same time. To get to the caves, take one of the regular **buses** (from the top of the main street in Archidona, where it intersects with Jondachi) towards Cotundo and ask the driver to drop you off at *las cavernas*; a **taxi** from Archidona costs around $2.

Local reserves

Archidona is also close to a pair of small private reserves. The **Reserva Ecológica Monteverde** ($2 entrance), 8km up the San Pablo road to the southeast of town, is a 60-acre reserve containing primary forest, hiking trails and places to swim and fish on the river. There are simple cabins (❺) with cold showers overlooking the Río Hollín; enquire at the *Residencial Regina* (T06/2889144) on Rocafuerte, north of the plaza in Archidona, or call T02/2891041 in Quito. Around 7km further along the same road, the **Reserva El Para** is slightly larger, with good birding. Taxis from Archidona charge about $6 to the Reserva Ecológica Monteverde and $10 to the Reserva El Para.

The **Izu Mangallpa Urcu Foundation** (T06/887487, Wwww .izu-mangallpa-urcu.freehomepage.com), run by the Mamallacta Alvarado family, protects sacred Kichwa lands on Galeras mountain. Visitors can stay in traditionally built cabañas, with bedding and mosquito nets, by the family farm 1km outside Archidona, beyond the village of Mariposa. For $40 a day

---

Caves and petroglyphs around Tena

While famed for the Cavernas de Jumandy (see p.313), the Tena region has many other less-visited **caves**, the majority of which are on private property meaning you'll need the owner's permission to visit them. The area is also littered with **petroglyphs**, rough but lyrical etchings of shapes, creatures and faces onto rocks and boulders, dating from several thousand years ago up until the sixteenth century. No one is exactly sure of their significance, but they are often found near waterways or on high ground, places of strategic and habitational importance. One of the best groupings, composed of at least sixty petroglyphs, is **Los Petroglifos del Valle Sagrado**, located on the hillside north of **Cotundo**, a village about 10km north of Archidona. The Fundación Sinchi Sacha (T06/2889044, in Quito 02/2230609, Wwww .sinchisacha.org) is developing a guidebook and an archeological park with trails around them; you can find out more information and hire a guide at their Centro de Turismo in Cotundo.

Anyone interested in **caving** should talk to Gabriel Guallo in Tena, who takes trips to the so-called "Grand Canyon" system near Mondayacu about 10km north of Archidona, as well as deep into the Cavernas de Jumandy. He's a good guide, but better on day-trips ($40) than more logistically difficult overnighters; contact him at Las Grutas de Gabriel, Abdón Calderón and Juan León Mera (T06/2887894 or 09/8839922).

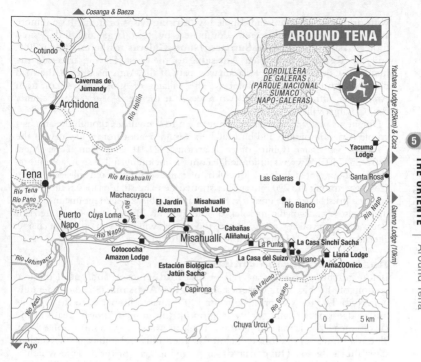

Cotundo

Cavernas de
Jumandy

Archidona

Río Hollín

CORDILLERA
DE GALERAS
(PARQUE NACIONAL
SUMACO
NAPO-GALERAS)

Yachana Lodge (25km) & Coca

Yacuma
Lodge

Tena

Río Misahuallí

Las Galeras

Santa Rosa

Río Tena
Río Pano

Machacuyacu

El Jardín
Aleman

Misahualli
Jungle Lodge

Río Blanco

Río Napo

Gareno Lodge (10km)

Puerto
Napo

Cuya Loma

Río Jatas

Río Napo

Cabañas
Aliñahui

Misahuallí

Cotococha
Amazon Lodge

La Punta

La Casa Sinchi Sacha

Río Jatunyacu

Estación Biológica
Jatún Sacha

La Casa del Suizo

Ahuano

Liana Lodge

AmaZOOnico

Río Arajuno

Capirona

Río Arajuno

Río Gusano

Río Anzu

0   5 km

Chuva Urcu

▼ Puyo

(all-inclusive) guests are treated to guided forest hikes, treks into Sumaco Napo-Galeras national park, talks about medicinal plants, weaving and handicraft demonstrations, traditional dances, myths, storytelling and talks on shamanism. To get there, take a taxi from Archidona for around $1.50.

Practicalities

Buses to Tena from Baeza or Coca pass through Archidona along the main road, so tell the driver if you want to be dropped off in town. Local buses from Tena to Archidona leave from the corner of Amazonas and Bolívar, stopping at the north end of this main street.

Most people stay in nearby Tena, which is far better geared to tourism, but there are a couple of decent **hotels** in Archidona should you want to make a base there. The *Palmar del Río Gran Hotel* on Napo and Transversal 13, south of the plaza (☎06/2889274; ❷), is a good-value choice for its clean tiled rooms, private bath and cable TV. A few kilometres south of Archidona, off the main road by the Río Inchillaquí, the European-run *Hacienda Hakuna Matata* (☎06/2889617, ⓦwww.hakunamat.com; ❼–❽) is set on a generous parcel of private land containing petroglyphs, sandy river beaches, swimming spots, a pool, comfortable screened cabins and a good **restaurant**. Horseriding, hiking and trekking in nearby jungle are also offered and the owners will pick you up for free from Archidona or Tena.

North of Archidona to Baeza

In the 65km from Archidona to Baeza, the road snakes its way up through a stunning landscape of increasingly compressed and precipitous hillcrests choked with dripping vegetation and dappled with rising wisps of steam. It's a remote and sparsely populated region, dominated by two large and little-visited protected areas, the **Parque Sumaco Napo-Galeras** to the east (see p.299), and the **Reserva Ecológica Antisana** to the west. Having traversed the luxuriant Cordillera de los Huacamayos, part of the Antisana reserve, the road descends from its highest point to the village of **Cosanga**, 47km from Archidona, sitting between the two reserves at the head of the green, cloudy Río Cosanga valley.

Despite its pretty location, there's not much to the village, though the area as a whole is rich in birdlife, and birdwatchers would benefit from a few days at the *Cabañas San Isidro* (Quito office, Carrión N21-01 and Juan León Mera ☏02/2547403, ⓦ www.sanisidrolodge.com; ❾ including full board), a comfortable, well-appointed **lodge** with 30km of trails, set in forested hills 3km from Cosanga. Among the 290 bird species spotted here are such rarities as the white-rimmed brush-finch, the greater scythebill and the black-billed mountain-toucan; there's also a cock-of-the-rock lek on the grounds. **Buses** from Quito, Tena or Baeza can drop you at Cosanga, where the owners will pick you up free of charge; alternatively, take a taxi directly to the lodge from Baeza for $15.

Reserva Ecológica Antisana

Before reaching Cosanga, the Tena–Baeza road winds in and out of the low section of the beautiful **Reserva Ecológica Antisana** ($5, though rarely collected). The reserve spreads out for 1200 square kilometres to the west, its knife-edge ridges rising steadily to prop up the unseen Andean peaks in the far distance – the icecapped summit of Volcán Antisana (5758m) among them. The road traverses the forested, cloud-daubed hills and gullies of the verdant **Cordillera de los Huacamayos**, an outlying arm of the reserve which is best accessed on the **Sendero de Jumandy**, once the footpath between Archidona and Baeza, but now the only trail into this remote area. Leaving

▲ Toucan, Yuturi Lodge

from the antennas at Km50, near the Virgen de los Huacamayos shrine, the stone path, only rehabilitated for 3km, ends at an oil duct, but the birding is excellent and scenery breathtaking. The **hike** there and back takes around two hours at a fast pace.

The Papallacta–Baeza road parallels the northern edge of the reserve, but the main road access into the **highland section** of Antisana – one of the best places in the country to see condors – is on its western side, via the village of Píntag about 30km southeast of Quito. This is also the route mountaineers attempting to climb **Volcán Antisana** take. It's not a technically difficult climb, but complicated and dangerous for frequent bad weather, lack of shelter and the series of crevasses on the approach; if you're climbing it, come fully equipped and acclimatized and hire an experienced mountaineering guide.

Misahuallí

For many years **MISAHUALLÍ**, a bustling little port at the confluence of the ríos Misahuallí and Napo, was *the* place in the Oriente in which to organize a jungle tour. The road linking Tena to Coca, completed in the late 1980s, changed that, slashing the port's commercial trade, while its surrounding forests were cleared or severely disturbed by settlers and oil prospecting. What primary forest remains in the upper Napo has shrunk to such an extent that larger animals, particularly mammals, have all but disappeared from the region. The oil industry continues to probe ever deeper into the east, opening up far remoter regions to visitors, where the big reserves protect thousands of acres of pristine rainforest and all its wildlife.

Luckily for Misahuallí, its lingering reputation as a good meeting point for arranging jungle trips at the drop of a hat has kept the port in business. With its constant trickle of tourists, almost every hotel, restaurant, craft shop and racketeer offers forays into the jungle, and the section of the Napo around here has more tourist **lodges** and cabañas than any other part of the river (see box, pp.320–321). Competition is fierce, keeping prices consistently low – another of the port's attractions for budget travellers – and the large number of **tour operators** (see box, p.318) offer similar activities and facilities, such as guided jungle hikes, swimming under waterfalls, gold panning and canoeing down rivers, with accommodation either at campsites or in simple cabins. English-speaking **guides** are pretty thin on the ground, so meeting them before you set out is always a good idea; check they have a Ministerio de Turismo-issued guiding licence and that they can produce written authorization from the community concerned if they plan to visit the Waorani. Tours to the remoter Cuyabeno or Yasuní reserves, the Río Tiputini or more distant rivers are more expensive and need to be at least four or five days long to be worthwhile. Before you leave Misahuallí by canoe you should register your **passport** at the Capitanía.

Having chosen your jungle trip, there's not a lot else to keep you busy in Misahuallí itself. You can take a dip in the river, or visit the Jardín de Mariposas, a **butterfly farm** (daily 9am–12.30pm & 2–5pm; $1.50) located a couple of blocks north of the square on Rivadeneira, where you can see over a dozen colourful species in the various stages of the lifecycle. Ask at the Ecoselva office (see p.318) for someone to lead you around the farm. Outside town, there's a good short hike up to some small **waterfalls** and **bathing pools** on the Río Latas, a favourite place for local children. Take a bus from the central square towards Puerto Napo and ask the driver to drop you off for "*las cascadas*", around 7km from Misahuallí. They'll leave you at the trailhead ($2.50 entrance fee); the biggest falls are about a ninety-minute hike away, but most people settle for the streams and pools along the way.

Misahuallí tour operators

Unless otherwise stated, prices for **tours** below are per person per day, but always make sure you know exactly what you're getting for your money (see also "Guided tours", p.280). The quality of the guides can vary enormously within a single outfit.

El Albergue Español At the hotel of the same name, ⓦ www.alberguespanol.com. Offers jungle, river and indigenous life tours (from $40) to their lodge (see *Cabañas Lodge El Albergue Español* p.318), which can include an ayahuasca shamanic ritual, and a six-day "Francisco de Orellana expedition" descending from Quito into the Amazon basin (from $250). Also owns the 800-hectare Reserva Jaguar, next to a locally protected forest, with good trails for guided hikes.

Ecoselva On the north side of the *parque central* ☏ 06/2890019, ✉ ecoselva@yahoo .es. Owner Pepe Tapia González speaks good English, leads tours (from $35) to the Río Arajuno, Cuyabeno and Yasuní and has a good knowledge of the jungle. He also welcomes volunteers to help work on his butterfly farm in town and to teach English in the local school (contribution $325 for one month minimum).

Viajes and Aventuras Amazonicas At *Hostal La Posada*, on the east side of the park ☏ 06/2890005 or 09/2098427. Several adventurous tours, often involving camping, such as one to San Francisco on the Río Indillama, south of the Río Napo. Cheaper tours explore areas closer to Misahuallí. From $35 per day; tubing also offered for $5–10.

Selva Verde Northwest corner of plaza ☏ 06/2890071. Ecuadorian-Kichwa specializing in community and ethnotourism, with trips to a Kichwa community on the Río Bueno, a Waorani community on the Shiripuno and to the *Churi Pacari* cabins on the Río Pusuno, as well as to local attractions, such as caves, waterfalls, AmaZOOnico or gold panning (all from $35). Longer tours to Cuyabeno and Iquitos are also available. The lead guide, Luis Zapata, speaks English, Spanish and Kichwa. They also run a charter boat service.

Teorumi José Antonio Santander and Guillermo Rivadeneyra ☏ 06/2890313 or 08/7016852, ✉ teorumi@yahoo.com. Owner Teodoro Rivadenayra, born in the nearby community of Shiripuno, is a Kichwa guide who studied biology in the UK at Leeds Univerity. With excellent English and a deep understanding of the region's natural history, his tours (1–10 days) include hiking through primary forest, visiting waterfalls, swimming and fishing. Longer tours (four days minimum), deeper into the rainforest, involve camping in tents. From $45 per day.

Arrival and information

Buses from the terminal in Tena arrive at Misahuallí's main square every 30–45 minutes (a 45min trip); the last bus back is at 6pm. If you're coming from Puyo, get off at Puerto Napo and wait at the north side of the bridge to pick up the bus from Tena. One daily Cooperativa Amazonas bus has a direct service from the terminal terrestre in Quito leaving at 11.30am, and returning from Misahuallí at 8.30am (7hr). Public **boat** services downstream from Misahuallí have been discontinued, but motorized canoes are available for **charter** down at the beach, though with typical rates at $15 for 30 minutes and $25 per hour, this is expensive unless you are in a group – just going to AmaZOOnico will set you back $70. Selva Verde tour operator runs charter services and accepts traveller's cheques with a ten percent service charge. Have your waterproofs and sun cream ready, bring something comfortable to sit on and wrap your gear up in plastic bags, as the boats are very low in the water and it can be choppy (if it rains, prepare to be soaked). You have to register your passport at the **Capitanía** (☏ 06/2890143), beyond the square towards the dock, before embarking. If you want to change **traveller's cheques**, you'll find the odd shop or tour agencies around the main square offering unfavourable rates, but you're better off going to Tena.

Accommodation

Accommodation in town is aimed at the budget traveller, though there are a few more luxurious places on the outskirts of town, as well as a number of jungle lodges in the vicinity (see box, pp.320–321). All of the hotels below have decent **restaurants**.

El Albergue Español Juan Arteaga ☎06/289004 or 08/4691271, ⓦwww.alberguespanol.com. The downstairs rooms are of the concrete-box mould, with private bath, hot water and fan, but those upstairs share an attractive wooden balcony and sitting area, along with commanding views of the Río Napo. Tours are offered to their cabañas and private reserve down the river. There's also laundry service, UV water purification and a restaurant. ❸

Centro Recreación Ecológico Misahuallí 50m before town on the main road ☎06/2890061. Large resort complex in a nine-hectare site at the entrance to town with either tiled en-suite rooms with hot water, fans and TV or cabañas a short walk away, which only have cold water, but cost the same. Local tours offered. ❸

France Amazonía 200m before town on the main road ☎06/2890009. One of the smarter accommodations available, offering very pleasant rooms with big-screened windows and private bath, set around a pretty garden and kidney-bean swimming pool. ❺

Marena Inn Juan Arteaga, next door to *El Albergue Español* ☎06/2890002. Rooms at this hotel are plain but contain fridges, private bath, TV and hot water. There's also a pool and the top-floor restaurant has attractive views. ❸

Misahuallí Jungle Lodge Ramírez Dávalos 332 and Páez, Quito ☎02/2520043,

ⓦwww.misahuallijungle.com. At the confluence of the Napo and Misahuallí rivers, just across the water from Misahuallí, this lodge consists of wooden cabins with private bath, fans, satellite TV, as well as hot water, a pool, games room and a restaurant all set in 145 hectares of steaming forest. Guided jungle hikes, including explanation of medicinal plants and forest survival techniques, and local tours are offered. ❽

El Paisano One block north of the square ☎06/2890027. Simple rooms with mosquito nets, a hammock and private bath with hot water, set around a pretty little cobbled garden with a restaurant, which offers vegetarian dishes and such cross-over curiosities as yuca omelette. ❷

La Posada East side of the square ☎06/2890005. Straightforward hotel featuring small, bright rooms with hot water and private bath. The restaurant has vegetarian food and is a nice place to watch the monkeys and vultures scrutinize the park for scraps. Tours offered. ❷

Shaw On the plaza above the *Eko Kafé* ☎06/2890019, ⓔecoselva@yahoo.es. Cheap and simple en-suite rooms with hot water overlooking the town park. The street-level café serves vegetarian food and organic coffee, and features a book exchange and craft store. Tours offered through Ecoselva (see p.318). ❷

Estación Biológica Jatún Sacha

Founded in 1986 with just two square kilometres of territory, the **Estación Biológica Jatún Sacha** ("big forest" in Kichwa) has grown into one of Ecuador's leading tropical field stations, protecting almost twenty square kilometres in its own private reserve. Located eight kilometres east of Misahuallí, the reserve is a luxuriant oasis in an area settlers and Kichwa people have cleared and cultivated since the 1970s; the rising poulation has put pressure on wildlife – mammals, in particular, have suffered badly from overhunting. Seventy percent of its land is undisturbed primary forest boasting an astounding degree of biodiversity. Crammed into its confines are 525 species of bird and 823 species of butterfly, alongside hundreds of different tree species.

Tourists are welcome to drop in for **day-visits** ($8), which should be enough time to walk the forest trails, including a very good **self-guided tour** on a well-labelled trail (guide available for $11). Occupying a transitional zone between the Andes and the lowlands proper, the terrain is quite hilly, cut up by creeks and

The **lodges around Misahuallí** are easier to get to than those on the lower Napo downstream of Coca and generally less expensive. Many have small pockets of primary forest attached, but in this more populated region there will be nothing like the vast virgin forests of the big reserves in the eastern Oriente. Even so, there are still plenty of birds and butterflies and dripping forest greenery. Lodges are marked on the map on p.315; prices quoted below include full board.

Cabañas Aliñahui Inglaterra 1373 and Amazonas, Edif. Centro Ejecutivo, 7th floor, Office 702, Quito ☎02/2274510, ⓦwww.ecuadoramazonlodge.com. In an enviable spot overlooking the Río Napo, about halfway between Misahuallí and Ahuano, *Aliñahui* ("beautiful view" in Kichwa) is also known as *Butterfly Lodge* in reference to the 750 species that set the place ablaze with colour. Cabins have balconies, solar-powered lighting, private bath and hot water and stand in fruit orchards. Paths around the grounds lead to spectacular lookouts on the cliff edge. Activities include naturalist and birding hikes, canoe trips and visits to Jatún Sacha. ➐

Cabañas Shiripuno Comunidad de Shiripuno ⓦhttp://shiripuno.free.fr. Just 2km from Misahuallí (reached by a short boat ride), these rustic bamboo and palm leaf cabins are run by the Shiripuno community, who also share cultural activities, including cooking and hunting, with guests. You can get more information from Agencia Teorumi in Misahuallí (see p.318). ➋

La Casa Sinchi Sacha Reina Victoria N26-166 and La Nina, Quito ☎02/2527240, ⓦwww.sinchisacha.org. Operated by a non-profit organization seeking the sustainable development of Kichwa communities. The lodge, which can sleep 24 people, has a shared bathroom with cold water and a 20-metre observation tower; it sits on the banks of the Napo, a ten-minute canoe ride downstream of Ahuano. Jungle hikes, canoeing, rafting and visits to the local Río Blanco community are offered. ➑

La Casa del Suizo Julio Zaldumbide 375 and Toledo, Quito ☎02/2566090 or 2509115, ⓦwww.casadelsuizo.com. The biggest and most comfortable hotel along the Río Napo, dwarfing the village of Ahuano, offers a less demanding way to experience the jungle and is very popular with families. Cabins have electricity, hot water, ceiling fans, porches with hammocks and river views. Covered walkways running through gardens link cabins to a large restaurant, bar and barbecue set around a lovely pool. Excursions include an easy half-day hike at Pangayacu, the "Misacocha Adventure" (a forest walk after which you float back on your own handmade balsa raft), visits to a ceramic workshop in Ahuano and trips to nearby AmaZOOnico. ➒

Cotococha Amazon Lodge Amazonas N24-03 and Wilson, 2nd Floor, Office 3, Quito ☎02/2234336, ⓦwww.cotococha.com. Forty minutes from Tena, 10km along the road to Ahuano, the lodge comprises seventeen spacious riverside cabins of traditional Kichwa design with smartly finished interiors, including private baths, hot

streams, so bring sturdy boots. The steely nerved can slip on a harness and scale the **observation tower**, a metal mast penetrating the canopy, and you can also visit the **Amazon Plant Conservation Centre** and see the foundation's ongoing work in agroforestry and silviculture. To **stay** in simple bunks in screened cabins with shared bathrooms ($33 per person including full board), contact Fundación Jatún Sacha in advance at Eugenio de Santillán N34-248 and Maurian, in Quito (☎02/2432240, ⓦwww.jatunsacha.org), near the Universidad Tecnológica Equinoccial (UTE). **Volunteers** ($465 per month plus $47 application fee) are welcome and can work on the reserve's various programmes, from reforestation and general maintenance, to teaching English, conservation and biology.

Regular **buses** from Tena via Puerto Napo pass Jatún Sacha on the way to La Punta and Santa Rosa. The nearest comfortable accommodation is *Cabañas* water, insect screens, comfortable beds (21 person capacity) and oil lamps. Jungle hikes, inner-tubing, rafting ($60), kayaking and visits to nearby Kichwa communities are offered. An all-inclusive three-day/two-night package starts at $190 per person.

Gareno Lodge Reservations through Guaponi on Ⓦwww.guaponi.com. A lodge southeast of Santa Rosa on the edge of Waorani territory in the community of Gareno. There are four traditonal cabins with private bathrooms, (some) hot water, balconies, hammocks and views over the Gareno river. Hikes are offered into the nearby primary forests by local guides. This is a good choice for birding and *the* place to spot the rare harpy eagle. Ⓖ

Jungle Lodge El Jardín Alemán 3km from Misahuallí on the road to Pusuno Ⓣ06/2890122 or 02/2462213, Ⓦwww.eljardinaleman.com. Set in spacious, colourful grounds close to its private pockets of primary and secondary forest nearby for jungle hikes, this German-run lodge has fresh double rooms with private bathroom, a whirlpool, games room and satellite TV. Jungle tours include guided walks, canoe trips and visits to a nearby Kichwa community for cultural presentations. Ⓖ

🏃 **Liana Lodge** Part of AmaZOOnico (see p.321) Ⓣ09/9800463, Ⓦwww .amazoonico.org. Beautifully crafted cabins on the east shore of the Río Arajuno, draped by vines at the fringes of the forest. Each has a balcony, two spacious rooms, large screened windows, private bath and hot water. The dining area and kitchen are constructed using the gnarled wood of the *pindja* tree. Activities include guided walks, birding, visits to a Kichwa family and shaman, fishing and going to AmaZOOnico's animal refuge, which the profits help support. The staff can also put you in touch with the nearby Kichwa community of Runa Huasi (see p.313). Two-night packages from $109 per person including meals, tours and transport in a motor canoe from Puerto Barantilla.

🏃 **Yachana Lodge** Vicente Solano E12-61 and Vía Oriental, Quito Ⓣ02/523777, Ⓦwww.yachana.com. This award-winning lodge sitting in eight square kilometres of primary and secondary forest and agricultural land, two hours downstream of Misahuallí, offers comfortable rooms and family cabins, lit by lanterns and equipped with private bath, porches, hammocks and has views of the river. The local community, heavily involved with the running of the lodge, lead guided forest walks, give talks on local culture and take visits to the associated community development projects the lodge supports. A four-day/three-night package costs $525.

Yacuma Ecolodge Juan León Mera 721 and Baquedano Ⓣ02/2900323, Ⓦwww .yacuma-lodge.com. Twelve wood-and-thatch cabins on the banks of the Río Napo, aimed at budget-minded travellers. Combines guided hikes and canoe rides with tubing, swimming and fishing. Packages cost from $210 for three days/two nights, up to $350 for five days/four nights.

Aliñahui (see box above), about thirty minutes' walk to the east of Jatún Sacha (which the buses also pass).

AmaZOOnico

Just beyond Ahuano, the Río Arajuno joins the Río Napo. Nestling among the trees a few hundred metres up the Arajuno, you'll find **AmaZOOnico** ($2.50), an animal refuge and rehabilitation centre. If you haven't had any luck seeing the big fauna of the rainforest you can't do much better than to come here, where monkeys of the capuchin, squirrel, spider and woolly varieties, coatis, kinkajous, caiman, turtles, jaguarundi, tapirs, boas, peccaries, ocelots and capybara are all cared for. Despite laws forbidding trade in wild animals or keeping them as pets, smuggling and trafficking of animals is rife and many animals come to the centre in pretty poor shape. A third are deemed suitable for release back into the wild, within the ten-square-kilometre **Bosque Protector Selva Viva** that envelopes the centre in lush forest, but many of the animals recover enough to roam freely around the zoo. A visit consists of an hour's guided tour of the centre along the muddy trails that link the pens, with commentary in English, Spanish, French, German or Kichwa. Between December and June, you've a good chance of seeing newborn coatis, squirrel and capuchin monkeys.

Accommodation is offered at the *Liana Lodge* nearby (see box, pp.320–321) which helps fund the zoo and protected forest. **Volunteers** wanting to help care for the animals are welcome, but should be prepared for hard work and be unflinching when it comes to the less romantic side of the job. They can stay at the refuge for free, but should apply first (T09/9800463, Wwww.amazoonico .org) and be able to speak one other language besides English. If you reserve in advance, they can make arrangements to pick you up from Puerto Barantilla, reached on the Santa Rosa **bus** from Tena (6 daily; 1hr 45min), alighting at Km45 at the Puerto Barantilla/Liana Lodge/AmaZOOnico sign. It's also possible to charter a **boat** from La Punta or Ahuano for around $35.

The southern Oriente

Ecuador's **southern Oriente** is less developed than its northern counterpart in every way, with fewer roads, fewer towns, fewer tourists and less oil activity. The region's two main population centres are **Puyo**, the provincial capital of Pastaza, and **Macas**, 129km further south, capital of the province of Morona-Santiago. Settlement by colonists is largely confined to a long, thin strip flanking the *Troncal Amazónica* (the Amazon highway), which runs from north to south through the region, in the *selva alta*, parallel with the eastern flank of the Andes. This road, mostly paved between Puyo and Limón, is virtually the only road in the southern Oriente, with access east into the heart of the tropical rainforest possible only by boat along the numerous rivers coiling through the forest, or by chartered light aircraft. **Indigenous groups** – principally the Kichwa in Pastaza, the Shuar in Morona-Santiago and pockets of Achuar in the east – communally own most of this territory.

Tourism in the southern Oriente is considerably less evolved than in the north; with the exception of the luxurious *Kapawi Ecolodge*, close to the Peruvian border, you'll find none of the fancy lodges and cabañas of the kind scattered up the Río Napo. Instead, the southern Oriente has excellent opportunities for culturally focused **ecotourism**, offered by tour operators based in Puyo and Macas in association with host indigenous groups. In Puyo, the Organización de Pueblos Indígenas de Pastaza (OPIP) has developed a variety of programmes opening up tracts of rainforest and local communities to visitors. In Macas, which has more tour operators, guides take tourists on multi-day trips to remote Shuar communities, often with an emphasis on learning about their customs, mythology and healing rituals, while exploring the jungle.

The main **route** into the southern Oriente is the hundred-kilometre road from the *serrano* city of Ambato down to Puyo, from where you can branch south to Macas or north to Tena. A less-serviced alternative is the controversial new road from Guamote (south of Riobamba) to Macas, traversing Parque Nacional Sangay on one of the most scenic routes to the lowland east (see p.274 for more details). There are also direct daily **flights** from Quito to Macas.

Puyo and around

Seventy-nine kilometres south of Tena, and by far the biggest urban centre in the southern Oriente, **PUYO** bears out its name (derived from the Kichwa word for "cloudy") and seems to be permanently suffused with a grey, insipid light that gives the town a gloomy air. Founded in 1899 by Dominican missionaries, very little remains of its traditional timber architecture, and these days most of the city's buildings are modern and concrete. Although not particularly appealing in its own right, Puyo does boast several attractions on its outskirts, most notably the fabulous **Jardín Botánico Las Orquídeas**. It also serves as a convenient launchpad for a range of **jungle tours**, commonly to the **Fundación Ecológica Hola Vida**, a tract of secondary rainforest 27km south of town, and to the site of **Indi Churis**, a further 7km south, to meet local Kichwa families. Puyo is also the **transport hub** of the southern Oriente, with frequent bus connections north to Tena and Coca, south to Macas and west to Baños and Ambato, in the sierra.

Arrival and information

The **bus station** is 1km west of the centre on the road to Baños, from where it's a short taxi ride ($1) or fifteen-minute walk into town. Some buses drop passengers at the Gasolinera Coca instead, at Avenida 20 de Julio and Cotopaxi, about six blocks north of the centre, also served by plenty of taxis. Downtown Puyo is compact and entirely manageable on foot, but if you need a **taxi** you'll find plenty of yellow ones and white *camionetas* lined up on 9 de Octubre and Atahualpa, charging around $1 for journeys within the town.

For **tourist information**, head for the Oficina de Turismo (Mon–Fri 8am–12.30pm & 2–6pm; ☎03/2885122, ⓦ www.pastaza.net) on the first floor of the Municipio, on the corner of 9 de Octubre and Francisco de Orellana. It doesn't have much by way of maps and brochures, but the staff do have copious files detailing attractions around Puyo and throughout the province of Pastaza. Otherwise, the hotels are a good source of advice. **Traveller's cheques** can be cashed at Casa de Cambio Puyo, at Atahualpa and 9 de Octubre. The Banco del Austro, Atahualpa and 10 de Agosto, has a Visa and MasterCard **ATM** and offers cash advance, while the Banco Pichincha, Francisco de Orellana and Atahualpa, also has an ATM. The **telephone office** is on Francisco de Orellana and General Villamil, and the **post office** is on 27 de Febrero and Atahualpa. There are several places around the centre offering **internet access** for around $1 per hour; try ciber@té opposite *Hostal Araucano*, or Compu-Business on Atahualpa and 10 de Agosto, which has broadband. The Lavendería La Mocita on the corner of 27 de Febrero and Bolívar **launders** clothes by the kilo.

Accommodation

The real cheapies in Puyo aren't too nice, leaving a cluster of fairly unremarkable but comfortable enough hotels, all around the same mid-range price bracket.

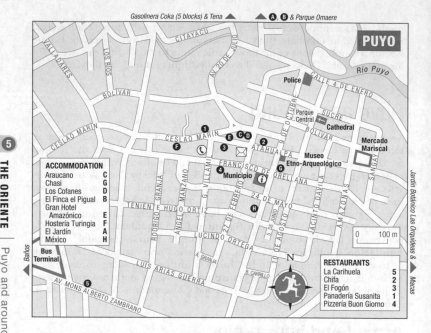

PUYO

Río Puyo

Police

Parque
Central

Cathedral

SUCRE

BOLIVAR

Mercado
Mariscal

CESLAO MARIN

ATAHUALPA

Museo
Etno-Arqueológico

FRANCISCO DE ORELLANA

Municipio

24 DE MAYO

TENIENTE HUGO ORTIZ

LUCINDO ORTEGA

LUIS ARIAS GUERRA

AV. MONS ALBERTO ZAMBRANO

Bus
Terminal

Baños ▲

Jardín Botánico Las Orquídeas & ▶ Macas

0   100 m

N

ACCOMMODATION
Araucano	C
Chasi	
Los Cofanes	G
El Finca el Pigual	D
Gran Hotel	B
Amazónico	E
Hostería Turingia	F
El Jardín	A
México	H

RESTAURANTS
La Carihuela	5
Chifa	2
El Fogón	3
Panadería Susanita	1
Pizzería Buon Giorno	4

Araucano Ceslao Marín 576 ☎03/2885686.
Friendly *hostal* popular with backpackers, with a
good restaurant and a choice of rooms with
shared or private bath (water rationed in the dry
season), generally decreasing in price the higher
up the building you have to go. Has tourist information and offers tours into the rainforest.
Breakfast included. ❷–❹

Chasi 9 de Octubre and Francisco de Orellana
☎03/2883059. Charmless hotel best used only as a
stand-by. The small rooms with private bathroom and
TV are functional and clean but the games arcade
downstairs ensures a near constant racket. ❷

Los Cofanes 27 de Febrero 629 ☎&℻03/2885560.
Superior hotel offering immaculate rooms in a
modern block, all with cool, tiled floors, freshly
painted walls, firm beds, fans and cable TV. ❺

Finca el Pigual End of Calle Tungurahua, Barrio
Obrero ☎03/2887972, ⓦwww.elpigualecuador.com.
Well-appointed, upmarket *hostería* set in beautiful
grounds on the left bank of the Río Puyo, reached by
a suspension bridge. Boasts a pool, steam baths,
sauna and a good restaurant. ❼

Gran Hotel Amazónico Ceslao Marín and
Atahualpa ☎03/2883094, ⓦwww.site.gran
hotelamazonico.com. Clean hotel offering decent
en-suite rooms with hot water and cable TV. Also
has parking, laundry service, restaurant and tour
agency. ❺

El Jardín Paseo Turístico del Río Puyo, near Parque
Omaere ☎03/2887770, ⓦwww.eljardinhostal.com.
Large, lodge-style timber building set in peaceful
gardens on the banks of the river. Offers comfortable rooms with private bath, laundry service, free
internet access and a great restaurant. ❺

México 9 de Octubre and 24 de Mayo
☎03/2885668. Good-value and centrally located
hotel, offering comfortable en-suite rooms with
private bath, hot water and cable TV. Parking
available. ❸

Turingia Ceslao Marín 294 ☎03/2885180, ⓦwww
.hosteriaturingia.com. Secure, German-owned
hostería of long standing, featuring modern and older
bungalows with private and shared bath, with wi-fi,
all set in pleasant gardens with pool, jacuzzi and spa
complex. ❺

The town and its outskirts

Sitting near the coiling Río Puyo's southern banks, Puyo's focal point is the
manicured **Parque Central**, featuring a paved esplanade dotted with flowering
trees, ornamental lampposts and a red-roofed bandstand from where you're

treated to fine views onto the surrounding countryside. Towering over the east side of the square is the modern, angular **cathedral**, with flashing white walls trimmed in brown. There's little else to grab your attention in town, save the **Museo Etno-Arqueológico** (Mon–Fri 8am–12.30pm & 2–6pm; $1), located on the third floor of the Casa de la Juventud, at Atahualpa and 9 de Octubre. Displays include traditional day-to-day objects used by indigenous communities of the region, such as blowpipes, cane spears, fishing nets, musical instruments, and *mucahuas* used to drink *chicha* out of, along with a modest archeological collection of pre-Hispanic ceramics and tools.

At the north end of 9 de Octubre, a ten-minute walk from the city centre, steps head down to the **Río Puyo**, snaking between dense foliage and crossed by a rickety suspension bridge leading to the **Parque Pedagógico Etno-Botánico Omaere** (daily 8am–5pm; $3). The park offers a bite-sized chunk of native forest laced with well-maintained paths, along with a medicinal plant nursery and several examples of typical indigenous dwellings of the Shuar, Kichwa and Waorani communities. A visit here can be combined with a leisurely stroll along the **Paseo Turístico**, a pleasant riverside trail that continues from Omaere for a couple of kilometres as far as the road to Tena. The not-to-be-missed **Jardín Botánico Las Orquídeas** (daily 8am–5pm, last entry at 4pm; $6; reservations on ☎03/884855, ⊛www.jardinbotanicolasorqudeas.com), located in the suburb of Intipungo, southeast of the centre, is an outstanding private botanical garden, with over two hundred species of native Amazonian orchids poking out of a lush tangle of vegetation spread over a couple of hills. Visitors are guided through the garden by its enthusiastic owner and creator, Omar Tello, who points out the tiniest and most exquisite flowers hiding under the foliage; at a brisk pace you could get round most of the paths in an hour, but allow at least two to get the most out of it. The garden is a five-minute taxi ride ($3) from the centre, or you can take the hourly bus #2 from opposite Cooperativa San Francisco, between Atahualpa and 27 de Febrero.

Another attraction on the outskirts of town, 9km north of Puyo on the road to Tena, is the **Zoocriadero El Fátima** (daily 9am–5pm; $2), a zoo with a mixture of walk-in enclosures where you can pet some of the smaller animals, and large, fenced-off areas mimicking the larger mammals' natural environment. All the wildlife is from the Oriente, and includes tapirs, capibara, caimans, monkeys, guatusas and many colourful birds. You can get here on any bus to Tena (from Gasolinera Coka), or else by taxi for about $4–5.

Eating and drinking

There's not a huge choice of places to eat in Puyo, but in addition to those listed below you could also try the restaurants of the *Hostería Turingia* and the *Amazónico* hotel, which are reasonably priced and among the town's better dining establishments.

La Carihuela Av Mons Alberto Zambrano near the bus station. Good restaurant offering tasty, mid-priced pastas, salads, meats and fish, always with vegetarian options as well as inexpensive *almuerzos* and *meriendas*.

Chifa Atahualpa and 27 de Febrero. This popular *chifa* serves up big portions – the shrimp dishes are especially good – in comfortable surroundings with glitzy floors and burgundy seating.

El Fogón Atahualpa and G. Villamil. Bargain grillhouse with great barbecued and rotisserie chicken, served in generous portions.

El Jardín Paseo Turístico del Río Puyo, near Parque Omaere ☎03/2887770, ⊛www.eljardinhostal.com. It's worth making the trip from the centre to this *hostal's* superior restaurant, where well-prepared chicken, trout, pasta and vegetarian dishes are served in a rustic timber dining room.

Panadería Susanita Ceslao Marín and Atahualpa. Good little bakery, which makes a useful breakfast venue for its great fruit juices and fresh bread. Pizzeria Buon Giorno 27 de Febrero and Francisco de Orellana ☎03/2883841. Modest but

spotless little dining room serving delicious, great-value pizzas cooked by a friendly *señora*. Delivery service is available. Closed Sat & Sun.

Tours from Puyo

Tourism in the Puyo region is still fairly undeveloped, though a number of opportunities for ecotourism have been opening up in recent years, mainly under the initiative of **OPIP** (Organización de Pueblos Indígenas de Pastaza), an indigenous organization controlling the bulk of Pastaza's territory. Some of the attractions are open to drop-in visitors, but OPIP prefers tourists to be accompanied by local indigenous **guides**, available at their associated tour agency, Papangu (see below), or other affiliated operators as listed.

One popular **day-tour**, usually kicking off with a visit to the Zoocriadero El Fátima, is to the **Fundación Hola Vida**, a tract of secondary rainforest 27km south of Puyo near the village of Pomona. This can also be visited independently by taxi from Puyo for about $10 each way. On a two- to three-hour hike through the forest, you can visit a stunning thirty-metre waterfall, bathe in crystalline rivers and take in splendid views over the Amazonian plain from a *mirador*. Tours here often then continue to the nearby **Proyecto Indi Churis** (☎03/2887309 or 2887988), where you can sample traditional Oriente dishes like *maitos* (meat or fish steamed in palm leaves), take part in a blowgun demonstration, participate in an evening cleansing ritual using medicinal plants, hike to a viewpoint and float on a river in a dugout canoe. Your visit can be extended by staying with a local family or sleeping in the project's cabañas. Independent travellers can get here by taxi ($13), or on one of two daily **buses**, which also pass Hola Vida, leaving from the stop by the Mercado Mariscal at 6.15am and 1pm (1hr); the last bus returns at 2.30pm.

For a more costly but truly off-the-beaten-track jungle encounter, there are a number of **far-flung indigenous communities** (Kichwa, Záparo, Shuar, Achuar and Waorani) that have set up ecotourism projects which you can visit by making arrangements with Puyo operators. Many of the villages are reached by light aircraft from Shell (see box, p.331), lengthy motor canoe rides with a return trip by plane, or – most adventurous of all – several days' paddling in a dugout canoe. You'll need at least four days to make the most of the further communities, even if flying. While facilities are rudimentary, you'll get guided hikes in pristine forests with true experts and treated to a real insight into authentic rainforest life few outsiders experience.

Tours to indigenous communities

Amazonia Touring Atahualpa and 9 de Octubre ☎03/2883219 or 2583024. Offers a range of tours of one to seven days, from a run round local attractions to visits to faraway Waorani (Shiripuno, Kinwaro and Toñampari) and Kichwa (Curaray) communities.

Coka Tours 27 de Febrero and Atahualpa ☎03/2886108. Offers local trips, tours to Kichwa, Shuar and Waorani communties and jungle expeditions including to the black-water systems of Cuyabeno. From $35 per person.

Madre Selva Ceslao Marín 668 and 9 de Octubre 2nd floor ☎03/28990449, ⊛www.madreselva ecuador.com. Does jungle tours, community ecotourism, rafting, tubing, canyoning, caving and biking from $25 per person. Run tours to Waorani areas, Kichwa communites around Cotococha and Chuva Urcu, south of Puyo, as well as to Shuar communities near the Cueva de los Tayos. Friendly staff and some basic English spoken.

Papangu 27 de Febrero and Sucre ☎&℻03/2887684, ⊛http://papangu .yuricrea.it. Offers trips to Kichwa villages, particularly the famous Sarayaku community, which is counting on tourism to help win its battle against oil development in its territory (see box, p.289). The community can currently only be visited via airplane, as colonists in favour of development in villages around Sarayaku do not allow them to pass on the river. Your support will assist the struggle to save their lands. From $99 per person per day.

Pashpanchu Expediciones CC Foncesa, Ceslao Marín ☎08/2784301, ⓦwww.pashpanchu .pastaza.net. Provides canoe and hiking trips (up to six days, sleeping in tents), observing wildlife and plants, and visiting indigenous communities. $30–40 per day.

Macas and around

MACAS, 129km south of Puyo, is the most appealing town in the southern Oriente, mainly for its pleasant climate, laid-back atmosphere and beautiful views onto the surrounding countryside. While there are a few worthwhile sights in and around town, Macas is best visited as a base for organizing excursions into the hinterlands to the east.

Arrival and information

Arriving in Macas by **bus**, you're dropped at the centrally located bus station on the corner of Avenida Amazonas and 10 de Agosto. **Flights** from Quito, operated by TAME (☎02/2509375 in Quito, ☎07/2701978 in Macas; ⓦwww .tame.com.ec) and Saero (☎02/3301152 in Quito, ☎07/2702764 in Macas; ⓦwww.saereo.com) land at the tiny airport on Amazonas and Cuenca, four blocks north of the bus terminal.

There's no official **tourist office** in town, but you can pick up a brochure listing attractions and tourist services at the Municipio on the plaza (☎07/2700143, ⓦwww.macas.gov.ec), and you can get information and see displays on Parque Nacional Sangay at the **Interpretation Centre** at Juan de la Cruz and Guamote, a couple of blocks south of the bus terminal. For **money**, Banco del Austro, corner of 10 de Agosto and 24 de Mayo, has a Visa and MasterCard ATM, but there's nowhere to change traveller's cheques. The Pacífictel **telephone office** is on 24 de Mayo and Sucre, the **post office** is on 9 de Octubre, on the Parque Central, and **internet facilities** are available at Cyber Vision opposite *Casa Blanca*.

Accommodation

None of Macas' dozen or so **hotels** could be described as upmarket, but there are plenty of comfortable, good-value options, most offering similar rooms at similar prices. The best is probably the *Casa Blanca*, at Soasti 14-29 (☎07/2700195; ❹), offering spacious, clean rooms with tiled floors, private hot-water showers, cable TV and breakfast. Other popular choices include the good-value *Milenio*, Amazonas and Tarqui (☎07/2700805; ❸), for its wooden floors and clean en-suite rooms with private baths and hot water; *Esmeralda* at Cuenca 612 (☎07/2700130; ❸), with comfortable beds, clean, white walls, breakfast, cable TV and views of Sangay from its rooftop terrace; and the long-established *Splendit* at Soasti and Bolívar (☎07/2700120; ❸), which has quiet rooms with private bath and hot water.

The town and around

A good place to take in the lie of the land is on the steps of the modern, concrete **cathedral** on the Parque Central, giving views across the low roofs

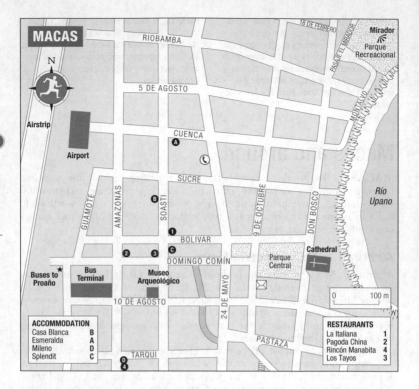

MACAS

N

Airstrip

Airport

Buses to Proaño

Bus Terminal

Museo Arqueológico

RIOBAMBA

5 DE AGOSTO

CUENCA
A

SUCRE

GUAMOTE

AMAZONAS

SOASTI

BOLÍVAR

DOMINGO COMÍN

10 DE AGOSTO

TARQUI

PASTAZA

24 DE MAYO

9 DE OCTUBRE

DON BOSCO

18 DE FEBRERO

PASAJE EL MIRADOR

Mirador
Parque Recreacional

MONTALVO

Río Upano

Parque Central

Cathedral

0   100 m

ACCOMMODATION
Casa Blanca	B
Esmeralda	A
Mileno	D
Splendit	C

RESTAURANTS
La Italiana	1
Pagoda China	2
Rincón Manabita	4
Los Tayos	3

of the town onto the eastern flanks of the sierra; on very clear days you can see the smouldering cone of Volcán Sangay, some 40km northwest. Behind the cathedral, the shelf on which Macas is built drops abruptly down to the **Río Upano** whose restless waters curl around the eastern edge of the town. For the best views eastwards, head five blocks north from the cathedral to the **Parque Recreacional**, a small, pretty space with a *mirador* looking down to the seemingly endless blanket of vegetation, stretching into the horizon in a fuzzy green haze. In the foreground, just across the river, you can see the whitewashed buildings of **Sevilla–Don Bosco**, a Salesian mission station with a handsome church, about a 45-minute walk from town. Back in the centre, the **Museo Arqueológico y Cultural de Morona Santiago** (Mon–Fri 9am–noon & 2–4.30pm; free) is on the top floor of the Casa de la Cultura at 10 de Agosto and Soasti. It has a fascinating display of Shuar artefacts, including feather adornments, headdresses made of animal heads, blowpipes, basketwork, large clay funerary urns traditionally used to bury dead children and a replica of a *tsanta* (shrunken head). There are good **artesanías** at the Fundación Chunkuap' shop on the corner of Bolívar and Soasti, which sells items local Achuar communities make, including ceramics, woven baskets and bags and blowpipes.

Outside town, the **Fundación Rescate Fauna Silvestre Eden** (daily 8am–5pm; $1) is an animal rescue centre where tapirs, peccaries, turtles, boas and parrots, among others, are all cared for. It's a short walk north of Proaño, a village that can be reached by a bus ride from Macas (hourly; 15min).

Eating, drinking and nightlife

The best **restaurant** in town is the classy *Pagoda China*, on the corner of Amazonas and Domingo Comín, its extensive Chinese menu is pricier than most here but worth it. Otherwise, try: *Los Tayos* on the corner of Soasti and Domingo Comín, an inexpensive and busy restaurant offering all the standards; *La Italiana*, on Bolívar and Soasti, a good place for pizza and pasta; or the busy *Rincón Manabita*, on Amazonas and Tarqui, which dishes up hearty staples such as chicken and rice, as well as good-value set breakfasts, lunches and dinners. For Oriente specialities, head for the bargain canteens clustered on Domingo Comín between Soasti and 24 de Mayo, where you'll find *ayampaco* (meat or fish wrapped in palm leaves) and the occasional *guanta* cooking over charcoal grills on the pavement. There's not a great deal to do in the evenings, but if you're looking for **nightlife**, try the underground *Acuario* disco on Sucre and Soasti, or the *Damasco Bar*, on 24 de Mayo and Tarqui.

Parque Nacional Sangay

To the west of Macas, the huge **Parque Nacional Sangay** ($10) protects over five thousand square kilometres of pristine wilderness, ranging from the ice-streaked peak of Volcán Tungurahua to the steaming Amazon basin. The lowland section is easily accessed from Macas, not least on the new road to Guamote in the sierra (see p.274 for more details and bus information), which

---

Tours around Macas

Most **tours from Macas** typically take in day- and night-hikes through the forest (often around four hours long), bathing in lakes and waterfalls, river trips in dugout canoes and visits to Shuar communities, occasionally with singing and dancing or the option of participating in a traditional purification ritual. **Costs** are generally around $40 per person per day, going up to around $50–80 per day for tours including a short flight to the remote areas to the east (see "East of Macas", p.330); much of the final day of the tour may be taken up by a lengthy bus journey returning to town. Expect community facilities to be basic, with **accommodation** in traditional bamboo huts or tents, and an emphasis more on adventure and low-impact cultural exchange than material comforts. Some operators offer English-speaking **guides**, but few are really fluent; if having an English-speaking guide is a priority, shop around and insist on meeting the guide before booking the tour to try to ensure you'll get on well with them.

Cabañas Yuquipa Contact the *Pancesa* bakery at Soasti and 10 de Agosto ☎07/2700071 or 2700768. Near the Shuar community of San Vicente, 12km north of town, these rustic cabins with composting toilet are built by the Río Yuquipa. Packages from around $35 a day include meals and guided jungle walks.

Insondu Mundo Shuar Bolívar and Soasti ☎07/2702533 or 08/8582559, ⓦwww .mundoshuar.com. Specialize in one- to four-day expeditions to Shuar communities at Yaupi that can take in hiking, canoeing, caving, swimming and fishing. Can also organize bike tours. Prices around $50–70 per person plus airfares where applicable.

Planeta Tours Domingo Comín and Soasti ☎07/2701328, ⒺPlaneta_ms@hotmail .com. Limit their tours to small groups and offer three-day trips into Parque Nacional Sangay, as well as expeditions to Shuar communities in Kunkup and Yaupi. Around $45 per person per day.

Tsuirim Viajes Don Bosco and Sucre ☎07/2701681 or 09/7372538. A range of scenic and cultural tours around Macas lasting one to five days, as well as trips to Yuquipa, Miazal, Alto Macuma, Chiguaza caverns, Arapico falls and Parque Nacional Sangay. Prices range from $50–80 per person per day, all inclusive.

runs across the width of the park. For more on the highland regions of Parque Nacional Sangay, see p.222.

Independent hiking here is a challenging undertaking, only suitable for fully self-sufficient hikers with IGM maps, a compass and good orienteering skills. It's usually possible to arrange to hire a **guide** at the **Interpretation Centre** in Macas at Juan de la Cruz and Guamote, a couple of blocks south of the bus terminal (☎07/2702368, ⓦ www.parquesangay.org.ec), where you can also pick up more information about the park and its attractions. Another option is to go on one of the guided hiking programmes some of the **tour operators** in Macas (see box, p.306) offer; locals with an intimate knowledge of the forests and trails usually lead these.

East of Macas

The swaths of primary rainforest in the hinterland east of Macas are among the most pristine in Ecuador. **Independent travel** in the area (besides being discouraged by indigenous groups) is almost impossible to arrange, apart from along the single road branching east just north of Méndez (see p.331) to the little village of **San José de Morona**, a ten-hour bus ride from Macas. The strip along this route has been partially cleared and colonized, so doesn't exactly take you into the heart of the jungle. The best way to visit the area is on a **guided tour** with an agency working in close cooperation with the indigenous communities it visits or whose territories it travels through.

Tour companies based in Macas (see box, p.329) visit three main targets east of town. Closest to Macas is **BUENA ESPERANZA**, reached by a short drive (2hr) northeast from Macas followed by a one-hour hike. Accommodation here is usually in a traditional open-sided Shuar dwelling. The Shuar hosts demonstrate the use the *cervátana* – a long, cane blowpipe used for hunting – and encourage visitors to have a go. Activities around here include hiking through the rainforest, with the possibility of a canoe trip.

The Shuar community of **MACUMA** is the focus of longer (usually five-day) tours which start with an hour's bus ride northeast of Macas to the end of the road near the community of Cuchaentza. From there it's three or four hours' hike through primary forest to Macuma. You'll learn about Shuar culture and food, hunting and fishing techniques, and see music, dance and handicraft demonstrations; other activities include jungle walks to waterfalls and paddling in dugout canoes on the Río Macuma.

Another accessible Shuar village is **KUNKUP**, two hours by road north of Macas and one hour's hike along the banks of the Río Palora. The community has benefited from an internationally sponsored resource-management plan, and now has a sizeable primary forest reserve, a capybara-breeding project, solar power and a community-based tourism programme.

Further afield is the Shuar community of **YAUPI**. It's reached on a 35-minute flight from Macas, or a gruelling seven-hour bus journey to Puerto Yaupi, followed by a motor-canoe ride upstream. From here, groups normally set out on a two-hour hike to the beautiful **Lago Kumpak**, where they lodge with Shuar families living on its shores. Canoe rides on the lake often feature in tours here – at night to look out for the glowing-red eyes of caiman and by day to spot birds, colourful fish and lizards. Most programmes also include day- and night-hikes through the rainforest and a canoe trip down the Río Yaupi to visit the **Cueva de los Tayos**, one of several enormous limestone caves in the region, inhabited by *tayos*, nocturnal **oilbirds** that nest in huge colonies in lightless places. At dusk, the birds fly out in a cacophony of shrieks and screams to feed on large fruits that are plucked with their heavy hooked beaks. From

Kapawi Ecolodge

Due east of Macas, in one of the most remote tracts of the Ecuadorian rainforest, the **Kapawi Ecolodge** (☎02/6009333 or 09/08344032, ⓦwww.kapawi.com) represents a unique model of community-participatory ecotourism. The luxurious jungle lodge, dramatically situated on the edge of a lagoon surrounded by primary rainforest, was created in 1996 by a private operator, Canodros, in close association with the **Achuar** people of eastern Pastaza, represented by the Federación de Nacionalidades Achuares del Ecuador (FINAE). The land occupied by the lodge was initially leased by Canodros, with management and ownership gradually passing into the hands of the Shuar people, who have owned and operated *Kapawi* in its entirety since January 2008. From the outset, the project has gone to great lengths to minimize the environmental impact of the lodge: most electricity is provided by a photovoltaic system; solar-heated water is used for hot showers; only biodegradable detergents are used; and all non-biodegradable waste is flown out to be properly disposed of.

The complex is composed of nineteen waterfront thatched **cabañas** built in the traditional Achuar style, without a single iron nail, along with two central buildings incorporating a bar, lounge and dining room. **Guided hikes** with English-speaking naturalist guides and **canoe trips** in the pristine area around the lodge provide exceptional opportunities for spotting wildlife, including freshwater dolphins, caimans, anacondas and monkeys, as well as over five hundred species of birds. Programmes also include visits to local Achuar communities, where guests are invited to share *chicha* and to sit and talk with the help of an interpreter. **Prices** start at $880 per person for three nights, going up to $1102 for four nights and $1578 for seven nights, including the flight from Shell to *Kapawi*.

the cave, tour groups normally continue downstream to join the road from San José de Morona, and catch a bus back to Macas (about 10hr).

Another less commonly offered possibility is to fly from Macas to the community of **MIAZAL**. Programmes here normally involve a seven-hour hike through glorious forest to a set of remote hot springs and a canoe ride down the **Río Mangosiza**, sleeping en route with Shuar families. Visitors either fly back or return by bus to Macas from Puerto Morona (9hr).

South to Gualaquiza

From Macas, the **Troncal Amazónica** road trails down into the southernmost reaches of the Oriente, eventually climbing back up to the highlands at the town of Zamora, 324km away. The sporadic farming villages and small towns dotted along its length offer little scope for getting into the rainforest further east, and – with the exception of the little town of **Gualaquiza**, 184km south of Macas – tend to be pretty uninviting places for a stopover.

Limón and Gualaquiza

South of Macas, you'll pass through Sucúa and then Méndez before finally reaching **LIMÓN** (General Leonidas Plaza on some maps), about 115km from Macas. It has a pleasant climate, tidy streets and is becoming a popular bolt hole for Cuencanos on weekend breaks, and a vogue arts shop in the centre selling locally produced paintings, ceramics and indigenous crafts caters to their tastes. The owners can provide you with **information** on local attractions, including waterfalls, caves and petroglyphs near the settlement of Indanza to the south, and help you find a guide to visit them. If you need a **place to stay**, try *Dreamhouse* on Quito and Bolívar (☎07/2770166; ➋) for modest but comfortable rooms with shared bath.

Eight kilometres south of Limón, the road forks in two; the right fork climbs dramatically up into the sierra to Cuenca, 100km west, while the left one continues 70km south to **GUALAQUIZA**, sitting at the confluence of the Zamora and Bobonaza rivers, against a backdrop of forested hills. Gualaquiza's quaint, colonial-style church and cobbled streets make it the most attractive little town along the road from Macas, but apart from enjoying the views and taking a stroll by the river, there's not much to do here and no compelling reason to stop over. The area around town is full of caves, waterfalls and pre-Columbian ruins, but finding them is an adventure best left to well-equipped, self-sufficient souls, preferably with the help of a local guide; for more information head to the municipal tourist office on the plaza (☎07/2780109). If you do stay in Gualaquiza, you'll find spacious, comfortable **rooms** at *Guadelupe* on Pesantez and García Moreno (☎07/2780113; ➋), and a couple of basic **places to eat** around the main square. *Copacabana*, on the third floor of the new building opposite the bus terminal, has a large dining area, a nice open balcony with views and a good menu.

South of Gualaquiza, the road heads into the tiny province of Zamora Chinchipe, through remote gold-mining territory dotted with macho, rough-edged mining settlements such as **Yantzaza**, before reaching the hill town of **Zamora**, 120km down the road, where it joins the highway to **Loja** in the sierra (see p.254).

Travel details

Buses

Coca to: Ambato (9 daily; 10hr); Baños (3 daily; 10hr); Guayaquil (3 daily; 15hr); Lago Agrio (every 15–30min; 3hr); Loja (1 daily; 30hr); Pompeya (3 daily; 3hr); Puyo (7 daily; 8hr); Quito (4 nightly via Loreto, 12 daily via Lago Agrio; 9–11hr); Santo Domingo (3 daily; 10hr); Tena (26 daily; 6hr).
Lago Agrio to: Ambato (6 daily; 9hr); Baeza (every 30min–1hr; 5hr); Coca (every 15–30min; 3hr); Cuenca (1 daily; 16hr); Esmeraldas (1 daily; 14–15hr); Guayaquil (2 daily; 14hr); La Punta (every 15min; 40min); Loja (1 daily; 24hr); Machala (1 daily; 18hr); Puyo (1 daily; 11hr); Quito (every 30min–1hr; 7hr); Santo Domingo (2 daily; 10hr); Shushufindi (every 15min; 3hr); Tena (2 daily; 7hr); Tulcán via La Bonita, check security (2 daily; 7hr).
Macas to: Cuenca (12 daily; 10hr); Gualaquiza (2 daily; 8hr); Guamote (3 daily; 5hr); Guayaquil (2 daily; 13hr); Morona (1 daily; 10hr); Proaño (hourly; 15min); Puyo (20 daily; 5hr); Quito (5 daily; 11hr); Sucúa (every 45min; 1hr); Yaupi (1 daily; 7hr).
Puyo to: Ambato (18 daily; 2hr 30min); Baños (every 30min; 1hr 45min); Guayaquil (10 daily; 8hr);

Macas (20 daily; 4hr); Quito (every 30min–1hr; 5hr); Riobamba (16 daily; 3hr); Tena (20 daily; 3hr).
Tena to: Ahuano (9 daily; 1hr 30min); Ambato (17 daily; 5hr); Archidona (every 20min; 15min); Baeza (26 daily; 2hr 30min); Baños (14 daily; 5hr); Coca (7 daily; 6hr); Guayaquil (2 nightly; 11hr); Lago Agrio (2 daily; 7hr); Misahuallí (every 45min; 45min); Pacto Sumaco (1 daily, 4hr); Puyo (every 30min–1hr; 2hr 30min); Quito (22 daily; 5–6hr via Baeza); Riobamba (6 daily; 6hr); San Pedro de Sumino (12 daily; 3hr); Santa Rosa (12 daily; 1hr 45min).

Boats

Coca to: Añangu (2 weekly; 3hr); Nuevo Rocafuerte (2 weekly; 10hr); Pañacocha (2 weekly; 5hr); Pompeya (2 weekly; 1hr 30min).

Flights

Coca to: Quito (Mon–Fri 8–10, Sat 5 daily, Sun 3 daily; 30min).
Lago Agrio to: Quito (Mon–Fri 6–7, Sat 2, Sun 2; 30min).
Macas to: Quito (1–2 daily; 30min).

6

The northern lowlands and coast

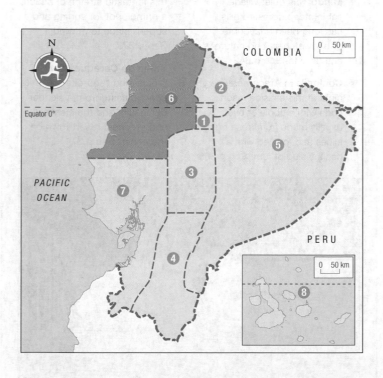

CHAPTER 6 # Highlights

✳ Private cloudforest reserves
The most accessible and
comfortable places to
experience a cloudforest
– a misty, half-lit universe
of tangled vines, creepers,
mosses, orchids, fluorescent
butterflies and endemic birds.
See pp.338–342

✳ Mindo This quiet village,
set in steep, forested hills,
has long been a favourite
of birdwatchers and nature
enthusiasts. See p.342

✳ Cocktails in Atacames Every
night at this seaside resort
ends with a tipple or two,
usually made from fresh fruit
juices and fortified with a
healthy slug of rum. See p.365

✳ Beach hideaways Holing
up in a secluded retreat with
its own deserted beach is a
great way to recharge your
batteries and escape the
crowds. See p.367, p.369
& p.371

✳ Surfing at Canoa Powerful
breakers relentlessly pound
this fantastic stretch of beach,
a prime spot for surfing and a
superb place to unwind.
See p.372

✳ Bahía de Caráquez Self-
proclaimed "eco-city" of white
condos rising from a slender
peninsula, and the cleanest
and greenest resort town on
the coast. See p.374

▲ Surfer, Canoa beach

The northern lowlands and coast

The north coast and lowlands, lying west of the Andes and north of the road from Manta to Quevedo, are among the most culturally – and biologically – diverse regions of the country. A few hours by bus away from the highland chill seems to put you in another universe – one of steaming forests bursting with exotic plants, birds and animals, giving out to long sandy **beaches** bathed by a warm ocean. Even the people seem different; you'll notice a much more relaxed and uninhibited atmosphere than in the sierra, further enhanced by a unique blend of Afro-Ecuadorian and indigenous Chachi and Tsáchila cultures.

Of the several **routes** to the northern lowlands from the sierra, the old road from Quito to the coast, the **Calacalí–La Independencia road**, passes through some of the best birdwatching territory in the country, including the village of **Mindo** and a handful of excellent private reserves protecting some of the last remaining **cloudforests** in the western Andes. Another road, which *should* be completed by the time you read this, will run broadly parallel between **Otavalo** and **Quinindé**, opening up communities and cloudforests hitherto too remote for casual visits. The main arterial route heads from Quito to **Santo Domingo de los Colorados**, set amid a broad sea of banana and oil-palm plantations, but skirts a few tropical wet forests too, including the little-explored **Reserva Ecológica Mache-Chindul**, which protects coastal hills swathed in impenetrable forests. From Santo Domingo a network of paved roads connects the major coastal centres of Esmeraldas, Pedernales, Bahía de Caráquez, Manta, Portoviejo and Guayaquil via Quevedo. The northernmost coast can be accessed by the fast, paved highway from Ibarra to the isolated port of **San Lorenzo**, lost in a knot of mangrove swamps; this road has largely replaced the famous old railway route, now defunct except for short fragments. Unlike the dry and scrubby shoreline to the south, the much lusher **north** enjoys high levels of rainfall, especially during the wet season (Dec–May), when monthly precipitation averages 300mm, but can easily reach 600mm; this can mean road washouts and travel disruption, so plan ahead.

A hundred kilometres down the coast from San Lorenzo, the rough oil-refining port of **Esmeraldas** lies just north of the area's best-known **beach resorts**, the biggest and brashest of which is **Atacames**, famous for its bars and nightlife and jam-packed during summer months and holidays with *serranos*

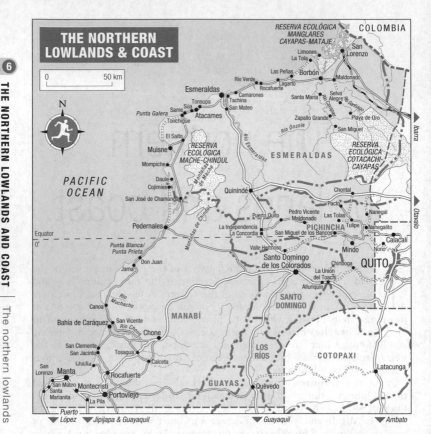

THE NORTHERN
LOWLANDS & COAST

seeking sunshine and warm waters. The less-developed beach centres are a bit
further afield, including the car-free sand-bar island of **Muisne**, 40km down the
coast, and the laid-back surfing zone of **Canoa**, more than 150km south;
between them, many tranquil, deserted beaches and hideaway hotels dot the
coastline. At the southern end of the region, **Bahía de Caráquez** is an elegant
resort town and a good base for visiting mangrove and tropical dry forests, and
the lively port of **Manta** is the area's economic powerhouse.

The northern lowlands

Rarely found on travel itineraries, major towns in the **northern lowlands** such
as Santo Domingo and Quevedo tend to be sweaty commercial centres
enveloped by acres of agricultural land. Still, a few small fragments of **tropical
coastal wet forest** do survive nearby in a handful of reserves, while at higher

elevations on the western flank of the Andes there are a number of sizeable and enchanting **cloudforests** – misty worlds of dense, mossy and vine-draped vegetation coloured by orchids, heliconia, birds and neon butterflies. The coastal and mountain forests make up part of the **Chocó and Tropical Andes bioregions**, respectively – regarded as the richest and most diverse places on earth. Species here were cut off from the Amazon rainforests to the east by the uplift of the Andes mountains 100 million years ago. Since that time, they have evolved quite differently from their eastern counterparts and the result is an amazing degree of biodiversity and endemism. But with logging, agriculture and human encroachment taking a substantial toll, only seven percent of Ecuador's original western forests remain. The area has been classified by Conservation International as one of the world's biodiversity "hot spots" – among the planet's most ecologically important and threatened regions.

Serviced by a near-constant stream of buses, the **main route** to the northern lowlands begins south of Quito and starts its descent of the western Andes at Alóag, heading down towards **Santo Domingo de los Colorados** – around which you can see tropical wet forests at **Tinalandia, Bosque Protector La Perla** and **Reserva Biológica Bilsa** – from where there are highways to all the major coastal centres. Leaving aside the soon-to-be-completed Otavalo–Quinindé road which passes through the remote Intag region, the attractive and peaceful **Calacalí–La Independencia road** is the alternative to the main route; leaving north of Quito, it passes close to some excellent **private cloudforest reserves** as well as the birding centre of **Mindo** before descending into farmland, where it joins the main highway between Santo Domingo de los Colorados and Esmeraldas. Fewer buses travel this road and most cloudforest reserves are not accessible by public transit alone anyway; contact their offices in Quito before setting out, both to reserve a room and to sort out travel arrangements.

The Calacalí–La Independencia road

The **Calacalí–La Independencia road** provides access to some of the last pristine **cloudforests** in the western Andes, largely protected by private reserves that offer good lodging and excellent **birdwatching**. After leaving Quito to the north, the road meets the equator at La Mitad del Mundo before it sweeps west to bypass **Calacalí**, home to its own small equator monument, and begins a dramatic descent from scrubby hillsides (at 2800m) to thickly matted forests carpeting steep ridges and hills – the rich greenery broken only by curling wisps of clouds. Most of the reserves lie within transitional zones from 1000m to 2500m, where the humid air adds high levels of moisture to the forests.

Sixty kilometres from Quito around the village of Nanegalito are several private reserves, among them **Maquipucuna, Yunguilla, Santa Lucía** and **Urcu Puyujunda**; beyond them to the northwest, the **Bosque Protector Los Cedros**; and around the Tandayapa valley, the **Bellavista Cloud Forest Reserve** and **Tandayapa Lodge**. Some 25km further west from Nanegalito, the road passes the turn-off for **Mindo**, a pleasant village renowned for its birdlife and set in the verdant hills of the **Mindo–Nambillo** protected forest. The road continues its descent into rich agricultural land, passing small farming towns such as **San Miguel de los Bancos** and **Puerto Quito** before meeting the highway linking Santo Domingo to the coast at Esmeraldas.

Pahuma Orchid Reserve

About 22km beyond Calacalí (at Km42), the **Pahuma Orchid Reserve** protects 6.5 square kilometres of rich cloudforest, from the summit of **El Pahuma** ("flattened peak") down to the highway. Across the road from the car park, a **botanical garden** (daily 8am–5pm; $5 including the reserve and trails) displays three hundred of the five hundred beautiful varieties of orchid found in the reserve, which you can also explore on 6km of hiking trails, including one ancient trail up to the Pahuma peak (guide $5 per person per half-day). For **accommodation** you can either sleep in private double rooms at the **Nature Centre** (❸) by the garden, or in dormitory bunks ($8), or hike up to the rustic *Guarida del Oso* cabin (bunks $5), where you'll need your own food, water and sleeping bag. You'll also need to be self-sufficient if you want to **camp** ($3) in a clearing on the summit of El Pahuma. For more **information** call ☎09/8947481 (Spanish-speaking only) or contact Fundación Ceiba in Quito (☎02/2432173, ⓦwww.ceiba.org).

Reserva Biológica Maquipucuna

Originally geared for research but now open to the public, eighty percent of the 45-square-kilometre **Reserva Biológica Maquipucuna** ($10) is undisturbed primary **cloudforest**, ranging from 1200m to 2800m across four ecological zones and bounded by another 140 square kilometres of protected forests. Together the areas are home to a considerable amount of **wildlife**, with two thousand plants, 330 birds and 45 mammals, among them pumas, ocelots, tapirs, agoutis and nineteen types of bats – you may even spot the elusive Andean **spectacled bear**.

Traversing the northern end of the reserve are five **trails** from fifteen minutes to seven hours long (English-speaking guides available with advance reservation), while near the lodge you'll find an introductory self-guided trail and the cool waters of the **Río Umachaca**, ideal for a quick dip after a long hike. During mealtimes, you can quiz the resident biologist and research scientists based at the nearby laboratory. The reserve is also dotted with **archeological sites** relating to the **Yumbos** people, who lived in the area before the arrival of the Incas, including fragments of an ancient trail that once connected the sierra to the lowlands, with path-side walls several metres high.

Practicalities

From Quito the reserve is a two-and-a-half-hour journey, which for the unpaved section at the end may require **four-wheel-drive** in the wet season (Jan–May). Once through Nanegalito, take the right turn to Nanegal and just before you reach that village, the turning for Maquipucuna is signposted to the right. It's 6km away, past the village of Marianitas. Alternatively, catch a Transportes Minas **bus** to Nanegal from the Ofelia terminal (Mon–Fri 7.30am, noon, 1.30pm, Sat 7am, 10.30am, noon, 1.45pm & Sun 7am, 10am, 1.30pm) and walk or hire a *camioneta* (around $10); or arrange transport with Fundación Maquipucuna in Quito (see below).

Bedrooms in the attractive wood-and-thatch **lodge** ($60 per person in four-person rooms with shared bath, $85 with private bath; meals included) have screens rather than walls, allowing the rich forest soundtrack to waft in. Budget travellers can stay in the **research facilities** by the organic garden ($45, including board) or **camp** for $5. **Volunteers** are welcome to clear trails, reforest pastures, tend the garden and help with nearby community projects; to make **reservations**, contact the Fundación Maquipucuna in Quito, Baquerizo E9–153 and Tamayo (☎02/2507200 or 09/4218033, ⓦwww.maqui.org).

Yunguilla

On the eastern side of the Maquipucuna reserve, a short *camioneta* ride from Calacalí, the community of **Yunguilla** ($3.50 entrance) runs an ecotourism project and invites visitors to stay at its *Casa Tahuallullo* ($35, including meals), a simple cabin with two rooms and space for eight, or to stay with local families. Also available are guided walks into the **cloudforest** and along pre-Columbian pathways, long-distance treks for up to five days, insights into local traditions, culture and legends, and produce from the community's jam- and cheese-making cooperatives. For more information and **reservations**, contact Germán Collahuazo (☎09/1144610 or 02/2906021, ✉yunguilla@yahoo.com) or try Ⓦwww.turismosostenible.ec.

Bosque Nublado Santa Lucía

On a small plateau affording stunning views of the green-blanketed hills and cloud-filled valleys below, ⚘ **Santa Lucía Lodge**, which enjoys a wonderful isolation and tranquillity enhanced by its lack of electricity and, thanks to its 1900m altitude, absence of annoying insects, is part of an award-winning community-run ecotourism project, which helps fund the conservation of 6.5 square kilometres of communally owned **cloudforest** (*bosque nublado*). Eighty percent of this is primary forest and harbours more than 386 **bird** species, including dozens of hummingbirds, such as the rare violet-tailed sylph, and golden and club-winged manakins, along with leks (courtship display grounds) for the cock-of-the-rock; **mammals** such as pumas, ocelots and Andean spectacled bears are also present. Forest **trails** traverse various elevations to maximize your sightings of birds and plants, passing by waterfalls and mountain streams perfect for bathing, and there's a 12-metre observation tower for closer examinations of the canopy. A six-hour hike along a pre-Columbian path links Santa Lucía to neighbouring Yunguilla (guides $25 per day or $35 for a bird specialist).

Practicalities

Reached by a stiff one- to two-hour **hike** beyond Maquipucuna, on a trail that coils 700m up a forested ridge, the lodge has a choice of double rooms ($56 per person per night) or dorms ($28), both with shared bathrooms, or there are private cabins with en-suite bath ($68 per person). The food is delicious and plentiful (much of it grown in the organic garden), and clean hot and cold water flows all day. Prices include full board, entrance to the reserve, and if you're not in the dorm, mules to carry luggage, and a local guide. The community is also keen to take on **volunteers** (two-week minimum) at substantially reduced rates to help with projects for reforestation, organic farming, agro-forestry, conservation monitoring, trail clearance and English teaching; Spanish is not required but certainly useful. Contact the lodge for **reservations** and information (☎02/2157242, Ⓦwww.santaluciaecuador.com).

Bosque Protector Biológica Los Cedros

As one of the most remote and exciting reserves in the western Andes, the **Bosque Protector Biológica Los Cedros** encompasses 64 square kilometres of pristine rain and cloudforests contiguous with the Reserva Ecológica Cotacachi-Cayapas (see p.150). Home to hundreds of tropical **birds** inhabiting the misty canopy, the reserve's greenery is a tight weave of vines, lianas, roots, bromeliads, heliconia and more than two hundred varieties of **orchids** (best seen mid-Jan to end Feb), including many newly discovered species. The reserve's also a base for an internationally supported primate research programme into the **brown-headed spider monkey**, Ecuador's only endemic monkey, of which there are only fifty breeding pairs left in the wild. The network of **trails** to and across the reserve gets muddy in the rainy season (Jan–April), but hiking is possible year round.

Practicalities

Although only 60km northwest of Quito, the reserve is a three-and-a-half-hour **bus** ride followed by a four- or five-hour uphill hike or mule ride. From the Ofelia terminal in Quito, take a Transportes Minas bus (5 daily at 6am, 10am, 12.45pm, 3.30pm & 6pm; 6am best if you want to arrive the same day at the reserve; 3hr 15min) to Chontal, where there are a couple of simple hotels and a few home-stay possibilities. By the time you read this, there should also be a bus service to Chontal on a new road from Otavalo. Contact the office in advance for full details and to arrange transport or mules if necessary.

The reserve's rustic but comfortable **accommodation** – a wooden lodge where a nearby mountain stream powers the hydroelectric system and provides fresh water – comes with hot showers and three delicous home-cooked meals a day ($50 per person). **Volunteers** are welcome for a minimum of one month ($450 per month contribution), and **reservations** should be made in advance through the Centro de Investigaciones de los Bosques Tropicales (CIBT), PO Box 17-7-8726, Quito (T02/2865176, W www.reservaloscedros.org).

Tulipe

At Km61, 3km beyond Nanegalito, there's a turning north to **TULIPE**, a small village tucked 9km away in a clutch of green subtropical hills, which appears to have once been a ceremonial centre of the Yumbos culture (800–1660 AD), traders overseeing routes between the Andes and the coast. Just below the road are the **ruins** ($2 entry) of six "*piscinas*", large sunken areas with steps and channels leading into them, supposed to have been filled with water and used as celestial "mirrors" to observe the movements of the sun and stars, or to perform rites of worship and purification. Judging from the number of pyramidal structures perched on the hilltops around the area, this was a major centre, and when the Incas conquered the region in the early sixteenth century, they added to the complex by building their own ceremonial bath on slightly higher ground to the east. An on-site museum here explains the site and has displays on the Yumbo culture.

To get to Tulipe, catch a Transportes Minas **bus** bound for Chontal from the Ofelia terminal in Quito (5 daily at 6am, 10am, 12.45pm, 3.30pm & 6pm; 2hr 30min). The nearest good **lodging** is at Bosque Nublado Urcu Puyujunda (see below) and the Bellavista reserve (see p.341). If you have to, you'll find a couple of basic hotels in Nanegalito.

Bosque Nublado Urcu Puyujunda

From Tulipe, a dirt road branches west up towards the village of Las Tolas, before which is a left-hand fork leading to the **Bosque Nublado Urcu Puyujunda**. This ecotourism project is perched on a peaceful ridge-top with gorgeous valley views and has six simple cabins equipped with private cold-water bathrooms ($119 per three-day trip, including lodging, meals, transport and guide). Among its five square kilometres of Chocó forest are found ancient walls, foundations and unexcavated remains of the lost Yumbos culture – easily explored on the reserve's trails. Other activities include guided hikes, horseriding, fishing, biking and cow milking on community farms partly funded by visitor contributions. **Volunteers** are welcome for reforestation, community education, farm work and biological and archeological research (from $85 per week). For **information** and reservations, contact the office in Quito, Marcella E8-45 and Los Shyris (☎02/2265736, ⓦwww.cloudforestecuador.com).

Bellavista Cloud Forest Reserve

The **Bellavista Cloud Forest Reserve** comprises seven square kilometres of knife-edged mountains and deep gorges between 1400m and 2600m, incised by streams and waterfalls and clothed in dense cloudforests, epiphytes, mosses, bromeliads and orchids. Twenty well-marked **trails** provide access to the diverse wildlife of the Tandayapa valley, including 320 **bird** species such as the masked trogon, tanager-finch, moustached antpitta, plate-billed mountain toucan and countless hummingbirds, making this a popular choice for birdwatchers – as well as any nature-lover. The lodge itself is dominated by a four-storey geodesic dome perched high on a mountain ridge, and gives astounding views over the valley and effectively doubles up as an observation tower above the forest canopy. You can also arrange horseriding trips, guided birdwatching walks and excursions to local ruins.

Practicalities

Bellavista is a two-hour **drive** from Quito. Take the Mindo road past Nanegalito to Km52, where a signposted ridge road takes you up to Bellavista, 12km away; small vehicles can continue past Nanegalito to Km77 and take the road doubling back to the left after the sign for the Corps of Engineers. **Buses** to Pacto, Mindo, San Miguel de los Bancos and Puerto Quito leave the Terminal Terrestre in Quito and pass Nanegalito, from where you'll have to hire a **camioneta** ($15).

Double **rooms** in the dome (❾) have balconies and private hot-water bathrooms, while above and accessed by ladder are shared sleeping areas ($57 per person). Further accommodation is available in three nearby houses, one of brick and wood, one bamboo and one secluded in the woods, each with private bath (❾). **Camping** ($7) includes use of the reserve facilities and access to the on-site restaurant (breakfast $8.50, lunch and dinner $18 each), while self-catering accommodation is available at the nearby research station ($17), though you can't buy food in the vicinity.

A full three-day package, including transport, meals and a guided forest walk, starts at $171 per person. **Volunteers** (around $5 per day) are welcome to work on general maintenance and path clearing, as are visiting researchers to undertake studies. For more **information** and reservations (required) visit the office in Quito, Jorge Washington E7-23 and 6 de Diciembre (☎02/2232313, ⓦwww.bellavistacloudforest.com), or call Bellavista direct (☎02/2116232; the owner-manager is English).

Tandayapa Bird Lodge

Located at 1700m and set on the edge of seven square kilometres of lush cloud-forest in the Tandayapa valley, **Tandayapa Bird Lodge** is known as one of the best birdwatching spots in Ecuador. The owners provide advice on the best sites, times of day and weather conditions for seeing any of the more than three hundred **bird** species inhabiting the valley, including 21 endemics found only in the Chocó bioregion, such as the rare **white-faced nunbird**, first discovered nesting nearby. Dozens of colourful hummingbirds flock to the feeders around the lodge and there are a number of **trails** of varying length and difficulty that crisscross the cloudforest, as well as canopy platforms and balconies that allow close observation of life in the trees. One highlight is the "forest floor species feeding station", a hide that allows you close access to shy ground birds such as the **moustached antpitta**, a bird so reclusive it was identified for the first time in Ecuador in 1996.

Practicalities

The lodge has comfortable private double **rooms** ($185, including full board) and singles ($109), plus a library and bar where an ornithologist is always on hand at the end of the day to answer questions over a cocktail. Multi-day packages are also available, including guided walks and transport to and from Quito. By **car**, take the road past Calacalí to Km52 and turn left beyond the *Paraíso del Pescador* onto a track that continues 6km to the lodge. **Buses** to Nanegalito regularly pass this turn-off, from where you can walk or hitch a ride, or continue to Nanegalito and take a **camioneta** for around $6. For reservations and information contact the office in Quito at El Condor Oe4-145 and Avenida Brasil (T02/2433676 or 09/9231314, Wwww.tandayapa.com).

Mindo

Set at 1250m on the forested western slopes of Volcán Pichincha, **MINDO** resembles an Alpine village transplanted to the tropics, with steep-roofed, chalet-like farmhouses punctuating its lush and beautiful landscape. Its pleasant subtropical climate attracts an increasing number of visitors seeking to spend a few days hiking, horseriding, "canopying" (zipping over the forest canopy on wires) or taking part in *regatas* – floating down rivers on inflatable tubes. But above all, the town is most renowned as a base for **birdwatching** in the surrounding hills, part of the biologically diverse **Chocó Endemic Bird Area**, which BirdLife International has officially designated an "Important Bird Area", the first in South America.

  Mindo has been held in high regard among birdwatchers ever since ornithologist Frank M. Chapman described the local avifauna in his seminal 1926 book, *The Distribution of Bird-Life in Ecuador*. One reason for Mindo's prolific biodiversity is its location in a transitional area between higher-altitude temperate zones and the lower humid tropical forests. This sector encompasses several habitats and harbours some 370 bird species, many of them endemic, including the velvet-purple coronet (one of 33 hummingbirds), yellow-collared chlorophonia and the endangered long-wattled umbrella bird – resembling a crow with an unmistakeable, dangling black wattle and a large Elvis quiff for a crest. With a good guide, you may see at least thirty endemic species and many dozens of other birds on a three- to four-day **tour** of Mindo's forests, which also hold several **leks** (courting grounds) for the Andean cock-of-the-rock and the club-winged manakin.

  There are also several hundred types of **butterflies** and a wealth of orchids here. There are between 25 and 32 species of colourful *lepidoptera* at **Mariposas de Mindo**, about 2.5km along the signposted track from the southwest corner of the town square (daily 9am–6.30pm; $3; taxi $5), bred for export around the world. The best **orquideario** ($2), at the *Armonía* hotel, cultivates around 200 orchid varieties, which can grow up to 5m, though many are so small they require a magnifying glass to be seen in any detail. A block from the park on 9 de Octubre, **Jardín Nathaly** ($3) exhibits a smaller assemblage of both orchids and butterflies. For more on reserves and excursions outside town, see "Activities around Mindo", p.345.

▲ Butterfly, Mariposas de Mindo

Arrival and information

Mindo is 6km down a winding road branching south of the Calacalí-La Independencia highway. Flor del Valle runs daily **buses** right into town from the Ofelia station in Quito (Mon–Fri 8am & 3.45pm, Sat 7.40am, 8.20am, 9.20am, 4pm, Sun, 7.40am, 8.20am, 9.20am, 1.45pm, 5pm; 2hr 30min trip). From Santo Domingo, Transportes Kennedy offers three daily buses to Mindo, and from the Terminal Terrestre in Quito there are plenty of buses that pass the turn-off to Mindo. From here, you can take a lift into town ($3, or less by *colectivo*), or make the ninety-minute walk. From Mindo, buses leave for Quito from Avenida Quito (daily 6.30am & 2pm), with some extra afternoon buses at weekends. Seats fill up quickly, so buy your tickets early.

Information is available from the municipal office on the corner of the park (under construction at the time of writing) and from other private offices on Avenida Quito.

Accommodation

Mindo has more than sixty **hotels** and sleeping capacity for over 1500 people. We've included some of the best options both in and outside of town. The more upmarket places tend to be out of town and have their own private reserves.

In town

Arco Iris 9 de Octubre on the *parque central* ☎02/3900405. Inexpensive option offering rooms either with private bath and hot water, or shared bath without, as well as a little TV lounge. ❷–❸
Armonía South end of the football pitch ☎02/3900431 or 09/9435098, ⓦwww .birdingmindo.com. Has a few modest rooms with shared baths and nicer secluded cabins with their own facilities at the back of the Orquideario. ❷

El Bijao Av Quito ☎02/3900430. This friendly and helpful place has simple wooden rooms fitted with screens and repellent coils to ward off mosquitoes, and a choice of shared or private bathrooms with hot water. The communal space features hammocks, a library and games, and there's a swimming pool, sauna and jacuzzi out back. The on-site restaurant is good and serves cheap fish, chicken or vegetarian dishes and set menus, as well as pancakes for breakfast. ❷

Birdwatcher's House Los Colibris ☏ 02/3900444, ⓦ www.birdwatchershouse.com. Cosy, spick-and-span en-suite rooms in a striking wood-and-thatch house with its own restaurant. Hot water, sauna, jacuzzi and parking are among the perks. ⑥

La Casa de Cecilia A few blocks northeast of the main square ☏ 09/3345393 or 02/3900413. Occupying a pleasant riverside location with a nice swimming spot, this good budget hotel has simple, clean rooms, kitchen facilities and can arrange excursions and volunteer work. ②

El Descanso Los Colibris ☏ 02/3900443, ⓦ www.eldescanso.net. An attractive, well-kept wooden house with a garden, offering good rooms and a cheaper shared loft ($12). Breakfast included. ⑤

Jardín de los Pájaros Los Colibris ☏ 09/1756688. Friendly hotel offering pleasant double rooms with private baths and hot water, and a nearby cabin ideal for families. Breakfast included and meals cooked on request. ④

San Vicente Five minutes' walk uphill southeast of the square ☏ 02/2236275. Friendly, family-run hacienda renowned for its guava jam, offering simple rooms with shared bath, in a building overlooking a rushing stream. Price includes full board and entrance to its forest. ⑥

Las Tangaras Av Quito ☏ 02/3900466, ⓦ www.lastangaras.com.ec. Enormous new complex with a floodlit swimming pool, sauna, whirlpool and steam room. The rooms have hot water, private bath, satellite TV and DVD. There's also an on-site restaurant and staff can help arrange trips and guides. ⑦

Out of town

El Carmelo 1km southwest of the football pitch ☏ 02/3900409, ⓦ www.mindo.com.ec. Double rooms, treehouses and cabins for up to six, as well as a pool, forest reserve and campsites ($8 per person). Regular price includes breakfast. Substantial discounts available Sun–Thurs, otherwise ⑦

Casa Divina 1.2km on the road to *Mindo Garden* ☏ 09/0509626, ⓦ www.mindocasadivina.com. Beautiful two-storey cabins set in a small private reserve with hiking trails and lookouts. The comfy en-suite rooms sleep one to four and come with proper bathtubs, porches and hammocks. The owners are helpful and keen on local conservation initiatives. ⑨

Mariposas de Mindo 2.5km on the road to *Mindo Garden* ☏ 02/3900493 or Quito 2440360, ⓦ www.mariposasdemindo.com. Quiet wooden cabins with private bath and hot water in the pleasing gardens of the butterfly farm. Breakfast included. ⑥

Mindo Garden 1.5km beyond *El Monte* ☏ 09/7331092, ⓦ www.mindogardens.com. Set in a peaceful garden full of flowering plants, featuring plush cabins within the sound of the river, games room and good restaurant. Breakfast included. ⑦

El Monte 2km along *Mindo Garden* road ☏ 09/3084675, ⓦ www.ecuadorcloudforest.com. A comfortable lodge just a 15min drive from Mindo (transport arranged when you reserve in advance), featuring three two-storey cabins sleeping up to four, with private baths and hot water but no

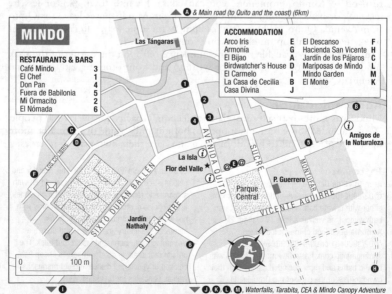

▲ Ⓐ & Main road (to Quito and the coast) (6km)

MINDO

Las Tángaras

RESTAURANTS & BARS
Café Mindo	3
El Chef	1
Don Pan	4
Fuera de Babilonia	5
Mi Ormacito	2
El Nómada	6

ACCOMMODATION
Arco Iris	E	El Descanso	F
Armonía	G	Hacienda San Vicente	H
El Bijao	A	Jardín de los Pájaros	C
Birdwatcher's House	D	Mariposas de Mindo	L
El Carmelo	I	Mindo Garden	M
La Casa de Cecilia	B	El Monte	K
Casa Divina	J		

Amigos de la Naturaleza

La Isla
Flor del Valle ★

AVENIDA QUITO

SUCRE

MONTUAR

P. Guerrero

Parque Central

VICENTE AGUIRRE

SIXTO DURÁN BALLÉN

Jardín Nathaly

9 DE OCTUBRE

0   100 m

▼ Ⓘ

▼ Ⓙ, Ⓚ, Ⓛ, Ⓜ, Waterfalls, Tarabita, CEA & Mindo Canopy Adventure electricity. Price includes board and guided activities and entrance into the forest. **9**

Sachatamia Lodge Km78 on the Calacalí road, east of Mindo turn-off ☎02/3900906, ⓦwww .sachatamia.com Smart, comfortable rooms in a polished, well-appointed lodge with views across its 1.2-square-kilometre private reserve, which includes a canopy cable traverse. Breakfast included. **7**

Eating and drinking

Many hotels, particularly the pricier ones, have decent **restaurants**, and there are several well-priced restaurants on Avenida Quito; these include *Don Pan*, an inexpensive pizzeria and bakery, *Mi Ormacito* and *El Chef*, which does good, cheap set menus. For decent trout, tilapia and fruit juice, among other snacks and dishes, try *Fuera de Babilonia*, north of the park. P. Guerrero, on the park, is a grocery stocking the best in locally made yoghurts, cheeses, jams, biscuits, *manjar de leche* and other goodies. Popular venues for an evening **drink**, include the relaxed *El Nómada* bar, on Aguirre, south of the square.

Activities around Mindo

There are many good hikes around Mindo in the **private reserves** adjoining the larger Bosque Protector Mindo-Nambillo (out of bounds to the general public), which usually have **hiking trails** you can use for a small fee. One of the most popular is to the **Cascada de Nambillo** waterfall ($5 or $3 for students; 4hr round-trip), an attractive spot where you can swim in a cooling river pool. With concrete changing rooms, a waterslide and plenty of family groups at weekends, don't expect a secret pristine paradise.

The latest Mindo craze is whizzing along zip lines high above the forest canopy, attached to the cable by a harness. The larger, locally operated **Mindo Ropes and Canopy**, about 2.5km up the road to the Nambillo waterfall ($15 full tour; ⓦwww.mindoropescanopy.com), features 12 cables ranging from 125m to 500m, totalling 2650m, and short guided hikes in the forest between cable platforms. The Costa Rican-run **Mindo Canopy Adventure**, about 100m further along ($2.50–15; ⓦwww.mindocanopy.com), has a collection of 13 zip lines ranging in length from 20m to 400m, making a total aerial canopy tour of 2500m.

Less adrenalized forest-lovers might prefer to push on another 1.5km or so to the more sedate **Tarabita de Mindo** (Thurs–Sun; $5) a 530-metre cable-car ride across a ravine to a private reserve, the **Santuario de las Cascadas**, where trails lead to seven waterfalls ($3 entrance); for tickets and information, go to *Café Mindo* on Avenida Quito. The environmental group Los Amigos de la Naturaleza de Mindo runs the **Centro de Educación Ambiental** (CEA), a short walk beyond *Mindo Garden* hotel, which includes simple, but attractive **cabañas** (**8**; three meals included) in a forest on the fringes of the reserve, where they maintain several good hiking trails (including one to the Cascada de Nambillo), and offer treks and tubing trips. Volunteers are also welcome ($200 per month) for conservation and educational work; for information and reservations ask at the Amigos de la Naturaleza office or at P. Guerrero groceries (☎02/2170115, ✉amigosmindo@yahoo.com). Another popular hike (3hr each way) is to the **Cascada de Azúcar**, inside the La Isla reserve, which you can rappel down with a guide for $15 and **camp** nearby for $5; for tickets and information contact the La Isla office on Avenida Quito (☎09/3272190, ✉laislamindo@yahoo.com).

You can hire **horses** at hotels such as *El Carmelo de Mindo*, *El Monte* and *San Vicente*, and you can rent fairly battered **mountain bikes** for $6 per day from Bici Star on 9 de Octubre by the square. Many places in town can provide you with equipment for **tubing** down local rivers (*regatas*) or arrange **guides** (make sure they have a licence from the Ministerio de Turismo) for hikes. Local ornithologist guides aren't nearly as prevalent, but there are few as expert albeit more expensive, as Vinicio Pérez (fixed fee of $100 per day or $150 with transport), who speaks good English and comes with a guarantee to see a hundred different bird species. Ask for him at *Birdwatcher's House* (T02/3900444 or 09/9476867, W www.ecuadorbirding.com).

West from Mindo

From the forested hills around Mindo, the Calacalí–La Independencia road continues its descent to the coast, entering open subtropical farmland punctuated by the odd palm tree. This region has long been the domain of cattle ranchers and farmers, who colonized it with *fincas* and homesteads and bought supplies in the three bustling centres along the route: **San Miguel de los Bancos**, 11km beyond the Mindo turn-off, **Pedro Vicente Maldonado**, 30km further on, and **Puerto Quito**, 23km west on the banks of the Río Caoni. With its warm climate and proximity to the capital, rolling scenery streaked by rivers and hidden waterfalls and acres of cheap land ripe for exploitation, developers are finally becoming aware of the tourism potential of the area. Regular **buses** ply the road from the Terminal Terrestre in Quito, and leave Santo Domingo about every twenty minutes for San Miguel de Los Bancos; if you get stuck anywhere en route, each of the three towns along the way provides accommodation.

By the time the old coastal road reaches the main Santo Domingo–Esmeraldas road, 28km on from Puerto Quito, you're in the lowlands proper, where the sun beats down with tropical intensity and huge **African palm** plantations and their oil-extracting factories begin to appear beside **fruit farms** and **banana** plantations. Santo Domingo, the commercial centre of the northern lowlands, is 49km southwest of the junction, while Esmeraldas, the biggest port on the north coast, is 130km north.

Practicalities

The smartest of several **resorts** along the road is **Arashá**, at Km121 and 4km west of Pedro Vicente Maldonado (T02/2449881, W www.arasharesort.com; packages ❾ with meals, one spa treatment and transport to and from Quito), a collection of luxurious thatched cabins with modern, tiled interiors set amid carefully landscaped gardens and a large spring-water pool. The centrepiece of the complex is a spa offering treatments including massages, body wraps, facials, aromatherapy baths and jacuzzi baths with mineral salts. The resort also arranges excursions into the surrounding countryside to spots such as **Laguna Azul**, a lake fed by a thirty-metre waterfall, and visits to Tsáchila communities.

Two kilometres before Puerto Quito, a minor road on the left at Km140 leads to **Aldea Salamandra** (T09/1981711, or Quito 02/2237353; $26 per person with board and excursions), an ecologically minded retreat with composting latrines and simple thatched cabañas and treehouses by the Río Caoni. Excursions include trips to fruit farms, cacao-picking to make your own chocolate, tubing on the river and bathing in the waters of a small lowland tropical reserve a ten-minute walk away, and **volunteers** are welcome to help with reforestation, harvesting and maintenance programmes (weekly $55 or monthly $200 contribution). A plusher option and popular with nationals is *La Isla* (T02/2463641 or 09/4499125, W www.hosterialaisla.com; ❼ including meals), a couple of kilometres past *Aldea Salamandra*, on a river island in a pretty setting with a fishing lake and swimming pool.

Santo Domingo de los Colorados and around

Getting to and from the major transport hub of **SANTO DOMINGO DE LOS COLORADOS** is far easier than finding anything to do once you're there. The city is encircled by a ring road linking a number of fast radial roads – east to Quito, north to Esmeraldas, west to Pedernales, southwest to Manta, Bahía de Caráquez and Portoviejo and south to Guayaquil via Quevedo.

When the road from Quito was completed almost fifty years ago, the door was unlocked to large tracts of forest, which were rapidly felled to make way for intensive agriculture, notably the enormous banana and oil-palm plantations that contribute a significant chunk to the national economy. Since then, Santo Domingo has grown at a phenomenal rate and is by far the most important commercial centre in the northern coastal interior. Its narrow, crowded and polluted streets – although recently improved after an injection of civic cash on being made the capital of the new Santo Domingo province – hold few attractions to sightseers, though the town does make a serviceable base for seeing nearby forest reserves, the last remaining pockets of coastal tropical wet forest, most of which have accommodation, guides and trails.

Birdwatchers on their way to these reserves might consider taking the old road from Quito to Santo Domingo via **Chiriboga**. It's a little-used dirt track (4WD recommended) servicing the Trans-Ecuadorian Oil Pipeline and passes through various transitional forests containing hundreds of bird species as it plunges from an altitude of 3000m before joining the main road from Alóag near La Unión del Toachi at 1200m. There are few facilities on this road, but you can stay at the rustic **Bosque Protector Río Guajalito** scientific station sct amid five square kilometres of forest, home to the rarely seen hoary puffleg hummingbird ($2 entrance; ☎09/5872237, ⓦwww.geocities.com/bp_guajalito, ⓔjavierrobayo @gmail.com; reservations required). There's a thirty-person dorm ($15 per person including meals) or you can **camp** for $5 per tent.

Arrival and information

The **bus** terminal, 1.5km north of the town centre along Avenida de los Tsáchilas, is serviced by dozens of companies with many routes across Ecuador. To reach the centre, either take a **taxi** ($1.50) or one of the local buses, many of which run along the main street and access the terminal. For **money**, Banco de Guayaquil has a Visa ATM on Avenida Quito north of town; Banco del Pacífico has a MasterCard and Cirrus ATM on the corner of 29 de Mayo and Ibarra; and Banco Pichincha has an ATM on the Chone roundabout. **Internet facilities** are available around the centre, particularly on Avenida 29 de Mayo.

Accommodation

You'll find a glut of cheap **hotels** around the noisy 29 de Mayo, many of which don't have hot water. Rooms away from the street are usually preferable, unless they lack windows, in which case they're likely to be a bit musty.

Covi Center 29 de Mayo and Cuenca ☎02/2754237. Affordable hotel offering clean rooms with private baths, phones and cable TVs, especially its quieter units at the back, though there's no hot water. ❷

Grand Hotel Santo Domingo Av Río Toachi and Galápagos ☎02/2767947, ⓦwww.grandhotelsd .com. This immaculate hotel is easily the best place in the centre, with smart and comfortable rooms. Breakfast is included, plus there's a jacuzzi, sauna and pool. ❽

Jennefer Av 29 de Mayo and Latacunga (no phone). Worth paying a bit more to get an electric shower and cable TV in some of the more spacious rooms. Avoid the small, cheap rooms at the back. **❷**

Sheraton Opposite the terminal, Av A. Calazacón ☎02/2751988. This secure establishment with clean, decent rooms with hot water and a popular restaurant downstairs is the best bet if you're catching an early-morning bus and want to stay close to the terminal. **❸**

Zaracay Av Quito Km1.5 ☎02/2750316, ⓦwww .hotelzaracay.com. On the outskirts of town and set in extensive grounds, with comfortable rooms (some with a/c) that include breakfast, plus a pool, tennis court and restaurant. **❽**

The Town

The only thing really worth a look here is the **market** along Avenida 3 de Julio, west of the main square of **Parque Zaracay**; it's busiest on Sunday, but bustles all week with locals buying food, clothes and other goods – though the covered section, thronged with butchers, isn't for the squeamish. The streets get even more crowded during the July 3 **fiesta** for Santo Domingo's cantonization, when an agricultural fair packs the *recinto ferial* exhibition hangar opposite the *Zaracay* hotel.

In the 1960s, tourists began coming to Santo Domingo to see the **Tsáchila** people, whom the Spanish labelled **Los Colorados**, meaning "coloured" or "redheads", due to their bowl haircuts pasted down with bright-red *achiote* dye. Although the city takes part of its name from this Spanish moniker, these days you're unlikely to see any urban Tsáchila wearing traditional dress or sporting their celebrated hairstyles – except for the stereotypes on local billboards and statues. The destruction of the forests around Santo Domingo has had a deep effect on the Tsáchila, the majority of whom have been forced to abandon their traditional way of life. The seven remaining Tsáchila communities are in the environs of the city. You'll see roadside signs for Tsáchila **curanderos**, shaman healers who now offer their services to outsiders, along the way to Quevedo, and the **Ecomuseo Etnográfico Shino Pi Tsáchila**, a museum explaining the culture and history of the people, is in the Búa community, 15km from Santo Domingo on the Chone road. You can visit some communities with tour

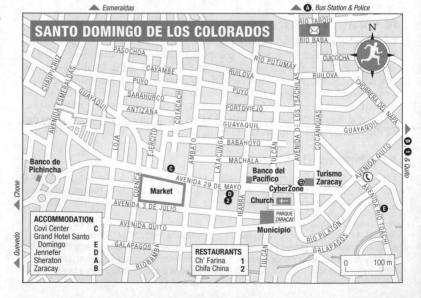

agencies in Santo Domingo, such as Turismo Zaracay, 29 de Mayo and Cocaniguas (☏02/2750546), and at the *Zaracay* hotel, which also offers **tours** to local forest reserves and an oil-palm plantation.

Eating

The more expensive hotels serve the best **food** in town, notably the *Grand Hotel Santo Domingo* and then *Zaracay*. There are also a few reasonable eateries outside the centre on **Avenida Quito**.

Ch' Farina at Km1 Av Quito ☏02/2763500 or 2750295. Located outside the centre, part of a decent pizza chain that does deliveries.

Che Luis Av Quito, on the way out of town. Moderately priced grillhouse serving steaks, chicken and other barbecued food.

Chifa China 29 de Mayo and Latacunga. The best of the local *chifas*, tucked in the courtyard of the *Jennefer* hotel.

Grand Hotel Santo Domingo Av Río Toachi and Galápagos. Its superior restaurant has a wide-ranging menu and very good dishes for around $8 per main course, including vegetarian meals, breakfasts and *criollo* specialities at the weekend. There are great set menus for $4.50 on Sundays.

Around Santo Domingo

Although a huge amount of lowland forest around Santo Domingo has been flattened for farming, pockets remain within striking distance of the city. Pressure to develop "unproductive" land – a euphemism for forests – has been considerable since the late 1950s, as colonists eyed more space for banana, palm and cacao plantations. Under government statute such undeveloped areas were up for grabs to anyone who intended to make them "productive", a policy that led to the destruction of more than ninety percent of Ecuador's northwestern forests. A handful of conservationists were nimble enough to buy forestland and set up their own private reserves, which are now among Ecuador's last **coastal tropical wet forests** in the Chocó bioregion.

Nurturing astounding wildlife diversity, these forest reserves are located in several areas: between Alóag and Santo Domingo; at the **Bosque Protector La Perla**, on the road to Quinindé; at the private **Reserva Biológica Bilsa**, adjoining the little-explored, state-run **Reserva Ecológica Mache–Chindul**, west of Quinindé; and at the **Bosque Protector Río Palenque**, on the Quevedo road.

La Hesperia and the Reserva Otonga

The Alóag–Santo Domingo road is one of the busiest routes to the coast, with **buses** passing by every few minutes, but there are a few scraps of dense **tropical forest** in secluded parcels off the highway. As you descend from the sierra, the first of these you'll come to is **La Hesperia** (turning at Km58; ⓦ www.volunteersecuador.com), just a ten-minute drive off the highway, a hacienda with its own seven-square-kilometre **forest reserve**. Recently developed for ecotourism, it has comfortable accommodation in three houses: one with private bathrooms and hot water ($45 per person), another with shared bathrooms ($35) and the last for volunteers ($20); camping is also available ($6). The private reserve abuts the larger Bosque Protector Toachi-Pilatón, and there are great opportunities for hiking, birdwatching and trout fishing in the Río Pilatón, while back at the hacienda you can hire a horse, get involved in the farming activities or serve as a volunteer. Reservations are required; call ☏09/9800521 or 02/2241877, or contact Fundación Jatun Sacha in Quito (☏02/2432240, ⓦ www.jatunsacha.org).

East of Alluriqín, at the small settlement of **La Unión del Toachi**, an access road leads south to the remote **Reserva Otonga**, whose forests are rich in wildlife and thought to contain several endemic species. The site is reached by a two-hour drive in a *camioneta* or *ranchera*, followed by a two-hour **hike** to the reserve station, which offers simple **accommodation** in a dormitory for thirty people (bring a sleeping bag). For more information, contact the reserve's Italian administrator, Dr Giovanni Onore (Ⓔgonore@puceuio.puce.edu.ec, Ⓦwww .parks.it/world/EC/riserva.otonga).

Tinalandia

Sixteen kilometres east of Santo Domingo on the road to Alóag, a signposted driveway leads to **Tinalandia** (Ⓦwww.tinalandia.com; ❽), a hacienda converted into a hotel in the 1950s, when its nine-hole golf course quickly made it one of the best-known lowland country hotels in Ecuador. Today its lush primary forest is renowned for its excellent **birdwatching** ($10 reserve entrance to non-residents), in which more than 350 species have been spotted around the grounds, including such rarities as the ochre-bellied flycatcher and the scaly-throated foliage-gleaner. Most of the delicately ageing **rooms** and **cabins** have hot water and are a kilometre uphill from the entrance, and the **restaurant** serves good food. Considering the resort's popularity with birding enthusiasts, try to make advance **reservations**, either directly (Ⓣ09/9467741) or through the office in Quito (Ⓣ02/2449028).

Bosque Protector La Perla

Forty kilometres northwest of Santo Domingo on the road to Quinindé (official name Rosa Zárate), and a few kilometres short of the unremarkable agricultural centre of La Concordia, the **Bosque Protector La Perla** (Ⓣ&Ⓕ02/2725344; $5, including guide) is a private 2.5-square-kilometre tropical wet-forest reserve with abundant birdlife set amid African oil-palm and banana plantations. At the reception hut near the signposted entrance off the main road, a Spanish-speaking **guide** (best reserved in advance) can direct you to all the best spots for birdwatching along several forested **trails**. You can't stay at the nearby hacienda, but **camping** ($5), bathroom and shower facilities are available at the site.

Alternatively, the nearest and best accommodation is the large *Athos* hotel, in **La Concordia** on the Calle Principal (Ⓣ02/2725488, Ⓦwww.hotelatos.com .ec; ❻), with air-conditioned en-suite rooms, though there are other cheaper options in town. You could also stay at one of the pleasant country hotels at **Valle Hermoso**, a town 2km off the Santo Domingo–Quinindé highway on the road towards San Miguel de Los Bancos, 19km southeast of La Concordia. The *Hostería Valle Hermoso* (Ⓣ02/2773208; ❺), set in 120-hectare grounds with lakes and waterfalls on the banks of the Río Blanco, is one of the better choices.

You can get to La Perla on any **bus** running between Santo Domingo and Quinindé or Esmeraldas, or take a **taxi** from La Concordia for a few dollars; they gather around the town's main square.

Reserva Biológica Bilsa

In the Mache hills west of Quinindé, 90km northwest of Santo Domingo on the road to Esmeraldas, is one of the last major tracts of Ecuadorian coastal humid tropical forest, the 30-square-kilometre **Reserva Biológica Bilsa**, which adjoins the enormous Mache-Chindul reserve. The reserve's forests range from 300m to 750m in altitude, high enough for heavy layers of fog to loom over the upper ridges, saturating the vegetation and allowing for great biodiversity. More than thirty new **plant** species have been discovered here, and it also has some of coastal Ecuador's greatest diversity of **birds** – one of the few places in the country where the rare long-wattled umbrella bird makes frequent appearances. **Mammals** at the reserve include jaguars, ocelots and the diminutive jaguarundi, while substantial numbers of mantled howler monkeys bawl across the canopy. The on-site **Center for the Conservation of Western Forest Plants** produces thirty thousand trees each year for reforestation projects, promotes environmental awareness and teaches land management to local communities.

Accommodation is in simple double or triple rooms with shared baths and latrines ($30 with three daily meals), and **volunteers** are welcomed to help with community and reforestation projects (minimum one-month service; $475 contribution). **Reservations** are essential and should be made through the Fundación Jatún Sacha in Quito at Eugenio de Santillán N34-248 and Maurian (T02/2432240, Wwww.jatunsacha.org), which can also make arrangements to access the reserve. This involves taking a bus to Quinindé, a *camioneta* to the village of La Y de la Laguna and a four-hour mule trek to the research station.

Reserva Ecológica Mache-Chindul

At the western edge of the Bilsa reserve, 700 square kilometres of coastal tropical wet forest are protected as the **Reserva Ecológica Mache–Chindul** (officially $5, but there's no guard post to collect it). It's characterized by extraordinary biodiversity and an unusually high level of endemism – more than ten percent of all its species are thought to be unique, though research is still in its early stages. Covering the northern half of the Mache-Chindul coastal mountains, which reach 800m in altitude, this remote area is one of the least-visited places in the country and has been inhabited for centuries by only a few small groups of **Chachi** and **Afro-Ecuadorian** peoples, who were largely overlooked until a road was built between Santo Domingo and Quinindé in 1948. Colonists have since slowly been encroaching, chopping down trees and selling Chachi lands illegally to lumber companies – hence the creation of this reserve in 1996.

With no tourist infrastructure inside the reserve, the easiest **access** is through the Reserva Biológica Bilsa, whose forests blend into those of Mache-Chindul. All other access points are quite remote and involve making long hikes, hauling food and camping gear, and hiring a guide or possibly even a mule ($10–15 per day, $20 for both). You can do so at the village of Boca de Tazones, 15km south of Atacames, the communities southeast of El Salto, 15km east of Muisne and 23km south of Tonchigüe, and San José de Chamanga, halfway between Muisne and Pedernales.

Bosque Protector Río Palenque

At Km56 on the Quevedo–Santo Domingo road, the **Bosque Protector Río Palenque** ($5) guards a square kilometre of tropical wet forest, ostensibly a small tract of land, though squeezed into its confines are at least twelve hundred species of plants (thirty of which are unique), 350 species each of birds and butterflies and gardens for orchids, bamboo and medicinal plants. The Fundación Wong (T04/2208670, Wwww.fundacionwong.org; reservations required) manages the reserve and encourages visitors to explore the forest and to **stay** at the Science Centre.

Quevedo

With no other sizeable community within a hundred kilometres, **QUEVEDO**, south of Santo Domingo, is a major commercial centre amid a sprawling agricultural landscape. After Babahoyo, it's the second town of little Los Ríos province, whose fertile soils are enriched by the regular flooding of its many rivers in the wet season, and support rice fields and a broad swath of banana plantations. At the crossroads of the Portoviejo–Latacunga and the heavily used Santo Domingo–Guayaquil roads, it can be a convenient place to break a long journey, but there's little else to detain you and you're unlikely to encounter any other tourists.

Quevedo has a large new **bus** terminal on the peripheral roads 2km northwest of the town centre, with regular buses to many destinations, including Quito (hourly; 5hr), Guayaquil (every 10min; 3hr), Santo Domingo (every 30min; 1hr 30min) and Manta (every 40min; 5–6hr). The Banco de Guayaquil, just off the main square on Bolívar and Sexta, has a Visa and MasterCard **ATM**. The **post office** is on 7 de Octubre and Avenida June Guzmán de Cortés.

For inexpensive **hotels**, try *Ejecutivo*, on 7 de Octubre and Segunda (❸), which has adequate rooms with cable TV and air conditioning. Quevedo's most luxurious spot, the business-oriented *Olímpico*, a taxi ride south of the centre on Avenida Jaime Roldos and Decimanovena (☎05/2750455 or 2750210, ℉2751314; ❼), offers spacious rooms with air conditioning, minibars, phones and TVs, plus an enormous ten-lane pool and a good **restaurant**. You'll find other affordable restaurants along 7 de Octubre, including several of Quevedo's many *chifas* (there is a significant Chinese community here).

The northern coast

Viewed by many Ecuadorians as the nation's playground, the **northern coast** is home to dozens of popular beach resorts, all within a day's drive of the capital. Busloads of *serranos* trundle down from the highlands to fill the resorts during weekends and holidays, making the most of the fun-loving and relaxed *costeño* spirit. Despite its popularity, the north coast is still relatively undeveloped, and you'll be able to find peaceful hideaways even at the busiest times. The area also holds mangroves, rocky cliffs, tropical wet forests, scrubby tropical dry forests, hidden fishing villages and forgotten ports, as well as some of the least explored parts of Ecuador outside the Oriente.

At the coast's northern tip near Colombia, **San Lorenzo** acts as the launching pad for trips to several little-visited destinations. The coast from La Tola down to **Esmeraldas** features long and often deserted beaches, whose potential has only recently been discovered. On the other side of Esmeraldas are some of Ecuador's most popular resorts, such as **Atacames**, loaded with beachfront bars, music and cocktails, or the smaller villages of **Tonsupa**, **Súa**, **Same** and **Tonchigüe** where fishing boats are giving way to beach towels and hotels.

Past the rocky **Punta Galera** is **Muisne**, a less hectic resort on an offshore sand bar, from where a road loops inland and back to the sea at **Pedernales** and the closest beaches to Quito. Further south, oceanside cliffs and sleepy coves make good geography for a cluster of hideaways, and the long beaches return at the surfing hangout of **Canoa**, extending all the way to **San Vicente**. Across the Río Chone estuary, **Bahía de Caráquez** is one of Ecuador's smarter resorts, while **Manta** is the country's exuberant second port and boasts a few beaches of its own. **Portoviejo** is the staid inland provincial capital of Manabí province, whose locals favour the nearby resorts of **Crucita**, **San Jacinto** and **San Clemente**.

Four main **roads** from the highlands run to the north coast; from Ibarra to San Lorenzo, running parallel to the largely disused railway; from Quito via Calacalí or Aloag; and from Latacunga via Quevedo. A fifth route from Otavalo via Quinindé is also nearing completion. Once you're at the sea, it's easy to get around on the paved coastal road, the Vía del Pacífico (E15), which runs the length of the shore. After heavy rains, washouts on roads to and around the coast are common and journey times are likely to be much greater.

The area has two distinct seasons, but the **climate** changes slightly the further south you go. Daytime average temperatures hover around 26°C (79°F) across the region throughout the year, with greater rainfall and humidity north of Pedernales; to the south there's very little rain from June to November. The **wet season** (Dec–May) features clear skies interrupted by torrential afternoon rains that can wash out roads.

Mosquitoes tend to be more of a problem at this time, and Esmeraldas province has one of the highest incidences of malaria in the country, so take plenty of insect repellent; see Basics, p.32. During the **dry season** the days are a little cooler and consistently cloudy, without as much rain. The most popular resorts get very crowded during national holidays and the **high season** (mid-June to early Sept & Dec–Jan), when hotel rates can be double the low-season prices and rooms are harder to come by.

San Lorenzo

A small, run-down town at the north-western tip of the country, surrounded by sea inlets and mangrove swamps, **SAN LORENZO** isn't exactly inviting with its ramshackle houses and pervasive sense of anarchy and disarray, evident in its dirty, potholed streets strewn with rubbish and periodically turned into muddy soup by the rain. Still, the town's considerable number of **Afro-Ecuadorians** – largely the descendants of colonial African slaves and later labourers from the plantations and mines of Colombia – do provide a distinct cultural flavour, refreshingly different

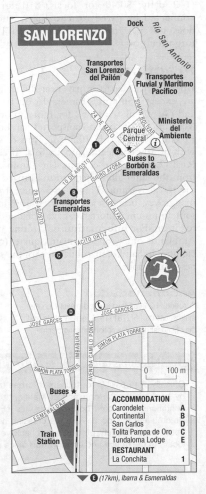

SAN LORENZO

Dock

Río San Antonio

Transportes San Lorenzo del Pailón

Transportes Fluvial y Marítimo Pacífico

24 DE MAYO

SIMÓN BOLÍVAR

Ministerio del Ambiente

Parque Central

Buses to Borbón & Esmeraldas

10 DE AGOSTO

ISIDRO AYORA

ELOY ALFARO

26 DE AGOSTO

Transportes Esmeraldas

TÁCITO ORTIZ

N

JOSÉ GARCÉS

JOSÉ GARCÉS

IMBABURA

AVENIDA CAMILO PONCE

SIMÓN PLATA TORRES

SIMÓN PLATA TORRES

SIMÓN PLATA TORRES

0   100 m

Buses

ESMERALDAS

Train Station

ACCOMMODATION	
Carondelet	A
Continental	B
San Carlos	D
Tolita Pampa de Oro	C
Tundaloma Lodge	E
RESTAURANT	
La Conchita	1

▼ **E** *(17km), Ibarra & Esmeraldas*

from the rest of the country, part of what sociologists call the "Pacific lowlands culture area", extending down the coast from Panama to Esmeraldas province in Ecuador. One of its manifestations is the colourful sound of the **marimba**, the wooden xylophone whose driving rhythms are a key feature of music and dance on the north coast. The town has several groups that stage occasional performances, and it hosts an annual international marimba **festival** during the last week of May. You'll also get plenty of fun and music at the town's main fiesta from August 6–10.

San Lorenzo's fortunes have long been tied to the railway from Ibarra. When the train opened in 1957, the population of this forgotten port doubled virtually overnight, but the anticipated economic boom never materialized; the train operated at a loss from the day it opened, and it became increasingly difficult to fund the repairs caused by frequent landslides and rockfalls. Damage from El Niño storms put an end to the full service in 1998, and it doesn't look likely to reopen any time soon. The surviving portion of the **railway** runs only 25km inland to San Javier de Cachaví, and is serviced fairly regularly by a train that leaves when demand is sufficient (1–2 daily; $0.40 for locals, $10 for foreigners). San Lorenzo is now connected by paved road to Ibarra and Esmeraldas; coastal through-traffic does not pass nearby, meaning San Lorenzo is once again becoming a forgotten port.

Practicalities

Buses arrive, depart or pass near the train station, where most company offices are, except Transportes Esmeraldas on 10 de Agosto which runs buses to Quito and Guayaquil; see p.352 for more information. At the **dock**, Trans Fluvial y Marítimo Pacífico and Transportes San Lorenzo del Pailón run four daily **boats** to Limones (7.30am, 10.30am, 1pm & 4pm; 1hr 30min, returning after 1hr) with hourly connections to La Tola; three daily to San Pedro beach and Palma Real (7.30am, 2pm & 4pm; 1hr 15min and 1hr 30min respectively, returning from the latter after 1hr); and to Tumaco in Colombia (7am & 1pm), but note the travel warning. This is also where to come to arrange boat **tours** of the mangroves, beaches and sites around town. Boat travel is exhilarating, but sometimes uncomfortable; have a hat and sunblock handy and take something to sit on. For **information** on visiting nature reserves, try the Ministerio del Ambiente office on the main square (☎06/2780184). There are few **bank** facilities in San Lorenzo, but a few of the shops on Imbabura change Colombian pesos into dollars.

Accommodation

Carondelet 24 de Mayo and Isidro Ayora, on the main square ☎06/2781119. A friendly place and the cheapest habitable option, offering clean, slightly poky rooms with mosquito nets and private baths. ➋

Continental Imbabura and Isidro Ayora ☎06/2780125, ℱ2780304. Half the rooms have

---

The Colombian border: travel warning

Offically, it's possible for tourists to **cross into Colombia** from San Lorenzo, either by boat to Tumaco or inland at Mataje, but in light of the increasingly dangerous conditions of remote border areas, it's strongly advised that you **do not enter** Colombia at this point – use the crossing north of Tulcán instead. To find out more about current safety precautions, check your embassy's **travel advisories** or ask locally at the **police and immigration** office in San Lorenzo (near the town entrance).

a/c, private baths and hot water, making it relatively luxurious, and romantic murals of life in San Lorenzo help lend a dash of cheer to the place. ❸–❹

San Carlos Imbabura and José Garces ☎&℻06/2780284. A simple hotel offering rooms with fans and mosquito nets; a few come with private bath, but no hot water. ❷–❸

Tolita Pampa de Oro Tácito Ortiz and 26 de Agosto ☎06/2780214. Comparatively spacious rooms with mosquito nets, fans and TV. If you can, try and hold out for one with a private bath and windows, which are leagues better than the interior rooms. ❷

Tundaloma Lodge Km17 on the Ibarra road ☎09/7788743, ⓦwww.tundaloma.com. The best local accommodation, a 20min taxi ride outside of town, comprises a group of comfortable wooden cabins sleeping four each, equipped with private bathrooms and warm water. They're on a steep hillside overlooking forest, so the birdwatching is good. ❻

San Lorenzo doesn't have many **restaurants**, other than grimy restaurants doling out the usual fish dishes, though *La Conchita* on 10 de Agosto is a cut above the rest, while the *Carondelet* hotel has passable meals and breakfasts.

Around San Lorenzo

Most travellers bypass San Lorenzo in favour of the beach resorts west of Esmeraldas, skipping the poor and largely comfortless coast on the way, with its rough lumber towns such as **Limones** and **Borbón** and tumbledown fishing villages like **La Tola**. Nevertheless, there are good opportunities here to see the mangroves of the **Reserva Ecológica Manglares Cayapas-Mataje**, and intrepid travellers can also visit the lowland forests of the **Reserva Ecológica Cotacachi–Cayapas** and the fascinating **Chachi** and **Afro-Ecuadorian** communities at its fringes. Community ecotourism projects, such as those in **Playa de Oro** and **San Miguel**, also make good bases, though you'll usually have to give them plenty of notice to prepare for your arrival; there's also basic accommodation in some of the river settlements.

There are two **routes** from **San Lorenzo to Esmeraldas**, 110km to the southwest. The fastest by several hours is the new **inland road** to Esmeraldas via Borbón and Maldonado. The other route involves **taking a boat** via Limones and La Tola and then a **bus** along the coast. Although slower and less comfortable, this latter route is far more scenic and passes through the tangled mangrove swamps of the Reserva Ecológica Manglares Cayapas-Mataje.

Reserva Ecológica Manglares Cayapas-Mataje

The **Reserva Ecológica Manglares Cayapas-Mataje** (officially $5; unlikely to be collected) comprises 513 square kilometres of **mangrove swamps**, a labyrinthine network of natural channels and canals between densely forested islands, stretching from the Colombian border to the estuary at La Tola. Five types of mangrove grow here, trees uniquely adapted to the salt water and loose sandy soils of the coast, whose knotted roots give protection from the tides, trap sediments and nurture a wealth of plants, fish, crustaceans and shrimp. Pelicans, frigatebirds, egrets and herons nest in their branches, taking advantage of this abundance of food.

You can travel through the mangroves and visit **Playa de San Pedro**, a twelve-kilometre sandy beach on an island at the northwest of the reserve, and **La Tolita Pampa de Oro** (see p.356) by taking a passenger boat from San Lorenzo, or by arranging a **tour** with one of San Lorenzo's boat companies, such as Coopseturi, at the Trans Fluvial y Marítimo Pacífico office at the dock (☎&℉06/2780161 or 2781603; ask for Andres Carvache), which offers **day-tours**, with boat trips from $30 per person, in groups of four. For other local **guides** try Olím Ferrín (☎06/2786091) of La Tola, or Julio de la Cruz from San Lorenzo (☎06/2781058), or Antonio Alarcón (☎09/7707459).

La Tolita Pampa de Oro

The archeological sites of the **La Tolita** people, who inhabited the region from 500 BC to 500 AD, offer little to see beyond a few earthen mounds, though at **La Tolita Pampa de Oro**, at the south end of the reserve on an island near La Tola, gold and platinum ornaments of exquisite craftsmanship have been unearthed. There is good reason to suppose the breathtaking **gold mask**, now the symbol of the Banco Central del Ecuador and housed in its museum in Quito, originated here, even though it was allegedly discovered near Sigsig in the highlands. With almost forty mounds distributed on a long east–west axis, the site may have played a major ceremonial or astronomical role; archeological work is ongoing and a simple **museum** exhibits some of the latest finds. The closest mainland access to La Tolita is the village of La Tola.

Limones

In the western corner of the reserve, the port of **LIMONES** (officially named Valdez) is accessible only by boat and seldom visited by gringos. Although it's even more dilapidated than San Lorenzo (to which 4 **boats** daily; 1hr 30min), you'll have to change boats here if you want to get to La Tola (hourly; 30min), from where buses head down the coast to Esmeraldas. You may also be able to catch a boat from Limones heading upstream to Borbón. If you need to stay, try *Colón* (☎06/279311; ❸) on Montúfar between 5 de Junio and Eloy Alfaro.

La Tola and Olmedo

Facing the Reserva Ecológica Manglares Cayapas-Mataje across the wide estuary of the Río Cayapas, **LA TOLA** is the fishing village from where you catch the bus to Esmeraldas after the boat ride from San Lorenzo via Limones. Across the river is the La Tolita site, which you can visit by hiring a launch, and a short bus ride outside town are the **Majagual** mangroves, thought to be the tallest in the world at more than 60m. There are trails through the mangroves here, but you'll need rubber boots if you want to stay dry.

　Boats run between La Tola and Limones every hour ($4; 30min). La Tola has a basic **hotel**, *Don Aris* (❸), if you get stuck, but try to get to Las Peñas if you can.

　In **OLMEDO**, a couple of kilometres down the Esmeraldas road, a women's cooperative runs an ecotourism project, the *Cabaña de los Manglares* (contact Luz de Alba on ☎06/2780239 in advance; ❸) which has clean bathrooms and a huge veranda strung with hammocks and supported on stilts above the tidal waters. Inexpensive **meals** are available and local **tours** include visits to the mangroves, archeological sites and beaches, plus fishing from a canoe.

Borbón

Forty kilometres southwest of San Lorenzo, unappealing **BORBÓN** is a rough-and-ready timber town sitting at the confluence of the ríos Cayapas and Santiago. The once bustling river port is best known as the hometown of the octogenarian Papa Roncón, Ecuador's greatest marimba player. Borbón is also the embarkation point for the Afro-Ecuadorian and Chachi communities upriver and the tropical forests of the Reserva Ecológica Cotacachi-Cayapas.

Buses from San Lorenzo leave every 30min (1hr journey) during daylight; there's also a regular service to Esmeraldas (every 30min; 3hr). **Boats** depart in the morning for various destinations along the Río Cayapas, but there is no public service up the Río Santiago. If you're looking to travel independently up these rivers and stay with local communities rather than at the lodges, you'll need to bring a mosquito net, some means of water purification and possibly some food too, to bolster their modest supplies; take nothing for granted. Borbón has several simple but not particularly salubrious **hotels**, though *Brisas del Río Santiago* (☎06/2786211; ❶), on 5 de Agosto, the main street, has fans, mosquito nets and an owner happy to advise about river travel upstream. *Castillo*, also on 5 de Agosto (☎06/2786613; ❷), has private baths, nets and fans.

Río Cayapas

The **RÍO CAYAPAS** rises south of Borbón to enter dense, lowland tropical forests, where the simple, open-sided stilted homes of the indigenous **Chachi** people occasionally appear at the green fringes of the riverbanks. Also known as the Cayapa, the Chachi have lived on the ríos Cayapas and Santiago at least since the time of the Spanish conquest. Some maintain that the Chachi came from the sierra, fleeing the Incas or Spanish conquistadors, while others claim they were a coastal people forced inland by the descendants of black slaves (see p.361). Whatever their history, some thirty thousand Chachi lived in Esmeraldas province before the Spanish arrived, but the region was so inaccessible they were spared the worst of the old world oppression and disease. Still, only five thousand Chachi remain today, living alongside Afro-Ecuadorians; both farm plantains, hunt and fish for survival. Since the 1940s and 1950s, these communities have been under pressure from the logging industry and more recently from multinational agribusiness, looking to exploit the forests around them. However, **ecotourism** is now emerging as a good alternative means for these communities to receive income while maintaining their forests. **Boats** leave Borbón for various destinations up the river between 10am and 11.30am; arrive early to get a place.

Santa María and around
Two hours by boat from Borbón is **SANTA MARÍA**, a missionary village inhabited by Chachis and Afro-Ecuadorians, who offer demonstrations of basket- and mat-weaving. Just downstream, **Punta Venado** is unusual for being abandoned for most of the year. As the major Chachi ceremonial centre, it fills with local people at Christmas and Easter, when its vine-choked houses and overgrown plazas are cleared for religious observances, music, dancing and drinking. Roughly 30 minutes further upstream is *Kumanii Lodge* (in US ☎1-800-747-0567, ⓦwww.kumanii-lodge.com; ❼ full board), a group of cosy thatched cabins with private bathrooms and mosquito nets; tours to local communities and dugout canoe lessons are offered. At **Zapallo Grande**, a well-tended village about two hours from Santa María, you can buy local **craftworks**, including baskets, textiles, mats and pottery at a local artesanía shop.

San Miguel
Five hours south of Borbón at the confluence of the ríos Cayapas and San Miguel, **SAN MIGUEL** is the last major settlement before the Cotacachi-Cayapas

Reserve and lies within reasonable proximity of it. The local community has developed the **San Miguel Eco Project**, focused around a handsome **lodge** overlooking the village and featuring a very pleasant veranda and screened bedrooms with mosquito nets. Staying here will give you the opportunity to go on **forest walks** with an expert local **guide** inside little-visited areas of this extraordinary reserve, as well as trips to a Chachi village. For information and reservations, contact Fundación Verde Milenio in Quito (☎02/2906192, ✆www .verdemilenio.org; ❽ including board, transport and excursions). They also offer less comfortable accommodation at the reserve's guard post, which has a basic **refuge** ($4) with small dorms and a kitchen (but no running water or electricity) and space for **camping**.

Río Santiago

Less travelled than the Río Cayapas, the **Río Santiago** winds through dense forests and provides the only access to the remote northwest section of the Cotacachi-Cayapas Reserve. The first settlement upriver of Borbón, **MALDONADO** is a village just off the Borbón–San Lorenzo road, close to the wet forests of the **Bosque Humedal del Yalare**, a good place for birdwatching. From Maldonado, a road heads inland as far as **Selva Alegre**. From there, a boat travels upstream to Playa de Oro, where a community of around fifty Afro-Ecuadorian families have set up an ecotourism project; the boat leaves on Saturdays around noon ($10 for tourists; 45min) and you should make arrangements for your return journey at the same time. A chartered **motor canoe** (*flete*) from Borbón ($80) or Selva Alegre ($50) might be better value if you're in a group.

The locals of **PLAYA DE ORO**, who still depend on the shrinking forests for food, welcome visitors at *Tigrillo Lodge* (✆www.touchthejungle.org; $50 per person including meals, guiding and excursions; two weeks' advance reservation essential), thirty minutes upstream from the village or at cabins in the village, which aren't as quiet, comfortable or secluded. They give jungle tours in the community's 10,000-hectare reserve ($10 entrance), which is unusual for its emphasis on the protection of small forest cats, such as ocelots and jaguarundi.

Las Peñas

From La Tola, battered buses service the coastal road to Esmeraldas (7 daily, 3hr), joining the Vía del Pacífico 2km beyond **LAS PEÑAS**, itself 8km southwest of La Tola. When the road from Ibarra to the coast was paved a few years ago, Las Peñas, once a quiet fishing village with a few simple huts and wooden boats hauled onto the grey sand, suddenly became the most easily accessed beach from the sierra at just four hours' journey by bus. Now, beach bars and restaurants line the seafront for hundreds of metres and concrete hotels rise above the haze of the surf. The place still sees few gringos, but fills at weekends and holidays with *serranos* from Ibarra when prices lurch upwards. The pick of the **hotels** is *Cumbres Andinas* (☎06/2786065; ❷), 300m northeast of the entrance, offering straightforward rooms with optional private bath and fan, but new places are appearing all the time.

Río Verde

Beyond Las Peñas, the coastal road continues past **Lagarto** (Km99 from Mataje on the Colombian border), **Montalvo** (Km104) and **Rocafuerte** (Km111), renowned for its seafood. On this stretch you'll see plenty of pelicans, cattle egrets and frigatebirds. Seven kilometres past Rocafuerte is **RÍO VERDE**, the location of Moritz Thomsen's books *Living Poor* and *Farm on the River of Emeralds* (see p.535) and a locally popular beach hangout, though still off the beaten track for foreigners. *Hostería Pura Vida*, 2km across the bridge in Palestina (☎06/2744203; ❺–❻), is the best place to stay, on a peaceful patch of beach with en-suite rooms and pastel-painted cabins. **Camarones** (Km144) is a quiet shrimping village and at **Las Piedras** (Km146), the road runs right along the shore, where you can see fisherman sifting the shallows with their nets. The **airport** for Esmeraldas at **Tachina** is a couple of kilometres further on; the city itself is on the other side of the Río Esmeraldas estuary, reached by the crossing at **San Mateo**, 10km upstream. There's a police **checkpoint** here, where you may have to show your passport.

Esmeraldas

ESMERALDAS is the largest industrial port on the north coast and capital of Esmeraldas province, whose economy is mainly driven by an oil refinery at nearby Puerto Balao, which links up to the **Trans-Andean oil pipeline**, snaking 500km from the Oriente. Despite the city's shaky infrastructure and the slums that fester on the hillsides fringing the centre, *serranos* are still drawn here by the lively atmosphere and beaches at **Las Palmas**, an upmarket suburb at the north end of town, where the city's bars, discos and the more expensive hotels and restaurants are found.

Arrival and information

A new **bus terminal** at the Codesa roundabout at the south end of the city deals with all provincial and long-distance traffic. We have left the bus office locations marked on the map, but some are likely to close down and all tickets can be bought in the terminal anyway. A **taxi** will charge $2 to take you to the centre. In town, **city buses** travel up Avenida Libertad to Las Palmas, and buses to and from San Lorenzo pass the **airport** (served by flights from Quito) at Tachina – 25km by road, or a 45-minute taxi ride ($8). There's basic tourist **information** at the Ministerio de Turismo office at Cañizares and Bolívar (☎06/2711370). Esmeraldas has a well-deserved reputation for **crime**; stick to the busy central areas, not including the Malecón which is unsafe, and don't wander around after dark. Take a taxi if carrying valuables.

Accommodation

Finding a cheap **hotel** in Esmeraldas is easy, but most are uninspiring and travellers usually push on to one of the popular beach resorts to the southwest. Pricier options are in Las Palmas, where the better hotels can be found, and only the top places have hot water.

Apart Hotel Esmeraldas Libertad 407 and Ramón Tello ☎06/2728700 or 2728701. The best and costliest hotel in Esmeraldas proper, frequented mainly by businessmen, offering nice tiled rooms with private hot-water baths and cable TVs. Despite a renovation, the building still feels a bit tired, but the restaurant is good. Breakfast included. **⑥**

Asia 9 de Octubre and Malecón ☎06/2723148. Large hotel which is a little bit dreary, but close to the coastal bus offices and clean enough. Choice of en-suite rooms, the fancier ones coming with a/c and cable TV. Garage. **③–⑥**

Cayapas Kennedy and Valdez, Las Palmas ☎06/2721318. Rooms come with a/c and hot water, though the ones upstairs enjoy better lighting. Also has a neatly pruned garden and a fine restaurant. **⑥**

Costa Esmeraldas Sucre 911 and Piedrahita ☎06/270640. Despite the thin mattresses, the ample rooms are all decent value, especially considering they come with ceiling fans, private baths, TVs and phones – though a/c is extra. **②**

Miraflores Bolívar 6-06 and 9 de Octubre ☎06/2723077. Acceptable rock-bottom choice whose small and simple rooms with shared baths are brightened by scrupulously polished wooden floors and plastic floral arrangements. Located on the main square, so the front rooms are noisy. **②**

Suites Costa Verde Luís Tello 809 and Hilda Padilla, Las Palmas ☎06/2728714 or 2728717, ☎2728716. Comfortable suites appointed with kitchenettes, minibars, dining spaces, satellite TVs and balconies with flowery window boxes, as well as less expensive rooms without the trimmings. Breakfast included. **⑦**

The Town

The tree-filled **parque central** is the focal point of this city of 125,000, and bustles with street vendors, shoeshiners and fruit-juice sellers. The town's only real attraction is the **Museo del Banco Central**, in a sprightly new building on the corner of Bolívar and Piedrahita (Mon–Sat 9am–4.30pm; free), housing a good collection of regional pre-Columbian artefacts, particularly the wonderfully expressive ceramics of the La Tolita culture. The **Centro Cultural Afro-Indio-Americano** on Montalvo and Maldonado (Mon–Fri 8am–noon & 2–6pm; free) is where to find out more about Afro-Ecuadorian culture and history. The busy **market**, a block west of the *Apart Hotel Esmeraldas*, is an education in exotic fruits. The biggest city **fiesta** is the **Independence of Esmeraldas** on August 5, which includes dancing, processions and an agricultural fair, while around Carnaval there's the **Festival Internacional de Música y Danza Afro**, held on Las Palmas

Land of emeralds

Esmeraldas town and province derive their name from the first visits of Spanish conquistadors, who entered coastal villages around here in 1531 and supposedly found **emeralds** the size of "pigeons' eggs"; the moniker stuck, despite years of fruitless expeditions for phantom emerald mines.

Before the Conquest, the Esmeraldas coast was so heavily populated with **indigenous tribes** that Bartolomé Ruiz, who passed through the area on orders from Francisco Pizarro five years earlier, was afraid to land and anchored in the bay instead. The native population declined rapidly during the sixteenth century, probably due to the introduction of foreign diseases, Spanish military probes and the arrival of Africans as slaves and soldiers, which dramatically changed the region's ethnic and cultural character.

The **Afro-Ecuadorians** here, possibly the descendants of escaped slaves from Guinea who survived a shipwreck off the Esmeraldas coast in 1553, had control of much of the region by the early seventeenth century, which hardly bothered the Spanish, who preferred to leave alone its impenetrable forests and hostile denizens. **Pedro Vicente Maldonado**, who became the provincial governor in 1729 at the age of 25, made the most successful exploration of the region in the colonial era, building the first road down from the highlands to the coast as far as Puerto Quito.

Little else is known about the region during this period, save for an account by Irish explorer **William B. Stevenson**, who in 1809 followed Maldonado's footsteps and uncovered the settlement at Esmeraldas, which then comprised 93 houses on stilts. Even then, the legend of the emeralds lived on, as Stevenson wrote that the province derived its name "from a mine of emeralds which is found no great distance from Esmeraldas-town...I never visited it, owing to the superstitious dread of the natives who assured me that it was enchanted and guarded by an enormous dragon".

beach, featuring marimba players, and traditional Afro-Hispano-American music and dance.

Eating, drinking and nightlife

Restaurants in Esmeraldas serve up tasty seafood blended with delicious tropical flavours drawn from Afro-Ecuadorian cuisine. **Encocados**, fish steeped in spiced coconut milk, is a speciality you'll find at most restaurants and roadside stalls. Although downtown Esmeraldas has a number of cheap restaurants with decent food, the best choices are in Las Palmas at the smarter hotels and along Avenida Kennedy, such as *Los Helechos* and *La Cascada*. Otherwise, there aren't many good restaurants to choose from, though *Chifa Asiático*, Cañizares and Sucre, doles out cheap and reliable Chinese food in spacious air-conditioned surroundings, and *Las Redes*, at the park on Bolívar, is a good little place for breakfast and seafood. For **nightlife**, head to Las Palmas where the **bars** and **clubs** lining the beach blast music out into the small hours. Popular spots include *Rock Julian's*, near the beach, which is Ecuador's version of a warehouse rave.

Listings

Airline TAME, Bolívar and 9 de Octubre ☎06/2721913; airport ☎06/2475040. Buses heading to San Lorenzo pass the airport.
Banks Banco de Guayaquil, Bolívar and Montalvo (MasterCard and Visa ATM); Banco del Austro, Bolívar and Cañizares (Visa ATM); Banco Pichincha, Bolívar and 9 de Octubre (Diners, Visa and Master-Card ATM).
Buses All tickets and services should be available from the new terminal; city-centre offices may be phased out. Aerotaxi for Ibarra via Quito, and to Guayaquil; Panamericana has comfortable buses to

Quito; Reina del Camino services Santo Domingo, Portoviejo and Manta; Trans CITA has the most regular service to Ambato; Trans Esmeraldas has regular and efficient services to Quito, Santo Domingo and Guayaquil, plus buses to Machala, Manta, Salinas, Huaquillas and Cuenca; Trans Gilberto Zambrano goes regularly to Santo Domingo; Trans Occidentales for Quito and Guayaquil; Trans Pacífico and Trans La Costeñita send alternate buses regularly to Borbón, San Lorenzo and Muisne via Atacames, Same and Súa, with a handful continuing to Pedernales;

La Costeñita also goes to La Tola; River Taviazo also runs a coastal service, calling at less frequented places such as Mompiche.

Hospital On Av Libertad, at the north end of town on the way to Las Palmas. Offers 24hr emergency treatment.

Police and immigration Policía Civil Nacional, in Batallón Montufar Complex, a few kilometres south of the centre on the main road (☎06/2780537).

Post office Libertad, between Pichincha and Espejo.

The coast west to Muisne

The expanses of pale sand streaking **west of Esmeraldas** sustain some of the country's most popular seaside resorts. During the **high season** (mid-June to Sept & Dec–Jan), a deluge of vacationers descends from the highlands, but the real crush comes during Carnaval, Semana Santa, Christmas and New Year, when the price of a room – if you can find one – can double. **Atacames** is the most famous and raucous resort, while others such as **Súa** and **Same** offer a more tranquil atmosphere, but can be just as busy at peak times. The beaches break around the dry and rocky headland of the **Punta Galera**, whose cliffs and secluded coves provide the quietest and most isolated beaches in the region, giving way to mangrove forests around **Muisne**, one of the remoter seaside resorts of the province. Regular **buses** travel between Muisne and Esmeraldas.

Atacames

Relaxed by day and brash, noisy and fun at night, **ATACAMES** is one of Ecuador's top beach resorts, always crowded during holidays and at Carnaval, when it's literally standing room only on its dusky beach. The town is divided by the tidal waters of the **Río Atacames**, which parallel the shore for about 1km, resulting in a slender, sandy peninsula connected to the mainland by a footbridge and, further upstream, a road bridge.

Arrival, information and transport

Trans La Costeñita and Trans Pacífico **buses** run between Esmeraldas and Muisne and call every twenty to thirty minutes at the town's central bus stop on Cervantes. **Tricicleros** ($0.50) ferry you from the bus stop to the beach, though they travel via a road bridge, so it can be quicker to **walk** by way of the footbridge. Long-distance buses usually stop at their own offices; buy your **ticket** early if you're heading back to Quito (6hr 30min trip). Trans Esmeraldas, at Juan Montalvo and Luis Vargas Torres, has three daily and two nightly buses to Quito and two to Guayaquil (8hr), while Trans Occidentales, not far from the footbridge, has five to Quito and a night bus to Guayaquil. Aerotaxi and Panamericana have less frequent services to Quito.

An iTur office at the *municipio*, 1.8km out of town towards Esmeraldas (Mon–Fri 8am–5pm; ☎06/2731912), provides **information**, maps and advice for local trips; by the time you read this it should have a new office on the recently spruced up Malecón del Río. For **banks**, Banco Pichincha, Cervantes and Espejo, provides Visa and MasterCard cash advance, and there's an ATM for Visa, MasterCard and Diners cards on Malecón and Tolita. Su

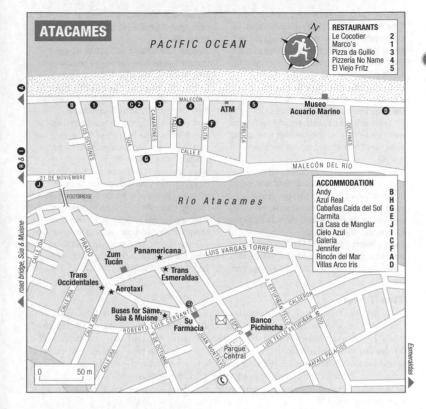

ATACAMES

PACIFIC OCEAN

MALECÓN
ATM
Museo
Acuario Marino

CAMARONES

TAGUA

TOLITA

CALLE E

PÚBLICA

DELFINES

MALECÓN DEL RÍO

21 DE NOVIEMBRE

FOOTBRIDGE

Río Atacames

CALLE 2DA

PRADO

Zum
Tucán

Panamericana

LUIS VARGAS TORRES

J. ESTUPIÑAN TELLO

CALDERÓN

OLMEDO

Trans
Occidentales

Trans
Esmeraldas

Aerotaxi

CALLE 3RA

CALLE 4RA

CALLE 5RA

Buses for Same,
Súa & Muisne

ROBERTO

LUIS CERVANTES

9 DE OCTUBRE

Su
Farmacia

JUAN MONTALVO

ESPEJO

Banco
Pichincha

LUIS TELLO ESTUPIÑAN

RAFAEL PALACIOS

Parque
Central

0   50 m

road bridge, Súa & Muisne

Esmeraldas

Farmacia, on the main road near the bus stop, changes traveller's cheques and is open late daily. The Zum Tucán **laundry**, on Vargas Torres, washes clothes by the kilogram. The **police** are located over the road bridge, first on the right on Avenida Las Acacias.

Accommodation

Despite having more than two hundred hotels rooms can be hard to come by during high season (July–Sept & holidays); expect to pay up to double the low-season rates. Weekends are also busy, but otherwise hoteliers are happy to bargain. If travelling alone, you may have to pay for all the beds in your room unless you're willing to share. In the wet season, having a **mosquito net** is a bonus. Unless you're a party animal, get a hotel with a bit of protection from the noise – that is, not overlooking the beach bars on the Malecón. The more expensive cabin complexes are often further from the racket, while the simple budget hotels crowd the centre.

Andy Malecón and Los Ostiones ☏06/2760221. Apricot-coloured high-rise at the epicentre of the resort. The sea-view rooms with balconies are great if you can take the noise, but the interior ones aren't really worth the cash. ❸

Azul Real 21 de Noviembre ☏06/2731740, ⓦwww.hotelazulreal.com. Lot with a car park, restaurant and pool and a stack of a/c rooms with cable TV and hot water. Not particularly inspirational, but clean and decent value. ❹

Cabañas Caída del Sol Malecón del Río ☎06/2731202 or 02/2957406 in Quito. Clean and roomy cabins back from the beach, equipped with private baths, fans, TVs, fridges and kitchen sinks. Good value in the low season, but prices more than double at busy times. ❸

La Casa de Manglar 21 de Noviembre ☎06/2760181. Simple rooms, mostly with bunks and shared baths, set in a peaceful location near the beach and town. You can put your feet up and watch life on the river from the rooftop terrace or make use of their internet café on the ground floor. ❸

Cielo Azul South end of 21 de Noviembre ☎06/2731813, ⓦwww.hotelcieloazul.com. Beach-front location and upmarket rooms equipped with cable TV, hot water, fridge and mosquito nets. The pool, hammocks and free wi-fi also help make this a comfy, well-sited choice. ❻

Galería Malecón ☎06/2731149. Popular for its central beachfront location and good restaurant, though the rooms are dark and poky. High-season

and weekend rates require payment for the whole room, most of which sleep four people. English spoken. ❷

Jennifer Calle Tolita ☎06/2731055. Bare and characterless brick bungalows, but good for the price, featuring fans, cable TV, bathrooms and fridges – and kitchenettes for a little more. ❷

Rincón del Mar Towards south end of beach ☎06/2760360. Pleasant cabins with fans, mosquito nets and private bathrooms, set well away from the noise and right on the beach. A few units have fridges and kitchenettes, and there's a pool too. English spoken. ❸

Villas Arco Iris At northern end of Malecón ☎06/2731069. Quiet spot abutting the beach, offering a palm-shaded avenue of attractive cabins with a/c, some with kitchens and fridges, and all with hot water and mosquito nets. Porch-side hammocks and swimming pool also make for good on-site relaxation, but a large new beachside block at the end of the garden rather spoils the view. English spoken. ❺

The Town

Most of the bars, hotels and restaurants in Atacames are on the peninsula and the shops and services are on the other side of the river, along the main road from Esmeraldas and around the little **parque central**. By the beach, the **Malecón** is the place for night-time action: salsa, merengue, pop and techno pummel the air from rival speakers, while partiers dance – or stagger – to the beat and knock back fruity cocktails. On weekdays and during the low season the crowds evaporate, but you can always count on a smattering of bars being open.

Apart from the beach and the bars, there's not much more to Atacames, though the **Museo Acuario Marino**, opposite the *Tahiti* hotel towards the northern end of the Malecón (Mon–Fri 9am–7pm, Sat 9am–10pm, Sun 9am–6pm; $1), presents starfish, turtles, caiman, seahorses and piranhas in fairly miserable conditions. Far more uplifting are the **humpback whales** visible off the coast between June and September (boats usually depart from Súa); *Tahiti* (☎06/2731078) on the Malecón is among many hotels offering whale tours. **Diving** trips are offered by Fernando Valencia, the owner of *Tahiti* (number above).

The sea here has a strong **undertow** that has claimed a number of victims, despite the occasional presence of volunteer lifeguards. **Crime** is also an unfortunate element of the quieter beach areas, so stay near the crowds, avoid taking valuables onto the beach and stay off it completely at night. The beachside **market**, mostly stocked with trinkets and sarongs, sometimes has black-coral jewellery for sale – a species under threat and illegal to take out of the country.

Eating, drinking and nightlife

The numerous **restaurants** along the Malecón serve up nearly identical **seafood** meals for $3–7, whether they come *apanado* (breaded), *frito* (fried whole), *a la plancha* (filleted and grilled or fried), *al vapor* (steamed) or *encocado* (in coconut sauce). *Marco's* is a reliable option, but there are many similar fish restaurants to choose from. **Pizza** ranks next in the popularity stakes, and the

▲ Atacames nightlife

best pizzerias are *Da Giulio*, *No Name* and *Le Cocotier*, all on the Malecón. The traditional Atacames **breakfast**, reputed to be a great hangover cure, is *ceviche* freshly prepared at the little street stalls on Calle Camarones. At night, the same stalls dish up shish kebabs and barbecued meat. *El Viejo Fritz* (also called *Der Alte Fritz*) on the Malecón, serves a good breakfast, tasty comfort food such as burgers, frankfurters and baked camembert and the odd German speciality too.

Every night most of the town's occupants gravitate towards the Malecón, promenading along its busy central section before making a beeline to any of the dozens of **beach bars** lining the sands, each laden with pyramids of fruit and bottles of rum. Current bar favourites are *Caída del Sol* and *Azul Marina*, but this can change as quickly as the merengue beat. Most of them have their own dancefloors, but more conventional **discos** playing techno and dance can be found on the other side of the street.

Súa

From **SÚA**, the exuberance of Atacames, 4km to the east, shimmers in the distance as a tiny mosaic of colour against the scrolling uniformity of the sand. Set in a cosy bay, this once-tiny fishing village can get as crowded as its more renowned neighbour in the high season, when inflatable bananas tear through the waves behind powerboats and sputtering waterbikes destroy any vestige of the town's tranquillity. Off season, Súa is quiet and friendly, though a bit less idyllic than it used to be.

At the heart of the village, the **Malecón** presents a small strip of hotels, restaurants and shops overlooking the **beach**, which is diminutive at high tide. Cradled by green hills that protect it from the full force of Pacific rollers, Súa's waters are far calmer than those of Atacames. Seasonal boats leave Súa in the morning for **humpback whale-watching** off the coast (June–Sept; $15 per person).

Practicalities

Regular **buses** between Esmeraldas and Muisne deposit passengers on the main road, a five-minute walk from the beach, from where **tricicleros** take visitors several hundred metres through the back of the village to the Malecón, where they're dropped off at the east side of the bay, by the *Chagra Ramos* hotel. There are no banking facilities in Súa.

Accommodation in Súa is less expensive and diverse than in Atacames, and it can be difficult finding a room at the height of the holidays. *Chagra Ramos* (☎06/2731006; ❸), at the east end of the bay, offers large villas that are good value for their private baths and sea-view balconies facing the setting sun, while older cabañas have ceilings that are a bit low and close; it also has a popular restaurant and you can also hire waterbikes and banana boats. Down the beach, *Las Buganvillas* (☎06/2731008; ❸) is a friendly budget choice draped in the eponymous flowers, with en-suite rooms and a swimming pool. Heading back from the beach a few blocks, *Cabañas Los Jardines* (☎06/2731181; ❺) has a pool, clean, family-sized rooms with bunks, double beds and private baths. You may need to find the owners at Bazar Barcelona on the Malecón to get in. A few reasonable seafood **restaurants**, juice stalls and beach **bars** line the Malecón; *Caracol* is a good choice.

Same

The main road leaves the coast beyond Súa to skirt the Cerro Don Juan before swinging back to the beaches at **SAME**, 11km west. Of all the resorts in the Atacames area, Same is the most exclusive and the least prone to overcrowding, where rows of palms shade a beautiful, soft **beach** of clean, grey sand caressed by a warm sea. Developers have long recognized its potential, but strip away their interventions – such as the Jack Nicklaus-designed golf course sitting under the white holiday villas cresting the hills – and Same is just a tiny village with little more than a handful of basic shops.

Practicalities

Buses between Muisne and Esmeraldas can drop you at Same; for the beach, ask the driver for "*el puente de Same*" and he'll stop at a track that leads to Same's bridge, which crosses a little stream over to the more affordable hotels and the beach – otherwise you may be deposited more than 1km from the beach at the golf course.

There's very little cheap **accommodation** in town – one reason why it's quieter than Atacames. The most affordable choice is *Azuca*, on the main road at the south end of town (☎06/2470343 or 09/9626443; ❷), offering three large, simple rooms in a pleasant house with a good Colombian restaurant. At the entrance to the beach on the left, *La Terraza* (☎06/2470320; ❹–❺) features attractive beachfront cabins under palm trees, furnished with porches, hammocks and private baths; some have air conditioning. There's also a restaurant that serves mid-priced pasta and seafood. You'll find a smarter version of the same at *Cabañas Isla del Sol* further down the beach (☎06/2733470, ⓦwww.cabanasisladelsol.com; ❼), but with kitchenettes, fridges, hot water, cable TV and a pool. For **food**, the ⚵ *Seaflower*, just back from the beach near the bridge, has an excellent German-run gourmet **restaurant** that's one of the best in the region, offering delicious seafood in enormous portions, accompanied by salads and fresh-baked bread for $9–12 per main course.

Tonchigüe

Same's beach stretches 3km down to Tonchigüe, passing expensive cabañas and villas, the best of which is the gorgeous **El Acantilado** (☎06/2733466, ⓦwww.hosteriaelacantilado.com; ❼, discounts for Rough Guide users), perched on a sandy cliff 1km south of Same. Surrounded by gardens ablaze with flowers, it has a games room, decent restaurant and cabins for up to eight people and suites for up to four, with hot-water bathrooms, fridges and fans, and some with beautiful ocean vistas. Reservations are advised in high season, particularly for the rooms with views.

Two kilometres further, **TONCHIGÜE** is a fishing village where tourism hasn't yet made a significant dent and its beach is strewn with blue fishing boats, tangled heaps of netting and fishy detritus. The cheap, out-of-the-way **accommodation** might be within a walk or bus ride of the more popular beaches, but it's strictly no-frills stuff. The en-suite rooms at *Mary*, on the Malecón (☎06/2470057; ❷), are the best of a basic bunch, while *Luz del Mar*, on 26 de Noviembre (☎06/2471118; ❷), has private baths and temperamental plumbing.

Punta Galera and Playa Escondida

A turning off the Vía del Pacífico at El Puente de Tonchigüe follows a secondary road along the coast around the rugged **Punta Galera**, a rocky cape where the coastline bends west then south. After 10km along this road, the secluded Canadian-run 🏕 **Playa Escondida** (☎06/2733122 or 2733106, ⓦwww .playaescondida.com.ec; ❸–❻; average daily expenditure with full board is around $30 per person) is a serene, ecologically minded beach hideaway. It offers charming but rustic cabins with shared or private showers and composting toilets, overlooking a pretty cove – effectively a private beach – backed by a 100-hectare tract of semi-tropical, semi-deciduous forest teeming with birds and wildlife like *guantas* and anteaters. On its tawny beach, marine turtles clamber ashore to lay eggs and whales are occasionally spotted out at sea. There's good walking at low tide along the craggy shoreline and you can arrange tours to the mangroves around Muisne. **Campers** will find plenty of shade and can pitch their tents for $5 per person, while **volunteers** contribute $10 per day for food and lodging, and help with general maintenance, housekeeping or conservation efforts within the reserve. A kilometre or so further west is *Cumilinche Club* (☎06/2733496, ⓦwww.cumilincheclub.com.ec; ❻, must pay for the whole cabin in high season ❽), seven thatched beach bungalows, including bathrooms, hot water and lounge, set in palms and forests by the shore.

Transportes Costeñita (7am, 12pm & 4pm) and River Taviazo **buses** (8am & 2pm), marked for Galera, Quingue or Estero de Plátanos, leave from the Malecón in Esmeraldas and pass all the coastal towns on the way, including Atacames (after 45min–1hr) and Tonchigüe (30min after that). Otherwise, you can rent a **camioneta** in Tonchigüe for about $5.

Muisne

Located some 35km south of the big resorts, luxury seaside villas and condominiums, **MUISNE** lies just beyond the range of most *serrano* vacationers, giving the place a slightly abandoned feel. Nonetheless, the relaxed and friendly air draws a reasonable amount of travellers down to this unusual, rather exotic resort, sitting on a seven-kilometre palm-fringed sand bar amid the **mangrove swamps** just off the mainland, reached only by boat from the small town of **El Relleno**, across the Río Muisne.

As you dock, first impressions are not promising. The salty breeze, equatorial sun and high humidity bring buildings out in an unsightly rash of peeling paint and mouldy green concrete, giving the place a dilapidated appearance – upkeep and construction are expensive, as materials have to be laboriously hauled in from the dock.

Brains over prawn

In the last twenty years about 20,000 hectares of mangroves surrounding the town have been cut down to create **shrimp farms** – ugly pools resembling sewage treatment facilities – which have dealt a severe blow to the birds, marine life and people who relied on the trees for food and sustenance. A handful of entrepreneurs have become millionaires, but most people have lost their way of life and many now work in the shrimp farms to survive or have migrated to city slums elsewhere. Government measures to stop the destruction – three to thirty days in jail for felling a mangrove – have largely remained unenforced and ineffective, meaning only about 3000 hectares of constantly threatened mangrove forests survive.

The organization **Fundecol** (☎06/2248201 or in Quito 02/2522714, ⓦwww .fundecol.org) attempts to protect the trees through security patrols, political activism, education and by running **tours** of the area ($30); local hotels offer similar trips. The Fundación Jatun Sacha manages the **Congal Biological Station** in five square kilometres of primary mangrove forest 2km from Muisne, developing ecologically sound aquaculture and running reforestation programmes; for **volunteering** work at Congal, contact Jatun Sacha in Quito (☎02/2432240, ⓦwww.jatunsacha.org).

The island itself splits into two distinct parts, connected by the double boulevard of **Isidro Ayora**, which runs 2km from the docks to the beach. The town's main shops and services cluster around the dock, where the police, post office and hospital are located, a close distance to the modest **parque central** on Isidro Ayora. Muisne's main attractions lie at the boulevard's other end, where crashing breakers and a broad, flat **beach** are fronted by a handful of inexpensive hotels, restaurants and the odd bar, all shaded by a row of palms

For **security** reasons, do not take valuables onto the beach, walk on it at night or venture into deserted areas. From time to time you may notice pinprick-like stings when swimming in the ocean; these are caused by tiny **jellyfish** (*aguamala*), whose sting doesn't last much longer than ten minutes. Locals claim a splash of vinegar relieves the pain – ask at a beachside restaurant.

Practicalities

Boats from El Relleno whisk people the short hop over the Río Muisne to the main town ($0.20), from where armies of rival **tricicleros** wait to ferry passengers over the cobbles from dock to beach ($0.50 per person). **Buses** arrive and depart from El Relleno; there are regular services to Esmeraldas (every 30min; 2hr 30min), passing the resorts to the north, and El Salto, from where you can catch southbound buses to Chamanga (1hr 30min from Muisne), the connecting point for Pedernales (1hr). A long-distance bus departs nightly for both Quito (8hr) and Guayaquil (9hr). The **telephone** office (daily 8am–8pm) is on Isidro Ayora, 50m east of the plaza. There are no **money-changing** facilities or ATM, so bring all the cash you need.

The best **place to stay** is the friendly *Playa Paraíso* on the beach, 150m south of the entrance (☎06/2480192; ❸), for its bright, fresh rooms or cabins with large mosquito nets and clean, shared bathrooms, plus a pretty garden, lounge and bar. Another friendly spot is *Spondylus*, the last hotel on the beach to the south (☎06/2480279; ❷–❸), featuring a colourful exterior, hammocks, TV lounge, a resident parrot and pleasant rooms – some with private baths for a bit more. The **restaurant** here only operates in the high season, but the one at *Playa Paraíso* dishes up ample breakfasts, including omelettes and fruit salads, as well as vegetarian meals. The beachfront is graced with several good **seafood** restaurants just north of the entrance, *Las Palmeras* and *Santa Martha* being among the most popular.

Muisne to San Vicente

The turning for Muisne off the Vía del Pacífico is at **El Salto**, a collection of grimy roadside stalls, shacks and *comedores*, 11km to the east. From El Salto, the main road speeds south for 56km through land dotted with only the odd stilt hut, passing a turn-off to **Mompiche** (Km27) and then **Chamanga** (San José de Chamanga in full, 2km from the main road), from where there is regular transport to **Pedernales**.

Beyond Chamanga and into **Manabí**, the province of the central seaboard, the climate and scenery soon change from the lush greenery of Esmeraldas to an increasingly dry, scrubby landscape. South of Pedernales is a sparsely populated area of small settlements, the largest being **Jama**, 45km down the road, and a rolling shoreline interspersed with deserted beaches and the occasional secluded hotel. A further 41km away, after turning inland past shrimp farms and through agricultural land, the road rejoins the coast at **Canoa**, an attractive beach resort with good surfing. The beaches continue south from here for almost 20km down to **San Vicente**, a bustling town opposite the high-rises of Bahía de Caráquez, across the Río Chone estuary.

Mompiche

On the sheltered south side of the Ensenada de Mompiche, where a beautiful seven-kilometre ribbon of dark sand curls around a broad bay, backed by a shock of emerald-green trees, is the little fishing village of **MOMPICHE**. It was once one of the most peaceful spots on the coast, protected by its relative isolation and accessible only by boat or on foot, but since it was linked by a 6km road – albeit a poor one that may require a four-wheel-drive vehicle after heavy rains – to the Vía del Pacífico, the town's wooden cabins, fishing boats and simple stores have been joined by an outbreak of hotels. As word spreads, it's also set to grow in stature as a **surfing** resort, as it not only has an excellent left point break at **Punta Suspiro** at the south end of the bay, but other possibilities nearby. Walk south along the beach and take the dirt road for about fifteen minutes to a gap in the fence on the right, where a trail leads to **Playa Osteonal**, a long, secluded fossil beach. Further south is the **Playa Negra**, a beach of strangely heavy black sand. The track finishes at the crossing for **Portete**, where you may be able to find a canoe ($0.25) to take you over to long palm-fringed beaches. The best time of year for surfing here is between December and January.

Practicalities

River Taviazo runs four **rancheras** a day from Esmeraldas to Mompiche, passing the other beach resorts on the coast. Most **hotels** are near the beach on the sheltered side of the bay. Starting at the entrance to the beach is *Estrella del Mar* (☎02/2330315 in Quito or 09/1355788; ❸), with straightforward en-suite rooms, hammocks and a restaurant. A short walk east is *DMCA Surf Hostal* (📧martindmca@hotmail.com; ❷–❸), a funky surfers' hangout featuring a choice of rooms with or without private bath and balcony, plus a TV lounge, DVD library, hammock terrace, meditation space and tattoo parlour. Surf equipment available for rent ($15 per day) and camping is possible for $2.

Continuing to the east of the village, *Gabeal* (T09/9696543; **6**, discounts in low season) has a choice of rooms from tiled floors to simple cabins of bamboo and concrete with palm-leaf thatched roofs and private bathrooms; camping is $3. The most romantic and isolated spot is *Las Piqualas*, 3km along the beach on the other side of the bay (T09/9472458, W www.playa-ecuador.com; **6**; breakfast $4, lunch and dinner $10 each), with spacious beach cabins with porches and hammocks, clutched by palms and run by a friendly Spanish couple. It's a 45-minute walk from Mompiche and only accessible by car at low tide or you could get here by boat from Muisne (30min; $15 for two people); it's best to book ahead and make arrangements with them.

Pedernales and around

Since the end of the 1980s, when two viruses decimated its shrimp industry, **PEDERNALES** has been trying to reinvent itself as a holiday destination. It still has a long way to go, despite being one of the nearest seaside resorts to Quito and sitting on a 52-kilometre stretch of beach. With its crowded, narrow streets and rather grubby sands, Pedernales itself has remained largely impervious to interest from international travellers, though it is a hub for transport along the coast to more beautiful, palm-shaded spots north and south.

The focus of town is the **parque central**, whose centrepiece is a **stone** that La Condamine engraved in Latin during his 1736 mission to the equator to determine the Earth's shape. The **church** is also worth a look for its colourful stained-glass window and mural overlooking the square. From the park, the streets fall steeply to the sea for a half-kilometre west to the **beach**, where unremarkable hotels, bars and restaurants cater mainly to national tourists. The town's two biggest **fiestas** are for its cantonization, March 13, and the *fiesta del café*, August 16, honouring the days when coffee was the principal crop.

Practicalities

The **bus terminal** is on Juan Pereira, two blocks northeast of the main square. Every twenty minutes, buses leave for Santo Domingo (3hr), from where there are regular connections to Quito. There are also direct buses to the capital (4 daily; 5hr), Guayaquil (6 daily; 8hr), San Vicente (every 30min–1hr; 2hr 30min) and Chamanga (every 30min–1hr; 45min). For Cocosolo and Cojimíes, **busetas**, **colectivos** and **taxis** leave from the park when full (roughly every 30min; 30min) at the corner of Eloy Alfaro and López Castillo; at low tide they drive along the beach and at high tide, take the slower road inland which adds 10km to the journey. The Pacífictel **telephone office** is on Eloy Alfaro, off the square behind the church.

The best **place to stay** is 20km up the beach at Cocosolo (see below), but if you have to stop in town, try *Playas* (T05/2681125; **3**) behind (cast) the bus station at Juan Pereira and Manabí, with good-value rooms, private baths and cable TVs. The hotels along the beach range from smartish cabaña complexes to lowly wooden shacks, and the nicest is *Mr John*, Avenida Plaza Acosta and Malecón (T&F05/2681107; **3**), offering bright, fresh rooms, fans, cable TVs and private baths with electric showers.

The local **restaurants** are mostly simple seafood *comedores*, but *La Choza* and *Costeñito 2* on the beachfront are a class above the rest. In town, *Costeñito* at García Moreno and Manabí is the nicest of a sorry bunch.

Cojimíes and Cocosolo

From Pedernales a gorgeous strip of sand – used as a freshly made road serviced by *camionetas* at low tide – unfurls for more than 30km north to the shabby and forgotten little town of **COJIMÍES**, squeezed onto the tip of an ever-dwindling tongue of sand, eroded by water on three sides. Over the centuries, the peninsula has given up more than a kilometre of land, and the town has been entirely relocated from its original pre-Hispanic site, which was called Quiximíes. At low tide, locals occasionally boat out to the **sandbanks** in the middle of the estuary and use them as private beaches for parties and barbecues. Ask around at the landing beach north of town about going on a **fishing** trip ($15 per hour). You can take boats over the estuary to Bolívar and Daule, from where it's a long walk to the main road, or you could charter one to Mompiche.

There are a few basic **hotels** in Cojimíes if you get stuck, but the most charming place to stay in this area is *Cocosolo*, 13km to the south (☎08/9998964 or 09/9215978, ⓦ www.hotelcocosolo.com; ➏ with breakfast), a lonely hotel which has stood for more than thirty years under the coconut fronds, enjoying peaceful isolation during high tide. You can stay either in its eccentric collection of sea-blue cabins, built on long stilts in the grove, or in the main house, which has several spacious en-suite rooms with hot water, near the garden, fish pond and swimming pool. **Camping** ($6) includes use of the hotel's facilities and restaurant; the owners can arrange fishing **tours** or excursions to the estuary mangroves and forested areas nearby. **Camionetas** regularly pass on the beach at low tide; at high tide they can drop you on the inland road behind the hotel.

Punta Blanca and Punta Prieta

Some 36km south of Pedernales, the road swings away from the shore to traverse the white cliff of **PUNTA BLANCA**, and the darker Punta Prieta, whose colour differences help fishermen navigate. In the 800m between the two cliffs is a cluster of secluded **hideaways** with access to quiet and beautiful stretches of beach. The first is *Punta Blanca Lodge Tent Camp* (☎09/9227559, or 05/2410272, ⓦ www.hotelpuntablanca.com; ➐ breakfast included), a unique and unusual place with large family tents under a roof, offering seaside views and equipped with double beds, desks, chairs and electric lights – in effect, hotel rooms with tarpaulin walls and zip doors. Set in neatly clipped gardens, the camp has clean, shared bathrooms with hot water and an attractive restaurant and bar with ocean views; more conventional suites in the hotel block have air conditioning and private baths (➑). **Tours** of the inland forests of the Reserva Mache Chindul are available, as well as fishing, diving and canoeing expeditions.

A few hundred metres up the road, *Latitude 7* (ⓔ jmelat7@yahoo.es; ➌), features a collection of artfully built wooden cabins, equipped with fridges, cookers (you can buy food on site), some with private bathrooms and hot water, or shared composting toilets, located in dry forest a short distance from the beach. A bit run-down and irregularly open, the place is nonetheless extremely peaceful and provides periodic silk-screening and jewellery workshops, plus sailing, *parapenting*, horseriding and fishing trips. A good pizzeria is operational here if it's not too busy; otherwise guests are invited to cook for themselves.

A short hop further south at **PUNTA PRIETA**, the ⚑ *Punta Prieta Guest House* (☎09/3423811, or in Quito, 02/2862986, ⓦ www.puntaprieta.com; ➎–➏) is the most charming and secluded of the three hotels, offering attractive cabins, comfortable rooms with private baths and hot water or airy suites with windows on three sides, king-size beds and fridges, all set in fragrant *palo santo* forest on an outcrop with stupendous views and access to two tranquil beaches. Delicious, reasonably priced **meals** are available in a stunning cliff-top restaurant where frigatebirds and pelicans fly right by the windows. **Campers** can stay for $4.

Don Juan to Río Muchacho Organic Farm

Further along, the Pacific Highway winds down from low hills to reveal **Don Juan**, a picturesque village in a cove washed by a pale-green sea, where there are a few basic hotels. Don Juan is the access for the **Reserva Lalo Loor**, which lies in an important transitional zone protecting rare tropical dry forest habitat, as well as semi-deciduous and wet forest on the highest reaches. It's managed by the Fundación Jatun Sacha, which seeks **volunteers** for on-site projects (☎02/2432240, ⓦwww.jatunsacha.org). Passing some huge shrimp farms, after 5km the route reaches the market town of **Jama**, the largest settlement between Pedernales and Bahía de Caráquez, which has a distinctly Wild West feel, and claims to have a greater proportion of inhabited colonial buildings than any town in Ecuador.

About 30km south of Jama, the highway passes the turn-off to the **Río Muchacho Organic Farm** (ⓦwww.riomuchacho.com), reached by a ninety-minute walk in the dry season. In an area damaged by deforestation, the farm is an oasis of sustainable agriculture and a leading environmental and ecotourism project. Visitors can learn about tropical permaculture, milk cows, help with reforestation, pick, roast and grind coffee, fish for river shrimp or opt for more relaxed activities, such as making tagua jewellery and utensils from gourd or smearing on local clay for a facial. **Accommodation** is available in cabins by the river or in the main house (starting at $7 per person or $15 including full board). A popular way to visit is on a three-day tour ($105 per person, including a horse ride to the farm, all meals and activities, with discounts for groups), though many people come as **volunteers** ($350 per month contribution) for farm work, reforestation or teaching in an environmental primary school, or even to learn about organic farming on a month-long intensive course. Make reservations in advance through their office in Canoa (see p.372) or with Guacamayo Bahía Tours in Bahía de Caráquez (☎05/2691107; see p.377).

Canoa

Down the coast from Jama and sitting at the upper end of a huge beach extending 17km south to San Vicente is **CANOA**, which has shifted from sleepy fishing village to laid-back beach resort, thanks largely to its fantastic surf and clean sands. With only a single paved street linking its shaded **square** to the sea, the town's low-level hubbub is submerged under the continuous roar of breakers rising and falling on the shore.

It's a lovely place to relax, with long, empty expanses of coastline and ample waves for **surfing** (good from Dec–April, best Jan–Feb; many hotels have boards for rent). At low tide you can take a **horse ride** or a walk to the sandy cliffs rising up through the haze in the north, where there's a **cave** to explore; it's best done with a local guide for safety. Trips to the **Río Muchacho Organic Farm** (see above) can be arranged at their office on 30 de Noviembre and Javier Santos, the second street on the right if walking up the main street from the beach.

Buses between Pedernales and San Vicente pass through Canoa every thirty minutes and stop at the main square.

Accommodation, eating and drinking

In addition to Canoa's well-priced **accommodation**, there are also several more expensive, self-contained hotels outside town to the south. Wherever you stay, it's worth asking about discounts during low season.

Canoa has plenty of simple seafood **restaurants** to choose from on the Malecón and main street, the best being *Torbellino* (closes 5.30pm), down from the square, which dishes up cheap and tasty fish and shrimp, and *Café Flor*, at the south end of town, 50m west of the San Vicente road, for its vegetarian dishes, pizza and seafood. *Surf Shak*, on the Malecón, does pizzas, burgers, weekend barbecues and drinks. The restaurant at *Bambú* is good and reliable for its lunches and dinners and does delicious breakfasts of fruit salads and pancakes. For **cocktails** and dancing, try the *Coco Bar* on the main street a block from the beach.

Hotels

Bambú On the beach at the north end of the village ☎09/9263365, ⓦwww .hotelbambuecuador.com. The town's best rooms – bright and breezy with little balconies overlooking a garden and the sea. There are also less expensive cabins with shared baths, and you can sleep in a hammock or camp here for a few dollars with the use of the facilities. Longboards and bodyboards are available for rent and there's a good bar and restaurant. ❸

Hostería Canoa 1km south of town ☎05/2616380, ⓦwww.hosteriacanoa.com. Colourful a/c cabins garlanded with bright bougain-villea and set around a pool, with an on-site sauna and jacuzzi. Breakfast included. ❼

Coco Loco On the beach, two blocks south of entrance ☎09/5447260, ⓦwww.hostalcocoloco .weebly.com. Friendly place, with a range of accommodation from dorm beds ($5) to en-suite doubles with sea views. There's hot water, a good bar and restaurant and a self-catering kitchen. Offers surfing lessons, and riding, fishing and biking trips. ❸–❹

País Libre Three blocks behind *Bambú* ☎05/2616387. An enormous, four-storey thatched cabaña-cum-hotel popular with *serranos*, offering nice rooms (those on the upper floors have great views) with mosquito nets and optional en-suite electric showers, plus a small swimming pool and disco. ❹

Paraíso Canoa Main street, 130m from the beach ☎08/2973272. Tidy, if bare, en-suite rooms with TV, fan, mosquito net and some with hot water. ❸

La Posada de Daniel By the square, 150m back from the beach ☎09/7508825, ⓦwww .laposadadedaniel.com. Cabins sleeping up to nine people (most are doubles), with private baths, fans, mosquito nets and balconies affording views of the village and shore. Also features a lounge, bar, restaurant, internet service and swimming pool. The proprietor, once a junior champion, gives surfing lessons; horseriding is also available. ❸

Shelmar 50m walk back from the beach, on the main street ☎09/8644892. Offers simple, clean rooms with fans and hammocks, some with private bath and hot water. Bicycles available for rent. ❶–❷

La Vista On the beachfront, three blocks south of entrance ☎09/2288995, ⓦwww.lavistacanoa .com. All rooms face the sea and have private bath and hot water, brick walls, wooden floors, glass windows, mosquito nets and balconies – a relief for those fed up with flimsy cabins. The restaurant specializes in surf and turf and the owners are friendly. ❹

San Vicente

Although on the same magnificent beach as Canoa, dusty **SAN VICENTE**, some 17km away, has none of its neighbour's charm, thanks largely to the busy thoroughfare running right next to the beach, jammed with noisy buses and *rancheras*. Still, there are several holiday hotels, mainly catering to nationals, including a few rather expensive resorts just outside town on the road back to Canoa. The best thing about the place is the **view** across the Río Chone estuary to Bahía de Caráquez, where row upon row of high-rise buildings balance on a finger of sand poking out to sea.

Practicalities

From the dock along the beach, **car ferries** run to Bahía de Caráquez every twenty minutes (15min trip; 6.30am–5.30pm, then every 40min till 10pm; $3), and foot passengers travel for free. **Pangas** (small boats) cross into the night for $0.35, and the *panga* dock is closer to the town centre. A bridge across the

BAHÍA DE CARÁQUEZ

ACCOMMODATION
Bahía Bed & Breakfast	E
Centro Vacacional Life	C
La Herradura	B
Italia	D
La Piedra	A
La Querencia	F

RESTAURANTS
Arena Bar	3
Brisas del Mar	2
El Buen Sabor	6
Colombiu's	4
D'Camarón	1
El Muelle Uno	5
La Terraza	7

PACIFIC OCEAN

CIRCUNVALACIÓN

EDUARDO RODRÍGUEZ

SERGIO P. ACOSTA

PADRE LEANNEN

DANIEL HIDALGO

MUÑOZ DÁVILA

CINCINATO ESTRADA

MALECÓN-VIRGILIO RATTI

CARLOS HURTADO

HORACIO GOSTALLE

OCTAVIO VITERI

MALECÓN VIRGILIO RATTI

MARAÑÓN

MATEUS

Parque San Vicente

BOLÍVAR

INTRIAGO

E Ceibos Tours

CHECA

Parque Manuel Nevares

ARENAS

Guacamayo Bahía Tours

Banco de Guayaquil

RIOFRÍO

MORALES

MONTÚFAR

Parque Infantil

Parque Obelisco

Car Ferry to San Vicente

ASCÁZUBI

Municipio

Market

Banco Pichincha

ANTE

Mirador La Cruz (150m)

P.F. CEBALLOS

Parque Sucre

AGUILERA

Panga Dock

Museo Banco Central

PEÑA

MARIANA DE JESÚS

MALECÓN ALBERTO SANTOS

VINUEZA

Río Chone Estuary

N

Puerto Amistad

0   250 m

Capitanía

F, Bus Terminal (400m) & Chone

estuary should be complete by 2011, which should make it a much easier business to get to Bahía. **Buses** regularly leave the centre for Pedernales via Canoa (every 30min till 7.45pm; 2hr 30min), from where you can get connections to Chamanga, the beach resorts to the north, Santo Domingo and Quito. Many other destinations are serviced from a new **bus terminal** (by the market about 1km up the road to San Isidro; $0.50 by tricycle taxi): to Guayaquil (8 daily; 6hr 30min), Manta (3 daily; 3hr 30min), Portoviejo (hourly; 2hr 30min) and Quito (2 daily; 8hr). There is an airport opposite the car-ferry dock, but currently no scheduled passenger services.

If you can't make it to Bahía or Canoa for a **hotel**, along the Malecón from the *panga* dock, the *San Vicente* (☎05/2674182; ❷) is very basic but adequate. Opposite the filling station, you'll find air-conditioned, en-suite rooms and a pool at *Vacaciones* (☎05/2674116; ❸).

Bahía de Caráquez and around

One of Ecuador's most agreeable coastal resort towns, **BAHÍA DE CARÁQUEZ,** an upmarket place of spotless, white high-rise apartment blocks, broad tree-lined avenues and leafy parks, sits on a slender peninsula of sand extending into the broad mouth of the Río Chone. Yachts from around the world bob and sway in the town's marina.

Following mudslides and a damaging earthquake in 1998, Bahía (as it's called for short) started afresh, proclaiming itself a *ciudad ecológica*, an **eco-city**, and set up a number of ambitious projects, including recycling, permaculture, composting, reforestation, conservation and environmental-education programmes. Even the *tricicleros* paint their "eco-taxis" green, adorning them with signs reading "*Bienvenidos Bahía Eco-Ciudad*". The Día del Mangle **fiesta** on February 28 marks the declaration with music and events such as mangrove planting in the area.

Bahía lies near several wonderful natural attractions, including **tropical dry forests**, empty **beaches** and **mangrove islands** teeming with aquatic birds. The vast shrimp farms in the estuary displaced more than sixty square kilometres of mangrove forest during the 1980s and 1990s, with the obvious exception of the world's first **organic shrimp farm**, a pollution-free enterprise that also helps in reforestation. Local **tour agencies**, some of which have played a major role in the local environmental movement, organize a number of good excursions in the area (see "Listings", p.377).

Arrival, information and transport

Bahía de Caráquez's main avenues run north–south, parallel to the estuary on the east side. The **Malecón**, the main road around the edge of the peninsula, is known by several other names at various points: at the southeast entrance to town, it's **Malecón Alberto Santos**; beyond the parks, **Malecón Virgilio Ratti**; and around the tip of the peninsula, the **Circunvalación**.

The **bus terminal** is 1km south of the centre on Malecón and Barrio Astillero; for bus information see "Listings", p.377. The **car ferry** from San Vicente comes in at Malecón and Ascázubi, while *panga* boats dock a little further south at Malecón Alberto Santos and Ante. A bridge across the estuary should be complete by 2011. The Bahía airport is over the water in San Vicente, but offers no scheduled passenger services. There are plenty of **taxis** ($1 within town) and **tricicleros** ($0.50) around the docks and bus station, though the cheaper hotels are within easy walking distance. **Yachts** can moor ($270 per month or $9 per day) at the American-run marina, **Puerto Amistad** (☎05/2693112, ⓦwww.puertoamistadecuador.com), on Malecón and Vinueza, which offers a range of services to its clients, and a restaurant open to all.

Maps and **information** are available at the municipal tourist office upstairs on Bolívar and Padre Leannen (Mon–Fri 8.30am–5pm, with lunch break; ☎05/2691044 or 2693240, ⓦwww.bahiadecaraquez.com), or you can try Guacamayo Bahía Tours (see "Listings", p.377), which should have English-speaking staff on hand.

Accommodation

Most of the smarter **hotels** are found on the northwest side of the peninsula; wherever you stay, it can be difficult to find a room during the high season and national holidays.

Bahía Bed & Breakfast Ascázubi and Morales ☎05/2690146. Charming but gloomy old house enlivened by a cheerful paint job and portraits on the wall. The priciest rooms have private baths, fans and TVs. Includes breakfast and provides maps and tourist information. ②–③
Centro Vacacional Life Octavio Viteri 504 and Muñoz Dávila ☎05/2690496. Great value for its

large brick cabins housing a bedroom, bathroom, kitchen and dining room, in quiet gardens with table football and pool table nearby; usually fully booked by private groups during high season. ③
La Herradura Bolívar and Hidalgo ☎05/2690446, ⓕ2690265. Smart seafront hotel evoking the feel of a hacienda by its wrought-iron furnishings, wagon wheels, barrels, horse harnesses and potted

plants. There's hot water and many rooms have a/c. **❼**

Italia Bolívar and Checa ☎05/2691137, ℗2690449. Rooms are a bit small and not amazing value, but they do have hot water, fans, phones, cable TVs and private baths. **❹**

La Piedra Malecón Virgilio Ratti 803 and Bolívar ☎05/2690780, ⓦwww.cialcotel.com. Clean, comfortable rooms and sun loungers surround an outdoor pool right by a patch of private beach.

Spacious bathrooms have proper tubs and hot water, while rooms boast telephones, a/c and cable TVs. Substantial discounts in low season. **❼**

La Querencia Velasco Ibarra and Eugenio Santos, south of the Capitanía ☎05/2690009. Blue-and-white budget hotel near the bus terminal in a family house. Some rooms have private baths, though without hot water. Fluffy towels provided and meals cooked on request. **❷**

The Town

Bahía is a pleasant town for a stroll – or taking a cruise with a *triciclero* ($5 per hour) – following the **Malecón** around the peninsula and viewing the busy river estuary on the east side, or the rough rollers coming to shore on the west. Locals swim and surf here, but to find more generous expanses of sand, take a taxi to the **beaches** south of town like **Punta Bellaca** (7km away; arrange return journey in advance). A good complement to the seaside promenade is the short push up to **Mirador La Cruz**, on top of the hill at the foot of the peninsula, which affords grand views of the city and bay.

In town, the renovated **Museo Bahía de Caráquez del Banco Central** (Tues–Fri 9am–4.30pm, Sat–Sun 11.30am–2.30pm; $1, Sun free) houses pre–Columbian artefacts, such as a Valdivian belt of highly prized *spondylus* shells from 3000 BC, plus a replica balsa raft, as well as temporary art exhibitions.

Eating

Along with the superior **restaurants** of the smarter hotels such as *La Piedra* and *La Herradura*, there are several very good places to eat, especially on the Malecón around the docks.

Arena Bar Bolívar and Arenas. Long-time stalwart of Canoa nightlife transplanted to Bahía, losing none of its beach cred: bright colours, tree-trunk tables, surfboard on the wall and great pizzas and cocktails. Opens 5pm.

Brisas del Mar Hidalgo and Malecón Ratti. Cheap and simple seafood restaurant serving good fish and *ceviche* dishes.

El Buen Sabor Malecón, near the dock. A local favourite with riverside views, specializing in *parrilladas*, tasty barbecued food, as well as traditional seafood.

Colombiu's Bolívar and Ante. Features large, delicious and affordable Colombian and Ecuadorian dishes and good seafood served on a leafy terrace under a sackcloth awning

D'Camarón Malecón Ratti and Acosta. Simple, inexpensive seafood restaurant specializing in all things shrimp, enjoying breezy outdoor seating and bracing sea views.

El Muelle Uno Malecón, by the dock. Fair-priced restaurant serving generous, savoury fish and barbecue lunches and dinners, plus vegetarian options like baked potatoes and cheese.

Puerto Amistad Malecón and Vinueza. The restaurant of the yacht club and marina, serving great international food at moderate prices, including hamburgers, 12oz rib-eye steaks and fish and chicken in fancy sauces, such as whisky and almond. Non-members are welcome.

La Terraza Malecón, near the dock. The seafood-and-grills menu might have few surprises, but it's cheaper than most, and the set lunches are good value too.

Listings

Banks Banco de Guayaquil, Riofrío and Bolívar, and Banco Pichincha, Bolívar and Ascazúbi, both have a Visa and MasterCard ATM.

Boats and ferries When the bridge across the estuary is finished (by 2011), it should be easy to take a bus or taxi to San Vicente. In the meantime, the car ferry leaves the dock on Malecón and Ascázubi for San Vicente (every 20min, 7am–5.50pm, then every 40min till 10pm; $3 cars, foot passengers free), while *panga* boats depart regularly from the municipal docks for San Vicente until late ($0.35) Yachts can moor at Puerto Amistad (see "Arrival and Information").

Buses Reina del Camino runs buses to Quito (4 daily; 8hr) and Guayaquil (every 1hr 30min; 5hr), including a less frequent executive service (2 daily to Quito; 3 daily to Guayaquil). Coactur has services for Portoviejo (every 30min; 2hr), where you can change for Manta. Buses heading north along the coast leave from San Vicente, over the estuary; when the bridge is complete these services may depart from Bahía so ask around. For Puerto López and the south coast, take a Guayaquil bus and change at Jipijapa.

Tour operators Guacamayo Bahía Tours, Bolívar 906 and Arenas (☎05/2691107 or 2691412, ⓦ www.guacamayotours.com), is a recommended tour agency and an excellent general source of local tourist information (English spoken). Their most popular tour is a 3-day visit to Río Muchacho Organic Farm (see p.372), but they also run "eco-tours" to their various projects (including EcoCamaronera Bahía, the world's first organic shrimp farm), offer volunteering placements, whale-watching trips, excursions to tropical dry forests, mangroves, estuaries, beaches, Isla Corazón, La Segua, Isla de la Plata and Parque Nacional Machalilla. E Ceibos Tours, corner of Bolívar 200 and Checa (☎05/2690801, ⓦ www.ceibostours.com) do trips to Isla Corazón, whale watching, birding trips to the mangroves of Simbocal, Cerro Seco dry forest, La Segua and other local points of interest. They also offer volunteering opportunities on local ecological projects.

Río Chone estuary, Isla Corazón and La Segua

Among the touring highlights from Bahía is a trip around the **Río Chone estuary**, where the network of red mangroves supports more than 4000 **frigatebirds** (rivalling the population of the Galápagos Islands), petrels, oystercatchers and sandpipers among many others. During the mating season (Aug–Dec, sometimes till Feb), it's possible to see the male frigatebirds' characteristic scarlet pouches inflating to woo circling females.

Further upriver, the **Isla Corazón** features an "ecological path" through the mangroves, where you can see crabs, shrimp and wetland birds, including the rare **roseate spoonbill**. One enjoyable element of this trip is taking a **dugout canoe** on the tiny creeks between the trees to view one of Ecuador's largest frigatebird colonies. **Dolphins** are occasionally seen in the estuary, and between June and September **whales** can be spotted rolling and diving off the coast.

Even further upriver are the wetlands of **La Segua**, a 1742-hectare reserve home to at least 164 bird species, including the wattled jacana, whose males unusually take on full responsibility for feeding and raising chicks.

Jororá, Punta Bellaca and Chirije

On the coast south of Bahía de Caráquez, **Jororá** and **Punta Bellaca** comprise one of the few **tropical dry forests** in the country outside the Parque Nacional Machalilla. Anteaters, sloths and iguanas can be found in this area, which is rich in fragrant *palo santo* trees, barbasco (a plant whose roots yield a poison used for insecticide) and ceiba trees – easy to identify with their great buttressed trunks. During the rainy season (Jan–May), the forests are luxuriant.

About 17km south of town, **CHIRIJE** is an isolated beach surrounded by tropical dry forest, which once acted as a seaport for the Bahía culture (500 BC to 650 AD). Archeologists and volunteers are welcome to help with the ongoing excavations, and artefacts found at the site are exhibited in a small on-site **museum**. You can stay here in attractive, solar-powered **cabañas** (☎09/9171935, ⓦ www.chirije.com; ⓐ) nestled among gardens and greenery;

activities include trekking on forest trails, birdwatching, snorkelling and surfing (lessons available). A beachside restaurant supplies good local specialities, including *biche*, a peanut and seafood soup. For tours and reservations call ℡09/9171935 or write to Ⓔinfo.chirije@gmail.com.

Saiananda Parque

On the main road 6.5km south of Bahía, **Saiananda Parque** (daily 9am–4pm; $2) features peacocks, ostriches, ñandu (a small flightless Argentinian bird), macaws, monkeys, deer and sloths, which roam around grounds that include bonsai, cactus and succulents gardens. The park has an excellent waterside vegetarian **restaurant** that looks down the estuary towards the peninsula; call ahead to reserve (℡05/2398331). You can also stay in comfortable rooms with fan, private bath and free wi-fi (Ⓔcharmsen@saiananda.com; ❻); they offer kayaking trips, tours to nearby islands and massages. Local **buses** from Bahía pass every ten minutes, or you can hire a **boat** to take you to the park's pier.

San Jacinto and San Clemente

In the 50km or so between Bahía de Caráquez and Manta, the coastline lurches between inaccessible cliffs and lengthy stretches of sandy beach. The **fishing villages** along here have become popular beach resorts with nationals and day-trippers from Portoviejo, and can get quite crowded during holidays and weekends.

Twenty kilometres south of Bahía are two fishing villages connected by 3km of beach and backed by bleak salt pampas. Despite their attractive beach, they seldom receive foreign visitors, but do have a number of inexpensive hotels to satisfy local demand, which can be considerable in July and August. In **SAN CLEMENTE**, the hotel with the most character is *Las Acacias*, 500m north of the village shrine and 300m back from the beach (℡05/2615050; ❸), a beautiful old wooden house with spacious verandas and clean and simple rooms with shared or private baths. Of the hotels strung along the beach between the two villages, the smartest is *Chediak* (℡05/2615499; ❺), with mosquito nets, hot water and sea views. In the larger **SAN JACINTO**, *Cabañas Ecológicas Casa Mar*, at the town entrance near the church (℡05/2633636, Ⓔmanabi1@espoir.org.ec; ❸), are a group of pleasant cabins with kitchens, dining rooms and one or two bedrooms set in small gardens with a gym and volleyball courts. The owner runs local tours, including one to a tropical dry forest. There are many other hotels besides, some of which shut up shop during the low season.

Buses to Portoviejo leave or pass every twenty minutes, with a less frequent service to Bahía de Caráquez. Pick up through buses on the main road.

Crucita

About 14km south of San Jacinto, and 30km northwest of Portoviejo on a fast paved road, the cliffs at the south end of **CRUCITA** fall away to a long **beach**, which is no more than a few metres wide at high tide, but becomes a broad expanse of dark sand when the waters recede. Fronting the beach is the **Malecón**, a shadeless and not very picturesque seafront promenade lined with hotels and restaurants. Still, the rugged cliffs and excellent wind conditions have made the village a minor centre for **airborne activities** such as paragliding and kite surfing; for information, talk to the owners of the *Voladeros* hostel.

The most frequent **bus** service to Crucita is from Portoviejo (every 15min; 45min–1hr), but you can also get there from Manta on buses that pass through

Portoviejo (12 daily; 1hr 30min); the last bus back to Portoviejo leaves at 8pm from the main square.

The best **place to stay** is *Venecia* (T05/2340301, Wwww.hosteriavenecia .com; ❺), a modern hotel building on the central Malecón, featuring fresh en-suite rooms equipped with Direct TV, air conditioning and hot water. There's a small indoor pool, and suites come with balconies, sea views and fridges. Nearby at Malecón 100, the friendly *Zucasa* (T05/2340106; ❺–❻) has a pool, wooden cabins with porches and hammocks or less expensive and exciting concrete rooms. Other options include *Hipocampo*, south Malecón (T05/2340167; ❷–❸), with straightforward en-suite rooms, the ones upstairs being brighter and having seaside views, and, at the Malecón's southern end, *Voladeros* (T05/2340200, Ehvoladeros@hotmail.com; ❸), a friendly little hostel offering simple rooms with optional en-suite baths and a swimming pool. The owner offers paragliding lessons and tandem flights ($300 for 4 days of training, equipment included). The many **restaurants** along the Malecón tout the standard list of seafood items.

Manta and around

About 50km south of Bahía de Caráquez, set in a broad bay dotted with freighters, cruise ships and fishing boats, **MANTA** is a city of some 183,000 people and Ecuador's largest port after Guayaquil. Divided by the Río Manta between the throbbing commercial centre to the west and the poorer residential area **Tarqui** to the east, the city is a manufacturing centre – but it's the **seafood industry** that really drives the economy. Fish and shrimp processors and packers line the roads entering Manta, and the business of netting swordfish, shark and dorado is lucrative enough to draw US and Japanese fishing fleets to these abundant waters. President Rafael Correra refused to renew the lease for a major US **air base** here used for drug surveillance – unless Ecuador could build a base in Miami, which unsurprisingly was rejected. Plans are now afoot to build a large oil refinery to take up the economic shortfall created by the closure of the base.

Manta is also known as a lively, holiday destination; its main **beach** is relatively clean, regularly patrolled, lined with restaurants and packed at weekends. As a bustling modern port more manageable in size and temperament than Guayaquil, Manta is a good place to refuel and make use of the banks, cinemas and services of a busy urban centre. A new road skirting the coast to the southwest also makes it a gateway to undeveloped villages and beaches, as well as the more established resorts of the southern coast beyond Puerto Cayo, where the road joins the Ruta del Sol (see p.422).

Some history

Fishing has always been important to Manta. In the pre-Columbian era the settlement here was known as **Jocay**, or "fish house", and from around 500 AD until the arrival of the Spanish, the region was the home of the **Manta people**, expert fishermen and navigators who tattooed their faces and held sway over the coast from Bahía de Caráquez to Salango, near Puerto López. The Manta were great traders and sailed on large balsa rafts as far north as Mexico, exchanging goods for their *spondylus* shells, which were used by many cultures as ornaments and deemed so valuable they were as good as money. Shortly after becoming the first European to cross the Pacific equator, Pizarro's navigator, **Bartolomé Ruiz**, encountered one of these rafts off the Manabí coast; it was

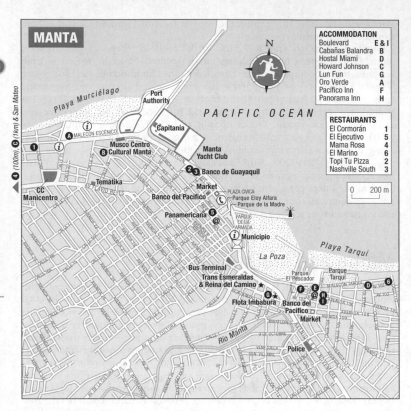

large enough to carry twenty men and thirty tons of merchandise, including gold, silver and emeralds.

The Manteño culture suffered greatly under the brutal conquistador **Pedro de Alvarado**, who swept through the region in 1534, hanging the chief and putting others to the dogs or burning them alive for failing to supply him with gold, jewels or food. Most others perished in the forced march to Quito (see p.490); the town that once had twenty thousand people had only fifty inhabitants by 1546. From the 1560s onwards, Manta began its long recovery and was soon the preferred **settlement** for colonists, rather than the nearby administrative capital of Portoviejo. Save for a few **pirate raids** in the seventeenth century, which drove some citizens inland to found towns such as Montecristi, Manta's place as the commercial capital of the central coast was assured.

Arrival, information and transport

Excepting the main highways, the city's streets are numbered sequentially from the river – Manta starts at Calle 1, Tarqui at Calle 101 – while avenues running parallel to the seashore use the coast as the starting point. **Buses** enter the city through Tarqui along the main road, Avenida 4 de Noviembre, which crosses the river and continues into Manta as the Malecón. The central bus station at Avenida 8 and Calle 7 is used by all local and long-distance buses except for those coming from Quito that have their own offices, such as Flota Imbabura, at Calle 2 and Malecón (*ejecutivo* service to Quito); Reina del Camino (regular services to Quito and Guayaquil) and Trans Esmeraldas (one nightly bus each for Esmeraldas and Quito), both at Malecón and Calle 4; and Panamericana, at Avenida 4 and Calle 12 (*ejecutivo* service to Quito). There are plans to relocate the bus station outside town on a peripheral artery, 6km from the centre. The **airport** is a few kilometres east of Tarqui, and can be reached by taxi for $3–4.

Taxis cost $1.50 to anywhere in the city, and **local buses** service the main thoroughfares and central bus station. If staying in Tarqui, you can easily catch one from Avenida 105 into the city centre or to Playa Murciélago – a far more attractive prospect than walking a kilometre over the busy road bridge.

Tourist **information** and maps are available at the municipal tourism office, Avenida 4 and Calle 9 (Mon–Fri 8am–5pm; ☎05/2611471, ⓦwww.manta.gov.ec), or from the Ministerio de Turismo, Malecón and Calle 7 (Mon–Fri 8.30am–5pm with break for lunch; ☎05/2622944). Open daily at the entrance to Playa Murciélago is the student-run Centro de Información Turística (☎05/2624099).

Accommodation

There are plenty of good choices for **accommodation** in Manta, with most of the more expensive hotels located at the smarter end of town near the beach, and cheaper places around downmarket Tarqui. There are few decent low-budget places, but you can expect fair **discounts** at many hotels in the low season.

Manta

Cabañas Balandra Av 7 and Calle 20 ☎05/2620316, ⓦwww.hotelbalandramanta.com. Commodious rooms or cabins sleeping four or five set amid gardens, with a/c, fridges, phones, cable TVs and private baths with hot water, plus use of a swimming pool. ❽

Howard Johnson Plaza Km1.5 Vía Barbasquillo ☎05/2629999, ⓦwww.ghlhoteles.com. Smart luxury chain hotel west of the centre with facilities such as pool, gym, restaurant, as well as great sea views. An architectural oddity means you take a lift downstairs from reception to your rooms. ❾

Lun Fun Av 11 and Calle 2 ☎05/2622966, ⓦwww.lunfunhotel.com. Despite its unenviable position in wasteland near the bypass, this plush hotel has it all – cable TV, hot water, a/c, free airport transfer and a fridge and phone in every room, plus wi-fi. Amiable Chinese–Ecuadorian owners speak English and run a good on-site Chinese restaurant. Breakfast included. ❼

Oro Verde Malecón and Calle 23 ☎05/2629200, ⓦwww.oroverdehotels.com. Immaculate five-star hotel on Playa Murciélago with supremely comfortable rooms, pool, sports and sauna facilities, casino, internet, delicatessen and an excellent restaurant. Breakfast included. ❾

Tarqui

Boulevard Av 105 and Calle 103, also at Av 106 and Calle 104 ☎05/2611654, ⓦwww.hotelesboulevardmanta.com. Complex of four neighbouring hotels offering fairly spacious rooms, some with a/c. The more luxurious wing has an indoor pool, sauna and restaurant, and rooms with a/c, hot water and cable TVs, and there's an outdoor pool nearby. Facilities can be used by all residents. ❺–❻

Hostal Miami Av 102 and Calle 107 ☎05/2622055. Unlike the nearby *Hotel Miami*, a friendly place abounding with replicas of Manteño-culture artefacts and offering decent, if slightly dog-eared, rooms with private baths around a courtyard. Some have balconies and are the same price as the less impressive interior rooms. One of the town's few good budget choices. ❷

Pacífico Inn Av 106 and Calle 101 ☎05/623584. Unmissable building towering over the stinking river inlet, where the rooms vary widely by traffic-noise levels, smell and light, but all come with private bath, cable TV and hot water. A/c costs extra. ❸–❺

Panorama Inn Av 105 and Calle 103 ☎05/2611312. Friendly hotel with options for low budgets, from rooms with fans and private baths to those with hot water, a/c and cable TVs. Rooms in the main building are a little tired, but the newer, costlier ones over the road are set around a nice swimming pool and perfectly comfortable, if bare. ❷–❹

▲ Manta

Manta town

Manta's tourist focus is the **Playa Murciélago**, a broad beach 1.5km north of the town centre, where from December to April the surf is good enough for the town to host international bodyboarding and windsurfing competitions. Swimmers should take care year round, as there is a strong **undertow**; there's usually plenty else going on here at weekends, from music to volleyball. The **Malecón Escénico**, a strip of restaurants and bars with a car park, fronts the beach. The police advise against wandering to quiet spots beyond the *Oro Verde*, where robberies have been reported. A string of fabulous beaches graces the coast west of town (see p.384), starting with **Playa Barbasquillo** and **Playa Piedra Larga**.

Opposite the Malecón Escénico at Calle 19, the **Museo Centro Cultural Manta** (Tues–Sat 9am–5pm, Sun 10am–3pm, $1, free Sun; Ⓦwww .museodemanta.com) has an interesting collection of artefacts from the Valdivian culture, which flourished here from 3500–1500 BC, and the later Manteño culture, including fish-shaped ocarinas and beautiful zoomorphic jugs and flasks. Heading east down the Malecón, you'll soon pass the **Capitanía**, by the entrance to Manta's main **port**, frequented by warships, the odd millionaire's yacht and countless container ships. Cruise liners tend to call between November and February, when the artesanía market at the **Plaza Cívica**, Malecón and Calle 13, is at its busiest and thronging with indigenous traders from Otavalo, who offer a decent selection of woven goods, jumpers and hammocks alongside more familiar coastal wares such as tagua carvings and Panama hats.

A block east is Manta's leafiest corner, the main square of **Parque Eloy Alfaro** and the **Parque de la Madre**. Away from the shore, the old heart of the port features narrow streets and wooden buildings rising up the hill.

Tarqui

As you cross into **Tarqui** past the old fishing harbour known as **La Poza**, currently being filled in to construct a conference centre, the stench of rubbish wafting out of the sluggish Río Manta is a fitting welcome to the less salubrious part of town. The **Playa Tarqui**, with its calm waters, is the town's second beach. It's dirtier and more dangerous than Murciélago, and not a recommended place to spend the day, though the **astillero**, where wooden boats are built, and the **fish market** are worth a look. At Tarqui's **market**, Calle 103 and Avenida 108 and surrounding streets, produce sellers compete with vendors pushing all sorts of domestic bric-a-brac. Avoid the area east of Calle 110, which is regarded as unsafe.

More conventional retail activity can be found at **El Paseo Shopping**, the largest and best of the city's malls, 2km out of town on 4 de Noviembre (take a bus or taxi), which also has a food court and an eight-screen **cinema**.

Eating, drinking and nightlife

The beaches in Manta and Tarqui abound with seafood **restaurants** and **bars**. At **Playa Murciélago**, the Malecón Escénico has a string of restaurants with near-identical menus and prices; the food is generally cheap and good. **Playa Tarqui** is fronted by rustic, thatched-roof bar-restaurants at the so-called **Parque del Marisco**, which dole out a lot of *ceviche* of questionable cleanliness. For a **drink**, try the American-run *Nashville South*, Malecón and Calle 14, which serves cold beer, food and snacks. Manta **nightlife** mainly gravitates towards Avenida Flavio Reyes, within a short walk of the Manicentro shopping centre; the most popular clubs of the moment are *Madera Fina*, Reyes and Calle 23, and the faster-paced *Temática* at Reyes and Calle 20.

Restaurants

El Cormorán Av 24 and Calle M-2. Well-presented restaurant regarded as one of the town's better places for fish and *ceviche*. Closed Sun.

El Ejecutivo On the eleventh floor of Edificio Banco Pichincha, Av 2 and Calle 12. Has great views of the city and bay and excellent food and service, with $5–6 main courses such as chicken in red-wine sauce with buttered new potatoes, accompanied by artichoke-heart salad. Closed Sat & Sun.

Lun Fun Av 11 and Calle 2. Upmarket hotel restaurant serving the best Chinese food in town, plus other international food.

Mama Rosa Av Flavio Reyes, Barrio Umiña. Huge menu based around moderately priced Italian food, covering pizza, pasta, risotto and grills, with red-check tablecloths and outdoor garden seating to boost the romance levels.

El Marino Malecón Tarqui and Calle 110. Popular spot for its great seafood, though the menu is limited and the place closes at 5.30pm.

Topi Tu Pizza Malecón and Calle 15. Thriving two-level pizzeria mocked up as a bamboo beach bar.

Listings

Airlines Flights to Quito: with Icaro, Edif Oro Mar, Malecón and Calle 23 (☎05/2627344); TAME, Edif El Vigía, Malecón and Calle 13C (☎05/2622006); and Aerogal, Av Flavio Reyes and Av 20 (☎05/2628899).

Banks Banco del Pacífico, Av 2 and Calle 13, and in Tarqui at Av 107 and Calle 103, has a MasterCard and Cirrus ATM and changes dollars traveller's cheques; Banco Pichincha, Av 2 and Calle 12, does Visa cash advance. There are also ATMs at El Paseo and Manicentro shopping malls.

Car rental Avis, Flavio Reyes and Av 24 ☎05/2622434; Budget, Malecón and Calle 16 ☎05/2629919.

Language school Ecuador Spanish Schools, Edif Barre, 3rd floor, Av 24 and Calle 15 (☎05/2610838, ⓦwww.ecuadorspanishschools.com).

Police and immigration Av 4 de Noviembre and Calle 104 ☎05/2920900; for emergencies ☎101.

Tour operators Blue Marlin Lodge (☎04/2402490, ⓦwww.bluemarlinmanta.com) runs sports-fishing trips; Delgado Travel, Av 6 and Calle 13 (☎05/2622813), does tours of the city and to *Hacienda San Antonio* (☎05/2622106, ⓦwww .sanantoniohotel.com.ec, ⓞ), on the coast west of Manta; and Metropolitan Touring, Av 4 and Calle 13 (☎05/2623090), provides local and national tours. The tourist office at Playa Murciélago offers trips to Parque Nacional Machalilla.

West of Manta

The coastline **west of Manta** is still relatively undeveloped but contains a few quiet fishing villages and some beautiful beaches, most of which are more suitable for **surfers** than swimmers (best surfing is Dec–April). **San Mateo**, 16km away, is one such village, with good surfing but with potential crowding. A few kilometres further along at **Santa Marianita**, the steady winds and large beach are perfect for **kitesurfing**. The dramatic headland and lighthouse at **SAN LORENZO**, 38km from Manta, provides a worthy backdrop to some terrific surfing at nearby **Las Piñas** beach (a 300-metre ride on good days). The best **place to stay** in San Lorenzo is *El Faro Escandinavo* (T09/1122336, W www.elfaroescandinavo.com; ●), offering a pool, internet and air-conditioned bungalows with hot water and cable TV right by the beach. The beachfront cabins, some air-conditioned, at *La Cueva* (T09/1047027, W www.la-cueva.com; ●) are cheaper and more rustic, but popular. Trans Jipijapa and Trans Manglaralto **buses** service this coastal road on the way to the modest high-season resort of Puerto Cayo (see p.433).

Montecristi

Eleven kilometres inland from Manta, the main road to Portoviejo passes **MONTECRISTI**, a small town nestled at the foot of the green Montecristi hills and founded by beleaguered refugees from Manta after they had lost everything in the pirate raids of the early seventeenth century. The central street, Avenida 9 de Julio, leads uphill from the highway for almost a kilometre to the main square at the head of the town. **Buses** from Manta marked "Montecristi" go right to the main square, while others stop on the main road, from where it's a ten-minute walk uphill.

Montecristi might look quite ramshackle were it not for its beautiful white **church** with elegant double staircase overlooking the town's attractive **central square**, which is resplendent against the backdrop of the cloud-draped hills.

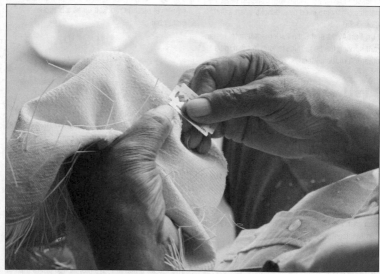

▲ Finishing a Panama hat, Montecristi

Where did you get that hat?

Few injustices can be more galling than having your nation's most famous export attributed to another country, yet this is what Ecuador has suffered with the "**Panama hat**". In the mid-nineteenth century, straw hats from Ecuador were traded in Panama along with vast quantities of other goods and quickly became a favourite with **gold prospectors** and labourers on the **Panama Canal**. It was precisely the question "where did you get that hat?" that started the association with the country of purchase rather than the country of origin – an error that was cemented when it was introduced to Europe at the **1855 World Fair** in Paris as the "Panama hat". The indignant words "Genuine Panama Hat Made in Ecuador" are now stamped on hats in an attempt to reclaim sovereignty over the product without upsetting the world-renowned name.

The tradition of hat-making probably goes back a long way in coastal Ecuador; **Valdivian** ceramic figurines from as long ago as 4000 BC seem to be wearing pointed straw hats. The first **conquistadors** also wrote about the broad, wing-like hats the locals wore, calling them **toquillas**, after *toca*, a Spanish word for a wimple. The Spanish soon began to wear them to stave off the sun's glare, praising their lightness, coolness and even their ability to carry water, due to the hat's ultra-fine weaving, but changed the shape into more conventional European styles. In the 1830s, factories employing more modern methods were set up in the highlands around **Cuenca** and Azuay and slowly began to surpass the traditional weavers on the coast. The hat reached its apogee as a fashion icon in the 1940s, when for a short time it became Ecuador's top export.

The straw, nicknamed **paja toquilla**, grows between Panama and Bolivia, but only the conditions in Ecuador's Manabí and Guayas provinces provide a suitable material for hat-making. The toquilla plant can grow up to 6 metres high after three years, but the best leaves are newer shoots harvested from around the base in monthly cycles. The leaves are split, cleaned, boiled, sundried and bleached with sulphur powder, then cut into straw. **Weavers**, mainly rural villagers from Manabí and Azuay provinces, get to work early in the morning or late at night, both to avoid the sun, which stiffens the straw prematurely, and so it's not so hot that their hands get sweaty. The brim is woven and tightened and the excess straw **trimmed** before the hats are washed, dried and **softened** with a mallet, while more sulphur powder is beaten into the fibres to bleach it before another final trim. The hats are then pulled over wooden blocks and ironed with more sulphur powder, then **blocked** into final shape by hand, which is more of an art than it sounds; most hats are now steam pressed by machine into shape in a few seconds. The making of a highest grade **superfino** takes several months and as many mastercraftsmen, the last experts of a dying art; perhaps it's no wonder the very best hats can fetch more than $10,000 in the US.

A number of miracles have been attributed to the effigy of the Virgin inside – there's a lively **fiesta** and street markets and processions around November 20–21 in her honour. The town is also the birthplace of **Eloy Alfaro**, the influential Liberal president at the beginning of the nineteenth century; his dignified statue adorns the square and his house, on Eloy Alfaro and 23 de Octubre, has been made into a **museum** honouring him (daily; free).

Montecristi's main claim to fame is as the manufacturing centre of the **Panama hat**, and at one time, almost every house in town had its own workshop. Dwindling demand has driven many locals to more profitable jobs in fishing and canning factories, or other crafts, such as tagua carving and straw-basket weaving, which supply the many **craft shops** on Avenida 9 de Julio.

Panama-hat workshops

Locals have been producing Panama hats here for well over a century, and you can still see top-quality artisans at work. José Chávez Franco's **workshop** is on Rocafuerte 386 (☎05/2310343), between Eloy Alfaro and 10 de Agosto (walk up past the church and turn right), or try the very senior Don Rosendo Delgado Garay, Rocafuerte 500 and Chimborazo (walk up past the church, turn left and the sign on his house is visible to the right). The bulk of the weaving work is actually done in villages nearby, and unfinished hats are sent for "cutting" and the final touches in Montecristi (see p.384). Ask Sr Chávez about tours to local villages **El Aromo** and **Piles**, where you can see toquilla plantations and weavers at work.

Panama hats can cost from a few dollars for a simple model, a *tropical* or *grueso*, to more than $400 for a *superfino* that takes three or four months to make, but this is still cheaper than virtually anywhere else in the world.

Portoviejo

About 35km east of Manta and connected to it by a fast road, **PORTOVIEJO** sits rather uneasily as the inland capital of coastal Manabí province. Ecuadorians know the province as the relaxed and fun-loving place of beach resorts and peaceful fishing villages, but Portoviejo is seen as its boring overseer, staffed by office workers toiling in the heat and dust. It's not of great appeal to visitors, who usually end up here by accident rather than design to change buses or money.

Francisco Pacheco founded Portoviejo on March 12, 1535, under the orders of the conquistador **Diego de Almagro**, who wanted to bring order to the region after the destruction wrought by Pedro de Alvarado a year earlier (see p.380). Although founded on the coast, it was relocated "seven leagues inland" later that year, only to suffer a terrible fire in 1541. Nevertheless, the town soon

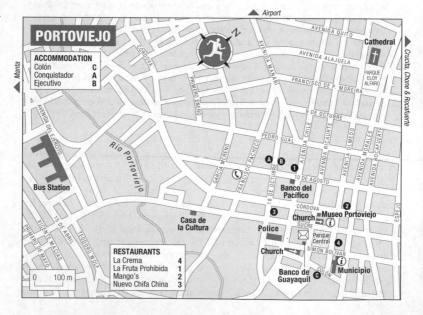

became an important agricultural centre, and in the 1570s even the few nearby indigenous communities that had survived the Conquest were doing well enough to own horses and commercial farms – while still having to pay crushing tribute to their Spanish overlords. During the post-colonial era Portoviejo flourished as a business centre, and while it's now second to Manta in commercial activity, it's still a key administrative centre and the site of an important state university.

Little of the town's colonial architecture has survived, but the most prominent landmark is the enormous modern **cathedral** on the Parque Eloy Alfaro, its concrete walls and striped brown, yellow and orange dome gleaming in the sun. One of the town's few other attractions, the **Casa de la Cultura**, Sucre and García Moreno (Mon–Fri 8am–noon & 3–6pm) puts on temporary art exhibitions, while the **Museo Portoviejo y Archivo Histórico** (Mon–Fri 9am–5pm; free), Olmedo and Sucre, exhibits Valdivian artefacts and other more recent pieces from the city's past. The **Jardín Botánico** on Avenida Universitaria, the road to Crucita, beyond the Universidad Técnica de Manabí ($1, including guided tour by students), comes as part of a 40-hectare reserve, divided into areas for palms, cacti, wet and dry forest, introduced species, animal rehabilitation, and for a tree nursery. On the road to Manta, El Paseo Shopping is a large modern shopping mall with an eight-screen **cinema**, showing blockbusters in English with Spanish subtitles.

Practicalities

Portoviejo's **bus terminal** is 1km west of the centre over the Río Portoviejo. The town isn't too safe generally, and particularly not in this area, so get a **taxi** ($1 most city destinations). The **airport**, Aeropuerto Reales Tamarindos, is 2km northwest of the centre, and TAME, on avenidas América and Chile (☎05/2632429, at airport 2637186), flies to and from Quito every day. Banco del Pacífico, América 101 and Avenida Manabí, changes dollars traveller's cheques and has ATMs here and at Avenida Chile and 10 de Agosto for Master-Card and Cirrus; Banco de Guayaquil on the *parque central* has a Visa ATM. Basic **tourist information** is available during office hours from the municipal office at the *municipio* (☎05/2631800).

If you have to **stay** here, try to avoid the cheap hotels around the bus station and head to the centre. Best in town is *Ejecutivo*, 18 de Octubre and 10 de Agosto (☎05/2630840, ⓦwww.hotelejecutivoportoviejo.ec; ❻–❼), complete with showy lobby, rather haughty receptionists and rooms or suites with full amenities. Opposite, *Conquistador* (☎05/2651472; ❸–❹) is good value for its private baths, phones, cable TVs, big double beds and choice of air conditioning or fan, though the rooms are showing signs of age. *Colón*, on Colón and Avenida Olmedo (☎05/2634004; ❸–❺), also has inexpensive en-suite rooms with cable TV and optional air conditioning, but avoid the dank interior rooms.

Restaurants in Portoviejo's centre, such as *La Crema*, on the *parque central* and the clean and efficient *Mango's*, on the corner of Córdova and Morales, feed city workers cheap and hearty lunches, but are closed evenings and weekends. *La Fruta Prohibida*, on Av Chile 607 and 10 de Agosto, serves healthy fruit salads, juices, shakes and snacks, while *Nuevo Chifa China*, on 18 de Octubre and Córdova, dishes up reliable Chinese food. There are also fried-chicken diners and the odd yogurt bar at the intersection of Avenida Rocafuerte and Pedro Gual, halfway between the two main squares.

Travel details

Buses

Bahía de Caráquez to: Guayaquil (every 1hr 30min; 5hr); Portoviejo (every 30min; 2hr); Quito (4 daily; 8hr).

Esmeraldas to: Ambato (11 daily; 8hr); Atacames (every 20min; 1hr); Borbón (hourly; 3hr 15min); Chamanga (every 40min; 3hr); Cuenca (1 daily; 15hr); Guayaquil (hourly; 7–8hr); Ibarra (4 daily; 9hr); La Tola (7 daily; 3hr); Machala (3 daily; 12hr); Manta (4 daily; 10hr); Mompiche (4 daily; 3hr); Muisne (every 20min; 2hr 30min); Pedernales (4 daily; 6hr 30min); Quito (hourly; 6hr); Same (every 20min; 1hr 30min); San Lorenzo (hourly; 4hr 30min); Santo Domingo (every 15–30min; 3hr); Súa (every 20min; 1hr 10min); Tonchigüe (every 20min; 1hr 35min); Tonsupa (every 20min; 50min).

Manta to: Bahía de Caráquez (every 2 hours; 3hr); Crucita (12 daily; 1hr 30min); Esmeraldas (4 daily; 10hr); Guayaquil (every 30min–1hr; 3hr); Jipijapa (every 30min; 1hr); La Libertad (hourly; 6hr); Montecristi (every 10min; 20min); Pedernales (4 daily; 6hr); Portoviejo (every 10min; 45min); Puerto López (hourly; 2hr by coast, 2hr 30min inland); Quevedo (13 daily; 5hr); Quito (hourly; 8hr); Santo Domingo (hourly; 6hr).

Pedernales to: Chamanga (every 30min; 1hr); Guayaquil (2 daily; 7–8hr); Quito (4 daily; 5–6hr); San Vicente (every 40min; 2hr 30min); Santo Domingo (every 20min; 3hr).

Portoviejo to: Bahía de Caráquez (hourly; 2hr); Crucita (every 15min; 45min–1hr); Esmeraldas (4 daily; 10hr); Guayaquil (every 30min–1hr; 4hr); Manta (every 10min; 45min); Pedernales (9 daily; 5–6hr); Quevedo (every 40min; 5hr 15min); Quito (hourly; 7hr); Santo Domingo (every 40min; 5hr).

San Lorenzo to: Borbón (every 30min; 1hr 15min); Esmeraldas (hourly; 4hr); Guayaquil (3 daily; 10–13hr); Ibarra (9 daily; 3hr 30min); Quito (2 daily; 7hr).

Santo Domingo to: Ambato (every 45min; 4hr); Bahía de Caráquez (2 daily; 5hr); Coca (4 daily; 12hr); Cuenca (3 daily; 8hr); Esmeraldas (every 15min; 3hr); Guayaquil (every 30min; 4hr 30min); Huaquillas (6 daily; 10hr); Lago Agrio (5 daily; 12hr); Machala (10 daily; 8hr); Manta (every 30min; 6hr); Muisne (4 daily; 6hr); Pedernales (every 30min; 3hr); Portoviejo (hourly; 5hr); Quevedo (every 15min; 1hr 30min); Quito (every 10min; 3hr); Salinas (2 daily; 8hr); San Miguel de los Bancos (every 20min; 3hr); Tulcán (3 daily; 7hr).

Boats

Limones to: La Tola (hourly; 30min); San Lorenzo (4 daily; 1hr 30min).

San Lorenzo to: Limones (4 daily; 1hr 30min); San Pedro (3 daily; 1hr 15min); Palma Real (2 daily; 1hr 30min).

Flights

Esmeraldas to: Quito (1–2 daily; 30min).
Manta to: Quito (6–7 daily; 35min).
Portoviejo to: Quito (1 daily; 30min).

Guayaquil and the southern coast

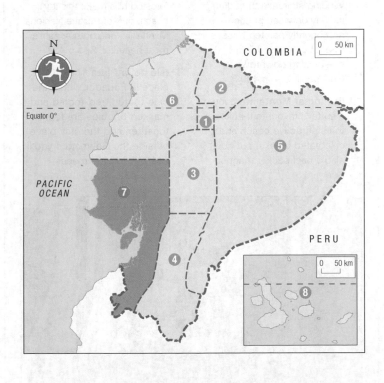

CHAPTER 7

Highlights

* **Malecón 2000** The centrepiece and symbol of a resurgent Guayaquil, this beautiful tree-lined riverside promenade takes in gardens, fountains, cafés, shops and landmarks. See p.398

* **Cerro Santa Ana** A showpiece of urban regeneration, built around a winding staircase threading its way between pristine and brightly painted houses to a fabulous viewpoint overlooking downtown Guayaquil. See p.400

* **Surfing at Montañita** Long a surfer's favourite thanks to its attractive beach and celebrated breaks, but now also a backpacker magnet. See p.423

* **Whale-watching from Puerto López** See humpback whales breach, roll and call to each other as they swim into warm coastal waters to mate and calve between June and September. See p.429

* **Playa Los Frailes** Virgin white sands and azure waters cradled by cliffs and backed by forested hills make this idyllic beach, part of Parque Nacional Machalilla, one of the coast's most beautiful. See p.432

* **Isla de la Plata** The only place in Ecuador where the blue-footed, red-footed and masked boobies are found together, and the only place outside the Galápagos you'll see waved albatrosses. See p.432

▲ Malecón 2000, Guayaquil

Guayaquil and the southern coast

S prawling over the west bank of the murky Río Guayas, the focus of Ecuador's southern coast is the port of **Guayaquil**, Ecuador's biggest city and an economic powerhouse that handles most of the country's imports and exports. Traditionally considered loud, frenetic, dirty and dangerous, Guayaquil has benefited from a huge injection of cash and a slew of urban regeneration schemes over the last decade or so, and these days is an enjoyable place to spend time in. Its beautiful riverside promenade, Malecón 2000, is a particular highlight, and the city's upbeat, urban tempo makes an exciting change of pace from rural Ecuador.

In contrast to this dynamic metropolis, Ecuador's **southern coast**, stretching south to the border with Peru and north to Puerto Cayo in southern Manabí, is largely rural and quiet, sporting a mix of mangrove swamps, shrimp farms and sandy beaches dotted with dusty villages and low-key resorts. Inland, monotonous banana plantations and brittle scrubland hold little appeal, though they do give way to lush forests further north. South of Guayaquil, the coastal highway heads 250km down to Peru, passing a few minor attractions on the way. Just south of town is the bird-rich **Reserva Ecológica Manglares Churute**, protecting one of the last major **mangrove swamps** left on the southern coast. Further south, Machala – capital of **El Oro** province and famous as the nation's "banana capital" – is low on sights and ambience, but serves as a useful launchpad for outlying targets such as the scenic hillside village of **Zaruma** or the fascinating petrified forest of **Puyango**, and is also handy as a stop on the way to the border crossing at **Huaquillas**.

West of Guayaquil, the neighbouring towns of **Santa Elena** and **La Libertad** are handy gateways to the self-styled **Ruta del Sol**, a 137km stretch of coast sporting a succession of long, golden beaches lapped by turquoise waters. Apart from the flashy, high-rise town of **Salinas**, just west of La Libertad, most are fairly undeveloped and backed by small resorts or down-at-heel fishing villages. Few places see many gringos along here, with the exceptions of laid-back **Montañita**, a grungy surfing hangout, the eco-resort of **Alandaluz**, with its tasteful bamboo cabins and private stretch of beach, and the dusty, tumbledown port of **Puerto López**, a base for summer **whale-watching** and year-round visits to **Parque Nacional Machalilla**. This park is the southern coast's most compelling attraction, taking in stunning, pristine beaches, dry and humid

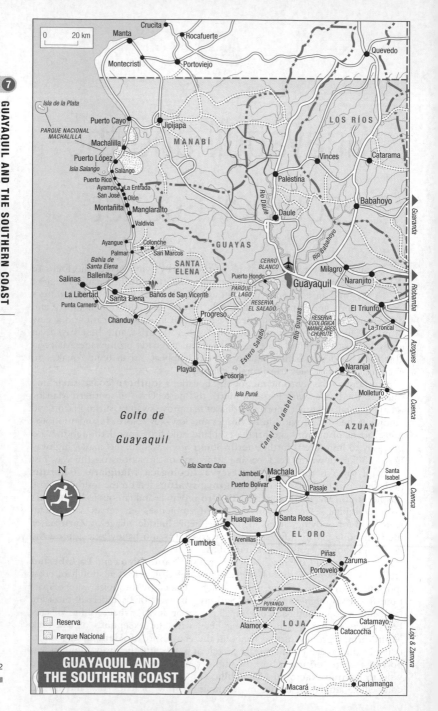

GUAYAQUIL AND THE SOUTHERN COAST

tropical forests and, most famously, the **Isla de la Plata**, an inexpensive alternative to the Galápagos for viewing boobies, frigatebirds and waved albatrosses.

The **best time to visit** the southern coast is between December and April, when bright blue skies and warm **weather** more than compensate for the frequent showers of the rainy season – the time of year when coastal vegetation comes to life and dry tropical forests become luxuriant and moist. Outside these months, the dry season features warm weather (around 23°C), but often depressingly grey skies. Not all the south coast's beaches are safe for swimming and many, like Manglaralto and Montañita, have dangerous currents and riptides that should be approached with great caution. Another consideration is the irregular and unpredictable **El Niño** weather phenomenon, when unusually heavy storms can leave the coast severely battered, washing away roads and disrupting communications.

Guayaquil

GUAYAQUIL was for years regarded as one of Ecuador's most dangerous cities, but following major regeneration programmes and public safety campaigns it has dramatically improved, with the central district now an unthreatening and surprisingly likeable place. When strolling the sparkling waterfront, it's hard to imagine among the whisper of fountains and leafy walkways that not long ago the area was considered completely out of bounds. The improvements aren't just cosmetic either: a reinvigorated cultural scene, thanks largely to important new exhibition spaces, and an ambitious overhaul of public transport point to an enduring and far-reaching transformation. Add all this to Guayaquil's natural energy and intensity and you have a winning combination. Still, beyond the heavily patrolled attractions and glittering renovations, shades of the city of old continue to lurk; never take valuables onto the streets and always use a taxi after dark.

Away from downtown, the several upmarket residential suburbs (mostly gated communities with plenty of armed guards to keep the numerous poor and slum districts at bay), reflect Guayaquil's status as the country's wealthiest city, thanks mainly to its massive port that handles major national exports, including bananas, shrimp, cacao and coffee. It's also Ecuador's largest city, with a population of more than 2.3 million people to Quito's 1.6 million, and there is a deep-seated rivalry between the two cities. As far as historical attractions go, Guayaquil lags far behind the capital, with only a smattering of colonial buildings still standing (most of the others having been destroyed in a 1942 earthquake). Nonetheless, Quito has nothing like Guayaquil's gleaming riverside development, the **Malecón 2000**, which incorporates gardens, shopping centres, restaurants, a landmark museum, cinema and gallery and several of the city's most famous monuments; it links downtown to the **Cerro Santa Ana**, a once-dangerous slum now ingeniously reinvented as a beacon of urban renewal, and **Las Peñas**, the city's most charming historic district. The effect of the regeneration projects cannot be underplayed; the city is no longer a place visited out of necessity, but a destination in its own right.

Some history
Conquistador Francisco de Orellana founded the city as **Santiago de Guayaquil** on July 25, 1537, its name supposedly honouring the local

GREATER GUAYAQUIL

Manta

Terminal Terrestre

Río Daule Terminal

Mall del Sol   Airport

See 'Urdesa' map

San Marino Shopping

Malecón del Salado

See 'Guayaquil' map

Salinas & Ruta del Sol

Babahoyo, Machala & the Highlands

Río Guayas

Metrovia line 1
Metrovia line 3

0   1 km

Huancavilca chieftain **Guayas** and his wife, **Quil**, who killed themselves rather than be captured by the Spanish. From its earliest years it was the most important entry point into Ecuador (known then as the "Audiencia de Quito") and quickly grew into a flourishing little port. Its fortunes were held back by the repeated attacks of pillaging British, French and Dutch **buccaneers**, regular **fires** engulfing its timber buildings and the deleterious mix of **tropical climate** and inadequate **sanitation**, which made it a hotbed of smallpox, yellow fever and typhoid. Nevertheless, during the seventeenth and eighteenth centuries Guayaquil gradually took on the shape of a proper city, with new roads, bridges, schools, hospitals and markets, mostly funded by burgeoning exports of **cacao**, **fruit** and **wood**.

On October 9, 1820, it became the first city in Ecuador to declare its **independence** from Spain, and it was from here that **General Sucre** conducted his famous military campaign, culminating in the liberation of Quito on May 24, 1822. Shortly afterwards, Guayaquil went down in history as the site of the legendary meeting between the two liberators of South America, **Simón Bolívar** and **José de San Martín**, whose campaigns from opposite ends of the continent were then drawing together in the middle (see p.493). In the decades following independence, Guayaquil grew rapidly and asserted its considerable role in the new republic – Ecuador's first bank was founded here in 1859, soon followed by a major public library and university. The tide of success turned in 1896, when the worst **fire** in its history wiped out seventy percent of the city in 36 hours.

Guayaquil was quickly rebuilt and became prosperous once more in the twentieth century, aided by the dramatic **banana boom**, which began in the late 1940s. The city's pivotal role in the country's international trade (and the huge increase in commerce at that time) funded new port facilities in 1963 and the construction of the massive three-kilometre **Puente de la Unidad Nacional**, the largest bridge on the Pacific coast of South America. In the last couple of decades numerous **shanty towns** have emerged on the city's periphery, as thousands of people have migrated from the countryside in search of work; **crime** levels soared to the point where, in 1998, a state of emergency and nightly curfews were imposed for several months. These measures, along with a stronger police presence, have improved security in downtown areas such as the Malecón 2000, but vigilance is still required.

Arrival

With its smart new bus terminal and airport, **arriving** in Guayaquil is no longer the daunting, chaotic experience it once was and getting to your hotel should be straightforward. Buses arrive at the gleaming **Terminal Terrestre** (☏04/2837600), 7km north of the city centre on Avenida Benjamín Rosales Aspiazu, complete with an attached shopping mall and several ATMs. **Local city buses** use a separate area at one end of the terminal; many (for example, the #2) will take you into the centre, as will the Metrovía (see p.395), opposite the terminal – but it's far easier and much safer to take a taxi to your hotel for $4–5.

The busy new **airport** – Aeropuerto José Juaquín de Olmedo – is a couple of kilometres southwest of the bus terminal toward the city. It serves domestic flights (Aerogal, Icaro and TAME) from Quito, Cuenca, Loja and the Galápagos Islands, as well international flights from several cities, including Miami, New York, Amsterdam and Madrid. The airport is well served by ATMs, internet facilities and an information desk (☎04/2169000). Taxis ($5–7 to the centre) are readily available from outside the arrivals gate; buses to the centre can be flagged down outside the terminal on Avenida de las Américas (again, try #2), but when carrying luggage, it's easier and safer to take a taxi. If leaving Ecuador from the airport, you're required to pay **$25 departure tax** in cash.

Guard against **petty theft** by staying alert when arriving in town and getting your bearings, not wandering the streets with your valuables and by always taking a taxi at night.

Information

The most convenient place to go for **tourist information** is the **Dirección Municipal de Turismo**, upstairs in the *municipio*, Pichincha 605 and Clemente Ballén (Mon–Fri 9am–5pm; ☎04/2599100, @diturgye@guayaquil.gov.ec), where you'll find a good spread of brochures, maps and general city information; it also has a small information kiosk in front of the building on Clemente Ballén (Tues–Fri 9am–5pm, Sat 9am–1pm). The **Ministerio de Turismo** office on Avenida Francisco de Orellana in Ciudadela Kennedy Norte (Mon–Fri 9am–5pm; ☎04/2684274) is helpful but too far from the centre to be useful. The regional **Ministerio del Ambiente** office, Av Quito 402 and Padre Solano (Mon–Fri 8.30am–4.30pm; ☎04/2397730), has information on the nearby Reserva Ecológica Manglares Churute (see p.406). The (Spanish only) **website** ⓦwww.guayaquil.guides.com is a good source of information, and the Dirección de Turismo is currently developing a new website ⓦwww.visitaguayaquil.com, which will include information in English.

Orientation and city transport

It can be initially hard to get a handle on the city as a whole, but getting your bearings in the central area is quite straightforward. The downtown core lies within a compact grid on the west bank of the Río Guayas. The riverside avenue is called the Malecón Simón Bolívar, usually shortened to the **Malecón**, while three blocks away is the main square of the **Parque Seminario**, sometimes still known by its old name of **Parque Bolívar**. The principal artery running through the city is **Avenida 9 de Octubre**, running from the Malecón up to the imposing **Parque del Centenario** and beyond.

Most sights are no more than a ten- or fifteen-minute walk from the Parque Seminario, though you might consider the city's excellent new **Metrovía** ($0.25), an ecofriendly bus system with its own lanes. There are currently two lines: Line 1 runs north–south through the city between the terminals at Río Daule, opposite the Terminal Terrestre, and El Guasmo, in the south, splitting into two parallel branches in the downtown section, with northbound buses following the axis formed by Pedro Carbo and Vicente Rocafuerte, and southbound buses going down Boyacá. Line 3 (Line 2 is still to be built) branches northwest from the centre (where it connects with Line 1), up to the terminal at Bastión Popular.

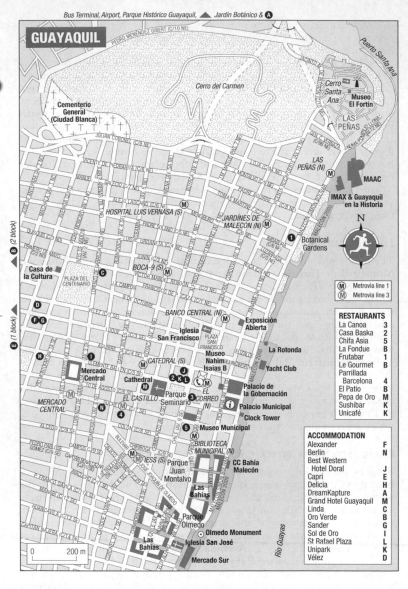

GUAYAQUIL

RESTAURANTS

La Canoa	3
Casa Baska	2
Chifa Asia	5
La Fondue	B
Frutabar	1
Le Gourmet	B
Parrillada	
Barcelona	4
El Patio	B
Pepa de Oro	M
Sushibar	K
Unicafé	K

ACCOMMODATION

Alexander	F
Berlin	N
Best Western	
Hotel Doral	J
Capri	E
Delicia	H
DreamKapture	A
Grand Hotel Guayaquil	M
Linda	C
Oro Verde	B
Sander	G
Sol de Oro	I
St Rafael Plaza	L
Unipark	K
Vélez	D

Ⓜ Metrovia line 1
Ⓜ Metrovia line 3

Avoid the confusing regular buses and take a **taxi**; taxi drivers in Guayaquil do not use meters, so ask in your hotel about the going rate for journeys around the city (a typical short one should be $1–2) and be sure to set a price with your driver before you leave. It's safest to take a cab belonging to a cooperative, whose name and phone number are displayed on the side of the car – you should be able to flag one down easily on most city-centre streets. Alternatively, call one of the 24-hour companies such as Aeropuerto (☎04/2294944), Carrousel (☎04/2110610) or Radio Taxi El Paraíso (☎04/2201877).

Accommodation

Guayaquil is packed with **hotels**, but few are geared towards tourists. Top-end establishments attract mainly corporate clients and nearly all have separate, much higher, rates for foreigners; single rooms are also hard to come by. The lower-end hotels are very good value but often double up as "motels" – places where couples are charged by the hour, but they're usually clean and safe. Many of the cheaper hotels only have cold-water showers, while air conditioning is offered in all expensive and most mid-priced hotels. Given the cacophony of Guayaquil's streets, it's always worth asking if there are any back, or even internal, rooms available.

Alexander Luque 1107 ⚊04/2532000, ⓦwww .hotelalexanderecuador.com. Very polished little hotel with well-furnished rooms featuring a/c and cable TVs. All the doubles are quiet, rather dark interior rooms, while the suites overlook the street. Parking is also available. ❻

Berlin Sucre and Rumichaca ⚊04/2524648. Adequate budget rooms with ceiling fans, TVs, small air vents and cold-water showers. Pretty spartan, but clean and spacious, with some rooms giving onto the street. ❷

Best Western Hotel Doral Chile 402 and Aguirre ⚊04/2328490, ⓦwww.hdoral.com. Some rooms are a bit gloomy and the muzak pollutes the communal spaces, but the "king-size" rooms have bright decor, huge beds, big cable TVs, a/c and heavily lined curtains to keep out the light. ❼

Capri Luque 1221 and Machala ⚊04/2530093, Ⓕ2532710. Small, good-value hotel with parking, offering neat rooms with cool floor tiles and white-washed walls. All rooms have cable TVs, a/c, fridges and private bathrooms – but those on the street are noisy. ❹

Delicia Clemente Ballén 1105 ⚊04/2324925. Dozens of rather bare, box-like rooms with shared or private baths and fans or a/c. Modest, but clean, friendly and safe. Popular with backpackers. If it's full, try its sister hotel, *Niucanche*, nearby on Pío Montúfar 107, for the same sort of thing. ❷

Dreamkapture Hostel Villa 21, Calle Juan Sixto Bernal, near intersection of Benjamín Carrion and Francisco de Orellano ⚊04/224 2909, ⓦwww .dreamkapture.com. Colourful and pleasant French–Canadian-run hostel out of the centre in the Alborada district, offering a range of small shared rooms (from $9 per bunk) or tidy doubles with shared (❹) or private bath (❺). Also has a small garden with a tiny pool, a kitchen for guests and an on-site travel agency. Can arrange tours to their lodge on the edge of the Reserva Ecológica Manglares Churute (see p.406).

Ecuahogar Out of the centre at Villa Manzana S-31, Av Isidro Ayora, Sauces 1 ⚊04/2248357. Well-managed youth hostel offering clean rooms with or without a/c and a choice of private or shared baths. Security boxes and the on-site café-restaurant are convenient. Dorm beds for $15 (including breakfast) also available. Breakfast included. ❻

Grand Hotel Guayaquil Boyacá and Clemente Ballén ⚊04/2329690, ⓦwww.grandhotelguayaquil .com. Large, upmarket hotel boasting a gorgeous outdoor pool with a cascading waterfall. Good rooms and furnishings, as well as a roof deck, sauna, massage rooms, steam baths, wi-fi and 24-hour café open to non-guests. Breakfast and 30min internet use included. ❽

Linda Lorenzo de Garaicoa 809 ⚊04/2562495. Smart new *hostal* with immaculate rooms featuring cool marble floors and comfortable beds, on the Parque del Centenario. ❺

Orilla del Río Outside the centre, Ciudadela Entreríos, Mz K1, #8 & 9, Calle 7, between Av Río Guayas Pío Montúfar 107 ⚊04/2835394, ⓦwww .orilladelrio.com.ec. In a comfortable residential district not far from the Parque Histórico, this cosy

---

Guayaquil street addresses

A confusing new street-numbering system coexists with standard street names, centred on two axes: east–west along 9 de Octubre, and north–south down Avenida Quito, with the city divided into quarters. Numbers ascend as you head away from these axes, but as each quarter has its own set of numbers, there are four Avenida 1s (each suffixed by different compass ordinals), or Calle 2s and so on, making for a bewildering entanglement of numbers and letters. For ease of use, we've stuck here to the old-fashioned names, though we've included the numbering system on our map.

converted home features immaculate en-suite rooms, cable TV, a/c and fridge, plus luggage storage, games room, living room and an outdoor jacuzzi. Breakfast included and transfers available. **7**

Oro Verde 9 de Octubre and García Moreno ☎04/2327999, ⓦ www.oroverdehotels.com. Guayaquil's premier city-centre hotel, this is a large, modern and impeccably decorated establishment with several restaurants, a pleasant outdoor pool, wi-fi and stylish, contemporary rooms. **9**

Sander Luque 1101 ☎04/2320030, ⓦ www.sanderguayaquil.com. Well-priced hotel offering clean, simple rooms with fans or a/c and private bathrooms. Mostly doubles, but also has some twin rooms, while the triples and family rooms are particularly good value. **4**

Sol de Oro Lorenzo de Garaicoa 1243 ☎04/2532067. Friendly hotel offering well-furnished rooms with cable TVs and a/c. Pricier

suites on the top floor are huge and boast excellent views over the city. A good mid-price choice, with a complimentary breakfast and its own garage. **6**

St Rafael Plaza Chile 414 and Clemente Ballén ☎04/2327140, ⓕ 2324195. All rooms have cable TV, fridge, a/c and decent bathrooms, and the price includes breakfast and 15 minutes free internet. A real bargain, considering the location. Includes wi-fi. **5**

Unipark Clemente Ballén 406, Parque Seminario ☎04/2327100, ⓦ www.uniparkhotel.com. Large, plush hotel with a vast, marble lobby, pleasant piano bar and modern, well-appointed rooms. Private parking and wi-fi available. **9**

Vélez Vélez 1021 and Av Quito ☎04/2530356. Simple but impeccably clean singles, doubles and triples with bare, pale-cream walls and floors and en-suite bathrooms with cold water. Some rooms have a/c, others have ceiling fans. Also has its own garage. **3**

The City

For sightseeing, the most impressive part of Guayaquil is the **Malecón 2000** riverside development, which includes the excellent **Museo Antropológico y de Arte Contemporáneo (MAAC)**. Close by are the rejuvenated district of **Cerro Santa Ana** and its spectacular viewpoint, and the tiny but attractive district of **Las Peñas**, featuring 1900s architecture and a string of art galleries. Other potential sights include the enjoyable **Museo Municipal** and a few private **museums** showcasing a wealth of religious art and pre-Columbian artefacts; all these museums have air conditioning, providing delicious relief from the heat. Out of the centre, worthwhile excursions include the **Parque Histórico Guayaquil**, an enjoyable exploration of the city's past and its regional environment, and the **Jardín Botánico**, which houses a fine collection of orchids. Slightly further afield, the **Reserva Ecológica Manglares Churute** (see p.406), the **Bosque Protector Cerro Blanco** (see p.415) and the mangroves at **Puerto Hondo** (see p.415) make rewarding **day-trips** from Guayaquil.

The Malecón 2000

The busy **Malecón Simón Bolívar** skirts the western bank of the wide, yellow-brown Río Guayas; it always heaves with traffic but the long pedestrianized section by the waterfront, known as the **Malecón 2000**, is the most pleasant place to stroll in town. Skilfully designed, diligently maintained and the most beloved public space in the city, it features a large, paved esplanade filled with trees, botanical gardens, contemporary sculpture and architecture, shopping malls and restaurants. It also connects some of Guayaquil's best-known monuments along a **promenade** (daily 7am–midnight), which security guards regularly patrol, enclosed by railings and accessed only at guarded entrance gates – making it one of the safest places to spend a day in Guayaquil.

Its centrepiece is the **Plaza Cívica**, reached by gates at the end of 9 de Octubre or 10 de Agosto. As you enter the gates, you're faced with **La Rotonda**, an imposing statue of South America's liberators, José de San Martín and Simón Bolívar, shaking hands against a background of tall marble columns topped by billowing South American flags. The monument, which looks stunning when illuminated at night, commemorates the famous encounter between the two generals here on July 26 and 27, 1822 (see p.493). It's designed so two people whispering into the two end pillars can hear each other – though the din of the traffic somewhat undermines the effect.

South of La Rotonda are sculptures dedicated to the four elements, with fire and earth doubling up as timber-and-metal **lookout towers** crowned by sail-like awnings. The views from the top are striking: on one side the urban sprawl stretches to the horizon, while on the other the low, fuzzy vegetation across the river lies completely free of buildings. Looking north, the huge bridge of **Puente de la Unidad Nacional** stretches across to the suburb of Durán, from where the famous Quito–Guayaquil trains used to leave. Beyond the sculptures and past the Yacht Club, the 23-metre Moorish **clock tower** marks the southern end of the Plaza Cívica.

South of the clock tower is the **CC Bahía Malecón** shopping centre (daily 10am–8pm) and the dignified **Plaza Olmedo**, dedicated to statesman and poet **José Joaquín de Olmedo** (1780–1847), the first mayor of Guayaquil and a key agitator for the city's independence. At the southern end of the promenade, the **Mercado Sur** (daily 9am–10pm; $1), a splendid construction of glass and wrought iron, is floodlit at night to dazzling effect and is a wonderful space for temporary exhibitions and events. Opposite, indigenous flower sellers surround the elegant **Iglesia San José**, and south of the Mercado Sur lies a small clothes and **artesanía market**, though you'll have to bargain hard to get a good deal. The real clothes bargains are to be found over the road from the Malecón at the sprawling **Las Bahías market**, sited on several blocks around the pedestrianized streets on both sides of Olmedo, near the bottom of the Malecón 2000.

North of the Plaza Cívica is a succession of sumptuous **botanical gardens**, fountains, ponds and walkways; each garden is themed on a historical period or Ecuadorian habitat, such as the Plaza de las Bromelias, a lavish concoction of cloudforest-like trees swathed in mosses and bromeliads. At the northern end of the promenade is an IMAX cinema (Mon–Thurs $4, Fri–Sun $5; ⓦwww .imaxmalecon2000.com). Below it, in the same building, **Guayaquil en la Historia** (daily 10am–6.30pm; $3) displays the evolution of the city, with fourteen beautifully crafted miniature reconstructions of various scenes, accompanied by information in English.

A little further on, the **Museo Antropológico y de Arte Contemporáneo (MAAC)** (Tues–Sun 9.30am–5pm, $3; Sun 10am–5pm, $1.50) is a flagship arts complex. Exhibition space for contemporary art is balanced by an excellent collection of fine pre-Columbian ceramics, golden objects and ceremonial paraphernalia, while **MAAC Cine** puts on a mixed programme of art-house, documentary and classic films (check ⓦwww.ochoymedio.net for details).

Guayaquil fiestas

The city's biggest **fiestas** are July 24, Simón Bolívar's birthday, and July 25, the foundation of the city, celebrated together in a week of events and festivities known as the **fiestas julianas**, complete with processions, street dancing and fireworks. Another important bash is October 9, for the city's **independence**, which is combined with the **Día de la Raza** on October 12, commemorating Columbus's discovery of the New World. New Year's Eve is celebrated with the burning of the *años viejos*, large effigies, on the Malecón at midnight.

Las Peñas and Cerro Santa Ana

The Malecón ends in the north at the picturesque barrio of **Las Peñas**, itself at the foot of Cerro Santa Ana. There's little more to it than a short, dead-end road – Numa Pompilio Llona – paved with uneven, century-old cobblestones, but the colourful wooden houses here make this one of the prettiest corners of Guayaquil. Many of the houses have been beautifully restored, but part of the area's charm derives from the flaking paint and gentle disrepair of those that haven't. A couple of cannons standing by the entrance point towards the river, honouring the city's stalwart resistance to seventeenth-century pirates, and the street is dotted with a few small art galleries; the best is the **Casa del Artista Plástico** of the Asociación Cultural Las Peñas.

Rising above Las Peñas, the **Cerro Santa Ana** was a very dangerous slum until a regeneration project transformed a swath of its ramshackle buildings into an eye-catching sequence of brightly painted houses, restaurants, bars and shops built around a winding, 444-step staircase to a viewpoint at the top of the hill: the **Plaza de Honores**, home to a colonial-style chapel and **lighthouse** modelled after Guayaquil's first, from 1841.

With its discreet balconies, ornate lampposts and switchback streets leading from intimate plazas, the development does a fair job of evoking the image of a bygone Guayaquil – despite the plastic "tiled" roofs, heavy presence of armed guards and large locked gates blocking out the slums at its margins. Yet the spectacular **views** from the Plaza de Honores and the top of the lighthouse are definitely worth a visit, particularly after a day on the Malecón as the sun dips on the seething city below. Just below the Plaza de Honores, the open-air **Museo El Fortín del Santa Ana** holds cannons, seafaring paraphernalia, the foundations of the fortress of **San Carlos**, built in 1629 to defend the city from pirate attacks, and a reconstructed pirate ship, half of which is a bar. Further below, down by the river, the **Puerto Santa Ana** is the city's latest regeneration project, currently being developed as a marina complete with waterside cafés, restaurants and apartments.

Parque Seminario and around

Guayaquil's central square, the **Parque Seminario** (also known as Parque Bolívar) is famous for its impish iguanas, which make occasional appearances out of the surrounding trees and shrubs. The huge, gleaming-white **cathedral**, a neo-Gothic confection of spires, arches and lancet windows, dominates the west side of the square; the building dates from 1948 and is built solidly of concrete – fire destroyed the original 1547 cathedral and subsequent incarnations.

One block southeast, on Sucre and Chile, the engaging **Museo Municipal** (Tues–Sat 9am–5pm; free) focuses on the history of the city and region. In the lobby sits one of its most stunning pieces: an enormous, six-hundred-year-old tree trunk embellished with dozens of carvings of human figures, produced by the seafaring Manteño-Huancavilca culture, the first people in what is now Ecuador to have any contact with the Spanish. Other striking pieces include a ten-thousand-year-old mastodon tooth, pre-Columbian pottery, a diorama of the great fire of 1896 and displays on the seventeenth-century English buccaneers who attacked the city.

Facing the waterfront three blocks east of the Parque Seminario, roughly opposite the clock tower, the large, Neoclassical **Palacio Municipal** is one of the most beautiful buildings in the city, featuring grey walls set off by dazzling white balconies and stucco mouldings and a central arcade topped by a glass-and-metal vaulted roof. Next door is the **Palacio de la Gobernación**, similar to its neighbour but smaller, plainer and less well kept. Directly across the street is the **Museo Nahim Isaias B**, at Clemente Ballén and Pichincha (Tues–Sat 9am–5pm; $1.50, free Sat), whose collection of pre-Colombian ceramics and a few gold items are displayed in a gallery overlooking a former banking hall.

Plaza San Francisco and around

Five blocks north of the Museo Municipal lies the small, tree-filled **Plaza San Francisco**, at Pedro Carbo and Vélez, where the grey-and-white **Iglesia San Francisco** towers over its flowerbeds and benches. The original church was destroyed in the 1896 fire, though the current building, erected six years later, preserves its colonial look. In contrast to the church's restrained design, across the road is a large, fantastical statue of a fish-cum-hummingbird covered in bright mosaics, a bright and modern design echoed a few blocks away at the **Exposición Abierta**, around the corner on Icaza and Panama, a collection of huge, brightly coloured murals on the side of the Banco del Pacífico building.

Parque del Centenario and around

From the Plaza San Francisco, the frenetic Avenida 9 de Octubre leads seven blocks west to the **Parque del Centenario**, an immense square spread over four blocks and landscaped with flowers and trees, but constantly choked with traffic. Its centre is marked by a towering column crowned by the statue *Liberty*, its arms outstretched and images of independence heroes arrayed around its base. On the west side of the square, at the corner with 9 de Octubre, is the **Casa de la Cultura** (Tues–Fri 10am–5.30pm, Sat 9am–3pm; $1), which exhibits pre-Columbian items in its poorly presented and not very engaging Sala Arqueológica, and a small but lovely gold collection in its **Sala de Oro**. The museum used to have more than five hundred pieces until a dramatic theft in 1987 reduced the collection to just 63 items.

A ten-minute walk north from the plaza along Moncayo (near a rough area and more safely travelled by taxi) brings you to the city cemetery, also known as the **Ciudad Blanca** ("White City") for its many rows of dazzling white tombs and mausoleums housing the remains of the local elite; at the end of an avenue lined with palms is the tomb of former president Vicente Rocafuerte, a Guayaquil native. Here and elsewhere in the cemetery, the funerary sculpture is remarkably indulgent, much of it carved from Italian marble. There's a **flower market** just opposite the cemetery, near entrance 6.

Malecón del Salado

Twelve blocks west of the Parque del Centenario, 9 de Octubre meets the green banks of the Estero Salado, a tributary of the Río Guayas and site of another swanky new riverside development, the **Malecón del Salado**. With its sleek, steel (pedestrian-only) suspension bridge, stylishly designed promenades and observation platforms and array of cafés and restaurants, this is a fun place to spend an hour or two. On weekends you can take a 45-minute boat trip down the river ($3), where the dilapidated wooden houses leaning over the water stand in striking contrast to the Malecón's modernity.

Parque Histórico Guayaquil

Northeast of town towards the wealthy suburb of Samborondón the **Parque Histórico Guayaquil** (Wed–Sun 9am–4.30pm; $3/$4.50 Sun, holidays and special events; ⓦ www.parquehistoricoguayaquil.com) is a well-designed and slickly operated park divided into three sections. A **forest-life** zone features walkways through mangroves, spacious enclosures holding native animals

RESTAURANTS
Anderson's 2
El Español 3
Riviera 1
Saitama 4

including tapirs, caimans, ocelots, spider monkeys, sloths and a harpy eagle and an observation tower for birdwatching. The **traditions** zone represents coastal culture and the *montuvio* way of life by a traditional farmstead (*granja*) with crops of cacao, banana, coffee, rice, *paja toquilla* (the straw used to make Panama hats) and *mate*, as well as a reconstructed cacao-plantation hacienda dating to 1883, half of which is original. The **urban architecture** zone displays some of the last fragments of Guayaquil's late nineteenth-century buildings, which have been reassembled and restored and now overlook the **Malecón 1900** – the riverside as it might have looked in the early 1900s. On Sundays, actors in period costume promenade along the waterfront, and plans are under way for a paddle steamer to ferry passengers back through time from the Malecón 2000. City **buses** #97 and #4 pass near the park entrance on Avenida Esmeraldas, but it's probably easier to get a **taxi** from downtown ($4–5).

Jardín Botánico de Guayaquil

On a lofty position on top of the Cerro Colorado, beyond the Ciudadela Las Orquídeas on the north side of town, the **Jardín Botánico de Guayaquil** (daily 8am–4pm; $3) has an excellent collection of orchids, as well as several hundred other plants on a peaceful site with great views over the city. You can wander through the gardens at your leisure, or hire a guide for $5 to show you around. As well as the numerous plants, there's a butterfly house, koi pond and geology area with rock and mineral exhibits. The #63 **bus** leaves from the Parque del Centenario and takes you within a fifteen-minute walk of the garden; if going by **taxi** (30min; $4–6), arrange a pick-up time for the return journey.

Eating

Downtown **restaurants** fall into two broad categories: those serving cheap and simple *almuerzos*, and those (usually attached to the smarter hotels) offering good-quality, but overpriced, menus. A more concentrated collection of restaurants, as well as bars and nightclubs, lines Avenida Estrada, the main drag of the affluent suburb of **Urdesa**; take buses #52 and #54 from the Malecón, #10 from Parque del Centenario, or go by taxi (20min; $3–4). You'll find plenty of **fast-food** outlets at the CC Malecón mall, including several taco and seafood bars, as well as others at the northern end of the promenade. The big shopping centres like Mall del Sol (see "Shopping", p.404) feature huge food courts with dozens of familiar international fast-food chains.

Downtown

La Canoa *Hotel Continental*, Chile 510 and 10 de Agosto. One of the best places to sample proper Ecuadorian cuisine, including *caldo de manguera* (pork tripe soup), *seco de chivo* (goat stew), *ceviche, bolones* and *guatita*, all at affordable prices and in a spacious, well-attended dining room. Open 24hr.

Casa Baska (also called *Tasca Vasca*) Clemente Ballén 422, Parque Seminario ☎04/2534599. Authentic Spanish restaurant with bare brick walls and a long list of mouthwatering tapas scrawled on a board: manchego cheese, serrano ham, croquettes, sardines in olive oil, seafood broth and lots more. It's all delicious, but quite pricey. Closed Sun.

Chifa Asia Sucre and Pedro Carbo. The smartest of three neighbouring Chinese restaurants, *Chifa Asia* has a clean, pleasant dining room and serves cheap and tasty Chinese and Ecuadorian food.

La Fondue *Oro Verde* hotel, 9 de Octubre and García Moreno. Small restaurant mocked up in a Swiss chalet interior, with the help of dangling cowbells and waitresses dressed as Alpine milkmaids. Despite the gimmicks, the fondues and *raclettes* are pretty good and cost around $8.

Fruta Bar Malecón and Martiínez ☎04/2300743. Sporting a beach-themed decor and welcome a/c, this snack bar serves refreshing and delicious juices, milkshakes, fruit salads and sandwiches. A bit pricey, but worth it.

Le Gourmet *Oro Verde* hotel, 9 de Octubre and García Moreno. Rather formal, award-winning restaurant with a sophisticated French menu and a Gallic head chef. Expensive, but not a bad place for a blowout.

La Pepa de Oro *Grand Hotel Guayaquil*, Boyacá and Clemente Ballén. Not as expensive as its smart appearance suggests, and has a sizeable choice of dishes from *platos típicos* to standard international food such as pizza, burgers, *fajitas* and sandwiches, to more exciting numbers, including fried tilapia in beer batter. Open 24hr.

Parrillada Barcelona Sucre and Boyacá. Large, slightly grubby canteen specializing in roast chicken, which you can see on a big rotisserie over hot coals by the door. No frills but very cheap.

El Patio *Oro Verde* hotel, 9 de Octubre and García Moreno. Modern, stylish café-restaurant with interesting decor, a buzzing atmosphere and good international food – a fun place to eat, though not cheap. Open 24hr.

Sushibar *Uniparkhotel*, Clemente Ballén 406, Parque Seminario. Affordable, first-rate sushi served in a classy bar-restaurant next to the hotel's front desk. From early evening onwards a pianist tinkles away in the background, adding to the atmosphere.

Unicafé *Unipark Hotel*, Clemente Ballén 406, Parque Seminario. Large, attractive dining room with blond wood chairs and bright colours. Does an appealing, if expensive, lunch and dinner buffet in addition to its national and international menu. Popular with business types.

Urdesa

Anderson Estrada 505 and Ébanos. Cast-iron candelabras, subdued lighting and a smoochy soundtrack make for an intimate, if slightly dated, feel to this restaurant, where the fish and seafood really stand out. Fairly pricey, except for the savoury crêpes which start at $3. Closed Sun.

El Español Corner of Estrada 302 and Cedros. For a quick snack or sandwich, this upmarket chain is a good choice for its tasty hams, salamis and cheeses served in a variety of rolls with a range of fillings, salads and condiments.

Parrillada del Ñato Estrada 1219 between Laureles and Costanera ☎04/2387098. A Guayaquil institution that gets carnivores slavering over colossal steaks and enormous portions of grilled meats (mains around $10) – though pizza and seafood are also available.

Riviera Estrada 707 and Ficus ☎04/2883790, ⓦwww.rivieraecuador.com. Excellent Italian restaurant, with snappy service and a full menu including fresh-made pasta, antipasti, risotto, profiteroles and tiramisu. Automatic parmesan graters and mini-chairs for your bags contribute to the air of pampering. Deli service also available.

Saitama Estrada 417 and Diagonal ☎04/2886725. A great place for reasonably priced sushi, with Asian decor, a pleasant vibe and friendly staff. Sushi is beautifully displayed and large orders are served in a big wooden boat.

Bars and clubs

Much of the city's nightlife goes on in the more affluent suburbs north of the centre, though if you're on the Malecón after sundown a stroll up Cerro Santa Ana or Las Peñas will reveal clusters of inexpensive drinking holes, good spots for bar hopping.

Artur's Café Numa Pompilio Llona 127, Las Peñas. An atmospheric place for an evening drink, in a tall old house by the river, with several little patios offering fantastic views onto the illuminated Malecón. Also serves tasty *platos típicos*, including *seco de gallina* (chicken stew), *humitas* and *empanadas*.

Diva Nicotina Escalón 10, at the bottom of the Cerro Santa Ana staircase. One for tobacco fans, this friendly bar stocks a fantastic range of Ecuadorian cigars, in all shapes, sizes and flavours, including chocolate, rum and coconut. The leaves are grown in neighbouring Los Ríos province and hand-rolled in a factory nearby. Cuban classics are also available.

Fizz y Santé Av Francisco de Orellana 796 and Agustín Cornejo, opposite the World Trade Center, Kennedy Norte. One of the current, mainstream night-time favourites, with a bar (*Santé*), which regularly features live music (when it's $15 cover), and a disco (*Fizz*) playing dance and Latin music next door.

Liverpool Coffee Station Las Monjas 402 and La Cuarta, Urdesa. If you're craving music in English (or from England), check out this cheerful bar, which has a Beatles night on Thursdays and live music in English on Fridays. Other live acts Tues, Wed & Sat. Dining also available. Mostly attracts an older crowd. Closed Mon.

El Manantial Estrada 520 and Las Monjas, Urdesa. Pleasant bar best enjoyed sitting outside on balmy evenings and downing a pitcher or two of beer, accompanied by scrumptious seafood snacks.

La Paleta Numa Pompilio Llona 176, Las Peñas. Arty two-floor bar appealing to an older demographic, with good wine, nibbles and tapas on offer, chill-out music and a relaxed vibe. Wed–Sat from 8pm.

Resaca Malecón 2000 and Junín. A great riverside location with outdoor seating or, failing that, large waterfront windows makes this trendy bar a prime venue for sipping a beer or cocktail against a backdrop of Guayaquil by night. Live music or karaoke on Saturday. Not a bad place to grab a bite either.

Performing arts and film

Guayaquil has a thriving **theatre** scene, best seen at the modern, well-designed theatre of the **Centro Cívico**, south of the city centre on Avenida Quito and Venezuela (taxi $3–4), which also has an excellent concert hall with regular **classical music** performances by the Orquesta Sinfónica de Guayaquil and visiting musicians. Check the local newspapers *El Universo* or *El Telégrafo* for listings.

Two cinema chains, **Cinemark** (Ⓦ www.cinemark.com.ec) and **Supercines** (Ⓦ www.supercines.com), have theatres in many of the city's shopping malls, with the best ones at San Marino Shopping and the Mall del Sol; see "Shopping", below, for details on how to get there. For independent and art-house films check the listings of **MAAC Cine** at the north end of the Malecón 2000 (see p.398), or there's the nearby **IMAX Cinema** (see p.399).

Shopping

For Western goods, the best option is the Mall del Sol near the airport (take bus #63-Las Orquideas from García Aviles and Aguirre, or a taxi for $3), or the new San Marino Shopping (take bus #52 from the Malecón, or #131-1 from García Aviles and Aguirre). Other good **malls** are Garzocentro, Avenida Guillermo Pareja and Agustín Freire; Policentro in the Ciudadela Kennedy; and Riocentro Los Ceibos, Km6.5 on the coast road. The chaotic **outdoor market**, Las Bahías (daily 8am–8pm), is spread over several blocks around the pedestrianized streets on both sides of Olmedo, at the southern end of the Malecón 2000, and has cheap clothes, bags, cosmetics, electrical equipment, bootleg DVDs and more.

Mercado Artesenal, Baquerizo Moreno and Juan Montalvo, near Las Peñas, has weavings, knitwear and other artesanía stalls; and Ecua-andino (⊤04/6002636, ⓦwww.ecua-andino.com) sells quality Panama hats.

Listings

Airlines Aerogal, Junín 440 and Córdova ⊤04/2310346, airport ⊤2284218; American, Edif San Francisco 300, Malecón 2000 and 9 de Octubre ⊤1800/247546, airport ⊤2282082; Avianca, Loc 19, Galerías Colón, *Hilton Colón*, Av Francisco de Orellana, Kennedy Norte ⊤1800/003434, airport ⊤04/2690235; Continental, Edif Banco La Previsora, 9 de Octubre 100 and Malecón ⊤1800/222333, airport ⊤04/2287311; Copa, 9 de Octubre and Malecón, Edif Banco La Previsora ⊤04/2303211, airport ⊤2286336; Iberia, 9 de Octubre 101 and Malecón ⊤04/2329558, airport ⊤2284151; Icaro, Local 5, Ground Floor, World Trade Center, Av Francisco de Orellana ⊤04/2631169, at airport ⊤3905060; KLM, Galerías Colón, office 10, *Hilton Colón*, Av Francisco de Orellana ⊤04/2692876, airport ⊤2691252; Lan, Galerías Hotel Hilton Colón ⊤04/2692850; Lufthansa, Malecón 1401 and Illingworth ⊤04/2324360; Taca, Edif Banco La Previsora, 9 de Octubre and Malecón ⊤04/1800/008222; TAME, Edif Gran Pasaje, 9 de Octubre 424 ⊤04/2310305, airport ⊤2169163; Varig, Nueva Kennedy, Calle E 106 and Calle 4 E ⊤04/2290249.

Banks and exchange Downtown: Banco del Pacífico, Pedro Carbo and Icaza (MasterCard and Cirrus ATM); Banco de Guayaquil, Icaza 105 and Pichincha (Visa cash advance, Visa and MasterCard ATM), also ATM at Aguirre and Chile; and Banco del Austro, Boyacá and 9 de Octubre (Visa ATM and cash advance). The bus terminal, airport and all large shopping centres have ATMs.

Car rental Most car-rental outfits have offices just outside the airport; some have a downtown branch too. Avis, at airport ⊤04/2169092; Budget, at airport ⊤04/2169026; Expo, at airport ⊤04/2169088; Hertz, at airport ⊤04/2169035; Localiza, at airport ⊤04/2281462.

Consulates Canada, Janquin Orrantia and Marengo ⊤04/2563580; Peru, Edif Centrum, 14th floor, Av Francisco de Orellana, Kennedy Norte ⊤04/2280114; UK, General Córdova 623 and Padre Solano ⊤04/2560400 ext 318; US, 9 de Octubre and García Moreno ⊤04/2323570, emergencies ⊤04/2321152.

Hospital Clínica Kennedy on Av San Jorge and la Novena ⊤04/2289666.

Internet Cybercafés can be found downtown, in the suburbs and in shopping centres; most have international calling facilities, such as Cyber One, Rendón and Córdova and Enl@ce.com, Vélez and Moncayo.

Laundry Lavandería Carmita, Boyacá 925 and V. M. Rendón, does same-day wet washes by the kilogram.

Police and immigration Av Río Daule, Prolongación de Av de las Américas ⊤04/2297004.

Post office Main office on Pedro Carbo and Ballén, just off the Parque Seminario.

Swimming pool Piscina Olímpica, Vélez and Masote, a few blocks from the Parque del Centenario (Mon–Fri 2–6pm, Sat & Sun 10am–6pm), offers two enormous outdoor pools, one for competitions and one for the general public.

Telephone office Pacifictel, off the Parque Seminario, Ballén and Chile.

Tour operators Canodros, Urb Santa Leonor, Mz 5, Solar 10 (⊤04/2285711, ⓦwww.canodros.com), owns a large Galápagos cruise boat and operates the *Kapawi Ecolodge* (see p.331); Discovery, Malecón 2000 and Martínez (⊤04/2304824, ⓦwww.crucerosdiscovery.com), offers cruises (every 2hr; 2hr 30min) to Isla Santay, an island in the Río Guayas, as well as party cruises; Galasam, Edificio Gran Pasaje, 9 de Octubre 424 (⊤04/2547585, ⓦwww.galapagos-islands.com), runs low- to middle-budget Galápagos cruises and offers jungle and regional tours; Klein Tours, Miguel Alcívar 410 and Ángel Barreira (⊤04/2681700, ⓦwww.kleintours.com), has higher-end Galápagos cruises and land tours; and Metropolitan Touring, Millenium Gallery, World Trade Center, Local #9, Av Francisco de Orellana Ciudadela. Atarazana Calle 11NE #103 y Av. 1NF (⊤04/2286565, ⓦwww.metropolitan-touring.com), is a long-established agency for cruises and general countrywide tours. Regional and local specialists, organizing tours of the Santa Elena peninsula, Ruta del Sol and elsewhere in the region (from $35 per day), include Guayatur, Aguirre 108 and Malecón (⊤04/2325542, ⓦwww.guayatur.com) and *Dreamkapture*, Villa 21, Calle Juan Sixto Bernal, near intersection of Benjamín Carrion and Francisco de Orellano, ⊤04/224 2909, ⓦwww.dreamkapture.com.

Travel agents The largest, and best for booking flights include Delgado Travel, Edif San Francisco, Córdova 1021 and 9 de Octubre, 3rd floor (⊤04/2561669); and Metropolitan Touring, Millenium Gallery, World Trade Center, Local #9, Av Francisco de Orellana Ciudadela. Atarazana Calle 11NE #103 y Av. 1NE (⊤04/2286565, ⓦwww.metropolitan-touring.com).

South to Machala and the border

On its way **south to the border** 244km away, the major coastal highway from Guayaquil passes one of the most important mangrove estuaries on the coast, the **Reserva Ecológica Manglares Churute**, where you can arrange to take boat rides through the swamps or walk in the surrounding forest. Further south, the road slices through endless **banana plantations** as you enter the country's banana-growing heartland. Ecuador didn't start exporting the fruit until 1945, but the boom that followed was so dramatic the crop became the country's most important agricultural export within two years, and has remained so ever since. A large portion of banana cultivation occurs in the province of El Oro, whose capital **Machala** is the main service centre of the industry. It's a busy, workaday town holding little of interest, but does serve as a handy base for trips to the charming hillside town of **Zaruma**, 86km east, and the petrified forest of **Puyango**, 100km south. It's also a convenient stop on the way to Peru, a one-hour bus ride south; most travellers choose to spend the night here before crossing the border at the dusty, ramshackle town of **Huaquillas**.

Reserva Ecológica Manglares Churute

About 45km southeast of Guayaquil on the road to Machala is the prominent visitor centre of the **Reserva Ecológica Manglares Churute** (daily 8am–2pm; $10), which protects 350 square kilometres of **mangrove** swamps. They're best viewed on a boat ride through the labyrinthine estuaries and channels that thread through the mangroves, whose dense tangle of interlocking branches looms out of the water. Originally covering a much larger coastal area (many were cleared to make way for shrimp farms), the mangroves are part of a unique ecosystem providing a habitat for many different fish and crustaceans and more than 260 **bird** species, including the purple gallinule, muscovy duck, pinnated bittern, glossy ibis, roseate spoonbill and horned screamer, now only found here in western Ecuador. Occasional sightings have been made of

▲ Banana plantations, Machala

Chilean flamingos (Jan–Feb), and bottlenose **dolphins** (June–Nov) are frequently seen frolicking around the boats.

From the visitor centre, a rudimentary path (1hr) leads inland for a walk along the slopes of Cerro El Mate, a low hill with a lookout point, to **Laguna El Canclón**, a wide, grey lake encircled by low-lying hills and rich in birdlife. Another path, **Sendero La Cascada** (2hr), takes you through dense, dry forest by some enormous royal palms and up the slopes of a hill covered in lush vegetation. Snakes, *guantas* and howler monkeys – which you're more likely to spot if with a guide – inhabit the dry and humid forests. The path is at the end of a track branching west from the coastal highway, 5km north of the visitor centre; guides can take you there in a jeep.

Practicalities

To get to the **visitor centre** from Guayaquil take any **bus** to Machala or Naranjal from the Terminal Terrestre and ask to be dropped at the Centro de Visitantes de la Reserva Churute – the sign is on the left-hand (east) side of

Banana republic

Ecuador exports more than four million tonnes of **bananas** yearly, making it the biggest producer of the world's most popular fruit. Most of Ecuador's bananas are grown on private, medium-sized **plantations**, effectively controlled by a few huge **companies**, namely US-owned Dole and Chiquita, Del Monte and Ecuador's own Noboa. With an 18-kilogram box of fresh-picked plantation bananas selling for $3–4, the trade is a highly profitable business.

Ecuador's extraordinary success in this sector is due in large part to the appalling **pay** and **working conditions** of its labourers, who are among the worst paid in the world. For a full day's labour (12–15hr), the typical banana worker can expect a salary of just a few dollars, perhaps enough to buy two or three bunches of the fruit in a Western supermarket. Such meagre wages also have to cover outlay for the workers' own tools, uniforms, transport to the plantations and drugs should they fall ill or have an on-site accident. Most can't afford **housing** and must share small rooms on the estates or live in squalid, jerry-built shacks.

Only one percent of the country's 250,000-strong workforce is **unionized** and most workers are effectively denied the right to form unions or bargain collectively; instant dismissals are common for any involvement.

There are more than three hundred varieties of banana, but the most commonly grown is the **Cavendish**. Since all Cavendish plants come from the same genetic source and are cultivated in close proximity to one another, pests, mould and disease can quickly wipe out a plantation, so the crops must be regularly sprayed with pesticides and other chemicals. Many workers complain of pesticide **poisoning**; throughout the 1990s Ecuadorian crops were treated with DBCP, a highly toxic chemical thought to cause birth defects, infertility and liver damage.

To compete with Ecuador, other countries' producers are forced either to degrade conditions for their own workforce or relocate – in other words, Ecuador is winning the race to the bottom. Supermarkets seem content to turn a blind eye to workers' low pay, non-existent welfare and even **child labour**, which has been documented on Ecuadorian plantations. **Consumer awareness** is one way to counter such corporate inaction, as is the use of **alternative products** such as organic and fair-trade bananas, which give workers a much better deal. In Machala, **UROCAL** is the organization most involved with such projects and staff are happy to show **visitors** around its members' farms, as long as you cover any costs incurred and preferably make a donation for their time. Get in touch at ©urocal@eo.pro.ec or ©urocal @ecuanet.net.ec.

the road, fifty minutes after leaving the city. You can **camp** outside the visitor centre ($3) or sleep in simple cabins ($5), though most people visit as a day-trip. **Boat rides** (3–4hr; $40 per boat) need to be booked at least a couple of days in advance through the Ministerio del Ambiente in Guayaquil, Av Quito 402 and Padre Solano (☎04/2397730 or 2560870), where you can also pick up **information** on the reserve and, with a day's notice, request a **guide** ($5; no English spoken).

Just outside the eastern limit of the reserve is *Monoloco Lodge* (☎04/2242909 or 09/7250120, ⓦ www.monoloco.ec), an alternative base for visiting Manglares Churute's inland sections. It has simple, inexpensive accommodation in shared or private rooms (from $18 per person including all meals), as well as horseriding ($10) and trekking ($15) through the reserve; arrange transport through *Dreamkapture*, its sister hotel in Guayaquil (see p.397).

Machala

Despite being founded in the sixteenth century, **MACHALA** looks like a city that's sprung up haphazardly in the last two or three decades. Shabby concrete buildings covered in flaking, white paint line its streets, belying the town's prosperity as the nucleus of Ecuador's banana industry (see box, p.407). There's plenty of hustle and bustle here, but little in the way of tourist attractions – most visitors are here en route to Peru, one hour south. The only time you might want to make a special trip is during the last ten days of September for the annual **World Banana Festival**, a huge commercial fair with festivities and events, including the World Banana Queen beauty competition.

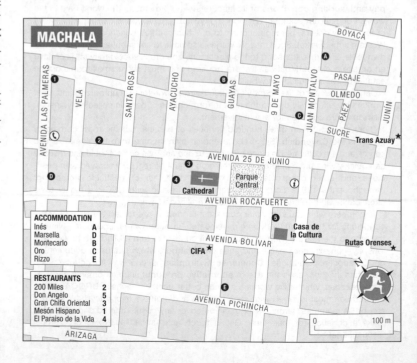

Arrival and information

Buses to Machala drop passengers at the bus company's depot; most are a few blocks east of the central square, an easy walk to the city's hotels. There's a **Ministerio de Turismo** information office on the mezzanine of the Edificio Mil, Juan Montalvo and 25 de Junio (Mon–Fri 8.30am–5pm; ☎ & ⓕ 07/2932106). The city centre is entirely walkable on foot, but if you need a **taxi** you can flag one down around the central square, or on any of the main arteries such as 25 de Junio or Vicente Rocafuerte; journeys within the central core cost $1.

Accommodation

Accommodation in Machala is quite pricey for what you get, with not a great choice on offer. There are a couple of decent budget places and if you're willing to indulge, you can treat yourself to the luxurious *Oro Verde*.

Inés Juan Montalvo 1509 ☎ 07/2932301, ⓕ 2931473. Small, dated though perfectly fine rooms, most with a/c and cable TV (plus some cheaper ones just with fan ❸) in a whitewashed house set back from a busy market area. There's a courtyard and private parking. ❹

Marsella Av Las Palmeras and 25 de Junio ☎ 07/2932460. A good option in the mid-price range for its clean en-suite rooms with a/c and hot water. ❺

Montecarlo Guayas and Olmedo ☎ 07/2931901, ⓕ 2933104. Spacious, light rooms with freshly painted walls, cool stone floors and slightly dated furnishings. All have en-suite baths, a/c and cable TV, though they can be a bit noisy. Breakfast included. ❺

Oro Sucre and Juan Montalvo ☎ 07/2937569, ⓕ 2933751. Probably the best mid-priced rooms in town, with firm beds, good-quality bedding, clean bathrooms, a/c, cable TVs and its own garage. Breakfast included. ❻

Oro Verde Circunvalación Norte and Calle Vehicular V-7 ☎ 07/2933140, ⓦ www .oroverdemachala.com. Classy hotel resembling an old timber-clad plantation manor, with beautiful gardens and a pool. It's sometimes possible to get a room at the national rate (a third off the foreign rate) if you beg hard enough. A short taxi ride 3km from the centre. ❾

Rizzo Guayas 1923 ☎ 07/2933651. Showing its age, but the rooms – all with private baths and a/c – are adequate and the pool is very inviting. ❻

The Town

Machala's centre is marked by the large, leafy **parque central**; the modern green-and-white **cathedral** on its west side boasts an eye-catching facade with a tall, thin clock tower flanked by two blue domes. A couple of blocks south and around the corner on Bolívar, the **Casa de la Cultura** contains the city's only museums, as well as permanent and temporary art exhibits of variable quality. On the ground floor, the **Museo Marino** (Tues–Fri 9am–noon & 2–5pm; $0.50) comprises a small roomful of glass cabinets crammed with fish, marine birds, molluscs, shells, corals and whale and dolphin bones; upstairs, the **Museo Arqueológico** (same hours and ticket) displays pre-Columbian coastal ceramics, while the **Museo Paleontológico** has an impressive collection of fossils from the Puyango petrified forest (see p.412).

There's little else to do in Machala except wander around the outdoor fruit and vegetable **market** – bounded by Boyacá, 9 de Mayo, Sucre and Páez – and marvel at the prodigious quantities of bananas for sale. If you enter or leave the town by the main artery formed by the extension of 9 de Mayo, look out for the **Monumento Al Bananero**, a towering statue of a workman carrying a mound of bananas.

Eating, drinking and nightlife

Machala's dining scene holds few surprises, though a good range of fresh **fish** and **seafood** can be found in nearby Puerto Bolívar (see p.410), a fifteen-minute bus ride away. There are few decent **bars** in town and you'll find a large modern **club**, *Twister*, at Km1.5 on the road to Pasaje, or a younger crowd at *La Ego* on Tarqui and Rocafuerte.

200 Miles 25 de Junio and Santa Rosa. Smart, modern and reasonably priced restaurant with attractive decor and fresh, well-cooked fish and seafood.

Don Ángelo 9 de Mayo and Rocafuerte. Unassuming local canteen that's been going for years, serving cheap and reliable *comida típica* like *locro de papa* and *seco de chivo*, plus staples like spaghetti and fried chicken and fish.

Gran Chifa Oriental 25 de Junio, between Guayas and Ayacucho. Modest but agreeable Chinese restaurant – a good bet for a cheap, filling meal.

Mesón Hispano Av Las Palmeras and Sucre. Delicious charcoal-grilled meat served on ministoves in a bright, attractive dining room, complete with potted ferns and whirring fans. Plenty of vegetarian options are also available, at the same bargain prices as their meat counterparts.

Oro Mar at *Oro Verde* hotel, Circunvalación Norte and Calle Vehicular V-7. If you feel like a splurge, head here for delicious international food served in a dining room overlooking the pool. Reached by taxi for about $1.50.

El Paraíso de la Vida Ayacucho between Av Rocafuerte and 25 de Junio. Inexpensive vegetarian restaurant with a pleasant dining room overlooking a little patio. Curiously, most items on the menu are veggie pseudo-meat dishes like "beef steak" and "loin".

Listings

Airline TAME, Juan Montalvo and Av Bolívar ☎07/2930139.

Banks and exchange Banco de Guayaquil, Av Rocafuerte and Guayas, has a MasterCard and Visa ATM; Banco del Austro, across the street, has Visa service; Banco del Pacífico, Av Rocafuerte and Junín, has a MasterCard and Cirrus ATM; and another branch of Banco de Guayaquil is nearby at Junín and 25 de Junio.

Consulate Peru, Villa Machala, Urb Unioro Manzana, 14 Bolívar and Colón (Mon–Fri 8am–1pm; ☎07/2920680).

Internet Aquinet, Sucre and Vela; Oro Net, 9 de Octubre and Buenavista; Ciber Yogurt, 9 de Mayo and Pichincha.

Laundry Lavandería Diviño Niño, next door to Casa de la Cultura on Av Bolívar.

Post office Juan Montalvo and Av Bolívar.

Telephone office Pacifictel, corner of avs 25 de Junio and Las Palmeras.

Moving on from Machala

With no central bus station, Machala's various **bus** companies operate out of their own mini-terminals, most of which are clustered together a few blocks east of the *parque central*. Key destinations include: Huaquillas, on the Peruvian border (serviced by CIFA, Guayas and Bolívar, and Ecuatoriano Pullman, Colón and 25 de Junio); Piura, in Peru (CIFA, see above); Guayaquil (frequent service with Ecuatoriano Pullman, as above, and various others); Cuenca (Transportes Azuay, Sucre and Junín); Loja (Transportes Loja, Tarqui and Bolívar; those going via the village of Alamor can drop you at **Puyango** for the petrified forest) and Quito (Panamericana, Colón and Bolívar, and Occidental, Buenavista and Olmedo). For the gold-mining village of **Zaruma**, take an hourly bus with Cooperativas TAC, on Colón between avenidas Rocafuerte and Bolívar, or with Transportes Piñas, on Colón and Avenida 25 de Junio

Puerto Bolívar and its islands

Just a fifteen-minute **bus** ride west of Machala (take services marked "Línea 1" from Avenida 25 de Junio and Guayas, on the central square) is **PUERTO BOLÍVAR**, a busy international port exporting vast quantities of bananas and shrimp around the world.

It's a little ramshackle and dilapidated and the best reason to come here is probably to take a boat ride, run by a couple of operators from the pier on the

Malecón, out to one of the islands close to the shore. The Asociación de Ecoturismo Rescate Ecológico offers guided trips in Spanish to the **Isla del Amor** and surrounding islands (reservations a day in advance on ☎07/2929105; $20 per group), where you can get close-up views of mangroves and their sea-bird inhabitants, both from the boat and from a raised walkway leading from a docking area through the swamp. Other boat companies provide similar services; ask around the docks and bargain. Motor canoes also leave from the dock for the car-free **Isla Jambelí** (5 daily, 25min; $2.50), a larger island with a wide, sandy **beach** with little shade and a few basic restaurants and hotels, the best of which is *La Casa en la Luna* (☎07/2964116; ❷), with shared bath and no hot water. The beach gets very busy on summer weekends, but you'll almost certainly have it to yourself through the week.

If you're looking for a bite to **eat**, try the fresh seafood at *Waikiki*, opposite the pier; it's one of the many *picanterías* (small, simple fish restaurants) forming a strip known as the **Jardín Comedor** between the church and pier.

Zaruma and around

Off the tourist trail and about 86km inland from Machala sits **ZARUMA**, one of the prettiest little towns in Ecuador. It has the country's finest collection of early twentieth-century timber buildings and is a charming place to wander around; steep, narrow streets are lined with brightly painted wooden houses and a gorgeous **timber church**, built in 1912, overlooks the central square.

Conquistadors first established a settlement here in 1549 to exploit the area's large **gold** deposits, and their mines flourished until the eighteenth century when they closed down because the seams were thought to be exhausted. Yet almost a century later, a Quito geologist analysing local rocks discovered a high gold content, sparking another **gold-mining** boom in 1880. Mining continues but on a much smaller scale, as the gold deposits are running out.

You'll find assorted mining paraphernalia at the captivating **Museo Municipal** (Wed–Fri 8am–noon & 2–6pm, Sat 8am–3pm, Sun 8am–noon; free), just off the main square, opposite the church, along with curiosities, including whale vertebrae, antique sewing machines, irons, phones and gramophones. You can also visit a disused mine, the **Mina de Sexmo** (Tues–Sat; free) on the outskirts of town (down the hill from the *Hotel Cerro de Oro*, then first right), where you don protective boots and hat and are guided round the tunnels.

Rounding out Zaruma's attractions are the **Museo Indígena Selva** (daily 8am–noon & 1–6pm; $1) on Honorato Márquez beyond the bus depots, with its unsettling collection of insects, stuffed animals and desiccated snakes, and the public **swimming pool** set in a fantastic hilltop location above the town – a lovely place to head on a warm, sunny day.

The nearby towns of **Piñas**, 13km west, and **Portovelo**, a few kilometres south of Zaruma (both easily reached by bus from Zaruma), retain less of their historic mining character, though each has a good museum. In Piñas, the **Museo Mineralógico Magner Turner**, in the Barrio Campamento Americano (daily; $1; ☎07/2949345), is one of the best mining museums in the country, and includes a large bunker, 150m of mineshafts and various mineral and gem exhibits. In Portovelo, the **Museo Rubén Torres** displays a modest array of antiques and pre-Columbian artefacts. Also in the region are several **reserves** managed by the Fundación Jocotoco (Ⓦwww.fjocotoco.org), protecting vital forest habitat harbouring some 630 types of birds, many of which are restricted-range endemic species. The closest to Zaruma is **Buenaventura**, a 1500-hectare reserve beyond Piñas on the road to Machala, which features a 6km forest trail and a small lodge for visitors (❾ including three meals); contact Mariana Arcentales for more information (Ⓔ fjocotoco @andinanet.net) or Javier Roballo in Loja (☎09/7101536).

Practicalities

Zaruma is a three-hour **bus** ride from Machala, and Transportes TAC provides a regular service from its depot on Colón, between avenidas Rocafuerte and Bolívar, as does Transportes Piñas, nearby on Colón and Avenida 25 de Junio. For onward travel, the main depots in Zaruma are on Honorato Márquez, the main road out of town. TAC runs buses to Guayaquil (5 daily; 6hr) and to Loja (3 daily; 4hr 30min), which is also served by Trans Piñas, a few doors down (3 daily). Both companies, as well as Trans Azuay, run an early-morning bus to Cuenca (6hr).

There's a reasonable choice of **accommodation**. On the way into town on Avenida Alonso de Mercadillo, the *Roland* (☎07/2972800; ❺) offers comfortable, carpeted en-suite rooms, the best of which have great views down the valley. In the centre, the *Aguila Dorada*, at Sucre 156 (☎07/2972230; ❸), also has good-value rooms with private baths, electric showers and cable TVs, but no rooms at the back overlooking the valley, while the nearby *Cerro de Oro* (☎07/2972505; ❸) has similar facilities for a similar price. For **restaurants**, try the *Chifa Chamizal Central*, set in a pretty red house with a terrace on Calle San Francisco off Sucre, for inexpensive Chinese food, international dishes and seafood, or the simple *Cafetería Uno* on Sucre, good for local specialities. **Internet** access is available at Zarumanet, Colõn and 10 de Agosto ($1.50 per hour).

Puyango petrified forest

One hundred kilometres south of Machala, spread over a dusty, semi-arid river valley close to the Peruvian border, is the **Puyango petrified forest** (daily 8am–5pm; $5), the largest of its kind in South America. It contains dozens of enormous **fossilized tree trunks** up to 120 million years old, many of which you can see from the 8km of marked paths wending through the mineralized wood. At the visitor centre, where you pay and register your visit, you can hire a **guide** (usually one of the warden's sons) to show you around the site; they don't speak English, but will point out many hidden fossils you'd otherwise miss, such as the imprints of ferns concealed by riverside plants. The most impressive relics are the giant tree trunks, types of **araucaria**, which grew in the region millions of years ago; many are in fragments but a few are almost whole, the largest being 11m long and 1.6m in diameter. The area is also inhabited by more than 150 species of **birdlife**, including beautiful red-masked parakeets.

A small **museum** (usually locked; ask the staff for entry) near the visitor centre houses a stash of incredible exhibits, including many marine fossils dating from when much of the region was covered by the sea, now 50km away. The collection includes fossilized pieces of fruit, including a *chirimoya* (a custard apple – you can still see the pips), a ray, small tortoise and octopus with clearly visible eyes. Perhaps the most intriguing pieces are the large, perfectly oval stones you can hold in your hands – and which the staff believe are dinosaur egg fossils.

Practicalities

The forest is three hours from Machala by **bus**. Take a bus from Machala to Alamor, either with Cooperativa Loja, from Tarqui between avenidas Bolívar and Rocafuerte (3 daily), or Cooperativa CIFA, from Avenida Bolívar and

Guayas (2 daily). Ask to be dropped at the Puente de Puyango, from where a track leads 5km west to the visitor reception area, through a handsome valley with plenty of opportunities for birdwatching. There are a few bunk **beds** ($5) for visitors next to the warden's quarters, and a rudimentary **campsite** in a pleasant spot near the river, close to a lovely natural pool for bathing. It officially costs $20 per tent, but this is invariably waived as none of the planned facilities has yet been built, nor shows any sign of materializing. A tiny **shop** near the visitor reception area has basic provisions, but you should bring as much of your food as possible. The nearest village to the site is Puyango, near the bridge where the bus drops you, with little more than a cluster of houses and a few small food stores.

Huaquillas and the Peruvian border

Some 73km southwest of Machala, **HUAQUILLAS** is a chaotic, jerry-built, mosquito-ridden border town. Its main commercial street is lined by hundreds of hectic market stalls selling cheap clothes, shoes, bags, food and electrical goods, while enormous shop signs hang over their canopies from dilapidated buildings on either side. Most visitors crossing the border avoid **staying** here by spending the night in Machala, but if you need a place to sleep you'll find clean, modest rooms with private bathrooms, air conditioning and cable TVs at the *Hotel Hernancor* on 1 de Mayo and Hualtaco (☎07/2995467; ❺), while the cheaper *Rodey*, Teniente Córdovez and 10 de Agosto (☎07/2995581; ❷), has only fans. There are a number of inexpensive canteens, but good **restaurants** include *La Habana*, T. Córdovez and Santa Rosa, for its affordable seafood, grills, breakfast and *almuerzos*, and *El Flamingo*, Avenida de la República and Costa Rica, for cakes, shakes and ice creams. **Internet** facilities are available at Hot Net, Avenida de la República and Santa Rosa.

If you're just arriving in Ecuador from Peru, **buses** from Huaquillas leave from company depots within a few blocks of the international bridge. Cooperativa CIFA, on Santa Rosa and Machala, has the most regular service to the biggest nearby city, **Machala** (every 10–20min; 1hr), where you'll find banking facilities and onward transport, and also sends buses to **Guayaquil** (5 daily; 4hr 30min), as do Ecuatoriano Pullman on T. Córdovez, and Rutas Orenses on R. Gómez. Panamericana, on T. Córdovez and Santa Rosa, runs regular buses to **Quito** (7 daily; 12hr), while Transportes Occidentales, on R. Gómez, has five daily buses to Quito. Use Transportes Azuay, T. Córdovez and Santa Rosa, for **Cuenca** (8 daily; 5hr).

Crossing the border

The Río Zarumilla, hugging the southwestern edge of Huaquillas, forms the **border**, and is crossed by the international bridge leading to the small town of **Aguas Verdes** in Peru. Before crossing it, you'll need to get your **exit stamp** at the **Ecuadorian immigration** office (open 24hr), 2km east of Huaquillas on the road from Machala ($2 by taxi). If you're coming here straight from Machala, bus drivers will drop you at the office on the way into Huaquillas (remind them as they sometimes forget), but won't wait for you while you get your exit stamp, usually a fairly fast and painless process. From here, hop on a bus or take a taxi to the bridge, which you'll have to cross on foot. On the other side, Peruvian officials may check your passport, but **entry stamps** are normally obtained at the main **Peruvian immigration office** at **Zarumilla**, a few kilometres away. It can be reached by **mototaxis** for about a dollar or by various other forms of transport that continue on to

HUAQUILLAS

PERU

Aguas Verdes

International Bridge

0   50 m

ACCOMMODATION
Hernancor   A
Rodey   B

RESTAURANTS
El Flamingo   2
La Habana   1

N

Panamericana ★ ★★ ①
Trans Occidentales ★ ★ Rutas Orenses
Trans Azuay
Ecuatoriano Pullman
Municipio

Police

@ Hot Net ②

MACHALA
CIFA ★

Ecuadorian Immigration (2km) & ▶ Machala (73km)

Tumbes, 27km south: regular **buses**, which won't wait for you while you get your passport stamped; **taxis** ($6, including wait at Zarumilla; firm bargaining required); or **colectivos** (about $0.75), though drivers are sometimes reluctant to wait at Zarumilla. Once in Tumbes, it's easy to find a direct **bus** to Piura, Trujillo or Lima.

It's quite a stressful experience, with a bevy of moneychangers, bus touts, bag carriers and taxi drivers jostling for your business and plenty of thieves around as well – keep your wits about you and never lose sight of your bags. Change as little **money** as possible, as the rates aren't good unless you bargain hard. Official moneychangers in Ecuador wear IDs, but always check calculations and cash received before handing anything over.

Playas and the Santa Elena Peninsula

West of Guayaquil, the busy E-40 highway heads to the westernmost tip of the mainland, marked by the **Santa Elena Peninsula**. It's an especially crowded route on Friday evenings when droves of Guayaquileños flee the uncomfortable heat of the city for the cooling breezes of the Pacific. Just fifteen minutes down the road, the highway provides access to a couple of enjoyable attractions that you could take in en route to the coast, or as a day-trip from Guayaquil, including the **Bosque Protector Cerro Blanco**, a small, well-managed forest reserve, and **Puerto Hondo**, a little village perched by a mangrove swamp that you can explore by boat. A further 45km west, a side road branches south to the easy-going, somewhat shabby little town of **Playas**, the closest beach resort to Guayaquil and always heaving with visitors on summer weekends (Dec–April).

Continuing west along the main road, you enter increasingly dry and scrubby terrain as you approach the Santa Elena Peninsula, the site of three towns – **Santa Elena**, **La Libertad** and **Salinas** – merging into one other almost seamlessly. The peninsula is of great **archeological** interest, as it was originally occupied by the country's most ancient cultures, such as the **Las Vegas** and the **Valdivia**. Some of the most important archeological sites have impressive museums attached to them, including the fabulous **Amantes de Sumpa**, near Santa Elena, sporting the tomb of two eight-thousand-year-old skeletons locked in an embrace. However, the peninsula is best known for its **beaches**, in particular the glitzy and often crowded resort of Salinas. A few quieter, calmer alternatives are **Ballenito** and **Punta Carnero**, and the small inland attraction of the thermal baths of **San Vicente**.

Bosque Protector Cerro Blanco

Just 16km out of Guayaquil, the **Bosque Protector Cerro Blanco** (Sat & Sun 8.30am–3.30pm or other days through prior reservation; $4; Ⓦwww .bosquecerroblanco.com) protects around fifty square kilometres of dry coastal forest, providing a vital refuge for **wildlife** such as howler monkeys, collared anteaters, brocket deer, a few jaguars and more than two hundred species of birds – including a group of endangered great green macaw, whose regional numbers had been reduced to a mere eight after the gradual depletion of their habitat. With luck, they can be spotted flying from the coastal mangroves up to the hills of the reserve around 6am, and back to the mangroves around 6pm.

Guides can accompany you on a choice of three **trails** through the reserve (1hr 30min–4hr round-trip). **Sendero Buena Vista Largo** is the longest and the best, rising from sea level at the reserve's entrance up to 600m in the hills north of the highway, offering lovely views out to the mangroves opposite the reserve. With advance permission it's possible to camp up in the hills at the far end of the trail, so you can wake up at dawn and catch the birds at their loudest and most visible.

Information on the reserve's flora and fauna is available in the **Centro de Interpretación**, and nearby there's a **Centro de Rescate** (animal rescue centre), originally set up to provide a home to abandoned animals before their reintroduction to the wild. Many of these were bought as pets and have become too tame to survive in the wilderness, so the centre has become something of a zoo, whose occupants include capuchin monkeys, wildcats, caimans and a cageful of great green macaws that can no longer fly.

Practicalities

Entrance to the reserve, which is run by the Fundación Pro-Bosque, is a thirty-minute **bus** ride from Guayaquil (every 10min), on any service to Playas, Santa Elena, La Libertad or Salinas from the main bus terminal. Look for the big sign for the Bosque Protector Cerro Blanco on the right-hand (north) side of the highway, where the driver will drop you off. From here it's a fifteen-minute walk up a clearly marked track to the information centre. On weekends you can just turn up, but on weekdays you should book ahead on ☎04/2874946 or 2874947. Should you want to **stay**, there's a pleasant two-room bamboo lodge (❸) and a free **camping** area with decent facilities; the site also has a small **café-restaurant** which opens on weekends. Many of the trail **guides** ($7–12 per group; some speak English) are biology students from Guayaquil University. There are usually several about, but it's worth phoning ahead to book one, particularly if you want to take the Sendero Buena Vista Largo walk.

Puerto Hondo and Parque El Lago

A kilometre west of the entrance to the Cerro Blanco forest reserve, **PUERTO HONDO** is a dusty, tumbledown little port strung around the head of a narrow saltwater estuary. You can visit **mangrove swamps** on one-hour motorized canoe rides ($7) with members of a guide association set up by the Pro-Bosque foundation here, making it a far cheaper alternative to the Reserva Ecológica Manglares Churute east of Guayaquil (see p.406); the swamps offer the chance to see the same ecosystem and many wetland birds. You can just turn up and arrange a ride at weekends, only needing to make advance reservations during the week, but it's worth phoning ahead anyway on ☎04/2874946 or 2874947.

The next stop along the road to the coast is the **PARQUE EL LAGO** (daily 8am–6pm; $0.50), a nationally designated recreation area covering tropical dry forest of the Chongón and Bedén river basins. The centrepiece is a large lake for boating and fishing, which Guayaquil's picnicking families share with more than 160 species of wetland birds. Visitors can also follow walking trails through the forests, rent a bike ($1 for 30min) or go on a short horse ride ($1 for 15min). Buses heading towards the coast can drop you at the entrance on the roadside.

All **buses** heading towards the coast via Cerro Blanco pass by the turn-off to Puerto Hondo, a five-minute walk south of the highway down a potholed street, as well as the roadside entrance to Parque El Lago.

Playas

About 45km west of Puerto Hondo, along the E-40 highway, is the dreary little town of **Progreso** where a major side road branches 26km south to the seaside town of **PLAYAS**. As the closest sandy beach to Guayaquil, Playas (whose official but largely ignored name is General Villamil) bulges with city visitors during the summer months and has slowly metamorphosed from a sleepy fishing village into a flourishing holiday resort over the last few decades. There's nothing slick about it; despite relying heavily on tourism Playas has a lived-in, unpretentious feel and a slow pace of life, with most traffic in its faintly shabby streets provided by ageing locals on clapped-out bicycles.

Arrival and information

Arriving by **bus** from Guayaquil (2hr), Transportes Villamil will drop you off at the depot behind the town plaza, while Transportes Posorja unloads at the intersection of Avenida Paquisha and Guayaquil; both points are just three blocks from the seafront. There's an **ATM** (Visa and MasterCard) at the Banco de Guayaquil on the main square, opposite the church.

Accommodation

Accommodation in Playas falls into two different areas: a cluster of lower-end hotels and *residenciales* in the centre and several upmarket choices dotted along the coast-hugging Avenida Roldos. Expect discounts in low season. The latter places can be reached on the unsigned pick-up trucks that serve as taxis ($1, less if you bargain hard) from Avenida Guayaquil, off the main square.

Arena Caliente Corner Av Paquisha and Estrada ☏04/2761580, ⓦ www.hotel-arenacaliente.com. The smartest place in the centre with a pleasant pool and clean, tiled rooms, equipped with a/c, private bath and hot water. Also has a popular restaurant. ⑥

Hostería Bellavista Av Roldos, 2km from the centre ☏04/2760600, ⓦ www.hosteriabellavista .net. Efficiently run operation with the best facilities in town, including spa, massage, steam room, gym, squash court, pool and access to a quiet stretch of beach. Discounts for stays longer than three days. ⑦

El Delfín Av Roldos, 1.5km southeast of the centre ☏04/2760125. Just a short distance from the sea and with very welcoming owners, this spot offers charming, wood-panelled rooms with private bath and hot water. ③

Marianela Av Roldos and Paquisha ☏04/2761507. One of the cheapest places to stay in town; four of the rooms have good sea views, but the rough wooden floors and ancient beds are very basic. ②

Playas Calle 8, just off the seafront ☏04/2760611. Decent, if tired, doubles with private baths, including a few with TVs and a/c. ④

El Rey David Calle 9 and Av Jambeli ☏04/2760024. Smarter than most, with clean rooms and a/c, but overpriced and without sea views. ⑤

Hostería El Tucán Av Roldos, 1km southeast of the centre ☏&ⓕ 04/2760866. Good-quality rooms with a/c, plus a sauna and large, gorgeous pool. The mini zoo here might not be to everyone's taste. ⑦

The Town

The chief attraction is the long and pleasant **beach**, where you'll still see fishermen hauling in their nets and may be able to spot a couple of traditional, single-sail balsa rafts, which were characteristic of the area for many centuries, though most have now been replaced with motorboats. There's nothing to do in Playas apart from lie on the sands or swim in the sea (sometimes a bit choppy), though if you feel like exploring you can walk 5km northwest along the beach to the **Punta Pelado**, whose usually deserted sands are backed by rugged cliffs.

Eating

All the hotels out of the centre have their own **restaurants** specializing in fresh fish and seafood. In town, don't miss the Lebanese-owned *Rincón de Mary*, on Avenida Roldos, whose owner prepares *kibe* (minced beef with herbs and spices in breadcrumbs) at very reasonable prices as well as fabulous falafel, tabbouleh and creamed aubergine; drop in and give advance notice if you want something more elaborate. There's also the attractively rustic *La Cabaña Típica*, on the beachfront close to the *Rincón de Mary*, with delicious *ceviches*, or the nearby string of *cevicherías* and *picanterías* on the beach and at the intersection of avenidas Paquisha and Roldos, selling cheap, fresh fish.

Museo Real Alto and Baños de San Vicente

Seventy kilometres west of Progreso on the E-40 highway, a prominent billboard announces the turn-off to the **Museo Real Alto** (Tues–Sun 9.30am–4.30pm; $2), an archeology museum 11km down the road to the tiny fishing village of Chanduy. Marking the site of one of the oldest permanent settlements in South America, established by the **Valdivia** culture in about 3000 BC, the museum boasts illuminating displays on the excavations at the site. It's impossible to reach by public transport, so unless you're willing to take a **taxi** from La Libertad (around $10, with an hour's wait), you may want to skip it and head for the easier-to-reach and more visually impressive Museo Los Amantes de Sumpa in Santa Elena (see p.417).

Back on the highway, a few kilometres beyond the turn-off to the Museo Real Alto, another well-signed road leads 8km north to the municipal **Baños de San Vicente** thermal baths complex (daily 7.30am–6pm; $1.50), though the institutional-looking pools (26°C–41°C) and mud baths set in a barren, rocky landscape are not enormously inviting. **Buses** for the complex leave the market in La Libertad (Mon–Fri 7.10am & 10.10am, with an extra bus Sat–Sun 1.10pm), passing Santa Elena's *parque central*, or you can arrive by **taxi** from Santa Elena (around $7 or $14 return with waiting time).

Santa Elena and Ballenita

Twelve kilometres beyond the turn-off to Baños de San Vicente, the E-40 hits the little town of **SANTA ELENA**, sited on the eponymous peninsula, and recently made the capital of its own little province, also called Santa Elena.

Unremarkable in almost every way, the town's sole attraction is the fascinating archeological museum of **Los Amantes de Sumpa** (Tues–Sun 9.30am–4.30pm; $1) on the western outskirts of town, signposted from the main road a couple of blocks south of the road to Salinas. The museum is built on the site of one of the oldest burial grounds in South America, established from 6000 BC by the ancient **Las Vegas** culture, one of the first groups on the continent to start shifting from a totally nomadic lifestyle towards semi-permanent settlements.

About forty years ago, some two hundred human skeletons were excavated here, including the remains of **the lovers of Sumpa** – the skeletons of a man and woman, about 25 years old when they died, buried facing each other, the woman with her arm raised over her head, the open-mouthed man with an arm on her waist. Their tomb, on display at the museum, makes an unforgettable sight, and the accompanying displays on the Las Vegas and other coastal cultures are excellent, ranging from funerary offerings such as shells, knives and colourful pebbles to a reconstruction of a typical *montuvio* house. Santa Elena is served by frequent buses from Guayaquil, and a taxi from the centre out to the museum should cost no more than $1.50. Alternatively, take a Salinas-bound bus and ask the driver to drop you at the turn-off to the museum, a short walk away.

Ten kilometres northwest of Santa Elena, **BALLENITA** is a small village with a long, crescent-shaped beach lapped by calm waters, which chiefly appeals as a quieter alternative to Salinas. There's nothing to do here except swim, sunbathe and clamber around the rock pools looking for shellfish, and there's nowhere to stay in the centre. A kilometre north of the village, however, high on a bluff overlooking the sea, is one of the most delightful **hotels** on the peninsula, the ✕ *Farallón Dillon* (T04/2953611 or 09/9771746, W www.farallondillon.com; ❻), whose tasteful rooms boast fine ocean views. Even if you're not staying here, it's worth eating in the hotel's restaurant, which must be the most exuberantly decorated dining room on the coast, with every available surface sporting objects and curiosities nautical, including a huge nineteenth-century lens from a French lighthouse, gaudy figure-heads and the prow of a whaling boat; even the access to the toilets is via an antique submarine door. The collection continues in the **nautical gallery** next door where you'll find antique sextants, brass navigation instruments and the ribs of *La Capitana*, a Spanish galleon which sank off Chanduy in 1654 with its cargo of three million pesos. Outside there's a terrace for spotting **humpback whales**, which swim off this stretch of coast (June–Sept) and a pleasant swimming pool. You can get to Ballenita on regular buses from La Libertad.

La Libertad and Punta Carnero

West from Santa Elena towards Salinas, a roadside petrol refinery signals your arrival in **LA LIBERTAD**, the largest town on the peninsula and the site of a busy produce market. With its untidy streets and unattractive beach, there's no reason to stop off here other than to catch a connecting bus (every 30min during daylight hours) north up the coast road, the *Ruta del Sol*, from the **bus station** on Avenida 8 and Calle 17, Barrio Eloy Alfaro. Other destinations are serviced by bus companies from their offices in the town centre clustered near 9 de Octubre and Guayaquil: Coop Libertad Peninsular and CICA run alternate buses to Guayaquil (every 15min; 2hr 30min); and Trans Esmeraldas has three nightly buses to Quito (10hr).

Five kilometres south of La Libertad – but reached by a longer, more circuitous road branching off the highway a few kilometres west of town – is the infinitely more appealing **PUNTA CARNERO**, a lonely, windswept promontory commanding superb views of the fifteen-kilometre stretch of beach flanking it. Pounding waves and strong currents make swimming at the beach unadvisable, but this is still a fabulous place to treat yourself to sun and solitude. Comfortable **accommodation** can be found at the *Hostería del Mar* (T04/2948077; ❻) on the road up to the cliff top, with a large pool overlooking the ocean. Further up the road the more upmarket *Punta Carnero* (T04/2948057 or 09/4305153; ❼) has a glass-walled restaurant looking down to the beach, a beautiful swimming pool and air-conditioned rooms with pleasing sea views. You can reach Punta Carnero by **bus** with Trans Libertad from La Libertad (every 20min), and

Cooperativas Mar Azul from Salinas (every 15min); ask the driver to drop you off at the road leading up to the promontory.

Salinas

The highway ends 5km west of La Libertad and 170km from Guayaquil at **SALINAS**, Ecuador's swankiest beach resort. Arriving at its graceful seafront avenue, the Malecón, feels like stepping into another world: gone are the ramshackle streets characteristic of Ecuador's coastal towns, replaced by a gleaming boulevard lined with glitzy, high-rise condominiums sweeping around a large, beautiful bay. Closer inspection reveals the streets behind the Malecón are as dusty and potholed as anywhere else, but this doesn't seem to bother anyone – it's the **beach** that counts here, with clean, golden sand and warm, calm waters safe for swimming. The best time to enjoy it is December, early January or March, during weekdays. Around Carnaval and on summer weekends it gets unbearably packed, while from April to November it can be overcast and dreary.

Arrival, information and transport

CLP **buses** from Guayaquil arrive in Salinas via the Malecón and continue to the avenue's western end; heading out of town, you need to catch one returning along Avenida General Enríquez Gallo. Blue-and-yellow **taxirutas** ($0.50), shared taxis, also go regularly to La Libertad along Gallo, from where you can catch onward buses. Tourist **information** is at the Cámara de Turismo, next door to the *Barceló Colón Miramar* hotel on the Malecón (Mon–Fri 9am–5pm; ☏04/2771690). A few years ago, the town's street names were changed from a straightforward numbering system to rather unwieldy names, which we use in our account and on our map – though some locals still stick to the old numbers.

Banks offering ATMs include Banco de Guayaquil (Visa and MasterCard), Malecón and Lupercio Bazan Malave; and Banco del Pacífico (MasterCard and Cirrus), General Enríquez Gallo and Leonardo Aviles. The **post office** is by the

▲ Salinas

police station at the east end of town. **Internet** access is available at Café Planet, General Enríquez Gallo and Digno A Nuñez; and Cybermar, Malecón and Fidón Tomalá Reyes. In the high season, **bicycles** can be rented from a couple of places along the beachfront ($5 per day). For **laundries**, the Lavandería de Todito, Rumiñahui and Aspiazu, washes clothes by the kilo.

Accommodation

Although the bulk of **accommodation** in Salinas is expensive, there are a few reasonable budget options. Expect substantial discounts in the low season.

Albita On Av Eduardo Aspiazu Estrada and Malave ⓉO4/2773211. Offers basic en-suite rooms enlivened by potted plants and a balcony with hammocks. ❹

Barceló Colón Miramar Malecón and Galápagos Ⓣ&ⒻO4/2771610, Ⓦwww.barcelo.com. Salinas' premier hotel, located in a landmark building at the east end of the Malecón, with impeccable rooms that all face the ocean. Full board. ❾

El Carruaje Malecón 517 Ⓣ&ⒻO4/2774282. Upmarket hotel with sea views (❼), whose rooms are smartly furnished and come with cable TVs and a/c. ❻

Francisco General Enríquez Gallo and Rumiñahui ⓉO4/2774106. Small and elegant hostel with immaculate, a/c rooms with cable TVs, giving onto a patio with a small pool. ❻

Las Rocas 24 de Mayo and General Enríquez Gallo ⓉO4/2771096. Good-value *hostal* with plain but clean rooms with optional private baths (❺) in a pretty, painted house. ❹

Yulee Eloy Alfaro and Mercedes del Jesús Molina ⓉO4/2772028. Lovely old house with bright-yellow walls, green shutters and a flower-filled courtyard, offering simple but comfortable rooms with shared (❸) or private baths (❺), or smarter ones with a/c, hot-water showers and cable TV (❻).

The Town

Salinas' main draw is its long, curving, golden **beach**, and warm(ish) ocean waters, safe for swimming in. Get here soon after breakfast and you'll have the sand and the sea virtually to yourself – but by afternoon in the high season you'll be sharing them with droves of vacationing Ecuadorians.

If you need a change of scene, try the **Museo Salinas Siglo XXI**, on the Malecón and Guayas y Quil (Wed–Sat 10am–6pm, Sun 9am–5pm; $2). It's divided into two sections: one giving an excellent overview of pre-Columbian cultures on the peninsula, including some beautifully crafted Guayala and Manteño-Huancavilca ceramics; the other with displays on nautical history, including items recovered from the galleon *La Capitana*, which sank off the coast near Punta Chanduy in 1654, taking with it more than two thousand silver bars and two hundred chests of coins. The small but captivating Museo de Ballenas (daily 10am–5pm, or when *Oystercatcher* restaurant is open; ring bell for attention or call ⓉO4/2778329; Ⓦwww.femm.org; donations welcome), attached to *Oystercatcher* restaurant on General Enríquez Gallo (a few blocks north of the *Barceló Colón Miramar* hotel), features a 12-metre skeleton of a humpback whale, skulls and bones of other cetaceans and preserved dolphins, all of which were washed ashore. At the other end of town, behind Cevichelandia on Peña Villao, is **Aquadventure** ($6; Ⓦwww.salinasaquadventure.com), Ecuador's largest water park.

At the western end of the Malecón near the Yacht Club, the **handicraft market** (daily Jan–March) sells jewellery, leather goods, tagua-nut carvings and sometimes Panama hats. A taxi ride away, powerful waves that churn the waters chocolate brown at high tide batter the rocky headland of **La Chocolatera**, the westernmost part of mainland Ecuador. La Chocolatera sits within the perimeter of a naval base where, at the entrance 2.5km from the shore, you'll have to ask permission and show your passport. Within the base, to the south is

Punta Brava, where there's a colony of sea lions, one of the northernmost on the continent. Beyond is the Mar Bravo, like La Chocolatera, a good spot for **surfing**, but considered too dangerous for bathing.

Deep-sea **sports fishing** is very popular around Salinas and can be arranged through Pesca Tours, on the Malecón and Rumiñahui (☏04/2772391, ⓦwww.pescatours .com.ec), who charge $400–500 for up to six people for a full day or $250–300 for a half a day in low season; the best time of year is between November and February but you can fish year-round. For local **birdwatching**, no one is more knowledgeable than Dutch naturalist Ben Haase (☏04/2778329, ⓔbhaase@ecua.net.ec), at the Museo de Ballenas and *Oystercatcher* restaurant. He leads tours to the Ecuasal salt pans south of town ($50), one of the best places in the country to see the Chilean flamingo as well as more than 120 other species, including many migratory birds, Franklin's gulls, masked water-tyrants and peregrine falcons, call ahead to acquire proper licences. Mr Haase can also offer advice on organizing **whale-watching** trips between June and September (around $25 per person).

Eating

Besides the **restaurants** below, you'll find some fast-food outlets along the central Malecón and a cluster of cheap and somewhat basic **cevicherías**, known as "Cevichelandia", around the municipal market at General Enríquez Gallo and Las Palmeras (Calle 16).

Amazon Malecón and Lupercio Bazán Malave. Attractive and moderately priced pizzeria and grill, also offering seafood, salads and vegetarian dishes.

Barceló Colón Miramar Malecón and Galápagos. Hotel restaurant that is one of the most stylish and expensive places to eat in town, serving everything from local seafood to national *comida típica* and elaborate international dishes.

La Bella Italia Malecón at Rumiñahui. Serves tasty pizzas and other Italian dishes in a dining room with wineglasses and napkins, as well as more standard Ecuadorian food in less formal surroundings at the front of the restaurant.

Don Kleber's Cevichelandia at General Enríquez Gallo and Las Palmeras (Calle 16). A good bet for a cheap seafood lunch – offering better quality and higher standards of cleanliness than some of its neighbours.

Mar y Tierra Malecón and Reinaldo Chávez. A quality choice for its excellent, if pricey, fish and seafood, served in a quirky boat-fronted (cannons and all) dining room that catches the sea breeze.

Oystercatcher General Enríquez Gallo, a few blocks north of the *Barceló Colón Miramar* hotel ☎04/2777335. Only open Friday to Sunday (10am–9pm) but worth the wait for some of the best oysters in town. You can also combine a meal with a visit to the Museo de Ballenas here (see p.421).

Ruta del Sol

From La Libertad, a paved road runs 137km up the coast to Puerto Cayo – a stretch promoted as the **Ruta del Sol**, offering fantastic views of long, empty beaches and passing a string of modest fishing villages and resorts. At Puerto Cayo, a branch of the highway heads inland to the unremarkable town of Jipijapa, while a new coastal road continues to Manta (see p.379). Along the Ruta del Sol sit the moderately interesting archeological museum at **Valdivia** and the attractive little seaside village of **Manglaralto**; most visitors give these a miss and head straight for laid-back **Montañita**, a favourite with surfers and a rapidly growing backpackers' beach hangout. A little further north, the dry, featureless landscape gives way to lush vegetation as you enter the **Cordillera Chongón-Colonche**, where the road veers inland from the coast through thickly wooded hills. The next gringo stop is **Alandaluz**, an ecologically focused resort, while further north **Puerto López** is a base for **whale-watching** trips (June–Sept) and visits to the **Parque Nacional Machalilla**, which takes in a major tract of tropical dry forest, fabulous beaches and the **Isla de la Plata** – favoured by bird lovers as a cheaper alternative to the Galápagos Islands.

Getting to the various points along the Ruta del Sol is easy on the many **buses** running up and down the coastal highway. In high season (Jan–April) there are regular direct services from Guayaquil to Montañita and Olón. Otherwise, there are frequent year-round services from La Libertad to Puerto López (continuing to Manta, beyond), stopping at all the villages en route; Puerto López can also be reached on direct year-round services from Guayaquil, as well as from Manta or Jipijapa, north of the town.

North of Santa Elena: Museo Cacique Baltacho and Ayangue

North of Santa Elena the road hugs the shore, skirting a string of long, slender beaches, and passing the run-down little villages of **Monteverde** and **Palmar**. The barren scrubland east of the road doesn't look too inviting, but reveals an oddity in a quiet corner of the forgotten town of **San Marcos** – the **Museo Cacique Baltacho** (irregular hours, ask around for the guardian; $0.50), a bizarre and striking single-room archeology museum in the shape of a giant half-submerged terracotta vase. Ancient tombs of the Huancavilca culture were discovered here and the museum, named after the region's chief at the time of the Conquest, displays local finds as well as a tomb reconstruction. Pick up a bus heading inland from the crossroads at Puente Palmar (10min journey).

Further up the coast, **AYANGUE** lies clasped in the arms of a hairpin bay, its soft, golden sands and shoal of bobbing fishing boats sheltered by two long headlands. Offshore, you can see **whales** from June to September, while a couple of nearby islands, Islotes El Pelado and El Viejo, provide alluring underwater scenery for **divers**. The village suffers from its proximity to Guayaquil during high-season holidays and weekends, when rooms are at a premium and the beach becomes choked. The most exclusive **hotel**, *Cumbres de Ayangue* (☎04/2916040, ⓦwww.cumbresdeayangue.com; ⓼), dramatically positioned at the tip of the southern headland, has its own secluded cove, a pool and smart en-suite rooms with cable TV, balconies and sea views. Cheaper alternatives are 1km away in Ayangue proper, including the friendly *Pangora* (☎04/2916126; ❺), an attractive beach house at the north end of the village with an open kitchen, or the more conventional *Sol y Mar* (☎04/2916014; ❸), a hotel block in the centre with en-suite rooms. Regular **camionetas** run the 3km from the highway to the village during daylight hours.

Valdivia

Just north of Ayangue, the impoverished village of **VALDIVIA** is best known for giving its name to the **Valdivia culture** that inhabited this region from 3500 BC, one of the earliest in South America to form permanent agricultural settlements and produce ceramics. Off the main square, the small **Museo Valdivia** (daily 9am–6pm; $1) has a fairly limited collection of ceramics and features a Japanese-style portico at the entrance – a nod to the contested theory that the Valdivia culture had close links to the Jomon culture of Kyushu, Japan, as extraordinary similarities in ceramic styles suggest. The museum shop sells replicas of pre-Columbian ceramics, which you can watch being made using traditional methods at the **workshop** here. The best **place to stay** nearby is 2km south of town at the *Valdivia Ecolodge* (☎04/2916128, ⓦwww.valdiviaecolodge.com; ❻) which has breezy open-sided, screened rooms with private baths and electric shower, a small pool and lovely views. Otherwise, it's easy enough to stop off for an hour or so and catch the next **bus** up the coast.

Manglaralto

Further north of Valdivia is the tidy, attractive village of **MANGLARALTO**, featuring a leafy square and a long, very beautiful **beach** – a quiet, remote alternative to the gringo-favoured Montañita and Alandaluz for a couple of days of oceanside relaxation; note that there are dangerous **riptides** off this part of the coast. Manglaralto has also been the focus of sustainable economic-development programmes by organizations such as **Pro-Pueblo**, a foundation which runs excellent projects in animal husbandry, organic farming, recycling, family planning, local sanitation and water distribution. It also has a small shop by the central square selling locally made crafts.

On the main street, Calle Constitución, just south of the square, *Marakayá* (☎04/2901294, ⓦwww.marakaya.com; ❺) has a few pleasant, well-kept **rooms**, which have mosquito nets and some air conditioning, and a café one block from the beach. *Manglaralto Sunset* (☎04/2901405, ⒺImanglaralto_beach@yahoo .com; ❹ weekdays, ❺ weekends), on El Oro a block north of the square, and *Manglaralto* (☎04/2901369; ❹), around the corner on Constitución and El Oro, both offer clean, en-suite accomodation with electric shower and complimentary breakfast. Further south along Constitución, rooms are available at *Los Cactus* (☎04/2901114; ❸), the family home of Paquita Jara, who also works with the Proyecto de Ecoturismo Comunitario (☎03/2656216 or 08/5446080, ⓦwww.piedrablanca.org), providing **guided walks** and **community stays** in the region.

Just 4km north of Manglaralto, **MONTAÑITA** is like nowhere else on the southern coast. Crammed into the centre are straw-roofed, bamboo-walled *hostales* and pizzerias advertised by bright wooden signs, while tanned, chilled-out gringos lounge around in shorts and bikinis and surfers stride up the streets with boards under arm. There's a certain 1960s, dope-fuelled atmosphere to

▲ Riding a wave, Montañita

Montañita that may not appeal to everybody, reaching a height during *la temporada* from January to April. Outside these months, visitors dwindle and the skies cloud over, but the hotels stay open all year catering to the steady stream of **surfing** addicts.

Arrival and information

Montañita is a small place, and everything is within easy walking distance of the seafront and the main street, Calle Principal. There's an **ATM** (MasterCard and Visa) inside the *Hotel Montañita*, but it often runs out of cash, particularly at weekends, so don't rely on it. Otherwise, the Farmacia San José changes travel-ler's cheques for a hefty commission. **Internet access** is at Montañita Express (around $2 per hr), off Calle Chiriboga; they also have a **tour agency**, offering rappelling, whale-watching (in season), trekking, mountain biking and horser-iding expeditions.

Accommodation

Accommodation is either in the village centre or by **La Punta**, a calmer location 1km north. There's plenty of choice, with new cheapies opening all the time, in which basic rooms, the occasional balcony and hammocks are generally standard. Discounts are often available in low season.

Arena Guadúa La Punta ☎09/3217064. Argen-tine-owned beachside surfer hangout offering thatched cabins, private baths and hot water, sea-view terraces, hammocks and mosquito nets. A funky beach bar provides breakfasts, snacks and cocktails. Breakfast included. ❻

Baja Montañita La Punta ☎04/2568840 or 09/1898542, ⓦ www.bajamontanita.com.ec. Resort-hotel in an enclosed complex with pool,

restaurant and en-suite rooms with hot water, plus suites featuring a/c and satellite TVs. A bit of a fish out of water in Montañita, though. ❽

Cabañas Nativa Bambú On the hill behind the village, across the main road ☎09/6087212 or 04/2901293. Attractive cabins with varnished floors, well-presented shared or private bathrooms, mosquito nets and terraces overlooking the village and sea – not far from the action but away from the noise. Tents are $5 per double and meals are available. **⑤**

Casa Blanca Chiriboga ☎09/9182501, ⓦwww .montanita-lacasablanca.com. Provides bamboo huts with hammocks, balconies and sea views (**⑤**) and less attractive brick-walled rooms (**❸**) with erratic hot-water showers.

Casa del Sol La Punta ☎04/2648287, ⓦwww .casasol.com. Agreeable, if pricey, rooms with private baths and hot water in a cosy, straw-roofed wooden building with balconies, terraces, hammocks, a TV room and restaurant. Surf lessons offered. **❻**

El Centro del Mundo On the beach ⓦwww .centrodelmundo-montanita.com, ⓔinfo @centrodelmundo-montanita.com (no phone). Popular hostel in an unmistakable tall bamboo house on stilts by the ocean, offering a choice of basic wooden rooms (**❷**) with optional en-suite bathrooms (**❸**), and mattresses in the attic for $3.50 per person.

Charo's Behind the plaza, on the beach ☎04/206004409/9386474, ⓦwww.charoshostal .com. Striking beachfront hostel with a green roof and concrete rooms disguised by wood and thatch. Clean, tiled en-suite rooms with hot-water showers. **❻**

Montañita Next door to *El Centro del Mundo* ☎04/2901299, ⓦwww.hotelmontanita.org. Imposing, modern hotel whose 36 clean, if bare, white-walled rooms have private baths, electric showers, mosquito nets and ceiling fans; also has an on-site swimming pool and terrace overlooking the sea. Fridays and Saturdays are more expensive. **⑤**

Paradise South On the other side of the river bridge from the centre ☎09/7878925. Quiet spot offering spacious grounds, a pleasant lawn, ping pong and pool table. Rooms are clean and compact, with optional bathrooms (**❸** without **⑤** with). The costlier rooms are upstairs and one has a/c.

The Town

The town's transformation from isolated fishing village to backpacker hangout has been brought about by some of the best **surfing** conditions in Ecuador; waves are strong, consistent and range from one to three metres in height, and there's a long right break lying off the northern end of the beach by the rocky promontory of **La Punta**. The best waves coincide with the summer months (Jan–April), when the water temperature averages 22–25°C. Every February, surfing fever reaches a peak during the **international surfing competition** held here over Carnaval, which attracts contestants from as far away as the US and Australia.

Surfboards (*tablas*) can be rented for about $18 a day at a number of places in the centre, such as Tikilimbo and Balsa House. Montañita's waves are best suited to experienced surfers, but beginners can get in on the action by taking one-to-one **lessons** with the Montañita Surf Club on the waterfont ($20 for a 2hr lesson; they also rent out boards and equipment).

Eating, drinking and nightlife

There's a wide choice of **café-restaurants** in the centre, all of them cheap and most offering a seafood menu supplemented by pizzas, pasta, pancakes and tropical fruit juices. One highlight is *Doña Elena*, on the main street, who serves great sea bass caught by her fisherman husband. *Hola Ola* on Chiriboga does pretty good falafel, hummus and breakfasts. These are all good places to sit and people-watch as you wait for the sun to go down and Montañita's **nightlife** to heat up, when bars rock to the likes of the Doors and parties unfold on the beach.

Olón and San José

Perched on top of the rocky headland north of Montañita, the impressive boat-shaped **Santuario del Inmaculado Corazón de María** – where an effigy of the Virgin is supposed to have wept blood in 1990 – gives spectacular views across to the neighbouring village of **Olón**, graced by a long white beach. The community manages the **Cangrejal de Olón**, a small reserve protecting mangrove and hibiscus forest, at the estuary of the Río Olón; ask locally if you want to visit. Continuing north, the landscape becomes noticeably lusher, with rolling greenery replacing the scrub and dry forests of the south. Such fecundity makes fruit-farming, not fishing, the economic engine of local villages like **SAN JOSÉ**, despite its glorious stretch of beach (mind the dangerous **undertow** if bathing). You can **stay** here at *Cuna Luna* (☎04/2780735; ❼) in clean and comfortable en-suite rooms with hot water, boasting plenty of polished wood and, occasionally, French doors or balconies right onto the beach. For more seclusion and tranquillity, try the ⚕ *Samai Center* (☎04/2780167 or 09/4621316, ⓦwww.sacred-journey.com; ❻, with full board available for $15 extra) a spa and "spiritual retreat" tucked away in the verdant hills 1km above the village; its cosy rooms and cabins, most with private bath and set within 12 hectares of private forest, command gorgeous views down to the sea. Treatments include massages, facials, herbal steam baths, shamanic healing, reflexology, plus tarot and feng shui consultations. There's also a purpose-built ceremonial centre, where visiting shamans lead rituals using sacred plants; the US owner (dubbed the "gringo shaman" by the national press) and his Ecuadorian wife regularly work with expert Kichwa shamans from the Andes and Oriente.

Cordillera Chongón-Colonche

Further north up the coast, the village of **La Entrada** is so called because it marks the entrance into the **Cordillera Chongón-Colonche**, a range of 800-metre-high hills covered by one of the last remnants of coastal forest in the region. This once extended up the whole of Ecuador's coastline north of the Santa Elena peninsula, but aggressive logging of native hardwoods such as *guayacán*, *cascol* and *guasmo* has reduced these coastal forests to a tiny fraction of their original area; the Parque Nacional Machalilla (see p.431), a further 30km up the road, protects the largest remaining tract.

As you enter the forest, the road veers inland into the heart of the Cordillera, and suddenly you're surrounded by dense vegetation dripping with moisture – a dramatic contrast to the dusty landscape further south. Eleven kilometres north of La Entrada, you pass a signed track branching west to *Atamari* (☎09/9821916 or 04/2780430, ⓦwww.resortatamari.com; ❾), perched on a cliff high above the sea, with spectacular views up the coast and access to two beautiful, deserted beaches. This upmarket, French-run establishment has private, well-equipped cabañas, a large pool, a lovely restaurant and bar and also offers PADI **diving courses** and dive trips. Any bus serving the coastal route can drop you off at the track leading up to the hotel, a fifteen-minute uphill walk.

Ayampe

Not far beyond La Entrada sits the unassuming village of **AYAMPE**, home only to a handful of farming families and set back from a huge, empty beach pounded by powerful breakers, its golden sands forming a striking contrast with the deep-green vegetation inland. It's a beautiful, little-known spot that has only recently begun to attract visitors to its small selection of generally good **hotels**.

Accommodation

Cabañas La Iguana ☎04/2780605, ⓦwww .designalltag.com/ayampe. Just to the south, beyond the cemetery, this Cuban-run spot has good, clean rooms set around a pretty garden and great vegetarian food, but BBQ and cooking facilities are available. Also offers mule tours along the Ayampe River. ❸

Cabañas La Tortuga ☎04/2780613 or 09/3834825, ⓦ www.latortuga.com.ec. Set on the seafront, this place has airy cabins with spacious bathrooms, hot water, mosquito nets, terrace and hammocks. ❺
Almare ☎042780611, ⓦ www.hotelalmare-ecuador .com. This is the smartest place in the village and features comfortable rooms with private baths and hot water, tiled floors, smoked-glass sliding doors that open onto balconies and a large terrace with gorgeous views of the sea. ❻

Finca Punta Ayampe ☎04/2780616 or 09/9708329, ⓦ www.fincapuntaayampe.com. 1km south of the village and set amid fruit orchards and vegetable gardens on a hill with tremendous views. The main building, a tall open-sided wooden structure with a sun deck and open fire, has airy rooms with private baths and hot water; private four-bed cabins are also available with similar facilities. The owner offers local tours and can give surf lessons. ❺

Alandaluz to Salango

About 3km beyond Ayampe, the coast road emerges from the Cordillera Chongón-Colonche and passes ⚑ **Alandaluz** (☎02/2440790 or 09/4274684, ⓦ www.alandaluzhosteria.com; ❺–❼), on the edge of the village of **Puerto Rico**. This is an award-winning ecological resort comprising thirty attractive two- to four-bed cabañas scattered around tree-filled grounds, with a magnificent high-roofed dining room, bar and lounge in a central bamboo building. The cabins are made of local, easily renewable materials, some units have special compost toilets to produce fertilizer, fruit and vegetables grow in organic gardens and water is meticulously saved and recycled; there are also newer, stone-built accommodation with fireplaces, flush toilets and even hot tubs. It remains a lovely, laid-back place to hang out for a few days, whether you want to lounge around on a private beach, use it as a base for visiting Parque Nacional Machalilla up the road (see p.431), or take a tour to the resort's private **Cantalapiedra** nature reserve and stay in a wood-and-thatch tower sleeping thirteen people. Although **camping** is possible ($5 per person), accommodation is expensive by backpacking standards (more luxurious cabins; ❼). Nonetheless, *Alandaluz* has poured its profits back into the local community, establishing recycling centres, reforestation projects and workshops in sustainable farming and building methods, among various other programmes. Other accommodation nearby includes Swiss-owned *La Barquita*, 1km south (☎04/2780051 or 09/3698818, ⓦ www.labarquita-ec .com; ❺), offering pretty beachfront rooms (including shared rooms with bunks from $9 per person) with mosquito nets, private baths and hot water. The restaurant and bar is in a gleaming, varnished wooden boat, making for a unique individual centrepiece.

A further 7km up the road near **Río Chico**, the *Hostería Piqueros Patas Azules* (☎04/2780279 or 09/7356833, ⓦ www.hosteriapiqueros.com; ❻) has comfortable rooms, a good restaurant and bar, a medicinal plunge pool and its own stretch of beach with a scattering of hammocks and deckchairs. Attached to the hotel is a *sala arqueológico*, whose impressive display of artefacts from the Valdivia culture includes fragments of pots and tablets carved with images of animals, thought to have been used by local chiefs to imprint their own symbolic "signature". A bit further up the highway, the tiny village of **Salango** is the site of a small but well-designed **archeology museum** (daily 9am–noon & 1–5pm; $1), illustrating the area's continuous occupation from the Valdivia culture around 3500 BC to the Manteño culture up to 1550 AD. Especially engaging are the displays on ancient fishing techniques and seafaring practices, including a reconstruction of a single-sail fishing raft like those the Spanish encountered when they first visited this coast in 1526.

Puerto López

Beyond Salango, the coast road cuts across the brow of a hill and down to **PUERTO LÓPEZ**, a small fishing town strung along a wide, crescent-shaped bay. Enjoying an undeniably picturesque setting, the town's golden sands are set off by the turquoise waters of the ocean and the green hills rising on either side.

Arrival, information and transport

Puerto López is well served by **buses** from La Libertad in the south (every 30min; 2hr) and Manta in the north (hourly; 2hr), as well from Jipijapa, inland (every 30min; 1hr 30min), and Guayaquil (4hr). There are also several daily direct buses from Quito (9 or 10hr). Buses drop passengers on the main road, General Córdova, by the church and the market building. **Tricicleros** ($0.50–1) will cycle (or motor) you to your hotel, while **camionetas** linger around the market for longer journeys.

The Cámara de Turismo (Mon–Sat 9am–2pm; ℡09/3334975, ⓦwww .puertolopez.net), General Córdova and Machalilla, provides general tourist **information** and maps. For information on Parque Nacional Machalilla go to the park's visitor centre on Eloy Alfaro and García Moreno. The town's only **bank**, Banco Pichincha on General Córdova, has an ATM (though it sometimes runs out so bring plenty of extra cash). The Pacifictel **telephone office** is on the main road, a block north of the church, but you're better off making international calls from an **internet** café – there are many along General Córdova and the Malecón ($2 per hr). The **post office** is on the Malecón south of General Córdova, and **laundry** services are offered by

PUERTO LÓPEZ

ACCOMMODATION
Hostal Tuzco	G
Hostería Mandalá	A
Los Islotes	F
Itapoa	B
Mantaraya Lodge	J
Máxima	D
Monte Líbano	I
Pacífico	C
Punta Piedrero	H
Sol Inn	E

RESTAURANTS
Bella Italia	1
Café Ballena	6
Carmita	3
Flipper	4
Rey de las Hojas	5
Spondylus	2

0   100 m

PACIFIC OCEAN

Machalilla

P.N. Machalilla

Market

Trans Aray   Reina del Camino

J (3.5km), Ayampe & Montañita

7

several tour operators, including Bosque Marino, Malecón and General Córdova ($3.50 per load).

Accommodation

Puerto López offers plenty of choices for **accommodation**, but it can get busy during the whale-watching season (June–Sept), when you should book ahead.

Los Islotes Malecón and General Córdova ☎05/2300108, ✉hostallosislotes@hotmail.com. This tidy little Colombian-managed place has spacious en-suite rooms with tiled floors and electric showers. Rooms with a sea view are worth the extra buck. ❻

Itapoa Malecón and Calderón ☎09/3145894. This friendly family-run beachside hotel has a choice of jauntily painted, fairly rustic cane cabins, or newer brick-and-tile numbers, all with private bath and hot water. Jacuzzi, steam room and breakfast are included in the price. ❸

Hostería Mandalá ☎05/2300181, ✇www.hosteriamandala.info. At the far northern end of the Malecón, this friendly Swiss-and Italian-owned place with attractively furnished thatched-roof cabins with private baths and hot water is set in lavish botanical gardens. Its lovely restaurant overlooks the ocean and serves good international food, including Italian specialities. ❻

Mantaraya Lodge 3.5km south of town ☎02/2448985 or 09/4044050, ✇www .mantarayalodge.com. A "Mediterranean village" of terracotta roofs and whitewashed walls set on a hill overlooking the sea. All rooms have a terrace, bathroom and hot water, plus there's a games room, TV lounge and restaurant. Also offer a range of walking and boat tours in and around Parque Nacional Machalilla. ❽

Máxima González Suárez and Machalilla ☎09/9534282, ✇www.hotelmaxima.org. The generously sized double rooms and small dorms (from $6 per person) in this US-Ecuadorian-run hostel come with windows on three sides, mosquito nets, fans, private bath and hot water.

Perks include an open kitchen and a TV area with a free DVD library. ❷

Monte Líbano ☎05/2300231. A simple, family-run place at the far southern end of the Malecón, with clean rooms – some with private bath – and a pleasant upstairs terrace looking out to sea. A backpackers' favourite. ❷

Pacífico Malecón González and Suárez ☎05/2300133. Long-established hotel featuring clean, simple rooms with private bathrooms and fan (❹) or a/c (❺) set around a swimming pool. The priciest rooms (❼) have sea-view balconies. Tours offered to Isla de la Plata and Parque Nacional Machalilla.

Punta Piedrero ☎05/2300013. This modern hotel at the southern end of the beach has spacious, if a little gloomy, en-suite rooms in a quiet, beachfront location. There's also a terrace with hammocks and parking is available. ❸

Sol Inn Juan Montalvo and Eloy Alfaro, ☎05/2300248. Relaxed and friendly backpacker hotel with bamboo-sided rooms, mosquito nets, fans and optional private bathrooms. A little garden, book exchange, kitchen, laundry service and plans for an internet café make this a good budget choice. Cheap dorm beds (from $6) also available. ❷

Hostal Tuzco General Córdova and J. León Mera ☎05/2300120 or 1200132, ✉jgsalazar1 @hotmail.com, ✇www.tuzco.com. Tidy little *hostal* with its own restaurant across the street, and a cheaper annexe with bunks for $6. Rooms have hot water, fans and mosquito nets; upstairs rooms with TV and mini-fridge cost a few dollars more. Also offer local trips and hikes in Parque Nacional Machalilla. ❸

The Town

At close quarters Puerto López is a rather untidy place with potholed streets, crumbling buildings and a far-from-spotless beach. Still, the town itself is improving all the time, and the surge of morning activity from busy fishermen and the swarm of children playing in the breakers after school give the place a spirited atmosphere.

Most visitors come to explore the surrounding beaches and forests and the **Isla de la Plata**, all part of the nearby **Parque Nacional Machalilla**; its headquarters and information centre are based here at García Moreno and Eloy Alfaro. Puerto López is also one of the country's main centres for **whale–watching** (June–Sept), when hundreds of humpbacks arrive off the coast and tour operators (see box, p.430) fight over the hundreds of visitors who come to see them.

Eating and drinking

The best place to **eat** traditional, straightforward seafood is *Carmita's*, Malecón and General Córdova, a friendly restaurant run by the same family for more than 35 years, serving freshly caught fish at great prices. Especially recommended are the *pescado al vapor* (steamed sea bass in tomato, onion and herb sauce) and *spaghetti con mariscos*. Other seafood standby options are *Spondylus* and *Rey de las Hojas*, both on the Malecón, while around the corner *Flipper* does a bargain $1.50 *almuerzo*. The ever-popular US-run *Café Ballena* (daily noon–9.30pm, closed mid-Nov to Dec), on the southern Malecón, serves home-made bread, sandwiches, pizza, salads and great apple pancakes; sip on a smoothie, nibble a chocolate brownie, take a book from the exchange and chat to the friendly owners, who are only too happy to share tips on making the most of the area. There's good Italian food at *Bellaitalia* (daily 6–10pm), Montalvo and Calderón, whose Bolognese owners dish up fantastic pizza, pasta and other specialities in a seductive candlelit garden.

Nightlife can be on the slow side in low season, but when the hotels fill, expect *Café Ballena* to be a focus of cocktail consumption. *Clandestino*, Córdova and Montalvo, is relaxed on school nights, but spirited at weekends.

Tours from Puerto López

There are currently seventeen **tour operators** in Puerto López, just about all of them strung along General Córdova or the Malecón. Most offer the same basic journeys at identical prices; they can't always provide English-speaking guides and sometimes make do with asking a member of the tour to translate for everyone else.

The most popular tour is the ninety-minute **boat ride to Isla de la Plata** ($35; see p.432), including a guided hike around the island, followed by lunch and snorkelling from the boat. Boats usually set off at 9am and return at 5pm, and the crossing can be rough, so take sea-sickness tablets if you're susceptible. On top of the cost of the tour you'll have to pay for your national **park fee** (mainland $12, Isla de la Plata $15, combined $25; ticket valid for five days), which is taken care of by the operator.

Whale-watching tours (June–Sept; $25) are an exciting way of seeing humpback whales as they travel up the Pacific coast from the Antarctic to give birth in warmer waters. It's easy to spot the enormous spouts they blow out as they surface and to hear their loud "singing" noises; it's also usually possible to get quite close-up views. Both of these trips often require a minimum of four people per boat; if you arrive at a quiet time, it may take several days to get a group together, with the best chances being at weekends. A less expensive sea jaunt is to nearby **Isla Salango**, where you can go snorkelling and fishing for $15–25, plus park fee. For all boat trips, be sure to take a warm outer layer as the wind can be surprisingly cold out at sea.

Some operators, including Naturis (℡05/23002188, ⑳www.naturis.com.ec) and Mantaraya (℡05/2300233, ⑳www.mantarayalodge.com), both at General Córdova and Juan Montalvo, also visit the coastal and inland areas of **Parque Nacional Machalilla** ($15–35 depending on duration of tour); these include the archeological excavations at **Agua Blanca** (see p.431), the **Sendero Bola de Oro** (see p.432) or the **Sendero El Rocío** (see p.432). Horseriding, mountain-biking excursions and sports fishing are other possibilities, offered by several operators.

With a few days' advance notice, Exploramar (℡05/2300123, ⑳www.exploradiving .com), General Córdova and Malecón, can organize **scuba-diving** day-tours ($95) with a PADI instructor and two tanks for certified and non-certified divers. Some dives take you down to Ecuador's only coral reef – where you can see many colourful fish as well as octopuses, urchins and sea cucumbers – while other options include a five-day open-water course ($420). Machalilla Tours, Malecón 119 and Eloy Alfaro (℡05/2300206), provides **surfing** lessons and excursions ($15) and rents **bikes** and **kayaks**.

Parque Nacional Machalilla

Parque Nacional Machalilla, mainland Ecuador's only coastal national park, protects the country's last major tract of tropical dry forest – now a mere one percent of its original size. The forest is notable for the remarkable contrast between the vegetation at sea level and that covering the hills rising to 800m above the coastline. The **dry forest**, panning in from the shore, comprises scorched-looking trees and shrubs adapted to scarce water supplies and saline soils, including many different cactuses, gnarled *ceibas*, *barbasco* trees and *algarobbo* (able to photosynthesize through its green bark). Also common are highly fragrant *palo santo* trees, whose bark is burned as incense in churches. A short hike east into the hills brings you into the wholly different landscape of **coastal cloudforest**, moistened by a rising sea mist that condenses as it hits the hills, where a dense covering of lush vegetation shelters ferns, heliconias, bromeliads, orchids and bamboos, as well as a great variety of animals and birds. The two different habitats can be observed on a ten-kilometre trail leading from the community of **Agua Blanca**, north of Puerto López, up to the **San Sebastián** cloudforest area. Agua Blanca sits near one of the most important archeological sites on the coast, the former settlement of **Sangólome**. Beyond this, the park takes in a number of pristine beaches, of which the most spectacular is **Playa Los Frailes**. Offshore areas include the tiny **Isla Salango** and the famous, bird-rich **Isla de la Plata**, the most popular destination in the park.

Pay your **entrance fee** at the park's **visitor centre** in Puerto López at the brown-and-white thatched building opposite the market, on Eloy Alfaro (daily 8am–noon & 2–5pm; ☎05/2300170). The three types of tickets, all good for five days, allow access to the mainland ($12) or Isla de la Plata ($15), or provide entrance to both ($25). **Arriving** at the coastal sections of the park is easy on any of the buses running north along the coast road (see "Transport", p.428). Inland targets, such as the villages of Agua Blanca and Río Blanco, are not served by buses, but can be reached by *camioneta* ($5–6) from Puerto López, or on tours (around $35) offered by some of the town's operators and hotels, including Naturis (see box opposite) and *Hostal Tuzco* (see p.429).

The **weather** is typically rainy, hot and sunny in summer (Jan–April), and dry, slightly cooler and overcast the rest of the year, with average year-round temperatures hovering around 23–25°C (73–77°F).

Agua Blanca and San Sebastián

Five kilometres north of Puerto López, at the hamlet of Buenavista, a side road leads east to **AGUA BLANCA**, an hour's walk from the main road. This humble village stands near the site of **Sangólome**, a former centre of the Manteño civilization (c.500 BC to 1540 AD), known for its finely crafted and polished black ceramics and large thrones supported by human or animal figures, several of which were found here. A small **museum** in the village (daily 8am–6pm) displays some beautiful ceramics excavated at Sangólome, while the **site** itself is a forty-minute walk away. There's not a great deal left to see, but the numerous low walls, foundations, temple remains and the ruins of a magnificent ceremonial hall give you an idea of the size and importance of the city, estimated to have housed around five thousand people. A $5 community **charge** ($3 each for two or more people) covers a two-hour **guided tour** (in Spanish) of the museum and archeological site, passing funerary urns, the Río Buenavista valley and returning via a viewpoint and a pungent sulphur lake, supposedly a tonic for bodily ills – if you can brave the stench. Unaccompanied visitors are not allowed at the archeological site, in order to prevent artefact theft.

You can also hire **guides** ($30 per day, plus about $15 per horse or mule if required) in Agua Blanca to take you on beautiful hikes through tropical dry forest, with many colourful birds, up to the lush **San Sebastián cloudforest**, home to black howler monkeys, snakes, *guantas* and anteaters. The route, one of the best ways to explore the interior of Parque Nacional Machalilla, is 10km each way, most comfortably spread over two days, **camping** at San Sebastián (come prepared for mud and rain, especially from Jan to April). Agua Blanca also has simple **lodgings** in rustic cabins (❶ shared bath; ❷ private bath). For reservations or further information contact the community on ☎09/4434864, ✉ casaculturalaguablanca@hotmail.com.

Bola de Oro

Nine kilometres inland from Puerto López, the small community of **RÍO BLANCO** is the starting point for a rewarding hike through dense, luxuriant cloudforest, rich in bird and animal life, up to the park's highest point (800m), known as the "Bola de Oro", or "gold nugget".You can hire a local guide ($30 per group) at Río Blanco the day before you plan to hike; they can supply you with mules ($15), though the final, steep portion of the trek can only be done on foot. The trail, quite hard-going in parts, is about a seven-hour round trip and can be very muddy, especially from January to April.You can break the trek by camping in a clearing at the Bola de Oro; otherwise, families in the village offer simple, inexpensive food and lodging. It's a forty-five-minute taxi ride from Puerto López if you just want to go in for the day.

Playa Los Frailes and Sendero El Rocío

Some 10km north of Puerto López, a signed dirt track branches west from the coast road, just south of the run-down village of Machalilla, to **Playa Los Frailes**, one of the most beautiful beaches on the Ecuadorian coast, with dramatic cliffs and forested hills framing its virgin white sands. Despite its popularity, the beach still feels like a wild, unspoiled place, particularly if you arrive in the early morning, when you're almost guaranteed to have it all to yourself. To get there, hop on any of the **buses** heading north from Puerto López and ask to be dropped at the turn-off to the beach, about fifteen minutes out of town. Just off the road at the national park kiosk, show your ticket or buy one if you haven't already paid your entrance fee. From here a footpath leads directly to Los Frailes in thirty minutes (the left fork), or you can follow a four-kilometre circular trail (the right fork) via the tiny black-sand cove known as **La Playita**, followed by **Playa La Tortuguita**, where spiky rocks rise from the turquoise waters. From La Tortuguita continue on the main footpath to Los Frailes, or follow the fork leading through dry forest dotted with fragrant *palo santo* trees up to a wooden *mirador* (lookout) giving spectacular views of the coast. This longer approach, via La Playita, La Tortuguita and the *mirador*, is by far the more rewarding and takes several hours to complete.

About 3km north of the turning for Los Frailes, you'll see signs for the **Sendero El Rocío**, an enjoyable two-kilometre trail beginning in the cultivated land of traditional coastal subsistence farms; it leads up to a viewpoint and into dry *palo santo* forest, emerging at an attractive beach. Locals act as guides for visitors; ask at the farms around the trailhead.

Isla de la Plata

Some 37km out to sea from Puerto López, and reached using one of the tour companies there (see box, p.430), **Isla de la Plata** is a small, scrubby island of just eight square kilometres, once the ceremonial centre of the Bahía culture

(500 BC to 650 AD). Its name comes from the legend that the English explorer Sir Francis Drake buried a chestful of silver here in the sixteenth century – never discovered, of course. Today, the island's fame derives more from its large population of **marine birds**, which are relatively fearless and allow close observation, attracting many visitors and giving it the sobriquet of "poor man's Galápagos". Yet this hackneyed phrase doesn't do the island justice; it's the only place in Ecuador – including the Galápagos – where blue-footed, red-footed and masked boobies are found together.

From the landing point in **Bahía Drake**, two circular **footpaths** lead around the island, each taking three to four hours to complete, including time spent watching the birds and listening to the tour guide's commentary. The most numerous bird species on the island is the **blue-footed booby**, though you can also see **frigatebirds**, **red-billed tropicbirds** and **waved albatrosses** (breeding season April–Oct; see p.525), as well as sea lions, which are colonizing the island in small numbers. Visits usually include some **snorkelling**, which provides a glimpse of a fabulous array of colourful fish. You might also spot dolphins and manta rays on the boat ride, as well as **humpback whales** (June–Sept).

Puerto Cayo to Jipijapa

Heading north of Puerto López along the coast, the sea is mostly hidden from sight until you reach **PUERTO CAYO**, 34km up the road. There are great views here onto a lovely broad beach hedged at the south by dramatic sandy cliffs – though the village itself is run-down and uninviting. A further 3km north up the coast, *Luz de Luna* (☎05/2616031 or 09/7088613, ⓦwww .hosterialuzdeluna.com; ⑥) makes an appealing place for a night, with comfortable rooms, a small swimming pool, access to a nice stretch of beach and a restaurant serving local *comida típica* cooked in a clay oven.

Just beyond Puerto Cayo, a road branches off the coastal highway (which continues on to Manta) and heads inland for 30km to **JIPIJAPA** (pronounced

▲ Waved albatrosses

"hippyhappa"). It's a dull town that doesn't live up to its delightful name but is the place to change **buses** if you're heading from or to Guayaquil. The terminal is 2km west of the centre, by the main road leading into town. You shouldn't have to wait too long to catch your connection, but if you arrive at night and get stuck here, your best bet for a **place to stay** is the *Jipijapa*, Santi-esteban and Eloy Alfaro (T05/2601365; ④), which has decent en-suite rooms and the option of air conditioning (⑤). For **restaurants**, there are several straightforward canteens and *chifas* around the centre, serving cheap meals of fried meat or fish. The Banco del Pichincha on the central plaza has a Visa and MasterCard **ATM**.

Travel details

Buses

Guayaquil to: Alausí (3 daily; 5hr); Ambato (hourly; 6hr 30min); Cuenca (every 40min; 4hr); Guaranda (12 daily; 3hr 30min); Huaquillas (every 30min; 4hr 30min); Jipijapa (every 30min; 2hr 30min); La Libertad (every 20min; 2hr 30min), change here for Puerto López; Loja (16 daily; 9hr); Machala (every 30min; 3hr); Manta (every 30min; 4hr); Montañita (Jan–April 6 daily; 3.5hr); Olón (Jan–April 6 daily; 3.5hr); Playas (every 20min; 2hr); Portoviejo (every 30min; 4hr); Puerto López (5 daily; 4hr); Quito (every 10–20min; 8hr); Riobamba (every hour; 5hr); Salinas (every 20min; 2hr 40min); Santo Domingo (every 10min; 6hr); Zaruma (10 daily; 6hr).

Jipijapa to: Guayaquil (every 30min; 2hr 30min); Manta (every 30min; 1hr); Puerto López (every 45min; 1hr 30min); Quito (3 daily; 9hr).

La Libertad to: Guayaquil (every 15min; 2hr 30min); Manglaralto (every 30min; 50min);

Montañita (every 30min; 1hr); Puerto López (every 30min; 2hr); Puerto Rico/Alandaluz (hourly; 1hr 40min); Punta Carnero (every 20min; 20min); Puerto López (2hr); Quito (3 nightly; 10hr); Salinas (every 10min; 10min); Santa Elena (every 10min; 5min); Valdivia (every 30min; 40min).

Machala to: Cuenca (every 15–45min; 4hr); Guayaquil (every 30min; 3hr); Huaquillas (every 20min; 1hr); Loja (8 daily; 6hr); Puyango (5 daily; 3hr); Quito (11 daily; 10hr); Zaruma (10 daily; 3hr).

Puerto López to: Guayaquil (5 daily; 4hr); Jipijapa (every 30min; 2hr 30min); La Libertad (every 30min; 2hr); Manglaralto (every 30min; 1hr); Manta (hourly; 2hr by coast, 2hr 30min inland); Salinas (2hr).

Flights

Guayaquil to: Baltra (4 Sun–Fri, 3 Sat; 1hr 30min); Cuenca (3–4 daily; 30min); Quito (around 23 Mon–Fri, around 12 Sat & Sun; 45min); San Cristóbal (1 Mon, Thurs, Sat & Sun; 1hr 30min).

8

The Galápagos Islands

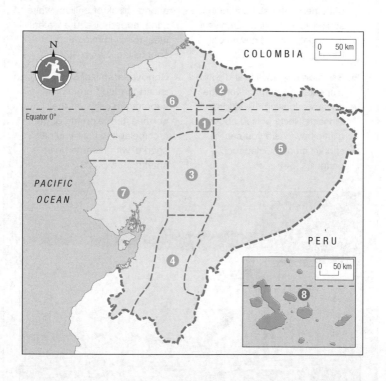

COLOMBIA

0   50 km

N

Equator 0°

PACIFIC
OCEAN

PERU

0   50 km

CHAPTER 8

Highlights

✳ **Puerto Ayora** A friendly, bustling little port, home to the islands' best hotels, restaurants and bars – and the Charles Darwin Research Station, the engine of Galápagos study and conservation. See p.457

✳ **Sulivan Bay** Explore a century-old pahoehoe lava flow patterned with petrified ripples, squiggles and swirls that give it the appearance of having only just cooled. See p.467

✳ **Bartolomé** A small island with a spectacular summit vantage point overlooking the landmark Pinnacle Rock, poised above a little bay where you can snorkel among Galápagos penguins. See p.467

✳ **Waved albatrosses** After ranging the oceans, the gentle giants of the Galápagos return to Española between April and December, and enact enthralling courtship displays before breeding with their lifelong partners. See p.482

✳ **Gardner Bay** One of the finest beaches in the islands, a long streak of brilliant white sand lapped by azure waters ideal for swimming and snorkelling. See p.482

✳ **Genovesa** An isolated island formed from a half-submerged crater at the northeastern extreme of the archipelago, where you can snorkel with hammerhead sharks. See p.483

▲ Galápagos penguin, Bartolomé

The Galápagos Islands

t's quite humbling that thirteen scarred volcanic islands, scattered across 45,000 square kilometres of ocean, 960km adrift from the Ecuadorian mainland and defying permanent human colonization until the twentieth century, should have been so instrumental in changing humanity's perception of itself. Yet it was the forbidding **Galápagos Islands** – once feared as a bewitched and waterless hell, then the haunt of pirates, and later still an inhospitable pit stop for whaling ships – that spurred **Charles Darwin** to formulate his theory of evolution by natural selection, catapulting science into the modern era and colouring the values and attitudes of the Western world ever since.

Three years before Darwin's arrival in 1835, Ecuador claimed **sovereignty** over the islands, but attempts to colonize the islands were unsuccessful until the mid-twentieth century, and even then only in very small numbers. It was inevitable after Darwin's discoveries and the global rise in recreational travel, that the Galápagos Islands' matchless wildlife would start to pull in large numbers of tourists, money, and then migrants close behind.

A total of about 40,000 people live in just eight main settlements on four inhabited islands. In the centre of the archipelago lies **Santa Cruz**, site of **Puerto Ayora**, the islands' most developed town, serviced by the airstrip on nearby Baltra island, where the majority of tourists begin a visit to the Galápagos. **San Cristóbal**, to the east, holds the provincial capital, **Puerto Baquerizo Moreno**, and the archipelago's other major runway. Straddling the equator to the west of Santa Cruz is the largest and most volcanically active of the islands, **Isabela**, whose main settlement, tiny **Puerto Villamil**, has an inter-island airport. Southerly **Floreana**, with its population of around a hundred people, has very little by way of infrastructure but does have a bizarre history of settlement.

The settled sites represent a mere three percent of the total land area of the archipelago. In response to the damage caused to flora and fauna by centuries of human interference, the rest of the land – more than 7600 square kilometres – has since 1959 been protected as a **national park**, with tourists restricted to the colonized areas and over sixty designated **visitor sites** spread across the islands. Most of these sites are reached by cruise boats only, or far less comprehensively by day-trips from the colonized areas, and visitors must be accompanied by a licensed

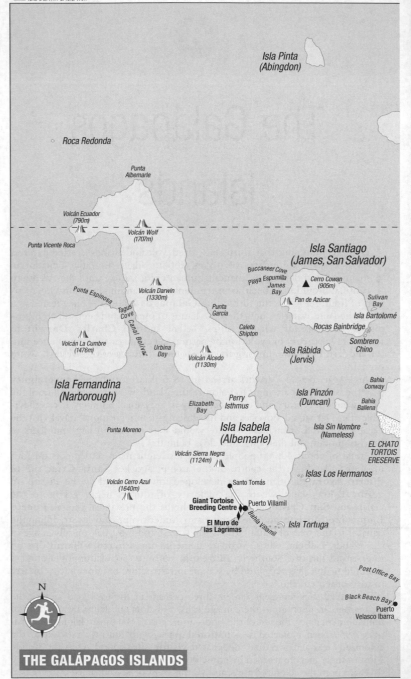

Isla Pinta
(Abingdon)

Roca Redonda

Punta
Albemarle

Volcán Ecuador
(790m)

Volcán Wolf
(1707m)

Punta Vicente Roca

Isla Santiago
(James, San Salvador)

Buccaneer Cove
Playa Espumilla
James
Bay

Cerro Cowan
(905m)

Pan de Azúcar

Sulivan
Bay

Punta Espinosa

Volcán Darwin
(1330m)

Tagus
Cove

Punta
García

Isla Bartolomé

Rocas Bainbridge

Canal Bolívar

Caleta
Shipton

Sombrero
Chino

Volcán La Cumbre
(1476m)

Urbina
Bay

Volcán Alcedo
(1130m)

Isla Rábida
(Jervis)

Isla Fernandina
(Narborough)

Elizabeth
Bay

Perry
Isthmus

Isla Pinzón
(Duncan)

Bahía
Conway

Bahía
Ballena

Punta Moreno

Isla Isabela
(Albemarle)

Isla Sin Nombre
(Nameless)

EL CHATO
TORTOIS
ERESERVE

Volcán Sierra Negra
(1124m)

Islas Los Hermanos

Volcán Cerro Azul
(1640m)

Santo Tomás

Giant Tortoise
Breeding Centre

Puerto Villamil

Bahía Vsiamil

Isla Tortuga

El Muro de
las Lágrimas

Post Office Bay

Black Beach Bay

Puerto
Velasco Ibarra

N

THE GALÁPAGOS ISLANDS

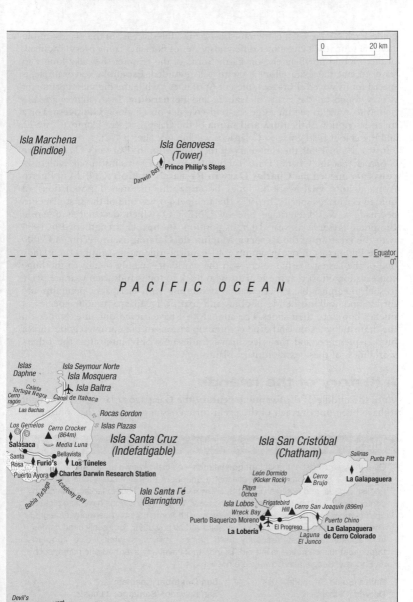

0   20 km

Isla Marchena
(Bindloe)

Isla Genovesa
(Tower)
Prince Philip's Steps
Darwin Bay

Equator
0°

PACIFIC OCEAN

Islas
Daphne
Isla Seymour Norte
Isla Mosquera
Caleta
Tortuga Negra
Cerro
Dragón
Isla Baltra
Canal de Itabaca
Las Bachas
Rocas Gordon
Los Gemelos
Cerro Crocker
(864m)
Islas Plazas
Salasaca
Media Luna
Isla Santa Cruz
(Indefatigable)
Isla San Cristóbal
(Chatham)
Salinas
Punta Pitt
Santa
Rosa
Bellavista
Furio's
Los Túneles
Cerro
Brujo
La Galapaguera
Puerto Ayora
Charles Darwin Research Station
León Dormido
(Kicker Rock)
Bahía Tortuga
Academy Bay
Isla Santa Fé
(Barrington)
Playa
Ochoa
Isla Lobos
Frigatebird
Hill
Cerro San Joaquín (896m)
Wreck Bay
Puerto Baquerizo Moreno
El Progreso
Puerto Chino
La Galapaguera
de Cerro Colorado
La Lobería
Laguna
El Junco

Devil's
Crown
Punta Cormorant
Isla Enderby
Isla Campeón
Isla Española
(Hood)
Isla Gardner
Gardner Bay
Isla Floreana
(Charles, Santa María)
Punta Suárez

guide. Each site has been chosen to show off the full diversity of the islands, and in a typical tour you'll encounter different species of flora and fauna every day, many of them found nowhere else on Earth. Some of the remoter sites take longer to travel to, but the extra effort is often well rewarded: **Española**, for example, is special for its waved albatrosses (present April–Dec), while the flightless cormorant is only found on the coasts of **Isabela** and **Fernandina**. Birdwatchers are also bound to want to see the large sea-bird colonies on far-flung **Genovesa**. For a fuller description of the **flora and fauna** of the Galápagos, see "Contexts", p.522, and the colour field guide to Galápagos wildlife (see after p.472).

It was also in 1959, the centenary of the publication of Darwin's *On the Origin of Species*, that the Charles Darwin Foundation (CDF) was instituted, which six years later opened the **Charles Darwin Research Station** (CDRS) in Puerto Ayora, whose vital work includes boosting the threatened populations of unique Galápagos species. In 1978 the archipelago was one of the first places to be made a World Heritage Site by UNESCO, which declared it a World Biosphere Reserve six years later. Its position was further strengthened in 1986 with the creation of the **Reserva Marina de Galápagos**, protecting 133,000 square kilometres of ocean within a 40-nautical-mile radius around the islands, one of the largest marine reserves in the world. It's mainly thanks to the huge conservation effort that the tourists who flock to the islands each year are privy to such incomparable experiences as swimming with Galápagos penguins and turtles, and walking beside boobies and marine iguanas as unique species of finches hop onto their shoes. The animals that have carved out an existence on the dramatic volcanic landscape conjure up visions of life completely devoid of human presence, and their legendary fearlessness only intensifies the other-worldliness of these extraordinary islands.

A history of the islands

Until the middle of the twentieth century, the Galápagos Islands were thought to have been out of reach of the prehistoric coastal peoples of the continental

The names of the Galápagos Islands

Over the years most of the **Galápagos Islands** – officially known as the **Archipiélago de Colón** – have come to own at least a couple of names, usually one given by English pirates, and another official Spanish name given in 1892, marking the fourth centenary of Columbus's discovery of the New World. Many islands have also picked up a number of other names along the way, with some boasting as many as eight. The official names are listed first below, followed by any other commonly used names in brackets; the most frequently used name – which is what we've adopted throughout this chapter – is in bold. Islands that have only ever had one name, such as Enderby, Beagle and Cowley, are not listed.

Baltra (South Seymour)
Darwin (Culpepper)
Española (Hood)
Fernandina (Narborough)
Genovesa (Tower)
Isabela (Albemarle)
Marchena (Bindloe)
Pinta (Abingdon)
Pinzón (Duncan)
Rábida (Jervis)

San Cristóbal (Chatham)
San Salvador (**Santiago**, James)
Santa Cruz (Indefatigable, Duke of Norfolk)
Santa Fé (Barrington)
Santa María (**Floreana**, Charles)
Seymour Norte (North Seymour)
Sin Nombre (Nameless)
Tortuga (Brattle)
Wolf (Wenman)

Galápagos time

Galápagos time is GMT minus 6 hours, 1 hour behind the Ecuadorian mainland.

mainland. In 1947, explorer and archeologist Thor Heyerdahl proved otherwise with his famous voyage from Peru to Polynesia on a balsa raft, the *Kon-Tiki*; in 1953 his excavations on the islands revealed over 130 shards of **pre-Columbian pottery** from coastal Peru and Ecuador, but no signs of permanent settlements, leading him to theorize the islands were used as a seasonal fishing base. Other early visitors could have included the great Inca **Tupac Yupanqui**, grandfather of Atahualpa; according to the early Spanish chronicler Pedro Sarmiento de Gamboa, Yupanqui may have journeyed to the islands in about 1485 following reports that they held gold, returning almost a year later with "some black men, much gold, a chair made of brass and the skin and jawbone of a horse". This unlikely plunder casts doubts on the story's veracity, handing the prize of first documented visitor to **Tomás de Berlanga**, Bishop of Panama, whose ship ended up here after being swept off course en route to Peru in 1535. He and his men spent a desperate week on the islands, having to chew cactus pads for their water, before the winds picked up so they could set sail again. He later wrote about how water from a well they had dug "came out saltier than that of the sea" and remarked the earth was "like dross, worthless" and the birds "so silly that they do not know how to flee". He also noted the islands' "many seals, turtles, iguanas, tortoises", references picked up by a Flemish cartographer, **Abraham Ortelius**, who named the islands "Galápagos" (Spanish for "tortoises") on his 1574 map, *Orbis Terrarum*. The islands' other name at that time, Las Encantadas ("enchanted" or "bewitched"), came from the strong currents and swaths of deep mist that made landing here so difficult, as if the shore itself was being moved by unearthly powers.

Pirates

Their reputation for being haunted made the Galápagos a perfect base for a number of seventeenth- and eighteenth-century **English pirates**, who came to the Pacific to pick off merchant ships as they sailed along the mainland coast. Among the most notorious was **John Cook**, who captured a Danish slave ship and renamed it the *Bachelor's Delight* after sixty female slaves were found in the hold, before using it to take three merchant ships off the coast of Peru in 1684. He then hid out in the Galápagos, only to discover he had a disappointing booty of thousands of sacks of flour and "eight tons of quince marmalade". Among his crew was **William Dampier**, who wrote the first comprehensive description of the islands in *A New Voyage Round the World*, and **William Ambrose Cowley**, the first man to chart the islands, naming them after English notables. In 1709 **Alexander Selkirk**, the inspiration for Daniel Defoe's novel *Robinson Crusoe*, turned up here after being rescued from the Juan Fernández Archipelago off the coast of Chile by English privateer **Woodes Rogers**. Selkirk helped Rogers sack Guayaquil before sailing to the Galápagos to make repairs and stock up on tortoises which, because they were able to stay alive for up to a year without food or water, were prized provisions for long sea voyages.

Whalers

The buccaneers' secret became well known after **James Colnett**, on the HMS *Rattler* in 1793, revealed in a report to the Admiralty that the Galápagos would be a convenient base for **whalers** to careen their boats and obtain provisions. Sperm whales were then one of the major sources of oil, a growing necessity in early industrial Britain, and the cold currents around the Galápagos guaranteed to attract large numbers. The whalers caused incalculable damage to the whale populations and decimated the Galápagos **tortoise** population too, through provisioning their vessels. Each ship may have loaded as many as 600 of the creatures before setting sail; an estimated total of around 200,000 tortoises were taken during the whaling era, bringing giant tortoise subspecies to extinction on Floreana, Rábida and Santa Fé islands. In the late nineteenth century, almost every whaling ship in the Pacific called at the islands to stock up. One of them, the *Acushnet*, carried the most famous whaler of them all, **Herman Melville**, who related his experiences in *Las Encantadas*, a book describing the islands as "five-and-twenty heaps of cinders" where "the chief sound of life... is a hiss".

The first settlers

The first documented **settler**, Irishman **Patrick Watkins**, demanded to be put ashore on Floreana in the early nineteenth century after quarrelling with his captain. Despite making a shelter and cultivating vegetables to sell to passing whalers, his ferocious appearance – matted red beard, blistered sunburnt skin and ragged clothes "covered with vermin" – was "so wild and savage…that he struck everyone with horror". Sailors assumed he spent all his time drinking

---

Darwin, the Galápagos and evolution

When **Charles Darwin** began his five-year voyage around the world in 1831, he was little more than an enthusiastic amateur naturalist set on a career in the clergy. His formative years had been directionless, and at Edinburgh University he found the lectures stultifying; even those in geology – a subject that became a passion in later life – he described as "incredibly dull". At Cambridge, studying divinity, he only just scraped through without honours. Yet it was there where he met Professor of Botany John Henslow, who recognized in the 22-year-old a talented mind with a flair for science. Henslow immediately recommended Darwin to Captain FitzRoy, who was seeking a naturalist on an expedition to chart the coast of South America. They set sail on **HMS Beagle** in December 1831.

Darwin suffered from terrible seasickness; whenever he could, he stayed on land and in the five-year voyage spent only eighteen months at sea. On September 15, 1835, the *Beagle* arrived at the Galápagos. "Nothing could be less inviting," he wrote, "the country is comparable to what one might imagine the cultivated parts of the Infernal regions to be." In the five weeks spent in the archipelago, he feverishly set about collecting samples and was taken aback by the "tameness" of the islands' creatures.

Darwin noticed countless things previous visitors hadn't. Still, it's clear his experiences on the islands only planted the seeds of ideas that were to blossom on his return to England. Indeed, already exhausted from four years of hard travel, Darwin's normally fastidious sampling was somewhat slapdash in the Galápagos. He failed to label the source islands of his bird collections ("it never occurred to me that, the productions of islands only a few miles apart, and placed under the same physical conditions, would be dissimilar"), and even misidentified the now celebrated **Darwin's finches**. It wasn't until his return to London, after the taxonomist John Gould had examined Darwin's samples and told him about the thirteen closely related species of finch, that the penny dropped. Despite giving acclaimed lectures about his geological discoveries and publishing the *Voyage of the Beagle* in 1839, he only hinted at the big ideas troubling him. For example, about the finches, he writes "there is not space in this work, to enter on this curious subject".

rum; in truth, he was hatching a plot to get off the islands, as no captain would take him. After two years, he managed to steal a ship, abduct four people to crew it and sail to Guayaquil, arriving ominously alone. Mainland life clearly wasn't for him – he was later imprisoned in Peru on suspicion of wanting to steal another boat to take him back to the Galápagos.

General José Villamil decided to claim the archipelago for the new-founded Republic of Ecuador in 1832. He gave the islands Spanish names and immediately set about colonizing Floreana with eighty soldiers condemned for mutiny whose death sentences had been commuted for a life of hard labour in the Galápagos. His idea was to start a trade in orchilla moss, used to make a deep-red dye, but the business never took off, and to add to his troubles, the government kept deporting hundreds of unruly criminals and prostitutes to the colony from the mainland. Eventually Villamil gave up and was replaced by the brutal **Colonel José Williams** who, despite keeping a large pack of ferocious dogs for protection, was chased off the islands after the colonists revolted. By 1852 the colony had been abandoned, setting a long-standing precedent of failure. The infamous **Manuel Cobos** (see p.472) came to a sticky end after a tyrannous rule over a settlement on San Cristóbal, and entrepreneur **José de Valdizán** was murdered in 1878 following a futile eight-year attempt to revive Villamil's colony on Floreana. **Antonio Gil** made a third attempt at the place in 1893, but after four years moved operations to Isabela, founding Puerto

Instead, he set about working over his ideas in near secret in his famous **Transmutation Notebooks**, the first of which begins: "Had been greatly struck… on character of South American fossils and species on Galápagos Archipelago. These facts origin (especially latter) of all my views." He saw the volcanic islands were relatively new and that life on the islands bore a resemblance to species in South America but were different in crucial ways. Darwin also realized life had come to the barren islands by air or sea and had adapted to the harsh environment through a process he termed "**natural selection**". In this, he maintained that at a given time certain members of a species are more suited to their surroundings than others and are therefore more likely to survive in it, so passing on their advantageous characteristics to their offspring. Over the course of time an entire population would come to develop those special features, eventually to such a degree as to become a new species – what Darwin called "**descent with modification**", rather than "evolution", which implied progressive movement towards the highest point of development. In his groundbreaking model, change was without direction and could result in a number of new species coming from a single ancestor.

It pained Darwin to know his ideas would upset the public and the Church, and he sat on his theory for nearly twenty years, quietly amassing the information to back it up. It took a letter from **Alfred Russel Wallace**, who had arrived at a similar conclusion (though without Darwin's intellectual rigour), to jerk him into action. In 1858 they offered a joint paper on their findings to the Linnaean Society in London and a year later Darwin published **On the Origin of Species**, which sold out in a day. It sent shockwaves throughout the Western world and opened up to science areas that had previously been the province of philosophers and theologians. Intense debate followed, but by the time of Darwin's death in 1882, the notion of evolution was well established. The most important, original and far-seeing part of his theory – natural selection – was still highly controversial; it was only in the 1930s that it received the full recognition it deserved, forming the basis of modern biology and forever changing humanity's view of itself.

Villamil, where he and his group eked out a living ferrying sulphur from a nearby crater to Guayaquil.

Scientists

While colonists were struggling, **scientists** were visiting in droves, largely thanks to the enormous publicity **Charles Darwin**'s 1835 voyage on the HMS *Beagle* had generated (see box, pp.442–443). Over the next century, scientific expeditions from around the world raced to build up wildlife collections for museums, often contributing to the damage wreaked by the whalers and settlers. In some instances, expeditions claimed a species was on the verge of extinction, so justifying the removal of the last few specimens they could find – only for future expeditions to do the same with any survivors. The 1905 voyage of the *Academy* gathered the largest collection, taking over 8500 bird specimens and 266 giant tortoises, including 86 from Isla Pinzón – from where four previous expeditions each believed they had taken the last surviving specimens – and one from Fernandina, the only tortoise ever recorded on this island.

The early twentieth century

In the early **twentieth century**, European colonists began appearing on the islands, the most extraordinary of whom were three groups of Germans – the Wittmers, the Ritters and a mad baroness plus lovers, protagonists of the so-called **Galápagos affair** (see box, p.480). During this period, international powers were starting to regard the islands as a place of considerable strategic importance,

Conservation in the Galápagos

No species has done more to upset the delicately balanced ecosystem of the Galápagos than **humans**. In one study of thousands of fossil bones, it was found that nearly every extinction of native species followed the arrival of Tomás de Berlanga, the first recorded visitor, in 1535. From that point onwards, the hunting of tortoises, fish, whales, fur seals and other animals has brought populations to the brink. Although our depredation of native species within the park has ceased, and fishing in the marine reserve is strictly controlled, a concerted conservation effort will always be needed to offset the impact of human colonization.

The introduction of foreign species

By far the worst human legacy on the islands has been the catastrophic introduction of **alien species**. When settlers arrived they brought with them plants, and domestic and farm animals that soon went wild, overrunning the islands and out-competing native species. **Pigs** trample vegetation, snaffle up land bird hatchlings and young tortoises and devour turtle eggs. Packs of feral **dogs** have attacked land iguanas, killing hundreds at a time on Santa Cruz and Isabela, and **black rats**, thought to be responsible for the extinction of endemic rice rats on four islands, killed every tortoise hatchling on Pinzón for most of the twentieth century. Wild **goats** are regarded as the biggest threat, denuding entire islands of vegetation, causing plant species to become extinct as well as depriving native species, particularly tortoises, of food, and encouraging soil erosion. Among some 490 accidentally introduced insect species are about 55 highly invasive types; these include two species of **wasp**, which eat indigenous butterfly and moth larvae, and the **fire ant**, only 2mm long and easy to transport unwittingly to new islands, which is having a devastating effect on native insects as well as attacking hatchling and adult tortoises. Introduced plants are also a major threat, disrupting the food chain from the bottom up. About ninety percent were introduced through agriculture, including **guava**, **blackberry**, **red quinine** and **elephant grass**, which are out of control on several islands, squeezing out native especially as a base from which to guard the entrance to the **Panama Canal**. By the time the canal was completed in 1914, a bidding war over the islands had already begun between several countries, including the US, Britain and France. However tempting the US's $15 million offer in 1911 for a 99-year lease was, Ecuador stuck firm – by this time the islands were a part of the national identity. After the Japanese attacked Pearl Harbor in 1941 it was clear the Panama Canal would need protection, and the Ecuadorian government granted the US permission to use Baltra as an air base. It was returned after the war and the runway there remains one of the island's main points of access.

Tourism, immigration and the issues today

Ever since regular flights began in the late 1960s, organized tourism has grown at a phenomenal rate to reach annual overseas visitor figures of around 173,000 in 2008 – up from about 70,000 in 2000 and a fourfold increase in twenty years, despite strict controls. The industry's success has also encouraged immigration to the islands, with the current population estimated at around 40,000, jumping from a little over 1000 in the 1950s. A government law passed in 1998 has failed to stem the flow. The success of tourism has been both a boon and bane. Revenues have undoubtedly helped insulate the Galápagos from the terrible economic crises suffered on the mainland, and provided a financial motive and backing for the crucial and highly successful conservation effort, as well as raising the profile of the islands around the world. But the

plants such as tree ferns, scalesia, guayabillo, cat's claw and others; sixty percent of native plants are thought to be under threat.

The Galápagos National Park Service (GNPS) and the CDF have been following a three-pronged approach to the problem of introduced species. **Eradication programmes** have done enough to allow some threatened native species to recover. Feral pigs, donkeys and goats have been eliminated from Santiago, and goats have been eliminated from six of the islands and islets. On Isabela, trained dogs kitted with leather boots to protect their paws from the lava surface are being used to track goats down; captured goats – the so-called "Judas goats" – are radio-collared and released, eventually leading hunters back to the herd. The second vital strand of the conservation effort are **repopulation programmes**, such as the one for giant tortoises, where eggs are gathered, incubated, hatched and raised until large enough to survive predatory attacks before being repatriated. Land iguanas and rice rats have undergone the same treatment, with positive results. A **quarantine system** in ports and airports has inspectors checking incoming cargoes for alien pests and seeds and the usual stowaway frogs, rats and insects.

Friends of Galápagos

The best thing you can do as a visitor to help the conservation effort is to join the **Friends of Galápagos**, a network of international conservation organizations. Membership entitles you to detailed news bulletins about the islands and ongoing conservation work, and information on events and appeals. The Friends provide vital funding for the CDRS and the GNPS, both at the heart of Galápagos conservation. In the UK, contact the Galápagos Conservation Trust (GCT), 5 Derby St, London W1J 7AB (☏020/7629 5049, ⓦ www.savegalapagos.org); in the US, contact the Galápagos Conservancy, 11150 Fairfax Blvd, Suite 408, Fairfax, VA 22030 (☏703/383-0077, ⓦwww.galapagos.org); check the GCT website for other national Friends organizations or join up in the islands at the CDRS.

wealth has also attracted large numbers of national migrants, and both tourists and residents put pressure on the islands' stretched resources and infrastructure. Then there are the imported goods; building materials, oil, agricultural fertilizers and produce are all part of the surge in cargo traffic that has resulted in a sharp increase in the number of potentially harmful alien species, up to a total of 1321 in 2007; in 1900 it was a little more than a hundred. See the box on pp.444–445 for more details.

Economic migrants who work outside the tourist industry can also create problems. **Farmers** cultivate a variety of introduced species, many of which have "escaped" into the wild, while **fisherman** do their best to make a living from the waters of the marine reserve within the regulations of the 1998 **Special Law for the Galápagos**, which allows only "local artisanal fishing" within it. The law did not go down well and the imposed quota on **sea cucumbers**, a delicacy in the lucrative Asian market, led to violent clashes with park authorities. Then again, overfishing had been so bad that current quotas are not even being met. Some poachers, both Ecuadorian and international, use outlawed methods, such as **long-lining**, which kills large numbers of sea birds as well as endangered fish. The Ecuadorian Navy and park wardens regularly detain illegal fishing boats, occasionally finding hundreds of **shark fins** (used in shark-fin soup) on board; the non-commercial part of the catch – sea lions, turtles, dolphins, pelicans, boobies and the shark carcasses themselves – are simply dumped at sea.

The combined threats to the Galápagos are so acute that in 2007 the UN declared it a **World Heritage Site in Danger**. The response of president Rafael Correa was to declare the conservation of the archipelago a "national priority". In a related move, the 2008 constitution made Ecuador the first country in the world to grant legal **rights to nature**, stating that it "has the right to exist, persist, maintain and regenerate its vital cycles, structure, functions and its processes in evolution". How this will be implemented in reality isn't yet clear, but it does show there is currently a strong political will to protect the Galápagos. Balancing the needs of all parties within this uniquely sensitive environment is one of the greatest challenges facing the islands today.

Geography and geology

The thirteen large islands (more than 10 square kilometres in area) and over forty small islands, islets and rocks (many of them unnamed) making up the **Galápagos Archipelago** cluster around the equator some 960km west of mainland Ecuador. The total land area of the archipelago is 7882 square kilometres; Isabela, the largest island, consisting of six separate volcanoes joined together by lava, takes up well over half of this. It also has the highest point on the archipelago, Volcán Wolf, at 1707m, bisected by the **equator** line.

The origins of the islands

The archipelago is purely **volcanic** in origin, and remains one of the most volatile such regions on the planet; the most recent eruption was La Cumbre on Fernandina in 2009. Unlike most of the world's volcanic areas, the islands don't lie on the borders of two tectonic plates, a fact that has puzzled scientists. The **hot spot theory**, in which a fixed area of extraordinary heat in the magma occasionally bubbles up to form a volcano, offers the most plausible explanation for this. The archipelago sits on the **Nazca plate**, which is moving eastwards and downwards to South America at a rate of 3.4cm a year: as the plate shifts, the volcano comes off the hot spot, becomes extinct and is eventually eroded by the elements and submerged beneath the sea. Meanwhile, new volcanoes appear over the hot spot. This would explain why the most easterly islands are the oldest and most weathered; San Cristóbal is thought to be between 2.3 and 6.3 million years old. In the west, Isabela and Fernandina are thought to have been created less than 700,000 years ago and are the most active and clearly volcanic islands. Two chains of extinct and eroded underwater mountains and volcanoes – the Cocos and Carnegie ridges, which extend for hundreds of kilometres northeast and east respectively of the Galápagos – are evidence the hot spot has been working for millions of years.

Volcanic formations

The beautiful **volcanic formations** you'll see on the islands are often quite different from those found on the mainland. This is due to **basaltic lava** which, rather than producing high cones such as Cotopaxi, makes **shield-shaped volcanoes**, such as the one at Fernandina. The broad tops of these can collapse into empty magma chambers below, leaving enormous **calderas**, huge depressions many times the size of the original vents, or **craters**, circular basins rimmed by lava walls at the volcano's summit; Volcán Sierra Negra on Isabela has a crater 10km across, one of the largest in the world. Like steam vents on the volcanoes, sulphur-encrusted **fumaroles** send puffs of gas into the air, as at Volcán Chico on the north side of Sierra Negra.

Much of the Galápagos landmass consists of **lava flows**, and you'll find two particularly interesting types on several islands. **Pahoehoe lava**, from the Hawaiian word meaning "ropey", describes the rippled effect caused when molten lava in contact with the air begins to solidify, but is then ruffled up by molten lava passing beneath it into tongue or rope-like shapes; Sulivan Bay, at Santiago, has excellent examples of this. **Aa lava**, named after the Hawaiian for "hurt", occurs when the surface of the lava flow buckles, breaks and then gets bulldozed by the continuing movement of the flow, resulting in layers of small, sharp rocks that can be very difficult to walk on. It can form a natural barrier to animals, as at the Perry Isthmus on Isabela, and castaways and buccaneers told of how this lava shredded their boots. If a lava flow hardens on the outside, and then the strength of the flow decreases, **lava tubes** are sometimes formed; there are several large enough to walk down on Santa Cruz.

Cones of various sizes and types frequently appear on the islands: **hornitos** (less than 1m high), resemble burst pimples solidified on a lava bed; the larger **spatter cones** give Bartolomé its spectacular lunar landscape; and the impressive **tuff cones** are often made up of stripy layers of rock-hard compacted ash. The **uplift** at Urbina Bay, on Isabela, is one of the more startling products of volcanic activity. In 1954, a five-kilometre stretch of reef was shunted 4m into the air by movements of magma beneath the crust, leaving its marine inhabitants drying in the sun. Islands including Plazas, Baltra and Seymour Norte are entirely the result of uplifts.

Visiting the Galápagos

High air fares and a heavy park-entrance fee for foreigners mean that just getting to the Galápagos is a relatively pricey undertaking – and that's before stumping up for a **boat tour** or specialist **scuba-diving tour**. Such tours, which last anything from three days to several weeks and vary greatly in levels of quality and price, are undoubtedly the best way to see the islands. Many people prearrange tours at home – the most expensive but hassle-free way – but **budget travellers** can cut costs by making arrangements in Quito or Guayaquil, or even waiting until their arrival in the Galápagos before choosing an operator. The tours sail between **visitor sites**, specially chosen to show off a representative portion of an island; often they comprise a tidy trail bordered by little black-and-white stakes, along which an accredited guide will lead you. Most cruises combine a variety of sites – usually stopping at two a day – which often have different endemic animals and plants popping up at each, but the popularity of the Galápagos does mean that even on longer tours to remoter islands, you'll probably be sharing the sites with several other groups. Boat tours mostly sail between islands by night, but **land-based tours**, where you sleep ashore and sail to nearby visitor sites in the day, are also available.

An alternative to a cruise is **independent travel** around the Galápagos, made possible by using **inter-island flights and ferries**, though these largely restrict you to the colonized areas, which rather misses the point of a trip here. Still, there are a few visitor sites close to the main settlements that you can reach on your own without a licensed guide. You can also take **day-trips** from the larger towns, namely Puerto Ayora and to a lesser extent Puerto Baquerizo Moreno, to a handful of sites around the central islands.

The most expensive, bureaucratic and complicated way to see the islands is to sail on **your own boat**; you'll need to have permission from the directorate of the Parque Nacional Galápagos prior to departure from a mainland port for the islands, then submit your vessel to inspections, quarantines and fumigations at that port; check their website for details ⓦ www.galapagospark.org.

When to visit

Wildlife spotting is good throughout the year, but certain species, like the waved albatross, are only seen at certain times of year; see the colour wildlife guide beginning after p.472, and p.522.

The Galápagos Islands do have a two-season **climate** governed by the strong **ocean currents** swirling around them. The **Humboldt current** (or Peru current) is particularly prevalent in the cool season, helped on by brisk southeast winds. It cools the sea and forms the **garúa mist**, hanging at 300m to 600m where the cool, moist air over the water meets the warm air above that's heated by the sun. The winds blow the mists onto the southeast (windward) sides of the islands, giving consistent precipitation at these altitudes, while the northern (leeward) sides receive very little rain. In the warm season, the winds fall off, allowing warm currents from Panama (the Panama flow) to displace the Humboldt current. Sea temperatures rise, the mist dissipates and normal rain clouds can form.

The islands are relatively dry all year, but during the **warm–wet season** (Jan–June) short and heavy bursts of rain break the sunny skies while temperatures nudge 30°C (86°F). You can also expect sea temperatures to be between 20°C and 26°C (68–79°F), reaching perhaps as high as 29°C (84°F) around the northeastern islands. This season is regarded as the best for **surfing**, particularly at the beginning till February. In the **cool–dry season** (July–Dec), the air temperature drops to around 22°C (72°F), the oceans become choppier and the skies are more consistently overcast, though very little rain falls on the lowlands. Sea temperatures can dip as low as 16°C (61°F), especially in August and September, so consider bringing a wet suit if you plan to snorkel. At this time of year, the *garúa* mists linger over the oceans and bathe the uplands in a near-perpetual fine drizzle, occasionally descending to sea level. The transitional months between seasons can show quite changeable weather combining any of these elements.

For tourism, the Galápagos **high season** begins around mid-June and lasts till August, starting up again in December and carrying on until mid-January. Exact

Galápagos essentials

Money:
- Take sufficient cash in US dollars; you need to pay the $100 park entrance fee in cash on arrival and tip guides and boat crew.
- Prices are higher than on the mainland for everything; there are usually high service charges for using credit cards.
- Shops and agencies on the islands generally prefer MasterCard, then Visa, though American Express and Diners are sometimes accepted.
- There are branches of Banco del Pacífico in Puerto Ayora and Puerto Baquerizo Moreno only, where you can change dollar or euro traveller's cheques (limit $1500 and €1200 respectively), use an ATM (MasterCard, Cirrus and Visa; $300 limit a day), and get cash advances on Visa and MasterCard.

Clothing:
- Shorts, t-shirt, hat and sunglasses are fine for sunny days; shorts are also needed for wet landings (wading ashore).
- Trousers and long sleeves for sea breezes, evenings and cooler, overcast dry-season days.
- Lightweight raincoat is usually sufficient for the odd cloudburst and *garúa* drizzle.
- Sturdy boots or shoes for the jagged lava.
- Swimwear and sandals for the beach.

Health items:
- Earplugs – excellent for blocking out your boat's engine noise at night.
- Seasickness medication for sufferers.
- Plenty of sunscreen, lip protection and skin creams.
- A water bottle for when you're at visitor sites.
- Insect repellent in the wet season or for the moister highland areas.
- Plenty of solution or eye drops for contact lens wearers; it can be very hot, dry, dusty and irritating to the eyes.

Photography and vision:
- A zoom or telephoto lens is not essential, but a big bonus for more dramatic photos.
- Plenty of film. If using digital, bring sufficient memory cards for your laptop, so you can regularly free space on your cards.
- A polarizing filter helps maintain vivid colours in harsh sunlight.
- Binoculars are useful, even though most of the time you'll be watching wildlife from close quarters.
- A small dry bag is good for keeping sea spray, rain and dust off your equipment, and a day pack to carry this, your water bottle and spare clothing at the visitor sites.
- A torch (flashlight) comes in handy for visiting lava tunnels or when staying in the remoter settlements, which have erratic electricity supplies.

Snorkelling and diving:
- Mask, snorkel and fins are great for seeing underwater fish and animals. Bring your own if possible, as they are often not supplied or may not fit if they are. You can also rent from diving operators in Puerto Ayora (see "Listings", p.462).
- From July to December a wet suit or jacket is a good idea for the cold water.
- Scuba divers should bring with them as much of their own equipment as practical (see p.454).

times vary, usually according to demand, with some operators only counting May to mid-June, and September, as **low season**.

Getting to the Galápagos

All **flights** to the Galápagos (a 3hr trip in total) depart from Quito and stop over in Guayaquil for around forty minutes. TAME flies twice daily to Baltra, a bus ride from Puerto Ayora on Santa Cruz; and on Wednesday and Friday to Puerto Baquerizo Moreno on San Cristóbal. Aerogal flies once or twice daily to Baltra, and once to Puerto Baquerizo Moreno on Monday, Tuesday, Thursday, Saturday and Sunday. Wherever you fly to, **prices** are fixed at $416 return from Quito and $345 from Guayaquil, with low-season discounts (May 1– June 14 & Sept 15– Oct 31) at $360 from Quito and $321 from Guayaquil. In the high season, a fifteen percent discount is offered to students holding a valid green ISIC. You can switch between Galápagos airports on your ticket for free, or fly out to one and return from another. You can also depart from Quito and return to Guayaquil (or vice versa) for slightly reduced fares. In high season it can be difficult to get a place, so make sure you're not being put on the waiting list. You should reconfirm inward and outward flights two days in advance and that the **luggage allowance** is 20kg. **Cargo boats** from Guayaquil and the mainland are prohibited from taking tourists to the Galápagos.

Having flown in from the mainland, those with a pre-booked cruise – the majority of tourists on most flights – will be given free transfer to their boat. If arriving in Baltra, your boat will either be waiting at the island's dock nearby, or at Puerto Ayora on Santa Cruz, a short hop by ferry from Baltra over the Canal de Itabaca to a connecting bus on the other side (45min). In Puerto Baquerizo Moreno, San Cristóbal, buses will take you the few minutes to the harbour. For more information on airport arrival, see p.458 for Baltra and p.470 for Puerto Baquerizo Moreno.

Park entrance fees

On arrival in the Galápagos you have to pay a $100 **park entrance fee** in cash at the airport. **Discounts** for foreigners only apply for under-12s ($50), under-2s (no charge), citizens of Andean Community or Mercosur countries ($50), registered foreign residents ($6) and students who have matriculated in an Ecuadorian university ($25). Your **passport** will be stamped and you'll be given a **receipt**; hold onto it as your boat operator will need it, even if you're just doing day-trips.

You will also need to pay $10 for the **Galápagos Transit Card**, which has been introduced to discourage illegal migration; usually it's bought at point of departure or tour companies can sort this out for you prior to arrival.

Important rules of the Galápagos

- Do not touch, feed, disturb or chase any animal.
- Do not move plants, rocks, shells or any natural objects.
- Do not take food onto the islands.
- Make sure you're not carrying soil or seeds from one island to another on your clothes or shoes.
- Never throw litter overboard or on the islands.
- Do not buy souvenirs made of plant or animal products from the islands.
- Declare any organic products in your possession to the quarantine services on arrival.
- Plants, fresh flowers and live animals may not be brought to the islands.

Galápagos cruises

Around eighty **boats** currently have licences to tour the Galápagos; these are divided into several categories of comfort and range from converted fishing boats for a handful of people to luxury cruisers for a hundred. The majority carry between ten and twenty passengers, and almost all boats rely on engine power to get them between islands, although several boost their speed with sails.

Boats and costs

Economy boats can cost as little as $80 per person per day in the low season or $100–150 in the high season. Many of these boats are poky, often having tiny bunk-bed cabins and shared bath, as well as uninspiring food and Class-I guides, who are Galápagos locals with the lowest level of naturalist training and only a fair amount of English. The boats are slower, tend to stick to the central islands and, if the weather's bad, generally suffer most from rocking and rolling. **Tourist boats** (around $150–$275 per person per day) should be a bit more spacious with slightly better facilities and Class-II guides, Ecuadorians with good education, often in related fields, who have at least five years' experience and can speak English, French or German fluently. **Tourist-superior boats** (from around $275–$350 per day) usually have more comfortable cabins still, sometimes with air conditioning, better food and Class-III guides, the highest level of accreditation, who have at least eight years' experience, degrees in biology, tourism or similar, and can speak fluent Spanish and English plus French or German. Many of the boats in the Galápagos are **first-class** or **luxury boats**, enjoying the best food, service, comfort and guides, who are always Class-III and invariably very highly qualified naturalists. Cabins typically have beds rather than bunks, private bath with hot water and air conditioning. They also tend to be faster – meaning less time on the move and often more time on the remoter islands – and a few have stabilizers to lessen the effects of rough seas. While the largest boats tend to have extra facilities (such as a pool), they take longer to disembark, giving you less time on shore. Tours on first-class and luxury boats are most often arranged in your home country (see Basics, pp.28–30 for details of specialist operators); for an eight-day cruise, costs start at around $2000 and can rise to over $4500, excluding flights and entrance fees.

If you're travelling alone you may be asked to pay a hefty **supplement** for your cabin, unless you're prepared to share. Other hidden costs include alcohol, rarely included in the price, and the **tip** at the end of the tour for the guide and crew; this will depend on the service you've received and what you can afford, but as a general rule an economy guide and crew will each expect around $25 per cabin per week, while operators of luxury boats suggest as much as $100 per person per week for the crew and $50 per person per week for the guide. If you can give the tip directly to the deserving, so much the better, as this avoids the possibility of unfair distribution of a general tip by an unscrupulous captain or guide.

Before you book

Before you plump for a tour, inspect the **itinerary** and make sure it takes in islands with the creatures you want to see. An eight-day tour is long enough for a good overview, but you still won't see absolutely everything, so plot the route on a map and use the colour field guide to Galápagos wildlife and the more detailed textual account beginning on p.522 to locate the whereabouts of some favourite species. To give you as much time at the sites as possible, don't pick tours that include more than a night in a single port, sail during the day (which means less time on the islands), or stop at too many sites you can

This list is not comprehensive but gives a good selection of **boat owners** themselves rather than general operators (a selection of the latter is listed in Chapter 1 "Quito" on p.115), who can make bookings on boats from a range of companies but will sometimes charge an extra commission; some are also agents for other companies. **Prices** listed are for an eight-day cruise in high season, per person, based on two sharing a cabin, not including air fare or park entrance fees. Agencies with offices in the Galápagos are listed under the relevant island.

Aida Maria Travel Amazonas N23-31 and Veintimilla ☎02/2546028, ⓦwww .galapagostours.net. One of the less expensive operators, with a fleet of three motor yachts (*Eden*, *Aida Maria* and *Rumba*), ranging from tourist class to first class, a diving boat (*Guantanamera*), a sailing catamaran (*Valkiria*) for tours of settled areas and a powerboat (*Maverick*) for land-based tours. From $1850.

Andando Tours/Angermeyer Cruises Mariana de Jesús E7-113 and Pradera ☎02/3237186, ⓦwww.andandotours.com. Andando is owned by a branch of the Angermeyer family, who came to the Galápagos in the 1930s. It has two good-looking first-class sailing yachts (*Mary Anne* and *Sagitta*) and also represents the owners of *Samba* and *The Beagle*. Look for news about the upcoming luxury sailing vessel *Mandalay*. From $2200.

Ecoventura Almagro N31-80, Edificio Venecia ☎02/22907396, ⓦwww.ecoventura .com; also branches in Guayaquil and the US. Operates three first-class motor yachts, *Eric*, *Flamingo I* and *Letty*, and a specialist diving boat, *Sky Dancer*. From $3225.

Enchanted Expeditions De las Alondras N45-102 and De los Lirios, Edificio Floralp ☎02/3340525, ⓦwww.enchantedexpeditions.com. A reliable and recommended operator running the luxury *Beluga* motor yacht and the first-class *Cachalote I*, an attractive 96-foot schooner for sixteen people. A good standard of service and guiding is complemented by some excellent cooking. From $2300.

Galasam Corner of Cordero N24-214 and Amazonas, Quito ☎02/2903909, ⓦwww .galasam.com; also in Guayaquil. Galasam has six boats covering a range of classes,

visit independently without a guide anyway. On the lower-end tours in particular, you should check exactly what you're getting: ask about what **food** you can expect (especially if you're vegetarian) and if water is free; whether there are **masks and snorkels** for all the passengers; if the **guide** speaks decent English; how much you will see on the first and last days; how many nights will be spent ashore; what the bathrooms and cabins are like; whether you'll have to share with strangers; and whether the boat will sail at night. Some **eight-day tours** are actually a combination of a four- and a five-day tour (with the swap-over day counting twice), which can waste time while new passengers are picked up. Most importantly, make sure your boat has adequate **safety equipment**, like life jackets, rafts and fire extinguishers. Following worries about safety standards on tour boats, the Ecuadorian government in 2000 stipulated that boats carrying more than fifteen passengers be required to hold an ISM (International Safety Management) certificate, which should be available for you to inspect on request.

Budget deals

Cruising the Galápagos Islands is not an activity well geared to **budget** travellers, but it is possible to minimize costs by getting a **last-minute deal**, especially in low season. Checking out the tour operators based in La Mariscal, Quito, is a good place to start, with the cheapest deals almost always found via companies that own their own boats. You'll get the best prices if you book at including the premium motor-catamarans *Queen of Galápagos* and *Millennium*, the first-class *Estrella de Mar I & II*, and *Cruz del Sur* and tourist-class *Princess of Galápagos*. From $1550.

Kem Pery Ramírez Dávalos 117 and Amazonas ☎02/2505599, ⩗www.kempery.com. Owns *Angelique*, a tourist-superior motor-sailer with capacity for sixteen people, which has a good reputation for inexpensive four-, five- or eight-day cruises. Special deals can be arranged combining a Galápagos trip with a stay at their jungle lodge in the Waorani reserve. From $2280.

Klein Tours Av Eloy Alfaro N34-151 and Catalina Aldaz ☎02/2267000, ⩗www.kleintours.com. Long-standing operator with two mid-sized first-class boats, *Coral I* and *Coral II*, as well as the luxury hundred-person cruiser, *Galápagos Legend*. From $2090.

Metropolitan Touring De las Palmeras N45-74 and De las Orquídeas ☎02/2988200, ⩗www.metropolitan-touring.com. One of the pioneers of tourism in the Galápagos, Metropolitan operates three large first-class boats: the ninety-person *Santa Cruz*, the forty-person *Isabela II* and the thirty-two-person *La Pinta*. It also offers land-based tours of the islands from its luxury hotel *Finch Bay* on Santa Cruz. From $3500.

Quasar Expeditions Jose Jussieu N41-28 and Alonso de Torres ☎02/2446996, ⩗www.galapagosexpeditions.com. A well-respected company offering top-level Galápagos tours on first-class and luxury yachts. Guiding, service and accommodation are excellent, and the boats *Grace* (from $4750), *Evolution* (from $4250) and *Alta* (from $4450) are among the most comfortable in the islands. The latter is also used for diving cruises. Itineraries are usually wide-ranging.

Rolf Wittmer Turismo Galápagos Foch E7-81 and Diego de Almagro ☎02/2563098, ⩗www.rwittmer.com. Rolf Wittmer, credited with being the first recorded native of Floreana island and son of the famous pioneering Wittmer family (see box, p.480), owns three first-class motor yachts, *Tip Top II*, *III* and *IV*, each with a sixteen-person capacity. From $2506.

Puerto Ayora in the Galápagos, where you'll be on the spot when the deals come up, and have the advantage of both meeting the guide and checking out the boat in advance. The downside is you could be waiting for several days or even weeks for a space; at busy times of year (July, August and over Christmas and the New Year), it's virtually impossible to get one. Many agencies in the Galápagos don't accept credit cards so it's a good idea to bring enough cash with you to pay for the cruise. For a typical eight-day tour on an economy boat count on paying $800–1000 in low season and a couple of hundred dollars more in the high season. Before you pay, ask about unexpected costs that can be associated with economy boats; for example, some don't have a water-maker and may charge for bottled water or supply town tap water, which needs purification. Less satisfactory options to cut costs are tours of four or five days, offered by many operators, or doing day-trips (see p.455), but these obviously won't give you the fullest picture of the islands. The largest discounts to be had are usually for first-class and luxury boats, though these may still be too expensive for shoestring travellers to afford.

The daily routine

Except for the most basic boats, life aboard a ship is relaxed and well organized. After an early breakfast, you'll set out in a dinghy (*panga*) for the visitor site and disembark with either a **wet landing** (wading ashore) or **dry landing** (on rocks or a dock). After three or four hours on the island, you'll return to the boat for lunch and a siesta before another visit in the afternoon; most days, there'll be a chance to have a swim or a snorkel. The boat usually sets sail for the next site after dinner, arriving early next morning; the engine noise and rocking of the boat may be disturbing on the first night, but even those without sea legs tend to get used to it.

Problems

The majority of tours pass without incident, but occasionally **problems** occur. Economy boats are usually the worst offenders; things that can go wrong include overbooking, petty theft, annoying engine noise and smells, food and water supplies running out, changes of itinerary, breakdowns and sexual harassment from guide or crew. One trick of operators is to swap boats at the last moment, so your tourist-superior boat has suddenly become a rickety old bucket; your contract should stipulate a refund if the category of boat changes and you should try to get a receipt from the agency and boat owner so it's clear what you've paid for. Even if the operator breaches the contract, getting a reimbursement can be hard work; if you feel wronged, report the operator to the Ministerio de Turismo and Capturgal (see p.458), who may be able to impose a fine on the operator and get you a **reimbursement**, and the Capitanía in Puerto Ayora. You can also tell the SAE in Quito (see p.77), which keeps a file of good and bad operators. In rare cases, irresponsible guides have disobeyed park rules, perhaps erring from the path, touching animals, bringing food onto the islands, disturbing nests or encouraging the crew to fish for food, which is illegal. This kind of behaviour should be reported to the Galápagos National Park Service.

Scuba-diving trips and tours

The Galápagos Islands are one of the best **scuba–diving** spots in the world. Marine turtles, hammerhead sharks, sea lions, fur seals, rays, eels, marine iguanas, sailfish, tuna, wahoo, barracudas, dolphins and even boobies are among creatures you might see. Unfortunately, diving here isn't easy and at times you'll have to contend with strong currents, surge, low visibility and cold water. As such, the islands are not considered a suitable place to learn to scuba dive from scratch, even though training courses are offered. There is a hyperbaric recompression chamber in Puerto Ayora (see "Listings", p.462), which is better than any facility on the mainland and is funded by a **$35 fee** to tourist divers. The fee doesn't entitle you to free treatment in an emergency; make sure you're properly insured as hyperbaric treatment is expensive. You should give your body at least 24 hours to adjust between diving and flying back to Quito.

Several companies organize **day-trip dives** from Puerto Ayora to a variety of sites for $80–120, including all equipment and a guide (see p.462 for details). These can be arranged with only a day's notice but are restricted to sites within range of port. There are plenty of such sites to choose from, including the reefs around Seymour Norte or Campeón near Floreana to wall dives at Daphne Minor or the Gordon Rocks near the Plazas. Less experienced divers will probably be asked to spend a couple of days diving at Academy Bay on Santa Cruz, where conditions are easier. **Diving-boat tours** cruise the islands, mixing one to four dives per day with land visits; you may even get to dive around islands such as Wolf and Darwin, where land visits are prohibited. On such tours you'll need to be an experienced diver with a certificate, and to bring most of your own equipment, usually with the exception of tanks (and air), weights and weight belts; in the cool season, your wet suit should be 6mm

▲ Galápagos sea lions, Isla Santiago

thick. Prices for eight-day diving tours start at around $2000 and rise to $4500 or more, depending on the level of luxury and standard of guiding; reservations should be made well in advance. In addition to the diving boats listed in the box on pp.452–453, you could also try diving specialists Scuba Galápagos (T 02/2503740, W www.scubagalapagos.com), who have a 12-person schooner, *Encantada*, and Deep Blue (T 02/2444558, W www.deepbluegalapagosdiving.com), operators of the 16-person motor vessel, *Deep Blue*. Luxury diving tours combining land visits are available with Aggressor Fleet (US T 1800/348-2628, W www.aggressor.com), who run two identical premier motor yachts, *Aggressor I* and *II*.

Day-trips and land-based tours

An inexpensive way to see the islands is to arrange **day-trips**, especially from Puerto Ayora. Costing around $60–90 per person, these usually include a guide of varying quality, lunch and a visit to one island. They're easy to organize as they're offered by many of the travel agencies in town, though you'll be limited to a handful of islands within striking distance of the port, namely Plaza Sur, Seymour Norte, Santa Fé and Floreana (if the boat leaves from Baltra, you may get to visit Bartolomé also). Some operators also offer **land-based** tours, where you sleep at night on shore and sail out to nearby visitor sites during the day – effectively a string of day-trips packaged together as a multi-day Galápagos tour. While this has the advantage of comfortable hotel accommodation and is usually less expensive than a conventional cruise (depending on the level of hotel used), the disadvantages are that sailing in the day makes for less time at the visitor sites and you'll be restricted to the busiest sites nearest to the population centres.

Independent travel between the islands

Independent travel between the islands will confine you to colonized areas and visitor sites close to towns you can visit without a guide. The most efficient but costly means of inter-island travel is by **flying** with EMETEBE (Ⓦwww .emetebe.com; see relevant town accounts for details). They have one nine-seater and one five-seater light aircraft, both of which make flights between San Cristóbal, Baltra and Isabela, daily from Monday to Saturday. Departure times are flexible depending on the requirements of passengers ($155 one-way, $260 return; each leg around 30min; book at least a day in advance). The luggage allowance is just 9kg (20lbs), and the charge for excess loads is $0.40 per kilogram.

Another option is to take a coop-run **lancha** or **fibra** (fiberglass motorboat), making daily trips from San Cristóbal to Santa Cruz (2hr journey) at 7am, returning 2pm; and from Isabela to Santa Cruz (2–3hr) leaving at 6am and returning 2pm. Tickets ($30 each way) can be bought from local travel agents. The ride can be rough and uncomfortable; bring plenty of water and sunscreen, check there are life jackets, and ideally take a boat with more than one engine. *Fibras* do not make any scheduled trips to Floreana and chartering is expensive. You may be able to hitch with a tour boat, or track down Claudio Cruz, who makes trips to Floreana from Santa Cruz at the weekends; ask for him at the port in Puerto Ayora or at Moonrise Travel (see p.463).

Isla Santa Cruz and around

The archipelago's centre and tourist hub, **SANTA CRUZ** is a conical island of just under 1000 square kilometres, whose luxuriant southeastern slopes are cloaked each year in *garúa* drizzle. Reaching an altitude of 864m, the island supports all Galápagos vegetation zones (see p.531), from cactus-strewn **deserts** around the coast, to tangled scalesia and miconia **forests** wreathed in cloud in the highlands, and sodden grassy **pampas** at the summit.

Santa Cruz's central location and proximity to the airport on Baltra have helped make it the most heavily populated island in the Galápagos. The majority of the 27,000 or so islanders live in the archipelago's largest town, **Puerto Ayora**, which is also the nerve centre of the conservation programme, headquarters of both the **Charles Darwin Research Station** and the **Parque Nacional Galápagos**. Home to more boats, tour brokers, hotels and restaurants than anywhere else in the islands, Puerto Ayora is also the best place for budget travellers to find last-minute places on cruises. There's plenty to do in the meantime, such as visiting **Bahía Tortuga**, the **Chato Tortoise Reserve** or exploring the island's several **lava tunnels**. Those itching to get to the wildlife can take day-trips by boat to the nearby islands in this central group, namely **Santa Fé**, **Plaza Sur** and **Seymour Norte**.

On the northwest side of Santa Cruz there are several worthwhile sites that can only be visited with guides by boat tours. Occasionally, day-trips sail there, but more commonly boats call at these spots having left the harbour at Baltra. A typical first stop is at **Las Bachas**, named for the barges the US abandoned on the beach here during World War II; their rusting skeletons still poke through the sand. It's a popular place for swimming, but also makes a good introduction to wildlife, with marine iguanas, hermit crabs, black-necked stilts, great blue herons and turtle nests – you may see turtle tracks from November to February – and flamingos tiptoeing around the saltwater lagoon behind the smaller beach. To the west is **Caleta Tortuga Negra**, a cove where Pacific green turtles (despite the cove's name) come to breed at the beginning of the warm-wet season. White-tipped reef sharks and rays can be spotted throughout the year, and the lagoon itself is fringed by mangroves, where herons and pelicans nest. On the northwestern tip of the island, the **Cerro Dragón** site consists of a gravel path winding up from flamingo lagoons to the top of the hill, passing land iguanas and their nests. Most have been repatriated since the extermination of feral dogs here in 1990. Heading further westwards, **Bahía Conway** (where in 1976 feral dogs attacked and killed a colony of five hundred land iguanas), and **Bahía Ballena**, a one-time whaling post, are seldom visited.

Puerto Ayora and around

Lying around the azure inlets of Academy Bay's rocky shore, **PUERTO AYORA**, on the southern coast of Santa Cruz, was home to fewer than a couple of hundred people until the early 1970s. Now, laden with souvenir shops, travel agents, restaurants and hotels, the current denizens enjoy a higher standard of living than any other province in the republic, giving it a distinct aura of well-appreciated privilege. There's a relaxed atmosphere to the place; tourists meander down the waterfront in the daytime, browsing through shops

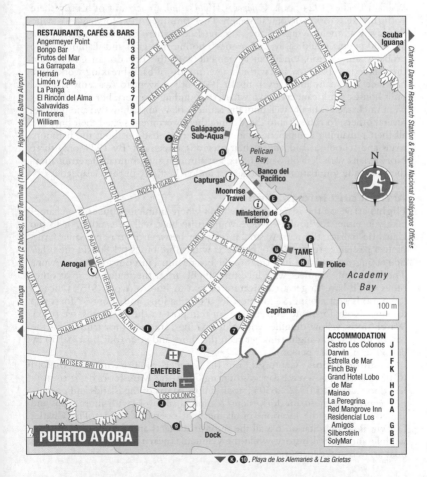

RESTAURANTS, CAFÉS & BARS

Angermeyer Point	10
Bongo Bar	3
Frutos del Mar	6
La Garrapata	2
Hernán	8
Limón y Café	4
La Panga	3
El Rincón del Alma	7
Salvavidas	9
Tintorera	1
William	5

ACCOMMODATION

Castro Los Colonos	J
Darwin	I
Estrella de Mar	F
Finch Bay	K
Grand Hotel Lobo de Mar	H
Mainao	C
La Peregrina	D
Red Mangrove Inn	A
Residencial Los Amigos	G
Silberstein	B
SolyMar	E

PUERTO AYORA

stuffed with blue-footed booby t-shirts and carvings of giant tortoises, while fishermen across the street in little **Pelican Bay** build boats and sort through their catches, watched by hungry pelicans. In the evenings, locals play five-a-side soccer and volleyball outside the Capitanía, and as it gets darker, the restaurant lights cast a modest glow over the bay and the bars fill with locals, tourists and research scientists, a genial mix that ensures Puerto Ayora has the best **nightlife** in the Galápagos.

Some history

The first record of human habitation in what is now Puerto Ayora is of a group of sailors, shipwrecked in 1905. They survived for three months by drinking sea-lion blood and chewing cactus pads, before discovering brackish water collecting in rock pools in Academy Bay, named after the California Academy of Sciences boat which – unbeknown to them – moored here only a few weeks earlier; they languished in the bay for a further three months until their rescue. Puerto Ayora itself was founded in the 1920s by a small group of Norwegians, lured to the Galápagos by ruthless promoters trading on the popularity of William Beebe's 1924 book, *Galápagos, World's End*, an account of his trip there with the New York Zoological Society. They promised the Norwegians – who gave away all their savings to go – a secret Eden where the "soil is so rich that 100,000 people could easily find homes", noting that gold and diamonds were probably around too. Under an agreement with the Ecuadorian government they landed on Floreana, but within a few months of back-breaking work some had died and many more given up. In 1926, others went to Academy Bay and built houses, a fish cannery and a wharf, so founding the port. For a time, things went uncharacteristically well until the cannery blew up, killing two and injuring several others. To rub salt into the wound, the government seized their boat and all their remaining equipment, claiming the settlers had not built the harbours, roads and schools as laid out in their previous agreement. By 1929, only three Norwegians were left on Santa Cruz, but through superhuman determination, they built the foundations for the largest and richest city in the Galápagos.

Arrival and information

Flights arrive on the island of Baltra, from where municipal **buses** (no charge) take you either to the dock where your cruise boat will be waiting, or to the Canal de Itabaca, the narrow stretch of water between Baltra and Santa Cruz. Here a passenger **ferry** ($0.80) connects with more buses ($1.80) on the other side taking you over the highlands to the bus terminal just outside Puerto Ayora. The buses only connect with incoming flights from the mainland, so at other times you'll have to get a **camioneta** or taxi to Puerto Ayora ($15). Once in town, **taxis** cost around $1 for most local destinations, and about $8 for a trip to Santa Rosa; for more information on transport to the highlands, see p.463. **Water taxis**, yellow dinghies with blue awnings, are useful for trips across the bay, or for day-and-night runs between the shore and your tour boat ($0.50 by day, $1 at night per person).

For **information**, Capturgal, on the corner of Darwin and Binford (☎05/2526206, ⓦwww.galapagostour.org), and the Ministerio de Turismo a few doors down (☎05/2526505), stock simple **maps** of the islands and population centres. At the main dock there's a municipal kiosk, with more maps and leaflets, including the locations of all the boat operators' offices. The Charles Darwin Research Station has all the nitty-gritty facts and figures of Galápagos wildlife and natural history, while the Capitanía, near the dock, keeps tabs on boat arrivals and departures.

Accommodation

The price of **accommodation** is higher than on the mainland, yet even the thriftiest backpackers should find something to suit them; in the low season you may be able to bargain down to the rate nationals pay, though many hotels insist on one price throughout the year. Higher-end hotels can quickly fill up in the high season, so reserve rooms well in advance. Hot water is generally only available in such establishments.

Residencial Los Amigos Av Charles Darwin ☎05/2526265. Popular, friendly and inexpensive place, where the cheapest rooms are upstairs, divided by thin plywood and mosquito screening (not the best sound insulators), and have shared bath with no hot water. Rooms downstairs come with private bath and better walls. ❷

Castro Los Colonos ☎05/2526508. Clean and comfortable rooms with private bath, a/c and hot water. Breakfast included. Reduced rates available in the low season. ❼

Darwin Av Herrera and Tomás de Berlanga ☎05/2526193. Pleasant and inexpensive hotel set around a little courtyard featuring en-suite rooms with hot water, but a/c costs extra. Good value. ❷

Estrella de Mar 12 de Febrero ☎05/2526427. Overlooking the bay, this is a good choice for its attractive rooms (those with bay views cost extra), with private bath, hot water and blue floors inlaid with red starfish and dotted with "Happy Hanukkah" foot mats. ❼

Finch Bay ☎05/2526297, ⓦwww.finchbayhotel .com. This award-winning, luxury eco-hotel at Punta Estrada (across the bay and reached by water taxi) is in a private location surrounded by mangroves. It has its own large pool, open-air hot tub, beach access and excellent restaurant. The comfortable rooms have a/c and unlimited water, as the hotel has its own desalinization plant along with garbage processing and recycling programmes. Tours can be arranged to nearby attractions. ❾

Grand Hotel Lobo de Mar 12 de Febrero and Av Charles Darwin ☎05/2526188, ⓦwww.lobodemar .com.ec. Remodelled to include a courtyard, swimming pool and a range of old and new rooms, some with gorgeous sea views, some with a/c and all with hot water. Internet and laundry services are available. ❽

Mainao Los Petreles/Matazarnos and Indefatigable ☎05/2527029, ⓦwww.hotelmainao.com. Blazing whitewash and little red awnings evoke the Mediterranean at this quiet backstreet hotel, featuring

comfortable, clean en-suite rooms with hot water and a/c; drinking water is provided and internet is also available. Breakfast is included and Rough Guide readers get a ten percent discount. ❽

La Peregrina Av Charles Darwin and Indefatigable ☎05/2526323. The price here includes a tasty breakfast of fruit salad, bread, juice and coffee, and its five bedrooms come with private bath (but no hot water) and a/c. ❻

🐢 **Red Mangrove Aventura Lodge** Av Charles Darwin and Las Fragatas ☎05/2526564, ⓦwww.redmangrove.com. Set at the water's edge amidst mangroves, this secluded, bohemian hotel was designed and built by its artist owners and has many idiosyncratic flourishes. Rooms are bright and fresh with views of bay or mangroves, and have hot water; there's a whirlpool on the veranda. Day-trips, windsurfing, kayaking, horseriding, mountain biking and tours to their highland camp (❾), and lodges on Isabela and Floreana can all be arranged. Breakfast included. ❾

Royal Palm Km18 vía Baltra ☎05/2527409, ⓦwww.royalpalmgalapagos.com. A luxury hotel set in an exclusive estate in the highlands with gorgeous views over the islands. There's lavish accommodation in villas, studios and suites, all with hot tub, satellite television, internet access, minibar, CD and DVD players. One of the most expensive hotels in the country. ❾

Silberstein Av Charles Darwin and Seymour ☎05/2526277, ⓦwww.hotelsilberstein.com. Once a well-known backpackers' hangout, the hotel now caters to rather more moneyed guests. The large rooms come with hot water and a/c, and there's a small swimming pool surrounded by a garden. ❽

SolyMar Av Charles Darwin ☎05/2526281, ⓦwww.hotelsolymar.com.ec. All the rooms here have private bath and hot water, as well as private balconies overlooking the bay, where marine iguanas bask during the day. The waterside terrace has a pool and hot tub. ❾

The Town and around

The main thoroughfare, **Avenida Charles Darwin**, runs along the **waterfront**, from the municipal dock at its southern end to the **Charles Darwin Research Station** at its northern end, where visitors can see giant tortoise corrals and extensive exhibits on the natural history of the islands. Just about everything you'll need is on Darwin: hotels, restaurants, the bank, travel agents, bars, discos, information, plus a number of less indispensable souvenir shops. The town's other important road is **Avenida Padre Julio Herrera** (also called Avenida Baltra), running inland from Darwin and the dock to become the main road to the highlands and the link to the Baltra airport.

If you have some time in the port, there are several good local excursions that don't require a guide. For some peace and quiet, you can't do better than visit one of the local beaches, such as the glorious **Bahía Tortuga**, or the **Playa de los Alemanes** and the nearby swimming hole, **Las Grietas**, both reached by water taxi. A tour in a **glass-bottomed boat** will reveal the joys of underwater nature as far as possible for those who don't want to snorkel (see "Travel agents and tour operators", p.463), while the Santa Cruz **highlands** (see p.463) also hold a number of natural attractions, including lava tunnels, craters and a tortoise reserve, which can be visited on day tours through many local agencies.

Charles Darwin Research Station

Even though it is primarily a science and conservation facility, just about every tour of the islands sooner or later washes up at the **Charles Darwin Research Station** (CDRS), twenty minutes' stroll from the town centre at the northern end of Avenida Charles Darwin. Past the **information booth** at the entrance, a path leads between some giant cacti to the **Van Straelen interpretation centre** (daily 9am–6pm; no charge), exhibiting information on geology, climate, conservation and many related aspects of Galápagos nature. A short video about the CDRS and the islands, introduced by a staff member, can be seen on request (daily 9am–noon & 2–4pm); details are available here about joining Galápagos conservation organizations. Past the visitor centre, you'll come to the **tortoise-rearing pens**, where predator-proof enclosures hold batches of miniature giant tortoises divided by age; the creatures are best seen when the covers are off (Mon–Fri 7am–4pm). Since 1965, a programme of tortoise repopulation has been ongoing, with eggs being carefully extracted from the wild and incubated here. After two or three years the hatchlings graduate to larger enclosures with the kind of terrain they might find in the wild; after four to six years they are deemed to have grown to an uneatable size (as far as predators are concerned) and repatriated to their home islands.

From the pens, a raised boardwalk weaves through the scrub past the **tortoise corrals**, where you can see fully grown giant tortoises. The most famous resident is **Lonesome George** (*Solitario Jorge*), the last surviving tortoise of the Pinta island subspecies, considered by many to be the rarest animal in the world. From 1906 until 1971 (when George was found) it was thought the Pinta tortoises were extinct; since then the search has been on to find him a Pinta partner, with a $10,000 reward on offer. At the moment, George is paired up with a couple of females from Volcán Wolf on Isabela, though – except for one fruitless liaison in 2008 – the unfortunate reptile has shown little interest in love. Recent research has suggested tortoises from Española – another subspecies from the opposite side of the archipelago – may in fact be George's closest relatives, so he may get on better with them. Despite his 75 years or so (with about another 75 to go), he's quite a shy animal, and the best time to see him is when he's being fed, on Mondays, Wednesdays and Fridays at 9am.

At the end of the walkway is an enclosure with half a dozen friendly tortoises, mostly former pets donated to the station. This is the best place to get up close and take photos – but be careful not to touch them or walk on their feeding area. Near the exit, you'll pass the CDRS kiosk, selling t-shirts, videos and souvenirs; this is the only place on the islands you can buy CDRS logo clothing, the proceeds of which go straight to the station. Near the exit you'll see a sign for a little **beach**, a hidden spot for lazing about and looking across the bay.

Bahía Tortuga

A three-kilometre walk through a cactus forest southwest of town brings you to **Bahía Tortuga**, a beautiful streaking beach of soft, white sand unfurling for almost a kilometre, washed by luminescent blue waters. People swim here but it's not safe, as the currents are very strong and there are no lifeguards around. A better spot for a dip is at the western end of the beach, beyond the rocky outcrop of lava, where there's a lagoon wrapped in mangroves; you may see marine iguanas, brown pelicans and even flamingos here.

To get there, head west out of Puerto Ayora on Charles Binford, which continues as a dirt road to a cliff, at the top of which is a **national park guardhouse** where you need to sign in. From here a paved trail undulates across a cactus forest to the beach. You can only get to the bay on foot, about forty minutes from town; there are no facilities, so bring water. The beach closes at 6pm.

Playa de los Alemanes and Las Grietas

A short water-taxi ride ($0.50) across the bay to the south towards the *Finch Bay Hotel* brings you to two popular swimming spots in an area surrounded by lagoons and saltbush teeming with birdlife. From the dock a path leads to an attractive protected beach ideal for swimming and snorkelling, the **Playa de los Alemanes**, named after the early German settlers that made their homes here when the island was first colonized. Beyond the beach, a gravel path leads for fifteen to twenty minutes to **Las Grietas**, inland saltwater grottoes surrounded by high lava walls, which are very popular with locals at weekends for bathing; on weekdays the pools are quiet.

Eating, drinking and nightlife

Among the many **restaurants** along Avenida Charles Darwin, there's a good proportion of relatively expensive places aimed squarely at tourists, and locally popular restaurants such as *El Rincón del Alma* and the downmarket *Frutos del Mar* (closed Mon), on the corner of Naveda nearby, serving bargain *almuerzos* and *meriendas*. For the best local **seafood** head to Charles Binford in the evening, where a string of *kioscos* (kiosks) simmer up cauldrons of *encocados* (an Esmeraldas speciality) and other *mariscos*, cooked in the style of the mainland coast. Of these, *William* (closed Mon) is the best, but anywhere you can see a crowd of satisfied customers washing down their rice and fish with a glass of cold beer is also likely to be good.

A pleasant mix of tourists, locals and resident research scientists brings a healthy international flavour to Puerto Ayora **nightlife**. *Limón y Café*, Avenida Charles Darwin and 12 de Febrero (daily until 1am), is a thatched **bar** with a good atmosphere, where you can shoot pool, sip a blue-footed booby cocktail, relax in a hammock and chat to dedicated beer-swilling regulars. The disco at *La Panga*, on Avenida Charles Darwin and Tomás de Berlanga (Mon–Thurs 8.30pm–2am, Fri & Sat 8.30pm–3am), tends to fill up quite late in the evening. Here, cheapskates can sink cocktails from "the Titanic Line" – dodgy-label spirits that do the damage at a fraction of the price of better-known brands. Upstairs is the *Bongo Bar*, a rooftop venue offering open-air seating, pool table and a small dancefloor. For good live *folklórica* music, ask a taxi driver to take you to *La Taberna del Duende* (Thurs–Sat), in a residential area towards the back of town, a popular, local *peña* done up in bamboo and straw matting.

Restaurants

Angermeyer Point ☎05/2527007. Built on decks over a rocky promontory, home to marine iguanas, this elegant, first-class restaurant is just a water-taxi ride from the dock. It serves excellent but pricey international food, including good seafood (sushi on Fridays) and fillet steaks, Sunday brunch, freshly baked bread and great cocktails. Deservedly popular, so reservations recommended.

La Garrapata Av Charles Darwin and Tomás de Berlanga. Highly regarded open-air restaurant with candlelit tables and a pleasing ambience, serving delicious seafood and grills. A little costlier than most places, but worth the extra expense.

Hernán Av Padre Julio Herrera and Opuntia. The town's favourite pizza parlour (a veggie thin-crust goes for $6), also serving other international comfort food, but the main triumphs are the excellent coffee and soft-serve ice cream, which is a real hit with locals. Full breakfast menu from 7.30am.

Salvavidas Muelle Municipal. While you tuck into an ample portion of fish and chips for around $5 or $2 an *almuerzo* at this decent seafood joint overlooking the dock, you can watch the herons getting their own nightly feed.

Tintorera Av Charles Darwin and Isla Floreana. Encouraging variety of dishes on the menu, including Thai and Indian curries, plus great desserts, freshly baked bread, home-made ice cream and breakfasts from 8am. Much of the food is locally sourced and it's a good place to meet people in a spot overlooking Pelican Bay. Closed Sat 3pm & Sun.

Listings

Airlines Aerogal, Av Herrera (☎05/2526798) and Baltra airport (☎05/2520405); EMETEBE, Av Charles Darwin above the post office (☎05/2526177) and Baltra (☎05/2521193); TAME, Av Charles Darwin and 12 de Febrero (☎05/2526527) and Baltra airport (☎05/2520111).

Banks Banco del Pacífico, on Av Charles Darwin and Charles Binford, changes dollar and euro traveller's cheques, has an ATM for MasterCard, Cirrus and Visa (daily limit $300), and offers cash advances for MasterCard and Cirrus.

Bike and sports rental Galápagos Tour Center, Av Padre Julio Herrera and Av Charles Darwin (☎05/2526245), rents out mountain bikes for $2 per hour or $15 per day, surfboards for $16 a day, and snorkelling equipment for $10 a day.

Cameras, film and repairs Galapagos On-Line, opposite the Capitanía on Av Charles Darwin, will burn discs from your memory cards. Galacolor, Tomás de Berlanga and Naveda, can do minor repairs and sells batteries, disposable cameras and film for just above mainland rates ($10 for slide film). Steer clear of film without a box – it's probably passed its expiry date.

Diving operators Galápagos Sub Aqua on Av Charles Darwin (☎05/2526350, ⓦwww.galapagos -sub-aqua.com) is a long-established outfit offering introductory dives at Academy Bay, day-trips and longer live-aboard tours, plus PADI training courses from beginner to divemaster. Scuba Iguana on Av Charles Darwin near the CDRS (☎05/2526497, ⓦwww.scubaiguana.com) has a similar range of services. English is spoken at both agencies. See also "Hospitals" below for information on the town's hyperbaric recompression chamber; it is very expensive – make sure you are properly insured and that your diving agency is affiliated.

Fibras and lanchas See "Independent travel between the islands", p.455.

Hospitals The public hospital is on Av Padre Julio Herrera and Av Charles Darwin. In emergencies, call ☎05/2526103. A better-staffed and equipped private clinic is Protesub (☎05/2526911, ☎09/9855911, ⓦwww.sssnetwork.com) on 18 de Febrero and General Rodríguez Lara, which primarily provides medical services for submarine and aquatic activities, and has a hyperbaric recompression chamber, but also offers general medical attention to the public.

Internet Connections cost around $2–2.50 an hour.

Language school Islas Galápagos Spanish Language Center; contact them via their Quito office at Darquea Terán 16-50 and Av 10 de Agosto (☎02/2223242, ⓦwww.islas-galapagos.com). Dancing and cooking classes, and family stays also available.

Laundry Peregrina, by *La Peregrina*, charges around $1 per kg (Mon–Sat 9am–noon & 3.30–5.30pm). Others are located on Av Padre Julio Herrera.

Post office On Av Charles Darwin, next to the Proinsular Supermarket. Servigalápagos (☎05/2526041) on Av Charles Darwin and Seymour, opposite the *Silberstein*, is a representative for DHL and Western Union couriers.

Shopping Souvenir shops line Av Charles Darwin, but on the waterfront near Tomás de Berlanga is an enjoyable crafts market. The general town market is on the road out of town at Av Padre Julio Herrera and Isla Duncan, and there's a supermarket next to the post office.

Travel agents and tour operators Moonrise Travel, on Av Charles Darwin, opposite the Banco del

Pacífico (☎05/2526403, ⓦwww.galapagosmoonrise .com), has a reputation for finding last-minute places on the more reliable tour boats quickly; it also runs day-trips to the nearby islands and tours of the highlands, including visits to their farm, Rancho Mariposa, where you can see wild tortoises. We Are The Champions Tours, Av Tomás de Berlanga (☎05/2526951, ⓦwww.wearethechampionstours .com), for last-minute cruises, day-trips, highlands, cycling and surfing trips. Aqua Tours (☎05/2526632) has a glass-bottomed boat, leaving the dock at 8.30am and 2.30pm for a 4hr tour, subject to demand.

The Santa Cruz highlands

If you're travelling independently, the **highland** sites are relatively easy to get to, though it's better to go with a **guide** (ask any tour operator; $20–30 per person depending on group size), both to navigate and to spot creatures and plants in the undergrowth. If you're on a **boat tour**, the itinerary may give you a half-day to explore the highlands, while tour agencies in Puerto Ayora offer **day-trips** there for around $20–30, often less if you can get a group together. **Buses** going to Santa Rosa (20min; stopping at Bellavista after 10min) leave hourly from the market on Avenida Padre Julio Herrera and Isla Duncan. The last bus back from Santa Rosa is at 9pm. Otherwise, wait at the market and catch a ride in a **shared taxi** for $1–2 to Bellavista or $3–4 to Santa Rosa; a normal taxi will cost $5–10 one-way, or $15 return with some waiting time. Traffic is sporadic, so allow plenty of time to hitch a lift back to town if necessary.

Bellavista, Cerro Crocker and around

The flora and fauna of the **highlands** of Santa Cruz are quite distinct from the parched coastal areas. Leaving Puerto Ayora, the main road over the island ascends from the lowland scrub and cactus fields. By the time you reach the little cattle village of **BELLAVISTA**, 6km north of the port, introduced elephant grass, plantains, papayas and avocados grow from the fertile red soil. From Bellavista, a trail leads north through farmland, miconia forests and pampa

Santa Cruz lava tubes

Huge underground **lava tubes** perforate Santa Cruz, and in places extend for several kilometres, enclosed by high jagged walls that disappear into the gloom. The tubes were formed when cooler outer parts of lava flows hardened into thick rock walls, providing insulation to keep a flow going inside; eventually the flow subsided, leaving long empty tunnels easily big enough to walk down. As they're on private land, you don't need an official guide to explore these volcanic curiosities, though tours can be arranged in Puerto Ayora. The floors can be slippery and rubble strewn, so a flashlight and sturdy shoes are a good idea.

One of the easiest to get to is near Bellavista (follow the "*los túneles*" signs from the village), where you can hire a flashlight ($0.50) to explore a tunnel ($2) several hundred metres long. Another set, known as El Mirador, is within walking distance 2.5km from town ($1 by taxi). There are also the Salasaca tunnels ($3), 5km northwest of Santa Rosa on the farm of Señor Arias; get in contact with him through one of the agencies to arrange a visit.

grass for about 8km (a 2hr 30min trek) to the summit of the island, **Cerro Crocker** (864m); when the mists disperse, the panoramic **views** are spectacular. About 5km into the walk you'll reach the crescent-shaped **Media Luna** and nearer the summit, **Puntudo**, both old volcanic cones grown over with thick vegetation. The trail can get very muddy and hard to follow in places, so getting a guide is a good idea.

Santa Rosa, the Chato Tortoise Reserve and around

Around 9km northwest from Bellavista, the farms of **SANTA ROSA** sit amid abundant fruit orchards and cedar trees that dwarf the native vegetation. From here, a track leads through 3km of farmland dotted with white cattle egrets and smooth-billed anis to the edge of the **Chato Tortoise Reserve** on the south-western corner of the island, among the best places in the Galápagos to see giant tortoises in their natural habitat. Here, the trail forks between a branch heading west through endemic scalesia forest up to **Cerro Chato** (about 3km), and east to a small lagoon (2km), where tortoises wallow in the company of white-cheeked pintails. Vermilion and Galápagos flycatchers are common sightings, but you'll need more luck to spot the secretive Galápagos rail. A **guide** is strongly recommended for visiting the reserve, not least because it is dangerously easy to get lost here; bring plenty of water, sturdy shoes and wet-weather gear.

A couple of kilometres beyond Santa Rosa on the way to Baltra, the road passes between **Los Gemelos**, a pair of yawning, forest-swathed pit-craters, formed when lava collapsed into underlying magma chambers. Trails lead from the road to viewpoints overlooking each, and **finches** and **flycatchers** inhabit the surrounding forests.

Islands around Santa Cruz

Among the small islands and islets surrounding Santa Cruz, there are five visitor sites, most of which can be reached on day-trips from Puerto Ayora, or being close to **Baltra** are often visited at the beginning or end of a cruise. Tour boats frequently call on **Seymour Norte**, **Plaza Sur** and **Santa Fé**, but few stop at the tiny lava reef of **Mosquera**. **Daphne Mayor** is one of the most restricted sites in the archipelago, due to a difficult landing on steep rocks prone to erosion.

Baltra and Mosquera

Stunted scrub and cactus growth, dry air and a parched landscape dotted with abandoned buildings isn't much of a welcome to one of the world's natural wonders, but **BALTRA** is many visitors' first taste of the Galápagos, before being whisked off to the dock to join a tour boat or catch the Santa Cruz ferry. The US Air Force occupied the island during World War II, blasting an airstrip into the rock so planes could swiftly be mobilized to defend the Panama Canal, but today it's controlled by the Ecuadorian Air Force. Except for **pelicans** and **sea birds** around the dock, there's not much to see on the island. The population of **land iguanas** was wiped out during the US occupation, though fortunately seventy specimens had been experimentally transferred in the early 1930s to Seymour Norte, immediately to the north. Following a repopulation programme by the CDRS, captive-bred iguanas were repatriated to Baltra in 1991.

Lying in the channel between Baltra and Seymour Norte and reached by tour boat, the tiny island of **MOSQUERA** is a shock of coral sand heaving with sea lions. You have free rein to walk about the island, enjoying the company of **herons** and **lava gulls**, and you can swim with the sea lions – but keep away from the bull male.

Isla Seymour Norte

SEYMOUR NORTE, directly north of Baltra (other name, Seymour Sur), is a small, low, flat island created by geological uplift, and makes frequent appearances on tour-boat itineraries. Passengers come ashore on black lava, where a trail leads past large colonies of **blue-footed boobies**. The island is also one of the best places in the Galápagos to see the **magnificent frigatebird**. Along the shore you'll also find barking **sea lions** and **marine iguanas**; take care where you put your feet as they nest here. An endemic variety of the *palo santo* tree, smaller than its relative with hairier, greyer leaves, borders the inland loop of the trail, and **land iguanas** (introduced here from Baltra in the 1930s) can occasionally be spotted tucked away in the vegetation.

Isla Daphne Mayor

Visible about 10km to the west of Baltra and Seymour, **DAPHNE MAYOR** (the larger of the two Daphnes) is composed of a tuff cone embedded with two craters. Since the early 1970s it's been the focus of research into **Darwin's finches** by two British scientists, Peter and Rosemary Grant, who have weighed, ringed, measured and photographed every finch on the island – about 25,000 altogether – and so documented evolutionary processes at work; Jonathan Weiner's book *The Beak of the Finch* tells the story of their studies (see p.539). Only small yachts are allowed to call at the islands, and even then only once a month. The dry landing is difficult, involving a leap onto a steep rock face, from where a slender trail leads up to the rim of the island; here you can gaze down into the craters. Colonies of **blue-footed boobies** nest in the furnace heat of these natural cauldrons, and **red-billed tropicbirds** tenant the crevices in the cliff walls.

Isla Plaza Sur

Less than a kilometre from the eastern coast of Santa Cruz, the two tiny Plaza islands, dramatically tilted to form sheer cliffs on the southern side, were formed by seismic uplift, when sections of the seafloor were thrust out of the water. Only **PLAZA SUR**, the larger of the two at less than 1.5km long and under 250m at its widest point, is open to visitors. Being within range of the Puerto Ayora day-trippers, the little island can get crowded, so a dock has been built to prevent tourists causing erosion on landing. Vociferous members of the thousand-strong colony of **sea lions** here see this as a territorial boundary, so take care boarding and disembarking; snorkelling and swimming are also better around neighbouring Plaza Norte, out of the sea-lion war zone. A rather more subdued group of elderly bachelors languish on a corner of lava (polished smooth over the years by their tired, defeated bodies) up on the cliffs, a tortuous climb over the rocks away from the macho action of the main colony.

The island has striking vegetation, a covering of juicy *Sesuvium* plants that turn crimson in the dry season, punctuated by chunky *Opuntia* cactus trees. When their succulent pads fall to the ground, **land iguanas** wriggle out of their torpor for a bite to eat. Before park rules were enacted, visitors often fed the iguanas fruit, and they subsequently learned to dash to the dock whenever a party landed; they're still often seen lurking around newly arrived groups, waiting in vain for a banana or orange.

A trail leads up to sheer cliffs, an excellent vantage point to spot **noddy terns**, **swallow-tailed gulls**, **Audubon's shearwaters** and **red-billed tropicbirds**, as well as the occasional **blue-footed** and **Nazca boobies**, **frigatebirds** and **pelicans**. Looking down into the swell, you may see yellow-tailed mullet, surgeonfish, manta rays and dolphins.

Isla Santa Fé

Visitors to **SANTA FÉ**, about 25km southeast of Puerto Ayora, disembark for a wet landing on the northeastern side of the island, at a stunning cove with brilliant-blue water and white sand, protected by a partly submerged peninsula. The bay is good for swimming – though give the bull sea lions here a wide berth – and snorkelling may yield up **spotted eagle rays** and **stingrays**, **white-tipped reef sharks** and other colourful reef fish.

There are two trails on Isla Santa Fé. The first is short and easy, circling through a forest of giant *Opuntia* **cacti** (a variety found only on the island), many reaching 10m in height with trunks 4m in circumference. The second is more strenuous, heading up a steep hill that affords spectacular views of the island. On both, you have a fair chance of seeing a species of **land iguana** unique to Santa Fé, having a paler colour and longer spines on its back than its counterparts on the other islands. With luck, you might also see one of the three surviving endemic species of **rice rat** rustling in the scrub – unlike on Fernandina, the only other island where they are found, this species often appears in the daytime. This is a good island to spot several other endemic species, including the **Galápagos hawk**, **dove** and **snake**.

Isla Santiago and around

About 25km northwest of Santa Cruz, **SANTIAGO** – officially called San Salvador – is the fourth-largest island in the Galápagos at 585 square kilometres, and the last unpopulated one to have been abandoned by human settlers. In the early nineteenth century, Captain Porter (p.482) is reputed to have set four goats free on the island, which swiftly set about multiplying, soon causing extensive damage to the island's native wildlife. Before trained hunters, aided by dogs and satellite tracking systems, could get to work on the island's 100,000 goats, its rampant feral pig population had to be eradicated, a mammoth task that took 28 years and was finally completed in 2001; the last goat was destroyed in 2005. As well as Santiago's four visitor sites, there are some interesting satellite islands, such as **Rábida**, **Bartolomé** and **Sombrero Chino**, and its proximity to Santa Cruz means the majority of boat tours stop somewhere in this area. Day-trip boats based in Baltra also occasionally call at Bartolomé.

Puerto Egas

Puerto Egas, in James Bay on the western side of the island, is Santiago's most visited site, good for snorkelling and spotting a healthy cross-section of wildlife. A few derelict buildings of the old port litter the bay, the relics of failed salt-mining operations from the 1920s and the 1960s, when Héctor Egas, the namesake of the port, left three men here to look after the property, vowing to return with more money to rekindle his bankrupt industry. One of his employees waited four years in vain for his boss to return, and became a minor attraction for early tourists – the vision of a castaway, with shaggy hair and a long, unkempt beard, who scoured the island for food.

A trail leads east from the port area to the old salt mine, a crater where flamingos are occasionally spotted. Along the shore to the west, the bay is an expanse of cracked and weathered black basaltic lava, with enough pools and crevices to sustain a wealth of intertidal wildlife. The **Sally lightfoot crabs**, **urchins**, **anemones**, **eels** and **octopuses** here make a handsome smorgasbord for a number of shore birds, **herons**, **oystercatchers**, **ruddy turnstones** and noddy terns among them. At the far western end of the trail, erosion has formed the **fur seal grottoes**, shimmering turquoise pools and inlets worn from lava tubes by the waves. Natural rock bridges straddle the breaches where **marine iguanas**, **fur seals** and **marine turtles** swim. The sloshing of water in one has earned it the title of "Darwin's Toilet". The tuff cone of Pan de Azúcar (Sugarloaf) volcano (395m) overshadows scrub and acacia trees often used by **Galápagos hawks** as perches.

Playa Espumilla, Buccaneer Cove and Sulivan Bay

North of Puerto Egas, on the other side of a lava flow, lies **Playa Espumilla**, a tawny beach couched in mangroves, favoured by **marine turtles** as a nesting ground. Feral pigs that dig up and eat turtle eggs have been a serious problem here in the past, but a recovery is expected following the completion of the eradication programme. A trail leads inland from the beach, weaving through the mangroves alongside a salty lagoon into thick vegetation, home to **Darwin's finches** and **flycatchers**.

Many boats cruise by **Buccaneer Cove**, roughly 8km north of Puerto Egas and a favourite hide-out of the seventeenth- and eighteenth-century freebooters looking to careen their boats and stock up on food and water. Fifty-metre tuff cliffs, spattered with guano, taper down to a short, dusky beach and then rise in the north forming pinnacles and spurs. Pre-Columbian pottery shards discovered here led archeologist and explorer Thor Heyerdahl to suggest mainland fishermen had used the cove as a campsite long before the arrival of the pirates, probably in the wet season when a freshwater stream ran down to the beach.

On the eastern side of Santiago, **Sulivan Bay**, named after Bartholomew James Sulivan, a lieutenant on the *Beagle*, is one for **lava** fans. A trail leads across a vast, century-old flow of pahoehoe lava, a petrified lake of rumpled ooze, intestinal squiggles and viscous tongues, punctuated by oddities like *hornitos*, solidified pimples made by bursts of gas, and moulds of tree trunks that vaporized in the heat. Two large tuff cones dominate the lava field, and in the cracks and crevices you'll see the layers of previous flows beneath. In this barren landscape, the pioneering *Mollugo* and the **lava cactus** *Brachycereus* are the only plants that can eke out life.

Isla Bartolomé

BARTOLOMÉ, positioned a few hundred metres off the east coast of Santiago, holds the best-known landmark of the Galápagos, the teetering dagger of **Pinnacle Rock**, a jagged remnant of an old tuff cone overshadowing a streak of pale sand at the southwestern end of the island. The many tours that come here usually combine a hike to the island's summit (114m) and a refreshing swim beneath the Rock, where you'll get some fine snorkelling and perhaps catch a glimpse of **Galápagos penguins** zipping by schools of colourful fish. If you don't see them here, you've a better chance of spotting them from a *panga* on the shaded cliffs each side of the bay.

The **trail to the summit** begins at the man-made dock on Bartolomé's northern point, before crossing a parched landscape relieved only by a scant covering of silvery *Tiquilia* – just about the only plant that can survive such dry, ashy soil – and the infrequent slitherings of a **Galápagos snake**. The trail loops round to the east and climbs up several hundred wooden steps to reach the top of the hill, from where there's the famous view of Pinnacle Rock. On the

▲ Pinnacle Rock, Isla Bartolomé

opposite side a stunning moonscape vista unfolds, with large spatter cones and **lava tunnels** dropping to the southeast to reveal the Daphnes, Baltra, Seymour Norte and Santa Cruz in the distance.

Bartolomé's second trail begins at the beach and leads through the mangroves and dunes across the island's isthmus to a second beach, patrolled by sharks and rays and out of bounds for swimmers. **Marine turtles** nest here at the outset of the warm-wet season.

Isla Sombrero Chino

Barely 100m from the southeastern tip of Santiago, the volcanic cone of tiny **SOMBRERO CHINO** does indeed bear more than a passing resemblance to a Chinese hat. Only small boats are allowed to call here, mooring in the blazing-blue channel between the islands, a terrific spot for snorkelling and where **Galápagos penguins** are occasionally seen. A trail on the island follows a white-coral beach, past a **sea-lion** colony to a cliff vantage point surrounded by scuttling **Sally lightfoot crabs** and **marine iguanas**. The pockmarked lava landscape is dashed with brighter blotches of **lava cactus**, while around the beach you'll find **saltbush** and colourful **Sesuvium**.

Isla Rábida

RÁBIDA is less than 5km south of Santiago and under five square kilometres in area. A wet landing at the north of the island onto a russet, sea-lion-strewn beach brings you to a trail leading through saltbush to a saline lagoon; **pelicans** sometimes build nests in the saltbush, while **white-cheeked pintails**, bachelor **sea lions** and **stilts** are lagoon residents. It's possible to see the odd **flamingo** sifting the murky waters for food here as well. A path rises up through **palo santo** and **Opuntia cacti** to a viewpoint above the carmine cliffs. There's good snorkelling near the cliffs or at the landing beach and plenty of colourful fish, diving **boobies** and pelicans to see.

Isla San Cristóbal and around

Out on the eastern side of the archipelago, with a shape resembling a "shrivelled appendix" according to 1940s travel writer Victor von Hagen, **SAN CRISTÓBAL** is the administrative seat of the Galápagos and at 558 square kilometres is its fifth largest island. **Wreck Bay**, at its western tip, is the site of the provincial capital, **Puerto Baquerizo Moreno**, a peaceful town slowly awakening to the rustle of tourist dollars since the island's airport opened in 1986. In its favour is the excellent **Centro de Interpretación**, which concentrates on the human and natural history of the islands, plus the nearby islets **León Dormido** (Kicker Rock) and **Isla Lobos**, which often feature in local excursions. On the rest of the island, points of interest include the highland town of **El Progreso**, site of Manuel Cobos's tyrannical colony, **Laguna El Junco**, the largest freshwater lake in the Galápagos, and **Punta Pitt**, the archipelago's easternmost point.

Cerro San Joaquín (summit measurements range from 730m to 896m), whose windward slopes are fertile enough to be farmed, dominates the southwestern half of the island. The northeastern area has the characteristic volcanic landscape of the archipelago, a collection of lava flows, spatter cones and other volcanic features.

Puerto Baquerizo Moreno

Founded by the colonist General Villamil in the mid-nineteenth century (see p.443), **PUERTO BAQUERIZO MORENO** was named after the first Ecuadorian president to visit the islands, in 1916. Despite being the capital, it's a sleepy town, virtually lifeless in the heat of the early afternoon, only coming alive fully when the sun sets over the bay. It may not get as many visitors as Puerto Ayora, but there is a burgeoning industry here: along the waterfront, a glut of travel agents, cafés, restaurants and souvenir shops all show a town keen to cut itself a larger slice of the tourism pie. Puerto Baquerizo Moreno is a bit short of things to do, but there's enough on the island to keep visitors busy for a few days. Just outside the port, the **Centro**

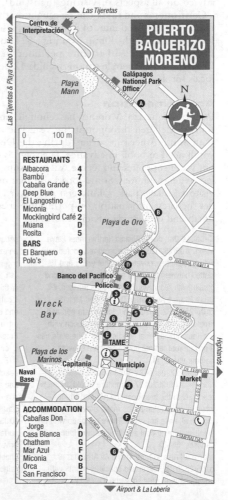

PUERTO BAQUERIZO MORENO

Las Tijeretas

Centro de Interpretación

Las Tijeretas & Playa Cabo de Horno

Playa Mann

Galápagos National Park Office

N

0   100 m

Playa de Oro

Wreck Bay

Banco del Pacífico

Police

Playa de los Marinos

Naval Base

Capitania

Municipio

Highlands

Market

Airport & La Lobería

RESTAURANTS
Albacora	4
Bambú	7
Cabaña Grande	6
Deep Blue	3
El Langostino	1
Miconia	C
Mockingbird Café	2
Muana	D
Rosita	5

BARS
El Barquero	9
Polo's	8

ACCOMMODATION
Cabañas Don Jorge	A
Casa Blanca	D
Chatham	G
Mar Azul	F
Miconia	C
Orca	B
San Francisco	E

de Interpretación has great displays of the archipelago's human and natural history, while spots on the coast nearby, such as **Tongo Reef** west of town, have become the focus of the Galápagos' growing reputation as a **surfing** hot spot. The waves are best from December to February at the beginning of the warm-wet season, when the water is also warmer.

Arrival, information and transport

From the **airport**, a taxi or truck into the town centre costs $1, although you can walk to it in twenty minutes on Avenida Alsacio Northía. **Fibras** from Santa Cruz arrive at the town's dock.

Tourist information is available from the municipal office at Avenida 12 de Febrero and Avenida Charles Darwin (Mon–Fri 7.30am–12.30pm & 2–5pm; ℡05/2222222, ⓦwww.sancristobalgalapagos.com) and the helpful Cámara de Turismo on Avenida Charles Darwin and Wolf (Mon–Fri 7.30am–noon & 2–5.30pm, ℡05/2520592, ⓦwww.galapagostour.org), which has leaflets and advice on all aspects of visiting the islands; English is spoken here.

Camionetas and **taxis** can be caught on the Malecón and charge a minimum fare of $1, and fixed rates of $2 to El Progreso, $6 to Lobería (return), $18 to El Junco (return with 40min waiting), $24 to La Galapaguera (return), $30 to Puerto Chino or $10 to hire per hour in the urban zone. Island **buses** to El Progreso pick people up on Avenida 12 de Febrero; service is irregular so ask locals for details.

Accommodation

Puerto Baquerizo Moreno has enough **hotels** to keep its modest flow of tourists sheltered throughout the year. The cheaper, funkier places can fill out with South American surfers during the December to February season, when you'll need to book in advance. The town is equipped with 24-hour electricity, but water shortages and feeble water pressure remain a problem for many of the less expensive hotels. Some locals also rent out **rooms** for short- and long-stay visitors (usually park volunteers) and advertise in the port's bars. **Campers** can get the latest information on permissible sites at the national park offices at the north end of Avenida Alsacio Northía.

Cabañas Don Jorge Alsacio Northía, near Playa Mann ℡05/2520208. Four ageing red-roofed cabins with kitchenettes, private bath, hot water and TV, slotted between the rocks and cacti in a secluded garden with sea views. Reservations advised. ❺

Casa Blanca Av Charles Darwin and Melville ℡05/2520392. A charming, family-run bed and breakfast with seven en-suite rooms, each with a/c, fan and individual artistic decor. One suite has a private roof terrace but several have lovely harbour views. ❼

Chatham Corner of Av Armada and Alsacio Northía ℡05/2520137. A mixture of old and new rooms, with the best boasting a/c and fridges, while dowdier alternatives make do with fans, though all have hot water. There's a patio with a small swimming pool and internet and laundry services. ❼–❾

Mar Azul Alsacio Northía and Av Armada ℡05/2520139. Clean and spacious rooms with private bath (electric showers), cable TV and fridge

set around two tranquil, leafy courtyards. There's an extra $10 charge for a/c and internet is available. ❺

Miconia Av Charles Darwin and Melville ℡05/2520608, ⓦwww.miconia.com. Great location in the heart of town overlooking the bay, and en-suite rooms with hot water, a/c, plus internet access, a small pool, gym and jacuzzi. Breakfast included. ❼–❾

Orca Playa de Oro at the north end of the Malecón ℡&Ⓕ05/2520233. Clean and quiet hotel near the beach, with en-suite rooms with fridge, cable TV and a/c, but you'll need to pay slightly more for the sea view. ❺

San Francisco Av Charles Darwin and Villamil ℡05/2520304. Inexpensive place popular with surfers, in a central location offering rooms with private bath, fans and TV. Pipes leading all over the cheerfully daubed indoor courtyard reflect the rather erratic plumbing. ❷

The Town

The one stand-out attraction of the town is the **Centro de Interpretación**, the Galápagos National Park's exhibition centre located about twenty minutes' walk north of the centre along Avenida Alsacio Northía (daily 9am–noon & 2–5pm; donation). The displays cover everything from geology, climate and conservation, to attempts at colonization in the 1920s, and have detailed explanations in Spanish and English. Impressive installations include a reconstruction of a ship's hold stuffed with overturned giant tortoises as they would have been stored by the pirates and whalers – one beast has its leg cut off for the boiling pot. Talks, lectures and concerts are held regularly in the open-air theatre and audiovisual projection room within the complex.

Behind the last exhibition room at the centre, a path leads up to **Cerro de las Tijeretas**, or **Frigatebird Hill**. It's only twenty minutes' walk through fragrant *palo santo* forests to a viewpoint at the top, where you'll have a fine panorama of the yachts in Wreck Bay, Isla Lobos to the north and León Dormido to the northeast. Below, a rocky cove echoes with jockeying **sea lions** while **frigatebirds** circle in the air above. They nest here in March and April and are seen less frequently during the cool-dry season. A series of paths network around the hill, so you can do a circuit; it's relatively easy to stay oriented. One trail leads to the **Tijeretas cove**, where you can snorkel, while others go down to the road back to town past the interpretation centre. Heading away from town to the north, you'll come to a secluded beach, the **Playa Cabo de Horno**.

Tongo Reef and La Lobería

At the weekends **surfers** make their way to the shoreline west of town to catch the waves. **Tongo Reef** is one of the more popular places, a twenty-minute walk past the naval base, but others include **Punta Carola** (beyond the Playa Cabo de Horno) and **El Cañón** (just northeast of Tongo Reef). You'll need to leave identification at the base, as this is a military area. Bring sandals you don't mind getting wet, as the volcanic rocks manage to combine extreme sharpness with extraordinary slipperiness. It's best to be with someone who knows the place as currents can be strong; ask at local travel agents about board hire and guides or instructors.

A good place near town to spot wildlife is **La Lobería**, thirty minutes' walk to the southwest. Here, a trail leads along a rugged coast of pitted black lava buffeted by ocean spray to a small beach, where you'll find sea lions, marine iguanas and many shore birds. Take Alsacio Northía south beyond the airport and follow signs to the right down a dirt road heading to the shore. Taxis are $6 return.

Eating, drinking and nightlife

Plenty of **restaurants** and **cafés** offer cheap ($2–4) two-course set-lunch *almuerzos*. Menus are rather similar, concentrating mainly on seafood, with the usual chicken and meat courses as backup. At the *Panadería Fragata,* a bakery on Avenida Alsacio Northía and Villamil, you can get your hands on fresh bread, sticky buns, ice creams and yogurts.

For **nightlife**, try the open-air bar of *El Barquero*, on Ignacio de Hernández and Manuel J. Cobos, a popular place for a cold beer. *Neptuno*, at the north end of the Malecón, is a disco with an energetic, youthful crowd, while *Polo's*, at Avenida 12 de Febrero and Ignacio de Hernández, has a pool table, relaxed atmosphere and dancefloor.

Albacora Av Alsacio Northía and Española. Popular for its cheap *almuerzos* and *meriendas*, the decor comprises cane walls, gravel floor and wicker lights flitting with finches. At night it twinkles with fairy lights.

Bambú Villamil and Ignacio de Hernández. In addition to the inexpensive *almuerzo*, you'll also find pizza and pasta dishes with vegetarian options.

Cabaña Grande Villamil and Av Charles Darwin. Locals come here in the evening to snack, sip a beer and watch TV. A toasted ham-and-cheese sandwich plus banana shake can be had for under $1.

Deep Blue Av Charles Darwin and Española. This intimate restaurant with a waterfront location is the place to sample *platos típicos*, particularly their fine *encebollados*, *ceviches* and even *guatita* (tripe). Mon–Sat 6.30am–7.30pm.

El Langostino Melville and Av Alsacio Northía. Widely regarded by locals as a top place to sample *ceviche*, best enjoyed with an ice-cold beer and

chifles (plantain chips) or *canguil* (popcorn). Other seafood also served.

Miconia Av Charles Darwin and Melville. The best and costliest restaurant in town overlooks the bay and offers a range of à la carte goodies, from tapas to *ceviche*, and excellent seafood.

Mockingbird Café Av Española and Ignacio de Hernández. A cosy internet café with a great line in chocolate brownies and organic coffee. Also features a book exchange.

Muana Av Charles Darwin and Melville. A good spot to sip a cold drink, have a snack or breakfast while watching the comings and goings along the bay.

Rosita Corner of Ignacio de Hernández and Villamil. Long-standing restaurant, with a patio shaded by a thatched awning. English names on the menu betray the place's success with the tourists, so expect to pay a little more for fish, meat and a range of *ceviche* dishes.

Listings

Airlines TAME have an office at the airport (☎05/2521351), as do EMETEBE (☎05/2520615) and Aerogal (☎05/2521118).

Bank Banco del Pacífico, on the promenade by Av Charles Darwin, changes dollar and euro traveller's cheques, has an ATM for MasterCard, Cirrus and Visa, and does cash advances for MasterCard and Visa.

Capitanía Av Darwin ☎05/2529113.

Fibras and lanchas See "Independent travel between the islands", p.455.

Hospital Alsacio Northía and Quito (☎05/2520118 in emergencies).

Internet Costs about $2–2.50 an hour.

Laundry Limpio y Seco, Av Alsacio Northía and Av 12 de Febrero.

Police Av Charles Darwin and Española (☎05/2520101 in emergencies).

Tour operators Chalo Tours, Española and Hernández (☎&℻05/2520953), offers bay tours to León Dormido and Isla Los Lobos, diving tours, surfing lessons, bike and kayak rentals, snorkels and fins and local excursions; Patagonia Eco Multi-sports, Teodoro Wolf and Av Charles Darwin (☎05/2520017), offers diving tours, snorkelling, kayaking, biking and camping trips; Agencia Sunfish on Av Charles Darwin sells boat tickets to Santa Cruz and Isabela as well as offering tours.

San Cristóbal highlands

The road heading east from Puerto Baquerizo Moreno rises swiftly into the misty highlands. After passing through about 8km of orange groves, you'll reach **EL PROGRESO**, a peaceful village of wooden, stilted houses, banana plants and fruit trees. It was founded in the 1870s by **Manuel Cobos**, an entrepreneur who tried to colonize the place with a hundred convicts. They planted orchards, sugar cane and vegetable gardens, built a sugar mill and enjoyed modest success for a short period – but, far away from the gaze of authority, El Progreso began to slip into brutal tyranny. Cobos paid his workers in his own invented currency only redeemable in his shop; he also owned the island's only boat, effectively making his workers prisoners and slaves. An increasingly savage overlord, he regularly beat them, once flogging six to death, and abandoned a man on Santiago and another on Santa Cruz, leaving them for dead. The Santa Cruz

A field guide to Galápagos wildlife

This field guide provides a quick reference to help you identify some of the more common birds, reptiles, mammals and marine invertebrates of the Galápagos Islands. Photos show easily identified markings and features, while notes give clear pointers about the kinds of habitat in which you are most likely to see each species, its rarity and general tips about sighting them. For information on visiting the Galápagos, see p.436–484, and for further details on the islands' wildlife, see p.522–532.

⚙ Habitat   ▽ Social Life   ✓ Sighting Tips

Birds

Blue-footed booby
Sula nebouxii (Piquero patas azules)

🐾 Common throughout the islands, which hold three-quarters of the global population, but prefers breeding on those south of the equator.

💭 Famous for their flamboyant courting display, seen throughout the year, in which they show off the blueness of their feet.

✓ Sexes are easy to tell apart: males have small black pupils and whistle, while females' pupils appear larger, and they honk.

Nazca booby
Sula granti (Piquero de Nazca)

🐾 Common throughout the islands and, like the blue-footed booby, nests on flat areas marked by a ring of guano.

💭 Colonies have their own yearly breeding cycle. Of the two eggs that are laid, only one will survive; the stronger chick will eat the other if it hatches.

✓ Outside of the nine-month breeding cycle, adults leave the colony scouring the high seas for food.

Red footed booby
Sula sula (Piquero patas rojas)

🐾 Nests in trees in colonies on the fringes of the archipelago.

💭 Prehensile feet are much better suited to movement in trees than on the ground. Breeding cycle is slow, lasting over a year.

✓ Best seen on Genevosa, home to the world's largest colony, but also found on San Cristóbal, Seymour Norte and Española.

Great and magnificent frigatebird
Fregata minor (Fragata común), *Fregata magnificens* (Fragata magnífica)

🐾 Around the coasts of most islands, nesting in low shrubs like saltbush, or in *palo santo* trees. There are some mixed colonies on Seymour Norte, San Cristóbal and Genovesa.

💭 Aerial virtuosi thanks to a very large wingspan and light, compact bodies. Males inflate a bright red gular sac to attract females during courtship.

✓ The magnificent is slightly larger than the great frigatebird and the males have black rather than pink-red feet. Female magnificent frigatebirds have blue eye-rings (greats have red) and black chins (greats have white).

 Habitat 　　 Social Life 　　 Sighting Tips

Galápagos penguin
Spheniscus mendiculus (Pingüino de Galápagos)

🐾 Nests in cracks and caves streaking coastal lava formations. It's the only penguin found north of the equator.

💭 Active before sunrise, they spend most of the day swimming with occasional breaks basking in the sun on rocky shores. If the water is cold and fish plentiful, they hunt in packs.

✔ Favour cooler waters off Isabela and Fernandina, but snorkellers often encounter them beneath Pinnacle Rock, Bartolomé or al Sombrero Chino and Rábida.

Flightless cormorant
Nannopterum harrisi (Cormorán no volador)

🐾 Nests in small colonies on rocky shores of Fernandina, and northern and western Isabela.

💭 Unusual aquatic courtship display with partners swimming past each other while snaking their necks and making throaty gurgles. Cannot fly, but feed on bottom-living fish such as eel and octopus.

✔ Unmistakable not just as the only cormorant in the Galápagos, but for its stunted and bedraggled wings, which they hold out to dry after fishing trips.

Lava gull
Larus fuliginosus (Gaviota de lava)

🐾 No colonies, preferring solitary nests by salty lagoons, or near the shore.

💭 Get nervous if their nests are approached, and will attack anything in its territory.

✔ Unafraid of humans, and often seen scavenging around harbours.

Swallow-tailed gull
Creagrus furcatus (Gaviota tijereta)

🐾 Favour cliff areas, but will also nest on rocky or sandy shores. Breed on all islands, except Fernandina and western Isabela.

💭 The world's only nocturnal gull, it flies far out to sea at sunset and locates its prey using its large eyes especially adapted for night vision and its unusual calls.

✔ Distinctive and attractive gull, whose scarlet eye-ring and red feet blaze against soft charcoal, grey and white plumage.

🐾 Habitat   💭 Social Life   ✔ Sighting Tips

Waved albatross
Phoebastria irrorata (Albatros de Galápagos)

🏵 Endemic to Isla Española.

💠 Has one partner for life and breeds annually between March and January. By December the young are ready to leave the colony and don't return for several years.

✓ The colony is deserted from January to March, and the best time to see the courtship dance is towards the end of the breeding season.

Red-billed tropicbird
Phaeton aethereus (Rabijunco piquirrojo)

🏵 High ledges or in crannies on steep cliffs.

💠 Suitable nesting areas are limited, leading to fights for space. When a bird finds a site it will start breeding, meaning that there's no fixed annual cycle.

✓ Largest colonies are found in Genovesa, South Plaza, Daphne and Seymour Norte.

Lava heron
Butorides sundevalli (Garza de lava)

🏵 Intertidal areas, mangroves and saltwater lagoons.

💠 Catch small fish, crabs and lizards in rock pools or in the webbed roots of mangroves. Usually breeds from September to March.

✓ Dark colouration and diminutive size allow it to blend in well with lava, but it's a common sight along Galápagos shorelines.

Striated heron
Butorides striatus (Garcilla estriada)

🏵 Nests on Santa Cruz, Pinta, Pinzón, Isabela and Fernandina.

💠 Solitary predator, usually waiting to strike on a perch by the water's edge.

✓ Easily confused with the lava heron, but has a black cap and a paler neck and breast.

🏵 Habitat   💠 Social Life   ✓ Sighting Tips

Galápagos hawk
Buteo galapagoensis (Gavilán de Galápagos)

🐾 Lowlands of most islands except San Cristóbal, Baltra, Seymour Norte, Daphne, Floreana, Wolf, Darwin and Genovesa.

🌿 Unusual breeding practice of "cooperative polyandry" in which four males pair with a single female, and team up to defend the territory and look after the young.

✓ Fearless and inquisitive, meaning you can often get quite close.

Galápagos mockingbird
Nesomimus parvulus (Cucuve de Galápagos)

🐾 Widespread on Genovesa, Wolf, Darwin, Isabela, Fernandina, Santa Cruz, Santiago, Pinta, Marchena and Santa Fé, with separate species on the islets of Floreana (*Nesomimus trifasciatus*), Española (*Nesomimus macdonaldi*), and San Cristóbal (*Nesomimus melanotis*).

🌿 Juveniles help their parents patrol territory and care for newborn offspring.

✓ A confident bird that will hop right up to you to take a look.

Galápagos dove
Zenaidia galapagoensis (Paloma de Galápagos)

🐾 Drier lowland areas on most islands.

🌿 Peak breeding season is between February and June; they nest in sheltered spaces under rocks or use old mockingbird nests.

✓ The doves on Darwin and Wolf are much larger and classed as a separate subspecies.

Cactus finch
Geospiza scandens (Pinzón del cactus), one of the thirteen species of Darwin's finches

🐾 All islands, except Fernandina, Genovesa, Wolf, Darwin and Española.

🌿 Specially adapted to feeding on *Opuntia* cacti, and gets all its water from cactus pulp.

✓ Has a longer bill proportionally than the other Darwin's finches.

🐾 Habitat 🌿 Social Life ✓ Sighting Tips

Woodpecker finch
Camarhyncus pallida (Pinzón artesano)

🌸 Mainly highlands, but also by the coast and in transitional areas.

👁 Uses twigs or cactus spines to pick grubs, larvae and insects from their holes.

✓ Found on Santiago, Santa Cruz, San Cristóbal, Isabela and Pinzón islands.

Galápagos short-eared owl
Asio flammeus (Búho orejicorto)

🌸 The highlands and on the coast next to sea-bird colonies on most islands except Fernandina, Wolf and Darwin.

👁 A diurnal hunter picking off small birds, this owl acquiesces to the Galápagos hawk when it's present, and hunts at dusk.

✓ Reliably seen around the storm petrel colonies on Genovesa.

Galápagos flycatcher
Myiarchus magnirostris (Papamoscas)

🌸 On all islands except Genovesa, Darwin and Wolf in the north.

👁 Like to nest during the rainy season (Dec–May) in holes found in trees and cacti.

✓ Will eat flies from the palm of the hand.

Reptiles

Giant tortoise
Geochelone elephantopus (Tortuga gigante)

🌸 Eleven subspecies with differing carapaces; the "saddle-back" shapes are suited to low, arid, sparsely vegetated areas, while the "dome" shapes prefer higher, lusher islands.

👁 Can survive for long periods without water, but like to wallow in pools and mud baths to cool down.

✓ On Isabela, Santa Cruz, Santiago, San Cristóbal, Española and Pinzón.

 Habitat   Social Life   Sighting Tips

Pacific green turtle

Chelonia mydas (Tortuga verde)

🌸 Oceanic, but come ashore at night to lay eggs on sandy beaches, and occasionally bask in the sun.

💬 Turtles from the Galápagos have been known to migrate as far as Costa Rica and Peru.

✔ Peak mating and nesting season is November to February.

Marine iguana

Amblyrhynchus cristatus (Iguana marina)

🌸 Rocky shorelines throughout the archipelago.

💬 The world's only ocean-going lizard. Excess salt is secreted through special nostril glands in a fine spray.

✔ During mating season (Jan–March), the males take on a reddish colouration; on Española it's an exotic red and turquoise, and the females turn red too.

Land iguana

Conolophus subcristatus, *C. pallidus* on Santa Fé, "*C. rosada*" on Wolf volcano, Isabela (Iguana terrestre)

🌸 Scrubby inland areas on Santa Cruz, Baltra, Seymour Norte, Plaza Sur, Fernandina, Isabela and Santa Fé.

💬 Basks in the sun and spends the night in burrows to maintain body temperature. Males are territorial and engage in battles with rivals over females.

✔ Plaza Sur and Santa Fé provide some of the best opportunities for sightings.

Lava lizard

Tropidurus (Lagartija de lava) one of seven species

🌸 Arid lowlands across the archipelago, except Genovesa, Darwin and Wolf.

💬 Perform a display of "press-ups" to affirm their territory to rivals. The pattern of press-ups varies between islands, even among the same species.

✔ On hot days, active during mornings and late afternoons, but will run for shade in the midday heat.

🌸 Habitat   💬 Social Life   ✔ Sighting Tips

Galápagos snake

Three species, *Philodryas biserialis*, *Alsophis dorsalis* and *A. selvini* (Culebra de Galápagos)

✿ Common on all islands except Genovesa, Darwin and Wolf.

♈ Grabs prey – mainly lava lizards, geckoes, finch chicks, rats and marine iguana hatchlings – in its jaws before constricting them to death.

✓ Snakes are small, around 1m long, and not dangerous to humans.

Mammals

Galápagos sea lion

Zalophus californianus wollebacki (Lobo marino)

✿ Throughout the archipelago. Favours resting on beaches.

♈ Bull sea lions ferociously guard territories (can be dangerous to humans too), where females rest and relax, forcing other males to set up "bachelor colonies" elsewhere.

✓ Juveniles are highly inquisitive and will often come to investigate snorkellers.

Galápagos fur seal

Arctocephalus galapagoensis (Foca)

✿ Prefers shaded spots on rockier, less accessible shores.

♈ Because of their thick coats, they favour cooler waters, shade, and do not like lying next to others.

✓ Usually encountered by tour groups at James Bay, Santiago and Darwin Bay, Genovesa.

Marine invertebrates

Sally lightfoot crab

Graspus graspus (Cangrejo de las rocas)

✿ Intertidal areas, particularly rocky shorelines.

♈ Follow the movements of the tide, scavenging for scraps and spooning up pieces of algae on specially adapted pincers.

✓ Skittish if approached, but if you stay still they will come to investigate.

✿ Habitat   ♈ Social Life   ✓ Sighting Tips

castaway survived for three years eating iguanas and cactus pads, and may have been rescued sooner had Cobos not left a sign visible to passing boats but inaccessible to the hapless victim, reading "Do not take this man away. He is twenty times a criminal." The bloody retribution came in 1904 when desperate colonists hacked Cobos to pieces on the spot where he'd recently had five people shot.

There's a simple **restaurant**, *La Quinta de Cristi*, in the village and a little further up the road is *La Casa del Ceibo* (T05/2520475 or 2520248; ❷), which takes the prize for the most peculiar **hotel** in the archipelago. A precarious bridge of rope and wire takes you 14.5m up into San Cristóbal's tallest tree – a 300-year-old ceibo – to a tree house equipped for three people, with sleeping mats, fridge, cooker, bathroom, hot water and a fireman's pole for the shortcut to the ground. Underneath, in a subterranean cave, is a video room. The restaurant, which is open at weekends, is no less eccentric, with walls constructed from over 20,000 bottles of beer, while the kitchen and paths are made of plastic crates. There's an irregular **bus** service to the village, but **taxis** can take you for $2, and around $0.25 if you share with locals returning to town. It'll take under an hour to get there on a **bike**, though it's uphill all the way.

Laguna El Junco
Ten kilometres beyond El Progreso, **Laguna El Junco** is a caldera lake at about 650m, often shrouded in mist in the dry season and surrounded by ferns, miconia, brambles and guava bushes. The quiet is occasionally broken by the squawk of a **moorhen** or splash of **white-cheeked pintails** and **whimbrels**. Fed by the mists and rain, it's one of the few freshwater lakes in the Galápagos, and if the clouds lift as you follow the **trail** around the rim you'll have some wonderful views over the island. **Buses** up this far are infrequent, but **taxis** will take you there and back for $18 with waiting time; several **tour operators** make trips to the lagoon too. If you do catch a bus, check when it returns so you don't have to walk the 18km back to Puerto Baquerizo Moreno. Bring sturdy shoes, a waterproof jacket and something warm for the fresher air.

La Galapaguera de Cerro Colorado and Puerto Chino
Beyond El Junco, the road descends to the southern shore, passing **La Galapaguera de Cerro Colorado**, one of two places to see **giant tortoises** on the island; the other is on the island's north side and visited from Punta Pitt on a cruise (see p.451). The former is the focus of a tortoise repopulation programme, where there's an **information centre** for visitors. The area is rich in *Calandrina galapagosa*, an endemic plant critically endangered by introduced species. Continuing the descent, the road meets the coast at **Puerto Chino**, where there's a beautiful, peaceful beach. **Camping** is allowed here with permission from the park authorities, but you'll have to be completely self-sufficient and have arranged transport in and out; it's easier to go with a tour operator, such as Chalo Tours, which offers a night's stay. A **taxi** to La Galapaguera costs $24 return, and to Puerto Chino $30 return.

Punta Pitt and La Galapaguera

Tour boats rarely visit the northeastern extremity of San Cristóbal. After a wet landing into a tight sandy cove, a fairly strenuous trail leads between thorny scrub and tuff cones, climbing to a pass with panoramic views. The real treat of **Punta Pitt** is that it's the only place in the Galápagos where all three species of booby are seen together. **Red-footed boobies** cling to muyuyo trees, while **blue-footed boobies** mark their patches on the ground with a ring of guano. **Nazca** boobies prefer spots closer to the cliffs, and **frigatebird** nests are also found in the *palo santo*. A trailhead at Salinas, west of Punta Pitt leads to **La Galapaguera** after about ninety minutes' hike, a good place to see **giant tortoises** in the wild. Unless your tour boat is stopping here, the only way to visit Punta Pitt and La Galapaguera is to arrange a **tour and guide** with a tour operator.

⑧ Isla Lobos, Playa Ochoa, León Dormido and Cerro Brujo

Thirty minutes' sail north of Puerto Baquerizo Moreno, **Isla Lobos** is a tiny island of rocky lava shores, covered with *palo santo* and speckled with **candelabra cacti**. It's heaving with **sea lions**, but along the short trail you'll also see **blue-footed boobies** and **frigatebirds**. Opposite, on the shore of San Cristóbal is **Playa Ochoa**, a fine white beach with a colony of **sea lions** backed by a tidal lagoon nurturing **flamingos** and the endemic **Chatham mockingbird**; newly arrived tour groups often fetch up here first for a swim and a snorkel as it's an enjoyable and easy introduction to the islands. Another hour by boat to the northeast brings you to **León Dormido** (it's said to resemble a sleeping lion), known as **Kicker Rock** in English. Dizzying tuff cliffs rise out of the ocean, cleft at one end by a narrow waterway, wide enough for a dinghy to go down. There's no landing site, but a cruise around the cliffs should reveal plenty of sea birds, including **frigatebirds**, **red-billed tropicbirds**, and **Nazca and blue-footed boobies**. It's a popular site for scuba diving and snorkelling. Visits to León Dormido sometimes return via **Cerro Brujo**, about thirty minutes to the east. On the west coast of San Cristóbal, this cone stands over a white beach alive with **sea lions**, **pelicans** and **waders**. All the above sites can be visited as part of a **day-trip** arranged through one of the tour operators in Puerto Baquerizo Moreno.

Western islands: Isabela and Fernandina

Straddling the equator, **ISABELA** is the largest island in the Galápagos at 4558 square kilometres, accounting for well over half the total land surface of the archipelago. The island comprises six **volcanoes**, fused together over time: from north to south, Ecuador (790m), Wolf (1707m), Darwin (1330m) and Alcedo (1130m) make up a narrow volcanic chain that tapers into the inaccessible aa lava flow of the Perry Isthmus, on the southwestern side of which Sierra Negra (1124m) and Cerro Azul (1640m) compose the squat base of the island. Several of the volcanoes are still active, the most recent eruptions being La Cumbre on Fernandina in 2009, Cerro Azul in 2008 and Sierra Negra in October 2005.

Much of Isabela's huge landmass is impassable, riven by fissures, blocked by jagged lava flows or tangled thickets and the rocky shores mean that there are few landing places on the island. Most of the visitor sites – **Urbina Bay**, **Elizabeth Bay**, **Punta Tortuga**, **Punta Moreno**, **Punta Vicente Rocafuerte** and **Tagus Cove** – are on its far western side, putting them in range only of the longer tours and faster boats. But it's worth the effort, because the upwelling of cold waters off the coast makes for a nutrient-rich zone, supporting such oddities as the **Galápagos penguin** and the **flightless cormorant**, also frequently spotted on nearby **Fernandina**. Plentiful stocks of fish also attract **whales**, large schools of **common dolphins** and gregarious **bottle-nosed dolphins** – an unexpected highlight of the western islands.

Puerto Villamil, on the island's southeastern coast, is far less developed than either Puerto Ayora or Puerto Baquerizo Moreno, but makes a quiet retreat away from the tour boats. From the town, you can also visit several interesting sites, as well as take a horse ride through the verdant highlands up to the awesome crater of **Sierra Negra** – provided it's not spitting ash and lava.

Puerto Villamil and around

PUERTO VILLAMIL, sitting under the cloud-draped slopes of the huge Sierra Negra volcano, was founded at the beginning of the nineteenth century and named after the general who annexed the islands for Ecuador in 1832. Now home to most of the Isabela's 2200 settlers, the quiet port isn't well developed for tourism, and visitors are infrequent enough to stick out. Just a small town of sandy roads and simple houses with fences of woven branches and cactus, fronted by a beautiful palm-fringed **beach**, it is nevertheless one of the most pleasant off-the-beaten-track places to stay on the islands, boasting several good attractions nearby that can be seen without guides.

Arrival, information and transport

EMETEBE **flights** arrive daily from San Cristóbal via Baltra. Their office is on Avenida Antonio Gil, opposite the police station (☎05/2529155). The airport is 3km outside town; there's no bus service and taxis rarely wait here ($2), so try and get a lift with someone. The hour-long walk along the road across the lava wastes is hot, uncomfortable and best avoided. *Fibras* leave for Puerto Ayora daily at 6am ($30; 2hr) Tickets can be purchased from local travel agents. For more information on *fibras* or *lanchas*, see "Independent travel between the islands", p.455.

You can pick up **maps** of town in Puerto Ayora, or at the *Hospedaje Las Gardenias* on Isabela. The **telephone office** is on the corner of Las Escalecias and Los Cactus, a few blocks back from the beach – look for its red-and-white aerial mast. **Internet** facilities are available next door at Easy Cybercafé, and at a couple of other locations around town for $2–2.50 an hour. Bring all the cash you need as there are no banks or ATMs. There are occasional **water** shortages in town.

Accommodation

The **hotels** in Puerto Villamil are generally of a good standard and cater to a range of budgets. Most of them can provide meals, given some advance notice, and help arrange local tours.

Casa de Marita ☎05/2529238, ⓦwww.galapagosisabela.com. This stylish beach house, shaded by palms on a gorgeous stretch of sand just east of town, offers an array of tasteful rooms, all bright, individual and equipped with a/c, mini-fridge, private bath and hot water. Breakfast is included and other meals are available by arrangement. Bicycles and snorkelling equipment available to rent and tours to island attractions can be arranged. ⓞ–⓼

Cormorant Beach House ☎05/2529192. This colourful two-storey house has a great beachfront location at the western end of town. There are four clean, affordable rooms, each with private bath, hot water and the option of a/c. Guests can also use the kitchen. ⓹

Las Gardenias Corner of Las Escalecias and Tero Real ☎05/2529115, ⓦwww.geocities.com/gardeniasisabela. A couple of blocks back from the beach in a peaceful spot, this cheap and simple hotel has three rooms with private bath and a triple with shared, plus a well-stocked kitchen and TV lounge. Meals and boxed lunches are available on request and tours can be arranged. ⓷

Red Mangrove Isabela Lodge Conocarpus, near the beach ☎05/2526564, ⓦwww.redmangrove.com. Neat beachfront cabins lined by flowery borders, each with two queen-size beds, private bath, hot water and a/c. Wireless internet and laundry available and a buffet breakfast is included. They also have a couple of cheaper rooms over the road with shared bath for $40 a night, which includes an "American" breakfast. Offers overnight stays in their highland camp (**8**) on Sierra Negra. **9**

Tero Real Las Escalecias ☎05/2529106. Inexpensive accommodation in six cabins set in a small garden with hammocks; each is equipped with fridge, private bath and hot water. Use of kitchen for guests and meals are cooked on request. **3**

San Vicente Cormorán and Las Escalecias ☎05/2529140, ✆www.sanvicentegalapagos.com. Popular and comfortable hotel offering cheerful en-suite rooms with a/c, hot water and TV, set in a little garden. Breakfast is included and tours by horse, kayak or boat are available. **4**

Around the port

A small dusty square, fronted by the *municipio* and a simple church, fixes the centre of town a block back from the waterfront, dock and Capitanía. Heading north of the square takes you towards the airport and highlands. There's not much going on in town, but plenty to see nearby. To the east is a path to **Concha de Perla**, a quiet and sheltered little bay with reasonable snorkelling. To the west, Avenida Antonio Gil heads west and passes small, secluded lagoons (*pozas*) – where you can spot waders, shore birds and sometimes flamingos – before a signposted track branches off north to the **Giant Tortoise Breeding Center**, about twenty minutes from the town centre. Work is ongoing here to breed the island's five unique tortoise subspecies, each based around the five largest volcanoes. On show are the rearing pens for the tiny hatchlings, and corrals for adult tortoises taken from the wild, including Cerro Azul tortoises rescued from the volcano when it erupted in 1998 and others saved from a serious forest fire on Sierra Negra in 1994.

The westward road along the coast (ignoring the turn-off to the tortoise centre) continues past several peaceful beaches, including the **Playa de Amor**, where there are some scenic trails perfect for local wildlife spotting. After about two hours' walk, you'll come to **El Muro de las Lágrimas** (The Wall of Tears), a testament to the suffering of three hundred prisoners who toiled here in the 1940s and 1950s; they had to build their own prison using sharp-edged lava boulders. Many died making the wall, which was some 190m long, 9m high and 6m wide at the base when the prison colony was abandoned after a revolt in 1959.

The best place to see marine life in the area is at **Las Tintoreras** (also known as **Las Islas de los Tiburones**), a handful of ragged black-lava grottoes poking out of the sea, a short boat ride from the port ($15–20). From the natural dock a trail leads past scuttling **marine iguanas** up to a lagoon and a narrow channel, where a "viewing gallery" allows you to see the sleek shapes of white-tipped **reef sharks** cruising back and forth. You can swim and snorkel in the lagoon – though don't swim in the channel itself, as it's not big enough for both you and the sharks – or back at the landing site. You may see **rays** and **marine turtles** here or in the gin-clear waters at **Cabo Rosa**, about an hour's ride away by boat from the port (local tour agencies and hotels can arrange this), where semi-submerged lava tunnels have created a striking, otherworldly landscape. The water is shallow here, so the approach is sometimes difficult in the dry season.

Sierra Negra

If you have a day to spare in Puerto Villamil, you can't do much better than go to the summit of **Sierra Negra** (1124m), which reveals a monstrous **crater** some 10km in diameter and 200m deep. It's best reached by horse from **Santo Tomás**, a highland farming community 14km northwest of the port, from where a muddy trail leads uphill over rugged terrain frequently cloaked in thick mist during the cool-dry season. Once at the rim, the heavy clouds curl dramatically over the southern lip before evaporating, leaving the gaping black crater stretching out in full view. On the north side of the rim you can walk to **Volcán Chico**, a collection of hissing volcanic cones that last erupted in 2005. The striking red and black lava coloured by wispy sulphur deposits is virtually lifeless, except for the odd candelabra cactus and a few hardy shrubs clinging to the walls of the fumaroles to suckle on the volcanic steam. This side of the volcano is usually in the sun and gives stupendous views of Fernandina and Isabela's four volcanoes beyond the Perry Isthmus.

Most hotels in town can organize this trip for you, including **guide** and **horse**, costing around $30 for a half day or $45 the whole day. Getting to the crater from Santo Tomás takes about ninety minutes by horse and it's a further thirty minutes' walk to Volcán Chico. Sheets of rubber and plastic sacks will probably serve for saddles if they're not wooden, so you can expect to get pretty sore. Wear long trousers for the horse ride and take a long-sleeved top and rain jacket to keep warm.

Eating and drinking

There's not a huge choice of **places to eat** in Puerto Villamil, but some of the best food on offer is the international cuisine available at *La Casa de Marita*, which requires arrangement in advance. Other options include *Costa Azul*, on Las Fragatas, offering well-prepared dishes in clean surroundings, and *La Choza*, across the street from the Capitanía, which is fairly pricey but serves tasty meals. *El Encanto de la Pepa*, on Conocarpus, has some great fish dishes (and more expensive chicken) in a comfortable little restaurant with plenty of character, and the *Peña La Playita* at the back of it, a small **bar** and disco. *Sea Lion*, at the end of the pier, is a great place for a cocktail at sunset, while on the beach near the *Cormorant Beach House*, *Beto's Bar* has lively music and does barbecues when there's a big enough crowd.

Tagus Cove and Punta Tortuga

A secluded cove of tuff cliffs on the Bolívar Channel, at the foot of Volcán Darwin, **Tagus Cove** is Isabela's most visited site. It's also a convenient anchorage that has been used for many years, as testified by the dozens of boat names etched and painted onto the cliffs; many are those of millionaires' yachts that stopped here on grand world cruises in the 1930s, but the oldest is from 1836, only a year after Darwin's visit.

From the landing point, a trail leads steeply up a breach in the cliffs into the scrubby vegetation typical of the dry coastal regions, including **lantana**, **lechoso**, **Galápagos cotton** and an endemic variety of **palo santo**, which provides a good habitat for a number of **Darwin's finches** and **flycatchers**. The path rises around the rim of **Darwin's Lake**, eventually giving wonderful views of its emerald surface. Strangely, this crater lake has both a higher salinity and water level than the sea, and no one knows exactly why; one theory is that seawater is absorbed upwards through porous rocks and concentrated in the "crucible" of the crater. The trail leads further up to a tuff cone from where you can see a maroon carpet of **aa lava** extending off to Volcán Wolf and Volcán Ecuador in the distance.

Around the cliffs by Tagus Cove, made stripy by thousands of compacted layers of ash, **blue-footed boobies**, **noddy terns**, **pelicans**, **penguins** and **sea lions** can all be seen. To its north, **marine turtles** make nests on the black-sand beach of **Punta Tortuga**. Mangroves back the beach, making it one of the few places to see the endangered **mangrove finch**.

Urbina Bay

Around 25km south of Tagus Cove, **Urbina Bay** shows one of the most dramatic results of tectonic activity. In 1954, a 1.5-square-kilometre section of sea reef was shunted up out of the water, an uplift of almost 4m in places. Skeletons of fish, lobsters and turtles strewn about the rocks told of the violence of the movement; you'll see some sun-bleached brain corals, shells and urchins, several hundred metres from the water's edge.

The trail here forms a long circuit, heading from a wet landing on a black beach inland to where **land iguanas** lurk beneath poison-apple trees (**manzanillo** – don't touch it), **palo santo**, **Vallesia** and **cordia**. In the rainy season, **giant tortoises** descend from Volcán Alcedo to the lowlands to lay eggs; feral goats have caused damage to the tortoises' habitat in this area. The trail then loops back along the shore, over the twisted black lava, home to **marine iguanas** and a few pairs of **flightless cormorants**.

Elizabeth Bay and Punta Moreno

On the west coast of the Perry Isthmus, it's possible to explore the narrowing, mangrove-crowded inlet of **Elizabeth Bay** by *panga* from your tour boat. This is a great place to spot marine wildlife; **turtles**, **reef sharks**, **sea lions** and **rays** all favour the cold, nutrient-rich waters. **Herons** look on from their perches in the tangled mangroves as **blue-footed boobies** dive-bomb the secluded channels, and **shearwaters** skim the surface of the sea. Tour boats usually anchor at the tiny Mariela islands at the mouth of the bay, a good place to see **Galápagos penguins**.

Punta Moreno, around 30km west of Elizabeth Bay, is one of the remotest and least-seen visitor sites in the islands. An enormous flow of **pahoehoe lava** unfurls into the distance, broken by fissures and peppered with brackish water holes ringed by reeds and buzzing with insects. These are the few sources of life in a virtually sterile landscape, supporting **flamingos**, **herons**, **moorhens** and **white-cheeked pintails**.

Punta Vicente Roca and Punta Albemarle

On the northwestern corner of the island, **Punta Vicente Roca** is a spectacular geological extremity of the collapsed Volcán Ecuador. There's nowhere to land in this stunning blue cove, but a *panga* ride close to the shore reveals breathtaking streaked tuff cliffs and a half-submerged cave, home to **blue-footed** and **Nazca boobies**, while flightless cormorants make good on less vertiginous patches. In the water, huge **ocean sunfish**, weighing around a tonne, feast on the jellyfish that congregate here – reason to take care when snorkelling in this otherwise enthralling spot, where dolphins, turtles and even whales are regulars.

Punta Albemarle marks the northernmost tip of the island and was a US radar base during World War II. As such, the military detritus doesn't look that inviting as you approach, but you'll also see (usually from the boat as it's a rough landing rarely attempted) **flightless cormorants** and what are thought to be the largest **marine iguanas** in the islands. It's also a good area for **whale** sightings.

Isla Fernandina

FERNANDINA, lying west of Isabela and dominated by the brooding shape of **Volcán La Cumbre** (1476m), is the youngest island in the archipelago, thought to be between 60,000 and 400,000 years old. It's also one of the most volcanically active islands, erupting ten times in the twentieth century alone, and most recently in April 2009. La Cumbre is crested by a huge caldera, 6km wide and 900m deep, the floor of which exploded in 1968, sending it crashing down by 300m. Fernandina has so far escaped the introduced species that have so damaged other islands, leading to the claim that it's the world's largest pristine island; take care you're not inadvertently transporting any organisms, such as seeds, on your clothes or the soles of your shoes.

Punta Espinosa, a spiky finger of lava at the northeastern tip of the island, is Fernandina's only visitor site. It's home to a sizeable colony of **marine iguanas**, their ashen bodies crammed head to foot on the black rocks. They lay eggs in pockets of sand and you'll see **Galápagos hawks** in the trees nearby waiting to pounce on any stray hatchlings. This is one of the best islands for **flightless cormorants**, which stand at the water's edge after a foray for food underwater, to dry out their useless wings. The **Galápagos penguin** can also be seen floating around the point, competing for fish with **sea lions**.

A trail here leads over rippled **pahoehoe lava**, studded with clumps of lava cacti, to a series of tide pools, a great place to spot **crabs**, **octopuses** and a range of shore birds, including **whimbrels**, **herons** and **oystercatchers**. A final trail heads eastwards to an imposing wall of **aa lava**, a jagged barrier to the slopes of Volcán La Cumbre.

Southern islands: Floreana and Española

Floreana and **Española** are regularly visited islands in the south of the archipelago, and also among its oldest, weather-beaten and eroded over several million years. Floreana, one of the first islands ever to have human settlers – all unsuccessful until the famous **Wittmer** family of the 1930s (see box, p.480) – is known for its interesting history, while Española is a favourite for its sea-bird colonies, especially the endemic waved albatross.

Isla Floreana

Arriving at the beginning of the nineteenth century, Patrick Watkins (see p.442) was the first in a long line of colonists to **FLOREANA**. As the sixth-largest island in the Galápagos (173 square kilometres), and just some 50km south of Santa Cruz, it was favoured for its good supply of both tortoise meat and fresh highland water. General Villamil began Ecuador's first official colony on the islands, the **Asilo de la Paz** ("Haven of Peace"), using convict labour in 1832. He gave up after five years, handing the settlement over to the brutal Colonel José Williams, who kept a pack of vicious dogs to keep his unruly charges at bay, but the hounds weren't protection enough and Williams fled the island after a rebellion in 1841. Almost thirty years later, José de Valdizán sought to rekindle the ill-fated venture, but after eight years his desperate settlers armed themselves and fought each other. Valdizán and several others were killed and the settlement fell apart. All this human interference has not been without effect on Floreana: its tortoise population is extinct, and feral cats so severely preyed on the **Charles mockingbird** that it's now only found on the islets Enderby and Campeón, off the northeastern shore.

There's a small settlement on the western coast of the island, **PUERTO VELASCO IBARRA**, home to around a hundred people. The *Pensión Wittmer* (☎05/2520150; ➐), for many years was the only **place to stay**, and run by

In the 1930s, a string of deaths and disappearances among a curious group of European settlers on Floreana – which became known as the **Galápagos Affair** after the book by John Treherne (see p.439) – made the islands more famous to the contemporary world than even Darwin had done a century earlier. The story began with the arrival in 1929 of two Germans, **Dr Friedrich Ritter** and his mistress **Dore Strauch**. Ritter, a determined, vain and deliberately compassionless man, was pumped up on the ideas of Nietzsche and Lao-tze, and had pretensions to being a great philosopher, rather than breadwinner in a suburban Berlin household. Dore fell under his spell as his patient, and they eventually conspired to run off to the Galápagos Islands, no easy holiday spot, but the perfect place to found a dark Utopia and play out the roles of "philosopher-heroes". Seeing himself as one of Nietzsche's *Übermenschen*, Ritter refused to bring a supply of morphine with him, welcoming the test of beating pain "by the power of the will". He had also had his and Dore's teeth removed, preferring the reliability of a set of steel dentures – which they shared. He refused to show any love to his mistress, leaving her weeping on the lava when she couldn't carry their supplies; he wouldn't even clean Dore's burn wounds after she'd knelt in red-hot coals. Towards the end he even beat her, but Dore claimed her devotion to him never faltered.

The couple lived alone on the island until 1932, when the **Wittmer family** – Heinz, Margret and their son Harry – arrived from Cologne. They were a far more practical bunch and stayed out of the way of their strange neighbours as much as they could. A couple of months later, a woman armed with a riding crop and a revolver, calling herself the **Baroness Wagner de Bosquet** and claiming to be an Austrian aristocrat, stormed onto the island with her two German lovers, Rudolf Lorenz and Robert Philippson. Her plan was to build a hotel for millionaires, the *Hacienda Paraíso*, which she set about doing, but before long it became clear to the previous settlers she was a compulsive liar and a sadistic megalomaniac. She took pleasure in treating Lorenz like a slave and regularly got Philippson to beat him. Soon she was treading on the other settlers' toes, intercepting their mail left at Post Office Bay, stealing supplies left for them by passing yachts and declaring herself "Empress of Floreana".

Matters came to a head during the long drought of 1934, when the Baroness and Philippson disappeared. According to Margret Wittmer, the Baroness said a friend was taking them to Tahiti, a story backed by Lorenz, who had managed to escape the household shortly before. But Dore claimed she heard a "long-drawn scream" coming from the hacienda and Ritter seemed unusually sure they had gone for good – even though all the Baroness's belongings were where she'd left them, including her beloved copy of *The Picture of Dorian Gray*. "She won't come back. Take my word for it," he told Margret Wittmer. He was right – neither the Baroness nor Philippson were ever seen again.

After their disappearance, Lorenz grew increasingly desperate to leave the island and persuaded a visiting Norwegian, Nuggerud, to sail him to San Cristóbal. Nuggerud wasn't keen: the sea was rough, he wanted to get back to his wife on Santa Cruz who was about to give birth to their first child and it was Friday 13th. Nevertheless, he relented; four months later, the desiccated bodies of both men were found on Marchena Island. Only a few days after this, Ritter fell gravely ill after eating a poisoned chicken cooked by Dore, who said she'd also eaten it, but was only mildly sick. His hatred for his mistress was remorseless and, just before he died, he wrote a final message to Dore: "I curse you with my dying breath." Dore returned to Berlin, where she died, shortly after telling her story in the book, *Satan Came to Eden*. Margret Wittmer, who was the last survivor of the original settlers, died in 2000 aged 95, but the deaths and disappearances on Floreana are no closer to being solved.

Margret Wittmer, one of the protagonists of the Galápagos Affair (see box opposite), but now taken over by her family. As well as providing meals for guests, the Wittmers can give advice on the **hikes** around the island, including down from the Asilo de la Paz, the site of the island's only water source; two daily work trucks depart for the highlands (30min; you'll want the 6am one if you want to explore). Alternative lodging can now be found at *Red Mangrove Floreana Lodge* (☎05/2526564, Ⓦ www.redmangrove.com; ❾ including breakfast; lunch and dinner $30 each), which offers clean but spartan pine cabins with bathroom and space for four, on the lava by the shore about ten-minutes' walk south of the port on the way to **La Lobería**, where there's a sea-lion colony. Apart from this, it's a very quiet island, with little to see and do, but an unbeatable place to get away from it all. If you're not on a tour, it's not straightforward to get to Floreana; for details about *fibras*, see "Independent travel between the islands", p.455.

Punta Cormorant and Devil's Crown

At **Punta Cormorant**, on the northernmost tip of Floreana, you'll land by *panga* on a beach made green from deposits of the mineral olivine. You won't actually see cormorants here, but a trail to the lagoon behind the mangroves does lead to a variety of wading birds, including **ruddy turnstones**, **whimbrels**, **stilts**, **white-cheeked pintails** and **phalaropes**; above all, this is the best place in the islands to see **flamingos**. Around this site are two species of plant found nowhere else in the world, the **cutleaf daisy** (*Leocarpus pinnatifidus*) and a type of **scalesia**.

The trail passes a viewpoint looking out to a tuff cone, and finishes at **Flour Beach**, so called for its very fine, white sand of ground coral. **Marine turtles** nest here, but it's better known for the schools of **stingrays** that settle in the

▲ Pink flamingos, Isla Floreana

shallows. You can't swim here, but opposite Punta Cormorant is **Devil's Crown** (also called Isla Onslow), a submerged cone sheltering beautiful coral reefs from the currents outside, which makes for excellent snorkelling and scuba diving. In addition to **surgeonfish**, **angelfish**, **parrotfish** and **wrasse**, you may see **white-tipped reef sharks** and even **hammerheads**.

Post Office Bay

A few kilometres west of Punta Cormorant is **Post Office Bay**, named such for a barrel near the beach that has been used for a makeshift mail drop since the end of the eighteenth century. British whalers, who left letters here to be picked up by homeward-bound vessels, began the practice, which was cleverly exploited during the Anglo-American war of 1812, when the canny US Navy Captain, **David Porter**, intercepted communications here, allowing him to round up one million tons of shipping in the region's waters.

The original **barrel** has long been replaced, but post is still left and delivered free of charge by visitors to the bay. The "post office" is now marked by a shrine of planks, with the names of yachts etched onto them, animal bones, driftwood and many other bits and pieces left by the regular tour boats and numerous day-trippers who visit. Nearby are the remains of a fish-canning factory Norwegian colonists set up and abandoned in the 1920s, and a short trail leading to a lava tube, for which you need caving gear to descend.

Isla Española

In the far southeastern corner of the archipelago, **ESPAÑOLA** is a remote island featuring regularly on tour-boat itineraries, a favourite for its sea-bird colonies and native wildlife. Isolation has given rise to a number of endemic species: Española's mockingbirds, lava lizards and colourful marine iguanas are found nowhere else in the world, while the **waved albatross**, the star of the island when in residence between April and December, has only one other home – even then in small numbers – at the Isla de la Plata off the mainland coast. Española's **giant tortoises** were nearly wiped out (down to only fourteen specimens in the 1970s) because of feral goats, which have since been eradicated. Under a long-term, CDRS-run repopulation programme, the thousandth Española tortoise reared in captivity was successfully repatriated to the island in March 2000.

Punta Suárez and Gardner Bay

Española's two visitor sites offer very different experiences. At **Punta Suárez**, on the western end of the island, noisy **sea lions** welcome visitors landing on a small beach. On the rocks, **marine iguanas**, unusual for rusty colourations that erupt into turquoise and red during the mating season, bask in the sun. **Hood mockingbirds**, even more gregarious than their relatives on other islands, will hop to your feet and tug at your shoelaces. From the beach, a long, looped trail heads up to a large plateau covered in **muyuyo**, **croton**, **lycium** and **atriplex** (salt sage), a scrubby costume of plants that bursts into green during the rainy season. The **waved albatross** nests among these bushes from April to December; it's a giant of a bird that flies alone above the seas for three months, before returning to the island to find its lifelong mate, perform its alluring courtship dance and breed (see also p.525). When it's time to hunt, the adults waddle to the high cliffs at the southern end of the island to launch themselves off, unfurling their 2.5-metre wings. Along the cliffs you'll also find **Nazca boobies**, **swallow-tailed gulls** and **red-billed tropicbirds**; in the west, a blowhole sends a tall jet of spray gushing through a fissure in the lava.

The trail then heads back across the plateau, through a field of **blue-footed boobies**, high-stepping and sky-pointing at each other in a cacophony of whistling and honking.

The second visitor site, **Gardner Bay**, on the northeast side of the island, holds one of the most spectacular beaches in the archipelago, a lightly curling strip of soft, white, coral sand, lapped by a dazzling blue sea. Bull **sea lions** energetically patrol the water while their many consorts doze on the sand. As an open site, you can walk the length of the beach without the rest of your group or the guide. It's a good spot for some swimming, but snorkelling is better around the offshore islets nearby, especially **Isla Tortuga**, where **eagle rays**, **white-tipped reef** and **hammerhead sharks** can be seen.

Northern islands: Isla Genovesa

Of the five islands that make up the remote northern group, only **Genovesa** is open to visitors. The tiny islands of **Darwin** and **Wolf**, at the far northwestern reaches of the archipelago, and **Marchena**, some 90km north of Santa Cruz, are occasionally visited by scuba divers, but only for offshore exploration, while **Pinta** is out of bounds to all but authorized scientists. Genovesa, lying approximately 95km northeast of Santa Cruz, reached after a night of sailing, is usually only visited by faster boats or as part of longer itineraries. It's well worth the extra effort, as it's one of the best **bird** islands in the Galápagos and home to the world's largest colony of **red-footed boobies**.

Isla Genovesa

Captains align solar-powered beacons on **GENOVESA** to find the safe route into **Darwin Bay**, formed by a pincer of imposing cliffs rising to 25m over the sea, the remnants of a large, sunken caldera. A wet landing onto a small beach brings you face to face with **Nazca boobies, frigatebirds, swallow-tailed gulls, mockingbirds** and **red-footed boobies**. Birds rule the roost here; there are no introduced species and very few reptiles. The **marine iguanas** on the rocks are among the smallest in the islands, and the absence of land iguanas and giant tortoises means Genovesa's **prickly pear cacti**, free from major predators, grow with soft spines. As a trail heads west along the shore past red-footed boobies, you'll also see **great** and **magnificent frigatebirds** nesting in saltbush and red mangroves, with **lava herons** and Galápagos doves hopping around the rocks searching for food. **Yellow-crowned night herons** loiter near the tide pools watching for chances to snatch **wrasse, blenny** and **damselfish**. Four types of **Darwin's finches** also inhabit the *palo santo* and *croton* scrub. Snorkelling in the bay can be thrilling for the schools of **hammerhead sharks** that sometimes congregate at its western arm.

Among the crevices and protrusions at the eastern end of the bay inhabited by **fur seals, swallow-tailed gulls** and **red-billed tropicbirds** is a natural dock and a gully, named **Prince Philip's Steps** after the Duke of Edinburgh's visit in the 1960s. **Nazca boobies** greet you at the top and another trail takes you through a *palo santo* forest, past more red-footed boobies and frigatebirds. On the far side you come out of the vegetation to stand above a broad lava flow overlooking the sea. Clouds of **storm petrels** swarm in the sky above their nests hidden in the lava fissures. They're the smallest of the sea birds – a perfect-sized meal for the superbly camouflaged **short-eared owls** which prey on them.

Travel details

Boats

Puerto Ayora to: Puerto Baquerizo Moreno (daily 2pm; 2hr); Puerto Villamil (daily 2pm; 2–3hr).
Puerto Baquerizo Moreno to: Puerto Ayora (daily 7am; 2hr).
Puerto Villamil to: Puerto Ayora (daily 6am; 2–3hr).

Flights

Baltra to: Guayaquil (3–4 daily; 1hr 35min); Puerto Baquerizo Moreno (1 daily Mon–Sat; 30min);

Puerto Villamil (1 daily Mon–Sat; 25min); Quito (3–4 daily; 3hr).
Puerto Baquerizo Moreno to: Baltra (1 daily Mon–Sat; 30min); Guayaquil (1 daily; 1hr 35min); Puerto Villamil (1 daily Mon–Sat; 40min); Quito (1 daily; 3hr).
Puerto Villamil to: Baltra (1 daily Mon–Sat; 25min); Puerto Baquerizo Moreno (1 daily Mon–Sat; 40min).

Contexts

Contexts

History

E xactly how and when the Americas were populated is still debated, but most authorities accept that humans first migrated from Asia over the Bering land bridge, formed by low sea levels during the last Ice Age, or along the coast aided by prevailing currents, between 40,000 and 12,000 years ago. The earliest evidence of human presence in Ecuador was discovered east of Quito at the El Inga archeological site and dates back to 10,000 BC.

Early cultures

Around this time, small **hunter-gatherer communities** collected seeds, berries, roots, insects and reptile eggs from the valley forests and roamed the high grasslands for bigger game. A set of arrowheads and spear points found at **El Inga** was carved from glassy black obsidian and basalt, materials taken from the huge lava wastes that then scarred the Andes; similar fragments made with hard volcanic materials have also been recovered from the Loja and Azuay areas in the southern sierra. On the coast at about this time other hunter-gatherer groups of the **Las Vegas** culture were emerging around the Santa Elena peninsula, and by 6000 BC they began seasonal cultivation of food crops and cotton – Ecuador's first known **agriculturists**.

Certain characteristics of Las Vegas culture, such as semi-permanent settlements and the fashioning of tools from polished stone, laid the basis for the **Valdivia** culture, which blossomed c.3500 BC and spread across the coast to southern Esmeraldas and El Oro over the next two thousand years, dominating the early **Formative Period** (4000–400 BC). The Valdivia culture is best known for its ceramics – among the oldest found in South America – especially its **Venus figurines**, stylized miniatures of women with long, flowing hair and often pregnant, which are believed to have been part of a fertility cult. They lived in oval, wood-and-thatch houses surrounding a central square, in villages strung along the coast and around river plains, where the soil was fertile enough to grow maize, cotton, cassava, peppers and kidney beans.

The **Machalilla** culture (1500–800 BC) that followed them preferred rectangular structures on stilts and practised skull deformation as a sign of status. They were more expert than their Valdivia counterparts at fishing and had surplus stores for trading with neighbouring groups. Their ceramic flasks, characterized by circular or stirrup-shaped spouts, are similar to those made by the Cotocollao, Cerro Narrío and Upano cultures, suggesting there was contact between them. Based around the Quito area, the **Cotocollao** people traded agricultural produce, such as quinoa, for coastal cotton, while the **Cerro Narrío** site in the southern sierra was an important trading centre between the coast and the Upano group based around Volcán Sangay in the upper Amazon basin. This communication across the regions seems to have intensified with the **Chorrera** culture (900–300 BC), which flourished on the coast at the close of the Formative Period, a sophisticated people who crafted some of the most beautiful ceramics of that age, distinctive for their iridescent sheen.

The subsequent **Regional Development Period** (300 BC to 800 AD) saw a splintering of cultures and the appearance of highly stratified societies.

The driving force behind these changes was a burgeoning economy and related interaction between cultures. As trading routes sprang up along the coast, seafaring cultures such as **Bahía** (from south of Bahía de Caráquez, dating from 500 BC to 650 AD), **Jama–Coaque** (north of Bahía, from 350 BC to 1540 AD) and **Guangala** (Guayas coast from 100 BC to 800 AD) transported their wares on balsawood rafts with cotton sails. The merchants of these cultures were part of the elite, acting as diplomats and facilitators securing necessary goods from afar. The merchants' most treasured possession, above even gold and platinum, was the deep-crimson **spondylus** (thorny oyster) shell, harvested from a depth of twenty to sixty metres by highly skilled fishermen. Prized ornaments and symbols of fertility, the shells were also a kind of universal currency, exchanged for anything from animal furs and armadillo shells to colourful cloths and beeswax. Such was the range of these traders that ceramics representing them – sitting **basketmen** figures, often adorned with necklaces, bracelets and earrings, with outsized baskets on their backs – have been found on the Pacific coast from Ecuador to Central America.

Meanwhile, in northern Esmeraldas and stretching into Colombia, the culture of **La Tolita** (500 BC to 500 AD) held one of the prime religious and trading centres on the South American coast, thought to have been at the island of La Tolita, in the mangroves near present-day San Lorenzo. Traders, craftsmen and worshippers from different regions swarmed to the site and the cross-fertilization of ideas led to the creation of exquisite ceramic styling and metalwork, including fine objects of platinum, silver, copper and gold.

In the **Integration Period** (800–1480 AD), when political leaders and chiefs (*curacas*) of local territories, defined through frequent skirmishes, exacted tribute and levied taxes from their communities, agricultural productivity surged through improved techniques in irrigation and terracing, and trading continued to boom. On the coast the **Manteño–Huancavilca** culture (500 BC to 1540 AD), occupying land from the Gulf of Guayaquil to Bahía de Caráquez, continued the seafaring traditions of their coastal forebears, while also producing distinctive artefacts like ceremonial U-shaped chairs supported by human or animal figures, and black ceramics. To their north, people such as the **Nigua**, **Chachi**, **Campaz**, **Caraque** and **Malaba** continued to live by hunting, fishing and farming small agricultural plots. Inland, to the south, the **Chono** – the ancestors of the Tsáchila (or Colorados) of today, defined archeologically as the **Milagro–Quevedo** culture – were known for fine weavings and gold adornments such as nose rings, headbands and breastplates. They also frequently warred with the fierce **Puná**, who occupied the island of the same name in the Gulf of Guayaquil.

In the highlands at this time, the major population groups occupied the elevated valley basins between the western and eastern cordilleras of the Andes, each basin (*hoya*) separated from the next by mountainous *nudos*, "knots" where the cordilleras tie together. From north to south these were the **Pasto**, occupying southern Colombia and Carchi; the **Cara** (or Caranqui), living around Ibarra, Otavalo and Cayambe, and responsible for enormous ceremonial centres such as the one at Cochasquí; the **Panzaleo** (also called the Quito), who inhabited the Quito valley, Cotopaxi and Tungarahua, and did much trade with the **Quijo** in the Oriente; the **Puruhá**, of the Chimborazo region; the **Cañari**, great gold and copper craftspeople who dominated the southern sierra; and the **Palta**, a tribe whose major centre was Saraguro near Loja and who had strong links with the Amazonian group, the **Shuar**.

The Incas

Around 1200, the **Incas** were an unremarkable sierra people occupying the Cuzco valley in Peru. After a string of military victories over neighbouring tribes in the fifteenth century, they grew into one of the most sophisticated civilizations of South America. In about 1460 the Inca **Tupac Yupanqui** set out to conquer present-day Ecuador with a force of 200,000 men. He brushed aside the Palta in the south in a matter of months, but met fierce resistance with the Cañari, and the warring left the whole region devastated. The Cañari had been so impressive in battle that when they were beaten many were recruited into the Inca professional army. Even the Cañari weren't as bellicose as the Cara in the north, who managed to keep the invaders at bay for seventeen years before a terrible massacre at Laguna Yahuarcocha in 1495, led by **Huayna Capac**, Tupac Yupanqui's son.

At its height in the early sixteenth century, the Inca Empire, known as **Tahuantinsuyo** ("Land of the Four Quarters", after its administrative division into four regions), extended from Chile and the Argentinian Andes to southern Colombia, a total area of some 980,000 square kilometres, linked by some thirty thousand kilometres of roads. It was a highly organized and efficient society that built great stone palaces, temples, observatories, storehouses and fortresses using masonry techniques of breathtaking ingenuity.

Just as impressive was its administrative system, allowing a relatively small number of people to hold sway over huge areas. **Indirect rule** was imposed on the conquered regions, with the local chief allowed to remain in power as long as he acknowledged the divine sovereignty of the Inca emperor. Lands were divided between the Incas (for the king, nobility and army), religion (for sacrifices, ceremonies and the priesthood) and the local communities, and tribute was paid in the cultivation of the imperial lands. Each year, subjects also had to honour the **mita**, a labour obligation requiring them to spend time working in the army or on public works. A shrewd policy stipulated the community could not be taxed on its own produce, a measure that did much to ensure contentment and stability in the colonies. Any troublesome subjects were forcefully resettled many hundreds of miles away – and indoctrinated and acculturated colonists were brought in as replacements. Many Palta, for example, were transported to Lake Titicaca in Bolivia, and swapped with communities there that had been under the Inca yoke for decades.

Considering that the Incas were rulers in what is now southern Ecuador for no more than seventy years, and in northern Ecuador for only thirty years, they had an enormous impact on the region. New urban and ceremonial centres were built, such as **Tomebamba** (now buried beneath Cuenca) and **Quito**, with roads connecting them to the rest of the empire, and fortresses were erected at strategic points across the country, as at **Ingapirca**. The language of the Incas, **Quechua**, was imposed on the defeated population and it's still spoken in various forms (as Quichua or Kichwa) by the majority of Ecuador's *indígenas*. The Incas also introduced sweet potatoes, peanuts and oca, and drove large herds of llamas north from Peru for their wool and meat.

By 1525 Huayna Capac was looking to establish a second capital at Quito or Tomebamba. Before he had a chance to act he was struck down by a virulent disease – probably **smallpox**, which had been brought to Central America by the Spanish and had swiftly spread southwards through the continent before them. Huayna Capac's likely heir also died from the disease and in the resulting confusion two other sons took charge of the empire: **Huáscar**, who, ruling the south from Cuzco, claimed he was the chosen successor; and **Atahualpa**, who asserted he'd been assigned the north, governed from Quito. Within a few years, friction between the two brothers erupted into a full-blown **civil war**, but Atahualpa had the advantage as the bulk of the imperial army was still in the north after the recent campaigns and under his command. Their forces clashed at Ambato, a pitched battle where more than thirty thousand soldiers from both sides, many of them conscripted locals, were killed. Atahualpa drove his brother south, laying waste to Tomebamba and the Cañari lands in revenge for their support of his enemy. With his superior troops, Atahualpa eventually got the upper hand, but even before he had heard of his generals' final victory over Huáscar in Cuzco, news reached him of a small band of bearded strangers that had landed on the coast nearby, plundering the villages and maltreating the natives.

The Spanish Conquest

In 1526 the Spanish pilot **Bartolomé Ruiz** sailed down the Ecuadorian coast on a reconnaissance mission and, near Salango, captured a large Manta merchant vessel laden with gold, silver and emeralds. His report convinced **Francisco Pizarro** that there were great riches to be had on the continent. After obtaining royal approval, Pizarro set sail from Panama in December 1530 with 180 men and 37 horses, landing at **Tumbes** in northern Peru in May 1532, with a few more troops brought by two other hardy campaigners, Sebastián de Benalcázar and Hernando de Soto. The Inca city, which marked the northernmost limits of the empire on the coast, lay in ruins from the civil war, and bodies hung from the trees nearby. The Spaniards soon learnt the civilization had been in the grip of a terrible conflict, and saw this made the perfect opportunity for conquest.

Pumped up by his victory over Huáscar's army of almost a hundred thousand, Atahualpa didn't regard the Spaniard's straggly band of a few hundred as much of a threat – even with their horses, an unknown quantity to the Incas. In a fatal miscalculation, the new emperor invited them to a meeting at **Cajamarca**, letting them past countless guardposts and strongholds and over mountainous terrain that would have been too steep for cavalry attacks. A day after his arrival in Cajamarca, Pizarro launched a surprise attack, taking Atahualpa hostage and massacring thousands of Inca soldiers and nobles in just a few hours. Many more were trampled to death in the stampede to escape the Spanish guns, steel armoury and cavalry. Atahualpa, seeing that his captors craved precious metals, offered to fill a room with gold and two huts with silver, in return for which Pizarro promised to restore him to his kingdom at Quito. Within a few months, six metric tons of gold and almost twelve tons of silver had been melted down, making rich men of the conquistadors. Nevertheless, they broke their promise and, fearing a counterattack, swiftly condemned Atahualpa to be burnt alive – a terrifying prospect for someone who believed his body must be preserved for passage into the afterlife – unless he became a Christian. In July 1533 the weeping Inca was baptized and then garrotted.

The Spanish quickly took Cuzco and southern Peru, and then turned their attention to Quito and the northern empire, modern Ecuador – a race was on to find the suspected treasures of its cities. In March 1534, the merciless governor of Guatemala, **Pedro de Alvarado**, gathered a formidable army, including several thousand Guatemalans, and landed on the Ecuadorian coast in the Manta area. Locals, who entreated him with offerings of food, were either slaughtered or thrown into chains and taken on his campaign. Despite torturing natives to find the best route into the highlands, he ended up going over the highest and most treacherous pass near Chimborazo, and lost many men and horses, as well as the race to Quito.

Sebastián de Benalcázar, meanwhile, had got wind of Alvarado's expedition early on, and swiftly summoned his own forces together, riding across the bleak Peruvian coast onto the Inca highway to Quito. In Tomebamba, where he found beautiful temples encrusted with emeralds and plated in sheets of gold, he forged an alliance with the Cañari, who were bent on exacting revenge for years of subjugation under the Incas. A couple of large Inca armies were still mobilized in the north, and in the cold páramo grasslands at Teocajas above Tomebamba, the tenacious Inca general **Rumiñahui** prepared his fifty thousand troops for attack. They fought bravely, despite a series of devastating cavalry charges, but it was clear it would take a miracle to beat the Spanish and their horses. He devised a number of ingenious traps, such as pits laid with sharp spikes hidden under the thick grasses, but each time their location was betrayed by informers. Rumiñahui battled with Benalcázar all the way to Quito and before the Spanish could get there he removed the treasures and torched the palaces and food stores. Then, joining forces with another general, **Zopozopagua**, he launched a night attack on the Spanish encamped in the city, but again was thwarted by superior military hardware. Eventually both Rumiñahui and Zopozopagua were caught, tortured and executed. **Quisquis**, the last of Atahualpa's great generals, valiantly fought his way from southern Ecuador to Quito, but when he found the city had already been taken, his army mutinied, hacking him to pieces rather than face death on the battlefields.

In August 1534 the Spaniards founded the city of **San Francisco de Quito** on the charred remains of the Inca capital, and a few months later they had conquered all of the northern part of the Inca Empire. The inaccessible north coast and much of the Oriente were deemed too difficult and unproductive to colonize and stayed out of their control for much of the colonial era. Still, the Conquest had had a devastating effect on the native populations of Ecuador through war, forced labour and Old World **diseases**. Smallpox, measles, plague and influenza cut the aboriginal population to 200,000 by the end of the sixteenth century, down from 1.5 million – an overall decline of over 85 percent.

The Colonial era

The Spanish were quick to consolidate their victories, with the Crown parcelling out land to the conquistadors in the form of **encomiendas**, grants that entitled the holders, the **encomenderos**, to a substantial tribute in cash, plus produce and labour from the *indígenas* who happened to live there. In return, the *encomenderos* were entrusted with converting their charges to Christianity, a task that was only a partial success; in many cases the *indígenas* merely superimposed Catholic imagery onto their existing beliefs, but eventually the two traditions fused in a syncretism that can still be seen today.

The *encomienda* system grafted easily onto the old Inca order, and the *encomenderos* were soon the elite of the region, which became the **Audiencia de Quito** in 1563. Roughly corresponding to modern-day Ecuador, the *audiencia* had rather vague boundaries, but included a huge swath of the Amazon following Francisco de Orellana's voyage (see box, p.294). It also enjoyed legal autonomy from Lima and direct links to Madrid, even though it was still a part of the Viceroyalty of Peru. During the early 1600s, there were more than five hundred *encomiendas* in the *audiencia*, run on the labour of about half the region's *indígenas*, who were effectively serfs on these estates, their labour often badly abused despite laws that were supposed to protect them.

Another quarter of the area's *indígenas* deserted the productive *encomienda* lands for the undesirable páramo and lowland forests, but they were rounded up at the end of the century and resettled in purpose-built "Indian towns", or **reducciones**, where colonists could more easily collect tribute and exploit their labour. The Spanish also borrowed – and corrupted – another Inca institution, the *mita*, a system that required these supposedly free *indígenas* to work for a year according to the needs of the colony. These workers, the **mitayos**, received a small wage but it was invariably less than the amount they owed their employers for subsistence purchases. Soon the *mita* system descended into debt slavery, as the *mitayos* worked indefinitely to pay off their unending deficits – which their children would inherit, so trapping them, too. The *audiencia* had such poor mineral resources – the small gold and silver deposits around Cuenca and Loja were exhausted by the end of the sixteenth century – that the *mitayos* were spared the agonies of working in mines: millions of their contemporaries died in the silver and mercury mines of Peru and Bolivia. Instead, most of the indigenous labourers were involved in **agriculture** (particularly the farming of introduced wheat, cattle, sheep and chickens) and **textiles**, an industry that boomed throughout the seventeenth century with the opening of hundreds of sweatshops, known as **obrajes**.

Events of the 1690s saw an abrupt halt to the economic success, as another wave of epidemics wiped out half the native population, droughts destroyed harvests and severe earthquakes shook the region. This triggered the demise of the *encomiendas*, which were replaced by large private estates, or **haciendas**, but for the *indígenas* the new system of **huasipungo** that the changes entailed brought little relief. In return for their labour on the haciendas, they were entitled to farm tiny plots of land in their spare moments, where they were expected to grow all their own food.

The last quarter of the remaining indigenous population escaped the rule of the Spanish altogether by living in the inaccessible tropical forests of the lowland Oriente or the north coast, the latter area under the control of a **black** and **zambo** (mixed black and indigenous) population, largely the descendants of escaped slaves, brought to work on the coastal plantations or fight in the Spanish army. The south coast had only a tiny workforce available, as more than 95 percent of the natives had been wiped out by disease, but even so, **Guayaquil**, founded by Benalcázar in 1535, was developing into an important trade and shipbuilding centre.

In the early 1700s the **Bourbon** kings of Spain, who had replaced the Hapsburg dynasty at the beginning of the century, were determined to tighten their grip over their enormous American territories. They embarked on a strategy of economic and administrative reform intended to boost productivity, such as transferring the *audiencia* to the newly established Viceroyalty of **Nueva Granada**, with its capital at Bogotá, Colombia, in 1717 (an arrangement that lasted three years), and then again in 1739. The expulsion of the **Jesuits** in 1767 by Charles III only damaged further the weak highland economy. The Jesuits – as well as teaching Christianity to the *indígenas* – had run the best schools and most productive and profitable workshops in the *audiencia*, but their very success had made them unpopular with the Crown. Yet while the highland textile economy suffered severe depression, the **cacao** industry on the coast was flourishing, with the commodity becoming the colony's largest export and plantations springing up all over the countryside north of Guayaquil. Employers were even willing to pay a proper wage to indigenous labourers, who were cheaper than imported slaves.

By the middle of the eighteenth century, a combination of developments brought about a general change of attitude in the Spanish colonies. The **criollos** – Spanish people born in the colonies – were nursing a growing resentment to the motherland that wasn't helped by the economic situation. High taxes, continual interference from Spain, and the fact that all the best jobs still went to the **peninsulares** – Spanish-born newcomers – only added to the discontent. At the same time, the **Enlightenment** was opening up new lines of political and philosophical thought which filtered down from Europe into the upper-class households of the *audiencia*, fostering ideas that sharply contradicted the semi-feudal organization of the colony. Scientific expeditions were a source of new knowledge, such as **Charles-Marie de La Condamine**'s mission (1736–45) to discern the shape of the Earth, which he did by measuring a degree of latitude on the equator north of Quito.

One of the first to articulate the new influences was **Eugenio Espejo**, an exceptional man who, despite being born of *indígena* and mulatto parents in a deeply racist society, obtained a university degree and became an outstanding doctor, lawyer, essayist and satirist. His outspoken views on republicanism and democracy cost him his life – he died in jail in 1795 – but he's still honoured as the progenitor of the country's independence movement.

The birth of the republic

Napoleon's successful invasion of Spain in 1808 sent shockwaves throughout its New World colonies. On August 10, 1809, a short-lived junta in support of the deposed king, **Ferdinand VII**, was established in Quito, but it failed in a matter of weeks when the backing of the rest of the *audiencia* was not forthcoming. Despite assurances of pardons, those involved were rounded up and sentenced to death. In August 1810, an incensed public stormed the prison where the condemned were held, but the guards massacred the junta's leaders before they could be freed. Even so, the disturbances led to a new **junta**, which ambitiously declared the independence of the *audiencia* in 1811, whether the rest of the colony was ready for it or not. With a band of ill-disciplined troops, the new government launched a foolhardy attack against the well-trained Spanish forces and were consequently routed at Ibarra in 1812.

After that defeat, it wasn't until 1820 that the independence movement regained momentum, this time in Guayaquil, led by **José Joaquín de Olmedo**, an intellectual and shrewd politician, where **independence** was declared on October 9. Urgent requests for assistance were immediately sent to the Liberator **Simón Bolívar**, who was marching south from Venezuela, and **José de San Martín**, who was sweeping north from Argentina, crushing the Spanish armies as they went. Bolívar quickly dispatched his best general, the 26-year-old **Antonio José de Sucre**, with a force of seven hundred men. Sucre scored a great victory at Guayaquil, but was thwarted at Ambato, until reinforcements sent by San Martín enabled him to push on to Quito. On May 24, 1822, he won the decisive **Battle of Pichincha**, on the slopes of the volcano above the city, and five days later the old *audiencia* became the **Department of the South** in a new autonomous state, **Gran Colombia**, roughly corresponding to the combined territories of Ecuador, Colombia, Panama and Venezuela today.

The early years of the republic were turbulent and disagreements over the state's border with Peru escalated into armed conflict in 1828. Guayaquil suffered extensive damage during a sea attack, but Sucre and **General Juan José Flores** defeated the Peruvian forces at the Battle of Tarqui in 1829. A year later on May 13, following Venezuela's split from Gran Colombia, Quito representatives also decided to declare their own republic, naming it **Ecuador**, after its position on the equator (other options were "Quito", which wasn't popular with those outside the city, and even "Atahualpia") and **General Flores**, a Venezuelan by birth who had married into the Quito aristocracy, became the country's first president.

The new nation didn't gel well at all. In the sierra the **Conservative** land-owning elites were happy to keep the colonial system in operation, while on the coast the **Liberal** merchant classes, rich on the country's sole export commodity, cacao, wanted free trade, lower taxes and a break with the old order. This dualism between the regions – and their great centres, Quito and Guayaquil – has coloured the politics and history of the country ever since.

Flores soon found his heavy-handed and Quito-oriented administration desperately unpopular on the coast, and cannily arranged for the Guayaquileño politician **Vicente Rocafuerte** to take the second term. Meanwhile Flores lurked in the background, pulling the strings as head of the military, and became president again from 1839 to 1845, when he was ousted by a junta from the coast. For the next fifteen years, the country descended into a political mire, with bitter fighting between the regions and the seat of government moving from Quito to Guayaquil to Riobamba and back to Guayaquil. Eleven presidents and juntas followed each other in power, the most successful being led by the Liberal **General José María Urbina**, who ruled with an iron fist from 1851 to 1856 and managed to **abolish slavery** within a week of the coup that swept him to the presidency. Moreover, he had strongly encouraged his predecessor, **General Francisco Robles**, to axe the tribute the *indígenas* were still being forced to pay after three centuries of abuse.

The turmoil of the era culminated in 1859 – later known as the **Terrible Year** – when the strain between the regions finally shattered the country: Quito set up a provisional government, Cuenca declared itself autonomous, Loja became a federal district and, worst of all, Guayaquil, led by General Guillermo Franco, signed itself away to Peruvian control. Peru invaded and blockaded the port, while Colombia hungrily eyed the rest of Ecuador for itself.

Conservative rule: 1861–95

Aiming to set the republic right, **Gabriel García Moreno** quashed the various rebellions with the help of Flores and seized power as president in 1861. Although born into a poor family in Guayaquil, García Moreno was educated in Quito and Europe and was both fiercely Conservative and a devout Catholic. He saw the country's salvation in the Church, and set about strengthening its position, establishing it as the state religion, signing control over to the Vatican, founding schools staffed only by Catholics, dedicating the republic to the "Sacred Heart of Jesus" and making **Catholicism** a prerequisite for citizenship. He was also ruthless with his many opponents, crushing them and several coup attempts with savage efficiency – for example, shooting the son of the Liberal rebel Vallejo before his father, then executing Vallejo himself.

His presidency did help foster growth in agriculture and industry, initiating a much-needed programme of road-building and beginning the Quito–Guayaquil railway, as well as creating the first national currency. Nevertheless he was hated by the Liberals for his authoritarianism and for strengthening the Church. One of the loudest critics was the writer, **Juan Montalvo**, who vilified his policies from the safety of self-imposed exile. In 1875, just after Moreno had been elected to his third term of office, an assassin murdered the president with a machete on the steps of the Palacio de Gobierno; when Montalvo heard, he exclaimed, "My pen has killed him!"

After García Moreno's death, Conservative power waned and an uprising brought military dictator **General Ignacio de Veintimilla** to the presidency, a man who was surprisingly popular, perhaps for his large-scale public works programmes and boisterous public fiestas. From 1884 to 1895 the country returned to constitutional governments, overseen by three progressive Conservative presidents who navigated between radical Conservatism and Liberalism. Yet their success in bridging the divide was limited, and all the while the Liberals were accruing power and influence as the late nineteenth and early twentieth centuries saw phenomenal growth in Ecuador's **exports**. For a time the country was the world's leading producer of cacao, and coffee, tagua nuts and Panama hats were also doing well – products all based on the coast around Guayaquil – and much of the money filled Liberal coffers.

The Liberal era: 1895–1925

A committed revolutionary and Liberal, **Eloy Alfaro** had been involved in guerrilla skirmishes with García Moreno's Conservative forces since his early 20s. He'd already fled the country twice before Liberal cacao lords sought his return and funded a military coup that brought him to power in 1895. Fervently anticlerical, Alfaro immediately set about undoing García Moreno's work and began measures that would permanently weaken the Catholic Church in Ecuador. In his two terms as president (1897–1901 and 1906–11), Alfaro defined the radical Liberal position, secularizing the state and education, expelling foreign clergy, instituting civil marriage and divorce and cutting links with the Vatican. He ploughed money into public works and saw through the completion of the Quito–Guayaquil railway with the help of US investors.

Yet he was under attack from both Conservatives and Liberal party factions sympathetic to his rival **General Leonidas Plaza** (president from 1901–05 and 1912–16). To fend off the revolts, largely instigated by Conservative rebels with the backing of the Church, Alfaro allocated forty percent of his entire budget to military expenditure. The split within the Liberal camp worsened, and when Alfaro's chosen presidential successor, Emilio Estrada, died suddenly just after his inauguration in 1911, the country fell into a bloody **civil war**. A year later, Plaza's forces defeated Alfaro, and he and his supporters were transported on the new railway to Quito, where they were murdered, dragged through the streets and burnt in the Parque Ejido. One good thing to come out of this period was the 1918 scrapping of debtor imprisonment that ended the colonial system of **debt peonage** against the *indígenas*.

The civil war had left the state weakened and cash-strapped, allowing power to shift to **la argolla**, a "ring" of wealthy cacao merchants and bankers, underpinned by the private Banco Comercial and Agrícola in Guayaquil. The bank provided loans to a succession of ailing administrations at the expense of rocketing inflation rates, and became so influential that it was said that any politician needed its full backing to be successful.

In the 1920s Ecuador descended into an **economic crisis**, a symptom of this arrangement, crippling inflation and a severe slump in cacao production. A devastating blight damaged the crop, and cacao prices plunged as the market was swamped by new producers, especially British colonies in Africa. The poor were hit very badly, and uprisings – one in 1922 by workers in Guayaquil and another in 1923 by *indígena* peasants on a highland estate – were suppressed with massacres. The bloodless **Revolución Juliana** of 1925 effectively marked the end of the old Liberal–Conservative tug-of-war and ushered in a disoriented era of coups and overthrows.

Political crisis: 1925–47

After two swift juntas, the military handed power to **Isidro Ayora** in 1926, who embarked on a programme of reforms, including the creation of the Banco Central in Quito to smash the influence of *la argolla*. The new bank couldn't temper the rate of inflation and popular discontent forced Ayora's resignation in 1931. Fuelled by the woeful economic condition at home and the Great Depression worldwide, the country's political cohesion finally crumbled away. In the 1930s a total of fourteen men took the presidency, and from 1925 to 1948, Ecuador had 27 governments.

Out of the turbulence of this era came the first of **José María Velasco Ibarra**'s five presidential terms, which began in 1934 and lasted less than a year, thanks to his removal by the military when he tried to assume dictatorial powers; in his career, he was to be overthrown by the army three more times. He went into exile until the 1940s, and chaos reigned.

In 1941, while government troops were tied up in Quito defending the presidency of **Carlos Arroyo del Río**, Peru invaded, quickly seizing much of the Oriente and occupying the provinces of El Oro and Loja in the south. The occupation only ended after the nations signed the **Rio Protocol** of January 1942, but 200,000 square kilometres of Ecuador's eastern territory – almost half of the country at the time – were ceded to Peru. Although the land was largely unexplored and uninhabited, the loss was a huge blow to national pride in a country that had identified itself with the Amazon since its navigation by Francisco de Orellana four hundred years earlier. It was disputed by Ecuador, thanks to an irregularity in the treaty, and the territory was included on all Ecuadorian maps until a peace treaty of 1998 between the two countries, finally brought the issue to a close.

Velasco ousted the disgraced Arroyo in 1944, but was deposed by the military in 1947. Three presidents soon came and went before Galo Plaza Lasso took the helm in 1948, adding some much-needed stability into the republic.

Prosperity and decline: 1948–72

Galo Plaza Lasso was the son of the former Liberal president Leonidas Plaza, but he also had strong links with the powerful Conservative families in the sierra, and so was well placed to form a stable government.

Committed to democracy, he strove for the freedom of speech and the press, and as a fair and popular president, he was the first since 1924 to complete his term of office.

The stability he had helped foster was due in large part to economic prosperity brought on by the **banana boom**. After World War II the world demand for bananas went through the roof, and while the traditional exporters in the Caribbean and Central America had trouble with crop diseases, Ecuador had huge parcels of ex-cacao land ready to be given over to bananas – and soon the country became the world's largest exporter, a position it retains today. Government reserves brimmed over and money was invested in infrastructure to open up more areas of the countryside to banana farms. Large areas around Santo Domingo were cleared for agriculture and **colonists** flooded to the coast – between 1942 and 1962, the population in the region rose by more than one hundred percent. As the industry was dominated by small and medium-sized farms, the new wealth spread through society far more completely than it had during the cacao boom.

The prosperity and well-being was such that Velasco even managed to complete his third term in office (1952–56), the only one that he did. His successor **Camilo Ponce Enríquez** also saw his term through, but in the late 1950s, as world demand for bananas slumped and export prices fell, **unemployment** began to rise and people took to the streets in protest.

Once again the master-populist Velasco was elected by a large majority, thanks to his oratory and promise of support to the urban poor. Exploiting the popularity of the recent Cuban revolution, he laced his speeches with anti-US attacks and won the support of the Ecuadorian left. Before long, pressure from the US on Latin America to cut ties with Cuba heightened tensions between leftists and anti-Communists. Hopes that the country had at last achieved political maturity were dashed as Velasco's coalition disintegrated under the strain, and rival groups resorted to violence. In a desperate search for revenue, Velasco put taxes on consumer items, sparking **strikes** across the country.

As a Cuba-style revolution threatened, the military (with probable CIA interference) installed Velasco's vice president, **Carlos Julio Arosemena Monroy**, in 1961, but he soon became unpopular with the establishment for refusing to sever links with Cuba and was branded a Communist. The damage to his credibility had been done by the time he relented in 1962, but by then he was a broken man and an alcoholic. A year later a **military junta** took power, jailing the opposition and suppressing the left, though it did pass the **1964 Agrarian Reform Law**, which at last brought the *huasipungo* system to an end, even if it didn't achieve a far-reaching redistribution of land. As banana prices plummeted in 1965, the junta ran up against serious cash-flow problems and was forced to step down the following year.

Elections in 1968 brought the 75-year-old Velasco back to power by the slenderest of margins. The economic situation was so serious that Velasco was forced to devalue the sucre (Ecuador's then currency) and raise import tariffs, but to temper these measures, he seized US fishing boats found inside Ecuador's territorial limits, the so-called **tuna war**. After two years, and relying heavily on the help of his nephew in the military, he assumed dictatorial powers (as he had done during two of his other terms) and clung to power until his overthrow by the military in 1972.

Military control and the oil boom: 1972–79

The military, led by **General Guillermo Rodríguez Lara**, seized control because it was anxious that the flighty populist, **Asaad Bucaram**, former mayor of Guayaquil, would be victorious in the upcoming elections, and because it aimed to be the custodian of the large **oil reserves** found in the Oriente. Texaco's explorations in 1967 had struck rich, locating high-quality oil fields near Lago Agrio, and by 1971 more than twenty international companies had swarmed to the Oriente on the scent of a fortune.

The junta was aggressively nationalist in stance, and determined that the state should get as much from the oil boom as possible. Contracts with foreign companies were renegotiated on more favourable terms, a state-owned petroleum company was set up, and in 1973 Ecuador joined **OPEC**. Money flooded into the public sector, stimulating employment, industrialization, economic growth and urbanization. The Oriente infrastructure was revolutionized, and in 1971 Texaco built a road to Lago Agrio, the first to leave the eastern Andean foothills. To keep Colombia or Peru from getting ideas about the oil-rich lands, colonists such as military conscripts were encouraged into the region by the thousands. The huge **environmental cost** of all the colonization and oil-industry activity is still being felt.

The junta pushed its nationalist stance too far when it declared that the state's stake in Texaco operations should be upped to 51 percent, discouraging further foreign investment and prospecting. Oil production fell by a fifth, but this was offset for the time being by a sharp rise in global prices. Yet even with the huge increases in revenues and booming economy, the government managed to overspend on its nationalization and industrialization schemes, racking up some impressive **debts** along the way. Trying to redress the balance, it slapped sixty percent duty on luxury imports, upsetting the private sector and sparking a failed coup that claimed 22 lives. Rodríguez Lara's position was weakened enough for a second, bloodless coup in 1976, led by a triumvirate of military commanders, who sought to return government to civilian rule, but on their terms.

The return to democracy: 1979–87

In August 1979, the military could no longer deny power to the centre-left coalition candidate, **Jaime Roldós Aguilera**, after his landslide election victory three months earlier and heavy pressure from US President Jimmy Carter. Since the oil boom, the **economic landscape** of the country had transformed: per-capita income was five times greater than before 1972, employment was up by ten percent and a new urban middle class emerged. Despite the new wealth, the position of the rural poor, the *indígenas* and the workers hadn't much changed and inequality was as entrenched as ever. Roldós' plans for wide-ranging structural reforms fell through as a bitter rivalry had developed between him and his party associate, Bucaram – the leader of an opposition-dominated congress – who set about blocking the Roldós agenda.

By 1981 the economic situation again looked precarious. The country had an enormous budget deficit, in large part due to overspending by Bucaram's congress. Worse still, trouble flared up on the Peruvian border, adding to the financial burden. Then, in May, three months after a ceasefire with Peru and only weeks after the presentation of a revolutionary law that would redistribute oil wealth to the people, Roldós was killed in an airplane crash near Loja. Many suspected it was an assassination, and recent claims from an insider allege the CIA was responsible (see *Confessions of an Economic Hit Man*, p.533).

Roldós's vice president **Osvaldo Hurtado Larrea** stepped in and tried to push on with the reform programme, but the economic situation rapidly deteriorated. Oil prices fell sharply, and gross domestic product shrank by more than three percent; **inflation** rates soared, **unemployment** climbed and the Unitary Workers' Front (*Frente Unitario de Trabajadores*) called four **general strikes**; El Niño floods caused US$1 billion of damage, while **blight** ravaged highland potato crops. Still, Hurtado did manage to take unpopular austerity measures to combat a **foreign debt** that had spiralled to US$7 billion, and to secure constitutional elections and the transition of power to a second democratically elected government – the first time in almost 25 years.

León Febres Cordero Rivadeneira and his broad-based centre-right coalition won the 1984 general election. Inspired by the Reagan and Thatcher administrations, the new government embarked on a "neo-liberal" programme favouring free markets, foreign investment, exports and the roll-back of state power. Yet the government was plagued by allegations of **corruption** and **human rights abuses**, and as the cost of living rose, public disquiet grew. In 1986, shortly after a failed coup attempt by air-force general **Frank Vargas**, Febres Cordero was held hostage by Vargas supporters and threatened with death unless the general was released. The president immediately complied, an act perceived as cowardly by the public. To add to the country's woes, in March 1987 a serious **earthquake** rocked the Oriente, killing hundreds, leaving tens of thousands homeless, and destroying 40km of the Trans-Andean oil pipeline. The economy was crippled as oil production stopped for six months while the pipeline was repaired, and Febres Cordero was forced to default payment on foreign debts totalling more than US$10 billion.

The failure of right-wing politics led in 1988 to social democrat **Rodrigo Borja Cevallo** winning a convincing victory with his *Izquierda Democrática* party (Democratic Left). Borja's reform programme, called **gradualismo**, steered the country away from the policies of Febres Cordero and aimed to protect human rights and press liberties, kick-start the nation's literacy programmes and rejuvenate relations with Peru. Yet runaway inflation led to a wave of national strikes, and in 1990 an umbrella organization of the nation's indigenous peoples, **CONAIE** (*Confederación de Nacionalidades Indígenas del Ecuador*), staged an uprising, calling for rights to land and territories, the right to self-government and the creation of a multinational Ecuadorian state. The same year, twelve Waorani communities received territorial rights to land bordering the Parque Nacional Yasuní in the Oriente.

Desperate to fix the economy, the public switched its support back to the right, voting in the 72-year-old **Sixto Durán Ballén** in 1992. He strove for modernization, privatization and reduction of state bureaucracy, but his administration was dogged by hostility from labour unions and CONAIE, as well as **corruption** scandals, and in 1995 his vice president, Alberto Dahik, fled the country to avoid prosecution over mismanagement of funds.

Off the rails: 1996–2006

The 1996 elections brought a shock when outsider **Abdalá Bucaram** – known as **El Loco** (the Madman) – the nephew of Asaad Bucaram, won by wooing the masses with an informal populist style, promising increased subsidies and a stronger public sector. His publicity stunts included releasing his own CD ("Madman in Love"), shaving off his Hitler-style moustache (he was an admirer), and offering to pay Diego Maradona $1 million of public money to play a soccer game in Ecuador. Before long, Bucaram betrayed his supporters with austerity measures that made utility prices skyrocket, and rumours of large-scale mismanagement of funds and **corruption** involving his family also began to circulate. In just a year, his popularity plummeted and trade unions called a general strike. Congress voted him out of office on grounds of "**mental incapacity**", but Bucaram stubbornly clung to the job, holing up in the presidential palace. For a few days in February 1997, he, his vice president Rosalía Arteaga, and the leader of Congress, Fabián Alarcón, all claimed to be the rightful president. Meanwhile huge crowds gathered around the building, chanting for Bucaram's removal. Ultimately, he fled to Panama, allegedly carrying suitcases stuffed with embezzled cash – according to some reports, he may have robbed the country of nearly a hundred million dollars.

Fabián Alarcón muddled through the commotion as interim president, faced with economic stagnation and corruption allegations, and in 1998 the Harvard-educated mayor of Quito, **Jamil Mahuad**, beat Alvaro Noboa, Ecuador's wealthiest banana baron and candidate of Bucaram's party. After an amazing start, signing a peace treaty with Alberto Fujimori, so ending decades of tension and hostility with Peru, nothing went right. The country's finances were in total disarray and even the government claimed it to be Ecuador's worst **economic crisis** in seventy years, with inflation at around fifty percent, oil prices down and $2.6 billion of El Niño damage to deal with, including the devastation of the banana harvest. In the face of paralysing strikes, Mahuad still pushed on with neoliberal **austerity measures**, terminating fuel subsidies – almost doubling the price of petrol, and quadrupling the cost of electricity. Just as it seemed the banking system was on the brink of collapse, he froze more than $3 billion of bank deposits, preventing people from withdrawing more than a few hundred dollars' savings – measures which didn't save banks from folding or stop a run on the sucre. Facing a **foreign debt** of $16 billion, Ecuador defaulted on a Brady-bond interest payment, the first country ever to do so.

By January 2000, Ecuador's economy had shrunk by seven percent from the previous year, inflation was running higher than sixty percent and the sucre had devalued by almost three hundred percent. In a desperate bid to save his presidency and stop the economy from completely falling apart, Mahuad announced the resignation of his entire cabinet and declared his intent to **dollarize** the national currency. CONAIE mobilized its supporters, and tens of thousands of *indígenas* filtered into Quito under the noses of troops posted to stop them. On January 21, 2000 the military unit guarding Congress stepped aside, and the indigenous groups stormed the building and announced the removal of Mahuad, the dissolution of Congress and the Supreme Court.

Only hours later, the military junta called for vice president **Gustavo Noboa** to take up the presidency; Mahuad went into exile. Regarded as honest and unaffected by the grandiose trappings of office, the portly, former university rector Noboa forged ahead with dollarization, implementing it in 2001 with the help of a $2 billion aid package. Though it helped economic stability and stopped hyperinflation, it came at the cost of rising prices and worsening conditions for the ever-increasing poor.

In the 2002 elections, another outsider, **Lucio Gutiérrez**, an ex-colonel involved in the 2000 coup, won with the backing of indigenous groups and unions by pledging to root out corruption and reverse monetarist reforms. Once in power, it wasn't long before he turned his back on his leftist supporters by cutting subsidies on food and cooking oil, and pleasing the US and overseas creditors by spending large chunks of oil revenue on servicing debt. As his popularity plummeted, he managed to cling to power only through mercurial coalitions with a range of unlikely political groups. His unconstitutional dismissal of the Supreme Court at the end of 2004, with the aim of replacing judges with cronies who would drop criminal charges against Abdalá Bucaram – a preliminary to the political return of the disgraced and exiled ex-president – was widely criticized as a "dictatorial act" and led in April 2005 to mass demonstrations and the withdrawal of support of the armed forces. Congress voted to remove him from office, and he fled from the presidential palace by helicopter, eventually finding asylum in Brazil. Claiming he had been illegally removed from power and that he would follow constitutional channels to get it back, he returned to Ecuador in October, whereupon he was arrested and imprisoned, only to be released in March 2006 when charges were dropped. His vice president, **Alfredo Palacio**, was sworn in as interim president and held together the many pieces of the fractious political system as best he could until the 2006 elections.

A new start?

After such instability, Ecuador was more than ready for a strong leader. In **Rafael Correa**, who became the country's 56th president in 2007 after winning run-off elections the previous year, it has exactly that. Describing himself as a humanist and social Christian, Correa is a leftist firebrand in the mould of Hugo Chávez (a personal friend) of Venezuela and Bolivia's Evo Morales – anti-neoliberal, against foreign and particularly US interference in sovereign affairs, sceptical about the motives of the World Bank and IMF, and strongly in favour of social justice, redistribution of wealth and the welfare state. In 2008, Ecuadorians voted by a two-thirds majority to approve the country's **twentieth constitution**, which aimed to redress structural inequalities and bolster civil rights, allowing civil union for same-sex couples and free healthcare for the elderly. It had environmentalists swooning too, by making Ecuador the first country in the world to extend "inalienable **rights to nature**", in the declaration that nature "has the right to exist, persist, maintain and regenerate its vital cycles, structure, functions and its processes in evolution". The constitution also allows Correa to run for another term, which means he could remain in power until 2017.

The president, who trained as an economist in the US, has not been afraid to throw his weight around. In December 2008, he claimed foreign loans taken by the military regimes were "illegitimate" and so defaulted on millions of dollars of debt payments. Meanwhile he has attempted to renegotiate Ecuador's "unacceptable" contracts with the oil multinationals, and expropriated two television channels from a group, which also owned Filanbanco, one of the collapsed banks from the Mahuad era, in an effort to repay something to the many who had lost their savings. He's ploughed billions into social projects, not least for the indigenous poor; having spent a year at a Salesian mission in Cotopaxi, he is a rarity as a Kichwa-speaking president. If relations with the **US** have been predictably strained, not helped by his refusal to renew the lease on the American air base in Manta, they could hardly be worse than those with **Colombia**. An incursion by the Colombian military against a rogue FARC base over the Ecuadorian border led to a breakdown in diplomatic relations and troop mobilizations by Ecuador and Venezuela, until the three countries settled their differences in an emergency summit.

His populist, no-compromise stance has clearly pressed the right buttons at home. He was **re-elected** in April 2009 with a majority vote, something that hadn't happened for thirty years. Whether he can convert his domestic support into far-reaching and long-lasting improvements for Ecuador remains to be seen. The number of people living in poverty has declined, but the rate is still high at 38 percent. Enormous foreign debt, deep-rooted corruption, fragile national security, high public spending in a shrinking global economy and severe pressures on the country's protected areas are just a few of the problems he faces.

Art, music, literature and film

Ecuador enjoys fantastic variety in its cultural life, a richness of ideas, styles and creative instincts born of the diversity of its regions and people. A bold pre-Columbian vein streaks through much of Ecuadorian culture, helped in no small part by the early involvement of native craftsmen in the production of artistic paraphernalia for the colony's religious centres, an element of a much wider process that resulted in the beguiling synthesis of Old and New Worlds found today. Since Independence, artists and writers, often far more political than their European counterparts, command huge respect in society and operate as the conscience and moral vanguard of the country, fighting tyranny, upholding the rights of the oppressed and championing the ideals of democracy and liberty. Ecuador is beginning to make a name for itself internationally in film, too, but from homes to offices, buses to taxis, the country throbs with music; it is the lifeblood of the people, bringing communities together in celebration and fiesta, and even transcends the rift between highlands and the coast.

Art

In many ways, pre-Columbian art resembles modern artesanía (handicrafts; see *Crafts and markets* colour section), in its combination of function and aesthetic. What we understand as fine art didn't make an appearance until after the Conquest, when it was employed in the process of converting the native population to Catholicism, being central both as a means of religious instruction and to provide icons of worship to replace indigenous pagan idols. The engine of artistic production in the new colony was the so-called **Quito School** (see box, p.88), founded by Franciscan friars in the 1530s, particularly the Flemings, **Jodoco Ricke de Marsalaer** (d. c.1574) and **Pedro "El Pintor" Gosseal**, who taught indigenous people how to paint and carve, in order to provide decoration for the new churches and monasteries springing up across the newly conquered lands. One of the key early exponents of painting was **Fray Pedro Bedón** (1556–1621), who had studied in Lima under the Italian Jesuit artist, Bernardo Bitti, himself the main source of the Renaissance and Mannerist styles of Spain, Flanders and Italy for local *indígenas* and *mestizos* to reproduce famous compositions from the Old World. The artworks were not mere copies, however, but imbued with a clearly discernible Andean flavour, reflecting the need to adapt images to local tastes – saints with indigenous physiognomy or dress, or images that substituted European flora and fauna for their Andean counterparts. The exuberant use of gold was also a departure from European modes, where it had not been fashionable since the Middle Ages. Artists of the Quito School also applied gilt to the clothing, haloes and icons of religious figures with alacrity, perhaps an echo of the widespread use of gold for sacred and royal objects in pre-Columbian times.

The last major artist of the Quito School, **Manuel Samaniego** (c.1767–1824), formed the bridge from religious to **secular** painting, if unknowingly. The author of an influential treatise on painting, he forsook the sombre, tenebrous tones of his predecessors, preferring a fresher, brighter and more colourful palette, and paid special attention to background landscapes, complete with native plants and buildings. The career of his apprentice **Antonio Salas** (1795–1860) was bookended by religious commissions, but his most famous works define the early **Independence** period, being potent and striking portraits of the heroes and leaders of the age, including wonderful likenesses of Simón Bolívar and first Ecuadorian president, General Juan José Flores. He was also the patriarch of a large and accomplished artistic family, including **Ramón Salas** (c.1815–80), an early proponent of **costumbrismo**, whose intimate watercolours wittily capture scenes of everyday life with all its assorted characters and types, emphasizing the customs and idiosyncrasies of the parochial. Such studies were a part of a growing interest in Ecuador itself, the newly created nation, and a burgeoning pride in its land and people, which was beginning to find expression in the paintings of nineteenth-century artists. Ramón's much better known half-brother, **Rafael Salas** (c.1824–d.1906), who was sent to be trained in Europe after his exceptional talent was recognized at an early age, was a leading figure in this direction, and among the country's first to make a **landscape** a subject in its own right. His works were surpassed only by **Joaquín Pinto** (1842–1906), a prodigy and polyglot with little formal training, whose unrivalled eye for the unusual and charming repeatedly triumphed in landscapes and *costumbrista* tableaux. Landscapes achieved new heights of technical finesse under the brush of **Rafael Troya** (1845–1920), who studied under visiting German artists and draftsmen and owed much to the naturalistic traditions of that country in his broad and idyllic panoramas that exhibited a hitherto unseen level of detail and chromatic subtlety.

In the early **twentieth century** the picturesque *costumbrismo* sketches of local people, particularly of *indígenas*, took on much stronger political and social overtones, developing into the **indigenismo** movement, which articulated native culture and imagery in terms of social protest. Its leaders were **Camilo Egas** (1899–1962), **Eduardo Kingman** (1913–98) and **Oswaldo Guayasamín** (1919–99). Of this trinity of modern Ecuadorian masters, all of whom have excellent museums dedicated to them, Guayasamín, the son of an *indígena* and a *mestiza*, now figures as the nation's favourite and most famous artist, regarded as the true champion of the oppressed, with copies of his work, the familiar twisted hands and hollowed faces of the downtrodden, flooding any street market where art is sold.

His domination of the art scene over the last few decades belies the richness of modern art in Ecuador, which has had links to a plethora of artistic movements and currents of thought. **Manuel Rendón** (1894–1982), the child of the Ecuadorian ambassador to France, grew up and trained in Paris and was exposed to new ideas, the avant-garde and non-figurative art from an early age. In Paris, he won praise from artists as eminent as Matisse, Braque and Modigliani and his exhibitions in Quito and Guayaquil in the late 1930s had a huge influence on later generations, along with the work of **Araceli Gilbert** (1913–93), an early Ecuadorian proponent of abstract and geometric art, and one of the country's few female artists. Following their line, **Enrique Tábara** (b.1930) has become a leader of the avant-garde and non-figurative art in Ecuador, a man who rubbed shoulders in Barcelona with Dadaists and Surrealists, such as André Breton and Joan Miró, and back home founded the influential Grupo VAN (Vanguardia Artística Nacional) with the likes of **Aníbal Villacís** (b.1927), **Estuardo Maldonado** (b.1930), **Hugo Cifuentes** (1923–2000) and Op artist **Luis Molinari** (b.1929) in opposition to the heavy political social realism of Guayasamín and others. Other important figures include **Juan Villafuerte**

(1945–77), whose prolific but short career included the celebrated "Transmutation Series" of monstrous and deformed figures designed to unsettle; **Oswaldo Viteri** (b.1931), who uses a wide variety of materials including Catholic livery, craft dolls, and folkloric objects to explore *mestizaje*, the cultural mix of Ecuador; and **Gonzalo Endara Crow** (1936–96), whose distinctive paintings blend myth, folklore and naturalism against backdrops of Ecuadorian scenery, prefiguring the popular naïve styles of the indigenous artists of **Tigua**.

In the contemporary scene there's also the **Artefactoría** collective founded in 1982 by Xavier Patiño, Jorge Velarde and Marcos Restrepo, loosely inspired by Surrealist ideas. While native culture has been so important to modern Ecuadorian art, it's notable that there have been relatively few well-known indigenous artists. One of them is **Ramón Piaguaje** (b.1962), a Secoya from the Cuyabeno area, who drew from childhood with his fingers in the sand and had no idea it was possible to create pictures in colour until an anthropologist supplied him with oils. He shot to fame after winning a major international prize with his beautifully toned and textured depiction of his rainforest home.

Music

Traditional **Andean** music (**música folklórica**) long predates the Conquest and is centred on **panpipes**, whose breathy, often melancholic tones are the quintessential sound of the Andes. There are several different sorts of panpipes, but the **rondador** is the only one that is exclusively Ecuadorian, a single row of pipes in a pentatonic (five-note) scale, typical of Andean music, but interspersed in intervals of thirds. If adjacent pipes are blown together a melody can be played in harmonious thirds, a very distinctive effect; rondador players commonly beat a drum at the same time. Other pipes you're likely to see are the **zampoña** (or **siku** in Kichwa), featuring two rows of pipes, which originate from the Lake Titicaca region on the borders of Bolivia and Peru, and the **antara** with a single row, from Nazca, Peru. The panpipes are usually complemented by wooden or bamboo flutes, namely the **pingullo** and **quena**, or the clay **ocarina**, another ancient Andean invention, as well as a **percussion** section with any combination of drums, such as the **bombo**, and shaken instruments like the maracas, rain stick, and **chajchas**, a collection of animal hooves tied together and shaken to make an elemental sound of wind or rain. **Stringed instruments** only appeared after the arrival of the Spanish, with guitars and violins being incorporated into the music. Adaptations were also made by Andean musicians, most obviously in the **charango**, a small ten-string guitar with a soundbox either made of wood or armadillo shell (when it's sometimes known as a **kirkincho**, after the Kichwa word), and the **hualaycho** or **chilleador**, a strummed charango with metal strings producing a strident sound. Brass is often added to the mix, usually in fiestas more than at **peñas** (folk music clubs), both of which are the best places to hear traditional music.

Since the Conquest, the interaction between traditional Andean music and European styles has given rise to many different genres and **dances**, often influenced by the imported sounds. At the most Andean end of the spectrum are **Sanjuanito**, musically related to the **huaynos** of Peru and Bolivia; **Yumbo**, thought to be a blending of indigenous styles from the highlands and the Oriente; the mournful plaints of **Yaraví**; and **Danzante**, most associated with villages of Pujilí and Salasaca. The European influence is more noticeable in **mestizo dances** like the Albazo, Tonada, Cachullapi, Fox Incaico, Chucchurillo and Capizhca. Then there are dances, identified as much with the coast as the highlands, which owe much more to the European side of the equation, such as the **Pasacalle**, a descendant of the jaunty Spanish Pasodoble, and the slow and poignant **Pasillo**, whose origins lie in the waltz. The Pasillo has been enormously popular since its appearance around the time of Independence and is regarded by many Ecuadorians, especially **mestizos**, as the definitive national dance, even though it also exists in Colombia, Venezuela and Central America.

The **Afro-Ecuadorians** of Esmeraldas, Imbabura and Carchi provinces have their own musical traditions, in part shared with the black communities of coastal Colombia, including dances such as the **Andarele** and **Bambuco**, which employ a different range of instruments. King of them is the **marimba**, a large, wooden instrument resembling a xylophone, producing a mellow yet uplifting tone, often accompanied by a **cunuco** (similar to a conga drum), **bombo** (drum), and **guasá** (a bamboo tube filled with dried seeds). The dry Chota Valley, one of the few highland areas with a significant black population, is home to **Bomba**, a fusion of the haunting pentatonic sounds of the Andes with the driving rhythms of Africa. It is played by **Bandas Mochas**, which originally only used instruments made from materials to hand, from cactus fibres for a trumpet to reeds for a flute, but now, thanks to wider availability and (slightly) better economic conditions, such oddities are complemented with conventional instruments. Among the indigenous people of the **Oriente**, there is a musical form called **Anent**, sacred songs usually sung to divine spirits by women as a kind of prayer to ensure the success of a given undertaking, whether it be for hunting, the health of the family or the fertility of the land. Hundreds of the songs exist, each passed down orally from mother to daughter across the generations.

In addition to this "Música Nacional" (national music) is the full range of Latin, tropical, rock, jazz, pop, techno and electronica from around the world, the music you're most likely to hear in clubs, bars and everyday places across the country. The most popular **Latin** styles include salsa, the stalwart dance music of salsotecas and discos; merengue and **bachata** from the Dominican Republic; the distinctly rural sounding **vallenatos** and **cumbias** of Colombia; and the romance and melodrama-soaked **boleros**, favoured by ageing bus drivers. Reggae and hip-hop are also making inroads, most notably in a Latin-fusion of Jamaican dancehall called **Reggaetón**, whose heavy lilting beat is the current favourite of teenagers in local discos.

Literature

Regarded as the nation's first great writer, even though he died 35 years before Ecuador came into existence as a country, **Eugenio Espejo** (1747–95) set the tone in national literature with his political polemics, satire and concern for social issues. Born to a Kichwa and a *mulata* (of mixed European and black ancestry), he overcame considerable racial discrimination to qualify as medic and then lawyer, but he's best known for his satirical works that called for the political independence of the Audiencia de Quito. His views frequently landed him in trouble with the colonial authorities, but in between arrests and trials, he became the first director of the Audiencia's first public library (later the National Library), and in 1792 founded Quito's first newspaper, albeit a short-lived one. The struggle for independence was continued by **José Joaquín de Olmedo** (1780–1847), both in action, as the leader of the 1820 insurrection, and in words in such works as the monumental epic poem *La Victoria de Junín, Canto a Bolívar* and *Oda al General Flores, Vencedor de Miñarica*, celebrating two military heroes and their battlefield successes.

The two giants of early republican literature were **Juan Montalvo** and his rival **Juan León Mera**, both born in Ambato in 1832, but very different in character and outlook. Mera was an autodidact and ultraconservative, while Montalvo was a liberal and ardently anticlerical, penning vitriolic attacks on the Catholic president, Gabriel García Moreno, and the dictator Ignacio de Veintimilla. A champion of democracy, his most important essays include *Siete Tratados* and *Las Catilinarias*, while his best fiction, *Capítulos que se le Olvidaron a Cervantes*, is a pastiche of Cervantes for a contemporary Ecuadorian audience. Mera's magnum opus was *Cumandá*, Ecuador's first great novel, about an Amazonian chief and his jungle dominion. It's a highly idealized and romantic depiction of indigenous life. It was far removed from the social realism introduced by **Fernando Chávez** in his seminal *Plata y Bronce* of 1927, which explored the myth of *indígena* as noble savage and examined the hardships suffered in a prejudiced society, a theme which hit its apogee with **Jorge Icaza's** (1906–78) masterful *Huasipungo* (1934), but persistently coloured much of the nation's writing throughout the twentieth century. In *Juyungo* of 1943, **Adalberto Ortiz** (1914–2003) explored similar territory but with particular reference to Afro-Ecuadorians and their relationship to *mestizos*, while **Jorge Carrera Andrade** (1902–78), essayist, diplomat and most notably a poet, composed elegant *microgramas* (among other things), a Hispanicized reworking of the Japanese haiku, on native life. From the latter half of the twentieth century onwards, one of the principal figures of Ecuadorian literature has been **Jorge Enrique Adoum** (b.1926), the onetime secretary of Pablo Neruda, whose enormous body of work encompasses poetry, novels, translations, essays and plays, his most celebrated work being *Entre Marx y una Mujer Desnuda* (1976), which won the prestigious Mexican Xavier Villaurrutia prize, the first time it had ever been awarded to someone outside Mexico.

Film

Ecuador's first feature film, *El Tesoro de Atahualpa*, was released in 1924 by the 19-year-old pioneer filmmaker **Augusto San Miguel**, who spent his father's inheritance on this and two other movies in two years. The last of these, *Un Abismo y Dos Almas*, was a brave and groundbreaking depiction of social prejudice and oppression, about a maltreated indigenous worker who challenges his master and the terrible retribution that results. The first **talkie**, *Guayaquil de mis Amores* (1930) by Francisco Diunmejo, was a song-and-dance spectacular featuring the best Ecuadorian musicians and Cuban dancers, which attracted huge crowds and established cinema as a medium of mass entertainment. Ecuadorian productions remained fairly infrequent until the industry began to pick up speed again in the 1990s, particularly with the work of **Camilo Luzuriaga**. As a follow-up to the qualified success of *La Tigra* (1990), about the relationship of three sisters on an isolated farm, Luzuriaga's adaptation of Jorge Enrique Adoum's novel *Entre Marx y Una Mujer Desnuda* (1996) is a valiant attempt to capture the many layers, ideas and oppositions of the original in film. The director making biggest waves at the moment is **Sebastián Cordero**, whose award-winning *Ratas, Ratones, Rateros* (*Rodents*; 1999) garnered international acclaim with its unflinching yet simple tale of an urban lowlife from Guayaquil and the destruction he wreaks on the lives of his young middle-class relatives from Quito who get mixed up with him. He continued the grittiness with *Crónicas* (*Chronicles*; 2004), about a vain and self-promoting Miami TV reporter who gets more than he bargained for when investigating a serial killer in a grimy town in Ecuador's coastal interior. Hollywood has come to Ecuador a few times, most notably in *Vibes* (1988), a fluffy comedy-fantasy with Jeff Goldblum and Cyndi Lauper, and for the tiresome *Proof of Life* (2000), about a love affair between Meg Ryan and Russell Crowe predicated on a guerrilla kidnapping – in both films the real star of the show is Ecuador's scenery.

Mainland geography and wildlife

In terms of both wildlife and geography Ecuador is one of the most diverse countries in the world. No larger than the US state of Nevada, this diminutive country is home to more than 1600 species of birds, 230 different mammals, 680 amphibians and reptiles, twenty thousand flowering plants and more than a million types of insects.

The mainland comprises three geographical regions and an extraordinary variety of habitats and ecosystems. In the **sierra**, mountain páramos, snow-tipped volcanoes and the Andean mountains form the north–south spine of the country. To the east, they slope down through primeval cloudforests into the tropical rainforests of the **Oriente** and the Amazon basin, forming an unassailable wall that prevents moist air from heading west, ensuring the rainforests have high levels of annual precipitation. On the west of the Andes, more cloudforests cloak the mountainsides down to the **coast** (*costa*, or *litoral*), which comprises dry and tropical forests, lowland hills and a shoreline of beaches and mangrove swamps.

The sierra

Around one hundred million years ago, the westward-moving South American tectonic plate collided with the eastward-moving Nazca plate, which holds the southern Pacific Ocean, and the **Andes** mountains rose along the edge of the South American landmass. In Ecuador, they consist of two parallel mountain chains, or cordilleras, separated by a broad central valley – which the German explorer, Alexander von Humboldt, named the Avenue of the Volcanoes in 1802. This central valley is itself divided into a series of fertile basins (*hoyas*), cut off from one another by "knots" (*nudos*) of intermediate hills. The basins have been populated for hundreds of years – in several cases, thousands of years – and even today are home to almost half the country's population.

A relatively young mountain range, the sharp, jagged peaks of the Andes, reaching almost 7000m in places, are not yet rounded by erosion and are still growing as the two underground giants continue to rumble against each other, making Ecuador geologically unstable and volatile. **Earthquakes** and **tremors** are common and Ecuador also has a number of active **volcanoes** – Cotopaxi, at 5897m, is one of the highest in the world. Ten of Ecuador's volcanoes exceed the snow line (5000m), and the summit of Chimborazo, at 6268m, actually surpasses Everest as the point furthest from the centre of the Earth by more than 2km, thanks to the planet's bulge around the equator. Eruptions of active volcanoes, such as Reventador, Tungurahua and Guagua Pichincha cause occasional disruption.

The **Andean climate** varies widely according to altitude, the time of year, and even the time of day. There are two seasons: dry (June–Sept) and wet (Oct–May), although even during April, the wettest month, downpours rarely occur every day. Whatever the time of year, daytime temperatures average highs of 20–22°C (68–72°F) and lows of 7–8°C (45–46°F), though there is huge local variation.

Below the snow line of the highest Andean peaks is a slender margin of tundra-like *gelodifitia*, where little else than mosses and lichens can survive the freezing nights and frigid soils. From around 4700m to 3100m, the climate of the **páramo** is less harsh, allowing for a wider range of life. Covering ten percent of Ecuador's total land area, the vegetation is dominated by dense tussocks of *Festuca* or *Calamgrostis* grasses, along with terrestrial bromeliads and ferns. In the wetter páramo, pockets of *Polylepis* forest grow, one of the few trees that can survive at this altitude. Plants tend to have small thick leaves to resist the nightly frosts and waxy skins to reflect the intense ultraviolet radiation during cloudless spells. Páramo soil is sodden, and excess water collects in the hundreds of lakes that spangle the undulating scenery. The first signs of **wildlife** also emerge in the páramo with mammals such as the Andean spectacled bear, South American fox and white-tailed deer, and birds like the Andean condor, Andean snipe, tawny antpitta and various hummingbirds.

Lower than the páramo are the **cloudforests**, clothing the sierra in dense vegetation between 1800m and 3500m. Wet, green, vibrant and extraordinarily beautiful, cloudforests feel like the prehistoric habitat of dinosaurs. Streaked by silvery waterfalls, the forests are shrouded in heavy mists for at least part of each day, as moisture from the lowland forests rises, cools and condenses. It's this dampness that creates such lush conditions, giving rise to an abundance of **epiphytes**, such as **lichens**, **liverworts**, **mosses**, **ferns** and **bromeliads**, which drape over the trees. They aren't parasites, but simply claim a branch space, set out roots and grow there as independent canopy residents. Many **orchids** are epiphytes, preferring moss-covered branches or exposed bark to normal soil. With more than 3500 species, Ecuador is thought to have more orchids than any other country in the world. In a ten-square-kilometre patch of eastern cloudforest alone, two hundred orchids have been counted, only a little less than Kenya's countrywide total.

Cloudforests are also home to an incredible range of animals such as woolly tapirs, spectacled bears and pumas, and they have an exceptional level of bird endemism – species unique to a place and not found anywhere else. At higher altitudes, the cloudforest is called **elfin forest** because the trees are restricted in growth by the permanent mist that blocks out the sunlight. Elfin forests are an impenetrably dense tangle of short, twisted, gnarled trees barely two metres tall.

The Oriente

The **Oriente** represents Ecuador's own piece of the **Amazon rainforest**, the largest tropical rainforest habitat in the world, with the greatest diversity of plants and animals on the planet – its unidentified varieties of beetles and insects alone are thought to outnumber all of Earth's known animal species. One study has even found a single hectare of Amazonian forest can contain up to 250 tree species, whereas in Europe and North America only ten different kinds of tree would occupy the same space. Another study has identified more types of ant living on a single tree stump than there are in the whole of the British Isles. The rivers and their banks, too, are home to a fantastic array of animals, including nearly two thousand species of fish, plus freshwater dolphins, giant otters, anacondas, caimans and many unique birds.

One reason for this extraordinary diversity is the Oriente's **climate** – it never suffers from a lack of heat or water, with high levels of precipitation all year round, particularly from April to July. Annual averages are frequently above

2500mm, while in some areas rainfall passes above 4000mm. Temperatures are consistent, hovering at around 23–26°C (73–79°F) all year.

Rainforest types

The different types of soil, terrain and rivers of the Amazon basin have allowed various kinds of rainforest to evolve. In the Oriente – and indeed the Amazon as a whole – the majority comprises **tierra firme rainforest** (also known as *terra firme* after the Portuguese term), with well-drained, nutrient-rich soils. Trees typically have huge, flaring buttress roots, tall slender trunks and branches radiating at the top like spokes on a bicycle wheel. Most grow to 25–30m, although some, such as the ceiba or kapok, exceed 50m, with the forest canopy creating a dark, permanently shaded and enclosed space underneath.

Because trees are often interconnected by vines, one falling tree – whether felled by a hurricane, lightning or human activity – can bring some of its neighbours down with it. Sunlight floods in, creating a different microclimate for the shadowy world under the canopy. Initially, fast-growing plants are favoured, and a dense tangle of competing shrubs, vines and spindly trees proliferates. Areas of disturbed forest, with an undeveloped canopy but dense ground cover and undergrowth, are known as **secondary forest**. Over time, it matures into fully developed **primary forest**, as the slower-growing trees out-compete and dwarf the pioneers and the canopy closes over, once again blocking sunlight from the forest floor, allowing only a sparse scattering of low-level plants.

Rainforest medicine and the case of ayahuasca

The indigenous people of the Oriente have accumulated knowledge about uses of plants' defence compounds for centuries, concocting **medicines** to treat ailments from headaches to digestive problems, muscular pains, toothache, insect stings, snakebites, ulcers, epilepsy, asthma, boils, blisters and baldness. A community's **shaman** is usually the keeper of the knowledge of how to extract, prepare and administer the drugs, his craft passed down by oral tradition. But as indigenous culture is diluted by outside influences, concern is mounting that shamanism will die out and knowledge will be lost, even though **shamanic tourism** is gaining popularity among visitors keen to experience rainforest rituals first-hand, and making such traditions commercially valuable.

As **ethnobotany** became popular in the late twentieth century, international pharmaceutical companies woke up to the potential treasure of medicinal rainforest plants. In 1986 Loren Miller, under the auspices of his one-man company the International Plant Medicine Corporation, obtained the US patent for *Banisteriopsis caapi*, otherwise known as the **ayahuasca** vine, found throughout the Amazon. A powerful hallucinogen, ayahuasca has been used for centuries as a fundamental ingredient in religious ceremonies and traditional medicines for bodily and spiritual cleansing. The exploitation of this sacred drug for commercial gain amounted, it was felt by many, to "bio-piracy" and was taken as an insult by more than four hundred cultures of the Amazon basin. It wasn't until 1996 that the patent was uncovered by **COICA**, a coalition of indigenous peoples from nine South American countries. COICA applied to the US Patent and Trademark Office for a re-examination of the patent in March 1999 and won a **landmark victory** in November that year. Yet, the patent was only revoked because of a legal loophole and the decision did not reflect the moral debate. It's possible that with cures to a number of diseases growing somewhere on the rainforest floor, the cash-strapped Ecuadorian government may yet court the help of overseas investors to exploit these natural resources.

The Oriente also holds large areas of flooded forest around different river systems, providing important alternative habitats for plants and animals. **White-water rivers** flow down from the Andes carrying great amounts of suspended sediment, enriching the soil during floods. Over time, accumulated sediment on the riverbanks forms ridges, or levees, which help prevent regular flooding, meaning the plants that thrive here have to withstand years without a flood. These areas of intermittently flooded forest are known as **várzea**, characterized by a dense understorey, a middle layer of *Cecropia* and a high layer of trees reaching over 35m, such as *Ficus insipida* and *Calycophyllum spruceanum*. Some *várzea* plants have developed floating seeds to aid their dispersal.

Black-water rivers usually originate within the rainforest area itself, so contain very little suspended sediment, but do have a lot of decomposing organic matter from fallen leaves and dead plants. The result is an acidic, tannin-rich water that looks like strong black tea. The open floodplains around black-water rivers give rise to the haunting **igapó forests**, which you can drift through on a canoe just beneath the canopy. *Igapó* trees are relatively short and have adapted to floods lasting many months, with roots that can survive underwater for long periods. Many trees here have developed a seed-dispersal strategy that relies on fish: their fruit falls into the water during floods, and their seeds germinate after having passed through the creature's digestive system.

The lush and palm-dominated **moretal** habitat occupies swampy and poorly drained areas near rivers and lakes, which often flood after localized rains. The most striking tree is a palm, *Mauritia flexuosa* (known as *morete* in Spanish, hence *moretal*), which grows to 30m, and the understorey is filled out with thick bursts of *Scheleea brachyclada* and *Croton tessmannii* among others.

Rainforest trees and plants

Rainforest trees usually have broad leaves, called drip tips, which thin to a narrow point at the end to facilitate water run-off. **Palm trees**, a good example of this, are extremely common and are used by indigenous peoples not just to make thatch for houses but also for ropes, weavings, hunting bows, fishing lines, hooks, utensils and musical instruments, as well as food and drink.

Many trees are cauliflorous, so their flowers and fruits grow from the trunk, rather than the canopy branches, enabling terrestrial animals – essential to the trees' reproduction – to access their **fruits** containing large seeds, a source of energy for monkeys, tapirs, rodents and peccaries. Other food simply falls to earth: the **brazil nut**, for example, hits the forest floor in large, woody pods, where the agouti, a type of rodent, gnaws through its tough shell. Many palms, such as the **coconut palm**, produce large, hard fruits encasing the seeds. Meanwhile, in the canopy, birds such as tinamous, guans, curassows, doves, pigeons, trogons, toucans and parrots eat smaller fruits and seeds.

Plants that don't rely on animals and birds for reproduction have developed **protective measures** to counter the attentions of hungry animals, self-defence tactics evident in rainforest leaves blemished by nibble marks. Some plants produce drugs, or **defence compounds**, and many tropical leaves are generously dosed with poisons such as curare, caffeine and cyanide. The **monkey pot tree**, for example, deters foragers by producing rotund "cannonball" fruits, each containing up to fifty long, thin seeds laced with toxic selenium. Other plants grow spines on their trunks to impale voracious caterpillars, while, less vindictively, the sap of the **rubber tree** congeals on exposure to air, so any insects that have gone to the trouble of chewing through the bark are only rewarded with an inedible goo.

Epiphytes flourish on, around and over the vegetation, and sometimes the treetops are so laden with squatters seeking access to the sun that it's hard to define the host under all its house guests. In the competitive world of the cloud-forest, even epiphytes can have their own epiphytes. Many bromeliads' leaves arrange themselves in overlapping rosettes, forming a bowl that catches and holds rainwater. Birds bathe in it, monkeys drink from it, and tree frogs, mosquitoes, flatworms, snails, salamanders and crabs can all complete their entire life cycle in these miniature aquatic habitats.

Lianas (a woody vine that roots in the ground) dangle downwards from trees, elaborately draping and entwining around their trunks. A liana may even loop its tendrils through the crowns of several trees, making intricate links in the canopy. Trunk-climbing vines start at the bottom of tree trunks and grow upwards, while strangler vines start at the top and grow down, encircling the tree and squeezing it tightly enough to choke it: the tree inside dies and decomposes, and the vine claims its place on the forest floor.

The coast

The western slopes of the Andes fall away to the **coastal region**, beginning with a large, fertile lowland river plain that extends for 150km to a range of hills, which rise up to 900m and form a ridge about 20km inland from the sea.

The **coastal lowlands** have a very warm **climate**, with temperatures fluctuating between 25°C and 31°C (77–88°F) throughout the year. Here, the humid rainy season runs from December to May, though the dry season is still fairly muggy. The north of the region is generally much wetter throughout the year than the south coast, which barely receives any rainfall during the dry season. At the coast itself, the climate is heavily influenced by oceanic currents, which from May to December are responsible for keeping temperatures down and skies overcast. From June to August, particularly between the northern Guayas and the southern Manabí provinces, the coast is shrouded in thick mist and illuminated by a grey light that leaches everything else of colour.

The northern coastal region was once thickly forested and included within it the **Chocó bioregion**, an area of extraordinary biodiversity extending up into Colombia. When the Andes were formed, the Chocó region in the west was cut off from the Amazon rainforests to the east. Since then, these highly humid western forests survived the Ice Age and followed an evolutionary path that diverged from that of their eastern counterparts, and it's thought that anywhere between one-fifth to a half of the nine thousand estimated plant and animal species here are endemic, such as the glorious scarlet-and-white tanager, the rufous-crowned antpitta and the banded ground cuckoo.

Unfortunately, in Ecuador less than five percent of the Chocó forests (which include coastal mangroves) have survived the twentieth century. Since the 1950s the destruction started apace with new roads leading to unplanned **colonization** and rapid **deforestation**. The region's fertility has given it the dubious honour of being the most intensively farmed area in Ecuador, with banana, rice, cacao, coffee and sugar-cane plantations. The latest threat to the Chocó comes from **oil-palm plantations**, which have felled about a thousand square kilometres of native forest, much of it primary growth. More than twenty animal species are in danger of extinction in the Chocó.

The southern coastal area forms part of the **Tumbesian bioregion**, which continues down into Peru. Originally, much of this distinctive landscape comprised **dry tropical forests** suited to the arid southern climate, but almost all of this habitat has now been cleared for agriculture, save a few pockets such as at the Parque Nacional Machalilla and the Bosque Protector Cerro Blanco. Trees and spiny shrubs, such as acacias and cacti, grow in abundance, as do some otherwise disappearing native trees, such as balsam and *tillo colorado*, long coveted for their fine wood. Plants in the region have adapted to the desert-like environment, and many trees such as the ceiba lose their leaves when water is scarce during the height of the dry season (July–Oct). Fewer birds live here than in the wet forests, but there are a significant number of range-restricted, endangered species endemic to this area, such as the grey-backed hawk, the ochre-bellied dove and the saffron siskin. Mammals include mantled howler monkeys, capuchins, coatimundi, ocelots and pumas.

Long, empty beaches fringe about one-third of Ecuador's 2000km of **coastline**, the rest comprising mangrove swamps, marshes, sandy cliffs, river

Mangroves and shrimp farms

As part of the natural ecosystem, **mangroves** act as an effective natural barrier between the land and the ocean, preventing erosion and forming a shield against tidal waves, cyclones and floods.

In the late twentieth century, mangrove forests along the coast of Ecuador began to be systematically cleared to make way for get-rich-quick **shrimp-farming** schemes. Production mushroomed in the early 1980s and shrimp became Ecuador's third most important export after bananas and oil, making the country the second-largest shrimp exporter in the world. To date, as much as seventy percent of the mangrove forests here have been destroyed to make way for breeding ponds. The effects of this clear-cutting have been disastrous, both for the environment and the local human populations, who once relied on the ecosystem for subsistence fishing.

While a few shrimp farmers reaped the benefits, many locals lost their livelihoods. Traditional fishermen, who once waded into the mangroves to collect fish and crustaceans, found little food or were denied access to their fishing grounds altogether. Many private enterprises brought their own people in to work on the shrimp farms, but the number of new jobs created fell far short of the number of people who had once survived off the land. Where a single hectare of mangrove forest provided sustainable food and livelihood for ten families, a typical shrimp farm spread over 110 hectares employed just a handful of people.

The shrimping industry in Ecuador has not even been a reliable source of income for the people involved in it. Farms are often high-risk ventures and the artificially cultured shrimp larvae are susceptible to outbreaks of disease and require large amounts of **antibiotics** and **pesticides**. These chemicals have further damaged the ocean ecosystem, and local wild marine animals are at risk from exotic diseases to which they have no immunity.

Additionally, the **mancha blanca** (white spot) virus of 1999 wiped out farms up and down the coastline, causing a two-thirds reduction in profits and the cessation of production in more than half the country's shrimp farms. The industry is now stabilizing, but is nothing like it was during the boom years. However, there is evidence that some out-of-business shrimp farmers may have learnt the lesson, turning to sustainable mollusc-farming projects that depend on the survival of the mangrove forests. Ecuador is also home to the world's first fully certified **organic shrimp farm**, a model of ecological production that could easily be replicated. In the meantime, it's up to consumers in the developed world to be aware that about a third of the shrimps they eat comes from farms in countries like Ecuador, responsible for mangrove destruction as well as human displacement and untold poverty and suffering.

deltas and estuaries. **Mangrove trees**, growing in shallow salt or brackish waters, are found especially along quiet shorelines and in estuaries. The most common type in Ecuador is the red mangrove, so named because of its reddish wood, and like all mangroves it has a convoluted mass of arching roots, which support it in the unstable sandy shoreline soils and are exposed at low tide. The mangroves build up rich organic soil in the knotted network of their roots and branches, supporting many other plants and wildlife. Frigatebirds, boobies and brown pelicans nest among the tangled branches and many types of fish, molluscs and crustaceans make homes in the protective shelter of the roots.

Mangroves play an essential role in the ecology of coastal areas, but much of Ecuador's mangrove treasury has been squandered, cut down to make way for the construction of profitable **shrimp farms** – only a few patches have been conserved. Around San Lorenzo near the Colombian border, the **Reserva Ecológica Cayapas-Mataje** harbours the tallest mangrove forest in the world (some over 64m) as well as lovely coconut forests, teeming bird colonies and rare mammals such as the miniature tree sloth, while **Manglares Churute**, south of Guayaquil, is home to flamingos, pelicans and occasionally bottle-nosed dolphins. Other nationally protected mangrove forests are at the estuary of the Río Muisne and Salado.

Wildlife

Few countries in the world come close to Ecuador for **wildlife**. Blessed with many thousands of colourful **birds** and **animals** crammed into a small area, Ecuador is a naturalist's dream – birdwatchers alone can rack up a list of several hundred after only a few days in the forests. To top it all off, a good number of them are found nowhere else – making Ecuador one of the most biologically important countries on the planet.

Birds

Ecuador is home to just over 1600 different **bird** species, representing a sixth of the planet's total. Because of its small size, the country also has the world's highest **diversity** of birds – even though Brazil is thirty times larger, the two countries are home to about the same number of bird species.

Cotingas
The most famous **cotinga** is the fabulous **Andean cock-of-the-rock**, which inhabits lower to mid-montane cloudforest, where several dozen birds gather in **leks** (bird courtship display areas) to reproduce. The chunky males, with spectacular scarlet-orange plumage outlined by black wings and tail and a showy crescent of feathers running over their heads, preen and pose for the females. Relationships are brief, lasting for only one or two couplings, after which the male continues to strut his stuff in the search for more mates. The **screaming piha** is another cotinga that lives in the rainforest, but its mating appeals are auditory rather than visual – its strident, piercing call is one of the most distinctive sounds of the forest.

Eagles
The **harpy eagle** is the world's largest, at over 1m in height, with sturdy, powerful legs as thick as human wrists and claws the size of human hands. Their

wings and back are black and their faces and bellies are grey. Remarkably agile despite their size, harpy eagles twist and turn through the canopy, making swift strikes at monkeys and sloths, plucking them off trees with their legs. They tend not to soar, but **crested eagles** and three species of **hawk-eagle** are easier to see circling high over the rainforest canopy.

Hummingbirds

Hummingbirds' names accurately reflect their beauty: **garnet-throated**, **sparkling-tailed** and **velvet-breasted**, to name but a few. Highly active, their wings can buzz at eighty beats per second as they dart backwards, forwards and hover on the spot to sip nectar with their bills. They're quite feisty and compete aggressively for flowers. Females flirt with dominant males and will mate with them even during the non-breeding season to gain access to the flowers in their territory. Hummingbird habitats range from the jungle to the páramo, with some species such as the sword-billed (which has a bill as long its body) and the booted racquet-tail found in the cloudforests. Cloudforest lodges with hummingbird feeders are the best places to see them up close.

Oropendolas

Trees favoured by the crow-sized **oropendolas** can be spotted at a distance because they tend to be out in the open and have pendulous, basket-like nests. The birds pick isolated trees to avoid egg-stealing monkeys, which don't like to traverse open ground. These birds come in two colour types – one displaying greenish hues, the other mostly black and russet, with yellow on the bill and tail. They are great singers, producing a wide range of sounds and songs.

Owls and potoos

The **spectacled owl**, one of Ecuador's largest, is dark brown with a brown-yellow lower breast and belly and bright yellow eyes ringed by white. The **black-and-white owl** has a horizontally black-and-white striped breast and feeds almost exclusively on bats.

The **common potoo**, another large nocturnal bird, is a visual challenge to detect in the daytime – it sits completely still in trees and, with its colouring and artful physical pose, looks exactly like the end of a branch.

Parrots and macaws

Most **parrots** are well camouflaged in the rainforest, but their harsh, banshee-like screeching makes them easy to locate. They usually mate for life, and it's possible to pick out the pairs by watching a flock. They crack tough nuts and seeds using strong jaws, while the upper jaw also functions as an extra limb for climbing and manoeuvring.

Macaws are the most spectacular members of the parrot family and their rainbow plumage, ranging from the magnificent **scarlet macaw** to the brilliant **blue-and-yellow macaw**, is easily seen even in the densest forest. About thirty percent of the South American parrots are considered to be at risk of extinction because of habitat loss and the highly profitable trade in exotic pets.

Tanagers

These small, gloriously colourful birds feed on fruit, nectar and insects and live in a variety of habitats, from the lowland jungle to the highland cloudforest. Montane species include the **golden tanager**, **beryl-spangled tanager** and

blue-winged mountain-tanager. In the Amazon you can't miss the flocks of exotic **paradise tanagers** with their neon-lime heads, purple throats, crimson lower backs, black upper backs and turquoise rumps.

Toucans

With their flamboyant oversized bills and colour-splashed bodies, **toucans** are easy to spot. The largest is the **white-throated toucan**, which has a black bill with a yellow stripe running down the middle, and baby-blue framed eyes. This species lives in the jungle along with **araçaris**, smaller, more colourful toucans. The highlands are where to find the wonderful **mountain toucans**.

Vultures and condors

Vultures thrive everywhere and wherever other animals die, as they only eat carrion. Their heads and necks are covered with bald skin rather than feathers so that caked blood from carcasses can be easily cleaned off. **Black vultures** are common around urban rubbish dumps, while the **greater yellow-headed vulture** dominates the rainforest niche.

The **Andean condor**, national bird of Ecuador, is the world's heaviest bird of prey, with a wingspan of 3m. Adults are black with a ruff-like white collar and bald pinkish head. Hunting has reduced their population to a maximum of 150 individuals. They live near and above the tree line, with the largest number soaring over the páramo around Volcán Antisana in the northeast.

Mammals

Ecuador is home to 317 species of **mammals**, representing about eight percent of the world's total. Many live in the forests and are shy of human presence, making them difficult to spot, though most jungle trips are rewarded with sightings of monkeys skipping through the canopy. The holy grail of the mountain forests is the Andean spectacled bear, but few visitors are lucky enough to see one.

Anteaters

Giant anteaters can weigh up to 40kg and amble along the rainforest floor looking for ant nests; when they find one, they poke their long tongues inside and trap the ants with gluey saliva. The other three species, such as the tiny **pygmy anteater**, live in trees, where they rip apart the nests of ants, bees and termites and lick up the residents.

Bats

Tent-building bats live in the rainforest and create homes by selecting a large leaf and nibbling a line down each side so that the leaf flaps droop downwards. Small groups of bats can be seen huddling together in a close-knit scrum underneath their protective tent.

The **common vampire bat** lives in the rainforest and subtropical forests of the Andean slopes up to 1500m, feeding entirely on the blood of mammals and prospering in the presence of domestic cattle and swine. They bite with sharp incisors, rarely waking their victims, and lick up the drops of blood dripping from the wound – vampire-bat saliva contains special anticoagulants so that the blood flows freely. There are very few cases of bats feeding on humans; it's thought they're only capable of biting through the webbed skin between fingers and toes.

Wild cats

Felines aren't easy to find, but they do scratch logs to proclaim their presence, so look for telltale marks.

Ocelots are small, with tawny fur and black spots, stripes and rosettes, living on a range of habitats with good cover, from rainforest to desert scrub, sometimes raiding chicken coops in villages. Pale-grey or yellow **pumas** also live in dry areas, while those in the rainforest are yellow-brown to dark red-brown.

Jaguars are tawny yellow with black spots. They've adapted to a range of habitats, from rainforest to arid scrub, hunting at any time of day for capybaras, deer, turtles, caimans, birds or fish. One of the best places to spot them is from a boat, as they lie on logs over the water, soaking up the rays in the morning sun.

Wild cat attacks on humans are very rare. If you meet a jaguar or a puma, don't run: stay facing it, make a lot of noise and wave your arms about.

Dolphins and manatees

Pink river dolphins, or *botos*, hunt for fish, turtles and crabs. Although nearly blind, they navigate and locate prey using a sonar system housed in a large bulge on their foreheads. Curious and intelligent, they'll approach swimmers but won't attack.

Amazonian manatees are highly endangered due to hunting, so you'll be fortunate to encounter one. These large, hairless, cigar-shaped herbivores are docile, browsing on aquatic plants and living under the water, only breaking the surface with their nostrils to breathe.

Monkeys

Ecuadorian **monkeys** live in trees and only hit the ground running to cross open space. **Marmosets** and **tamarins** are the smallest of them and sport flamboyant facial hair, ear tufts, tassels, ruffs, manes and moustaches. They communicate with timid chirps and bird-like whistles and can be seen in villages and towns.

Howler monkeys are far more often heard than seen. At dawn and dusk they band together for deafening howling sessions which carry across the canopy for kilometres. A male usually starts off the clamour with an escalating grunting session, which segues into long, deep roars. Females join in with their higher-pitched voices. **Red howlers** favour tall riverbank trees, so they're most easily spotted from a boat.

Otters

There are two **otters** in Ecuador, the **neotropical river otter** and the **giant otter**, which can grow up to 1.5m in length, not counting its metre-long tail. They have sleek reddish-brown coats, huge, fully webbed feet and intelligent, canine-type faces (their local name is *lobo del río*, or river wolf). They live in social groups in quiet waters, swimming, diving and feasting on fish, mammals and birds, and reputedly even anacondas.

Rodents

Rats and **mice** thrive in urban environments, **squirrels** leap acrobatically through the trees and **porcupines** root around on the rainforest floor.

The **capybara** is the world's largest rodent, weighing some 55kg, with stocky bodies and thin hind legs – they often sit on their haunches like dogs. Small herds live along Amazonian lakes, rivers and swamps, feeding on water lilies, water hyacinth, leaves and sedges. Humans, caimans, jaguars and anacondas all eat them – if they don't leap into the water and swim away first.

Sloths

Sloths live in the rainforest and feed on canopy leaves, digesting them in a multi-chambered stomach. Algae flourishes in tiny grooves on their body hair, turning the sloths an alien green and camouflaging them in the trees. They're hard to see from the ground, but eagles are masters at spotting them and swooping in to pick them off the branches. Once a month, sloths climb down from their trees and dig a hole in the ground in which to defecate.

Spectacled bears

Ecuador's only **bear** lives in forested mountain habitats from 1000m to 4000m. They're mostly black or brown, mottled white or cream with distinctive "spectacles" encircling part of each eye. By bear standards they're small – the males weigh about 80kg and the females 60kg. Each paw is equipped with short, sharp, powerful claws for climbing or tearing apart trees. Up in the trees they build platforms of branches, on which they rest or feed on fruits and honey.

Tapirs

The region's largest terrestrial mammals, **tapirs** have stocky bodies, muscular necks, elongated, overhanging upper lips and short tails and spend about ninety percent of the day eating a calorie-poor leaf diet. Their droopy upper lips are used to reach out and sweep food into their mouths.

The **Brazilian tapir**, the size of a Shetland pony, varies in colour from black to red to tan. They hang out in swamps in the rainforest and in grassy habitats up to 2000m, and if afraid leap into the nearest water and swim away – though if you can imitate their loud whistle, they will answer you. The extremely rare brown, shaggy **mountain tapir** lives in the montane forests and páramo.

Reptiles and amphibians

There are about eight hundred **reptile** and **amphibian** species living in Ecuador. They thrive in the Amazon and also in the Andean foothills, where many are endemic.

Caimans

Crocodilian **caimans** lie motionless along riverbanks waiting for fish and other water-dwelling animals, such as capybaras, snakes and birds, to come within striking distance of their powerful jaws. The best way to see them is from a boat at night. Hold a torch at eye level and scan the riverbank; the caimans are easy to find because their eyes shine red in the beam.

Frogs

Frogs thrive in the Amazon where the hot, damp conditions keep them warm and hydrated. Over 75 percent are nocturnal and a deafening chorus wafts each night from ponds, lakes, riverbanks and the depths of flooded forests, as the males compete to attract females with their throaty tones.

The **leaf dweller**, which looks just like a dead leaf, is fairly common but difficult to see, as it's only visible when on the move. Fast-flowing streams are where to look for **glass frogs**, which are completely transparent, revealing their tiny beating hearts and other organs under the skin. The well-known **poison-dart frog** is small and brightly coloured, and only active during the day.

Lizards and geckoes

Many **lizards** and **geckoes** live in the Amazon, such as the common **iguana**, which, with its heavily scaled head and spiny back, looks like a miniature dinosaur. The **basilisk**, or Jesus lizard, can be seen scurrying across still rivers, but they aren't really walking on water – the hind feet are just under the water's surface and are sprung upwards and onwards by an air bubble trapped beneath the basilisk's webbed foot.

Snakes

Plenty of **snakes**, both harmless and poisonous, slither through Ecuador's forests, but they are encountered only rarely. **Pit vipers** locate prey with heat receptors between their eyes and nostrils that can register changes in temperature of only 0.003°C. The teeth usually lie back horizontally but are erected to strike, bite and inject venom. Tan-coloured with dark diamond patterning, the two-metre-long, highly venomous **fer-de-lance** is the most notorious viper, an aggressive snake with a very painful bite that can kill. The **bushmaster** is the largest viper in the world, at up to 3m in length.

The **boa constrictor**, which can reach 4m in length, is found in a variety of habitats from wet lowland forest to arid grassland. Another constrictor, the **anaconda**, is the largest snake in the world, occasionally growing to over 8m and weighing in at more than 200kg. Highly intelligent, it lies in wait by rivers for unsuspecting capybara, tapirs, large birds and peccaries, watching their drinking habits for weeks at a time before striking.

Turtles

Aquatic side-necked turtles are frequently seen in the rainforest, sunning themselves on branches sticking out of the water. When defending themselves, they tuck their heads sideways into their shells. Turtles build nests of rotting debris, which incubate their eggs at a constant temperature.

Insects

In Ecuador there are at least a million different types of **insect**, and the rainforest is the best place to find them. At nightfall, they produce the unmistakeable rainforest soundscape – a cacophony of cheeps, clicks, trills, screeches and wheezes.

Ants

Many rainforest **ants** make their homes on plants, which provide shelter, protection and food via nectar. **Acacia ants**, for example, pay for their board on the acacia tree by defending it from unwelcome visitors and will attack beetles, caterpillars and other ants that try to land or climb on it. They also prune back other plants that grow too close or shadow their tree from the sunlight.

Army ant colony members can number over a million. Squadrons run eight to ten abreast along forest trails and cooperate to overpower other invertebrate creatures far larger than themselves. **Leaf-cutter ants** are highly visible as they trudge along forest trails in lengthy columns bearing relatively huge leaf clippings. The leaves are transported back to their vast underground nests, but instead of consuming them the ants chew them into a soft pulp to make a compost on which to grow a special fungus – their favourite food.

One ant to avoid is the **conga** or **giant hunting ant**, a large, aggressive-looking black creature whose sharp sting can cause pain and fever, lasting from a few hours to a few days.

Beetles

One of the most common beetles is the **giant ceiba borer**, its outer skeleton gleaming like iridescent metal – the wing covers are popular in the production of earrings. **Hercules**, **rhinoceros** and **elephant beetles** are hard to miss, as they're the little giants their names suggest. The **headlight** or **cucuyu beetle** is also easily spotted: two round, light-producing organs behind its head give it the appearance of a toy car. The beautiful **tortoise beetle** looks as though it's been dipped in liquid gold. If attacked, it pulls in its legs and head and seals itself to the ground.

Butterflies

Ecuador is home to 4500 species of **butterfly**, with the number of known ones growing almost daily. The most striking are the **morphos**, huge tropical visions in electric blue. Their brilliant colour doesn't derive from pigment, but from the way light is reflected and refracted by their complex wing scales. **Owl butterflies** have owl-like eyespots on their wings to direct hungry birds away from crucial body parts. **Clearwings** look like tiny fairies; with completely transparent wings, they're hard to see when motionless. **White-and-sulphur butterflies** are highly visible from rainforest rivers. Droves gather on riverbanks to lick salt and other nutrients from the ground. When disturbed by passing boats they swirl up in a confetti cloud of white, yellow and orange.

Fish

There are more than eight hundred species of **freshwater fish** in Ecuador, with an incredible diversity in rainforest rivers. The **pirarucu**, one of the world's largest freshwater fish, lives here – the real giants have all been fished out, but specimens of up to 2m are still caught. Watch for **leaf fishes** bobbing past your boat, hard to discern from dead leaves on account of their crumpled, blotchy appearance and lower jaw, which mimics a stem.

Forty percent of the fish are either **catfish** or **characins**. Many characins are fruit-eaters and wait for fruit to fall from trees in the flooded forests. The notorious **red piranha** is also a characin. Small but ferocious, they are only a danger to human swimmers in large groups when water levels are low and food supplies poor. Far more dangerous is the **electric eel**, which grows up to 1.8m and can produce a jolt of 650 volts.

The catfish to watch out for is the tiny **candiru**, which usually parasitizes other fish but has been known to follow urine currents of human swimmers, entering the urethra on occasion. Once inside, it lodges itself securely with an array of sharp spines and causes unmentionable discomfort. The offending fish is so firmly wedged it has to be surgically removed.

Galápagos wildlife

I n contrast to the diversity of life found on the mainland, few species have managed to make the 960-kilometre journey to the Galápagos. But it's the islands' small number of species in isolation that has fascinated generations of scientists. Like a self-contained puzzle, life on the Galápagos can be unravelled in a way impossible for the tangled mass of mainland biological relationships.

The origins of Galápagos life

The Galápagos Islands came into being as barren, lifeless heaps of lava cut off from the rest of the world by vast expanses of ocean. It's thought that the first life to make the crossing were seeds and spores of mosses, lichens and ferns, blown from the continent on the prevailing **winds** and deposited on the islands through rainfall. Insects, snails and spiders could also have been carried thousands of kilometres in the air, and when the winds were fierce enough they may also have blown land birds, such as hawks and finches, as well as bats to the archipelago. Many of the sea birds routinely fly long distances and need no vegetation for nests, making them likely candidates for early pioneers. As the unforgiving lava broke down into soil patches, a larger number of plants would have been able to colonize the island, in turn supporting more animals. It's thought up to sixty percent of plant species were brought to the islands by **birds**, either as undigested seeds in guano, or regurgitated, or attached to their feet and feathers.

The last route was **by the sea** – several currents converge on the islands, and may have brought species from the Pacific, Central and South American coasts. Swept up in the flow, marine turtles, penguins, seals and sea lions could all have swum to the islands aided by the currents, while giant tortoises – not natural swimmers – are, however, buoyant and can survive for long periods without food or water. The only satisfactory explanation for the arrival of other reptiles and rice rats (the only native land mammal) is on tree trunks and logs, or on floating rafts made of matted vegetation set adrift from the mainland after storms. Such a journey would have taken a couple of weeks, too long for most mammals and amphibians to survive without fresh water under a tropical sun, but well within the capabilities of reptiles such as iguanas.

The arrival of **humans** in the Galápagos provided a new means for foreign species to colonize the islands, and those such as dogs, rats, ants and goats, as well as plants like blackberry, red quinine and elephant grass now pose one of the greatest threats to the delicate ecology of the islands (see box, pp.444–445).

Separated from the rest of their kind, the marooned denizens of the Galápagos **evolved** as they adapted to their new environment, often ending up as quite different species to their mainland counterparts. These new plants and animals, found nowhere else in the world, are termed **endemic** species. Sometimes a single common ancestor has brought about a number of new species – as with Darwin's finches, a process known as **speciation**. In the Galápagos, though, the story doesn't end there: not only is the archipelago far from the continent, but the islands and islets comprising it are distant enough from each other to bring about their own endemic species. In a few instances, even the isolated habitats *within* an island can provoke speciation: for example, the five main volcanoes of Isabela are each populated by their own subspecies of giant tortoise.

Many Galápagos animals have evolved without the threat of **predators**, which accounts for their unusual fearlessness, and some have filled niches that would have been taken by other species on the mainland. The lack of mammals has meant that giant tortoises hold a similar role to mammal browsers, such as cows and sheep, while small land birds such as mockingbirds occupy niches similar to mainland mice.

Birds

The Galápagos Islands are an incomparable treat for birdwatchers. Despite a relatively small number of **bird species** for the tropics (there are 60 types of resident birds, and another 81 migratory species visit the islands), about half of the residents are endemic, and visitors are often able to walk within a metre of many of them. The naturalist William Beebe, who made two expeditions to the islands in the 1920s, tells of frantically searching for a flycatcher with his camera, only to find it perched on the lens "pecking at the brass fittings". A week's cruise of the islands, taking in a variety of habitats, will enable you to spot a healthy number of them, but consider the season if you want to see particular birds or behaviours. **Sea birds** make the most of good fish stocks in the cool-dry season, and migrants are in evidence from around October to February. Most **land birds** breed in the rainy season, when food is more abundant.

Sea birds

Since most **sea birds** are naturally strong long-distance fliers that thrive in island environments, only six out of the nineteen resident species are endemic. Sea birds are also among the most prevalent of Galápagos fauna, having numbers approaching a million.

Boobies

Among the best-known sea birds here are the **boobies**, probably named after the Spanish *bobo*, meaning "fool", perhaps for their ungainly waddling walk and relaxed attitude to being caught. In the same family as the gannet (*Sulidae*), the boobies are fantastic fishers; on spying their quarry they tuck their wings behind them and plunge from the sky, entering the water at terrific speed (an air sac in the skull softens the impact).

Of the three species, the **blue-footed booby** is the most widespread but least numerous, occupying small colonies all over the islands, where you'll hear the limp whistle of the males and boisterous honking of the females. Their wonderful courtship display of "skypointing" and "high-stepping", to show off the blueness of their feet, happens throughout the year. The female lays up to three eggs in the "nest" (little more than a ring of guano on a scraped patch of ground) and incubates them with her warm and veiny feet. If food is scarce, the first-born hatchling will tuck in on its less fortunate siblings, a way of guaranteeing that at least one will survive. The world's largest colony of **red-footed boobies** is on Genovesa, and despite numbering around a quarter of a million pairs in the archipelago, the red-foots are the least seen of the boobies, as they tend to inhabit the remoter islands; they're also the only tree-dwelling booby. The **Nazca booby** (formerly called the masked booby, but now considered a separate species) has rather lacklustre feet compared to its relatives, but makes up for it with its dazzling white plumage.

Flightless cormorants

Among the endemic sea birds, the **flightless cormorant** is one of the most peculiar-looking on the islands. Forgoing the ability to fly, these blazing-blue-eyed birds have developed large webbed feet and a sturdy lower body better suited to diving for food. Without an oily plumage, the birds hold their useless, bedraggled wings out to dry after each fishing expedition. Their snake-like necks are ideal for reaching into nooks and crannies for eels and octopus, and play a prominent part in their courtship ritual. Their nests are exotic collections of seaweed, twigs, fish bones, starfish and whatever else the male dredges up and offers as gifts to the nest-tending female during the incubation and brooding times. There are only around five hundred pairs of flightless cormorants in the world, all found on Isabela and Fernandina islands, where the fishing is good due to the cold Cromwell Current that comes from the west.

Frigatebirds

The two **frigatebird** species in the archipelago, the **great frigatebird** and the **magnificent frigatebird**, are among the most commonly seen sea birds, often spotted manoeuvring in the sky, blotting out the sun with their huge wingspans (up to 2.4m for the slightly larger magnificent frigates), while their twitching scissor tails keep them on course. The two appear similar at first, but are easy to tell apart: male magnificent frigatebirds have a purple sheen on their feathers, whereas great frigates have green; female magnificent frigatebirds have a blue eye-ring, whereas female great frigates have a red eye-ring and a white chest.

Once called **man of war birds**, they have a reputation for aggression, harrying other sea birds to disgorge their catch, which they'll skilfully intercept before it hits the water. Their own fishing technique involves a deft flicking with their long hooked beaks on the surface of the water, whipping out their prey while ensuring that their feathers stay dry (they have lost the ability to oil their plumage, and will drown if they get wet enough). In the mating season, the males inflate their brilliant red **gular sacs**, or throat pouches, flap their wings and call out to attract the attention of any passing females. At times, dozens of males will be competing for a mate when the colonies, freckled with colour, resound with their wavering calls. You can see the spectacle throughout the year at Seymour Norte or during March and April at Genovesa and San Cristóbal, though you may also be lucky at other times.

Galápagos penguins

The **Galápagos penguin** is another endemic sea bird and always an odd sight in tropical waters, being the only penguin that's found north of the equator. It's related to the Humboldt and Magellan penguins that mostly occupy the Humboldt Current off the coast of Chile, and like its relatives it also prefers the cold water, largely colonizing areas around Isabela and Fernandina islands. Using its small, muscular wings as paddles and its feet as rudders, the Galápagos penguin can propel itself at up to 40kmh through the water.

Gulls

The threatened **lava gull** is perhaps the rarest gull in the world, numbering around two hundred pairs. The dusky-coloured bird with white eyelids scavenges the ports, bays and beaches of the population centres, particularly at Puerto Ayora. The other endemic gull, the **swallow-tailed gull**, is far more attractive, having large black eyes set off from its black head by bright red eye-rings. It's one of the world's only nocturnal gulls, flying up to 35km out to sea and picking out phosphorescent shapes of squid in the darkness with its huge eyes, then turning home to locate land by the echo of its strange clacking call.

Waved albatrosses

The **waved albatross** is the emperor of the islands, the largest bird of the archipelago with a wingspan of 2.5m, weighing 4kg and living for up to forty years. Save for a few pairs that nest on the Isla de la Plata, the waved albatross is endemic to Española, and each year more than twelve thousand pairs come to nest and breed there from April to December. This bird chooses a mate for life and roams the island after months alone at sea to find its partner. Its beguiling courtship display, a lengthy mix of "bill circling", "sky-pointing", "gaping", "clunking" and "sway-walking" among other manoeuvres, is thought to cement the marriage bond.

Other sea birds

Other residents of the archipelago include the graceful **red-billed tropicbird**, the widespread **brown pelican**, the **brown noddy** and **sooty tern**, the **Galápagos petrel** (formerly the dark-rumped petrel, and now recognized as endemic), **Audubon's shearwater** and three species of **storm petrel**.

Shore and wetland birds

Rock pools, mangroves, beaches and shallow salty lagoons are common features of the Galápagos coast, providing habitats for as many as fifty bird species, many of them migrants such as the **wandering tattler**, which commutes from the Arctic. Only one of the shore birds is endemic, the **lava heron**, though there are several residents that have shown enough of the slow signs of evolution to have earned endemic subspecies status, such as the **yellow-crowned night heron**. **Striated** and **great blue herons** are the other resident heron species frequently seen around the coastal waters, gazing into pools with beady eyes. **Greater flamingos** tiptoe about the saltwater lagoons, sifting the silt and surface for water boatmen and shrimp. During the breeding season, care must be taken not to disturb these elegant birds, as they are prone to abandon nests if startled. There are fewer than 250 pairs in the Galápagos.

As well as resident waders such as the **American oystercatcher** and **black-necked stilt**, a number of familiar migrants are in evidence, including **turnstones**, **sandpipers**, **yellowlegs**, **sanderlings**, **whimbrels**, **phalaropes** and **plovers**. The **white-cheeked pintail duck** is equally at home by the coast or at the freshwater lagoons in the highlands, where the **purple** or **common gallinule** (moorhen) make their home. **Cattle egrets**, nesting in the mangroves, are more usually seen in the highlands in large flocks near livestock. This striking white bird has now managed to colonize much of the world, though it was found only in West Africa till the late nineteenth century.

Land birds

The **land birds** of the Galápagos have been of enormous interest to scientists ever since Darwin's discoveries. Unlike most strong-winged sea birds, which are accustomed to making long journeys, the land birds can only have been brought to the archipelago blown on the winds of freak storms. And yet, of the 29 resident species, a phenomenal 22 are endemic, so such abnormal bird-carrying gales must have occurred no less than fourteen times – quite a feat considering that none strong enough to achieve this has yet been recorded.

Most famous of Galápagos birds are **Darwin's finches**, the thirteen endemic and subtly different finches that proved to be of enormous importance to their namesake. These dowdy, sparrow-sized birds are notoriously difficult to tell apart, despite the all-important differences in beak size and feeding habits. Since the finches are so similar, more like each other than any other kind of finch, Darwin suspected that they were all descendants of a common ancestor. No doubt the archipelago's grouping of isolated islands allowed for this remarkable speciation, even though many of them now inhabit the same islands.

The **large ground finch** has the biggest beak and is able to crack open large, hard seeds, while the **warbler finch** probes plants and flowers with its sharp and slender bill and has been called "more warbler than finch". The **woodpecker finch** and endangered **mangrove finch** are celebrated for their ability to use tools, often fashioning a twig or a cactus spine to wheedle larvae and grubs from tight spots. A subspecies of the **sharp-billed ground finch** on remote Wolf and Darwin islands has earned the moniker **vampire finch** for pecking at Nazca boobies and feeding off their blood. The **small ground finch** has better interspecies relations, preening tortoises and iguanas for parasites, which it devours.

The archipelago has four endemic **mockingbirds**: the **Galápagos mockingbird** is fairly widespread, while the **Chatham mockingbird** only inhabits San Cristóbal, the **Hood mockingbird** Española, and the rare **Charles mockingbird** a couple of islets around Floreana. They are among the most confident and inquisitive birds on the islands, having no qualms about hopping around the feet of large groups of tourists.

Galápagos hawks are almost as fearless, having no natural enemies, and are content to let humans get to within a few metres of them. The Galápagos hawk practises a breeding system whereby the female has as many as four mates, who help her incubate the eggs and tend to the young. With the hawk, the **Galápagos barn owl** and the **short-eared owl** make up the archipelago's birds of prey. The latter is the more commonly seen, particularly on Genovesa, where it swoops on the young of the large sea-bird colonies. Other endemics include the elegant **Galápagos dove**, the secretive and miniature **Galápagos rail**, the **Galápagos flycatcher** and the **Galápagos martin**, the archipelago's only non-migratory member of the swallow family.

For all their intrinsic interest, the endemics can be a drab bunch, and indeed, the archipelago's two most colourful birds are residents. The **yellow warbler** and the dazzling male **vermilion flycatcher**, boasting a smart red-and-black plumage, are common favourites brightening up the dour scenery.

Reptiles

Above all fauna on the Galápagos, it's the **reptiles** that give the islands their distinctive prehistoric flavour. Until the arrival of humans, its isolation made the archipelago virtually impenetrable to mammal life, allowing the reptiles to take up their ecological niches. Although their appearance is "antediluvian", the Galápagos reptiles have undergone the same evolutionary processes as the islands' other creatures, resulting in a high level of endemism. Of the 23 reptile species, 21 are unique to the Galápagos and several of these are specific to particular islands. Five reptile families are represented on the archipelago: **tortoises**, **marine turtles**, **iguanas** (including lizards), **geckoes** and **snakes**.

Being **ectothermic** animals, reptiles cannot regulate their body temperature through physiology, such as sweating or dilating and constricting blood vessels as humans do. They need to heat their blood up to a certain level before they can become properly active – which is why you'll commonly see iguanas splayed on rocks absorbing the sun's rays for many hours, only moving into the shade if they get too hot. This system also allows them to survive on less food and water than other animals, a characteristic along with tolerance to salt water that made the journey across from the mainland that much easier.

Marine turtles

Although you may be lucky enough to see the **leatherback**, **hawksbill** or **olive ridley turtles** in Galápagos waters, only the **Pacific green turtle** is a resident, regularly nesting on the islands' beaches. The green turtles weigh up to 150kg and are graceful swimmers, motored by their large front flippers. They've been known to make regular journeys between the islands and the Ecuadorian mainland and can stay submerged for hours on end. Females mate with a succession of males inshore at the surface and dig large holes on sandy beaches to lay clutches of up to a hundred eggs. In less than two months, the hatchlings are ready to make their dash to the sea avoiding mockingbirds, frigatebirds, herons, ghost crabs and a host of other hungry predators awaiting a feast. They break out at night simultaneously to keep the number of casualties down to a minimum, but even when they've reached the sea they swim nonstop to avoid sharks and other predators lurking inshore.

Iguanas

The cracked volcanic shores make a fitting home to the demonic-looking colonies of **marine iguana**, the world's only seagoing iguana.

The marine iguana feeds on small tufts of seaweed or algae in rocky, intertidal areas. The larger males supplement this with the more plentiful supplies found underwater. Using their flattened tails to swim through the waves, they can dive to 12m and stay submerged for up to an hour, while they tear the weeds from the rocks, aided by their broad, blunt mouths. To compensate for such a salty diet, special glands above the eye allow the marine iguana to blow excess salt out of its nose in a fine spray, hence the salt crystals caked to their heads. They'll often "sneeze" at you if you get too close to them. In the mating season, starting in January on most islands, marine iguanas take on a fiery red colouration. On Española they have a blotched black-and-red appearance during the year and burst into bright red and turquoise in the months of breeding.

The larger **land iguanas** can live up to 60 years and prefer the drier areas of the central and western islands, as they rely on cactus pads and fruits for much of their food, rolling them on the ground first to get rid of the spines before chomping in. Three endemic species inhabit the Galápagos, one of which is confined to Santa Fé island; and another, identified as a new species only in 2009, is a pink iguana found only near the summit of Wolf volcano on Isabela. Introduced species have been very harmful to land-iguana populations: the creatures are now extinct on Santiago and were almost finished off on Baltra during World War II, though fortunately some had been moved to Seymour Norte previously and have since been reintroduced to their home island.

Tortoises

The **giant tortoises** of the Galápagos have come to symbolize the islands – and indeed, are the origin of their name. The lumbering and hoary beasts weigh up to 250kg and are the largest tortoises in the world. Only one other island on the globe in the Seychelles has a giant-tortoise population. The Galápagos once had fourteen subspecies of giant tortoise, and numbers could have been as high as 250,000. Unchecked slaughter during the height of the whaling era in the nineteenth century brought the population down to 15,000 and made three subspecies extinct. One other is set to be lost, too; **Lonesome George**, kept at the Charles Darwin Research Station on Santa Cruz, is thought to be the last surviving Pinta tortoise. A reward of $10,000 is on offer to anyone that can find him a mate.

Giant tortoises can be identified by two basic types of shell shape, but there's a degree of overlap between the subspecies with other shell shapes that fall somewhere in between. The **dome-shaped tortoise** is found in moister areas with thicker vegetation, while the **saddleback** shape allows a greater reach for the scarcer food on the drier islands.

Giant tortoises are **vegetarians** and enjoy the nourishment of more than fifty plant species. When food is abundant they eat heartily, but it takes as long as three weeks to digest a meal, and even when it finally passes through, it's easy to see what they've been eating. Their somewhat coarse digestion does allow them to gorge on the highly toxic poison apple (even touching it can cause skin irritation to humans) and prickly *Opuntia* cactus pads, despite the spines.

Tortoises are thought to live for more than 150 years, though no one knows for sure as they always outlive the research projects. They only become sexually mature around their 25th birthday. The mating season begins as the warm-wet season nears its end, when males compete for females by extending their necks – the highest head wins. The male mounts the female, fitting perfectly on her back due to the concave shape of his underside, and mates in a cacophony of grunts, wheezes and sighs lasting hours. Females then retreat to coastal areas to lay their billiard-ball-sized eggs, which can take up to eight months to hatch. It's the temperature of the nest that determines the sex of the hatchlings, rather than any specific chromosomal information. Apart from mating, tortoises are virtually silent unless they are alarmed, when they quickly draw their limbs and head into the shell, forcing air out of their nostrils with a sharp hiss.

The first amphibian

For millions of years, no amphibian has been able to colonize the Galápagos Islands. Salt water is murderous to them, drying out their delicate skins on contact, making a sea crossing to the islands impossible. Since 1998, however, a two- to three- centimetre **tree frog** (*Scinax quinquefasciata*) has become established on three of the populated islands, and is being found with increasing frequency at Puerto Ayora. It seems the tiny grey-and-black frog, common throughout the coastal mainland, stowed itself away among crates of vegetables brought over by boat and air. The abnormally wet 1997–98 **El Niño** event allowed the new arrivals to get a toehold on the islands – probably breeding in small pools of fresh water common around the houses, gardens and leaking pipes of the population centres – as well as the introduction of **kikuyo**, a plant that provides the perfect refuge for frog eggs and tadpoles. It's not clear if this species is a danger to the native wildlife; it must be devouring insects, and if it has poison glands, as many frogs do, it could pose a more serious threat to native predators, wiping out large numbers of them. The Galápagos authorities are still investigating the matter, but are anxious to get the frogs out of the wild. Eradication programmes have been started but the scheme to give a small bounty for each one caught had to be abandoned when it was found that locals were breeding them for cash.

Other reptiles

Seven endemic **lava lizards** dart around the island coasts, hunting for insects and spiders. The males can grow up to 30cm in length and are larger than the females, which are distinguished by the vivid-red colouration on their head or throats. They mark their territories by doing sequences of "press-ups" on their forelegs, and each island has its own unique pattern. The lava lizard is hunted by the three endemic types of **Galápagos snake**, unspectacular non-venomous constrictors about a metre long, which devour **geckoes**, small, wide-eyed nocturnal lizards that can stick to windows with their special toe pads. Five of the six native geckoes are endemic; three others have been recently introduced.

Mammals

The travails of making the crossing from the continent have proved too much for most **mammals**, and there is a noticeable absence of them on the islands. Just six native species inhabit the Galápagos, and of them only the **rice rats** made the gruelling sea journey on a vegetation raft (like many of the reptiles, which are far better suited to this kind of transport). Four of the seven rice-rat species are now extinct, wiped out by the introduced black rat, which out-competes them. The remaining three species are found on Santa Fé and Fernandina islands, islands that have so far been spared invasion by the black rat.

The **bats** took the air route: the ancestors of the endemic *Lasiurus brachyotis* were most likely blown over from the mainland like land birds, while the other native species, the **hoary bat**, is a known migrant and widespread throughout North America. There's nothing to stop mammal populations flourishing once they get to the Galápagos, as has been demonstrated by a number of **introduced species**, such as feral goats, cats, dogs and rats, which have been doing terrible damage to native wildlife, all brought to the islands by another late and supremely harmful mammalian arrival, *Homo sapiens*.

Sea lions and fur seals

The archipelago's endemic **sea lions** and **fur seals** may well have swum to the islands, aided by strong currents. A relative of the larger Californian sea lion, the **Galápagos sea lion** never fails to charm visitors to the island. Sometimes boisterous, sometimes lazy, the sea lions' yelping, sneezing, coughing and whooping has an unnerving human quality to it. You'll commonly see sleepy females piled together on the beach, while the large dominant bull, weighing up to 250kg and identifiably male for the pronounced bump on its forehead, aggressively patrols its territory barking loudly above and below the waves. Lesser males have no place at these heavily guarded "harems" and form colonies in less favourable locations, where they build up strength and size to make a successful challenge. The bull spends so much of its time guarding its territory that it doesn't feed, and eventually has to give way to a fitter male. These inquisitive, graceful and friendly animals will often check you out if you're swimming nearby, staring into your mask or tugging at your flippers. The bulls should be given a lot of space, though – they have a nasty bite and don't take kindly to humans who appear to be muscling in on their territory.

Galápagos fur seals are more shy and difficult to see, choosing the shade of craggy cliffs and rocks, where they can find a nook to keep out of the sun's glare. In spite of their name, they are in the same family (*Otaridae*) as the sea lion, having protruding ears and the ability to "walk" on their front flippers, unlike the *Phocidae*, the true seals. They're related to the southern fur seals of Antarctica and the southern mainland, and have thick coats like them, though in the heat of the Galápagos they must take care not to overheat. Their large, mournful eyes give them excellent vision for their nightly hunting trips and they avoid expeditions at full moon, when sharks have a better chance of seeing them. In the nineteenth century, their warm, double-layered pelt was highly sought after, and numbers declined from overhunting. They are now protected and colonies have recovered to around five or six thousand.

Whales and dolphins

One of the most thrilling moments during a Galápagos cruise is a sighting of **whales** or **dolphins**. Amiable **bottle-nosed dolphins** frequently surf the bow wave, jockeying for position at the front of a boat and jumping high in synchrony at either side. Huge schools of dark-grey and white **common dolphins** occasionally pass boats, skipping through the waves in long lines, while **striped** and **spinner dolphins** are seen less frequently. Whalers hunted the waters west of Isabela and Fernandina exhaustively during the first half of the nineteenth century, until populations all but disappeared around the 1860s. Today several whale species are found in these areas and the **sperm whale** is known to have breeding grounds in the area. The **humpback whale** is the most easily spotted, sometimes "breaching" – hurling its sixteen-metre body out of the water before crashing down in an avalanche of spray. Other baleen whales, those that sift for plankton and shrimp such as the **sei**, **minke**, **Bryde's** and **finback**, are more usually seen as a fin and a puff of spray in the distance. **Orcas** or **killer whales** feed on dolphins, fur seals, penguins and sea lions.

Fish and marine invertebrates

Bathed in cold upwelling currents and warm tropical waters, the Galápagos harbours 306 **fish** species, with 51 endemics. Plenty of interesting fish can be spotted with a snorkel and mask, but the most thrilling to swim with are the **sharks**. Regularly seen species include **white-tip reef sharks**, **hammerheads** and **black-tip sharks**, none of which is usually dangerous to humans. You'll need to scuba dive to see the **Galápagos shark**, which prefers deeper waters. There have been very few reports of a shark attack in the Galápagos, certainly none fatal, but follow the advice of your guide all the same. The colossal eighteen-metre **whale shark** is the largest fish in the world and feeds on plankton.

The **rays** include the **stingray**, **golden ray**, the beautiful **spotted eagle ray** and the **manta ray** (which can grow up to 6m across). The larger rays are frequently seen somersaulting out of the water before landing in clouds of spray. Among the more commonly seen bony fishes are the **blue-eyed damselfish**, the stripy **sergeant major**, the **moorish idol**, the **hieroglyphic hawkfish** and the **white-banded angelfish**, as well as several **blennies**, **wrasses** and **parrotfish**. The **four-eyed blenny** is so called because each eye has two facets, allowing it to see both in and out of the water. It can spend two hours flapping about the rocks as it hunts for insects and small crabs.

Many interesting organisms are visible around the shore between the tides. **Octopuses** lurk in rock pools, but can be difficult to see because of their ability to change colour. Among the most visible intertidal animals are the more than one hundred **crab** species scuttling over the rocks and beaches. The brightest is the **Sally lightfoot crab**, whose red casing gleams against the black lava. Its name comes either from a Jamaican dancer or its ability to zip over the water of a tide pool. Young Sally lightfoots are dark to blend in with the background. **Ghost crabs** live in holes dug in sandy beaches, while the soft-bodied **hermit crab** occupies abandoned shells, moving as it grows. **Fiddler crabs** are easy to identify by their outsized claw. **Sea urchins**, **sea cucumbers**, **starfish**, **anemones**, **molluscs** and **sponges** can also be found.

Land invertebrates

There are more than two thousand species of **land invertebrates** – animals without a backbone, such as insects and spiders – in the Galápagos, over half of them endemic. It sounds a huge number, but compared with more than a million species found in mainland Ecuador, it's clear that land invertebrates found the archipelago difficult to reach and colonize.

The arid climate of the islands has meant that many **insects** are nocturnal, escaping the noonday heat in dank and shaded hideouts. For this reason many are drably coloured. **Beetles** account for more than four-hundred species, **bugs** eighty or so and **flies** around one hundred, including the bothersome **horsefly** and **midge**. The **carpenter bee** is the only bee in the Galápagos, an important pollinator of native plants. Of the butterflies and moths, the yellow **Galápagos sulphur butterfly** and the **green hawkmoth**, which has a proboscis twice the length of its body, are among the most commonly seen of the two groups. The **Galápagos silver fritillary** has sparkling silvery patches on its wings, but perhaps the most colourful insect outside the eight butterfly species is the **painted locust**, frequently spotted around the coast in black, red and yellow. There are two **scorpions**, both of which can sting but are not dangerous, and more than fifty **spiders**, including a venomous relative of the black widow and the **silver argiope**, which weaves a silky "X" into the centre of its web. A thirty-centimetre, crimson-legged **centipede**, the poisonous endemic *Scolopendra galapagensis*, has a very painful bite, normally reserved for unlucky insects, lava lizards and small birds.

Ticks and **mites** annoy reptiles rather than humans, and tortoises and iguanas rely on finches to remove them. Of the tiny **land snails**, the *Bulimulus* genus has enjoyed extraordinary speciation with more than sixty known endemics descended from a single ancestor – putting Darwin's finches quite in the shade.

Plants

There are more than six hundred plant species in the Galápagos, around forty percent of which are endemic. Botanists have divided the islands into **vegetation zones**, each of which contains certain groupings of plants. Levels of rainfall play an important part in determining these zones and, generally speaking, the higher the altitude, the more moisture is received, allowing for a greater number of plant species. Usually the southern, windward side of an island receives far more rain than the leeward, which lies in a rain shadow, so in many cases the zones differ from one side of an island to another.

Coastal and arid zones

Going by altitude, the first zone is the **coastal** or **littoral zone** around the shore, dominated by salt-tolerant plants, notably four species of **mangrove** (red, black, white and button), which make important breeding sites for many sea and shore birds. When water is scarce **sea purslane** (*Sesuvium*) turns a deep red, covering shorelines in a crimson carpet, reverting to green in the wet season. **Beach morning glory** is a creeper that helps bind sand dunes together and produces large lilac flowers.

The **arid zone** is one of the largest zones, and is the most familiar to island visitors for its scrubby and cactus-filled semi-desert landscape. The **candelabra cactus** (*Jasminocereus*), whose distinctive barrel-shaped fingers can grow to 7m, and the **lava cactus** (*Brachycereus*), growing in small yellow clumps on black lava flows, are both endemic. The widespread **prickly pear cactus** (*Opuntia*) comes in fourteen endemic types on the islands and forms a major food staple for many birds and reptiles. The most striking of them has developed into tall, broad-trunked trees up to 12m in height, in part an evolutionary response to browsing tortoises. The lower shrubby forms are mostly found on tortoise-free islands, and in the northern islands, where pollinating insects are absent, the spines are softer to allow birds to do the job. The ubiquitous tree of this zone is the **palo santo**, recognizable for its deathly grey appearance. Its name translates as "holy stick", both because its fragrant resin is burnt as incense in churches (it can also be used as an insect repellent) and because its off-white flowers appear around Christmas. When the rains come, green leaves start sprouting on its branches. Virtually waterless ashy or sandy soils support the low-lying grey *Tiquilia*, as seen scattered around the dry slopes of Bartolomé. The genes of the **Galápagos tomato**, one of the world's only two tomato species, whose seeds germinate best having passed through the giant tortoise's digestive system, have been used to develop drought-resistant tomatoes in other countries. **Lichens** are also common in the arid zone, requiring very little moisture or soil, and grow on trees (such as the grey crustose lichen on the *palo santo*), rocks and even tortoise shells.

Transition and highland zones

The **transition zone** links the dry zone to the more humid areas of **highland zones**. It's dominated by **pega pega** (meaning "stick stick"), so called for its sticky leaves and fruit, **guayabillo**, an endemic that produces fruits similar to the guava, and **matazarno**, a tall tree used for timber.

The humid area starts at around 200m and is divided into four zones. The **scalesia zone** is lush and densely forested, perpetually soaked in *garúa* mist during the cool-dry season. It's dominated by **lechoso** (*Scalesia pedunculata*), a fifteen-metre-tall tree with a bushy leafy top, among the tallest members of the daisy and sunflower families, most often seen by visitors in the highlands of Santa Cruz. From one ancestor the *Scalesia* genus has developed into twenty forms according to the various environmental nuances of the islands. As in a cloudforest, the trees are covered with **epiphytes**, mainly **mosses**, **liverworts** and **ferns**, but also a few **orchids**, and one **bromeliad** (*Tillandsia*). At the higher end of this zone, the smaller **cat's claw** tree begins to take over, also hung heavy in epiphytes, which appear brown in the dry season, so giving it the name the **brown zone**. On Santa Cruz and San Cristóbal islands, the **miconia zone** is made up of a belt of **cacaotillo** (*Miconia robinsoniana*), an endemic shrub growing to about 5m, producing dark blue berries and resembling the cacao. Beginning at about 700m, the **pampa zone** is the highest and wettest zone, made up mainly of **grasses**, **sedges** and other plants adapted to boggy environments. The **tree fern**, reaching a height of 3m, is the tallest plant growing in this zone.

Books

With the possible exception of the Galápagos Islands, foreign writers have paid less attention to Ecuador than to its South American neighbours, and few Ecuadorian works are ever translated into English. That said, there's a reasonable choice of books available in English, covering subjects as diverse as archeology, exploration, travel and cookery, though not all are easy to find. One of the best places to buy English-language books is Quito, particularly at the excellent Libri Mundi bookshop (see p.114). Many of the titles listed below are also available from internet retailers such as Amazon, including some of the out-of-print books, which can be sourced from secondhand bookstores. Publishers are listed UK/US, unless there is only one, in which case this is indicated. Entries tagged with the 🏃 symbol are particularly recommended.

History and society

Michael Anderson *A Numismatic History of Ecuador* (Greenlight). Much more than a study of Ecuadorian coinage, the history of a relatively young nation's struggle for its own currency, intimately bound up in its political and cultural past – and particularly interesting in light of dollarization.

David Corkill *Ecuador: Fragile Democracy* (o/p). A clear and thorough summary of Ecuador's history and economy from the Spanish Conquest to the neoliberalism of the late 1980s.

Carlos de la Torre (ed.) *The Ecuador Reader: History, Culture, Politics* (Duke University). Enthralling compilation of voices, opinions and writings by Ecuadorian politicians, authors, artists, intellectuals and activists, interspersed with essays on Ecuador by outsiders, with up-to-date analysis on the latest trends and issues. A must for understanding contemporary Ecuador.

🏃 **John Hemming** *The Conquest of the Incas* (Pan/Harcourt Brace). Marrying an academic attention to detail with a gripping narrative style, Hemming's book is widely regarded as the best account of this devastating conquest. His

earlier work, *The Search for El Dorado* (Michael Joseph/Phoenix Press), pinpoints the origin of the myth of El Dorado.

Mark Honigsbaum *The Fever Trail: in Search of the Cure for Malaria* (Pan). A riveting story centring on three British explorers' long nineteenth-century search for the elusive cinchona tree – a native of Ecuador, first discovered in the Podocarpus area, and the only source of quinine – and their hapless task of bringing it to the colonies. Followed this with *Valverde's Gold* (Picador), an account of his search for the lost treasure of the Llanganates.

John Perkins *Confessions of an Economic Hit Man* (Ebury Press/Plume). Bestselling memoirs of a so-called "economic hit man", whose job it was to exert pressure through fair means or, more normally, foul on foreign leaders in the interests of US foreign policy and businesses. The Ecuadorian government, one of the alleged victims of his trade, was encouraged by him to take unpayable loans, effectively handing control of the economy to the US. He also claims that left-wing president Jaime Roldós refused to play along, and was assassinated as a result.

Sarah Radcliffe and Sallie Westwood *Remaking the Nation: Place, Identity and Politics in Latin America* (Routledge). Thought-provoking analysis of the complex and often contradictory factors informing perceptions of national identity in Latin America, using Ecuador as a case study. A fascinating insight into the country's self-image, as influenced by gender, age, class and ethnicity.

Wilma Roos and Omer van Renterghem *Ecuador in Focus* (Latin America Bureau/Interlink). A short and easy-to-read introduction to Ecuador, with chapters on

history, people, environment, economy and culture.

Mary Weismantel *Cholas and Pishtacos: Stories of Race and Sex in the Andes* (University of Chicago). Brilliantly explores the relationship and tensions between the races and sexes, set against the vivid backdrop of the Andes. The author underpins her analysis on two colourful figures of South American popular culture, the *chola* (a voluptuous highland *mestiza*) and the *pishtaco* (a mythical white ghoul that feeds on human fat), and draws on wide-ranging sources, from the reminiscences of potato sellers to highbrow novels.

Memoirs and travel

Ludwig Bemelmans *The Donkey Inside* (o/p). Classic narrative based on the author's travels through Ecuador in the 1940s. A little old-fashioned and conservative, but masterfully written and a lively read.

Joe Fisher *Cotopaxi Visions* (Quarry). Fast-paced, picaresque account of the author's quest for self-discovery and spiritual ecstasy in the Ecuadorian Andes in the 1970s. An entertaining read, even if you don't share Fisher's mysticism.

Albert Franklin *Ecuador: Portrait of a People* (Franklin Press). An affectionate and perceptive portrait of Ecuador in the early 1940s, as it stood, in the author's words, "at the threshold between the feudal world and the modern world".

Toby Green *Saddled with Darwin: A Journey through South America* (Phoenix). Elegantly written and loaded with wonderful anecdotes, an account of a madcap undertaking to follow Darwin's travels across South America on horseback. The author's total lack of riding experience was only one of the obstacles.

Grace Halsell *Los Viejos: Secrets of Long Life from the Sacred Valley* (o/p). In 1974 the author set off to live in Vilcabamba – in the supposed "valley of eternal youth" – for a year to try to find out what allowed its residents to live useful, meaningful and active lives well into old age. The result was an engaging glimpse of Vilcabamba before the arrival of the tourist boom.

Peter Lourie *Sweat of the Sun, Tears of the Moon* (University of Nebraska). Gripping account of the modern-day treasure seekers intent on retrieving Atahualpa's ransom from the Llanganates mountains, written by a young American who became embroiled in their obsessions in the 1980s.

Henri Michaux *Ecuador: A Travel Journal* (Northwestern University Press). Beautifully written – and sometimes ether-induced – impressions of Ecuador, based on the mystical Belgian author's travels through the country in 1977, and presented in a mixture of prose, poetry and diary notes.

Tom Miller *The Panama Hat Trail* (National Geographic). Blending lively travel narrative with investigative journalism, an engaging book tracking the historical and geographical course of the Panama hat, from the *toquilla* fields of the lowlands to the hat exporters and boutiques of the United States.

Karin Muller *Along the Inca Road: A Woman's Journey into an Ancient Empire* (National Geographic). With a research grant and a cameraman, Muller searches for the Royal Inca highway that once linked Ecuador to Chile and has dozens of adventures on the way, including a tear-gas riot and a land mine removal exercise, and being beaten with a guinea pig by a shaman for a diagnosis.

Neville Shulman *Climbing the Equator: Adventures in the Jungles and Mountains of Ecuador* (Summersdale). A writer and explorer journeys through rainforests, meets indigenous people and attempts to climb Chimborazo, in a compelling and informative narrative, with a foreword by Chris Bonington.

Diane Terezakis *Maíz y Coca Cola: Adventures, Scrapes, and Shamanism in the Amazon and Andes* (Xlibris). American city-girl seeks out the shamans and medicine men of Ecuador in an amusing voyage of self-discovery and altered states of consciousness.

🏃 **Paul Theroux** *The Old Patagonian Express* (Penguin). A cranky but entertaining account of the author's railway odyssey through the Americas, including a chapter on the time he spent in Quito (which he liked) and Guayaquil (which he hated), and attempting, and failing, to take the famous train ride between the two.

🏃 **Moritz Thomsen** *Living Poor* (Eland/University of Washington). An American Peace Corps volunteer writes lucidly about his time in the fishing community of Río Verde in Esmeraldas during the 1960s, and his mostly futile – sometimes farcical – efforts to haul its people out of poverty. Thomsen never left Ecuador and followed this book with three other autobiographical works – *Farm on the River of Emeralds* (Barrie & Jenkins/Vintage), *The Saddest Pleasure* (Sumach/Graywolf) and *My Two Wars* (US: Steerforth) – before dying in a squalid apartment in Guayaquil in 1991. He refused to help himself, even though he had a shoe box full of uncashed royalty cheques worth $40,000.

Celia Wakefield *Searching for Isabel Godin: An Ordeal on the Amazon, Tragedy and Survival* (Creative Arts Book Co). Fascinating account of the heartbreaking story of Isabel Godin, the Peruvian wife of Jean Godin, one of the key scientists on La Condamine's mission. Briefly left in Ecuador while her husband made further travel arrangements, she found herself separated from him for the next twenty years, kept apart by disaster, disease, treachery, sheer bad luck and the vagaries of international politics.

Robert Whitaker *The Mapmaker's Wife* (Bantam). The story of Isabel Godin again (as above), but with more of the science and history surrounding La Condamine's mission.

Mountaineering and hiking

Yossi Brain *Ecuador: A Climbing Guide* (Mountaineers). Covers climbing routes up Ecuador's most popular mountains and its lesser-known peaks.

Robert and Daisy Kunstaetter *Trekking in Ecuador* (Mountaineers).

Includes almost thirty beautiful, well-chosen routes, and plenty of maps, photos and elevation profiles.

Rob Rachowiecki, Mark Thurber and Betsy Wagenhauser *Ecuador: Climbing and Hiking Guide* (Viva).

New edition of a long-standing climbing and hiking guide to Ecuador, which details more than seventy routes throughout the country, concentrating on the sierra.

Richard Snailham *Sangay Survived* (Hutchinson). Brisk account of the attempt of six British-army climbers – the advance party of a geological survey – to climb Volcán Sangay in 1976, when an unexpected eruption left two of them dead and the rest of the team seriously injured and stranded on the volcano.

🏃 **Edward Whymper** *Travels Amongst the Great Andes of the Equator* (Rockbuy). Exploits of the pioneering mountaineer at the end of the nineteenth century, who managed to rack up a number of first ascents, including Chimborazo, Cayambe and Antisana. Best of all are the stunning illustrations of brooding peaks and highland life.

Wildlife and the environment

John Eisenberg and Kent Redford *Mammals of the Neotropics: Ecuador, Peru, Bolivia, Brazil* (University of Chicago). Useful guide to more than 650 species, including distribution maps, colour and monochrome photographs and background information on ecological and behavioural characteristics.

🏃 **Alexander von Humboldt** *Personal Narrative of Travels to the Equinoctial Regions of the New Continent during the Years 1799–1804* (BiblioBazaar). Written by perhaps the greatest of all scientist-explorers, who composed 29 volumes on his travels across South America. The sixth volume of his *Personal Narrative* touches on Ecuador, and includes the ground breaking botanical map of Chimborazo (which von Humboldt failed to climb after several attempts), showing the changes in the volcano's flora at different elevations.

Kevin Kling *Ecuador, Island of the Andes* (Thames & Hudson). A collection of stunning photographs of the peoples and landscapes of the Ecuadorian sierra, invested with a haunting, timeless quality that makes them linger in the mind.

John Kricher *A Neotropical Companion* (Princeton University). Excellent and thorough introduction to the flora, fauna and ecosystems of the tropics of Central and South America, aimed at the general reader.

David L. Pearson and Les Beletsky *Ecuador and the Galápagos Islands* (Arris Books/Academic Press). Substantial wildlife guide including 96 colour plates, which gives a good overview of much of the flora and fauna you're likely to stumble across on your travels. There's too much in Ecuador to be able to cover everything, but the species here are well selected and described in detail.

🏃 **Robert S. Ridgely and Paul J. Greenfield** *The Birds of Ecuador* (Cornell University). Long-awaited, monumental two-volume book (available separately) including a field guide with glorious colour plates of Ecuador's 1600 bird species. The country's definitive bird guide, and an indispensable resource for anyone interested in South American avifauna.

Robert S. R. Williams *Guide to Bird-watching in Ecuador and the Galápagos Islands* (Biosphere). Not the best choice for identification purposes, but still a useful field guide that offers details of 120 birding sites and maps, a checklist of Ecuadorian species and information on habitats and conservation.

The Oriente

Philippe Drescola *The Spears of Twilight: Life and Death in the Amazon Jungle* (HarperCollins). Drescola, a French ethnologist, spent two years living among the Achuar of the Oriente in the 1970s, a time vividly and intelligently recounted in this memoir.

Gines Haro *Yasuní Green Gold* (New Internationalist). Coffee-table book with a conscience, celebrating Yasuní and explaining the issues as part of a campaign to "keep oil underground" there.

Joe Kane *Savages* (Pan/Vintage). An affecting and sensitive book on the protests of the Waorani against "the Company", the monolithic multinational oil industry and its supporting agencies. It's sprinkled with a poignant humour generated from the gap in cultures between the author and his subjects.

José Toribio Medina (ed.) *The Discovery of the Amazon* (Kessinger). The most detailed account of Francisco de Orellana's voyage down the Amazon, with half the book given to the original source documents, translated into English.

Suzana Sawyer *Crude Chronicles* (Duke University). The deepest exposition on the flowering of the indigenous and environmental movements in Ecuador against the ravages of neoliberal politics and global economics. A benchmark work in this field.

Anthony Smith *Explorers of the Amazon* (University of Chicago). An entertaining introduction to the exploration of the Amazon, streaked with wry humour. Includes chapters on Francisco de Orellana, La Condamine and Alexander von Humboldt. *The Lost Lady of the Amazon* (Constable and Robinson/Caroll & Graf), is about the epic journey of Isabela Godin (see Celia Wakefield, in "Memoirs and travel").

Randy Smith *Crisis Under the Canopy* (Abya Yala, Ecuador). An in-depth look at tourism in the Oriente and its effect on the Waorani people.

Rolf Wesche *The Ecotourist's Guide to the Ecuadorian Amazon* (CEPEIGE, Ecuador). Focuses on old Napo province (Baeza, Tena, Misahuallí and Coca), and although the town and hotel accounts are out of date, there are some good descriptions of petroglyph sites, caves and hikes, as well as a selection of excellent 1:50,000-scale maps.

Rolf Wesche and Andy Drumm *Defending Our Rainforest* (Acción Amazonia, Ecuador/Island). Although some are out of date, includes practical details and descriptions of many indigenous ecotourism projects in the Oriente, accompanied by spirited analysis of why they could be the salvation of the forests and its people.

Galápagos

Johanna Angermeyer *My Father's Island* (Pelican). The author uncovers the hidden past of her relatives through lyrical reminiscences on the Angermeyer family's struggle to settle on Santa Cruz, Galápagos.

Carol Ann Bassett *Galápagos at the Crossroads* (National Geographic). Provocative book dissecting the colliding forces that threaten to destroy what is special about the islands. Chapters take the perspectives of tourists, fishermen and modern-day pirates among others to explain all the contemporary issues.

William Beebe *Galápagos: World's End* (Dover). This pleasing book, which combines eager prose with keen scientific observation, brought the Galápagos to the attention of a new generation of travellers in the 1920s, and its popularity sparked a number of ill-fated attempts to colonize the islands. Beebe was the director of the New York Zoological Society and went to the Galápagos as head of a two-and-a-half-month scientific expedition, but problems with the water supply meant that he spent only "six thousand minutes" there.

Isabel Castro and Antonia Phillips *A Guide to the Birds of the Galápagos Islands* (A & C Black/Princeton University). Comprehensive, easy-to-use bird guide with colour illustrations and detailed descriptions to help identification.

Ainslie and Francis Conway *The Enchanted Islands* and *Return to the Island* (Kessinger). Humorous stories of an American couple's thwarted attempts to settle in the Galápagos in the 1930s and 1940s.

Charles Darwin *Voyage of the Beagle* (Penguin). A hugely enjoyable book with a chapter devoted to the Galápagos; original insights and flashes of genius pepper Darwin's wonderfully vivid descriptions of the islands' landscapes and wildlife. As revolutionary science texts go, *On the Origin of Species* (Penguin) is arguably one of the most accessible, but it's heavy going compared to *Voyage of the Beagle*.

Adrian Desmond and James Moore *Darwin: The Life of a Tormented Evolutionist* (Penguin/W. W. Norton). The enormous, definitive and best selling biography of Darwin, so thorough and wide-ranging that it also serves as a compelling study of Victorian Britain as a whole.

Julian Fitter, Daniel Fitter and David Hosking *Wildlife of the Galápagos* (Collins/Princeton University Press). A great, portable wildlife guide with photos of more than 250 Galápagos species, including plants and insects, accompanied by succinct and informative text, plus maps of the visitor sites and coverage of history, climate, geography and conservation too.

Herman Heinzell and Barnaby Hall *Galápagos Diary: A Complete Guide to the Archipelago's Birdlife* (University of California). Charming and idiosyncratic guide to the islands' birds, using photos, colour illustrations and diary entries that highlight breeding habits and behavioural oddities.

John Hickman *The Enchanted Islands* (UK: Anthony Nelson). A succinct, well-researched and entertaining history of human life on the islands, especially strong on the many colourful episodes concerning early pirates and castaways.

Paul Humann (ed.) *Reef Fish Identification: Galápagos* (New World Publications). Colourful photos and concise information on Galápagos reef fish in a slim and manageable field guide.

Michael H. Jackson *Galápagos: A Natural History* (Academic & University Publishers Group/University of Calgary). The most complete guide to the natural history of the Galápagos Islands, containing a broad and readable overview of geography, geology, flora and fauna, and conservation. Includes some colour plates and a wildlife checklist.

Colney K. McMullen *Flowering Plants of the Galápagos* (Cornell University). Galápagos flora has often played second fiddle to the islands' famous animals, but this excellent field guide helps to redress the balance with its succinct descriptions of more than four hundred plants and their locations, and plenty of colour photos.

Henry Nicholls *Lonesome George* (Palgrave Macmillan). Everything you wanted to know about the world's most famous tortoise in a spirited and entertaining biography, which champions compassionate conservation.

Tui de Roy *Spectacular Galápagos: Exploring an Extraordinary World* (Hugh Lauter Levin Associates), *Galápagos: Islands Born of Fire* (Warwick), and others. Stupendous photos of Galápagos wildlife and landscapes.

Andy Swash and Robert Still *Birds, Mammals and Reptiles of the Galápagos Islands* (Christopher Helm/Yale). Excellent compact field guide with colour photos and sketches, including a fin guide to aid the identification of dolphins and whales.

John Treherne *The Galápagos Affair* (Pimlico). Excellent overview of the extraordinary events on Floreana in the early 1930s that led to unexplained deaths and disappearances, including a large appendix detailing the author's own theories.

Jonathan Weiner *The Beak of the Finch* (Vintage). The fascinating work of two British scientists who have spent twenty years cataloguing Darwin's finches – in effect, witnessing the processes of evolution at first hand.

Margret Wittmer *Floreana* (Anthony Nelson/Moyer Bell). One of Floreana's original colonists describes how she conquered the privations of Galápagos life, and gives her version of events in the "Galápagos affair".

Arts and popular culture

Dawn Ades *Art in Latin America: The Modern Era 1820–1980* (Yale University). Excellent and lavishly illustrated general history of Latin American art from Independence, with discussions of a number of Ecuadorian artists, including Guayasamín, Viteri, Troya, Galecio and Antonio and Ramón Salas.

Christy Buchanan and Cesar Franco *The Ecuador Cookbook: Traditional Vegetarian and Seafood Recipes* (Christy Buchanan). Paperback cookbook offering a series of delightfully illustrated and easy-to-follow vegetarian and seafood recipes from Ecuador in English and Spanish.

Thomas Cummins *Ecuador: The Secret Art of Pre-Columbian Ecuador* (Five Continents Editions). Fantastic illustrations of Ecuador's greatest and most unusual pre-Columbian artwork, plus essays from expert archeologists.

Pablo Cuvi *Crafts of Ecuador* (o/p; available by mail order from SAE). Sumptuously illustrated coffee-table book taking in the gamut of Ecuador's traditional artesanías, from textiles to woodcarvings, accompanied by solid background information on the history and development of these crafts.

Lynn Meisch *(et al.)* *Weaving and Dyeing in Highland Ecuador* (University of Texas). Comprehensive study about Ecuadorian textiles and weaving. Meisch also wrote *Traditional Textiles of the Andes* (Thames and Hudson), which has beautiful colour illustrations accompanying six interesting essays on weaving in the Andes; *Otavalo: Weaving, Costume and the Market* (Ediciones Libri Mundi,

Ecuador), which covers the history, methods and modern-day situation of Otavalo's weavers; and *Andean Entrepreneurs: Otavalo Merchants and Musicians in the Global Arena* (University of Texas).

Gabrielle Palmer *Sculpture in the Kingdom of Quito* (University of New Mexico). Meticulously and thoughtfully researched exposé of the development of colonial sculpture in Quito, illustrated by some gorgeous photographs.

Fiction

Demetrio Aguilera-Malta *Don Goyo* (Humana). A spell-binding novel, first published in 1933, dealing with the lives of a group of *cholos* who eke out a living by fishing from the mangrove swamps in the Gulf of Guayaquil, which are in danger of being cleared by white landowners.

Kelly Aitken *Love in a Warm Climate* (Porcupine's Quill). Collection of short stories by a Canadian writer, all set in Ecuador and told by a series of North American female narrators. Imaginatively and compellingly written, bristling with tensions and conveying a strong sense of place.

Susan Benner and Kathy Leonard (eds.) *Fire from the Andes* (University of New Mexico). Impressive anthology of short stories by contemporary women authors from Ecuador, Bolivia and Peru. The eight Ecuadorian stories touch on themes such as patriarchy, racial prejudice, poverty and ageing.

William Burroughs *Queer* (Penguin). Autobiographical, Beat-generation novel about a morphine addict's travels through Ecuador in an abortive search for *yage*, a hallucinatory drug from the Oriente.

Jorge Icaza *Huasipungo* (*The Villagers*; European Schoolbooks/ Southern Illinois University). Iconic *indigenista* novel written in 1934, portraying the hardships and degradation suffered by the Andean

indígena in a world dominated by exploitive landowners.

Benjamin Kunkel *Indecision* (Picador/Random House). Enjoyable coming-of-age novel about a 20-something trying to find direction in his life, who travels to Ecuador to see an old high-school crush. A little predictable, but there's plenty of humour and originality to maintain the pace, and the descriptions of Ecuador are always entertaining.

Adalberto Ortiz *Juyungo* (Lynne Rienner). A 1940s novel set in the tropical lowlands, about the life of a black labourer who kills two white men in self-defence. An atmospheric read, full of evocative detail.

Luis Sepulveda *The Old Man Who Read Love Stories* (Harvest). Captivating and deceptively simple story of an itinerant dentist's twice-yearly voyages into a Shuar community in the Oriente – vividly evoking the sensations of travelling in the rainforest, while unobtrusively raising environmental questions.

Kurt Vonnegut *Galápagos* (Flamingo/Delta). A darkly comic novel which, turning natural selection on its head, has a handful of passengers on a Galápagos cruise ship marooned on the islands as the only survivors of a war and global pandemic. "Big brains" had been the species' fallibility, and a million years' evolution takes humanity in a quite different direction.

Language

Language

Language

The official language of Ecuador is Spanish, though at least twenty other first languages are spoken by native Ecuadorians, including nine dialects of Kichwa (also known by its Spanish spelling of "Quichua") and a further eight indigenous languages of the Oriente. English and some other European languages are spoken in tourist centres and well-to-do hotels and agencies, but otherwise you'll need to know a bit of Spanish.

It's an easy language to pick up, especially in the Ecuadorian **sierra**, whose inhabitants are known for speaking fairly slowly and clearly, usually pronouncing all the consonants of a word. On the **coast**, the accent is much harder to decipher, with the "s" sound frequently dropped and whole word endings missing, so that "arroz con pescado", for example, becomes "arro' con pe'ca'o". Many beginners spend a week or longer getting to grips with the basics at one of Quito's numerous **language schools**, most of which offer great-value one-to-one lessons for about $5 per hour (see box, pp.74–75). Popular alternatives to Quito include Baños (see p.205) and Cuenca (see p.247), both home to a number of language schools.

Those who already speak Spanish will have no trouble adjusting to the way it's spoken in Ecuador, which conforms to standard textbook **Castilian**, spoken without the lisped "c" and "z". That said, it does have its own idiomatic peculiarities, one of which is the compulsive use of the word "nomás" ("just" or "only"), which crops up all over the place ("siga nomás" for "go ahead", or "siéntate nomás" for "sit down", for example). Something else that sets Ecuadorian Spanish apart from Iberian Spanish are the many indigenous words that pepper its vocabulary, particularly **Kichwa** words such as *guagua* (baby), *mate* (herbal infusion), *pampa* (plain), *soroche* (altitude sickness) and *minga* (communal labour). Ecuador also readily borrows from **English**, resulting in a slew of words regarded with horror by Spaniards, such as *chequear* (to check), *parquear* (to park), *rentar* (to rent), *sánduche* (sandwich) and *computador* (computer). This somewhat flexible approach to their own language makes Ecuadorians more than willing to accommodate a foreigner's attempts to speak Spanish, which are invariably rewarded with smiles and compliments no matter how clumsy or inaccurate.

Pronunciation

The rules of **pronunciation** are pretty straightforward and, once you get to know them, strictly observed. Unless there's an accent, words ending in d, l, r, and z are **stressed** on the last syllable, all others on the second last. All **vowels** are pure and short.

A somewhere between the "a" sound of back and that of father

E as in get

I as in police

O as in hot

U as in rule

C is soft before E and I, hard otherwise: *cerca* is pronounced "serka".

G works the same way, a guttural "h" sound (like the ch in loch) before E or I, a hard G elsewhere – *gigante* becomes "higante".

H is always silent

J is the same sound as a guttural G: *jamón* is pronounced "hamon".

LL sounds like an English Y: *tortilla* is pronounced "torteeya".

N is as in English unless it has a tilde over it, as with *mañana*, when it's pronounced like the "n" in onion or menu.

QU is pronounced like an English K.

R is rolled, RR doubly so.

V sounds more like B, vino becoming "beano".

X is slightly softer than in English – sometimes almost SH – except between vowels in place names where it has an "H" sound – for example México (meh-hee-ko).

Z is the same as a soft "C", so cerveza becomes "servesa".

If you're using a dictionary, remember that in Spanish CH, LL, and Ñ count as separate letters and are listed after the Cs, Ls, and Ns, respectively.

Words and phrases

We've listed a few essential **words** and **phrases** below, but if you're travelling for any length of time a dictionary or phrasebook, such as the *Rough Guide Dictionary Phrasebook: Spanish*, is a worthwhile investment.

Basics

yes, no	sí, no	with, without	con, sin
please, thank you	por favor, gracias	good, bad	buen(o)/a, mal(o)/a
where, when	dónde, cuándo	big	gran(de)
what, how much	qué, cuánto	small	pequeño/a, chico
here, there	aquí, allí	more, less	más, menos
this, that	este, eso	today, tomorrow	hoy, mañana
now, later	ahora, más tarde	yesterday	ayer
open, closed	abierto/a, cerrado/a		

Greetings and responses

Hello, Goodbye	Hola, Adiós	I don't speak Spanish	(No) Hablo español
Good morning	Buenos días	My name is…	Me llamo…
Good afternoon/night	Buenas tardes/noches	What's your name?	¿Cómo se llama usted?
See you later	Hasta luego	I am English	Soy inglés (a)
Sorry	Lo siento/discúlpeme	…American	…norteamericano (a)
Excuse me	Con permiso/perdón	…Australian	…australiano (a)
How are you?	¿Cómo está (usted)?	…Canadian	…canadiense (a)
I (don't) understand	(No) Entiendo	…Irish	…irlandés (a)
Not at all/You're welcome	De nada	…Scottish	…escosés (a)
		…Welsh	…galés (a)
Do you speak English?	¿Habla (usted) inglés?	…New Zealander	…neozelandés (a)

Accommodation

twin room	una habitación doble	...with two beds/ double bed	...con dos camas/cama matrimonial
room with double bed	una habitación matrimonial	...for one night/one week	...para una noche/una semana
single room	una habitación sencilla		
private bathroom	baño privado	It's for one person /two people	Es para una persona/ dos personas
shared bathroom	baño compartido	It's fine, how much is it?	¿Está bien, cuánto es?
hot water (all day)	agua caliente (todo el día)		
cold water	agua fría	It's too expensive	Es demasiado caro
fan	ventilador	Don't you have anything cheaper?	¿No tiene algo más barato?
air-conditioned	aire-acondicionado		
tax	impuesto	Can one...?	¿Se puede. . ?
mosquito net	tolda/mosquitero	...camp (near) here?	¿...acampar aquí (cerca)?
key	llave		
check-out time	hora de salida	Is there a hotel nearby?	¿Hay un hotel aquí cerca?
Do you know...?	¿Sabe...?		
I don't know	No sé	I want	Quiero
There is (is there)?	(¿) Hay (?)	I'd like	Querría
Give me...	Deme...	What is there to eat?	¿Qué hay para comer?
(one like that)	(uno así)	What's that?	¿Qué es eso?
Do you have...?	¿Tiene...?	What's this called in Spanish?	¿Cómo se llama este en español?
...a room	...una habitación		

Directions and transport

bus terminal	terminal terrestre	...the post office	...el correo
ticket	pasaje	...the toilet	...el baño
seat	asiento	Where does the bus to... leave from?	¿De dónde sale el camión para...?
aisle	pasillo		
window	ventana	What time does the bus leave?	¿A qué hora sale el bus?
luggage	equipaje		
How do I get to...?	¿Por dónde se va a. . ?	What time does the bus arrive?	¿A qué hora llega el bus?
Left, right, straight on	Izquierda, derecha, derecho		
Where is...?	¿Dónde está...?	How long does the journey take?	¿Cuánto tiempo demora el viaje?
...the bus station	...el terminal de buses		
...the train station	...la estación de ferrocarriles	Is this the train for... ?	¿Es éste el tren para...?
...the nearest bank	...el banco más cercano	I'd like a (return) ticket to...	Querría pasaje (de ida y vuelta) para...
		What time does it leave (arrive in...)?	¿A qué hora sale (llega en...)?

Numbers

1	un/uno/una	3	tres
2	dos	4	cuatro

5	cinco	70	setenta
6	seis	80	ochenta
7	siete	90	noventa
8	ocho	100	cien(to)
9	nueve	101	ciento uno
10	diez	200	doscientos
11	once	201	doscientos uno
12	doce	500	quinientos
13	trece	1000	mil
14	catorce	2000	dos mil
15	quince	first	primero/a
16	dieciséis	second	segundo/a
17	diecisiete	third	tercero/a
18	dieciocho	fourth	cuarto/a
19	diecinueve	fifth	quinto/a
20	veinte	sixth	sixto/a
21	veitiuno	seventh	séptimo/a
30	treinta	eighth	octavo/a
40	cuarenta	ninth	noveno/a
50	cincuenta	tenth	décimo/a
60	sesenta		

Days and months

Monday	lunes	March	marzo
Tuesday	martes	April	abril
Wednesday	miércoles	May	mayo
Thursday	jueves	June	junio
Friday	viernes	July	julio
Saturday	sábado	August	agosto
Sunday	domingo	September	septiembre
		October	octubre
January	enero	November	noviembre
February	febrero	December	diciembre

Food and drink terms

The following should more than suffice as a basic menu reader for navigating restaurants, food stalls and markets throughout the country.

Basics

aceite	oil	arroz	rice
ají	chilli	azúcar	sugar
ajo	garlic	la carta	the menu
almuerzo	lunch, set-menu lunch	cena	dinner

comidas típicas	traditional food	miel	honey
cuchara	spoon	mixto	mixed seafood or meats
cuchillo	knife	mostaza	mustard
la cuenta	the bill	pan (integral)	(wholemeal) bread
desayuno	breakfast	pimienta	pepper
galletas	biscuits	plato fuerte	main course
hielo	ice	plato vegetariano	vegetarian dish
huevos	eggs	queso	cheese
mantequilla	butter	sal	salt
merienda	set-menu dinner	salsa de tomate	tomato sauce
mermelada	jam	tenedor	fork

Cooking terms

a la parrilla	barbecued	duro	hard-boiled
a la plancha	lightly fried	encebollado	cooked with onions
ahumado	smoked	encocado	in coconut sauce
al ajillo	in garlic sauce	frito	fried
al horno	oven-baked	picante	spicy hot
al vapor	steamed	puré	mashed
apanado	breaded	relleno	filled or stuffed
asado	roast	revuelto	scrambled
asado al palo	spit roasted, barbecued	saltado	sautéed
crudo	raw	seco	stew (also means dry)

Soups

caldo	broth	sopa	soup
caldo de gallina	chicken broth	sopa de bolas de verde	plantain dumpling soup
caldo de patas	cattle-hoof broth		
crema de espárragos	cream of asparagus	sopa del día	soup of the day
locro	cheese and potato soup	yaguarlocro	blood-sausage soup

Meat and poultry

aves	poultry	cuero/cueritos	pork crackling
bistec	beef steak	cuy	guinea pig
carne	beef	jamón	ham
cerdo/carne de chancho	pork	lechón	suckling pig
		lomo	steak of indiscriminate cut
chicharrones	pork scratchings, crackling		
		pato	duck
chuleta	cutlet, chop (usually pork)	pavo	turkey
		pollo	chicken
churrasco	beef steak with fried egg, rice and potatoes	res	beef
		ternera	veal
conejo	rabbit	tocino	bacon
cordero	lamb	venado	venison

Offal

chunchules	intestines	menudos	offal
guatita	tripe	patas	feet, trotters
hígado	liver	riñones	kidneys
lengua	tongue		

Seafood and fish

anchoa	anchovy	corvina	sea bass
atún	tuna	erizo	sea urchin
bonito	pacific bonito, similar to tuna	langosta	lobster
		langostino	king prawn
calamares	squid	lenguado	sole
camarón	prawn	mariscos	seafood
cangrejo	crab	mejillón	mussel
ceviche	seafood marinated in lime juice with onions	ostra	oyster
		pescado	fish
concha	clam, scallop	trucha	trout

Snacks

bocadillos	snacks	salchipapas	chips, sausage and sauces
bolón de verde	baked cheese and plantain dumpling	sanduche	sandwich
canguil	popcorn	tamales	ground maize with meat or cheese wrapped in leaf
chifles	banana chips/crisps		
empanada	cheese or meat pasty		
hamburguesa	hamburger	tortilla de huevos	omelette (also called omelet)
humitas	ground corn and cheese wrapped in leaf and steamed		
		tortilla de maíz	corn tortilla
		tostada	toast
patacones	thick-cut fried banana/plantain	tostado	toasted maize

Fruit

cereza	cherry	manzana	apple
chirimoya	custard apple; cherimoya	maracuyá	passion fruit
		mora	blackberry
ciruela	plum	naranja	orange
durazno	peach	pera	pear
fruta	fruit	piña	pineapple
frutilla	strawberry	plátano	plantain
guayaba	guava	tomate de arbol	tree tomato
higo	fig	toronja	grapefruit

Vegetables

aceitunas	olives	legumbres	vegetables
aguacate	avocado	lentejas	lentils
alcachofa	artichoke	menestra	stew, typically beans and lentils
arvejas	peas		
cebolla	onion	palmito	palm heart
champiñón	mushroom	papa	potato
choclo	maize, sweetcorn	papas fritas	chips (french fries)
coliflor	cauliflower	pepinillo	gherkin
espinaca	spinach	pepino	cucumber
frijoles	beans	tomate	tomato
hongo	mushroom	verduras	vegetables
lechuga	lettuce	zanahoria	carrot

Desserts

cocados	coconut sweets	pastas	pastries
ensalada de frutas	fruit salad	pastel	cake
flan	crème caramel	postres	desserts
helado	ice cream	torta	tart
manjar de leche	very sweet caramel, made from condensed milk		

Drinks

agua (mineral)	(mineral) water	caipiriña	cocktail of rum, lime, ice and sugar
con gas	sparkling		
sin gas	still	cerveza	beer
sin hielo	without ice	chicha	fermented corn drink
aguardiente	sugar-cane spirit	cola, or gaseosa	fizzy drink
aromática	herbal tea	jugo	juice
hierba luisa	lemon verbena	leche	milk
manzanilla	camomile	limonada	fresh lemonade
menta	mint	mate de coca	Coca leaf tea
batido	milkshake	ron	rum
bebidas	drinks	té	tea
café	coffee	vino (blanco/tinto)	(white/red) wine
café con leche	coffee with milk		

Kichwa (Quichua)

Around twenty percent of Ecuador's population are **Kichwa** speakers, the language of the Inca Empire, which in one form or another is spoken by indigenous communities from southern Colombia all the way to northern Chile. There are many regional differences, however, so that a speaker from Ecuador would have as much difficulty understanding a Peruvian, as a Spanish-speaker would have understanding Italian. **Dialects** also differ between areas of Ecuador, with noticeable variations between speakers of the highlands and of the Oriente, and again between highland areas such as Cañar, Chimborazo and Imbabura.

Though there are regional differences, the basic **phrases** below should be understood by Kichwa speakers throughout the country. Spellings do vary; you may see "c" written for "k", or "hua/gua" for "wa", for instance. Most people will also know Spanish, but exhibiting an interest in speaking Kichwa can only help increase pride in a language that has long been stigmatized and suppressed by the Spanish-speaking establishment. It's little wonder that many speakers are rejecting the Spanish spelling of their language, "Quichua", which you'll still see commonly used. The effort spent taking some time to **learn** Kichwa will be repaid many times over in the access it will give you to Kichwa communities and the friendships you'll make. Lessons are offered at EIL, Hernando de la Cruz N31-37 and Mariana de Jesús, Quito (T02/2551937, Wwww.eilecuador .org), or you could try indigenous tour operators, such as Runa Tupari of Otavalo (see p.136), who will be able to fix you up with homestays. You could also make enquiries and pick up resource materials at Abya Yala, a cultural centre in Quito dedicated to protecting and promoting indigenous culture, at 12 de Octubre 1430 and Wilson (T02/2506251, Wwww.abyayala.org), or check the notice boards of the SAE (see p.77).

Useful words and phrases

Hello	Imanalla	No	Manan
Good morning	Alli puncha	I, my	Ñuka
Good afternoon	Alli chishi	You (informal)/	Kan/kikin
Good evening/night	Alli tuta	(formal)	
See you tomorrow	Kayakama	Excuse me	Kishpi chigway
See you later	Asha kashkaman	It's so cold!	Achachay!
Let's go	Akuichi	It's so hot!	Araray!
How are you?	Imanalla kangui?	What's your name?	Ima shuti kangui?
I am fine	Allillami kapani	My name is...	Ñuka shuti mikan...
Please	Jau man	Please sit down	Tiyaripay
Thank you (very much)	Pagui (shungulla)	Say it again please	Kutin nipay
Yes	Ari	How old are you?	Mashna watata charingui?

Numbers

1	shuk	11	chunka shuk
2	ishki	12	chunka ishki
3	kimsa	20	ishki chunka
4	chusku	21	ishki chunka shuk
5	pichka	100	pachak
6	sukta	1000	waranka
7	kanchis	2345	ishki waranka kimsa pachak chuksu chunka pichka
8	pusak		
9	iskun		
10	chunka	1,000,000	junu

Common words in names and places

alli	good	pachamama	nature, mother earth
allpa	earth, soil	pakarina	sunrise
chaka	bridge	pichu	chest
chullpi	corn	pirka	wall
churi	son	pishku	bird
wawa (guagua)	baby	rasu	snow
huarmi	wife	raymi	fiesta
huasi	house	ruku	old
inti	sun	rumi	stone
jaka	abyss	runa	indigenous person
jatun	big	sacha	forest
kari	man	sara	corn
killa	moon, month	sisa	flower
kincha	corral	sumak	beautiful
kucha (cocha)	lake	tayta	father, polite term for an older man
llakta	village, community	tullu	bone
makui	hand	uma	head
mama	mother, polite term for an older woman	urku	mountain
ñan	path, street	warmi	woman
ñaña	sister	wayna	lover
pacha	hour, weather	yaku	water, river

Glossary

adobe sun-dried mud brick

aguas termales hot springs

apartado postal box

artesanía traditional handicraft

balneario thermal baths resort

bargueño colonial wooden chest, inlaid with bone, ivory and other decorative materials in geometric patterns

barrio district, quarter or suburb

buseta small bus

cabaña cabin

calle street

camioneta pick-up truck

campesino literally from the countryside, used to describe *mestizo* rural farmers

canoa dugout canoe

casilla postal box

cc abbreviation of *centro comercial*, or shopping centre

chicha fermented maize drink

chiva open-sided wooden bus mostly found in rural areas

cholo coastal fisherman, but also used in the sierra to refer to *mestizo* artisans and traders in the Cuenca region, most commonly applied to women ("la chola Cuencana")

choza a rough-thatched hut or shack

colectivo collective taxi

cordillera mountain range

Criollo "Creole": used historically to refer to a person of Spanish blood born in the American colonies, but nowadays as an adjective to describe something (such as food or music) as "typical" or "local"

curandero healer

encomendero possessor of an *encomienda*

encomienda a grant of indigenous labourers to landowners during colonial times

fibra open fibreglass boat used as transport between islands in the Galápagos

finca small farm

flete small boat for hire

folklórica andean folk music

gringo slightly (but not always) pejorative term for an American specifically, but also used generally for any foreigner from a non-Spanish-speaking country

guardaparque park warden

hacienda farm or large estate

indígena used adjectivally to mean "indigenous", or as a noun to refer to an indigenous person

lancha launch, small boat

lek bird courtship display area

local "unit" or "shop" in a shopping centre

Malecón coastal or riverside avenue

Mestizo person of mixed Spanish and indigenous blood

minga Kichwa term for collective community work

mirador viewpoint

montuvio *mestizo* farm worker in the coastal interior

Municipio town hall or town council

nevado snowcapped mountain

pampa plain

panga dinghy, usually with a motor

páramo high-altitude grassland, found above 3000m

peña nightclub where live music is performed, often folk music

petrolero oil-worker

plata silver; slang for money

pucará fort

quebrada ravine, dried-out stream

quinta villa or fine country house

ranchera open-sided wooden bus mostly found in rural areas

sala room or hall

selva jungle or tropical forest

serrano from the sierra or highlands

shigra a bag made of tightly woven straw, often dyed in bright colours

s/n used in addresses to indicate "sin número", or without a number

soroche altitude sickness

SS HH abbreviation for *servicios higiénicos*, toilets

tambo rest-house on Inca roads

tarabita simple cable car

termas thermal baths, hot springs

triciclero tricycle-taxi driver

Travel store

Angermeyer Cruises

G A L A P A G O S

Cast off for the Galapagos Islands...

Travel

Andorra The Pyrenees, Pyrenees & Andorra Map, Spain

Antigua The Caribbean

Argentina Argentina, Argentina Map, Buenos Aires, South America on a Budget

Aruba The Caribbean

Australia Australia, Australia Map, East Coast Australia, Melbourne, Sydney, Tasmania

Austria Austria, Europe on a Budget, Vienna

Bahamas The Bahamas, The Caribbean

Barbados Barbados DIR, The Caribbean

Belgium Belgium & Luxembourg, Bruges DIR, Brussels, Brussels Map, Europe on a Budget

Belize Belize, Central America on a Budget, Guatemala & Belize Map

Benin West Africa

Bolivia Bolivia, South America on a Budget

Brazil Brazil, Rio, South America on a Budget

British Virgin Islands The Caribbean

Brunei Malaysia, Singapore & Brunei [1 title], Southeast Asia on a Budget

Bulgaria Bulgaria, Europe on a Budget

Burkina Faso West Africa

Cambodia Cambodia, Southeast Asia on a Budget, Vietnam, Laos & Cambodia Map [1 Map]

Cameroon West Africa

Canada Canada, Pacific Northwest, Toronto, Toronto Map, Vancouver

Cape Verde West Africa

Cayman Islands The Caribbean

Chile Chile, Chile Map, South America on a Budget

China Beijing, China, Hong Kong & Macau, Hong Kong & Macau DIR, Shanghai

Colombia South America on a Budget

Costa Rica Central America on a Budget, Costa Rica, Costa Rica & Panama Map

Croatia Croatia, Croatia Map, Europe on a Budget

Cuba Cuba, Cuba Map, The Caribbean, Havana

Cyprus Cyprus, Cyprus Map

Czech Republic The Czech Republic, Czech & Slovak Republics, Europe on a Budget, Prague, Prague DIR, Prague Map

Denmark Copenhagen, Denmark, Europe on a Budget, Scandinavia

Dominica The Caribbean

Dominican Republic Dominican Republic, The Caribbean

Ecuador Ecuador, South America on a Budget

Egypt Egypt, Egypt Map

El Salvador Central America on a Budget

England Britain, Camping in Britain, Devon & Cornwall, Dorset, Hampshire and The Isle of Wight [1 title], England, Europe on a Budget, The Lake District, London, London DIR, London Map, London Mini Guide, Walks In London & Southeast England

Estonia The Baltic States, Europe on a Budget

Fiji Fiji

Finland Europe on a Budget, Finland, Scandinavia

France Brittany & Normandy, Corsica, Corsica Map, The Dordogne & the Lot, Europe on a Budget, France, France Map, Languedoc & Roussillon, The Loire, Paris, Paris DIR, Paris Map, Paris Mini Guide, Provence & the Côte d'Azur, The Pyrenees, Pyrenees & Andorra Map

French Guiana South America on a Budget

Gambia The Gambia, West Africa

Germany Berlin, Berlin Map, Europe on a Budget, Germany, Germany Map

Ghana West Africa

Gibraltar Spain

Greece Athens Map, Crete, Crete Map, Europe on a Budget, Greece, Greece Map, Greek Islands, Ionian Islands

Guadeloupe The Caribbean

Guatemala Central America on a Budget, Guatemala, Guatemala & Belize Map

Guinea West Africa

Guinea-Bissau West Africa

Guyana South America on a Budget

Holland see The Netherlands

Honduras Central America on a Budget

Hungary Budapest, Europe on a Budget, Hungary

Iceland Iceland, Iceland Map

India Goa, India, India Map, Kerala, Rajasthan, Delhi & Agra [1 title], South India, South India Map

Indonesia Bali & Lombok, Southeast Asia on a Budget

Ireland Dublin DIR, Dublin Map, Europe on a Budget, Ireland, Ireland Map

Israel Jerusalem

Italy Europe on a Budget, Florence DIR, Florence & Siena Map, Florence & the best of Tuscany, Italy, The Italian Lakes, Naples & the Amalfi Coast, Rome, Rome DIR, Rome Map, Sardinia, Sicily, Sicily Map, Tuscany & Umbria, Tuscany Map, Venice, Venice DIR, Venice Map

Jamaica Jamaica, The Caribbean

Japan Japan, Tokyo

Jordan Jordan

Kenya Kenya, Kenya Map

Korea Korea

Laos Laos, Southeast Asia on a Budget, Vietnam, Laos & Cambodia Map [1 Map]

Latvia The Baltic States, Europe on a Budget

Lithuania The Baltic States, Europe on a Budget

Luxembourg Belgium & Luxembourg, Europe on a Budget

Malaysia Malaysia Map, Malaysia, Singapore & Brunei [1 title], Southeast Asia on a Budget

Mali West Africa

Malta Malta & Gozo DIR

Martinique The Caribbean

Mauritania West Africa

Mexico Baja California, Baja California, Cancún & Cozumel DIR, Mexico, Mexico Map, Yucatán, Yucatán Peninsula Map

Monaco France, Provence & the Côte d'Azur

Montenegro Montenegro

Morocco Europe on a Budget, Marrakesh DIR, Marrakesh Map, Morocco, Morocco Map,

Nepal Nepal

Netherlands Amsterdam, Amsterdam DIR, Amsterdam Map, Europe on a Budget, The Netherlands

Netherlands Antilles The Caribbean

New Zealand New Zealand, New Zealand Map

DIR: Rough Guide **DIRECTIONS** for short breaks

Nicaragua Central America on a Budget
Niger West Africa
Nigeria West Africa
Norway Europe on a Budget, Norway, Scandinavia
Panama Central America on a Budget, Costa Rica & Panama Map, Panama
Paraguay South America on a Budget
Peru Peru, Peru Map, South America on a Budget
Philippines The Philippines, Southeast Asia on a Budget,
Poland Europe on a Budget, Poland
Portugal Algarve DIR, The Algarve Map, Europe on a Budget, Lisbon DIR, Lisbon Map, Madeira DIR, Portugal, Portugal Map, Spain & Portugal Map
Puerto Rico The Caribbean, Puerto Rico
Romania Europe on a Budget, Romania
Russia Europe on a Budget, Moscow, St Petersburg
St Kitts & Nevis The Caribbean
St Lucia The Caribbean
St Vincent & the Grenadines The Caribbean
Scotland Britain, Camping in Britain, Edinburgh DIR, Europe on a Budget, Scotland, Scottish Highlands & Islands
Senegal West Africa
Serbia Montenegro Europe on a Budget
Sierra Leone West Africa
Singapore Malaysia, Singapore & Brunei [1 title], Singapore, Singapore DIR, Southeast Asia on a Budget
Slovakia Czech & Slovak Republics, Europe on a Budget
Slovenia Europe on a Budget, Slovenia
South Africa Cape Town & the Garden Route, South Africa, South Africa Map
Spain Andalucía, Andalucía Map, Barcelona, Barcelona DIR, Barcelona Map, Europe on a Budget, Ibiza & Formentera DIR, Gran Canaria DIR, Madrid DIR, Lanzarote & Fuerteventura DIR Madrid Map, Mallorca & Menorca, Mallorca DIR, Mallorca Map, The Pyrenees, Pyrenees & Andorra Map, Spain, Spain & Portugal Map, Tenerife & La Gomera DIR
Sri Lanka Sri Lanka, Sri Lanka Map
Suriname South America on a Budget
Sweden Europe on a Budget, Scandinavia, Sweden
Switzerland Europe on a Budget, Switzerland
Taiwan Taiwan
Tanzania Tanzania, Zanzibar
Thailand Bangkok, Southeast Asia on a Budget, Thailand, Thailand Map, Thailand Beaches & Islands
Togo West Africa
Trinidad & Tobago The Caribbean, Trinidad & Tobago
Tunisia Tunisia, Tunisia Map
Turkey Europe on a Budget, Istanbul, Turkey, Turkey Map
Turks and Caicos Islands The Bahamas, The Caribbean
United Arab Emirates Dubai DIR, Dubai & UAE Map [1 title]
United Kingdom Britain, Devon & Cornwall, Edinburgh DIR England, Europe on a Budget, The Lake District, London, London DIR, London Map, London Mini Guide, Scotland, Scottish Highlands & Islands, Wales, Walks In London & Southeast England
United States Alaska, Boston, California, California Map, Chicago, Colorado, Florida, Florida Map, The Grand Canyon, Hawaii, Los Angeles, Los Angeles Map, Los Angeles and Southern California, Maui DIR, Miami & South Florida, New England, New England Map, New Orleans & Cajun Country, New Orleans DIR, New York City, NYC DIR, NYC Map, New York City Mini Guide, Oregon & Washington, Orlando & Walt Disney World® DIR, San Francisco, San Francisco DIR, San Francisco Map, Seattle, Southwest USA, USA, Washington DC, Yellowstone & the Grand Tetons National Park, Yosemite National Park
Uruguay South America on a Budget
US Virgin Islands The Bahamas, The Caribbean
Venezuela South America on a Budget
Vietnam Southeast Asia on a Budget, Vietnam, Vietnam, Laos & Cambodia Map [1 Map],
Wales Britain, Camping in Britain, Europe on a Budget, Wales
First-Time Series FT Africa, FT Around the World, FT Asia, FT Europe, FT Latin America
Inspirational guides Earthbound, Clean Breaks, Make the Most of Your Time on Earth, Ultimate Adventures, World Party
Travel Specials Camping in Britain, Travel with Babies & Young Children, Walks in London & SE England

Books change lives

Poverty and illiteracy go hand in hand. But in sub-Saharan Africa, books are a luxury few can afford. Many children leave school functionally illiterate, and adults often fall back into illiteracy in adulthood due to a lack of available reading material.

Book Aid
International
www.bookaid.org

Book Aid International knows that books change lives.

Every year we send over half a million books to partners in 12 countries in sub-Saharan Africa, to stock libraries in schools, refugee camps, prisons, universities and communities. Literally millions of readers have access to books and information that could teach them new skills – from keeping chickens to getting a degree in Business Studies or learning how to protect against HIV/AIDS.

What can you do?

Join our Reverse Book Club and with your donation of only £6 a month, we can send 36 books every year to some of the poorest countries in the world. For every two pounds extra you can give, we can send another book!

Support Book Aid International today!

 Online. Go to our website at **www.bookaid.org**, and click on 'donate'

 By telephone. Start a Direct Debit or give a donation on your card by calling us on 020 7733 3577

Book Aid International is a charity and a limited company registered in England and Wales.
Charity No. 313869 Company No. 880754   39-41 Coldharbour Lane, Camberwell, London SE5 9NR
T +44 (0)20 7733 3577   F +44 (0)20 7978 8006   E info@bookaid.org   www.bookaid.org

Visit us online

www.roughguides.com

Information on over 25,000 destinations around the world

- **Read** Rough Guides' trusted travel info
- **Access** exclusive articles from Rough Guides authors
- **Update** yourself on new books, maps, CDs and other products
- **Enter** our competitions and win travel prizes
- **Share** ideas, journals, photos & travel advice with other users
- **Earn** points every time you contribute to the Rough Guide
  community and get rewards

BROADEN YOUR HORIZONS

Small print and
Index

A Rough Guide to Rough Guides

Published in 1982, the first Rough Guide – to Greece – was a student scheme that became a publishing phenomenon. Mark Ellingham, a recent graduate in English from Bristol University, had been travelling in Greece the previous summer and couldn't find the right guidebook. With a small group of friends he wrote his own guide, combining a highly contemporary, journalistic style with a thoroughly practical approach to travellers' needs.

The immediate success of the book spawned a series that rapidly covered dozens of destinations. And, in addition to impecunious backpackers, Rough Guides soon acquired a much broader and older readership that relished the guides' wit and inquisitiveness as much as their enthusiastic, critical approach and value-for-money ethos.

These days, Rough Guides include recommendations from shoestring to luxury and cover more than 200 destinations around the globe, including almost every country in the Americas and Europe, more than half of Africa and most of Asia and Australasia. Our ever-growing team of authors and photographers is spread all over the world, particularly in Europe, the US and Australia.

In the early 1990s, Rough Guides branched out of travel, with the publication of Rough Guides to World Music, Classical Music and the Internet. All three have become benchmark titles in their fields, spearheading the publication of a wide range of books under the Rough Guide name.

Including the travel series, Rough Guides now number more than 350 titles, covering: phrasebooks, waterproof maps, music guides from Opera to Heavy Metal, reference works as diverse as Conspiracy Theories and Shakespeare, and popular culture books from iPods to Poker. Rough Guides also produce a series of more than 120 World Music CDs in partnership with World Music Network.

Visit www.roughguides.com to see our latest publications.

Rough Guide travel images are available for commercial licensing at www.roughguidespictures.com

Rough Guide credits

Text editor: Harry Wilson
Layout: Sachin Tanwar
Cartography: Maxine Repath and Animesh Pathak
Picture editor: Sarah Cummins
Production: Rebecca Short
Proofreader: Karen Parker
Cover design: Chloë Roberts
Photographer: Greg Roden
Editorial: Ruth Blackmore, Andy Turner, Keith Drew, Edward Aves, Alice Park, Lucy White, Jo Kirby, James Smart, Natasha Foges, Róisín Cameron, Emma Traynor, Emma Gibbs, Kathryn Lane, Monica Woods, Mani Ramaswamy, Lucy Cowie, Amanda Howard, Lara Kavanagh, Alison Roberts, Joe Staines, Peter Buckley, Matthew Milton, Tracy Hopkins, Ruth Tidball; **Delhi** Madhavi Singh, Karen D'Souza, Lubna Shaheen
Design & Pictures: **London** Scott Stickland, Dan May, Diana Jarvis, Mark Thomas, Nicole Newman, Emily Taylor; **Delhi** Umesh Aggarwal, Ajay Verma, Jessica Subramanian, Ankur Guha, Pradeep Thapliyal, Anita Singh, Nikhil Agarwal, Sachin Gupta
Production: Vicky Baldwin

Cartography: **London** Ed Wright, Katie Lloyd-Jones; **Delhi** Rajesh Chhibber, Ashutosh Bharti, Rajesh Mishra, Jasbir Sandhu, Karobi Gogoi, Alakananda Bhattacharya, Swati Handoo, Deshpal Dabas
Online: **London** George Atwell, Faye Hellon, Jeanette Angell, Fergus Day, Justine Bright, Clare Bryson, Aine Fearon, Adrian Low, Ezgi Celebi, Amber Bloomfield; **Delhi** Amit Verma, Rahul Kumar, Narender Kumar, Ravi Yadav, Debojit Borah, Rakesh Kumar, Ganesh Sharma, Shisir Basumatari
Marketing & Publicity: **London** Liz Statham, Niki Hanmer, Louise Maher, Jess Carter, Vanessa Godden, Vivienne Watton, Anna Paynton, Rachel Sprackett, Libby Jellie, Laura Vipond, Vanessa McDonald; **New York** Katy Ball, Judi Powers, Nancy Lambert; **Delhi** Ragini Govind
Manager India: Punita Singh
Reference Director: Andrew Lockett
Operations Manager: Helen Atkinson
PA to Publishing Director: Nicola Henderson
Publishing Director: Martin Dunford
Commercial Manager: Gino Magnotta
Managing Director: John Duhigg

Publishing information

This fourth edition published January 2010 by
Rough Guides Ltd,
80 Strand, London WC2R 0RL
14 Local Shopping Centre, Panchsheel Park, New Delhi 110017, India

Distributed by the Penguin Group
Penguin Books Ltd,
80 Strand, London WC2R 0RL
Penguin Group (USA)
375 Hudson Street, NY 10014, USA
Penguin Group (Australia)
250 Camberwell Road, Camberwell, Victoria 3124, Australia
Penguin Group (Canada)
195 Harry Walker Parkway N, Newmarket, ON, L3Y 7B3 Canada
Penguin Group (NZ)
67 Apollo Drive, Mairangi Bay, Auckland 1310, New Zealand
Cover concept by Peter Dyer.

Typeset in Bembo and Helvetica to an original design by Henry Iles.

Printed in Singapore

© Harry Adès and Melissa Graham 2010

Maps © Rough Guides

576pp includes index
A catalogue record for this book is available from the British Library
ISBN: 978-1-84836-191-1

Help us update

We've gone to a lot of effort to ensure that the fourth edition of **The Rough Guide to Ecuador** is accurate and up-to-date. However, things change – places are "discovered", opening hours are notoriously fickle, restaurants and rooms raise prices or lower standards. If you feel we've got it wrong or left something out, we'd like to know, and if you can remember the address, the price, the hours, the phone number, so much the better.

Please send your comments with the subject line "**Rough Guide Ecuador Update**" to @mail@roughguides.com. We'll credit all contributions and send a copy of the next edition (or any other Rough Guide if you prefer) for the very best emails.

Have your questions answered and tell others about your trip at @www.roughguides.com

Acknowledgements

Harry Adès: I'd like to thank Matt Goldman, Carlos Villafuerte and Louise Williamson for their hard work and excellent research, and the many helpful people who have made this update possible, including Nicola Mears, Josef DeCoux, Mary Finn, Marcelo and all at the SAE, Chris Sacco, Piet Sabbe, Carlos Donoso, Frank Kiefer, Nessa Findlay, Molly Brown, Bonnie Burgess Olson, Francisco Izurieta, Miff & Humbs, BKS and gang, David Beyer and Jorge Pérez. Big thanks to Harry Wilson, a solid-gold editor whose diligence, receptiveness and good humour have kept the whole thing on track. Words cannot express my gratitude to Melissa Graham for sharing the load so valiantly – you've been a rock of strength! And a final special thank you to all at home, my family and especially Shahla and Sylvie, who make my days happy ones. Doggoss!

Melissa Graham: I'd like to give special thanks to the following people in Ecuador who kindly and patiently shared their time and knowledge: Carolina Piza of the Municipalidad de Guayaquil; César Cerda of RICANCIE; Bonnie Burgess Olson of Wildsumaco Lodge; Michelle Kirby and Andres Hammerman of the Black Sheep Inn; and Katrien of TribuTrek. Finally, warm thanks to Harry Adès, for his unflagging commitment and support, and our excellent editor, Harry Wilson.

The editor thanks the authors for their diligent, hard work and attention to detail; Sachin Tanwar and the Delhi team for their excellent typesetting; Sarah Cummins for her superb picture research and editing; Maxine Repath in London and Animesh Pathak in Delhi for their collective mapmaking skills; Karen Parker for her vigilant proofreading; and all other Rough Guides editors and colleagues for their overall guidance.

Readers' letters

Thanks to all the readers who have taken the time to write in with comments and suggestions (and apologies if we've inadvertently omitted or misspelt anyone's name):

Franklin Alvarado, Emmanuel B. Anama, Jr., Jan Joost Bierhoff, M. Baird, Steven Bond, Craig Butz, Dani Campson, Bjorn Clasen, Thomas Cushnie, Sandy Deal, Simon Debaat, Simon Deeble, David Doyon, Derek Drager Iris Edenheiser, Steve Dretz, Sue Fisher, Rachel Fitch, Kléver Albán Flores, Brindanna Fouhy, Marcus Franklin, James Garland, Kevin Geary, Frank Geboers, Sebastian Gerschefsk, Anne Guilmette, Angus Gregson, Sonya Hammons, Brendan Heath, Becky Hilton, Mary Holozubiec, David & Carole James, T. J. Komoly, Christopher Little, Judy Logback, Richard Loerky, Astley Milne, Alex Narracott, Oonagh Parish, Dianna Pettet, Natacha Pin-Abrantes, Claude-Eric Poulin, Sarah Ramey, Nicole & Martin Rechsteiner, Piet Sabbe, Rosmarie Scholler, Stefan Siclovan, Luke Smith, Pam and John Stack, Maik Cayapa Tapuy, Martien Tijssen, Peter Tucci, Michal Wasik, Margot Whitfield, Janet Williams and Rosemary Wilson.

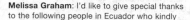

Index

Map entries are in colour.

N

O

P

Q

Map symbols

maps are listed in the full index using coloured text

▪▪▪▪▪	International boundary	☉	Statue/monument
▪▪▪▪	Provincial boundary	♀	Museum
▪▪▪▪	Chapter boundary	♦	Point of interest
═══	Road	⋀⋁	Spring/spa
┅┅┅	Unpaved road	⋓	Viewpoint
───	Track/seasonal road	✈	Airport
▥▥▥	Steps	★	Public transport stop
▬▬▬	Pedestrianized street	Ⓣ	Trole stop
------	Path	Ⓔ	Ecovía stop
▬•▬	Railway	Ⓜ	Metrobus stop
•----•	Cable car (TelefériQo)	🅿	Parking
───	Waterway	⊞	Hospital
⤳	Rock	@	Internet access
⋀⋀	Mountain range	☏	Telephone office
⛰	Cliff	ⓘ	Information office
▲	Peak	⊠	Post office
⋀⋀	Volcano	⊠—⊠	Gate
◠	Cave	⚱	Church (regional maps)
☀	Lighthouse	▪	Building
⚵	Waterfall	⊞	Church (town maps)
⊛	Crater	⬭	Stadium
⬢	Lodge	⊞	Cemetery
⚠	Campsite	⣿	Parks/reserves
)(	Bridge	⣿	Beach
∴	Ruins		